W9-CHR-457

COMPUTER FORENSICS

AND

INVESTIGATIONS

Bill Nelson, Amelia Phillips, Frank Enfinger, Chris Steuart

THOMSON

COURSE TECHNOLOGY

Professional ■ Trade ■ Reference

Computer Forensics and Investigations

is published by Course PTR, a division of Course Technology

Senior Editor:
William Pitkin III

Developmental Editor:
Lisa Ruffolo, The Software Resource

Technical Editor:
Mark Edmead

Product Marketing Manager:
Jason Sakos

Cover Design:
Mike Tanamachi

Senior Editor:
Lisa Egan

Production Editor:
Megan Belanger

Senior Manufacturing Coordinator:
Laura Burns

Associate Product Manager:
Nick Lombardi

Text Designer:
GEX Publishing Services

Product Manager:
Amy M. Lyon

MQA Technical Leaders:
Nicole Ashton, Marianne Snow

Editorial Assistant:
Amanda Piantedosi

Compositor:
Danielle Foster

Indexer:
Katherine Stimson

Course Technology reserves the right to revise this publication and make changes from time to time in its content without notice.

ISBN 1-59200-382-6

Library of Congress Catalog Card Number: 2003115726

Contents at a Glance

Contents

CHAPTER 6
Current Computer Forensics Tools   169

CHAPTER 9
Data Acquisition   **261**

CHAPTER 10
Computer Forensic Analysis   **297**

Preface

Computer forensics and investigations has been a professional field for many years, but most of the well-established experts in the field have been self-taught. The growth of the Internet and the proliferation of computers worldwide now increase the need for conducting computing investigations. Computers can be used to commit crimes, and crimes can be recorded on computers, including violations of company policies, records of embezzlement, e-mail harassment, murder, leaks of proprietary information, and even terrorism. Law enforcement, network administrators, attorneys, and private investigators now rely on the skills of professional computer forensics experts to investigate criminal and civil cases.

This book is not intended to provide comprehensive training in computer forensics. It will, however, give you a solid foundation by introducing computer forensics to those who are new to the field. Other books on computer forensics are targeted to experts, while this book is intended for novices who have a firm understanding of the basics of computers and networking.

The new generation of computer forensics experts needs more initial training because operating systems, computer hardware, and computer forensics software tools are changing more quickly now than in the past. This book covers current and past operating systems, such as Windows 9x, Mac OS, and Linux, and a range of computer hardware, from basic PC workstations to high-end network servers. While this book focuses on a few computer forensics software tools, it also reviews and discusses other tools that are currently available.

The purpose of this book is to guide you toward becoming a skilled computer forensics investigator. A secondary goal is to help you pass the appropriate certification exams. As the field of computer forensics and investigations matures, keep in mind that the certifications will change.

The International Association of Computer Investigative Specialists (IACIS) exam is the most well known and is intended primarily for law enforcement. However, IACIS makes exceptions for investigators outside of law enforcement who can prove their credentials. Chapter 5 reviews the certifications that are current at the time of publication, and Appendix A covers them in more detail.

THE INTENDED AUDIENCE

While this book can be used by people with a wide range of backgrounds, it is intended for people who have an A+ and Network+ certification or equivalent. A networking background is necessary so that you understand how PCs operate in a networked environment and can work with a network administrator when necessary. In addition, readers must understand how to use a computer from the command line, and how to use popular operating systems, including Windows 9x, Windows 2000, Windows XP, Linux, and Mac OS, and their related hardware.

This book can be used at any educational level, from the technical high school and community college to the graduate level. The current professional in the public and private sectors can also use this book. Each group will approach the problems from a different perspective, but all will benefit from it.

CHAPTER DESCRIPTIONS

The chapters in this book discuss the following topics:

Chapter 1, "Computer Forensics and Investigations as a Profession," introduces you to the history of computer forensics and how the use of electronic evidence came into being. It also introduces the legal concerns and compares public and private sector cases.

Chapter 2, "Understanding Computer Investigations," exposes you to an application that is used throughout the book. It also applies scientific techniques to an investigative case.

Chapter 3, "Working with Windows and DOS Systems," discusses the most common operating systems of our era. You examine what happens and what files are altered during computer startup and how each system deals with deleted and slack space.

Chapter 4, "Macintosh and Linux Boot Processes and Disk Structures," continues the operating system discussion from Chapter 3 by examining the next two most popular operating systems for PCs. It also covers CDs, DVDs, SCSIs, and RAID systems.

Chapter 5, "The Investigator's Office and Laboratory," presents an ideal view of how computer forensics labs should be equipped, from the very small private investigator to the regional FBI lab. It also covers the certifications for investigators.

Chapter 6, "Current Computer Forensics Tools," explores current computer forensics tools and evaluates their strengths and weaknesses. This is one of the longer chapters and covers tools that may not be readily available.

Chapter 7, "Digital Evidence Controls," emphasizes that digital evidence is extremely fragile and easily changed. The chapter covers how to record a crime scene and secure the evidence so that it can be used in court.

Chapter 8, "Processing Crime and Incident Scenes," begins by explaining search warrants and continues by discussing the nature of a typical computing-forensics case. It discusses when to use outside professionals, how to assemble a team, and how to evaluate a case.

Chapter 9, "Data Acquisition," explains how to prepare to acquire data from a suspect's drive and discusses the tools available for each of the command line and GUI operating systems.

Chapter 10, "Computer Forensic Analysis," covers investigative plans and how to set up your forensic workstation for a specific investigation. It also outlines the step-by-step process that you follow to retrieve the potential evidence.

Chapter 11, "E-mail Investigations," covers e-mail and Internet fundamentals and then examines e-mail crimes and violations. It also reviews some of the popular e-mail forensics tools that are currently available.

Chapter 12, "Recovering Image Files," explains how to recover image files on an evidence disk and examines image recovery tools, data compression, and restoring graphics. It also discusses steganography and copyright issues.

Chapter 13, "Writing Investigation Reports," explains how to create formal and informal reports for computer forensics investigations.

Chapter 14, "Becoming an Expert Witness," explores the role of the expert witness, including developing a curriculum vita and tracking your qualifications as you acquire them. It also describes the differences between an expert and a technical witness.

Appendix A, "Certification Test References," examines the certifications that are currently available.

Appendix B, "Computer Forensics References," contains an alphabetical list of Web sites and publications that are available for computer forensic investigators.

Appendix C, "Procedures for Corporate High-Technology Investigations," contains tables of commands that are referenced throughout the text.

FEATURES

To aid you in fully understanding networking concepts, this book includes many features designed to enhance your learning experience.

- **Chapter Objectives.** Each chapter begins with a detailed list of the concepts to be mastered within that chapter. This list provides you with both a quick reference to the chapter's contents and a useful study aid.

- **Illustrations and Tables.** Illustrations are provided to step you through various commands and forensics tools. Extra graphics are included for tools that are not included with the text or do not provide free demonstration versions. Tables are provided to detail useful commands.

- **Chapter Summaries.** Each chapter's text is followed by a summary of the concepts introduced in that chapter. These summaries provide a helpful way to recap and revisit the ideas covered in each chapter.

- **Key Terms.** All of the terms within the chapter that were introduced with boldfaced text are gathered together in the Key Terms list at the end of the chapter. This provides you with a method of checking your understanding of all the terms introduced.

TEXT AND GRAPHIC CONVENTIONS

Wherever appropriate, additional information and exercises have been added to this book to help you better understand the topic at hand. Icons throughout the text alert you to additional materials. The icons used in this textbook are described below.

The Note icon draws your attention to additional helpful material related to the subject being described.

Tips based on the author's experience provide extra information about how to attack a problem or what to do in real-world situations.

PHOTO CREDITS

Figure 1-2: 8088 computer courtesy of IBM Corporate Archives

Figure 6-10: BIAProtect portable forensics unit courtesy of Business Intelligence Associates (www.biaprotect.com)

Figure 6-15: Forensic Recovery of Evidence Data Center (FREDC) courtesy of Digital Intelligence, Inc.

Figure 6-16: Fred unit courtesy of Digital Intelligence, Inc.

ACKNOWLEDGMENTS

The team would like to express its appreciation to Will Pitkin, the Acquisitions Editor who has given us a great deal of moral support; Joe Virzi, the book representative who made this all possible; and Joe Dougherty, the President of Course Technology, for listening to our ideas. We would like to thank the entire Editorial and Production staff for their dedication and fortitude during this project, including Amy Lyon, the Product Manager, Megan Belanger, the Production Editor, Lisa Ruffolo, the Developmental Editor, as well as the testers in the Quality Assurance department, Marianne Snow and Serge Palladino. We also appreciate the careful reading and thoughtful suggestions of the reviewers: Russell Davis, Larry Dombrowski, Mark Edmead, and Michael Sthultz. We also would like to thank Franklin Clark, an investigator for the Pierce County Prosecutor in Tacoma, WA for his input, and Mike Lacey for his photos.

We also appreciate the careful reading and thoughtful suggestions of the reviewers: Russell Davis, Larry Dombrowski, Mark Edmead, and Michael Sthultz.

Bill Nelson

The writing of this book required extensive teamwork. This teamwork extended beyond my coauthors, Amelia, Frank, and Chris. It extended to our families, friends, and editors. Without this team effort, this book would not have succeeded.

I would especially like to express my gratitude to my wife Tricia for her support during the long hours I spent writing. Her support during and after this book production is appreciated very much. She did a wonderful job of minimizing life's daily distractions, allowing me to concentrate on my writing. In addition to Tricia's support, I need to mention my mother and father, Celia and Harry, for their sustained enthusiastic support through my writing journey. As for my coauthors, their team attitude shows what can be accomplished from a group of highly skilled professionals. Our brainstorming sessions provided inspiration, the sharing of knowledge, and even entertainment. I would like to especially thank my coauthor Amelia for prompting me to work on this book. Without her encouragement and positive attitude, we would not have accomplished this production.

I need to also extend my appreciation to my longtime professional friend, Franklin Clark, of the Pierce County Prosecutors Office in Tacoma, Washington. Frank was my key inspiration in the writing of this book. His guidance and wisdom in high technology investigations is second to none. I will continue to appreciate his friendship and counsel. And finally, I would like to express my appreciation to my lifelong friend Mike Lacey for his contribution of the many digital images used for this book.

Amelia Phillips

This book is dedicated to the memory of Thomas Leonard, founder of CoachU.com, Coachville.com, and a man who inspired me to do things I never thought I could.

I want to thank my co-authors for their fantastic fortitude and good humor throughout the learning experience we have had. Also thanks to all my friends for listening to me gripe for the last year.

Frank Enfinger

I want to express my appreciation to my wife for dealing with the kids and all the distractions as I spent long hours and sleepless nights creating the exercises for my chapters in this book. I also want to thank my children for the time I couldn't spend with them. My coauthors were very supportive, and I have enjoyed working with them.

Christopher K. Steuart

I would like to express my appreciation to my wife Josephine, son Alexander, and daughter Isobel for their enthusiastic support of my commitment to *Computer Forensics and Investigations,* even as it consumed time and energy that they deserved. I would like to thank my parents, William and Mary, for their support of my education and the development of the skills needed for this project. I thank my co-authors, Bill, Amelia, and Frank, for inviting me to join them in this project. I would like to express my appreciation to Lieutenant General (then Captain) Edward Soriano for seeing the potential in me as a young soldier and encouraging me in learning the skills and processes required to administer, communicate with, and command an organization within the structure of law, regulation, and personal commitment. I thank the faculty of Drake University Law School and particularly Professor James A. Albert for encouraging me to think and write creatively about the law.

ABOUT THE AUTHORS

Bill Nelson has been a computer forensics investigator for a Fortune 50 company for over six years and has developed high-tech investigation programs for professional organizations and colleges. His previous experience includes Automated Fingerprint Identification System (AFIS) software engineering and reserve police work. Bill has served as president and vice-president for Computer Technology Investigators Northwest (CTIN) and is a member of Computer Related Information Management and Education (CRIME). He routinely lectures at several colleges and universities in the Pacific Northwest.

Amelia Phillips is a graduate of Massachusetts Institute of Technology with BS degrees in Astronautical Engineering and Archaeology and an MBA in Technology Management. After serving as an engineer at the Jet Propulsion Lab, she worked with e-commerce Web sites, and began her training in computer forensics to prevent credit card numbers from being stolen from sensitive e-commerce databases. She designed programs for community colleges in e-commerce, computer forensics, and data recovery. Amelia also consults with developing nations to help provide retention, e-learning, and entrepreneurship programs as a result of grants obtained by her employer, Highline Community College.

Frank Enfinger is a tenured professor at North Seattle Community College as well as a Computing Forensic Specialist with a local police department. Prior to entering the computing industry, Professor Enfinger served a tour of duty in the United States Marine Corps. Over the years, Professor Enfinger has worked with computer technology for a number of corporate and government entities, including hospitals, Internet service providers, and environmental protection companies. Professor Enfinger has earned a degree and numerous certifications in the field of Computer Science and continues to work with evolving technologies.

Christopher K. Steuart is a practicing attorney maintaining a general litigation practice, with experience in information systems security for a Fortune 50 company and the U.S. Army. He has presented computer forensics seminars in regional and national forums including the American Society for Industrial Security (ASIS), Agora, Northwest Computer Technology Crime Analysis Seminar (NCT), and CTIN.

Read This Before You Begin

The following section lists the minimum hardware requirements that allow you to complete all the steps in this book. In addition to the items listed, you must be able to download and install demo versions of software.

MINIMUM LAB REQUIREMENTS

- Computers that boot to a true command line to run Digital Intelligence's DriveSpy and Image. Windows XP does not allow these programs to run.
- Lab computers that boot to Windows XP or 2000
- Computers that dual boot to Linux or UNIX
- At least one Macintosh computer

The steps in this text are designed with the following hardware and software requirements in mind. The lab in which most of the work takes place should be a typical network training lab with a variety of operating systems and computers available, including a Windows XP, 2000, or 9x computer and a Linux computer.

OPERATING SYSTEMS AND HARDWARE

Windows XP and 2000

Use a standard installation of the Home, Professional, or Server versions. The computer running Windows XP or 2000 should meet the following minimum requirements:

- 3 1/2-inch floppy disk drive
- CD-ROM drive
- VGA or higher monitor
- Hard disk partition of 10 GB or more
- Mouse or other pointing device
- Keyboard
- 128 MB RAM

Windows 9x

Some steps require access to a computer that can boot directly to a DOS prompt. You can also run many GUI programs on these machines, but they might require more memory than listed below. The computer running Windows 95 or 98 should meet the following minimum requirements:

- *Windows 95:* 8 MB RAM with 24 MB or more recommended
  Windows 98: 16 MB RAM with 24 MB or more recommended

- Hard disk partition of 1 GB or more

- Other hardware requirements are the same as those listed for the Windows XP computer

Linux

This text assumes that you are using the Red Hat Linux 7.3 standard installation. Some optional steps require the GIMP graphics editor, which must be installed separately in Red Hat Linux 7.3. Linux can be installed on a dual-boot computer as long as one or more partitions of at least 2 GB are reserved for the Linux OS.

- Hard disk partition of 2 GB or more reserved for Linux

- Other hardware requirements are the same as those listed for the Windows XP computer

COMPUTER FORENSICS SOFTWARE

This book heavily references two computer forensics programs: DriveSpy and Image, both developed by Digital Intelligence, Inc. DriveSpy and Image are DOS programs that run from a true DOS prompt rather than from a DOS shell. DriveSpy and Image both run on Windows 98 only. These software programs require a true DOS prompt. This necessitates a dual boot setup that includes Windows 98 if you wish to utilize the software.

This book also includes steps that involve the following software, which can be downloaded via the Internet. You can download freeware, shareware, or free demo versions of these programs. Because Web site addresses change frequently, use a search engine to find the following software online if the addresses are no longer valid.

- *AccessData Forensic ToolKit*: Download the demo version from *www.accessdata.com*.

- *Hex Workshop*: Download the trial version from *www.hexworkshop.com*. You can also use Norton Disk Edit or WinHex instead of Hex Workshop.

- *IrfanView*: Download from *www.irfanview.com*.

- *NTFSDOS*: Download from *www.sysinternals.com*.

- *SecureClean*: Download from *www.accessdata.com*.

- *Steganography tool (S-Tools suggested)*: Download from *www.stegoarchive.com*.

- *Tom's Root Boot Kit*: Download the freeware version from *www.tux.org*.

- *WinZip*: Download an evaluation version from *www.winzip.com/download.htm*.
- *JASC Paint Shop Pro*: Download a trial version from *www.jasc.com*.

In addition, you will use Microsoft Office Word (or other word-processing software) and Excel (or other spreadsheet software). For some chapter exercises, you will need to download supplemental data files from the Course PTR Web site. Simply go to *www.courseptr.com* and navigate to the page for this title. You can then download the data files directly from this page to your computer.

You will also need to have e-mail software, such as Microsoft Outlook Express or Eudora, installed on your computer.

1

COMPUTER FORENSICS AND INVESTIGATIONS AS A PROFESSION

After reading this chapter, you will be able to:
- Understand computer forensics
- Prepare for computing investigations
- Understand enforcement agency investigations
- Understand corporate investigations
- Maintain professional conduct

This chapter introduces you to computer forensics and investigations and discusses some of its problems and concerns. The field of computing investigations and forensics is still in the early stage of development. This book blends traditional investigation methods with classic systems-analysis problem-solving techniques and applies them to computing investigations. These disciplines combined with the implementation of computer forensics tools will make you a highly skilled computer forensic analyst.

UNDERSTANDING COMPUTER FORENSICS

Computer forensics involves obtaining and analyzing digital information for use as evidence in civil, criminal, or administrative cases. Until recently, legal professionals could not use digital evidence in court because it was not considered tangible evidence. Many court cases in state and federal courts and appellate decisions that were challenged and argued in the United States Supreme Court set precedents for using digital evidence. The **Fourth Amendment** to the United States Constitution, which protects the rights of the suspect, particularly as related to search and seizure, has also played a role in determining whether using digital evidence is a violation of privacy (see *www.usdoj.gov/criminal/cybercrime*).

Until 1988, investigators needed a separate search warrant to search for and seize computer evidence. A **search warrant** is a legal document that allows law enforcement to search an office, place of business, or other locale for evidence relating to an alleged crime.

The case described in the following summary was one that established a different precedent, so that separate search warrants may not be necessary. However, when preparing to search for evidence in a criminal case, many investigators still include the suspect's computer and its components in the search warrant to avoid problems. One of the breakthrough cases in the nation occurred in Pennsylvania. The case was the *Commonwealth v. Copenhefer* 555 PA 285,719 A.2d 242. When the detective summarized the case, he recognized that it established the legal foundation for the seizure and subsequent search of computers used in a crime. The detective investigated a homicide where the defendant saved incriminating information on his business computer. The defendant's attorney appealed to the Supreme Court to prevent the prosecution from using the evidence on his computer because the detective did not obtain a separate search warrant to search the computer. The courts sided with the prosecution.

The case involved a kidnapped woman who was eventually found dead and was probably murdered. Initial investigations by the Federal Bureau of Investigation (FBI), state police, and local police resulted in the discovery of a series of hidden computer-generated notes and instructions, each leading to another. The investigation also produced several possible suspects, including one who owned a nearby bookstore and had a history of hostile encounters with the victim and her husband.

In addition to finding physical evidence, investigators also examined a computer used by the victim's husband. They discovered a series of drafts and amendments to the text of a phone call the husband received, a ransom note, a series of other notes, and a detailed plan for kidnapping the victim. On direct appeal, the Supreme Court concluded that the physical evidence, especially the computer forensics evidence, was sufficient to support the conviction of the bookstore owner.

Comparing Definitions of Computer Forensics

According to DIBS USA, Inc., a privately-owned corporation specializing in computer forensics (*http://www.dibsusa.com*), computer forensics involves scientifically examining and analyzing data from computer storage media so that the data can be used as evidence in court. Investigating computers typically includes securely collecting computer data, examining the suspect data to determine details such as origin and content, presenting computer-based information to courts, and applying laws to computer practice.

In general, computer forensics investigates data that can be retrieved from the hard disk or other disks of a computer. Like an archaeologist excavating a site, computer investigators retrieve information from a computer or its component parts. The information you retrieve may already be on the disk, but it might not be easy to find or decipher. In contrast, **network forensics** yields information about which ports were used to access a computer or which ports a computer accessed to commit a crime. Network forensics uses log files to determine when someone logged on or last used their login ID. The network forensics investigator tries to determine which Uniform Resource Locators (URLs) a user accessed, how he or she logged on to the network, and from what location. This book discusses when network forensics should be used in your investigation.

Computer forensics is different from **data recovery**, which involves recovering information from a computer that the user deleted by mistake or lost during a power surge, for example. Computer forensics tries to recover data that users have hidden or deleted in a way that allows it to be used as evidence. The evidence can be incriminating or **exculpatory**, meaning it may clear the suspect. Investigators often examine a computer disk not knowing whether it contains evidence—they must search storage media, and if they find data, they piece it together to produce evidence. Investigators can also use electron microscopes and other sophisticated equipment to retrieve information from machines that have been damaged or purposefully reformatted.

Like companies specializing in data recovery, companies specializing in **disaster recovery** use computer forensics techniques to retrieve information lost by their clients. Disaster recovery also involves preventing data loss by using backups, UPS devices, and off-site monitoring.

Investigators often work as a team to make computers and networks secure in an organization. Computing investigations and forensics is one of three functions in a triad that makes up computing security. In the enterprise-network environment, the triad consists of the following parts:

- Vulnerability assessment and risk management
- Network intrusion detection and incident response
- Computing investigations

Figure 1-1 shows how these three parts of computing security are related. Each side of the triad represents a group or department responsible for performing the associated tasks. Although each function operates independently, when conducting a large-scale computing investigation, all three groups draw from one another. By combining each of these three groups into a team, all aspects of a high-technology investigation are addressed without calling in outside specialists.

Figure 1-1   Investigations triad

The **enterprise environment** refers to large corporate computing systems that may include one or more disparate or formerly independent systems. In smaller companies, one group might perform the tasks shown in the investigations triad, or they might contract with other companies to perform them.

When you work in the **vulnerability assessment and risk management** group, you test and verify the integrity of stand-alone workstations and network servers. This integrity check covers the physical security of systems, and the security of operating systems (OSs) and applications. People who work in this group test for known vulnerabilities of OSs and applications used throughout the network. This group mounts attacks on the network to connected computer workstations and servers to assess vulnerabilities. Individuals performing this task typically have several years of experience in UNIX and Windows NT/2000/XP administration.

Professionals in the vulnerability assessment and risk management group also possess skills in **network intrusion detection and incident response**. This group detects attacks from intruders by using automated tools and the manual process of monitoring network firewall logs. When an attack is detected, the response team tracks, locates, identifies, and denies the intruder further access to the network. If an intruder is launching an attack that causes significant or potential damage, this team collects the necessary evidence, which may be used for civil or criminal litigation against the intruders. **Litigation** is the legal process to prove guilt or innocence in court.

If an unauthorized user is using the network or if any user is performing illegal acts, the network intrusion detection and incident response group responds by locating the user or blocking the user's access. For example, someone at a community college recently sent inflammatory e-mails to other users on the network. The network team realized quickly that the e-mails were coming from a node on their own network, and dispatched a security team to the location. Historically, vulnerability assessment staff contributes significantly to high-end computing investigations.

The **computing investigations** group manages investigations and conducts forensic analysis of systems suspected of containing evidence relating to an incident or crime. For complex casework, the computing investigations group draws on resources from those involved in vulnerability assessment, risk management, and network intrusion detection and incident response. Computing investigations completes all case investigations.

Exploring a Brief History of Computer Forensics

Thirty years ago, most people did not imagine that computers would be an integral part of everyday life. Now computer technology is commonplace, as are the crimes where the computer is both the instrument of the crime and the location where evidence is stored or recorded.

In the 1970s, electronic evidence did not hold up in court because the fields of computing and computer forensics were new. Yet, electronic crimes were being committed, usually those involving white-collar fraud. Most computers in this era were mainframes, and they were used by an exclusive realm of highly educated and specialized people. People who used mainframe computers worked in banks, engineering, and academia. White-collar fraud began when people in those industries saw a way to make money by manipulating computer data.

One of the most well-known crimes of the mainframe era was the one-half cent crime. It was common for banks to track monies in accounts to the third decimal place or more. Banks used and still use the "rounding up" accounting method when paying interest. If the interest applied to an account resulted in a fraction of a cent, that fraction would be used in the calculation for the next account until the total resulted in a whole cent. It was assumed that sooner or later every customer would benefit. This method was corrupted on more than one occasion by computer programmers who would open an account for themselves and write programs so all the fractional monies went into their accounts. In smaller banks, this would amount to only a few hundred dollars a month. In larger banks with branch offices, however, the amount of money reached hundreds of thousands of dollars.

In the 1970s and early 1980s, when crimes such as the one-half cent crime were being committed, most law-enforcement officers did not know enough about computers to ask the right questions or to preserve evidence for trial. Many attended the Federal Law Enforcement Training Center (FLETC) programs that were designed to train law enforcement in recovering digital data.

As personal computers (PCs) gained popularity and began to replace mainframe computers in the 1980s, many different OSs emerged. Apple released the Apple 2E in 1982, and then launched the Macintosh in 1984. Computers such as the TRS-80 and the Commodore 64 were the machines of the day. CP/M machines (the 8088 series) and Zeniths were also in demand.

The disk operating system (DOS) was available in many varieties, including PC-DOS, QDOS, DR-DOS, IBM-DOS, and MS-DOS. Forensics tools at that time were simple, and most were generated by government agencies such as the Royal Canadian Mounted Police (RCMP) in Ottawa, who had their own investigative tools, and the United States Internal Revenue Service (IRS). Most of these tools were written in C and assembly language, and were not used by the general public.

In the mid–1980s, a new tool called X-Tree Gold appeared. It recognized file types and retrieved lost or deleted files. Norton Disk Edit soon followed, and became the best tool to find deleted files. You could use these tools on the most powerful PCs of that time; IBM-compatible computers had 10 MB hard disks and two floppy drives, as shown in Figure 1-2.

Figure 1-2   8088 computer

In 1986, Apple produced the Mac SE, a Macintosh that was available with an external EasyDrive hard disk with 60 MB of storage (see Figure 1-3). At this time, the Commodore 64 was a popular computer that still used standard audiotapes to record data, so the Mac SE represented a significant advance in computer technology.

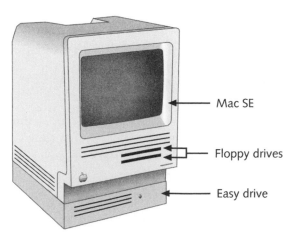

Mac SE

Floppy drives

Easy drive

Figure 1-3   Macintosh SE with external hard drive

By the early 1990s, specialized tools for computer forensics appeared. The **International Association of Computer Investigative Specialists (IACIS)** introduced training on the currently available software for forensic investigations and the IRS created search-warrant programs. However, no commercial software for computer forensics was available until ASR Data created Expert Witness for the Macintosh. This software can recover deleted files and fragments of deleted files. One of the partners later left and developed Encase, which has become a popular computer forensics tool.

As computer technology continued to grow, so did computer-forensics software. The introduction of large hard disks posed new problems for investigators. Most DOS-based software does not recognize a hard disk larger than 8 GB. Because contemporary computers have hard disks of 20 to 80 GB and larger, new forensics software is needed.

Other software, such as iLook, which is currently maintained by the IRS Criminal Investigation Division and limited to law enforcement, can analyze and read special data files that are copies of a disk. AccessData's Forensic Tool Kit (FTK) has become a popular commercial product that performs similar tasks in the law-enforcement and civilian markets. These tools and others are covered in Chapter 6.

As software companies become more savvy about computer forensics and investigations, they are publishing more forensic tools to keep pace with the technology. This book discusses as many tools as possible. You should also refer to trade publications and Web sites to stay current.

Developing Computer Forensics Resources

To be a successful computer forensics investigator, you must be familiar with more than one computing platform. In addition to older platforms such as DOS and Windows 9x, you should be familiar with Linux, Macintosh, and the current Windows platforms.

However, no one can be an expert in every aspect of computing. Likewise, you cannot know everything about the technology you are investigating. To supplement your knowledge, develop and maintain contact with computing, network, and investigative professionals. Keep a log of contacts, and record the names of other professionals with whom you have worked, their area of expertise, the last few projects you worked on together, and their particular contribution.

Join as many computer user groups as you can, both in the public and private sectors. In the Pacific Northwest, for example, **Computer Technology Investigators Northwest (CTIN)** meets monthly to discuss problems faced by law enforcement and corporations. This non-profit organization also conducts free training. You can probably locate a similar group in your area such as the **High Technology Crime Investigation Association (HTCIA)**, an organization that exchanges information about techniques related to computer investigations and security.

User groups can be especially helpful when you need information about obscure OSs. For example, a user group helped convict a child molester in Pierce County, WA, in 1996. The suspect installed video cameras in all the rooms of his house, served alcohol to young women to intoxicate them, and secretly filmed them playing strip poker. When he was accused of molesting a child, police seized his computers and other physical evidence. The investigator discovered that the computers used CoCoDos, an operating system that had been out of use for years. When the investigator contacted a local users group, they provided the standard commands and other information necessary to gain access to the system. On the suspect's computer, the investigator found a diary detailing the suspect's actions over the last 15 years, including the molestation of over 400 young women. As a result, the suspect received a much longer sentence than he would have if he had molested only one child.

Build a network of computer forensic experts and other professionals, and keep in touch via e-mail. Find and cultivate professional relationships with people who specialize in technical areas different from your own. If you are a Windows expert, maintain contact with experts in Linux, UNIX, and Macintosh.

Outside experts can provide detailed information that you need to retrieve digital evidence. For example, in a recent murder case, a husband and wife owned a Macintosh store. When the wife was discovered dead, probably murdered, investigators found that she had wanted to leave her husband, but didn't because of her religious beliefs. The police got a search warrant and confiscated the home and office computers.

When the detective on the case examined the home Macintosh, he found that the hard disk had been compressed and erased. He contacted a Macintosh engineer who determined the two software programs that had been used to compress the drive. Based on this information, the detective could retrieve information from the hard disk, including text files indicating that the husband had spent $35,000 in business funds to purchase cocaine and prostitution services. This proved to be a crucial piece of evidence that allowed the prosecutor to convict the husband of premeditated murder.

Take advantage of news services devoted to computer forensics, which you can access using your e-mail software. You can also post a description of a forensics problem on an automatic mailing list server such as listserv or Majordomo to solicit advice from experts. When you address mail to an automatic mailing list, it is broadcast to everyone on the list. In one case, an Intel computer contained digital evidence, but investigators couldn't access the hard disk without the password, which was hard-coded into the motherboard. When the detectives on the case began to run out of options and time, they posted a description of the problem on a listserv. Someone responded and told them that a dongle (a mechanical device) would bypass the password problem. As a result, they were able to convict the perpetrator.

PREPARING FOR COMPUTING INVESTIGATIONS

Computing investigations and forensics falls into two distinct categories: public investigations and private or corporate investigations (see Figure 1-4).

Private or corporate organizations
Company policy violations
Litigation disputes

Government agencies
Article 8 in the Charter of Rights
of Canada or
U.S. Fourth Amendment search
and seizure rules

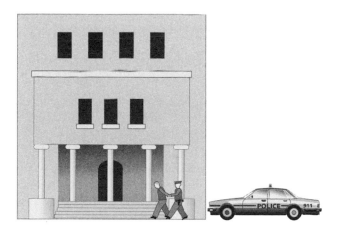

Figure 1-4 Public versus private sector investigations

Public investigations involve government agencies responsible for criminal investigations and prosecution. Government agencies range from local, county, and state or provincial police departments to federal regulatory enforcement agencies. These organizations must observe items such as Article 8 in the Charter of Rights of Canada and in the United States, Fourth Amendment issues relating to **search and seizure** rules (see Figure 1-5).

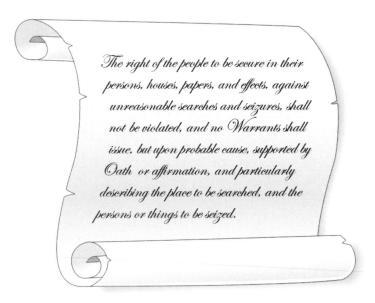

The right of the people to be secure in their persons, houses, papers, and effects, against unreasonable searches and seizures, shall not be violated, and no Warrants shall issue, but upon probable cause, supported by Oath or affirmation, and particularly describing the place to be searched, and the persons or things to be seized.

Figure 1-5   The Fourth Amendment

Criminal law protects the rights of the suspect, and as a computer investigator, you must be sure to follow these laws, especially the laws of search and seizure. The Department of Justice (DOJ) updates their infomation on computer search and seizure on a regular basis (see *http://www.usdoj.gov/criminal/cybercrime/*).

While public investigations typically involve criminal cases and government agencies, private or corporate investigations deal with private companies, non-enforcement government agencies, and lawyers. These private organizations are not governed directly by criminal law or Fourth Amendment issues, but by internal policies that define expected employee behavior and conduct in the workplace. Private corporate investigations also involve litigation disputes. Although private investigations are usually conducted in civil cases, a civil case can escalate into a criminal case, and a criminal case can be reduced to a civil case.

Understanding Enforcement Agency Investigations

When conducting public computing investigations, you must understand your local city, county, state or province, and federal laws on crimes relating to computers, including the standard legal processes and how to build a **criminal case**. In a criminal case, a suspect is tried for a criminal offense such as burglary, murder, or molestation. To determine if there was a computer crime, an investigator asks questions such as the following: What was the tool used to commit the crime? Was it a simple trespass? Was it a theft, a burglary, or vandalism? Did the perpetrator infringe on someone else's rights by cyberstalking or by harassing them?

Because computers and networks are only tools that can be used to commit crimes, and are therefore no different from a device a car thief uses to steal a car or the lock-pick a burglar uses to break into a house, many states have added specific language to their criminal codes to define crimes that involve computers. That is, many states have expanded the definition of laws such as burglary or theft to include taking data from a computer without the owner's permission, making computer theft the same as breaking into someone's house and stealing their silver.

 Until 1993, the laws defining computer crimes did not exist. To this day, many have yet to be tested in court.

NOTE

Other states have instituted specific criminal statutes that address computer-related crimes, but typically do not include computer-related issues in the standard trespass, theft, vandalism, or burglary laws.

Computers are involved in many serious crimes. The most notorious are those involving child molestation. Digital images are stored on the hard disks, Zip disks, floppy disks, and other storage media, and circulated on the Internet.

Other computer crimes concern missing children and adults because information about missing people is often found on computers. Drug dealers often keep information about their transactions on their computer or personal digital assistant (PDA). This information is especially useful because it helps law enforcement convict the person they arrested, and helps to locate the drug suppliers and other dealers.

In stalking cases, deleted e-mail, digital photos, and other digital evidence stored on a computer can help resolve a case.

Following the Legal Processes

When conducting a computer investigation for potential criminal violations of the law, the legal processes you follow depend on local custom, legislative standards, and rules of evidence. In general, however, a criminal case follows three stages: the complaint, the investigation, and the prosecution. Someone files a complaint, a specialist investigates the complaint and, with the help of a prosecutor, collects evidence and builds a case. If a crime has been committed, the case is tried in court. This process is outlined in Figure 1-6.

A criminal case begins when someone either finds evidence of an illegal act or witnesses an illegal act. The witness or victim, the complainant, makes a complaint to the police. Based on the incident or crime, the complainant makes an **allegation**, an accusation or supposition of fact that a crime has been committed.

A police officer or constable interviews the complainant and writes a report about the crime. The police department processes the report and the department's upper management decides to start an investigation or to log the information into a police blotter.

Figure 1-6   Public-sector case flow

The **police blotter** provides a record of clues to crimes that have been previously committed, and is an aid for all current and future investigations. Criminals typically repeat actions in their illegal activities, and these habits often appear in the police blotter. This historical knowledge is useful when conducting investigations, especially in the area of high-technology crimes.

Law enforcement is concerned with protecting the public good. As a result, not every good police officer is a computer expert. Some are computer novices, while others might be trained to recognize what they can retrieve from a computer disk. To differentiate the training and experience law officers receive, CTII has established three levels of law enforcement expertise:

- *Level 1*—Acquiring and seizing digital evidence, normally performed by a street police officer.

- *Level 2*—Managing high-tech investigations, teaching the investigator what to ask for, understanding computer terminology and what can and cannot be retrieved from digital evidence. The assigned detective(s) usually handle the case.

- *Level 3*—Specialist training retrieving digital evidence, normally performed by a data recovery or computer forensics expert, network forensics, or Internet fraud investigation.

If you are an investigator assigned to a case, recognize the level of expertise police officers and others involved have in the case. You should have Level 3 training to conduct the investigation and manage the case. You start by assessing the scope of the case, which includes the OS, hardware, and peripheral devices. You then determine whether resources are available to process all of the evidence. For example, determine whether you have the proper tools to collect and analyze the evidence, and whether you need to call on other specialists to assist in collecting and processing the evidence. After you have gathered the resources you need, your role is to delegate, collect, and process the information relating to the complaint.

After you build a case, the information is turned over to the prosecutor. Your job is finished when you have used all known and available methods to extract data from the digital evidence that was seized.

As the investigator, you must then present the collected evidence with a report to the government's attorney. Depending on your community and the nature of the crime, the prosecutor can be a prosecuting attorney, district attorney, state attorney, county attorney, Crown attorney, or a United States attorney. In large organizations, the actual prosecutor is typically a deputy or assistant attorney to the prosecuting attorney.

In a criminal or public case, if you have sufficient information that supports a search warrant, the prosecuting attorney may direct you to submit an **affidavit**, which is a sworn statement of support of facts about a crime or evidence of a crime to a judge requesting a search warrant prior to the seizure of evidence. Figure 1-7 shows a typical affidavit. It is your responsibility to write the affidavit, which must include **exhibits** (evidence) that support the allegation to justify the warrant. You must then have the affidavit **notarized** under sworn oath, verifying that the information in the affidavit is true.

After a judge approves and signs a search warrant, it is ready to be executed, meaning that you can collect evidence as defined by the warrant. After you collect the evidence, you process and analyze it to determine whether a crime actually occurred.

The evidence is then presented in court after which a verdict is handed down either by a judge, administrative law judge, or jury.

Understanding Corporate Investigations

Private or corporate investigations involve private companies and lawyers who address company policy violations and litigation disputes, such as wrongful termination.

When conducting a computer investigation for a private company, remember that business must continue with minimal interruption from your investigation. Because businesses are typically focused on continuing their usual operations and making profits, many in a private corporate environment consider your investigation and apprehension of a suspect secondary to stopping the violation and minimizing damage or loss to the business. Businesses also strive to minimize or eliminate litigation, which is an expensive way to address criminal or civil issues. Corporate computer crimes can involve e-mail harassment, falsification of data, gender and age discrimination, embezzlement, sabotage, and **industrial espionage**, which involves the selling of sensitive company information to a competitor. Anyone with access to a computer can commit these crimes.

Embezzlement is a common computer crime, particularly in small firms. Typically the owner is busy and trusts one person, such as the office manager, to handle daily transactions. When the office manager leaves, the owner discovers that some clients were overbilled, others were not billed at all, and money is missing. Rebuilding the paper and electronic trail can become tedious. Collecting enough to press charges may be beyond the owner's capabilities.

Corporate sabotage is most often committed by a disgruntled employee. The employee decides to take a job at a competitor's firm and collects critical files on a floppy or Zip disk before leaving. This can also lead to industrial espionage, which has intensified recently.

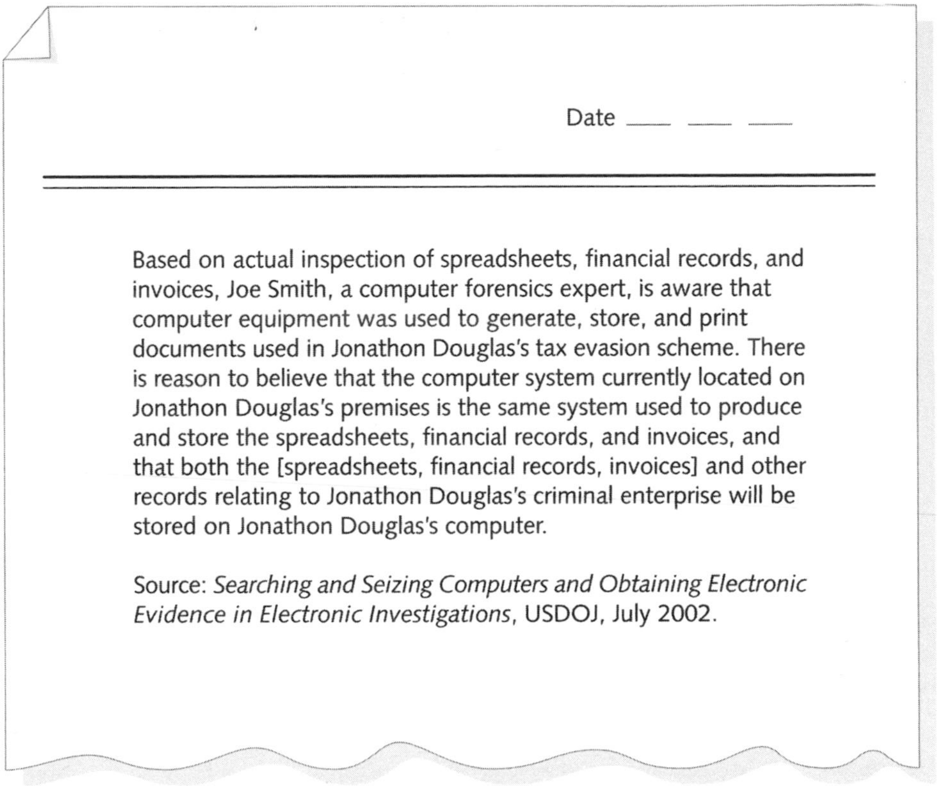

Date ____ ____ ____

Based on actual inspection of spreadsheets, financial records, and invoices, Joe Smith, a computer forensics expert, is aware that computer equipment was used to generate, store, and print documents used in Jonathon Douglas's tax evasion scheme. There is reason to believe that the computer system currently located on Jonathon Douglas's premises is the same system used to produce and store the spreadsheets, financial records, and invoices, and that both the [spreadsheets, financial records, invoices] and other records relating to Jonathon Douglas's criminal enterprise will be stored on Jonathon Douglas's computer.

Source: *Searching and Seizing Computers and Obtaining Electronic Evidence in Electronic Investigations*, USDOJ, July 2002.

Figure 1-7   Typical affidavit

Investigators will soon be able to conduct digital investigations on site without a lab and without interrupting work on a computer. Suppose that an assisted-care facility has an employee involved in an insurance scam. The person is overcharging the insurance company and then funneling the monies into their own bank account. The network server keeps track of patient billing and critical items such as medication, serious medical conditions, and treatments for each patient in the facility. To take that system offline for more than a short time could result in harm to one of the patients. Investigators cannot seize the evidence; instead, they acquire a disk image and any other information and allow the system to go back online as quickly as possible.

Organizations can help to prevent and address these crimes by creating and distributing appropriate policies, making employees aware of the policies, and enforcing them.

Establishing Company Policies

One way that businesses can avoid litigation is to publish and maintain policies that employees find easy to read and follow. The most important policies are those that set the rules for using the company's computers and networks. Published company policies provide the **line of authority** for a business to conduct internal investigations. The line of authority states who has the legal right to initiate an investigation, who can take possession of the evidence, and who can have access to the evidence.

Well-defined policies give computing investigations and forensics examiners the authority to conduct the investigation. Policies also demonstrate that an organization intends to be fair-minded and objective about how it treats employees, and that it will follow due process for all investigations. Without defined policies, a business risks exposing itself to litigation by current or former employees.

Displaying Warning Banners

Another way a private or public organization can avoid litigation is to display a warning banner on its computer screens. A **warning banner** typically appears when a computer boots or connects to the company intranet, network, or virtual private network (VPN) and informs the end user that the organization reserves the right to inspect computer systems and network traffic at will. (An **end user** is a person using a computer workstation to perform routine tasks other than systems administration.) Without explicitly stating this right, employees may have an assumed **right of privacy** when using a company's computer systems and network accesses. An assumed right of privacy is when an employee thinks that their transmissions at work are protected in much the same way that mail sent via the United States Postal Service is protected. Figure 1-8 shows a sample warning banner.

Figure 1-8 Sample warning banner

A warning banner establishes authority for conducting an investigation. By displaying a strong, well-worded warning banner, an organization does not need to obtain a search warrant or court order as required under the Fourth Amendment search and seizure rules. If a company owns the computer equipment, they do not need a search warrant to seize the machinery. This right to inspect or search at will applies to both criminal and company policy violations within a business with a well-defined policy.

Computer systems users can include employees or guests. Employees can access the intranet and guests typically can only access the main network. Companies can use two types of warning banners, one for internal employee access (intranet Web page access), and another for external visitor accesses (Internet Web page access). The following lists recommend the items that should be listed in all warning banners. Before applying these warnings, you should consult with the legal department of the sponsoring organization for any additional required legal notices for your area.

Depending upon the type of organization that you are part of, the following text can be used in internal warning banners:

- Access to this system and network is restricted.
- Use of this system and network is for official business only.
- Systems and networks are subject to monitoring at any time by the owner.
- Using this system implies consent to monitoring by the owner.
- Unauthorized or illegal users of this system or network will be subject to discipline or prosecution.

An organization such as a community college may simply state that systems and networks are subject to observation and monitoring at any time because members of the local community who are not staff or students may use the facilities. A for-profit organization may have proprietary information on their network and use all of the suggested items. Guests such as employees of business partners may regularly use the system.

The text that appears when a guest attempts to log on can be similar to the warnings in the following list:

- This system is the property of Company-X.
- This system is for authorized use only; unauthorized access is a violation of law and violators will be prosecuted.
- All activity, software, network traffic, and communications are subject to monitoring.

As a corporate computing investigator, make sure a company displays a well-defined warning banner. Without it, you have no authority to inspect systems for employee policy violations. Some might argue that written policies are all that are necessary. However, in the actual prosecution of cases, the warning banner is what won in the end. A prosecutor can more easily show a warning banner to a jury than a policy manual.

Many government agencies, such as the Department of Energy, Argonne National Labs, and Lawrence Livermore Labs, now require warning banners on all computer consoles on their system.

Designating an Authorized Requester

As mentioned earlier, investigations must establish a line of authority. In addition to warning banners that state a company's rights of computer ownership, businesses should specify an **authorized requester** who is authorized to conduct investigations. The executive management should define this policy to avoid conflicts of interest from competing organizations or departments. In large organizations, competition for funding or management support can become so fierce that people may weave false allegations of misconduct to prevent a competing department from delivering a proposal for the same pot of funds.

Executive management must also define and limit who is authorized to request a computing investigation and forensic analysis to avoid trivial or inappropriate investigations. The fewer groups that have authority to request a computing-related investigation, the better. Examples of groups that should be considered to have direct authority to request computer investigations in the corporate environment include the following:

- Corporate Security Investigations
- Corporate Ethics Office
- Corporate Equal Employment Opportunity Office
- Internal Auditing
- The General Counsel, Legal Department

All other groups such as Human Resources or Personnel should coordinate their request through the Corporate Security Investigations group for the purpose of separation of power in the employee's discipline.

Conducting Security Investigations

Conducting a computing investigation in the private sector is not much different from conducting one in the public sector. During public investigations you search for evidence to support criminal allegations. During private investigations you search for evidence to support allegations of abuse of a company's assets and in some cases, criminal complaints. Three types of situations are common in the computing enterprise:

- Abuse or misuse
- E-mail abuse
- Internet abuse

Most computing investigations in the private sector involve misuse of computing assets. This misuse is typically referred to as employee abuse. Computing abuse complaints center around e-mail and Internet misuse by employees, but may involve other computing resources such as using company software to produce a product for personal profit. Figure 1-9 shows how employees can abuse their company computer privileges.

Figure 1-9   Employee abuse of computer privileges

The scope of an e-mail investigation ranges from the excessive use of a company's e-mail system for personal use to making threats to others via e-mail. Some of the most common e-mail abuses involve transmitting offensive and lewd messages. These types of messages create a **hostile work environment** that can cause an employee to file a civil law suit against a company that does nothing to prevent it.

In addition to e-mail and general abuse, computer investigators also examine Internet abuse. Abuse of Internet privileges by employees range from excessive use, such as spending all day Web surfing, to viewing pornographic pictures via the Web while at work.

An extreme situation of Internet abuse is the online viewing of contraband pornographic images, such as child pornography. Viewing contraband images is a criminal act in most places and must be handled with the highest level of professionalism by the computing investigator. In later chapters, you learn the procedures and processes that are necessary to conduct these types of investigations.

By enforcing policy consistently, a company minimizes its liability exposure. The role of a computing investigator is to verify and help management correct abuse problems in an organization.

Be sure to distinguish between a company's abuse problems and potential criminal problems. Abuse problems violate company policy, but may not be illegal if performed at home. Criminal problems involve acts such as industrial espionage, embezzlement, and murder. However, actions that appear to relate to internal abuse might escalate to criminal or possible civil litigation. Because of this, you must treat all the evidence you collect with the highest level of security and regard. Later in this book, you learn the rules of evidence and apply them to computing investigations.

Similarly, your private corporate investigation may appear to involve a civil, non-criminal matter, but as you progress through your analysis, it may turn into a criminal matter. Because of this, you must always remember that all your work can come under the scrutiny of the legal system, either civil or criminal. By applying the same standards to civil investigations that are applied to criminal investigations, you eliminate any concerns. These standards are stressed throughout the book.

Corporations often employ what is called a **silver-platter doctrine**, which is credible evidence delivered from a non law-enforcement agent to a law-enforcement officer. Remember that a police officer is a law-enforcement agent. If you are a corporate investigator, your job is to minimize the risk to your company. After you turn the evidence over to law enforcement and begin working under their direction, all evidence is subject to Fourth Amendment rules.

Litigation is costly, so after you have assembled evidence, offending employees are typically disciplined or let go with a minimum of fanfare. However, in those cases in which you discover a criminal act has been committed involving a third-party victim, you generally have a legal and moral obligation to turn the information over to law enforcement.

In the next section, you will be exposed to situations in which the criminal evidence must be separated from any corporate proprietary information.

Distinguishing Personal and Company Property

Many company policies distinguish between personal and company computer property. One area that is difficult to distinguish involves PDAs and personal laptops. Suppose an employee purchases a PDA and hooks up the device to their company computer as shown in Figure 1-10. As they synchronize the information on their PDA with the information in their copy of Microsoft Outlook, they copy some of the data in their PDA to the company network. Because it is on the company network, does the information on the PDA belong to the company or the employee?

Now suppose that the company gave the employee the PDA as part of their holiday bonus. Can the company claim rights to the PDA? Similar issues come up when an employee brings in a personal laptop and hooks it up to the company network. What rules apply? These are issues that you will encounter as computers become more entrenched into daily life. These questions are still being debated and companies are establishing their own policies to handle this type of situation.

Figure 1-10   Personal versus company property

MAINTAINING PROFESSIONAL CONDUCT

Your **professional conduct** as a computing investigation and forensics analyst is critical because it determines your credibility. Professional conduct includes ethics, morals,
and standards of behavior. As a professional, you must exhibit the highest level of ethical
behavior at all times. To do so, you must maintain objectivity and confidentiality during
an investigation, enrich your technical knowledge, and conduct yourself with integrity.
By watching any current crime drama, you can see how attorneys attack the character of
witnesses. Your character should be beyond reproach.

NOTE
Maintaining objectivity means you must form and sustain unbiased opinions
of your cases. Avoid making conclusions about your findings until you have
exhausted all possible leads and considered every available fact. Your ultimate
responsibility is to find the digital evidence to support the allegation or exclude
the defendant from the criminal conduct. You must ignore external biases to
maintain the integrity of your fact-finding in all investigations. For example, if
you are employed by an attorney, do not allow the attorney's agenda to dic-
tate the outcome of your investigation. Your reputation and livelihood depend
on being objective in all matters.

You must also maintain the credibility of an investigation by keeping the case confidential.
Only discuss the case with people that need to know about it, such as other investigators
involved in the case or someone in the line of authority asking for an update. If you need

advice from other professionals, discuss only the general terms and facts about the case without mentioning specifics. All investigations you conduct must be kept confidential, until you are designated as a witness or required to release a report at the direction of the attorney or the court.

In the corporate environment confidentiality is critical, especially when dealing with employees who are released because they were running their company at work on company machinery and time. The agreement might have been to lay off the employee without benefits or unemployment compensation in exchange for no bad references. If you provide the details of the case and the name of the employee to others, your company could be sued for breach of contract.

In rare instances, your corporate case may become a criminal case as serious as murder. Because of the legal system, it may be years before the trial gets to court. If an investigator were to talk about the digital evidence, the case could be dismissed because of a technicality.

When working for an attorney on an investigation, the attorney-work-product rule and attorney-client-privilege communications applies. This means you can only discuss the case with the attorney. All communications about the case to other persons require the approval of the attorney.

In addition to maintaining objectivity and confidentiality, you can also enhance your professional conduct by continuing your training. The field of computing investigations and forensics is constantly changing. You should stay current with the latest technical changes in computing hardware and software, networking, and computing forensic tools. You should also learn about the latest investigation techniques that you can apply to your cases.

One way to enrich your knowledge of computing investigations is to record your fact-finding methods in a **journal**. The journal can help you remember how to perform tasks and procedures and use tools for both hardware and software. Be sure to include dates and significant details that serve as memory triggers. Develop a routine of regularly reviewing your journal to keep your past achievements fresh in your mind.

You should also continue your professional training. In addition to attending workshops, conferences, and vendor-specific courses which are conducted by software manufacturers for their product, you might also need to continue your formal education. You enhance your professional standing if you have at least an undergraduate bachelor degree in a computing field. If you do not have an advanced degree, consider graduate-level studies in a complementary area of study, such as business law or e-commerce.

Companies often supplement your education in exchange for a commitment to additional employment time.

TIP

In addition to education and training, membership in professional organizations adds to your credentials. These organizations typically sponsor training and provide information exchanges of the latest technical improvements and trends in computing investigations. Also monitor the latest book releases and read as much as possible about computer investigations and forensics (see Figure 1-11).

Figure 1-11   Ensure your future

As a computing investigations and forensics professional, your community expects you to achieve a high public and private standing and maintain honesty and integrity. You must conduct yourself with the highest levels of integrity in all aspects of your life. Any indiscreet actions on your part can cause you embarrassment, and can provide opportunities for an opposing attorney to discredit you during your testimony in court or in depositions.

Chapter Summary

- ☐ Computer forensics is the systematic accumulation of digital evidence in the investigation of a criminal or corporate-level violation. Computer forensics differs from network forensics, data recovery, and disaster recovery in scope and objective.

- ☐ Laws for digital evidence were established in the late 1980s.

- ☐ To be a successful computer forensics investigator, you must be familiar with more than one computing platform. To supplement your knowledge, develop and maintain contact with computing, network, and investigative professionals.

❏ Public and private computer investigations differ in that public investigations require a search warrant before the digital evidence is seized. Fourth Amendment rights also apply. During public investigations you search for evidence to support criminal allegations. During private investigations you search for evidence to support allegations of abuse of a company's assets and in some cases, criminal complaints.

❏ The silver-platter doctrine refers to handing the results of private investigations over to the authorities because of indications of criminal activity.

❏ A computer forensics investigator must keep an impeccable reputation at all times in case they are called into court to testify.

KEY TERMS

affidavit—The legal document that an investigator creates outlining the details of a case. In many cases, this document is used to issue a warrant or deal with abuse in a corporation.

allegation—A charge made against someone or something before proof has been found.

authorized requester—In a corporation or company entity, the persons who have the right to request an investigation such as the chief security officer or chief intelligence officer.

computing forensics—Applying scientific methods to retrieve data and/or information from digital evidence.

computing investigations—The detailed examination and collection of facts and data from a computer and its operating system used in an affidavit or warrant.

criminal case—A case in which criminal law must be applied.

criminal law—The statutes in your country or jurisdiction that determine what items must be addressed in an investigation.

Computer Technology Investigators Northwest (CTIN)—A non-profit group based in the Seattle-Tacoma, Washington, area comprised of law enforcement and private corporations whose aim is to improve the quality of investigations in the Pacific northwest.

data recovery—A specialty in which companies retrieve files accidentally or purposefully deleted.

disaster recovery—A specialty in which companies do real-time backups, monitoring, and data recovery.

end user—The person who uses a software package. In most cases this person has less expertise than the software designer.

enterprise environment—Refers to large corporate computing systems that may include one or more disparate or formerly independent systems.

exculpatory—Evidence that indicates the suspect is innocent of the crime.

exhibits—Items used in court to prove a case.

Fourth Amendment—The Fourth Amendment to the United States Constitution contained in the Bill of Rights. It dictates that you must have probable cause for search and seizure.

High Technology Crime Investigation Association (HTCIA)—A non-profit association for solving international computer crimes.

hostile work environment—An environment in which a person cannot perform his or her assigned duties. In the workplace, this normally includes actions such as sending threatening or demeaning e-mail or a co-worker viewing hate sites.

industrial espionage—Selling of sensitive company or proprietary information to a competitor.

International Association of Computer Investigative Specialists (IACIS)—An organization created to provide training and software for law enforcement in the computer forensics field.

journal—A notebook or series of notebooks in which you record the techniques you used and the people who assisted you with specific types of investigations.

line of authority—The people or positions specified in a company policy who have the right to initiate an investigation.

litigation—The legal process taken to prove a person's or entity's guilt or innocence in a court of law.

network forensics—Information obtained about which ports were used to access a computer or which ports a computer accessed to commit a crime.

network intrusion detection and incident response—Detecting attacks from intruders by using automated tools and the manual process of monitoring network firewall logs.

notarize—To have a document witnessed and a person clearly identified as the source before a notary public.

police blotter—A journal of criminal activity used to inform law-enforcement personnel of current criminal activities.

professional conduct—Behavior expected of an employee in the workplace or other such professional setting.

right of privacy—When an employee thinks that their transmissions at work are protected.

search and seizure—The legal act of acquiring evidence for an investigation. *See* Fourth Amendment.

search warrant—The legal document that allows law enforcement to search an office, place of business, or other locale for evidence relating to an alleged crime.

silver-platter doctrine—The policy of submitting to the police by an investigator who is not an agent of the court when a criminal act has been uncovered.

vulnerability assessment and risk management—Determining the weakest points in a system, then calculating the return on investment to decide which ones have to be fixed.

warning banner—Text that appears when someone logs on to a company computer that tells them the appropriate use of the machine or Internet access.

2

UNDERSTANDING
COMPUTER INVESTIGATIONS

After reading this chapter, you will be able to:
- Prepare a case
- Begin an investigation
- Understand data-recovery workstations and software
- Execute an investigation
- Complete a case
- Critique a case

This chapter explains how to manage a computing investigation. You will learn about the problems and challenges that examiners face when preparing and processing investigations, including the ideas and questions they must consider. This chapter also introduces you to popular computer-forensic software and explains how to use it. Throughout this chapter, you examine the details and differences among software packages, and learn how to use the software in different scenarios. You also explore standard problem-solving techniques.

As a basic computer user, you can solve most software problems by working with a graphical user interface (GUI). A forensics professional, however, needs to interact with primary levels of the operating system (OS) that are more fundamental than a GUI. You should be comfortable working at the command line. Many computer-forensic software tools involve working at the command line, and you should be prepared to learn how to use these tools.

You will work with floppy disks to perform the steps in this chapter. Once you know how to search for and find data on a small storage device, you can apply the same techniques to a large disk, such as a 20 GB hard disk.

PREPARING A COMPUTER INVESTIGATION

Your role as a computer-forensic professional is to gather evidence from a suspect's computer and determine whether the suspect committed a crime or violated a company policy. If the evidence suggests that the suspect committed a crime or violated a policy, you begin to prepare a case, which is a collection of evidence you can offer in court or at a corporate inquiry. To gather the evidence in a computer-forensic case, you investigate the suspect's computer, and then preserve the evidence on a different computer. Before you begin investigating, you must follow an accepted procedure to prepare a case. By approaching each case methodically, you can evaluate the evidence thoroughly and document the chain of evidence, or **chain of custody**, which is the route that the evidence takes from the time you find it until the case is closed or goes to court.

The following sections present two sample cases—one involving a computer crime and another involving a company-policy violation. Each describes the typical steps of a forensics investigation, including gathering evidence, preparing a case, and preserving the evidence.

Examining a Computer Crime

Law enforcement often finds computers and components as they are investigating crimes, gathering other evidence, or making arrests. Computers can contain information that helps law enforcement determine the chain of events leading to a crime or provide evidence that is more likely to lead to a conviction. For example, consider the following scenario in which computers are involved in a crime. The police raided a suspected drug dealer's home, and found a computer and several floppy disks in a bedroom (see Figure 2-1). Two computers were "bagged and tagged" as part of the search and seizure, meaning they were placed in evidence bags and then labeled with tags. The lead detective on the case wants you to investigate the computer to find data that could be evidence of a crime, such as drug-related files for the dealer's contacts, and then organize the data.

The acquisitions officer gives you documentation regarding items collected with the computer, including a list of the other storage media such as floppy disks, CDs, and DVDs that investigating officers found. The acquisitions officer also notes that the computer is a Windows XP system and that the machine was running when they discovered it. Before shutting down the computer, officers photographed all the open windows on the Windows desktop, including one showing Windows Explorer. The acquisitions officer provides you with the digital photos of the desktop.

In your preliminary assessment, you assume that the floppy disks, hard disk, and other storage media include intact files, such as e-mail messages, deleted files, and hidden files. You have a range of software to use in your investigation. Your office owns Digital Intelligence DriveSpy and Image, Norton Disk Utilities, Guidance Software EnCase, and AccessData Forensics Toolkit. In Chapter 6, you will learn the strengths and weaknesses of each of these software packages.

After your preliminary assessment, you determine the risks in this case. Because drug dealers do not usually make information about their accomplices readily available, the files on the

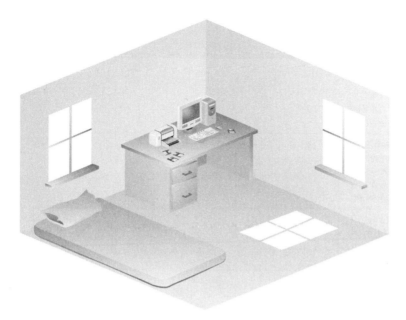

Figure 2-1   Crime scene

disks you received are probably **password protected**. You may need to acquire **password-cracking software** or find an expert who can help you crack the passwords.

Now you are ready to list the steps you need to take in the case, including how to address the risks and obstacles. Then you can begin the actual investigation and data retrieval.

Examining a Company-Policy Violation

Companies often establish policies regarding computer use by employees. Employees surfing the Internet, sending personal e-mail, or otherwise using company computers for personal tasks during work hours can waste company time. Because lost time can cost companies millions of dollars, computer-forensic specialists are often used to investigate policy violations. For example, consider the following scenario that involves a company-policy violation.

George Montgomery has worked at a firm for several years and lately has not been completing his projects on time. His supervisor, Steve Billings, receives reports from co-workers that George is spending time on his own business and not performing his assigned work duties. Steve files a complaint with the company Information Technology (IT) staff.

The IT staff monitors George's computer activity. Their information shows that he is saving files to a floppy disk on a regular basis. Steve knows that the work George is assigned to complete normally takes place on the file server. Steve begins to look around for floppy disks that do not look like standard company disks, which have labels showing the company logo.

As shown in Figure 2-2, George works in a cubicle with three other people, so it is fairly easy for Steve to observe him while talking to one of his co-workers.

Figure 2-2 Standard company cubicle

One day Steve spots a floppy disk on George's desk that does not include the company label. Steve confiscates the disk, takes it to his office, and locks it in his desk drawer. Steve calls IT to tell them he has the disk.

A computer-forensic examiner in IT can now acquire the floppy disk and systematically investigate this company-policy violation case.

TAKING A SYSTEMATIC APPROACH

When preparing a case, you can apply standard systems-analysis steps to problem solving, which are explained in the following list.

- **Make an initial assessment about the type of case you are investigating**. To assess the type of case you are handling, talk to others involved in the case and ask questions about the incident. Have law enforcement or company security officers already seized the computer, disks, and other components? Do you need to visit an office or other locale? Was the computer used to commit a crime or does it contain evidence regarding another crime?

2

- **Determine a preliminary design or approach to the case**. Outline the general steps you need to follow to investigate the case. If the suspect is an employee and you need to acquire their system, determine whether you can seize the employee's computer during working hours or if you have to wait until after office hours or the weekend. If you are preparing a criminal case, determine the information that law enforcement has already obtained.

- **Create a detailed design**. Refine the general outline by creating a detailed checklist of the steps you need to take and an estimated amount of time you need for each step. This will help you stay on track during the investigation.

- **Determine the resources you need**. Based on the OS of the computer you are investigating, list the software that you have and others that you might need.

- **Obtain and copy an evidence disk drive**. In some cases, you might be seizing multiple computers along with Zip disks, Jaz drives, CDs and other removable media. (For the examples in this chapter, you are only using floppy disks.) Make a forensic copy of the disk.

- **Identify the risks**. List the problems you normally expect in the type of case you are handling. This is known as standard risk assessment. For example, if the suspect seems knowledgeable about computers, he or she might have set up a logon scheme that shuts down the computer or erases the hard disk when someone tries to change the logon password.

- **Mitigate or minimize the risks**. Identify how you can minimize the risks. For example, if you are working with a computer where convicted criminals have likely password-protected the hard drive, you can make multiple copies of the original media before starting. Then you can destroy one or more copies during the investigation, but still achieve your goal of retrieving information from the disk.

- **Test the design**. Review the decisions you've made and the steps you've already completed. If you have already copied the original media, a standard part of testing the design involves comparing hash signatures to ensure that you made a proper copy of the original media.

- **Analyze and recover the digital evidence**. Using the software tools and other resources that you've gathered, and overcoming the risks and obstacles that you identified, examine the disk to find digital evidence. Later in this chapter, you will recover data from a floppy disk.

- **Investigate the data you recover**. View the information recovered from the disk including existing files, deleted files and e-mail, and organize them to help prove the guilt or innocence of the suspect.

- **Complete the case report**. Write a complete report detailing what you did and what you found.

- **Critique the case**. Self-evaluation is a critical part of professional growth. After you complete a case, review it, identifying successful decisions and actions, and how you could have improved your participation.

The amount of time and effort you put into each step varies depending on the nature of the investigation. For example, in most casework, you need to create a simple investigation plan so that you do not overlook any steps. However, if a case involves many computers with complex issues to identify and examine, a detailed plan with periodic review and updates is essential.

A systematic approach helps you discover the information you need for your case, and you should gather as much information as possible. "Never enough information" should be your credo when you start a computing investigation and begin hunting for a crucial piece of evidence. Eventually, however, you might feel that you have too much information, especially if it's not logically organized. How do you process this information during a high-technology computer or network investigation? Where do you start gathering information? Moreover, what exactly are you looking for? These are some of the key questions you must answer during each phase of a computing investigation.

Assessing the Case

Recall that identifying case requirements involves determining the type of case you are investigating. Doing so means you should systematically outline the details of the case, including the nature of the case, the type of evidence available, and the location of the evidence.

In the previous company-policy violation case, suppose you have been asked to investigate George Montgomery, who may be conducting his own business using a company computer. Recall that Steve Billings, George's supervisor, has already obtained a floppy disk that might contain evidence regarding George's business. By talking to George's co-workers, Steve has learned the nature of George's business. You can begin assessing this case as follows:

- *Situation*—Employee abuse case.

- *Nature of case*—Side business on the employer's business computer.

- *Specifics about the case*—The employee is reportedly conducting a side business on his assigned computer. The business involves registering domain names for clients and setting up their Web sites at local Internet Service Providers (ISPs).

- *Type of evidence*—Floppy disk

- *Operating system*—Microsoft Windows XP

- *Known disk format*—FAT12

- *Location of evidence*—One 3.5-inch floppy disk that a manager recovered from the employee's assigned workstation. The manager has received complaints from employee's co-workers that he is spending too much time on his own business and not performing his assigned work duties. Company policy states that all company-owned computing assets are subject to inspection by company management at anytime. Employees have no expectation of privacy when operating company-computing systems.

Based on these details, you can determine the case requirements. You now know that the nature of the case involves employee abuse of computers and that you are looking for evidence that an employee is conducting his own business using his employer's computers. On the floppy disk that Steve retrieved from the employee's computer, you are looking for any information related to Web sites, ISPs, or domain names. You know that the OS of the employee's computer is Windows XP, and that the floppy disk the manager retrieved uses the FAT12 file system. To duplicate the floppy disk and find deleted and hidden files, you need a reliable computing forensic tool, such as DriveSpy or Image Acquisition, also called Image, from Digital Intelligence. Because Image and DriveSpy run at the command line, you need to use a Windows 98 computer workstation to acquire the evidence from the floppy disk. (In Chapters 4 and 6, you will discover that the OS of the forensics machine is independent of the OS of the suspect machine.) Because the manager already retrieved the floppy disk, you do not need to obtain the disk yourself.

NOTE

In later chapters, you will see the advantages of using older OSs to acquire certain data.

You call this case the Domain Name case, and determine that your task is to gather data from the floppy disk that Steve found to confirm or deny the allegation that George is conducting his own business on company time. Remember that the employee is only suspected of abuse, and the evidence you obtain may be **exculpatory**—meaning it may prove his innocence. You must always maintain an unbiased opinion and be objective in all your fact-findings. If you are systematic and thorough, you will likely produce consistently reliable results.

Planning Your Investigation

Now that you have identified the requirements of the Domain Name case, you can plan your investigation. You have already determined the kind of evidence you need; now you can identify the specific steps to gather the evidence, establish a chain of custody, and perform the forensic analysis. These steps become the basic plan for your investigation, and indicate what you should do when. To investigate the Domain Name case, you should perform the following general steps. Most of these steps are explained in more detail in the following sections.

1. Acquire the floppy disk from George's manager.

2. Complete an evidence form and establish a chain of custody.

3. Transport the evidence to your **computing-forensic facility/lab**.

4. Secure your evidence in an approved secure container.

5. Prepare your computer-forensic workstation.

6. Obtain the evidence from the secure evidence container.

7. Make a forensic copy of the **evidence floppy disk**.

8. Return the evidence floppy disk to the secure evidence container.

9. Process the copied floppy disk with your computer-forensic tools.

TIP

The approved secure container you need in Step 4 should be a fireproof locker or cabinet that is locked and has limited access. Limited access means that only you and other authorized persons can open the evidence container.

The first rule for all investigations is to preserve the evidence, which means that it should not be tampered with or contaminated. Because Steve retrieved the floppy disk from George's workstation, you need to acquire the floppy disk from him. Ask Steve who had possession of the disk since it was confiscated so you can account for the floppy disk's chain of custody. When you talk to Steve, he confirms that the floppy disk has been locked in his desk since he obtained it from George's desk.

To document the evidence, you record details about the disk, including who recovered the evidence and when, and who possessed it and when. Use an **evidence custody form**, also called a chain-of-evidence form, which helps you document what has and has not been done with both the original evidence and the forensic copies of the evidence.

Depending on whether you are working in law enforcement or private corporate security, you can create a chain-of-evidence form to fit your environment. An evidence form should be easy to read and use. Evidence forms contain information for one or several pieces of evidence. Consider creating a **single-evidence form** and a **multi-evidence form** to complement your investigative administrative needs.

If necessary, document how to use your chain-of-evidence form. Clear instructions help the user remain consistent when completing the form. It also ensures that everyone uses the same definitions for collected items. Standardization helps to maintain consistent quality for all investigations and avoid confusion and mistakes about the evidence you collect.

Figure 2-3 shows a sample multi-evidence form used in a corporate environment.

A chain-of-evidence form typically contains the following information:

- *Case number*—The number assigned by your organization when an investigation is initiated.

- *Investigating organization*—The name of your organization. In large corporations with global facilities, several organizations might be conducting investigations in different geographic areas.

- *Investigator*—The name of the investigator assigned to this case. If many investigators are assigned, insert the lead investigator's name.

2

Corporation X			
Security Investigations			
This form is to be used for one to ten pieces of evidence			

Case No.:		Investigating Organization:	
Investigator:			
Nature of Case:			
Location where evidence was obtained:			

	Description of evidence:	Vendor Name	Model No./Serial No.
Item #1			
Item #2			
Item #3			
Item #4			
Item #5			
Item #6			
Item #7			
Item #8			
Item #9			
Item #10			

Evidence Recovered by:		Date & Time:	
Evidence Placed in Locker:		Date & Time:	

Item #	Evidence Processed by	Disposition of Evidence	Date/Time
			Page ___ of ___

Figure 2-3 Sample corporate chain-of-evidence form

- *Nature of case*—A short description of the case. For example, in the corporate environment, it might be "Data recovery for corporate legal" or "Employee Policy Violation Case."

- *Location where evidence was obtained*—The exact location where the evidence was collected. If you are using a multi-evidence from, a new form should be created for each location.

- *Description of evidence*—Describes the evidence, such as hard disk drive, 20 GB or one 3.5-inch floppy disk, 1.44 MB. On a multi-evidence form, write a description for each item of evidence you acquire.

- *Vendor name*—The name of the manufacturer of the computer evidence. List a 20 GB hard disk drive, for example, as a Maxtor or Floppy Disk Imation 2HD IBM Formatted 1.44MB. Later you will see how differences among manufacturers can affect data recovery.

- *Model number or serial number*—List the model number or serial number of the computer component. Many computer components including hard disk drives, memory chips, and expansion slot cards such as internal modems have model numbers but not serial numbers.

- *Evidence recovered by*—The name of the investigator who recovered the evidence. The chain of custody for the evidence starts with this information. If you insert your name, for example, you are declaring that you have taken control of the evidence. It is now your responsibility to ensure nothing damages the evidence and that no one tampers with it. The person placing his or her name here is responsible for preservation, transportation, and securing the evidence.

- *Date and time*—The date and time the evidence was taken into custody. This information establishes exactly when the chain of custody starts.

- *Evidence placed in locker*—Indicates which secure evidence container is used to sort your evidence, and when the evidence was placed in the secure locker.

- *Evidence processed by item number*—When it is time to analyze the evidence that is stored in the evidence locker, indicate the name of every person who handled and processed it.

- *Item #/Evidence processed by/Disposition of evidence/Date/Time*—When you or an authorized computing investigator obtain the evidence from the evidence locker for processing and analysis, list the specific item number, your name, and then describe what was done to the evidence.

- *Page*—The forms used to catalog all evidence for each location should have individual page numbers. List the page number, and indicate the total number of pages associated with this group of evidence. For example, if you collected fifteen pieces of evidence at one location, you will need to fill out two multi-evidence forms. The first form will be filled in as "Page 1 of 2." The second page will be filled in as "Page 2 of 2."

Figure 2-4 shows an evidence form for a single piece of evidence. The only significant difference is that a single-evidence form lists only one piece of evidence per form. The single-evidence form provides flexibility in tracking individual pieces of evidence for your chain-of-custody log. It typically provides space for a descriptive narrative, which is helpful when finalizing the investigation and creating a case report. Here you can accurately account for what was done to the evidence and what was found.

Use these forms as a reference to all actions taken for your investigation analysis.

You can use both the multi-evidence form and the single-evidence form in your investigation. By using two forms you can keep the single-evidence form with the evidence and the multi-evidence form in your report file. They also provide redundancy that can be used as a quality control for your evidence.

Metropolis Police Bureau			
High-tech Investigations Unit			
This form is to be used for only one piece of evidence.			
Fill out a separate form for each piece of evidence.			

Case No.:		Unit Number:	
Investigator:			
Nature of Case:			
Location where evidence was obtained:			

Item # ID	Description of evidence:	Vendor Name	Model No./Serial No.

Evidence Recovered by:		Date & Time:	
Evidence Placed in Locker:		Date & Time:	

Evidence Processed by	Disposition of Evidence	Date/Time
		Page ___ of ___

Figure 2-4 Single-evidence form

Securing Your Evidence

Computing investigations demand that you adjust your procedures to suit the case. For example, if the evidence for a case includes an entire computer system and associated media, such as floppy disks, Zip and Jaz cartridges, 4 mm DDS DAT tapes, and USB key-chain storage devices, you must be flexible when you account for all the items. Some evidence is small enough to fit into an evidence bag. Other items, such as the CPU cabinet, monitor, keyboard, and printer, are too large.

To secure and catalog the evidence contained in large computer components, you can use large **evidence bags**, tape, tags, labels, and other products available from police-supply vendors. When acquiring products to secure your computer evidence, make sure they are safe and effective to use on computer components. Be cautious when handling any computer component to avoid damaging the component or coming into contact with static electricity, which can destroy digital data. When collecting computer evidence, make sure that you use anti-static bags (see Figure 2-5). Consider obtaining an anti-static pad with an attached wrist strap, as shown in Figure 2-6. Both help to prevent damage to your computer evidence.

Figure 2-5   Anti-static bag

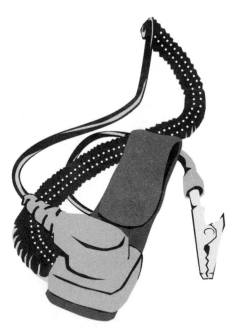

Figure 2-6   Wrist strap

Be sure to place computer evidence in a well-padded container. Padding prevents damage to the evidence as you transport it to your secure evidence locker, evidence room, or computer lab. Save discarded hard disk drive boxes, anti-static bags, and packing material for computer hardware when you or others acquire computer devices.

2

Because you may not have everything necessary to secure your evidence, you will be required to improvise. Securing evidence often requires you to build secure containers. If the computer component is large and contained in its own casing, such as a central processing unit (CPU) cabinet, you can use evidence tape to seal all openings on the cabinet. Placing evidence tape over the floppy disk drive opening, power supply electrical cord insert, CD drive, and any other openings ensure the security of your evidence. As a standard practice, you should write your initials on the tape before applying it to the evidence.

If you transport a CPU case, place a used floppy disk into the floppy disk drive to reduce possible damage to the floppy drive during transport.

Computer components have specific temperature and humidity ranges. If it is too cold, hot, or wet, computer components and magnetic media can be damaged. When collecting computer evidence, make sure that you have a safe environment to transport and store it until you reach a secure evidence container.

UNDERSTANDING DATA-RECOVERY WORKSTATIONS AND SOFTWARE

Now you know what is involved in acquiring and documenting the evidence. In Chapter 6, you will examine a complete setup of a computer-forensic lab, or the **data-recovery lab**, which is where you conduct your investigations and where most of your equipment and software are located, including the secure evidence locker.

To conduct your investigation and analysis, you must have a specially configured personal computer (PC) known as a **computer-forensic workstation**, which is a computer loaded with additional bays and forensics software.

Depending on your needs, most computer-forensic work can be performed on the following Microsoft OSs:

- MS-DOS 6.22
- Windows 95, 98, or Me
- Windows NT 3.5 or 4.0
- Windows 2000
- Windows XP

TIP

Chapter 6 covers the software resources you need and the forensics lab and workstation in detail. Visit *www.digitalintel.com* to examine the specifications of the Forensic Recovery of Evidence Device (F.R.E.D.) unit.

If you start Windows while you are examining a hard disk, Windows alters the evidence disk by writing data to the Recycle Bin file and damages the quality and integrity of the evidence that you are trying to preserve. Chapters 3 and 4 cover which files Windows automatically updates at startup. Windows XP and 2000 systems also record the serial number of the hard drives and CPUs in a file, which can be difficult to recover.

Of all the Microsoft operating systems, the least intrusive to floppy disks and hard disks is MS-DOS 6.22. In Chapter 6 you will create a forensic boot floppy disk. This special bootable floppy disk does not alter the data on a suspect's computer disk. When you acquire data from a hard disk, you should start the system from a forensic boot floppy disk. The only exception is when you have installed a write-blocking device on the suspect's hard disk. You can use one of several write-blockers that allow you to boot to Windows without writing any data to the evidence disk. One write-blocker is based on technology from ACARD (*www.microlandusa.com*). ACARD has developed a circuit card that is inserted between the computer's disk controller and the hard disk. Several ACARD models are SCSI-based devices that allow you to connect and access Enhanced Integrated Drive Electronics (EIDE) disks. (See Chapter 4 for more information on hard disk types.) This special write-blocker circuit card prevents the OS from writing data to the connected disk drive.

Other vendors sell write-blocker devices that connect to SCSI cards, Firewire, or USB 2.0 ports. Current vendors include Digital Intelligence with its SCSIBlocker, FireBlocker, and FireChief; and Guidance Software, producer of FastBloc and Image MaSSterSolo.

To avoid writing data to a disk, you will set up your forensic workstation for Windows 98 so that it boots to MS-DOS rather than Windows 98. You are using Windows 98 because Windows XP and 2000 can only access a DOS shell; they cannot boot directly to DOS. If you are not already familiar with MS-DOS, the following section introduces you to common MS-DOS commands. MS-DOS is the baseline for all computer-forensic analysis. Many computer-forensic acquisition tools work in the MS-DOS environment. These tools do not work in Windows or in an MS-DOS Command Prompt window in Windows.

Windows products are being developed that make performing disk forensics easier. However, because Windows has limitations when performing disk forensics, you must still become skilled in acquiring data in MS-DOS. At times, the only way you can recover data is with an MS-DOS tool. Remember that no one computer-forensic tool can recover everything. Each has its own strengths and weaknesses. Develop skills with as many tools as possible to become an effective computing investigator.

Setting Up Your Workstation for Computer Forensics

To set up your Windows 98 workstation to boot into MS-DOS, you need to modify the Windows 98 file MSDOS.SYS. You can add commands to this file so that Windows displays a Startup menu listing options for starting up your computer, including booting into MS-DOS.

The C: drive root directory for Windows 98 contains a system file named MSDOS.SYS. The properties for this file are typically set to Hidden and Read Only so it cannot be changed inadvertently. You can add two commands to this file so that it displays the Windows Startup menu, also called the Startup Boot menu.

To add commands to the MSDOS.SYS file:

1. Start Windows 98, if necessary. Click **Start**, and then click **Run**. The Run dialog box opens (see Figure 2-7).

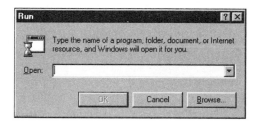

Figure 2-7   Run dialog box

2. In the Open text box, type **msconfig** and then click the **OK** button. The System Configuration Utility dialog box opens (see Figure 2-8).

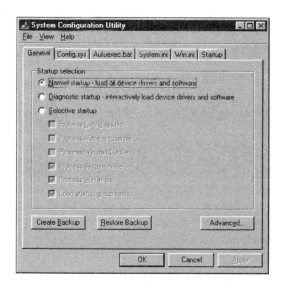

Figure 2-8   System Configuration Utility dialog box

3. On the General tab, you select startup settings. Configuring the Startup menu is an advanced setting. Click the **Advanced** button. The Advanced Troubleshooting Settings dialog box opens (see Figure 2-9).

4. Click the **Enable Startup Menu** check box so that Windows displays the Startup menu when you start the computer.

5. Click the **OK** button to close the Advance Troubleshooting Settings dialog box.

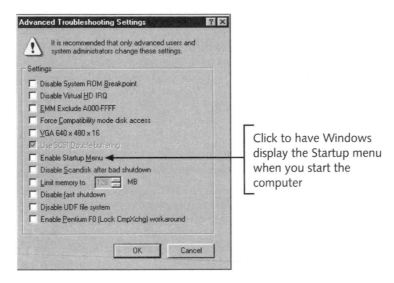

Figure 2-9   Advanced Troubleshooting Settings dialog box

6. Click **OK** to close the System Configuration Utility dialog box. Windows modifies the MSDOS.SYS file by turning on the Boot Menu switch.

7. If a message appears asking if you want to reboot or restart so the changes can take effect, click **Yes**.

Now you can open the MSDOS.SYS file, examine its settings, and add a command to the file to extend the amount of time the Startup menu appears before it closes and Windows starts as usual. Before you can modify the MSDOS.SYS file, you must change its Read-Only and Hidden properties.

To add a command to the MSDOS.SYS file:

1. If necessary, change the Windows view setting to show hidden files. Open a My Computer window, click **View** on the menu bar, and then click **Folder Options**. In the Folder Options dialog box, click the **View** tab. Under the Hidden files folder, click the **Show all files** option button, and then click **OK**.

2. In the My Computer window, navigate to the root folder on your hard disk, which is usually C:\. (If the drive where Windows is installed has a different drive letter, use that letter instead of C.) Right-click **MSDOS.SYS** and then click **Properties** on the shortcut menu. The MSDOS.SYS Properties dialog box opens.

3. In the Attributes section, click the **Read-only** box to remove the check mark. Then click the **Hidden** box to remove the check mark. Click **OK** to close the MSDOS.SYS Properties dialog box.

4. Start Notepad. (Click **Start**, point to **Programs**, point to **Accessories**, and then click **Notepad**.)

5. Click **File** on the menu bar, and then click **Open**. The Open dialog box opens. Navigate to the root drive, select **All Files (*.*)**, if necessary, in the Files of type list box, and then double-click **MSDOS.SYS**. The MSDOS.SYS file opens in Notepad.

6. Note that the BootMenu command is set to 1, which means it's turned on. A setting of 0 means it's turned off. The BootMenuDelay is also set to 5 seconds by default.

7. If your MSDOS.SYS file does not include a BootMenuDelay line, press **Enter** at the end of the file to add a new line, and then type **BootMenuDelay=59** as shown in Figure 2-10. If your file does have a BootMenuDelay line, extend the amount of time the Startup menu appears by changing the BootMenuDelay setting to **59**, which is the maximum number of seconds you can display the Startup menu.

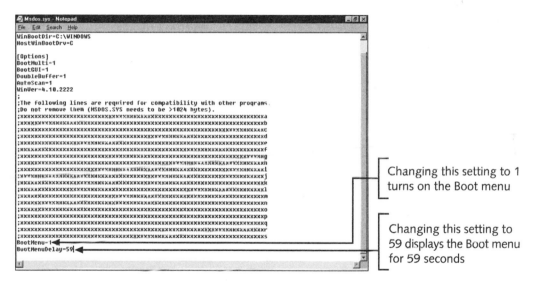

Figure 2-10   Modified MSDOS.SYS file after the Boot menu has been turned on

8. Click **File** on the menu bar, and then click **Save**. Close Notepad.

9. You now need to reboot your computer. If you are working in a computer lab, check with your technical support person to make sure you have permission to restart your computer.

10. Click **Start**, click **Shut Down**, and then click **Restart the computer**.

Next, you need to install your forensic tools on your forensic workstation. For this section you will use Digital Intelligence's DriveSpy and Image utilities, which can be purchased from Digital Intelligence's Web site at *www.digitalintel.com*.

To install DriveSpy and Image:

1. Your computer should have rebooted to Windows. Use Windows Explorer to create folders named **Chap02\Chapter** and **Tools** in the work folder for this book.

In the "Read This Before You Begin" section of this book, you created a folder on your system where you can store your work. This book calls this folder the "work folder." Create the Chap02\Chapter and Tools folders in your work folder.

TIP

2. Using Windows Explorer, copy the following Digital Intelligence files to the Tools folder in your work folder:

- Drivespy.exe

- Drivespy.hlp

- Drivespy.ini

- Image.exe

- Image.ini

Now you must create a command-line batch file that will append an additional path defining the location for the Digital Intelligence tools. By doing so, you can use the forensic tools from any folder on your hard disk. To do so, you create a text file in Notepad called Toolpath.bat.

To create the Toolpath.bat file:

1. Start Notepad. (Click **Start**, point to **Programs**, point to **Accessories**, and then click **Notepad**.)

2. Type the following command to define the path to your forensics tools. Replace *work folder* with the name of the work folder you are using to store your files for this book: **SET PATH=%PATH%;C:*work folder*\Tools** where C: is the drive where your work folder is located.

3. Click **File** on the menu bar, and then click **Save As**. The Save As dialog box opens. Click the **Save in** list arrow, and then navigate to C:\Windows. (If Windows is installed on a different drive, use that drive letter instead of C.) Click the **Save as type** list arrow, and then click **All Files**. In the File name text box, type **Toolpath.bat**. Click **Save**.

4. Close Notepad.

5. Shut down your computer by clicking **Start**, clicking **Shut Down**, and then clicking **Restart**.

6. The Windows 98 Startup Boot Menu appears, as shown in Figure 2-11. Use option 1 for a Normal boot to Windows 98, and option 5 for Command

Mode to boot to MS-DOS. You have approximately 59 seconds to respond to the menu. If you do not select one of the numbered mode options, the computer boots to Normal mode (Windows 98).

```
Microsoft Windows 98 Startup Menu
========================================

     1. Normal
     2. Logged (\BOOTLOG.TXT)
     3. Safe mode
     4. Step-by-step confirmation
     5. Command prompt only
     6. Safe mode command prompt only

Enter a choice: 1          Time remaining: 57




F5=Safe mode  Shift+F5=Command mode prompt  Shift+F8=Step-by-step confirmation [N]
```

Figure 2-11   Windows 98 Startup menu

7. To boot your workstation to the MS-DOS mode, in the Enter a choice prompt, type **5** to select Command prompt only as shown in Figure 2-12 and then press **Enter**.

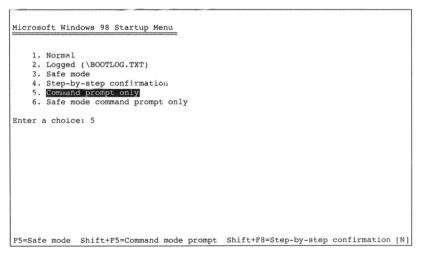

```
Microsoft Windows 98 Startup Menu
========================================

     1. Normal
     2. Logged (\BOOTLOG.TXT)
     3. Safe mode
     4. Step-by-step confirmation
     5. Command prompt only
     6. Safe mode command prompt only

Enter a choice: 5




F5=Safe mode  Shift+F5=Command mode prompt  Shift+F8=Step-by-step confirmation [N]
```

Figure 2-12   Selecting Command prompt only

Your workstation boots to the root level of your C:\ disk drive, and displays a C:\> command prompt. You have now set up your workstation so that you can perform some basic computer-forensic acquisitions and analysis.

EXECUTING AN INVESTIGATION

Now you are ready to return to the Domain Name case. You have created a plan for the investigation, set up your forensic workstation, and installed the software you need to examine the evidence. You can begin executing an investigation. Start by copying the evidence using a variety of methods. Recall that no one method retrieves all the data from a disk, so it is a good idea to use several tools to retrieve and analyze the data.

Start by gathering the resources that you identified in your investigation plan. You need the following items:

- Original floppy disk

- Evidence form

- Evidence container for the floppy disk, such as an **evidence bag**

- Bit-stream imaging tool; in this case you use the Digital Intelligence Image utility

- Computing forensic workstation to copy and then examine your evidence

- Secure evidence container

You will use the Digital Intelligence Image utility to copy a floppy disk later in this chapter. For more information on the Digital Intelligence Image utility, visit the Digital Intelligence Web site at *www.digitalintel.com*.

Gathering the Evidence

When you gather evidence, recall that you need anti-static bags and pads with wrist straps to ensure that you are grounded to prevent static electricity from damaging fragile electronic evidence. You also want to make forensic copies that are as close to exact duplicates as possible.

In the Domain Name investigation, you are ready to gather the evidence. You need to acquire George Montgomery's floppy disk from his manager, Steve Billings, and then secure the disk in an evidence bag. You perform the following steps to collect the evidence and transport it to your forensic facility:

1. Arrange to meet Steve so you can interview him and pick up the floppy disk. Depending on George's work schedule, you might have to meet Steve outside of the office so that George does not become suspicious. If you were analyzing a hard disk, you would need to arrange a time to enter the office and acquire the hard disk.

2. After interviewing Steve, fill out the evidence form, have Steve sign it, and then sign it yourself.

3. Store the floppy disk in an evidence bag, and then transport it to your forensic facility

4. Carry the evidence to a secure container, such as a locker, cabinet, or safe.

5. Complete the evidence form. As mentioned earlier, if you are using a multi-evidence form, you can store the form in the file folder for the case. If you are also using single-evidence forms, store those in the secure container with the evidence. Reduce the risk of tampering by limiting access to the form.

6. Secure your evidence by locking the container.

Understanding Bit-stream Copies

A **bit-stream copy** is a bit-by-bit copy of the original storage medium, and is an exact duplicate of the original disk. Recall that the more exact the copy, the more likely you can retrieve the evidence you need from the disk.

A bit-stream copy is different from a simple backup copy of a disk. Backup software can only copy or compress files that are stored in a folder or share a known file type. Backup software cannot copy deleted files or e-mail messages or recover file fragments.

Bit-streaming literally means that a disk is copied bit by bit, creating an exact image of the disk. The **bit-stream image** is a file that contains an exact copy of all the data on a disk or disk partition. To create an exact image of an evidence disk, it is preferable to copy the bit-stream image to a target work disk that is identical to the evidence disk, as shown in Figure 2-13. The manufacturer and model of the target disk must be the same as the manufacturer and model of the original evidence disk. The size of both disks should also be the same, although some software tools that create bit-stream images can accommodate a target disk that is a different size from the original evidence disk. These imaging tools are discussed in Chapter 9.

 Occasionally, the track and sector maps on the source and target disks do not match, even if you use disks of exactly the same size. Newer tools are available that adjust for the target-drive geometry.

TIP

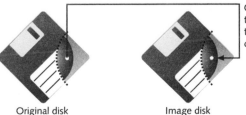

Creating a bit-stream image transfers each bit of data from the original disk to the same spot on the image disk

Original disk   Image disk

Figure 2-13   Transfer of data from original to image to target

Copying the Evidence Disk

After you retrieve and secure the evidence, you are ready to copy the evidence disk and analyze the data. The first rule of computer forensics is to preserve the original evidence. Conduct your analysis only on a forensic copy of the original media. A **forensic copy** is an exact duplicate of the original data. To make a forensic copy of a floppy disk, you must create a bit-stream data copy of the disk using an MS-DOS command or a specialized tool, such as the Digital Intelligence Image utility.

Making a Bit-Stream Copy of a Floppy Disk Using MS-DOS

One method of making a duplicate copy of your evidence floppy disk is to use the MS-DOS command Diskcopy with the verification switch /V, which verifies that the data is copied correctly. This command accurately copies one floppy to another floppy. Its only disadvantage is that it does not create a separate image file of the original floppy disk. Use the Diskcopy command only if you have no other tools available to preserve the original data. The Image tool from Digital Intelligence provides a reliable backup of your floppy-disk evidence.

To make a bit-stream copy of a floppy disk, retrieve the floppy disk from your secure evidence container, and provide the appropriate information on your evidence form. Then complete the following steps at the DOS prompt on your forensics workstation.

To make a bit-stream copy of a floppy disk using MS-DOS:

1. Because your evidence floppy disk is the original media, you must write-protect the floppy disk. Move the write-protect tab on the floppy disk to the open position.

2. If necessary, boot your forensic workstation to the MS-DOS prompt.

3. Insert the evidence floppy disk into the floppy disk drive of your workstation, which is usually drive A. The original disk is your source disk.

4. At the MS-DOS prompt, type the following command:

   Diskcopy A: A: /V

   Press **Enter**. Recall that the /V switch will verify that the data is copied correctly. You may be prompted to insert the source disk, press **Enter**.

5. When the disk is copied, you will be prompted to place a target disk into the A: drive. This is where you want to store the copy of the evidence disk. Remove the evidence disk and insert a blank unformatted or formatted disk into the floppy drive. The software will automatically overwrite everything. Follow the on-screen instructions and proceed with the data copy.

6. As the data is being copied to the target floppy disk, place the original floppy disk into your secure evidence container. When asked if you want to create another duplicate of the disk, type **n** for no. When asked if you want to copy another disk, type **n** for no.

7. Place a label on the working copy of the floppy disk, if necessary, and then write **Domain Name working copy #1** on the label.

Always remember to maintain your chain of custody for your evidence.

TIP

In a live investigation, you should place the original floppy disk into your secure evidence container as the data is being copied to the target floppy disk.

Acquiring a Bit-Stream Copy of a Floppy Disk Using Image

You can also make a bit-stream copy of a floppy disk using Digital Intelligence Image. This tool creates a file that contains every byte of data on a floppy disk, creating an image of the floppy disk rather than only a copy. The unique feature of this tool is that it preserves your data in a compact data file (also called an **image file**) on your disk. After you have created the image file of the floppy disk, you can copy the data to another floppy disk.

While newer tools are on the market that can read directly from the image file, with most computer-forensics tools, recall that the image file must be restored to a medium of the same size and type to access the data. In this way, working with image files is similar to restoring a file from a true backup utility that does not merely copy files.

When you use Image, you first acquire a bit-stream copy of a floppy disk and store that copy in a file on your hard disk. You complete this task in the following steps. Then you copy the file from your hard disk to a blank floppy disk, which you will do in the second set of steps.

As described earlier, in a live investigation, you would first retrieve the original floppy disk from your secure evidence container, and then fill out your evidence form before performing the following steps at your forensic workstation. Because the image file for this case is in your data files, you do not need to perform these steps. You can, however, practice the steps using one of your own disks.

To acquire a bit-stream copy of a floppy disk using Image:

1. Write-protect the original floppy disk by moving the write-protect notch to the open position.

2. If necessary, boot your computer to MS-DOS command mode.

3. Insert the original floppy disk into the floppy disk drive of your computer, which is usually drive A. This is the source disk.

4. At the command prompt, change to the Chap02\Chapter folder in your work folder on the hard disk by typing the following command and then pressing **Enter**. The following command assumes that your work folder is in the root directory, and the Chap02 folder is in the work folder. Substitute the names of the folders you are using on your computer as appropriate:

   cd work folder**Chap02****Chapter**

5. To acquire data from the original evidence floppy disk, type the following command, and then press **Enter**. If your disk is in a floppy drive other than A, substitute that drive letter in the following command:

image a: c:*work folder*\\Chap02\\Chapter\\Test.img

Replace *work folder* with the name of the work folder on your hard disk. If the drive letter of your hard disk is not C, substitute that drive letter for C.

This generates the bit-stream copy and stores it in the *work folder*\\Chap02\\Chapter folder.

6. Remove the original evidence floppy disk. In a live investigation, you would return the original disk to your secure evidence container.

You have now acquired the bit-stream copy of your evidence and stored it on your hard disk in a file called Test.img. The next step is to transfer the image of your evidence to a target disk such as a floppy disk to create a working copy.

Making a Bit-Stream Copy of Evidence Using Image

Now that you have created a bit-stream image copy of your original evidence floppy disk, you must create a working copy of the disk, one that you can analyze without contaminating the evidence. When you transfer the contents of the image file you created in the previous steps to a different disk, Image uncompresses the image file and creates an exact duplicate of the disk, including **slack space** and **free space** on the disk. Slack space is the disk area between the end of a file and its allotted space, while free space is any space on the drive not currently assigned to an existing file. (Both terms are covered in detail in Chapters 3 and 4.)

To create a working copy of the evidence disk:

1. If necessary, boot your computer to Windows.

2. Using Windows Explorer or My Computer, find the **C2Chap01.img** file in the Chap02\\Chapter folder in your data files (which you can download from *www.courseptr.com*).

3. Copy the **C2Chap01.img** file from your data files to the Chap02\\Chapter folder in your work folder on your hard disk.

4. Reboot your computer to MS-DOS mode.

5. At the MS-DOS prompt, change to the *work folder*\\Chap02\\Chapter directory, if necessary, by typing the following command and then pressing **Enter**:

cd *work folder*\\Chap02\\Chapter

6. Place a blank formatted floppy disk into the floppy disk drive of your computer, which is usually drive A.

7. At the MS-DOS prompt, type the following command, and then press **Enter**:

image C2Chap01.img a:.

8. Place a label on the working copy of the floppy disk, if necessary, and then write **Domain name working copy #2** on the label.

You have now created a working bit-stream copy of your original evidence floppy disk, which contains the same evidence as the original. Next you can analyze the working bit-stream copy of your evidence.

Analyzing Your Digital Evidence

When you analyze digital evidence, your job is to recover the data. If users have deleted files or overwritten them on a disk, the disk contains deleted files and file fragments, in addition to complete files. Remember that as files are deleted, the space they occupied becomes free space—meaning it can be used for new files that a user saves. The files that were deleted are still on the disk until a new file is saved to the same location, overwriting the original file. In the meantime, those files can still be retrieved. Most forensics tools can retrieve deleted files to be used as evidence.

To analyze digital evidence, you can use another MS-DOS tool from Digital Intelligence called DriveSpy, which is also a command-line tool. In Chapter 5, you will use GUI tools that can read the image files.

Overview of DriveSpy

DriveSpy is a powerful disk-forensic tool compact enough to fit on a floppy disk. DriveSpy searches for, analyzes, and extracts data from a floppy disk or a hard disk. DriveSpy is designed to work from the DOS command prompt, and has limited functionality from a Windows MS-DOS shell. It is best to use DriveSpy from a workstation booted into MS-DOS. If you are running DriveSpy using MS-DOS version 6.22, DriveSpy can read disk drives larger than 8.4 GB and disk partitions larger than 2 GB. If you run DriveSpy in MS-DOS 7.0 or later, you can store recovered data in larger disk partitions.

DriveSpy uses the following modes:

- *System mode*—DriveSpy operates at the workstation's BIOS level. It allows you to view and navigate to all the disk drives connected to the computer.

- *Drive mode*—DriveSpy accesses the physical level of the disk drive. Use this mode when you need to examine a disk not formatted for MS-DOS or Windows 9x. Specifically, Drive mode lets you view the raw data on a disk. (Chapter 6 provides more details about DriveSpy Drive mode.)

- *Part (or Partition) mode*—DriveSpy refers to the logical level of the disk drive. At the logical level, you view the actual file structure of a disk, that is, the disk's partition. In Part mode, DriveSpy can read MS-DOS and Windows 9x disks, and shows the directory structures and files for File Allocation Table (FAT) file systems. FAT is covered in greater detail in Chapter 3.

DriveSpy extracts files and other raw data from a disk, including deleted files and fragments of deleted files that have been partially overwritten. DriveSpy even performs a unique copy of a hard disk.

In this chapter, you have used Digital Intelligence's Image, a special utility that creates an exact copy of a floppy disk. Image stores the data from a floppy disk in either a compressed data file or a flat (non-compressed) file. Image also duplicates an evidence floppy disk on another floppy disk, which lets you preserve your original evidence. Recall that you should avoid working with the original medium. By creating a bit-by-bit copy, you can perform your forensics examination on the duplicate floppy disk.

Using Digital Intelligence DriveSpy

DriveSpy is a computer-forensic tool that recovers and analyzes data on FAT12, FAT16, and FAT32 disks, which are different formatting techniques used by Microsoft. Other versions of DriveSpy can read New Technology File System (NTFS) and Linux system disks. DriveSpy logs all of your actions and copies data from your forensic image disk. It searches for files that have been altered so that they appear to be of a different format, and it searches for keywords of interest to your investigation.

Recall that you copied the DriveSpy files to the *work folder*\Tools folder earlier in this chapter. To launch DriveSpy, the DriveSpy.exe file must be in the same folder as the DriveSpy.ini and DriveSpy.hlp files.

DriveSpy specifies drives by number, with the first drive being D0. Many systems have multiple partitions and multiple drives, which becomes important in your computer-forensic lab where several drives might be connected to the same machine. While DriveSpy identifies hard disks by number, it does not number the floppy disk and CD drives. With most versions of Windows (Windows Me being the most challenging), you can launch DriveSpy from Windows Explorer to access the DOS prompt.

To prepare to analyze the bit-stream copy of your evidence disk:

1. Retrieve the forensic copy of your evidence disk from your evidence container, and write-protect the floppy disk by moving the notch to the open position.

2. Start your computer-forensic workstation and boot into MS-DOS.

3. First, you need to run the Toolpath.bat file created earlier. Go to the *work folder*\Tools folder, where *work folder* is the name of your work folder. At the prompt, type **Toolpath.bat** and press **Enter**.
You return to a command prompt.

4. Insert the evidence disk that you labeled "Domain Name working copy #2" into drive A: of your workstation.

Now you are ready to start DriveSpy.

To use DriveSpy to analyze the bit-stream copy of your evidence disk:

1. Change to the *work folder*Tools folder on your hard disk, which is where you copied the DriveSpy files earlier in the chapter. At the MS-DOS prompt, type **DriveSpy** and then press **Enter**. The welcome screen appears, shown in Figure 2-14.

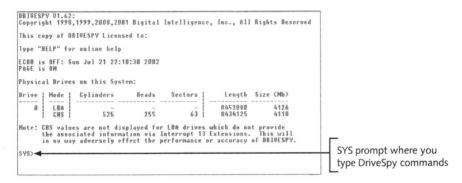

```
DRIVESPY V1.62:
Copyright 1998,1999,2000,2001 Digital Intelligence, Inc., All Rights Reserved

This copy of DRIVESPY Licensed to:

Type "HELP" for online help

ECHO is OFF: Sun Jul 21 22:10:30 2002
PAGE is ON

Physical Drives on this System:

Drive | Mode | Cylinders    Heads    Sectors |   Length   Size (Mb)
------ | ---- | ---------    -----    ------- | --------   ---------
    0  | LBA  |     -          -         -    |  8452080     4126
       | CHS  |    526        255        63   |  8434125     4118

Note: CHS values are not displayed for LBA drives which do not provide
      the associated information via Interrupt 13 Extensions. This will
      in no way adversely effect the performance or accuracy of DRIVESPY.

SYS>
```

SYS prompt where you type DriveSpy commands

Figure 2-14   Opening screen for DriveSpy

Note that DriveSpy provides the SYS prompt where you can type DriveSpy commands. You can use the DriveSpy Output command to log your actions, which you need for your final report for this examination. The log file keeps track of all the commands you use to obtain data from the forensics disk.

2. At the SYS> prompt, type the following command and then press **Enter**. Substitute the italicized text as appropriate:

Output *work folder*\Chap02\Chapter\C2Chap01.log

3. To access the floppy disk with DriveSpy insert the evidence disk that you labeled "Domain Name working copy #2" into Drive A: of your workstation, type **Drive A** and then press **Enter**.

4. DriveSpy changes to Disk mode, and summarizes the disk information for the disk in Drive A (see Figure 2-15).

   Recall that Disk mode reads the physical level of the disk, and does not show file structures such as directories (or folders) and files.

5. To access the Partition level of the floppy disk, type **Part 1** at the DA prompt, and then press **Enter**.

   Partition information appears, as shown in Figure 2-16, including the type of file system used on the disk, the number of sectors per cluster, the total sectors and clusters available in the partition, and its raw and formatted data storage capacity. The information also includes a useful map of where the start and end sectors are for the boot sector of the partition, the first and second FATs (FAT1 and FAT2), the root directory and the data storage areas of the partition. Chapter 3 discusses these file structures in detail.

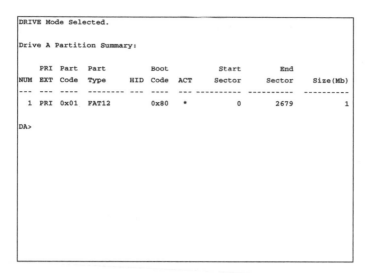

```
DRIVE Mode Selected.

Drive A Partition Summary:

      PRI  Part  Part               Boot            Start        End
 NUM  EXT  Code  Type      HID      Code  ACT       Sector       Sector      Size(Mb)
 ---  ---  ----  --------  ---      ----  ---   ----------    ----------    ----------
  1   PRI  0x01  FAT12              0x80   *             0          2679             1

DA>
```

Figure 2-15   Accessing the A: drive with DriveSpy

```
PARTITION Mode Selected.

Partition 1: Primary, (Active), FAT12 (0x01)
Defined in Partition Table at Absolute Sector: 0 (Entry Number 1)

Sectors/Cluster:       1
Total Sectors:         2880
Total Clusters:        2847
Raw Capacity:          1 Mb
Formatted Capacity:    1 Mb

                    |  Start      End    |
                    |  Sector    Sector  |
----------------    | -------   --------  |
Partition           |      0       2979  |
Boot Sector         |      0          0  |
FAT1                |      1          9  |
FAT2                |     10         18  |
Boot Dir            |     19         32  |
Data Area           |     33       2879  |


DAP1:\>
```

Figure 2-16   Accessing the partition level of a disk

   6. Type **Q** and then press **Enter** to exit DriveSpy.

You have successfully explored the investigation disk that contains your evidence. Next, you can run basic commands to navigate the DriveSpy folder and analyze and extract data from the evidence disk.

To analyze and extract data with DriveSpy:

1. Restart DriveSpy by typing **DriveSpy** at the MS-DOS prompt and then pressing **Enter**.

2. At the DriveSpy SYS prompt (indicating System mode), create the log file where DriveSpy can record all the tasks you perform while working in DriveSpy. Type the following command and then press **Enter**, substituting the name of the work folder on your system as necessary.

   output *work folder*\Chap02\Chapter\Ch2Chap02.log

3. At the DriveSpy SYS prompt, type **Drive A** and press **Enter** to switch to Drive mode.

4. At the DA (Drive A) prompt, type **Part 1** and press **Enter** to switch to Partition mode for Drive A.

5. At the DAP1 (Drive A, Partition 1) prompt, type the following command and then press **Enter**, substituting the name of the work folder on your system as necessary:

   dbexport *work folder* \Chap02\Chapter\C2Chap01.txt

   The Dbexport command creates a text file with the name you specify, such as C2Chap01.txt. This text file contains all of the entries of directories and files listed in the FAT, and is useful in identifying what is on the evidence disk. You can also open this text file in a word-processing, spreadsheet, or database program to sort and search for information.

6. Next, you copy all the allocated data from the evidence disk. Allocated data is data not deleted from the disk. At the DriveSpy prompt, enter the following Copy command with the recursive /S switch to copy all the allocated files in any subdirectories that might exist on the evidence disk to the Chap02 folder in your work folder. Replace the italicized text as necessary, then press **Enter**.

   Copy *.* /S *work folder*\Chap02\Chapter

   If a message appears asking if you want to view the results in page mode because they might be lengthy, press **Y**.

7. Type the following command to copy all deleted files from the evidence disk. Replace the italicized text as necessary, then press **Enter**.

   Unerase *.* /S *work folder*\Chap02\Chapter

   If a message appears asking if you want to view the results in page mode because they might be lengthy, press **Y**.

DriveSpy locates all the deleted files on the evidence disk that have not been overwritten. That is, it searches the FAT for all files where the filename starts with the MS-DOS delete symbol of a lowercase sigma (σ). Then DriveSpy copies the contents of the deleted files to the specified location, such as the Chap02 folder in your work folder.

To analyze the data:

1. Reboot your machine to Windows mode.

2. Use Windows Explorer or My Computer to open the floppy disk and note how many files it contains.

3. Right-click the first file and then click **Properties** on the shortcut menu. In the General tab of the Properties dialog box for the file, note the Created, Modified, and Accessed dates and times. List the filename and properties in a separate document or sheet of paper. Put an asterisk next to any that are during George's working hours (8 a.m. to 5 p.m.). Then close the Properties dialog box. Note the properties for each file on the disk.

4. Use Notepad to open each file. In a separate document or on a sheet of paper, note what each file contains. Close Notepad.

5. Use Windows Explorer or My Computer to open the *work folder*\Chap02\ Chapter folder and examine the contents. You should see several files in addition to the log and text files. These are the deleted files DriveSpy retrieved.

6. In Notepad, open **C2Chap01.txt** and examine the contents. Depending on your system, you might see the sigma (σ) to represent deleted files or a question mark (?) at the beginning of the filename. Close Notepad.

7. Examine the contents of the deleted files. Determine whether they contain information about George's own business.

8. In Windows Explorer or My Computer, right-click each file and examine the Created, Modified, and Accessed dates and times in the file's Properties dialog box. Record your findings in a separate document or sheet of paper.

You should find evidence that proves George was working on his own business during company work hours.

COMPLETING THE CASE

After you analyze a disk, you can retrieve deleted files and e-mail, items that have been purposefully hidden, and much more, which you will do later in this book. The files on George's floppy disk indicate that he was doing outside work on the company's machine.

Now that you have retrieved and analyzed the evidence, you need to find the answers to the following questions to write the final report:

- How did George's manager acquire the disk?

- Did George perform the work on a laptop, which is his own property? If so, did he perform his business transactions on his break or during his lunch hour?

- At what times of the day was George using the non-work related files? How did you retrieve that information?

- Which company policies apply?

- Are there any other items that need to be considered?

When you write your report, state what you did and what you found. The log file generated by DriveSpy provides you with a historical account of all the steps you have taken. As part of your report, depending on guidance you have from your management or legal counsel, include the DriveSpy log file to document your work. In any computing investigation, you should be able to repeat your steps and achieve the same results. Without this ability, your work product has no value as evidence.

Keep a written journal of everything that you do. Your notes can be used in court, so be mindful of what you write or e-mail even to a fellow investigator.

Basic report writing involves answering the five W's: who, what, when, where, and how. In addition to these basic facts, you must also explain computer and network processes. Typically your reader will be a senior personnel manager, a lawyer, or on rare occasions, a judge, and might have little computer knowledge. Identify your reader and write the report for that person. Provide explanations for processes and the inner workings of systems and their components and how they work.

Your organization might have predefined templates for you to use when writing reports. Depending on your organization's needs and requirements, your report must describe the findings from your analysis. The log file generated by DriveSpy lists all of your activity in the order that you had performed your examination and data recovery. Integrating a computing-forensic log report into your formal report will complement your formal report. Consider writing your narrative first and then placing the log output at the end of the report using references to the log report on your fact-findings. Writing technical reports for your investigations is covered in greater detail in Chapter 14.

In the Domain Name case, you would show conclusive evidence that George had his own business that registered other people's domain names, and provide the names of his clients and his income from this business. You could also show letters he wrote to clients regarding their accounts. The time and date stamps on the files are during work hours. As the investigator, you would either hand the evidence file to your supervisor or to Steve, George's boss. They would then decide on a course of action.

CRITIQUING THE CASE

After you close the case and make your final report, you need to meet with your department or group of fellow investigators and critique the case. Ask yourself critical questions such as the following:

- How could you improve your participation in the case?

- Did you expect the results you found? Did the case develop in ways you did not expect?

- Was the documentation as thorough as it could have been?

- What feedback has been received from the requesting source?

- Did you discover any new problems? If so, what are they?

- Did you use new techniques during the case or during research?

Make notes to yourself in your journal about techniques or processes that may need to be changed or addressed in future investigations. Then store your journal in a secure place.

CHAPTER SUMMARY

❑ Always use a systematic approach to your investigations. Determine the type of problem you are dealing with, create a preliminary plan, choose your resources, perform a risk analysis, and then implement the plan.

❑ When planning a case, take into account the nature of the case, the instructions from the requester, what additional tools and/or expertise you may need, and how you will acquire the evidence.

❑ Criminal cases and corporate-policy violations should be handled in much the same manner to ensure that quality evidence is presented. Criminal cases can go to court and company-policy violations can end there.

❑ When you begin a case, apply standard problem-solving techniques such as defining the problem, designing a solution, and carrying out that solution.

❑ You should create a standard evidence custody form to track the chain of custody of the evidence relating to your case. There are two types of forms: multi-evidence form and a single-evidence form.

❑ Always maintain a journal to make notes on exactly what you did when handling evidence.

❑ An image file is a bit-by-bit duplicate of the original disk. You should use the duplicate whenever possible.

❑ DriveSpy and Image are command-line forensic tools that can retrieve existing files, deleted files, and file fragments.

❑ You can create bit-stream copies of files using either the Diskcopy DOS utility or the Image tool.

KEY TERMS

allocated data—Data on a drive that has not been deleted or written over.

approved secure container—A fireproof container that is locked by key or combination.

bit stream copy—A bit-by-bit copy of the data on the original storage media.

bit stream image—The file used to store the bit-stream copy.

chain of custody—The route that evidence takes from the time it is obtained by the investigator until the case is closed or goes to court.

computing forensic facility/lab—A computer lab that is dedicated to computing investigations, and typically has a variety of computers, OSs, and forensic software.

computer-forensic workstation—A workstation set up to allow copying of forensic evidence whether on a hard drive, floppy, CD, or Zip disk. It typically has various software preloaded and ready to use.

data recovery lab—An alternate name for a computer-forensic lab.

evidence bag—A non-static bag used to transport floppy disks, hard drives, and other computer components.

evidence custody form—A printed copy of a form indicating who has signed out and physically been in possession of evidence.

evidence floppy disk—The original disk on which the electronic evidence was found.

exculpatory—Evidence that proves the innocence of the accused.

forensic copy—A copy of an evidence disk that is used during the actual investigation.

free space—Space on a drive that is not reserved for saved files.

image file—A file created by Image tool from Digital Intelligence.

multi evidence form—A chain-of-evidence form used to list all items associated with a case.

password protected—Files and areas of any storage media can have limited access by using a password to prevent unintentional use.

password cracking software—Software used to match the hash patterns of passwords or simply guess the words by using common combinations or by employing standard algorithms.

single evidence form—A form that dedicates a page for each item retrieved for a case. It allows the investigator to add more detail as to exactly what was done to the evidence each time it was taken from the storage locker.

slack space—Space on a disk between the end of a file and the allotted space for a file.

CHAPTER 3

WORKING WITH WINDOWS AND DOS SYSTEMS

After reading this chapter, you will be able to:

♦ Understand file systems

♦ Explore Microsoft disk structures

♦ Examine New Technology File System (NTFS) disks

♦ Understand Microsoft boot tasks

♦ Understand Microsoft Disk Operating System (MS-DOS) startup tasks

Chapters 3 and 4 provide an overview of computer data and disk drives. This chapter reviews how data is stored and managed on Microsoft operating systems (OSs). To become proficient in recovering data for computer investigations, you should understand file systems and their associated OSs, including legacy OSs, such as MS-DOS, Windows 9x, and Windows Me, and current OSs, including Windows 2000 and XP. In this chapter, you examine the tasks each operating system performs when it starts so you can avoid altering evidence when you examine data on a disk. Chapter 4 discusses Macintosh and Linux file systems and hardware devices such as Small Computer System Interface (SCSI) and Integrated Drive Electronics (IDE) disks.

UNDERSTANDING FILE SYSTEMS

To effectively investigate computer evidence, you must understand how the most popular operating systems work in general, and how they store files in particular. In addition to reading this section on file systems, you should also review any text that has A+ certification by the Computer Technology Industry Association (CTIA) for additional information regarding hardware and firmware startup tasks and operations.

A **file system** provides an operating system with a road map to the data on a disk. The type of file system an operating system uses determines how data is stored on the disk. A file system is usually directly related to an operating system, although some vendors combine file systems so that any operating system can read them. For example, disk drives configured in the older Linux Ext2 and Ext3 file systems can be accessed with most current Linux releases.

No matter which platform you use, you need to understand how to access and modify system settings when necessary. When you need to access a suspect's or subject's computer to acquire or inspect data related to your investigation, you should be familiar with the platform. This book examines Windows or DOS personal computers (PCs) in detail. For other computer systems, consult vendor-specific manuals and system administrators.

Understanding the Boot Sequence

To ensure that you do not contaminate or alter data on a subject's computer, you must understand how to access and modify a PC's complementary metal-oxide semiconductor (CMOS) and basic input/output system (BIOS). The computer stores system configuration and date and time information in the CMOS when the power to the system is off. BIOSs contain programs that perform input and output at the hardware level. To avoid altering evidence data on a Windows/DOS PC, you need to access CMOS and BIOS settings.

To avoid altering data on the hard disk, you must make sure that when the subject's computer starts, it boots to drive A. Booting to a hard disk overwrites and changes evidentiary data. You can ensure that a computer looks for system information in drive A by accessing the CMOS setup. To do this, you need to monitor the subject's computer during the initial **bootstrap** to identify the correct key or keys to use to access the CMOS setup. The bootstrap is contained in read-only memory (ROM) and tells the computer how to proceed. As the computer starts, the screen usually displays the key or keys to press to open the CMOS setup screen. For example, you might need to press the Delete key as the system starts to access the CMOS.

The key you press to access CMOS depends on the BIOS on your computer. Popular BIOS manufacturers Award and AMI use the Del or Delete (depending upon your keyboard) key to access CMOS. Other keys that are used are Ctrl+Alt+Ins, Ctrl+A, Ctrl+S, Ctrl+F1, F2, and F10. Figure 3-1 shows a typical CMOS setup screen.

On the CMOS setup screen, check the boot sequence for the subject's computer. If necessary, change the boot sequence so the operating system accesses drive A before any other boot device on the subject's computer. Each BIOS vendor screen is different. For example, in Figure 3-1, you press Tab to move to the appropriate line and then use the

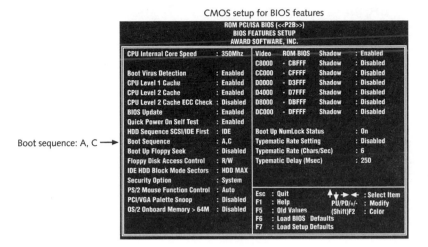

CMOS setup for BIOS features

Figure 3-1 Typical CMOS setup screen

Arrow keys to change the boot sequence. If necessary, refer to the BIOS vendor documentation or Web site for instructions on changing the boot sequence.

Examining Registry Data

When Microsoft created Windows 95, they consolidated initialization (.ini) files into the **Registry**, a database that stores hardware and software configuration information, user preferences, and setup information. The Registry was used in Windows 2000, Me, and 98, and is still used in Windows XP.

For investigative purposes, the Registry can contain valuable evidence. Current computer forensic tools do not examine the content of the Registry. Instead, you can use the Regedit program for Windows 9x systems and Regedit32 for Windows 2000 and XP. For more information on how to use a Registry editor, see the Microsoft Windows Resource Kit documentation for the appropriate operating system. You can find the information at *www.microsoft.com* or order the manual with a CD from Microsoft Press. In general, you can use the Find command on the Edit menu in the Registry editor to locate entries that might contain trace evidence, such as information identifying the last person to log on to the computer, which is usually contained in the user account information. Windows 9x systems may not record a user's logon information, but you can find other related user information such as Network logon data by searching for all occurrences of "username" or application licenses.

In Windows 95 and 98, the Registry is contained in two binary files, System.dat and User.dat, which are located in the Windows folder in the root directory. For Windows 2000 and XP, Registry information is contained in the \Winnt\Config and \Windows\System32\Config folders, respectively.

As a computing investigator and forensics examiner, you should explore the Registry of all Windows systems including Windows XP, 2000, and 9x. Be careful not to alter any Registry setting, because changing a setting could corrupt your system, possibly making it unbootable.

Disk Drive Overview

You should be familiar with disk drives and how data is organized on a disk so that you can effectively find data. Disk drives are made up of one or more platters coated with magnetic material, and data is stored on the platters in a particular way. Following is a list of the elements of a disk and the terms used to describe disk data structure:

- *Geometry*—The **geometry** reflects the internal organization of the drive.
- *Head*—The **head** is the device that reads and writes data to the drive.
- *Tracks*—**Tracks** are individual circles on a disk platter where data is located.
- *Cylinders*—A **cylinder** is a column of tracks on two or more disk platters.
- *Sectors*—A **sector** is an individual section on a track, typically made up of 512 bytes.

Figure 3-2 illustrates the major components of the drive. Understanding these parts of a disk drive will become more important as you progress through the study of computing investigations and forensics.

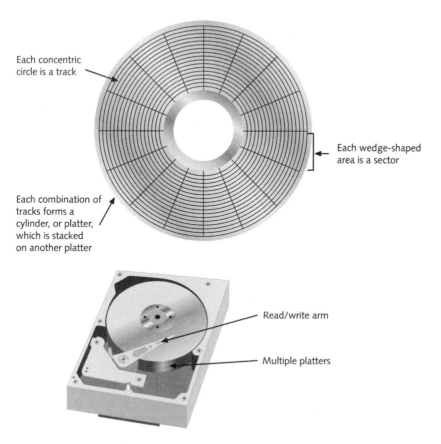

Each concentric circle is a track

Each wedge-shaped area is a sector

Each combination of tracks forms a cylinder, or platter, which is stacked on another platter

Read/write arm

Multiple platters

Figure 3-2   Disk drive structure

The typical disk drive stores 512 bytes per sector. The manufacturer of the disk engineers the disk to have a specified number of sectors per track. The number of bytes on a disk is determined by multiplying the number of cylinders (platters) by the number of heads (actually tracks) and by the number of sectors (groups of 512 or more bytes) as shown in Figure 3-3. The hard disk drive industry refers to this as cylinders, heads, and sectors (CHS).

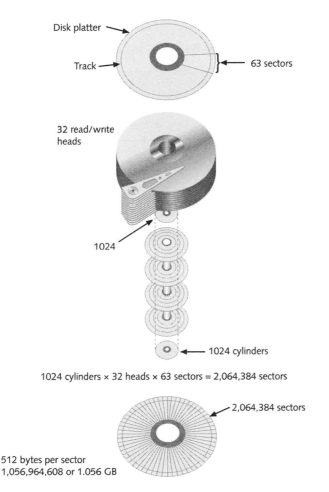

Disk platter

Track — 63 sectors

32 read/write heads

1024

1024 cylinders

1024 cylinders × 32 heads × 63 sectors = 2,064,384 sectors

2,064,384 sectors

512 bytes per sector
1,056,964,608 or 1.056 GB

Figure 3-3 CHS calculation

Tracks also follow a numbering scheme and are numbered starting from zero (0), which is the first value in computing. If a disk lists 79 tracks, you actually have 80 tracks, 0-79.

Other disk properties, such as **zoned bit recording (ZBR)**, **track density**, **areal density**, and **head and cylinder skew**, are handled at the hardware or firmware level of the disk drive. ZBR is how most manufacturers deal with the fact that the inner tracks of a platter are physically smaller than the outer tracks. Grouping the tracks by zones ensures that the tracks are all the same size.

Track density addresses the space between each track. As with old vinyl records, the smaller the space between each track, the more tracks you can place on the platter. On older disks, the space was wider, which allowed the heads to wander. This allowed specialists to retrieve data from previous writes to a platter.

Areal density refers to the number of bits in one square inch of a platter, as shown in Figure 3-4. Note that this includes the unused space between tracks. Head and cylinder skew are used to improve disk performance. As the read-write head moves from one track to another, starting sectors are offset to minimize the lag time.

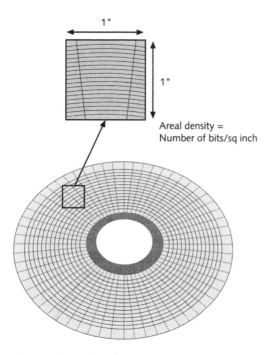

Figure 3-4 Areal density

 For more details on disk drives, visit *www.storageview.com*.

EXPLORING MICROSOFT FILE STRUCTURES

Because most PCs use Microsoft software products, you should understand Microsoft file systems so you will know how Windows and DOS computers store files. In particular, you need to understand clusters, file allocation tables (FATs), and the NTFS. The method an OS uses to store data determines where data can be hidden. When you examine a computer for forensic evidence, you need to explore these hiding places to determine whether they contain files or parts of files that might be evidence of a crime or policy violation.

3

In Microsoft file structures, sectors are grouped together to form **clusters**, which are storage allocation units of 512, 1024, 2048, 4096, or more bytes. Clusters combine to make larger blocks of data that work as one larger storage unit. Combining sectors minimizes the overhead of writing or reading files to a disk. The operating system groups one or more sectors into one cluster.

The number of sectors in a cluster varies according to the size of the disk. While a double-sided 3.5-inch floppy disk has one sector per cluster, a hard disk has four or more sectors per cluster.

Clusters are numbered sequentially starting at two because the first section of all disks contains a system area, the boot record, and a file structure database. Clusters are assigned by the operating systems and are referred to as **logical addresses**. Sectors, however, are referred to as **physical addresses** because they reside at the hardware or firmware level.

Disk Partition Concerns

Many hard disks are partitioned, or divided, into two or more sections. A **partition** is a logical drive. For example, an 8 GB hard disk may contain four partitions or logical drives. Some FAT versions do not recognize disks larger than 2.02 MB, so these disks have to be partitioned into smaller sections for the FAT to recognize the additional space. Someone who wants to hide data on a hard disk can create hidden partitions or voids—large unused gaps between partitions on a disk drive. That is, they can create partitions that contain unused space (the voids) between the primary partition and the first logical partition. This unused space between partitions is called the **inter-partition gap**. If someone hides data in an inter-partition gap, they could also use a disk editor utility such as Norton Disk Edit to alter information in the disk's partition table. Doing so removes all references to the hidden partition, concealing it from the computer's operating system. Another technique is to hide incriminating digital evidence at the end of the disk by declaring a smaller number of bytes than the actual size of the drive. Norton Disk Edit, however, lets you access these hidden or vacant areas of the disk.

One way to examine the physical level of a partition is to use a disk editor such as Norton Disk Edit, WinHex, or Hex Workshop. These tools allow you to view file headers and other critical parts of a file. Both involve analyzing the key hexadecimal codes that the operating system uses to identify and maintain the file system. Table 3–1 lists the hexadecimal codes that appear in a partition table and identifies the file system structure.

In some instances, you may need to identify the operating system on an unknown disk. You can use Norton Disk Edit, WinHex, or Hex Workshop to do this. The following steps show you how to download, install, and use Hex Workshop.

Table 3-1   Hexadecimal Codes in the Partition Table

Hexadecimal code	File system
01h	DOS 12-bit FAT
04h	DOS 16-bit FAT for partitions less than 32 MB
05h	Extended partition
06h	DOS 16-bit FAT for partitions greater than 32 MB
07h	NTFS
0Bh	DOS 32-bit FAT
0Ch	DOS 32-bit FAT for Interrupt 13 support

To use Hex Workshop:

1. If necessary, install Hex Workshop on your computer.

2. To download the trial version, use your browser to go to *www.hexworkshop.com* and follow the download instructions. Follow the online instructions to install and start Hex Workshop.

3. Insert a floppy disk in the floppy disk drive.

4. In Hex Workshop, click **Disk** on the menu bar and then click **Open Drive**. Click **OK**. Hex Workshop attempts to access your floppy disk and then the hard disk.

5. Figure 3-5 shows a typical Hex Workshop window for a hard disk. If you are working on a Windows 98 machine, the upper-right corner of the Hex Workshop window shows "MSWIN4."

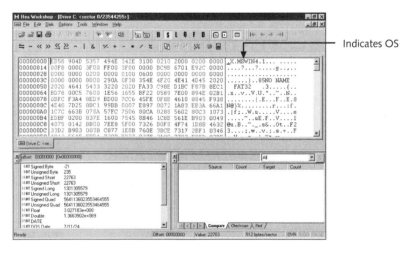

Figure 3-5   Hex Workshop showing OS

In addition to identifying the OS, tools such as Hex Workshop can identify file types. A file header allows the computer to identify a file type with or without an extension. In the following steps, you use Hex Workshop to identify file types. Before performing the steps, use Windows Explorer or My Computer to find a folder on your system that contains a bitmap (.bmp) file and a folder that contains a Word document (.doc).

To use Hex Workshop to identify file types:

1. To open a bitmap file on your computer, click **File** on the Hex Workshop menu bar, and then click **Open**. Navigate to a folder that contains a bitmap (.bmp) file, and then double-click a .bmp file. It should be the same on any OS.

2. As shown in Figures 3-6 to 3-8, the upper-right corner of the Hex Workshop window identifies the file type for most graphics. For .bmp files, it shows "BM6," "BM," or "BMF." The center section in the upper-left corner of the window shows "424D," which also indicates a .bmp file.

3. To open a Word document, click **File** on the menu bar and then click **Open**. Navigate to a folder that contains a Word document (.doc) file, and then double-click a .doc file.

4. As shown in Figure 3-9, the first line contains a row of zeros followed by "DOCF," which identifies the file as a Word document.

5. Close Hex Workshop.

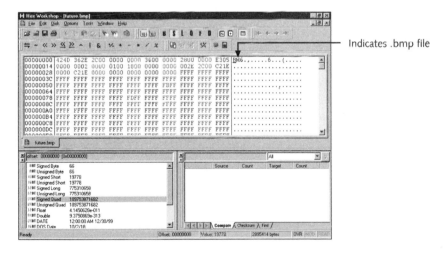

Indicates .bmp file

Figure 3-6   Hex Workshop showing .bmp file with "BM6"

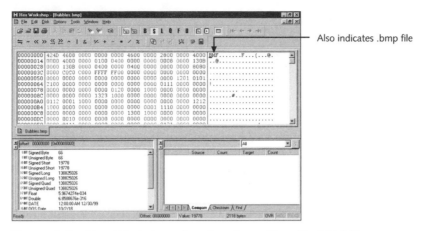

Also indicates .bmp file

Figure 3-7 Hex Workshop showing .bmp file with "BMF"

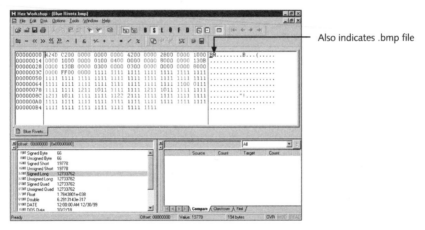

Also indicates .bmp file

Figure 3-8 Hex Workshop showing .bmp file with "BM"

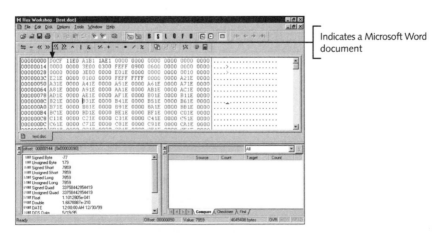

Indicates a Microsoft Word document

Figure 3-9 Hex Workshop showing .doc file

Boot Partition Concerns

On Windows and DOS computer systems, the boot disk contains a file called the **Master Boot Record (MBR)**, which contains information regarding the files on a disk and their locations, size, and other critical items. Several software products can replace the MBR provided by Microsoft operating systems. Third-party boot utilities, such as Partition Magic, let you install two or more operating systems on a single disk.

Because these boot utilities can interfere with some computer forensic data acquisition tools, you need many data acquisition tools. You cannot rely on any one vendor product to do computer forensic tasks.

Examining FAT Disks

The **File Allocation Table (FAT)** is the original file structure database that Microsoft originally designed for floppy disks. FAT is used on file systems prior to Windows NT and 2000. The FAT database contains filenames, directory names, date and time stamps, the starting cluster number, and attributes (archive, hidden, system, and read-only) of files on a disk. PCs use the FAT to organize files on a disk so that the OS can find the files it needs. The FAT is typically written to the outermost track on a disk.

There are three versions of FAT—FAT12, FAT16, and FAT32—and a variation called Virtual File Allocation Table (VFAT). Microsoft developed VFAT to handle long file-names when it released the first version of Windows 95 and Windows for WorkGroups. The previous version of FAT used by Microsoft DOS 6.22 had a limitation of eight characters for filenames and three characters for extensions.

FAT12 is used specifically for floppy disks, and therefore has a limited amount of storage space. It was originally designed for MS-DOS 1.0, the first Microsoft operating system, which only used floppy disk drives.

To handle large disks, Microsoft developed FAT16, which is still used on older Microsoft operating systems such as MS-DOS 3.0, Windows 95 (first release), and Windows NT 3.5 and 4.0. FAT16 supports disk partitions that have a maximum storage capacity of 2.02 GB.

When disk technology improved and disks larger than 2 GB were created, Microsoft developed FAT32, which is used on newer Microsoft operating systems such as Windows 95 (second release), 98, Me, 2000, and XP. FAT32 can access up to 2 terabytes of disk storage. One disk can have multiple partitions in FAT16, FAT32, or NTFS.

Cluster sizes vary according to the size of the hard disk and the file system. Table 3-2 describes the number of sectors and bytes assigned to a cluster on FAT16 and FAT32 disks according to hard disk size.

Microsoft operating systems allocate disk space for files by clusters. This practice results in **drive slack**, which is any space not used for active files. Drive slack includes **RAM slack** and **file slack**. For example, suppose you create a large text document that contains 5000 characters. That is, it contains 5000 bytes of data. If you save the 5000-byte

Table 3-2   Sectors and Bytes Per Cluster

Drive size	Number of sectors	FAT16	FAT32
256-511 MB	16	8 KB	4 KB
512 MB-1 GB	32	16 KB	4 KB
1-2 GB	64	32 KB	4 KB
2-8 GB	8	N/A	4 KB
8-16 GB	16	N/A	8 KB
16-32 GB	32	N/A	16 KB
More than 32 GB	64	N/A	32 KB

file on a FAT16 1.6 GB disk, a Microsoft OS automatically reserves one cluster for your 5000–byte file.

For a 1.6 GB disk, the operating system allocates about 32,000 bytes, or 64 sectors (512 bytes per sector), for your file. The unused space, 27,000 bytes, is the file slack space (see Figure 3-10). RAM slack is created in the unused space on a sector. The file in the previous example uses up 10 sectors or 5120 bytes. 120 bytes of a sector is not used. Any information in the RAM at that point such as login IDs or passwords are placed in RAM slack when you save a file. Later you will see how fragments of files and passwords can be retrieved from these areas.

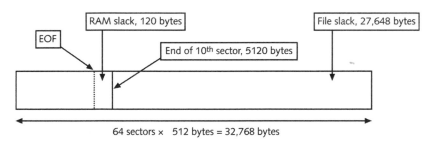

Figure 3-10   File slack space

The purpose of providing so much space is to minimize the fragmentation of files as they increase in size. The operating system adds your extra data to the end of the file. It lets the file expand to this assigned cluster until it consumes the remaining reserved 27,000 bytes of space.

When you run out of room for an allocated cluster, the operating system allocates another cluster for your file, which creates more slack space on the disk. As files grow and require more disk space, assigned clusters are chained together. Typically chained clusters are contiguous to one another on the disk. However, as some files are created, then deleted, and other files are expanded, the chain can be broken or fragmented. By using a tool such as Norton Disk Edit, you can view the cluster-chaining sequence and see how FAT addresses link clusters to one another (see Figure 3-11).

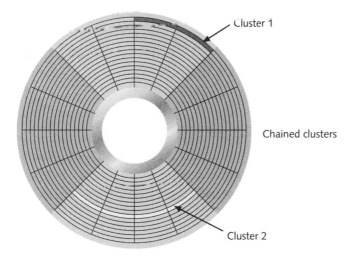

Figure 3-11   Chained clusters as a result of increasing file size

Figure 3-12 shows a FAT32 cluster assignment in Norton Disk Edit. FAT32 systems list the volume number along with other file information. In this figure, the primary master disk drive is represented as [0], or zero. The numbers to the right of each [0] define the content of the FAT32 cluster assignment. That is, the number listed to the immediate right of each [0] is the next cluster to which the file is written.

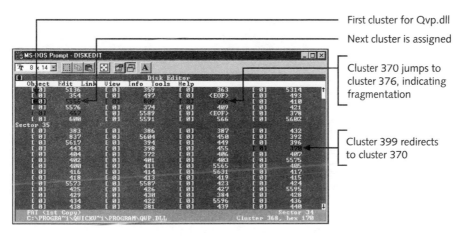

Figure 3-12   FAT32 cluster assignment

When the operating system stores data in a FAT file system, it assigns a starting cluster position to a file. Data for the file is written to the first assigned cluster. Recall that when the file runs out of room in this first assigned cluster, FAT assigns the next available cluster to the file. If the next available cluster is not contiguous to the current cluster, the file becomes fragmented. Within the FAT for each cluster on the **volume** (partitioned disk), the operating system writes the next assigned cluster, which is the number to the right of [0] in the FAT cluster assignment. Think of clusters as buckets that can hold a specific amount of bytes. When a cluster (or bucket) fills, the operating system allocates another cluster (bucket) to collect the extra data. The file shown in Figure 3-12 has a significant amount of fragmentation.

Another tool that lists the order of cluster assignments for a file is DriveSpy's **Chain FAT Entry (CFE)** command, shown in Figure 3-13.

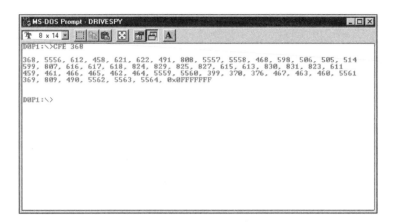

Figure 3-13   DriveSpy CFE command

Figure 3-13 shows each cluster assignment as a whole. In this view, you can also see that this file is fragmented. This figure also shows the **end-of-file marker** of 0x0FFFFFFF. This is the code typically used with FAT file systems to show where the file ends.

On rare occasions such as a system failure or sabotage, these cluster chains can break. If they do, data can be lost because it becomes disassociated with the previous chained cluster. FAT looks forward to the next cluster assignment, but does not provide pointers to the previous cluster. Rebuilding these broken chains can be difficult.

Many of the most recent disk forensic tools have automated most of the file rebuilding process. These improved features allow for easier recovery of lost data.

TIP

The FAT contains information about the files on the disk, including the filename, the cluster location on the disk, creation date and time, modified date and time, and the last accessed date.

Deleting FAT Files

When a file is deleted in Windows Explorer or through the MS-DOS Delete command, the operating system inserts the lowercase Greek letter sigma (σ) in the first letter position of the filename in the FAT database. The sigma symbol instructs the operating system that the file is no longer available and that a new file can be written to the same cluster location.

In Microsoft operating systems, when a file is deleted, only the reference to the file is removed. The data in the file remains on the disk drive. The area of the disk where the deleted file resides becomes **unallocated disk space** (also called disk free space). The unallocated disk space is now available to receive new data from either new files or other files needing more space as they grow. Most forensic tools recover any data still residing in this area.

EXAMINING NTFS DISKS

The **New Technology File System (NTFS)** was introduced when Microsoft created Windows NT. NTFS is the primary file system for Windows XP. Each generation of Windows NT, 2000, and XP have included minor changes in the configuration and features of NTFS. The design of NTFS originated from Microsoft's project for IBM with the OS/2 operating system, where the file system was called **High Performance File System (HPFS)**. When Microsoft created Windows NT, it provided backward capability so that NT could read OS/2 HPFS disk drives. Since the release of Windows 2000 and XP, this backward capability is no longer available.

To be an effective computing investigator and forensic examiner, you should maintain a library of old operating systems and application software. Also keep older hardware that is in good operating condition. You might need the old software and hardware to perform your analysis because there are some forensic tasks you can't perform with modern tools on older operating systems and hardware.

NTFS offers significant improvements over the older FAT file systems. NTFS provides much more information about a file, including security features, file ownership, and other attributes of the file. NTFS also allows for more control over files and folders (directories) than the older FAT file systems.

In NTFS, everything written to the disk is considered a file. On an NTFS disk, the first data set is the **Partition Boot Sector**. The Partition Boot Sector starts at Sector 0 of the disk and can expand to 16 sectors. Immediately after the Partition Boot Sector is the **Master File Table (MFT)**. The MFT is the first file on the disk, and is similar to the FAT in Microsoft's older operating systems. The MFT is covered later in this section.

An MFT file is created at the same time a disk partition is formatted as an NTFS volume. The MFT typically consumes about 12.5 percent of the disk when it is created. As data is added, the MFT can expand to take up 50 percent of the disk.

One of the most significant advantages of NTFS over FAT is that it consumes much less file slack space. Compare the cluster sizes in Table 3-3 to Table 3-2, which showed FAT cluster sizes.

Table 3-3   Cluster Sizes in an NTFS Disk

Drive size	Clusters	Size
0-512 MB	1	512 bytes
512 MB-1 GB	2	1024 bytes
1-2 GB	4	2048 bytes
2-4 GB	8	4096 bytes
4-8 GB	16	8192 bytes
8-16 GB	32	8192 bytes
16-32 GB	64	32,768 bytes
More than 32	128	65,539 bytes

The clusters are smaller for the smaller disk drives. This saves more space on all disks using NTFS.

NTFS also uses **Unicode**, an international data format. Unlike the **American Standard Code for Information Interchange (ASCII)** 8-bit configuration, Unicode uses a 16-bit configuration. For western language alphabetic characters, the first eight bits are identical to ASCII, and the remaining eight bits are null (that is, they are all binary zeros). Knowing this feature of Unicode comes in handy when you perform your first keyword search for evidence on a disk drive. (This is discussed in more detail in Chapter 10.)

Because NTFS provides many more features than FAT, more utilities are used to manage it. For example, the MFT stores file data differently from FAT. The next section of this chapter covers this feature.

NTFS System Files

Because everything on an NTFS disk is a file, the first file, the MFT, contains information about all files located on the disk. This includes the system files used by the operating system such as Windows XP, 2000, and NT. Within the MFT, the first 15 records are reserved for system files. Records within the MFT are referred to as **meta–data**. Table 3-4 lists the first 15 meta–data records you find in the MFT.

Table 3-4   Meta-data Records in the MFT

Filename	System file	Record position	Description
$Mft	MFT	0	Base file record for each folder on the NTFS volume. Other record positions within the MFT will be allocated if more space is needed.
$MftMirr	MFT 2	1	The first four records of the MFT are saved in this position. If a single sector fails in the first MFT, the records can be restored allowing for recovery of the MFT.
$LogFile	Log file	2	Previous transactions are stored here to allow for recovery after a system failure has occurred in the NTFS volume.
$Volume	Volume	3	Information specific to the volume such as label and version is stored here.
$AttrDef	Attribute definitions	4	A table listing the attribute names, numbers, and definitions.
$	Root filename index	5	This is the root folder on the NTFS volume.
$Bitmap	Boot sector	6	A map of the NTFS volume showing which clusters are in use and which are available.
$Boot	Boot sector	7	Used to mount the NTFS volume during the bootstrap process. Additional code is listed here if this is the boot drive for the system.
$BadClus	Bad cluster file	8	For clusters that have unrecoverable errors, an entry of the cluster location is made to this file.
$Secure	Security file	9	The unique security descriptors for the volume are listed in this file. This is where the Access Control List (ACL) is maintained for all files and folders (directories) on the NTFS volume.
$Upcase	Upcase table	10	This converts all lowercase characters to uppercase Unicode characters for the NTFS volume.
$Extend	NTFS extension file	11	Various optional extensions are listed here such as quotas, object identifiers, and reparse point data.
		12-15	Reserved for future use.

3

NTFS Attributes

When Microsoft introduced NTFS, the way its operating system stores data on disks had significantly changed. In NTFS, all files and folders (directories) have file attributes. Individual elements of a file such as its name, security information, and even the data in the file are considered file attributes. Each of these attributes has a unique **attribute type code**. Some attribute type codes have names and code.

NTFS attributes fall into two categories, **resident attributes** and **nonresident attributes**. Attributes contained within the MFT are referred to as resident attributes. In Windows 2000 and XP, all file and folder (directory) data is contained within the MFT. If more room is needed for file growth, the MFT assigns an inode to the file attribute. An inode links attribute records to other attribute records within the MFT.

 Linking data with inodes originated with UNIX. The inode linking used in an MFT works differently from UNIX or Linux inodes (discussed in Chapter 4). The MFT inodes only link records within the MFT, that is, to resident attributes.

TIP

Table 3-5 shows the fields (attributes) in each record within the MFT.

If the file is extremely large, such as a large database file, the MFT assigns the data to a nonresident attribute area of the disk. The file entry has links from the MFT to areas outside of the MFT in the free disk space area of the disk volume.

Data is linked to nonresident attributes by directly accessing cluster positions on the disk volume. That is, when a disk is created as an NTFS file structure, the operating system assigns logical clusters to the entire disk's partition. These assigned clusters are called **logical cluster numbers (LCNs)**. LCNs become the addresses that allow the MFT to read and write data to the nonresident attribute area of the disk.

When data is written to nonresident attribute disk space, an LCN address is assigned to the MFT file (record) entry. This file entry is given a **virtual cluster number (VCN)** for every LCN used to store data for each file in a nonresident disk. A VCN is associated with the LCN for the files that extend into the nonresident attribute disk space (see Figure 3-14).

The first VCN used for each file that extends into the nonresident attribute area of a disk volume starts at zero (0). The numbering of the LCN also starts at zero (0), which is the beginning area of the disk partition (the volume).

Table 3-5   Attributes in the MFT for Windows 2000 and XP

Attribute type	Purpose
Standard information	Time stamp data and link (inode) count information is listed here.
Attribute list	Attributes that do not fit within the MFT are listed here. This lists the location of the nonresident attributes.
Filename	The long and short name for the file is contained here. Up to 255 Unicode bytes are available for long file names. For POSIX requirements, additional names or hard links can also be listed here.
Security descriptor	Ownership and who has access rights to the file or folder is listed here.
Data	File data is stored here. Multiple data attributes are allowed for each file. When more space is needed for additional data an inode is assigned linking to a new MFT attribute record.
Object ID	The volume-unique file identifier is listed here. Not all files will need this unique identifier.
Logged tool stream	This field is used by the encrypted file system service that was implemented in Windows 2000 and XP.
Reparse point	This is used for volume mount points and for installable file system (IFS) filter drivers. For the IFS it marks specific files that are used by drivers.
Index root	Implemented for use of folders and indexes.
Index allocation	Implemented for use of folders and indexes.
Bitmap	Implemented for use of folders and indexes.
Volume information	Used by the $Volume system file. The volume version number is listed here.
Volume name	Used by the $Volume system file. The volume version label is listed here.

3

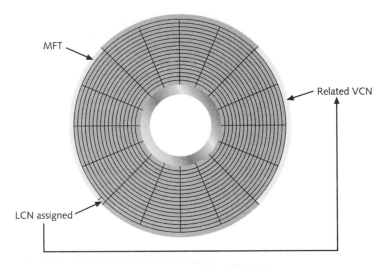

Figure 3-14   MFT relationship with VCN and LCN

NTFS Data Streams

Of interest to the computing investigator and forensic examiner are **multiple data streams**. Data can be appended to existing files when you are examining a disk. Data streams can obscure valuable evidentiary data, either intentionally or by coincidence.

In NTFS, a data stream becomes an additional data attribute of a file. From a Windows NT, 2000, or XP DOS shell, you can create a data stream by using the following command. Note that the data stream is defined in the MFT by the colon (:) between the file extension and the data stream label.

```
C:\ECHO text_message > myfile.txt:stream1
```

To display the content of a data stream, use the following MS-DOS command:

```
C:\ MORE < myfile.txt.stream1
```

Later you will learn how to search for specific keywords relating to your investigation. You might retrieve a file associated with a keyword, but not be able to open the file. A data stream does not appear when you open the file in a text editor. The only way you can tell whether a file has a data stream attached to it is by examining the MFT entry for that file. If you see a colon (:) with a name following it in the MFT, that is a data stream file.

NTFS Compressed Files

To improve data storage on disk drives, NTFS provides compression similar to FAT DriveSpace 3, a compression utility used by Windows 98. Under NTFS, individual files, folders, or entire volumes can be compressed. With FAT16 you can only compress a volume. When you are running a Windows XP, 2000, or NT system, the compressed data appears normal when you access it through Windows Explorer or applications such as Microsoft Word.

During an investigation, you typically work from a bit-stream image copy of a compressed disk, folder, or file. The operating system of your forensic workstation may only be able to see the compressed data as an unusual binary file. If you do encounter and identify compressed data, you need to decompress the data or use a computer forensic tool that can decompress automatically. Only a few advanced computer forensic tools can decompress and examine compressed data.

NTFS Encrypted File Systems (EFS)

When Microsoft introduced Windows 2000, they added encryption to NTFS. Microsoft refers to this built-in encryption as **Encrypted File System (EFS)**. An EFS implements a **public** and **private key** method of encrypting files, folders, or disk volumes (partitions). Encrypted files are only accessible by the owner or user who encrypted the data. The owner holds the private key, while the operating system holds the public key. (Encryption is covered in more detail later in this chapter.)

When a Windows XP or 2000 user implements EFS, a **recovery certificate** is generated and sent to the local Windows XP or 2000 administrator's account. The purpose of the recovery certificate is to provide a mechanism that will recover encrypted files under EFS if there is a problem with the original private key of the user. The recovery key is stored in one of two places. When the user of a networked workstation initiates EFS, it sends the recovery key to the local domain server administrator's account. If the workstation is standalone, it will send it to the workstation's administrator's account.

A user can apply EFS to files stored on his or her local workstation or on a remote server. Windows XP and 2000 will automatically decrypt the data when the user or an application initiated by the user accesses an EFS file, folder, or disk volume.

EFS data is only accessible by the owner of the data. Future plans include allowing the user to give other users the ability to access his or her EFS data. If a user copies a file that is encrypted with EFS to a folder that is not encrypted, the copied data is saved unencrypted.

EFS Recovery Key Agent

The Recovery Key Agent implements the recovery key certificate, which is the Windows XP or 2000 administrator account. There are two ways the Windows XP or 2000 administrator can recover a key. It can be recovered from Windows or from an MS-DOS command prompt. There are three functions available when using the MS-DOS command prompt, they are:

- CIPHER
- COPY
- EFSRECVR

For specific information on how to use these commands, use the question mark switch after each of these commands. With the exception of the COPY command, these only work on NTFS systems. Encrypted files are not part of FAT12, FAT16, or FAT32 operating systems.

- CIPHER /?
- COPY /?
- EFSRECVR /?

TIP

If you copy an encrypted file from an NTFS disk to a floppy disk, it is automatically unencrypted.

To recover an encrypted EFS file, the user can either e-mail it or copy the file to the administrator. The administrator can then run the recovery agent function to restore the file. For additional information, review the appropriate Microsoft Windows Resource Kit documentation (*www.microsoft.com*) for the latest procedures on how to recover EFS certificates.

Deleting NTFS Files

You typically use Windows Explorer to delete files from a disk. When a file is deleted from Windows XP, 2000, or NT, the operating system renames the deleted file and moves it to the Recycle Bin. Another method of deleting files is from the MS-DOS shell prompt using the DEL (delete) command. This method does not rename and move the file to the Recycle Bin, but eliminates it from the MFT listing in the same way that the FAT does.

When you delete a file using Windows Explorer, Windows allows you to restore the deleted file from the Recycle Bin. To do this, the operating system takes the following step when deleting a file or a folder using Windows Explorer:

1. Windows changes the name of the file and moves it to a subdirectory with a unique identity in the Recycle Bin.

2. Windows stores information about the original path and filename in the **Info2 file**, which is the control file for the Recycle Bin. It contains ASCII data, Unicode data, and the date and time of the deletion for each file or folder.

NTFS files that are deleted using an MS-DOS shell function in a similar way as FAT files. The following steps also apply when a user empties a Recycle Bin. When a file is deleted from an MS-DOS shell, the operating system performs the following tasks:

1. The associated clusters are designated to be free; that is, they are marked available for new data.

2. The $BITMAP file attribute of the MFT is updated to reflect the deletion of the file showing that this space is available.

3. The file attribute record for the file in the MFT is marked as being available.

4. Any linking inodes and VFN/LCN cluster locations to nonresident data are removed from the MFT.

5. A run list is maintained in the MFT of all cluster locations on the disk's non-resident attribute area. When the list of links are deleted, any reference back to the links are lost.

TIP

NTFS is more efficient than FAT for reclaiming deleted space. Deleted files are overwritten more quickly.

UNDERSTANDING MICROSOFT BOOT TASKS

You should have a good understanding of what happens to disk data at startup. In some investigations, you must preserve the data on the disk as the perpetrator of a crime or security incident last used it. Any access to a computer system after it was used for illicit reasons alters your disk evidence.

Altering disk data on a suspect computer lessens its evidentiary quality considerably. In some instances, improperly accessing a suspect computer could cause it to completely lose its worthiness as evidence, thus making the digital evidence useless for any litigation. Later, you learn how to properly handle and preserve digital evidence.

The following sections review the files that are activated when a Windows machine starts up. Knowing what happens when your computer starts helps you know what to look for when you to examine a disk drive.

Windows XP, 2000, and NT Startup

Although Windows NT is significantly different from Windows 95 and 98, the startup methodology for the New Technology operating systems—NT, 2000, and XP—are about the same. There are some minor differences in how specific system start files function, but they basically accomplish the same orderly startup.

All NTFS computers perform the following steps when the computer is turned on:

1. Power-on self test (POST)

2. Initial startup

3. Boot loader

4. Hardware detection and configuration

5. Kernel loading

6. User logon

Windows XP uses the files discussed in the following section to startup. These files can be located on either the system partition or the boot partition.

Startup Files for Windows XP

The **NT Loader (NTLDR)** file loads the operating system. NTLDR is located in the root folder of the system partition. When the system is powered on, NTLDR reads the Boot.ini file, which displays a boot menu. After you have selected the desired mode to boot to, it runs Ntoskrnl.exe and reads Bootvid.dll, Hal.dll, and the startup device drivers.

Boot.ini specifies the Windows XP path installation. The Boot.ini file is located in the root folder of the system partition, and contains options that allow you to select the Windows version.

If a system has multiple booting operating systems, NTLDR reads the **BootSect.dos** file, which contains the address, or the boot sector location, of each OS. The BootSect.dos file is a hidden file located in the root folder of the system partition.

The **NTDetect.com** file is located in the root folder of the system partition. When the boot selection is made, the NTLDR runs NTDetect.com, a 16-bit real-mode program. This real-mode program queries the system for the basic device and configuration data. It then passes its findings to NTLDR. This program identifies components and values on the computer system such as the following components:

- CMOS time and date value
- Buses attached to the motherboard, such as Industry Standard Architecture (ISA) or Peripheral Component Interconnect (PCI)
- Disk drives connected to the system
- Mouse input devices connected to the system
- Parallel ports connected to the system

NTBootdd.sys is the device driver that allows access to SCSI or ATA drives that are not related to the BIOS. Controllers that do not use Interrupt 13 (INT-13) use this file. This program runs in privileged processor mode with direct access to hardware and system data. The NTBootdd.sys is located in the root folder of the system partition. On some workstations a SCSI disk drive is used as the primary boot disk. The function of the NTBootdd.sys file is to provide a method for the operating system to directly communicate with the SCSI disk.

Ntoskrnl.exe is the Windows XP OS kernel. It is located in system-root\Windows\System32 folder.

Hal.dll is the hardware abstraction layer dynamic link library (DLL). The HAL allows the OS kernel to communicate with the computer's hardware. It is located in the system-root\Windows\System32 folder.

At startup, data and instruction code is moved in and out of the **PageFile.sys** to optimize the amount of physical random-access memory (RAM) that is available.

The Registry key HKEY_LOCAL_MACHINE\SYSTEM contains information that is required by the OS to start system services and devices. This System Registry File is located in the system-root\Windows\System32\Config\System folder.

Device drivers contain instructions for the OS for hardware devices such as the keyboard, mouse, and video, and are stored in the system-root\Windows\System32\Drivers folder.

TIP To identify the specific path for "system-root" at an MS-DOS prompt, type the **SET command** and then press the Enter key with no additional switches or parameters. The SET command when executed alone displays all current system-root paths.

Windows XP System Files

Next you need to examine the core operating system files used by Windows XP, 2000, and NT. These files are typically located in \Windows\System32 or \Winnt\System32.

Table 3-6 describes the essential files used by Windows XP. While a few of these are repeats, you should be aware of their key roles.

Table 3-6 Windows XP System Files

Filename	Description
Ntoskrnl.exe	The executable and kernel of the XP operating system
Ntkrnlpa.exe	The physical address support program for accessing over four gigabytes of physical memory (RAM)
Hal.dll	The hardware abstraction layer (described earlier)
Win32k.sys	The kernel-mode portion of the subsystem for Win32
Ntdll.dll	System service dispatch stubs to the executable functions and internal support functions
Kernel32.dll	Core WIN32 subsystem DLL file
Advapi32.dll	Core WIN32 subsystem DLL file
User32.dll	Core WIN32 subsystem DLL file
Gdi32.dll	Core WIN32 subsystem DLL file

Contamination Concerns for XP

When you start a Windows XP or older NTFS workstation, several files are immediately accessed. When any of these or other related operating system files are accessed at startup, the last access date and time stamp for the files changes to the present time. This change destroys any potential evidence that might be needed to show when a Windows XP workstation was last used. For this reason, you should have a strong working knowledge of the boot process so that you understand what occurs during a system startup.

Windows 9x and Me Startup

Windows 9x operating systems, Windows 95, and Windows 98 have similar boot processes. Windows Me is also similar, with one significant exception; you cannot boot to a true MS-DOS mode. When conducting a computing investigation and forensic examination, having the ability to boot to MS-DOS is much preferred, especially if you are running a later version of Windows 95 OEM SR2 (version 4.00.1111) or newer where the MS-DOS boot mode can read and write to FAT32 disk.

Windows 9x operating systems have two modes: **DOS protected-mode interface (DPMI)**, and **protected-mode graphic user interface (GUI)**. Many of the computer forensic tools currently available use the DPMI mode, and only work in MS-DOS mode. They must be run from MS-DOS, not an MS-DOS shell from Windows, because certain disk drive accesses used by these MS-DOS tools conflict with the GUI.

The system files used by Windows 9x have their origin in MS-DOS 6.22. The **IO.SYS** file communicates between a computer's BIOS and hardware and with MS-DOS code, the kernel. During the boot phase of a Windows 9x system, IO.SYS monitors the keyboard for an F8 keystroke. If F8 is entered during the boot up process, IO.SYS loads the Windows boot menu. The options on the Windows boot menu range from booting to Windows normally to running in Safe mode to perform maintenance.

Option number 5 listed in the Windows boot menu (see Figure 3-15) is Command prompt only. By selecting this option you can go directly into a Windows 9x version of MS-DOS.

Microsoft Windows 98 Startup Menu

1. Normal
2. Logged (\BOOTLOG.TXT)
3. Safe mode
4. Step-by-step confirmation
5. Command prompt only
6. Save mode command prompt only

Enter a choice: 1

Figure 3-15   Windows 9x boot options

You need to be familiar with either MS-DOS 6.22 or Windows 9x MS-DOS. **MSDOS.SYS** is a hidden text file that contains startup options for Windows 9x. In MS-DOS 6.22, the MSDOS.SYS file is the actual operating system kernel. In Windows 9x, MSDOS.SYS has a different role in that it has replaced the AUTOEXEC.BAT and CONFIG.SYS files from MS-DOS 6.22. The MSDOS.SYS file is usually located in the root directory of the C: drive.

3

Since MSDOS.SYS in Windows 9x is a text file, you can add switches to customize the boot process. Of interest to the computing investigator and forensic examiner are the two switches of BOOTMENU= and BOOTMENUDELAY=. By placing these two switches in the [Options] group of the MSDOS.SYS file, you can force the Windows boot menu to appear every time the system is booted.

Each switch requires a unique number value to function correctly. The BOOTMENU switch has only two values—zero (0) or one (1). Value zero is the default and turns off the Windows boot menu unless F8 is pressed during the boot up process. Value one forces the Windows boot menu to appear every time the system is booted.

To extend the duration of the Windows boot menu past its default time of a few seconds, you can alter the time before the boot process automatically continues by putting a value from one to fifty-nine after the BOOTMENUDELAY, as shown in Figure 3-16.

```
[Paths]
WinDir=c:\windows
WinBootDir=c:\windows
HostWinBootDrv=c

[Options]
BootMulti=1
BootGUI=1
DoubleBuffer=1
BootMenu=1
BootMenuDelay=59
;
;The following lines are required for compatibility with other programs.
;Do not remove them (MSDOS.SYS needs to be >1024 bytes).
;xxxxxxxxxxxxxxxxxxxxxxxxxxxxxxxxxxxxxxxxxxxxxxxxxxxxxxxxxxxxxxa
;xxxxxxxxxxxxxxxxxxxxxxxxxxxxxxxxxxxxxxxxxxxxxxxxxxxxxxxxxxxxxxb
;xxxxxxxxxxxxxxxxxxxxxxxxxxxxxxxxxxxxxxxxxxxxxxxxxxxxxxxxxxxxxc
;xxxxxxxxxxxxxxxxxxxxxxxxxxxxxxxxxxxxxxxxxxxxxxxxxxxxxxxxxxxxxd
;xxxxxxxxxxxxxxxxxxxxxxxxxxxxxxxxxxxxxxxxxxxxxxxxxxxxxxxxxxxxe
;xxxxxxxxxxxxxxxxxxxxxxxxxxxxxxxxxxxxxxxxxxxxxxxxxxxxxxxxxxxxf
;xxxxxxxxxxxxxxxxxxxxxxxxxxxxxxxxxxxxxxxxxxxxxxxxxxxxxxxxxxxg
;xxxxxxxxxxxxxxxxxxxxxxxxxxxxxxxxxxxxxxxxxxxxxxxxxxxxxxxxxxh
;xxxxxxxxxxxxxxxxxxxxxxxxxxxxxxxxxxxxxxxxxxxxxxxxxxxxxxxxxxi
;xxxxxxxxxxxxxxxxxxxxxxxxxxxxxxxxxxxxxxxxxxxxxxxxxxxxxxxxxj
;xxxxxxxxxxxxxxxxxxxxxxxxxxxxxxxxxxxxxxxxxxxxxxxxxxxxxxxxxk
;xxxxxxxxxxxxxxxxxxxxxxxxxxxxxxxxxxxxxxxxxxxxxxxxxxxxxxxxl
;xxxxxxxxxxxxxxxxxxxxxxxxxxxxxxxxxxxxxxxxxxxxxxxxxxxxxxxm
;xxxxxxxxxxxxxxxxxxxxxxxxxxxxxxxxxxxxxxxxxxxxxxxxxxxxxxxn
;xxxxxxxxxxxxxxxxxxxxxxxxxxxxxxxxxxxxxxxxxxxxxxxxxxxxxxo
;xxxxxxxxxxxxxxxxxxxxxxxxxxxxxxxxxxxxxxxxxxxxxxxxxxxxxxp
;xxxxxxxxxxxxxxxxxxxxxxxxxxxxxxxxxxxxxxxxxxxxxxxxxxxxxq
;xxxxxxxxxxxxxxxxxxxxxxxxxxxxxxxxxxxxxxxxxxxxxxxxxxxxr
;xxxxxxxxxxxxxxxxxxxxxxxxxxxxxxxxxxxxxxxxxxxxxxxxxxxxs
AutoScan=1
WinVer=4.10.2222
```

Figure 3-16   Windows 9x boot delay

The **COMMAND.COM** file provides a prompt when booting to MS-DOS mode (DPMI). With COMMAND.COM you can run a limited number of MS-DOS commands that are built into COMMAND.COM, called the internal MS-DOS commands, which are described in the following list:

- DIR for directory listing
- CD (CHDIR) to change directory location
- CLS to clear the screen of all output
- DATE to display the CMOS calendar value
- COPY to copy a file from one location to another
- DEL (ERASE) to erase a file
- MD (MKDIR) to create a subdirectory
- PATH to define where to find other commands and programs
- PROMPT to define what your MS-DOS prompt will look like
- RD (RMDIR) to erase a directory or folder
- SET to define or remove environment variables
- TIME to display the CMOS clock value
- TYPE to list the content to screen of a text file
- VER to get the MS-DOS version number you're working in
- VOL to display the volume label of the disk drive

As described earlier, system files in Windows 9x and Me that contain valuable information can easily be altered during booting, destroying their evidentiary value. Later you will discover how to test your forensic workstation to make sure it is not contaminating your evidence.

UNDERSTANDING MS-DOS STARTUP TASKS

Similar to Windows 9x, MS-DOS uses three files when booting: IO.SYS, MSDOS.SYS, and COMMAND.COM. Two other files are then used to configure MS-DOS at startup: CONFIG.SYS and AUTOEXEC.BAT. MS-DOS 6.22 boot files use the same names for the first three files. However, there are some significant differences between these files and those found in Windows 9x.

IO.SYS is the first file that is loaded after the ROM bootstrap loader finds the disk drive. IO.SYS then resides in RAM and provides the basic input and output service for all of MS-DOS functions.

The **MSDOS.SYS** file is the second program to load into RAM immediately after IO.SYS. This original MSDOS.SYS file is the actual kernel for MS-DOS, not a text file like the Windows 9x and Me MSDOS.SYS files. After MSDOS.SYS completes setting up the DOS services, it looks for the CONFIG.SYS file to configure the device drivers and other settings. MSDOS.SYS then loads COMMAND.COM. As the loading of COMMAND.COM nears completion, MSDOS.SYS looks for and loads AUTOEXEC.BAT.

COMMAND.COM for MS-DOS provides the same internal DOS commands in MS-DOS 6.22 as in Windows 9x.

CONFIG.SYS is a text file containing commands that are typically run only at system startup. These unique commands enhance the computer's DOS configuration.

AUTOEXEC.BAT is an automatically executed batch file, and contains customized settings for MS-DOS. In this batch file, you can define the default path and set environmental variables such as temporary directories.

MS-DOS accesses and resets the last access dates and times on files when powered up. In Chapter 5, you will create a boot floppy disk that prevents you from changing data on a suspect's hard disk.

Other DOS Operating Systems

Years ago there were several other microcomputer operating systems, such as Control Program for Microprocessors (CP/M), Digital Research Disk Operating System (DR-DOS), and Personal Computer Disk Operating System (PC-DOS). Of these operating systems, only DR-DOS is still commercially available. As mentioned in Chapter 1, you might encounter a very old computer that uses one of these operating systems. If you do, you will need to call upon your talents and those of your network of experts to research, explore, and test these old operating systems. This section describes the unique features and facts about each operating system.

In the 1970s, a company named Digital Research created the first non-specific micro-computer operating system, CP/M. Computers using CP/M originally had 8-inch floppy disk drives, and did not support hard disk drives. The central processing unit (CPU) in CP/M was the Z-80 from Zilog, which could access up to 64 KB of RAM. The file system was unique to CP/M. In the early 1980s, IBM provided an expansion card with a built-in Z-80 CPU. This allowed users to process the many applications available for CP/M at that time.

After Microsoft developed MS-DOS, Digital Research created DR-DOS to compete against MS-DOS. In 1988 DR-DOS was the final operating system produced by Digital Research, which used FAT12 and FAT16 file systems. DR-DOS has a richer command environment than MS-DOS, and its operating system files are organized differently. Rather than storing the operating system commands in the DOS directory, they are stored in the DR-DOS directory. DR-DOS is now primarily sold as an embedded OS for out-of-the-box ROM or Flash ROM systems.

When IBM created the first PC using the Intel 8088 processor, they needed an operating system. In the early 1980s, IBM contracted with Microsoft, then a startup company. In 1981, Microsoft purchased a program called 86-DOS from a small company called Seattle Computing. 86-DOS could run on the Intel 8088 16-bit processor, and was a modification of CP/M from Digital Research. Microsoft then provided 86-DOS to IBM for use on their PCs and IBM called it PC-DOS.

PC-DOS works much like MS-DOS. IBM maintained upgrades to PC-DOS until Microsoft released Windows 95. The operating system files in PC-DOS are slightly different from MS-DOS. For example, IO.SYS is called IBMIO.SYS and MSDOS.SYS is called IBMDOS.SYS. PC-DOS uses FAT12 and FAT16 file systems, so accessing data from PC-DOS is no different than working with MS-DOS.

DOS Commands and Batch Files

After Microsoft introduced Windows 95, the use of MS-DOS commands and batch files has steadily declined. However, some MS-DOS commands are still used, so you can apply them to batch files for your computing administrative functions.

Batch files can control the quality of your work because they repeat the same series of commands every time with no mistakes. Batch files are ideal for investigations with important tasks that may become repetitive because of large quantities of data you must sort through.

MS-DOS has several commands that you can combine into a single batch file, which then work like a single command. A simple batch file could copy a file from one folder to another folder or disk, and then compare the original file to the newly copied file. The MS-DOS commands to use for this batch file are COPY, FC (for File Compare), and ECHO. COPY copies a file from a source to a target. You use FC to verify that the file was copied properly. The ECHO command turns the screen output on or off. Figure 3-17 shows the batch file you are about to create. Cpverify.bat copies the WhatsNew.txt file to the Temp folder, and then verifies that the file was copied to that folder.

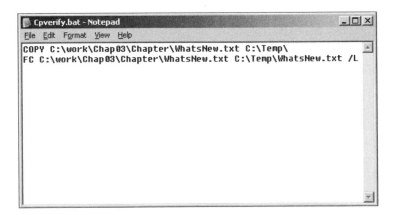

Figure 3-17   Batch file Cpverify.bat

To create Cpverify.bat:

1. On a Windows 98 machine, open Notepad and type **This is a test**.

2. Save the file as **WhatsNew.txt** in the Chap03\Chapter folder in your work folder.

3. Create a file in Notepad by clicking **File** on the menu bar and then clicking **New**.

4. Type **@Echo on** and press **Enter**.

5. If necessary, create a folder named **Temp** in the root directory. Type **Copy C:*work folder*\Chap03\Chapter\WhatsNew.txt C:\Temp** and press **Enter**, where *work folder* is the name of the work folder on your system.

6. Type **FC C:*work folder*\Chap03\Chapter\WhatsNew.txt C:\Temp\WhatsNew.txt   /L** and press **Enter**, where *work folder* is the name of the work folder on your system.

7. Save the file as **Cpverify.bat** in the Chap03\Chapter folder in your work folder.

8. Close Notepad.

9. Open the Command Prompt window.

10. Navigate to the folder where you stored Cpverify.bat by typing **cd ..*work folder*\Chap03\Chapter** and pressing **Enter**.

11. Run the batch file by typing **Cpverify** and pressing **Enter**. See Figure 3-18.

12. Exit the command prompt window.

MS-DOS provides functions such as parameter passing and conditional execution commands. The commands that are unique for batch files are listed in Table 3-7. These commands are a mix between internal and external MS-DOS commands.

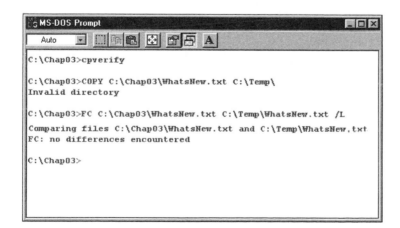

Figure 3-18   Results of Cpverify.bat

Table 3-7   DOS Batch Commands

Batch command	Function
@	Suppresses the display of the commands to the screen.
CALL	Initiates another batch file. When it completes the called batch file it returns control to the original batch file, e.g. CALL BATCH1.
CHOICE	Stops the batch file and waits for input from the keyboard. The key stroke input is then interrupted with the IF ERRORLEVEL command.
ECHO	Turns on or off the display of commands to the screen as they execute, e.g. ECHO ON or ECHO OFF.
FOR..IN..DO	Repeats a command or group of commands in For-Next loop.
GOTO	Jumps to a predefined label within the batch file. Labels are defined by any name value that is not already defined as an MS-DOS command and ends with a colon (:), e.g. LOOP:.
IF	Allows for a conditional execution of a command; if true, the command is executed, if false, it is skipped.
PAUSE	Halts the batch job execution, displays a message, and waits for any key to be pressed before continuing the batch file execution.
REM	Allows you to insert comments in the batch file. All text to the right of the REM command is ignored.
SHIFT	For parameters that are passed within a batch file. Moves all the parameters one parameter to the left.

You can pass up to ten command parameters from the command line to the batch file. Parameters in MS-DOS batch files are numeric values preceded by a percent sign (%), which tells the batch file that a parameter value is expected. The number indicates which parameter is passed. In Cpverify.bat, you could change the fixed file values to parameters to pass. The following is the original batch file:

```
@ECHO ON
COPY E:\UTILIT~5\PGP\WHATSNEW.TXT  C:\TEMP
FC E:\UTILIT~5\PGP\WHATSNEW.TXT  C:\TEMP\WHATSNEW.TXT /L
```

The following is the parameter-passing batch file:

```
@ECHO ON
COPY %1 %2
FC %1 %2 /L
```

When you run this new batch file, you enter the path and filenames at the prompt.

To modify Cpverify.bat:

1. Open a new text file in Notepad.

2. Type **Testing versatility of batch files**.

3. Save the file as **Testing.txt** in the **Chap03\Chapter** folder in your *work folder*.

4. Open **Cpverify.bat** in Notepad.

5. Delete the second line, type **COPY %1 %2**, and then press **Enter**.

6. Delete the third line, type **FC %1 %2 /L**, and then press **Enter**.

7. Save the file with the same name and in the same location, and then close Notepad.

8. Open a Command Prompt window.

9. Use the **cd** command to access the **Chap03\Chapter** folder in your *work folder*.

10. Type **Cpverify Testing.txt C:\Temp\Testing.txt** and then press **Enter**.

Cpverify copies the Testing.txt to the Temp folder, and then displays a message indicating that the original and copied files are the same. The advantage to using parameters is that you do not have to update your batch file every time you want to repeat a specific group of tasks.

Another useful command is GOTO, a simple branching command that instructs the batch file to jump to a predefined location, which is defined by a unique name that is preceded with a colon (:), as in the following example.

```
:GO_LOOP
    ECHO Sample GOTO loop
GOTO GO_LOOP
```

A loop structure repeats one or more commands until a specified condition is met. The preceding GO_LOOP command runs forever because it doesn't specify a condition that stops the loop. To specify a condition, you can use the **IF** command.

The IF command will test three possible conditions: ERRORLEVEL, the value of two strings to see if they are equal, and whether a file exists.

The ERRORLEVEL has five numeric error codes starting from zero (0). The commands that return these error codes are:

BACKUP	DISKCOMP	DISKCOPY
FORMAT	GRAFTABLE	KEYB
REPLACE	RESTORE	XCOPY

The meaning of each code is shown in Table 3-8.

The following code provides an example of how to use ERRORLEVEL in a batch file with XCOPY. You can use the XCOPY command to copy files and any subfolders to a specified location.

```
XCOPY C:\TEMP A:\
IF ERRORLEVEL 1 GOTO GO_ERROR
Other code skipped when the above error is encountered.
:GO_ERROR
ECHO Command failed! Check for floppy in drive A
```

Table 3-8 Error Codes

Code	Result
0	Indicates that the operation was successful.
1	Error of a read or write operation.
2	The user initiated Ctrl+C. (Recall that Ctrl+C is a common method to interrupt a command.)
3	Fatal termination of read or write occurred.
4	An error occurred during initialization.

The following code uses ERRORLEVEL with the EXIST command. You use this command in the format IF EXIST filename to verify whether filename exists. If it does, the next command or function on the same line is performed. If filename does not exist, the command on the same line is skipped, and the command on the next line is performed.

```
CD \MYDOCU~1
IF EXIST TEXT.DOC GOTO GO_DEL
Other code skipped when the above error is encountered.
:GO_DEL
DEL TEXT.DOC
```

In MS-DOS, you can also compare strings. The following example shows how to use the IF command to compare two values and then branch to another command:

```
REM TEST_IF.BAT
IF "%1"== "" GOTO ERR_MSG
IF %1==COPYFILE GOTO GO_COPY
IF %1==BYE GOTO END
:ERR_MSG
  ECHO You need to enter something!
  ECHO Run this batch file again!
  GOTO :END
:GO_COPY
  COPY C:\TEMP\TEXT.DOC A:
:END

  EXIT
```

To run this batch file, be sure to enter a matching parameter, as in the following code:

```
TEST_IF COPYFILE
```

Or

```
TEST_IF BYE
```

This example shows that if the user enters no parameters, which MS-DOS interprets as a null value, DOS tells the user to run the file again with the correct input. It stops running the file with the EXIT command and returns to the MS-DOS prompt.

NOTE MS-DOS parameters are case-sensitive. If you use all uppercase characters in a batch file, for example, you must type uppercase letters when you enter the parameters.

The FOR..IN..DO command allows you to define a group of variables, and then process those variables to perform a specific task. A parameter can be also passed to refine the batch file. The double percent sign with a single letter (%%A) defines a variable in MS-DOS batch files, as in the following example.

```
            REM CPFLOPPY.BAT
    FOR %%A IN (A: a: B: b:) DO IF "%%A"==%1" GOTO CP_FILE
            ECHO You forgot to specify which floppy drive to
use.
            ECHO Remember the floppy drive is either A: or
B:
    GOTO END
    :CP_FILE
            ECHO You have selected the %1 drive.
            COPY C:\TEMP\TEXT.DOC A:
    :END
```

With the FOR command, a batch file repeats a command or function until the correct value is entered. In the preceding example, the FOR %%A command branches to the DO IF statement if the user types the correct floppy disk drive letter. The allowed values for this example are a, A, b, and B. Use the CHOICE command if you want to build a batch file to accept input after the file has started running. CHOICE limits you to the options you have listed in the batch file, and does not pass a parameter. This command also uses the ERRORLEVEL command, though not like the other previously listed DOS commands. In the steps that follow you create a batch file that uses these options to format a floppy disk. The CHOICE command can branch to up to 255 different labels that are defined in its key switch value. The syntax for the CHOICE command is:

```
    CHOICE /C:key /N /S /T:choice,seconds prompt
```

Table 3-9 defines each switch and option in the CHOICE command.

Table 3-9   CHOICE Command Switches and Options

Switch or option	Function
/C:key	Defines the keys, or labels, that are displayed at the CHOICE prompt
/N	Suppresses the DOS question mark at the prompt
/S	Makes the input at the CHOICE prompt case-sensitive
/T:choice/seconds	Provides a delay in seconds for any previously defined /C:key value
Prompt	Defines the choices for the user

Recall that the ERRORLEVEL command has five basic responses from 0 to 4. Used with the CHOICE command, ERRORLEVEL responds with exit codes to allow you to branch to a specific label. The exit codes used are defined in Table 3-10.

Table 3-10   ERRORLEVEL Codes for the CHOICE Command

Code	Results
0	Terminated by user by pressing Ctrl+C or Ctrl+Break
1	First key parameter is selected with the /C:key switch
2	Second key parameter is selected with the /C:key switch
3-254	nth key parameter is selected with the /C key switch
255	Error parameter is selected with the /C key switch

The CHOICE command is an external MS-DOS command. Windows 9x stores the command in the \WINDOWS\COMMAND folder, while MS-DOS 6.22 stores it in the \DOS directory. To build a batch file on a floppy disk, you must copy the CHOICE command to the disk along with the batch file.

To use the CHOICE command in a batch file:

1. On a Windows 98 machine, open Notepad and create a new file named **MyChoice.bat**. Save the file in the Chap03\Chapter folder in your work folder.

2. Type the following code in the document:

```
@ECHO OFF
cls
ECHO.
ECHO   *** Floppy Disk Format Batch Job ***
ECHO.
ECHO Choose the drive containing the disk you want to for-
mat.
ECHO.
ECHO Floppy disk drives available:
ECHO.
ECHO "A:"
ECHO "B:"
ECHO.
ECHO Select drive and type of format:
ECHO.
ECHO Option        Drive & Format
ECHO ------        ----------------
ECHO    A          A: Quick Format
ECHO    B          A: Unconditional Format
ECHO    C          A: Quick Format with System Files
```

3

```
ECHO    D          B: Quick Format
ECHO    E          B: Unconditional Format
ECHO    F          B: Quick Format with System Files
CHOICE /C:ABCDEF "Choose Drive and Format option "
if errorlevel 255 goto Error
if errorlevel 6    goto F_for
if errorlevel 5    goto E_for
if errorlevel 4    goto D_for
if errorlevel 3    goto C_for
if errorlevel 2    goto B_for
if errorlevel 1    goto A_for
:Error
ECHO.
ECHO Run this batch file again,
ECHO but next time,
ECHO make a different selection.
ECHO.
GOTO End
:F_for
ECHO.
ECHO "B: Quick format with system files."
FORMAT B: /Q /S
ECHO.
GOTO End
:E_for
REM "B: Unconditional format."
FORMAT B: /U
GOTO End
:D_for
ECHO "B: Quick format."
FORMAT B: /Q
GOTO End
:C_for
ECHO "A: Quick format with system files."
FORMAT A: /Q
GOTO End
:B_for
ECHO "A: Unconditional format."
FORMAT A: /U
GOTO End
:A_for
ECHO "A: Quick format."
PDBLOCK 0
:End
```

3. Save the file and exit Notepad.

4. Open a Command Prompt window.

5. Using the cd command, navigate to the **\Chap03\Chapter** folder in your *work folder*.

6. Type **MyChoice.bat** and press **Enter**.

   The batch file displays commands on the screen that allow you to format the disk in the A: or B: drive in a variety of formats—quick, unconditional, or quick with system files.

7. In drive A: or B:, insert a floppy disk containing files you no longer need. Then type **C** or **F**, depending on the floppy disk drive you are using. Your choice is confirmed and the the floppy disk is formatted.

8. Once the formatting process is over, exit the Command Prompt window.

MS-DOS has many more commands, switches, and functions. It is highly recommended that you learn more of these commands as you progress through your training as a computing investigator and forensic examiner.

Chapter Summary

- ❏ The Microsoft operating systems (OSs) used FAT12 and FAT16 on older systems such as MS-DOS, Windows 3.X, and Windows 9x. The maximum partition size is 2.02 GB. Newer systems use FAT32. FAT12 is used almost exclusively on floppy disks.

- ❏ The Registry on older Windows OSs is used to keep a record of hardware attached, user preferences, network information, and installed software. Buried deep in the Registry is information such as passwords. It is contained in two binary files called System.dat and User.dat.

- ❏ The capacity of a hard disk is obtained by using the cylinders, heads, and sectors (CHS) method. To find the byte capacity of a disk, multiply the number of heads, cylinders, and tracks.

- ❏ Clusters are used to accommodate large files. Sectors are grouped into clusters and clusters are chained to minimize the overhead of reading and writing files to a disk. Clusters are logical addresses.

- ❏ The New Technology File System (NTFS) is more versatile because it uses the Master File Table (MFT) to track information such as security items, the first 750 bytes of data, long and short filenames, and a list of the nonresident attributes.

- ❏ File slack, random-access memory (RAM) slack, and drive slack are all areas in which valuable information may reside on a drive. These include items downloaded files, swap files, passwords, and login IDs.

- ❏ To be an effective computer forensic investigator, you need to maintain a library of older operating systems and applications.

- ❏ NTFS uses Unicode to store information. Unicode is an international code and uses a 16-bit configuration instead of the 8-bit configuration used by American Standard Code for Information Interchange (ASCII) and other older representation codes.

❏ Hexadecimal codes provide information about files and OSs. You can determine the file type by using various tools such as WinHex and Hex Workshop.

❏ NTFS uses inodes to link file attribute records to other file attribute records. Attributes fall into two categories—resident and nonresident attributes.

❏ NTFS can compress individual files, folders, or entire partitions. FAT16 can only compress entire volumes.

3

KEY TERMS

American Standard Code for Information Interchange (ASCII)—A coding scheme using 7 or 8 bits that assigns numeric values to up to 256 characters, including letters, numerals, punctuation marks, control characters, and other symbols.

areal density—The number of bits per square inch of a platter.

attribute type code—In NTFS, the code assigned to file attributes such as the filename and security information.

AUTOEXEC.BAT—An automatically executed batch file that contains customized settings for MS-DOS, including the default path and environmental variables such as temporary directories.

bootstrap—Information contained in the ROM that the computer accesses during its startup process that tells it how to access the OS and hard drive.

boot.ini—Specifies the Windows XP path installation.

BootSect.dos—If the machine has a multiple booting system, NTLDR reads bootsect.dos to determine the address of the sector location of each OS. This is a hidden file.

Chain FAT Entry (CFE)—A command used by DriveSpy that displays all the clusters in a chain that start at a specified cluster.

clusters—Storage allocation units composed of sectors. Clusters are 512, 1024, 2048, or 4096 bytes in length.

COMMAND.COM—Provides a prompt when booting to MS-DOS mode.

CONFIG.SYS—A text file containing commands that are typically run only at system startup to enhance the computer's DOS configuration.

cylinders—The intersection of tracks on two or more disk platters.

DOS protected-mode interface (DPMI)—Used by many computer forensic tools that do not operate in the Windows environment.

drive slack—Any information that had been on the storage device previously. It can contain deleted files, deleted e-mail, or file fragments. Both file slack and RAM slack constitute drive slack.

Encrypted File System (EFS)—Symmetric key encryption first used in Windows 2000 on NTFS formatted disks.

end-of-file marker—0x0FFFFFFF. This is the code typically used with FAT file systems to show where the file ends.

File Allocation Table (FAT)—The original file structure created by Microsoft. It is written to the outermost track of a disk and contains information about each file stored on the drive. The variations are FAT12, FAT16, and FAT32.

file slack—The slack space created when a file is saved. If the allocated space is larger than the file, the remainder is slack and can contain passwords, login IDs, and deleted e-mail.

file system—Provides an OS with a road map to the data on a disk.

geometry—The internal organization of the drive.

Hal.dll—Hardware abstraction layer dynamic link library. It tells the OS kernel how to interface with the hardware.

head and cylinder skew—A method used by manufacturers to minimize lag time. The starting sectors of tracks are slightly offset from each other to move the read-write head.

Heads—The devices that read and write data to the disk platters.

High Performance File system (HPFS)—File system used by IBM for their OS/2 OS.

IF—This command tests three possible conditions: ERRORLEVEL, the value of two strings to see if they are equal, and whether a file exists.

Info2 file—In Windows NT, 2000, and XP, the control file for the Recycle Bin.

inter-partition gap—Partitions created with unused space or voids between the primary partition and the first logical partition.

IO.SYS—This MS-DOS file communicates between a computer's BIOS and hardware and with MS-DOS code.

logical address—When files are saved, they are assigned to clusters. The clusters have been given numbers by the OS that start at two. The cluster number defines the logical address.

logical cluster number (LCN)—Used by the MFT of NTFS. It refers to a specific physical location on the drive.

Master Boot Record (MBR)—On Windows and DOS computer systems, the boot disk file, which contains information regarding the files on a disk and their locations, size, and other critical items.

Master File Table (MFT)—Used by NTFS to track files. It contains information about the access rights, date and time stamps, system attributes, and parts of the file.

meta-data—In NTFS, this refers to information stored in the MFT.

MSDOS.SYS—A hidden text file that contains startup options for Windows 9x.

multiple data streams—Ways in which data can be appended to a file intentionally or not. In NTFS, it becomes an additional data attribute of a file.

New Technology file system (NTFS)—Created by Microsoft to replace FAT. NTFS uses security features, allows for smaller cluster sizes, and uses Unicode, which makes it a much more versatile system. Used mainly on newer OSs such as Windows NT, 2000, and XP.

nonresident attributes—When referring to the MFT of the NTFS, all data that is stored in a location separate from the MFT.

NTBootdd.sys—A device driver that allows access to SCSI or ATA drives that are not referred to in the BIOS.

NTDetect.com—A command file that identifies hardware components during boot up and sends the information to NTLDR.

NT Loader (NTLDR)—Loads Windows NT. It is located in the root folder of the system partition.

Ntoskrnl.exe—The kernel for the Windows XP.

PageFile.sys—At startup, data and instruction code is moved in and out of the PageFile.sys. This is to optimize the amount of physical memory (RAM) that is available during startup.

partition—A logical drive on a disk. It can be the entire disk or a fraction thereof.

Partition Boot Sector—The first data set of an NTFS disk. It starts at Sector [0] of the disk drive and it can expand up to 16 sectors.

physical address—The actual sector in which a file is located. Sectors are at the hardware and firmware level.

private key—In encryption, the key held by the owner of the file.

protected-mode graphical user interface (GUI)—One mode in Windows 9x.

public key—In encryption, the key held by the system receiving the file.

RAM slack—The slack in the last sector of a file. Any data currently residing in RAM at the time the file is saved can appear in this area whether the information was saved or not. It can contain login IDs, passwords, and phone numbers for dial-ups.

recovery certificate—A method used by NTFS so a network administrator can recover encrypted files if the user/creator of the file loses their private key encryption code.

Registry—In Windows, the Registry contains information about the hardware, network connections, user preferences, installed software, and other critical information. Using the Regedit or Regedit32 from the Run dialog box lets you access the Registry.

resident attributes—When referring to the MFT, all attributes that are stored in the MFT of the NTFS.

sectors—Individual sections on tracks, typically made up of 512 bytes.

SET command—When used at the command-line prompt with no switches or attributes, this command displays all current system-root paths.

track density—The space between tracks on a disk. The smaller the space between tracks, the more tracks on a disk. Older drives with wider track densities allowed wandering.

tracks—The individual concentric circles on a disk platter.

unallocated disk space—The area of the disk where the deleted file resides.

Unicode—A 16-bit character code representation that is replacing ASCII. It is capable of representing over 64,000 characters.

virtual cluster number (VCN)—When a file is saved in the NTFS, it is assigned both a logical cluster number and a virtual cluster number. The logical cluster is a physical location, while the virtual cluster consists of chained clusters.

volume—Any storage media, such as a single floppy disk, a partition on a hard drive, the entire drive, or several drives. On Intel systems, a volume is any partitioned disk.

zoned bit recording—How most manufacturers deal with the fact that the inner tracks of a platter are physically smaller than the outer tracks. Grouping the tracks by zones ensures that the tracks are all the same size.

4

MACINTOSH AND LINUX BOOT PROCESSES AND DISK STRUCTURES

After reading this chapter, you will be able to:

♦ Understand Macintosh disk structures

♦ Explore Macintosh boot tasks

♦ Examine UNIX and Linux disk structures

♦ Understand UNIX and Linux boot processes

♦ Examine compact disc (CD) data structures

♦ Understand other disk structures

In Chapter 3, you explored the Microsoft operating systems, including Disk Operating System (DOS) and Windows, and the Microsoft file systems. Because computer forensics investigators must understand how most operating systems store and manage data, this chapter continues that exploration by examining the Linux and Macintosh operating systems. Chapters 3 and 4 provide a foundation for you to build from as you become more knowledgeable about current and legacy operating systems and their associated file systems.

In addition to Linux and Macintosh operating systems, this chapter discusses media and hardware such as CDs, Integrated Device Electronics (IDE) hard drives, small computer system interface (SCSI) hard drives, and the redundant array of independent disks (RAID) configuration. These devices store data in particular ways, which you should understand so that you can retrieve evidence data as necessary.

UNDERSTANDING THE MACINTOSH FILE STRUCTURE

The current Macintosh operating system is Mac OS X version 10.2, known as Jaguar. This section addresses older Macintosh OS 9 file systems. Jaguar and the Macintosh OS X, known as Darwin, is a complete **Berkeley Software Design (BSD) UNIX** implementation that was designed at the University of California at Berkeley. The Macintosh is a popular computer for schools and graphics professionals, and Apple's innovations continue to make the Macintosh popular in the personal computer (PC) market. As a result, computer forensic investigators must be familiar with the Mac OS file and disk structure. The Macintosh uses a **hierarchical file system (HFS)** where files are stored in directories, or folders, which can be nested in other folders. The **File Manager** handles the reading, writing, and storage of data to physical media. It also collects data to maintain the HFS, and manipulates files, folders, and other items. The **Finder** is another Macintosh tool that works with the operating system to keep track of files and maintain each user's desktop.

In the Mac OS, a file consists of two parts: a **data fork** and a **resource fork**. As shown in Figure 4-1, each fork contains information vital to each file.

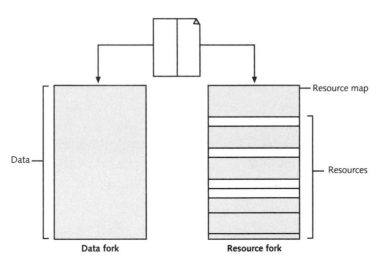

Figure 4-1   Mac OS resource fork and data fork

The resource fork contains the following information:

- Resource map
- Resource header information for each file
- Window locations
- Icons

The data fork typically contains data that the user creates, such as text or spreadsheets. Application programs, such as Microsoft Word or Excel, also read and write to the data fork. When you are working with an application file, the resource fork contains additional information such as the menu, dialog boxes, icons, executable code, and controls.

In the Mac OS, the resource or data fork can be empty. Because the File Manager is in charge of reading and writing to files, it can access both forks.

Understanding Volumes

A **volume** is any storage media that is used to store files. A volume can be all or part of the storage media for hard disks; however, in the Mac OS, a volume on a floppy disk is always the entire floppy. With larger disks, the user or administrator defines a volume (see Figure 4-2).

Volume clients

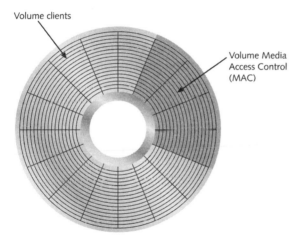

Volume Media
Access Control
(MAC)

Figure 4-2   Multiple volumes on a disk

Volumes have **allocation blocks** and **logical blocks**. A logical block is a collection of data that cannot exceed 512 bytes. When you save a file, the File Manager assigns the file to an allocation block, which is a group of consecutive logical blocks. On a floppy disk, an allocation block is typically one logical block. As the volumes increase in size, one allocation block may be composed of three or more logical blocks. Figure 4-3 illustrates the relationship between the two blocks.

File Manager can access a maximum of 65,535 allocation blocks per volume. If a file fork contains information, it always occupies one allocation block. For example, if the data fork only contains 11 bytes of data, it occupies one allocation block on a floppy disk or 512 bytes. That leaves more than 500 bytes empty in that fork.

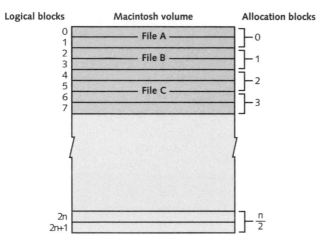

Figure 4-3   Logical and allocation block structures

The Macintosh file system has two descriptors of the end of file (EOF)—the **logical EOF** and the **physical EOF**. The logical EOF is the number of bytes that contain data. The physical EOF is the end of the number of allocation block for that file, as shown in Figure 4-4.

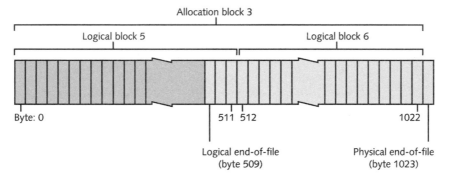

Figure 4-4   Logical EOF and physical EOF

Macintosh reduces file fragmentation by using **clumps**, which are contiguous allocation blocks. As a file increases in size, it occupies more of the clump. By adding more clumps to larger files, the volume fragmentation is kept to a minimum.

EXPLORING MACINTOSH BOOT TASKS

For older Macintosh operating systems, the first two logical blocks on each volume (or disk) are the boot blocks, which contain information about the system startup. The startup block contains information about the system configuration. Optional executable code for the system file can also be placed within the boot blocks. Typically system startup instructions are stored in the HFS system file, not the boot blocks.

The older Macintosh operating systems use a **Master Directory Block (MDB)**, also known as a **Volume Information Block (VIB)**. All information about the volume is stored in the MDB, and is written to the MDB when the volume is first initialized. A copy of the MDB is also written to the next-to-last block on the volume. This copy is updated whenever the extents overflow file or the catalog increases in size. The purpose of the copied MDB is to support disk utility functions. The **extents overflow file** is used by the File Manager to store any information not in the MDB or **Volume Control Block (VCB)**. The **catalog** is used to maintain the relationships between files and directories on a volume. (See *developer.apple.com/techpubs/mac/Files/Files-102.html* for more information.) When the operating system mounts the volume, some information from the MDB is written to a VCB, which is stored in system memory and used by the File Manager.

A File Manager utility manages files in the operating system. A system application called a **Volume Bitmap** tracks each block on a volume. That is, the Volume Bitmap knows which blocks are in use and which ones are available to receive data. The Volume Bitmap has information about the blocks' usage, but not about the blocks' content.

The File Manager stores file-mapping information in two locations: the contents overflow file and the file's catalog entry. The Volume Bitmap's size depends on the amount of allocated blocks for the volume.

The Mac OS 9 file system uses a B*-tree file system for the File Manager. **B*-tree** organizes the directory hierarchy and file block mapping for the File Manager. In the B*-tree, files are nodes (records or objects) that contain file data. Each node is 512 bytes long. The nodes that contain actual file data are called leaf nodes. The B*-tree also has nodes that handle file information called header nodes, index nodes, and map nodes. The **header node** stores information about the B*-tree file. The **index node** stores link information to the previous node and the next node. The **map node** stores a node descriptor and a map record. The **leaf node** is the bottom level of a B*-tree file that stores data for the individual files.

EXAMINING UNIX AND LINUX DISK STRUCTURES

In addition to Windows and Macintosh operating systems, contemporary computers and networks use UNIX and Linux. There are many flavors of UNIX on the market, including System 7, SGI IRIX, Sun Solaris, IBM AIX, BSD, and HP-UX. Linux is also available in many distributions, such as Caldera, Red Hat, and SuSe. All Linux references in this text are to Red Hat Linux because of its popularity and ease of use. Linux is probably the most consistent UNIX-like operating system available today because the Linux kernel is regulated under the **GNU General Public License (GPL)** agreement, which defines Linux as open source software, meaning that anyone can use, change, and distribute the software without owing royalties or licensing fees to another party; no single person or entity controls Linux. Being an open source operating system under the GPL also helps to maintain the stability and quality of Linux.

Table 4-1 lists several system files from popular UNIX operating systems.

Table 4-1   UNIX System Files

OS	System files	Purpose
AIX	/etc/exports	Configuration files
	/etc/filesystems	Static file system information
	/etc/utmp	Current logon information
	/var/adm/wtmp /etc/security/lastlog	Logon history information
	/etc/security/failedlogin	Failed logon information
HP-UX	/etc/utmp	Current logon information
	/var/adm/wtmp /var/adm/wtmpx	Logon history information
	/var/adm/btmp	Failed logon information
	/etc/fstab	Static file system information
	/etc/checklist	Static file system information (version 9.x)
	/etc/exports	Configuration files
	syslog	System log files
IRIX	syslog	System log files
	/etc/exports	Configuration files
	/etc/fstab	Static file system information
	/var/adm/btmp	Failed logon information
	/var/adm/lastlog /var/adm/wtmp /var/adm/wtmpx	Logon history information
	/var/adm/utmp /var/adm/utmpx	Current logon information
Linux	/etc/exports	Configuration files
	/etc/fstab	Other relevant files
	/var/log/lastlog /var/log/wtmp	Logon history information
	/var/run/utmp	Current logon information

Table 4-1 *continued*

OS	System files	Purpose
Solaris	/etc/passwd	Account information for local system
	/etc/group	Group information for local system
	/var/adm/sulog	Switch user log data
	/var/adm/utmp	Logon information
	/var/adm/wtmp /var/adm/wtmpx /var/adm/lastlog	Logon history information
	/var/adm/loginlog	Failed logon information
	messages	System log files
	/etc/vfstab	Static file system information
	/etc/dfs/dfstab /etc/vfstab	Configuration files

In the following steps, you use standard Linux commands to find information about your Linux system.

To find system information using standard Linux commands:

1. Boot your Linux computer and open a terminal window, if necessary. If your computer starts at a graphical desktop, click the **Red Hat** icon in the lower-left corner of the desktop, point to **System Tools**, and then click **Terminal**.

2. To find the name of your computer and the version of Linux it uses, type **uname –a** and press **Enter**. Record or capture a screen image of the results.

TIP

To capture a screen image in Linux, use the GIMP graphics program. In Linux Red Hat 8, click the Red Hat icon on the desktop, point to Graphics, and then click The GIMP. Close all windows and palettes except the main The GIMP window, if necessary. Click File on the menu bar, point to Acquire, and then click Screen Shot. Click the Single Window option button, if necessary, to capture a window, and then click the OK button. Click the window you want to capture. To save the image, right-click the captured image, point to File, and then click Save As.

3. Type **ls –l** and then press **Enter** to list the files in the current directory. Note the name of one file in the directory.

4. To determine the access time of a file (the last time a command was executed on the file), type **ls –ul** *filename* where *filename* is the name of the file you noted in Step 3. Then press **Enter**. Record or capture a screen image of the results.

5. Type **netstat –s** at the Linux command prompt, and then press **Enter**. A list appears showing protocol information that your computer uses to communicate with other systems connected to your Linux computer.

The standard Linux file system is called the **second extended file system (Ext2fs)**, which can support disks as large as 4 TB and files as large as 2 GB. Of the file structures studied so far, Linux is most closely related to Macintosh. (Recall that the most recent versions of Mac OS are built on BSD UNIX.) Linux, however, is unique in that it uses **inodes**, or information nodes, that contain descriptive information about each file or directory. Specifically, an inode is a pointer to other inodes or blocks. When the last pointer to a file is deleted, the file is effectively deleted. Instead of copying a file to every directory in which it is listed, using inodes lets Linux store the file in one location and create pointers to that file in other locations, as shown in Figure 4-5. For example, suppose you need to access the MyDatabase file when you are working in the Clients directory, the Accounting directory, and the General_Documents directory. Instead of making individual copies of MyDatabase in each directory, you create the file once in one directory, and then create pointers to MyDatabase from the other two directories.

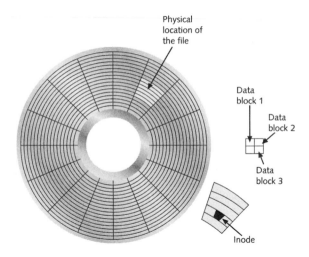

Figure 4-5   Using inodes to represent files

Each inode keeps an internal link count. When that number becomes 0, Linux deletes the file. To find deleted files during a forensic investigation, you search for inodes that contain some data and whose link count is 0.

The Linux file structure is made up of **meta-data** and **data**. Meta-data includes items such as the user ID (UID), group ID (GID), size, and permissions for each file. An inode contains the modification, access, and creation (MAC) times, not a filename. Inodes have a number that is linked with the filename in the directory called "file_name." To keep track of files and data, Linux pairs the inode number with the filename. The data portion of the Linux file structure contains the contents of the file.

UNIX and Linux Overview

In UNIX and Linux, everything is a file, including disk drives, the monitor for a workstation, any connected tape drives, a network interface, system memory, directories, and actual files. All UNIX files are defined as objects, which means that a file, like an object in an object-oriented programming language, has properties and methods (actions such as writing, deleting, and reading) that can be performed on the file.

UNIX consists of four components that define the file system: the boot block, super-block, inode, and data block. A block is a disk allocation unit that ranges in size from 512 bytes and up. The bootstrap code is located in the boot block. A UNIX or Linux computer has only one boot block, which is located on the main hard disk. The superblock contains vital information about the system and is considered part of the meta-data. The superblock indicates the geometry of the disk, available space, and the location of the first inode. It also keeps track of all the inodes. Linux keeps multiple copies of the superblock in various locations on the disk to prevent losing such vital information.

The superblock manages the UNIX or Linux file system, including configuration information about the file system, such as the block size for the disk drive, the file system names, blocks reserved for the inodes, free inode list, free block starting chain, volume name, and the last update time and backup time inodes.

The first data after the superblock on a UNIX or Linux file system are the inode blocks. An inode is assigned to every file allocation unit. As files or directories are created or deleted, inodes are also created or deleted. The link between the inodes associated with files and directories controls access to those files or directories.

The final component in the UNIX and Linux file system is a **data block**. As in the Microsoft file system structures, the Linux file system on a PC has 512-byte sectors. Typically a data block consists of 4096 or 8192 bytes with clusters of hard disk sectors. Figure 4-6 shows that when you save a file, the data blocks are clustered and a unique inode is assigned.

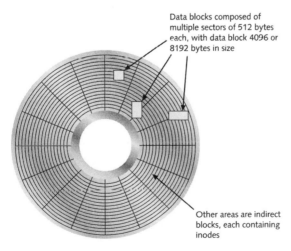

Figure 4-6   Clustering sectors and blocks to save a file in Linux

As with other operating systems, the size of a data block determines how much of the disk space is wasted. The larger the data block, the higher the likelihood of fragments. If you create a 512 KB database, 19 data blocks of 8192 bytes are clustered to save the file, and 3648 bytes are left empty, but allocated. Note that in addition to keeping track of the file size, the inode keeps track of the number of blocks assigned to the file.

When manufactured, all disks have more storage capacity than the manufacturer states. For example, a 20 GB disk may actually have 20.5 GB of free space because disks always have bad sectors despite the most careful procedures. While DOS and Windows do not keep track of bad sectors, Linux does in an inode called the **bad block inode**. The root inode is inode 2, while the bad blocks inode is inode 1. Some forensic tools ignore inode 1 and fail to recover valuable data for cases. Someone trying to mislead a computer forensic investigation can access the bad blocks inode in Linux and list good sectors in it, and then hide information in these bad sectors.

To find the bad blocks on your Linux computer, you can use the `badblocks` command, though you must log on with a system administrator account to do so. Linux also provides two other commands that provide bad block information—the `mke2fs` and `e2fsck` commands. While the badblocks command can destroy valuable data when you run it, the `mke2fs` and `e2fsck` commands include safeguards that prevent them from overwriting important information.

In the following steps, you check a floppy disk for bad blocks. You need a blank floppy disk or one that contains data you no longer need.

To check a floppy disk for bad blocks:

1. Boot your Linux computer to a graphical desktop. Insert a floppy disk in the floppy disk drive, but do not mount it. If your system is set to mount disks automatically, click the **Red Hat** icon in the lower-left corner of the desktop, point to **System Tools**, and then click **Disk Management**. Make sure the floppy drive is selected, and then click the **Unmount** button.

2. To open a terminal window, click the **Red Hat** icon in the lower-left corner of the desktop, point to **System Tools**, and then click **Terminal**.

3. At the command prompt, type **mke2fs –c /dev/fd0** and press **Enter**. Note that /dev/fd0 specifies the location of the first floppy disk drive on the system. If you are using a different floppy disk drive, such as fd1, use that location instead. Linux reads and displays disk information, including any bad blocks. After the command prompt appears, record or capture a screen image of the results.

4. To compare the results of the `mke2fs` and `e2fsck` commands, type **e2fsck –c /dev/fd0** and press **Enter**. (Replace "fd0" with your floppy disk drive, if necessary.) Linux again reads and displays disk information, including any bad blocks. After the command prompt appears, record or capture a screen image of the results.

5. Find information about the `badblocks` command. Type **man badblocks** and then press **Enter**. The first manual page for the badblocks command appears. Press **Pg Dn** to see additional pages. Record or capture a screen image of each page.

6. Be prepared to explain the value of finding bad block information on a Linux computer.

An assigned inode contains the following information about a file or directory.

- The mode and type of the file or directory

- The number of links to a file or directory

- The UID and GID of the file's or directory's owner

- The number of bytes contained in the file or directory

- The file's or directory's last access time and last modified time

- The inode's last file status change time

- The block address for the file data

- The indirect, double indirect, and the triple indirect blocks addresses for the file data

- Current usage status of the inode

- The number of actual blocks assigned to a file

- File generation number and version number

- The continuation inodes link

You can display information about files and directories using the Linux `ls` (list) command. The list command provides options for determining the type of information to display. Figure 4-7 shows some of the information you can display with the list command and the `-l` option, which you type as `ls -l`.

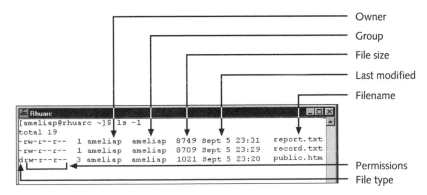

Figure 4-7   Information about the inode

In the following steps, you use the `ls` command and some of its options. You need to use a computer where Red Hat Linux is installed.

To use the `ls` command to find file information:

1. Boot your Linux computer and open a terminal window, if necessary. If your computer starts at a graphical desktop, click the **Red Hat** icon in the lower-left corner of the desktop, point to **System Tools**, and then click **Terminal**.

2. Navigate to your home directory, if necessary. For example, type **cd /home/*username*** where *username* is the name of your home directory. (Be sure to insert a space after the `cd` command.) Then press **Enter**.

3. At the command prompt, type **ls –A** and press **Enter**. (Be sure to insert a space after the `ls` command.) The `ls` command with the –A option lists all files including hidden ones, but not the current or parent directories. Note the files and directories listed.

4. At the command prompt, type **ls –a** and press **Enter**. Recall that Linux commands are case-sensitive. The `ls` command with the –a option lists all files including hidden ones and their parent and current directories. Record the results and compare them to the results from Step 3.

5. To find the inode number of files in the current directory, type **ls –i** and press **Enter**. What do you notice about the numbering scheme? Record the results.

6. To find detailed information about the files in the current directory, including size, permission, and modification time, type **ls –l** and press **Enter**. Record the results.

7. Be prepared to discuss the differences and similarities of what you observed.

To provide more information about a file or directory, UNIX and Linux file systems implement a continuation inode, which provides more room for higher-level features for files and directories. The continuation inode for a file or directory contains information such as the mode and file type, the quantity of links in the file or directory, the file's or directory's access control list (ACL), the least and most significant bytes of the ACL UID and GID, and the file or directory status flag. The status flag field of an inode contains unique information about how Linux handles a file or directory. It is a bit containing information that defines permissions, and is typically expressed in octal format. Table 4-2 describes the code values.

The last block for a UNIX or Linux file system is the data block, which is where the directories and files are stored on a disk drive. This location is directly linked to the inodes.

Table 4-2   Code Values for an Inode

Code values	Description
4000	UID on execution—set
2000	GID on execution—set
1000	Sticky bit—set
0400	Read by owner—allowed
0200	Write by owner—allowed
0100	Execution/search by owner—allowed
0040	Read by group—allowed
0020	Write by group—allowed
0010	Execution/search by group—allowed
0004	Read by others—allowed
0002	Write by others—allowed
0001	Execution/search by others—allowed

4

Understanding Inodes

Inodes provide a mechanism that links data stored in data blocks. The block is the smallest amount of data that can be allocated in a UNIX or Linux file system. The size of the block depends on how the disk volume was initiated. Block sizes can range from 512 bytes or larger. Many Linux implementations assign 1024 bytes per block.

The Linux Ext2 file system (Ext2fs) and Ext3 file system (Ext3fs) are improvements over the original Ext file system implemented when Linux was first released. One significant improvement with Ext3fs is that it adds linking information to each inode. In Ext3fs, if one inode becomes corrupt, data can be recovered more easily than in Ext2fs. In Ext3fs, each inode has additional information that links the other inodes in a chain of inodes.

When a file or directory is created on a UNIX or Linux file system, an inode is assigned. This first inode has thirteen pointers. Pointers one through ten link directly to data-storage blocks in the data block area of the disk. Each pointer contains a block address indicating where data is stored on the disk. These pointers are direct pointers because each pointer is associated with one block of data storage.

As a file grows, the operating system provides up to three layers of additional pointers, or inodes. The pointers in the first layer or group are called **indirect pointers**. The pointers in the second layer are called **double-indirect pointers** and the pointers in the last or third layer are called **triple-indirect pointers**.

To expand storage allocation, the operating system initiates the eleventh pointer of the original inode. The eleventh pointer links to 128 pointers inodes, and each of these pointers link directly to 128 individual blocks located in the data block area of the disk drive.

If all ten pointers in the original inode are consumed with file data, the eleventh pointer links to another 128 pointers. The first pointer in this indirect group of inodes point to the eleventh block. The last block of these 128 inodes is block 138.

The term indirect inodes refers to the eleventh pointer in the originating inodes pointing to another group of inode pointers. That is, it is indirectly linked to the original inode.

If more storage is needed, the twelfth pointer position of the original inode is used. The twelfth pointer links another 128 inode pointers. From each of these 128 pointers, another 128 pointers are created. This second level of inode pointers are then linked directly to blocks in the data block area of a disk drive. The first block pointed to for this double-indirect inode is block 139.

If more storage is needed, the thirteenth pointer links to 128 pointer inodes. Each of these 128 pointers points to another 128 pointers, and each second layer of pointers points to a third layer of 128 pointers. At this triple-indirect inodes level, data-storage blocks are linked.

Figure 4-8 shows how data is linked using inodes in a Linux file system.

To work with files and directories, you work at the Linux command line using a particular shell, which is a command-line interpreter that provides an interface for entering commands and viewing their results. Table 4-3 contains useful commands for most UNIX and Linux shells, including switches that are unique to a UNIX version.

Table 4-3   UNIX and Linux Shell Commands

Shell command	Associated switches	Purpose
`cat` file `more` file		Displays the contents of a file (similar to the MS-DOS TYPE command)
dd	Refer to man pages for available switches	Copies a disk drive by blocks, which is the same as creating a bit-stream copy of a disk drive
`df` `bdf` (`HP-UX`)	-k (Solaris)	Displays partition information for local or NFS mounted partitions
find	Refer to man pages for available switches	Locates files matching a specific attributes such as name, last modification time, or owner
netstat	-a	Identifies other systems that are connected via the network to a UNIX or Linux system
ps	ax (BSD) -ef (Sys V)	Displays the status of operating system processes
uname	-a	Displays name of the system

For more information on UNIX and Linux commands and their options, use the man command, which displays pages from the online manual. For example, to learn more about the ls command, type man ls at the Linux command prompt.

4

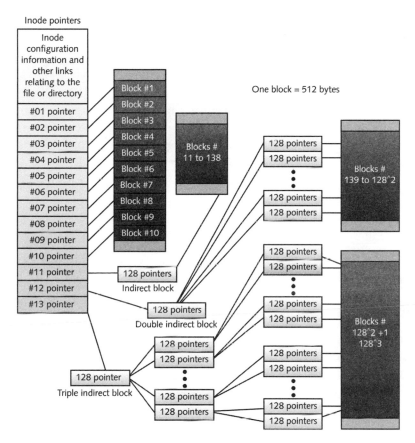

Figure 4-8   Linux file system inode pointers

UNDERSTANDING UNIX AND LINUX BOOT PROCESSES

As a computer forensics investigator, you will probably need to acquire digital evidence from a UNIX or Linux system that cannot be shut down, such as a Web server or file server, so you must understand the boot processes for UNIX and Linux to identify potential problems. When you turn on the power to a UNIX workstation, instruction code located in firmware on the system's central processing unit (CPU) loads into random-access memory (RAM). This firmware is called memory-resident code because it is located in read-only memory (ROM).

As soon as the memory-resident code is loaded into RAM, the instruction code checks the hardware. Typically the code first tests all components such as RAM chips to verify they are available and capable of running. Then it probes the bus, looking for a device that contains the boot program, such as a hard disk, floppy disk, or CD. When it locates the boot device, it starts reading the boot program into memory. The boot program, in turn, reads the kernel into memory. When the kernel is loaded, the boot program transfers control of the boot process to the kernel.

The first task of the kernel is to identify all devices. It then configures the identified devices and starts the system and associated processes. After the kernel becomes operational, the system is usually booted to single-user mode where only one user can log on. Typically single-user mode is an optional feature that allows the user to access various modes such as a maintenance mode. If the user bypasses single-user mode, the kernel runs system startup scripts that are specific to the workstation and runs multi-user mode. Users can then log on to the workstation.

As the kernel finishes loading, it identifies the root directory, the system swap file, and dump files. It also sets the hostname and time zone, runs consistency checks on the file system, mounts all partitions, starts network service daemons, sets up the network interface card (NIC), and establishes user and system accounting and quotas.

Review the documentation of the UNIX system you are examining for further information on the boot process.

Understanding Linux Loader

Linux Loader (LILO) is the Linux utility that initiates the boot process, which usually runs from the disk's MBR. LILO is a boot manager that allows you to start Linux or other operating systems, including Windows. If a system has two or more operating systems located on different disk partitions, LILO can be set up to start any one of them. For example, you might have Microsoft Windows 2000 on one partition and Linux on another. When you turn on the computer, LILO displays a list of available operating systems, and asks you which one you want to load.

LILO uses a configuration file named lilo.conf that is located in the /etc directory. This file is a script that contains the location of the boot device, the kernel image file such as vmlinux, and a delay timer that specifies how much time to allow you to select which OS you want to use.

UNIX and Linux Drives and Partition Scheme

UNIX and Linux view disk drives and their associated partitions in ways that are significantly different from MS-DOS and Windows. For example, in Windows XP, the primary master disk that contains the first boot partition is typically listed as drive C. In UNIX and Linux, disks and partitions within each disk are labeled as paths, with each path starting at the root (/) directory. For IDE disk drives, the Primary Master controller disk is defined as /dev/hda. The first partition on the Primary Master disk is defined as /dev/hda1. Device /dev/hda1 is equivalent to drive C in Windows or MS-DOS. If other partitions are located on the Primary Master disk, their numbered values are incremented; for example, the second partition on the Primary Master disk is /dev/hda2. If a disk has a third partition, it is /dev/hda3, and so on.

Disk drives that are connected to the Primary Slave or Secondary Master or Slave controller are defined as /dev/hdb. Any additional disk drives are incremented alphabetically. For example, if a third disk drive is mounted, it is listed as /dev/hdc, and so on.

If a SCSI controller is installed on a UNIX or Linux workstation, it has a similar designation as IDE disk drives and partitions. The first drive connected to the SCSI controller is identified as /dev/sda. The first partition for this drive is listed as /dev/sda1. Any additional partitions, such as a second partition, are incremented by one; for example, the second partition on a SCSI disk drive is /dev/sda2.

4

EXAMINING COMPACT DISC DATA STRUCTURES

Compact discs (CDs) and **digital video discs (DVDs)** have rapidly become the preferred way to store large amounts of data. Many people now use CD and DVD burners to transfer digital information from a hard disk to a CD or DVD. As a computer forensics investigator, you may need to retrieve evidence from CDs and DVDs, which are optical media that store information in a manner different from magnetic media. To create a CD, a laser burns flat areas (or **lands**) on the top side of the CD (the side without the label). Lower areas not burned by the laser are called **pits**. The transitions from land areas to pit areas have the binary value of one (1), or on. Where there is no transition, the location has a binary value of zero (0), or off.

The basic structure of a CD surface includes the following components:

- Label surface
- Protective layer
- Reflective layer
- Substrate layer

Figure 4-9 shows the physical makeup of a CD.

The **International Organization of Standards (ISO)** has established standards for CDs, including the ISO 9660 for a CD, Compact Disc-Recordable (CD-R), and Compact Disc-ReWriteable (CD-RW), and ISO 13346 for DVDs. ISO 9660 has an extension standard called Joliet, which allows for long filenames under Microsoft Windows 9x, NT, 2000, and XP. Under ISO 13346 for DVDs, the Micro-UDF (M-UDF) function has been added to allow for long filenames.

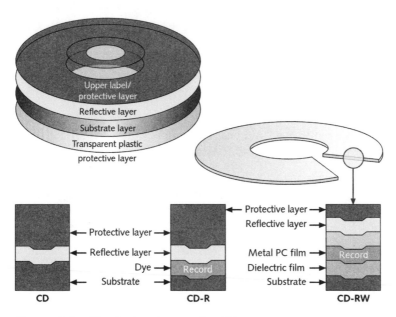

Figure 4-9   Physical makeup of a CD

A variety of products have been produced to make CDs more versatile. The writeable CD-R has a dye layer substance that changes when a laser heats it. The heat from the dye causes a change in the reflective ability of the media. This change in reflectivity is what changes the values of 1's and 0's.

The rewriteable CD-RW disks use a media that changes appearance depending on the temperature applied by a laser. This media is called a **phase change alloy** (also known as a Metal PC layer) that changes from **amorphic** (meaning non-crystalline) to crystalline. The amorphic condition is achieved when the laser heats the Metal PC layer to 600 degrees Celsius. When the laser cools it to 200 degrees Celsius, the Metal PC layer becomes crystalline. Each of these changes either reflect or deflect light, which signals that a bit is either set to 0 or 1.

On the surface of a CD, data is configured into three regions: the lead-in, program area, and lead-out. The lead-in area contains the table of contents in the subcode Q-channel. Up to 99 tracks are available for the table of contents. The lead-in also synchronizes the CD as it is spinning. Subcode channels are additional data channels that provide start and end markers for tracks, time codes for each frame, the table of contents in the lead-in area, and graphic codes.

The program area of the CD stores data. As with the lead-in area, up to 99 tracks are available for this area. The lead-out area is the end-of-CD marker for the storage area. Figure 4-10 shows the logical layout of a CD.

A unit of storage on a CD is a called frame, which includes a synchronized pattern, a control and display symbol, and eight error correction symbols. Each frame contains

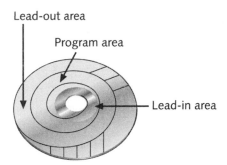

Figure 4-10   Logical layout of a CD

24 17-bit symbols, and are then combined into blocks that form a sector. A block on a CD is 2352 bytes for music CDs (also called CD-DAs) or 2048 bytes for data CDs. CD players 12X or slower use a **constant linear velocity (CLV)** method for reading discs, usually music CDs. Newer CD players 12X or faster read discs using a **constant angular velocity (CAV)** system.

Unlike CDs, DVD disk file structures use a Universal Disk Format (UDF) called Micro-UDF (M-UDF). For backward compatibility, some DVDs have integrated ISO 9660 to allow for compatibility with current operating systems.

UNDERSTANDING OTHER DISK STRUCTURES

This section covers media and hardware devices that you might encounter as part of an investigation, including SCSI disks, IDE/EIDE disks, and RAID configurations. While some of the devices were popular in the early days of computing, they have been upgraded to deal with high-end or high-speed devices. You should be familiar with the purpose of each device, its basic operation, and the problems it poses during a forensic investigation.

Examining SCSI Disks

Small Computer System Interface (SCSI) is an input/output standard protocol device. SCSI allows a computer to access devices such as hard disk drives, tape drives, scanners, CD-ROM drives, and printers. Its original purpose was to provide a common bus communication device for all computer vendors. When Shugart Systems created SCSI in 1979, it was designed to work with many of the leading computer manufacturers. As SCSI evolved, it became a standard for PCs, Macintosh, and many UNIX workstations. Older Macintosh systems such as the Mac SE only shipped with a SCSI port.

When you examine and process evidence on a computer system, you need to take an inventory of all connected devices to make sure that you collect all possible magnetic media to determine what you need to investigate. During this inventory, you should identify whether the computer uses a SCSI device. If so, determine whether it is an internal SCSI device, such as a hard disk drive, or an external device, such as a scanner or tape drive. If the computer is using external media devices, such as a tape drive with tapes or removable disk drives such as a Jaz drive, examine the content of these devices as part of your investigation. Determine whether you have the right SCSI card, cables, adapters, and terminators to examine a suspect SCSI drive. You also need the correct software drivers that allow your operating system to communicate with the SCSI device.

The **Advanced SCSI Programmer Interface (ASPI)** provides several software drivers that allow for communication between the operating system and the SCSI component. Currently, Windows XP, 2000, Me, and 9x have integrated ASPI drivers, which make adding a SCSI card to a Windows workstation easy. The Windows 98 Config.sys file typically contains ASPI drivers that allow you to read a CD from an emergency boot disk or Windows 98 startup disk. However, to access a SCSI device from MS-DOS, you must configure MS-DOS to install the appropriate SCSI driver. Most manuals or textbooks that have A+ certification from CompTIA contain information on how to do this.

When applying a SCSI device to your forensic workstation, you might have to change the port number on the hard disk, for example, to make sure duplicate port numbers are not assigned to other devices. If you are using a SCSI UltraWide card such as the Adaptec 29160, port 7 is typically reserved for the SCSI card itself. It is a good habit to verify which ports are used for your SCSI system.

One characteristic of a SCSI device is proper termination. A SCSI terminator is a resistor that is connected to the end of the SCSI cable or device. Newer SCSI devices typically use an integrated self-terminator. Some newer SCSI cards such as the Adaptec 29160 self-correct and allow for access to a SCSI driver. It may, however, take several seconds for the device to adjust.

One problem area on older SCSI disk drives is identifying which jumper group terminates and assigns a port number. Use Web search engines to find specification sheets that list this information for particular types of SCSI drives.

Examining IDE/EIDE Devices

Most forensic disk examinations involve Enhanced Integrated Drive Electronics (EIDE) disk drives. You might, however, also encounter the older IDE disk drive versions. When accessing these types of drives on your computer forensic workstation, you should know how the drives work.

All Advanced Technology Attachment (ATA)-33 through ATA-133 IDE and EIDE disk drives use the standard 40-pin ribbon or shielded cable. ATA-66, ATA-100, and ATA-133 can use the newer 40-pin/80-wire cable. These newer cables provide for considerably faster data transfer rates.

If you are examining a pre-ATA-33 IDE disk drive, it may not work correctly or be accessible to your workstation, although PCs are usually backward compatible with the older IDE drives. When you must access an older IDE disk drive, you may need to locate an older Pentium I or 486 PC and rely on your technical skills and those of other experts to investigate the disk.

For more information about ATA disk drive architecture and future developments, consult the Web pages of T13 (www.t13.org). T13, a committee of INCITS (www.incits.org), is the current authority on standards for ATA.

TIP

4

The Complementary Metal Oxide Semiconductor (CMOS) on current PCs use logical block addressing (LBA) and enhanced cylinder, head, and sector (CHS). When you connect an ATA-33 or newer disk drive to a PC, the CMOS automatically identifies the proper setting of the disk, which is convenient when you are installing hard disks on your workstation. However, this automatic identification feature can pose problems during an investigation. If you need to make a duplicate copy of an old pre-ATA-33 256 MB disk drive, for example, you need the CHS for the drive. Suppose you have a spare 4.0 GB drive that you plan to use to store a copy of the 256 MB disk. When you connect the two drives and power up your workstation, you enter CMOS and manually set CMOS to match the same CHS as the 256 MB disk drive. When you reboot your workstation and access CMOS, you will find that the CHS you applied did not take effect. To solve this problem, use a disk-imaging tool such as NTI SafeBack, Columbia Data Systems SnapCopy, or Guidance Software EnCase. These tools force the correct CHS configuration onto the target disk drive so that you can copy evidence data correctly.

Another solution is to obtain a 486 PC. The CMOS and basic input/output system (BIOS) used in the 486 do not automatically adjust the CHS of the newer ATA disk drives, but do allow you to set the CHS manually. However, one disadvantage of using a 486 PC is that the IDE ATA controller does not recognize disk drives over 8.4 GB. If you need to manually configure the CHS of a disk drive larger than 8.4 GB, you can explore other alternatives. One solution is to acquire an Enhanced Industry Standard Architecture (EISA) card that is engineered to connect to an Institute of Electrical and Electronics Engineers (IEEE) 1394 Firewire device. Several vendors make EIDE disk drive bays that connect to Firewire, and one vendor in Taiwan produces an EISA Firewire card. However, locating this manufacturer and communicating with them may be more costly than purchasing one of the other products that can force CHS changes to a larger target disk drive.

Another option when you are using a 486 PC is to acquire an older ISA SCSI card and an A-Card IDE adapter card. A-Card, a Taiwan manufacturer, sells SCSI-to-IDE adapter cards for various SCSI models. A-Card sells one card designed for UltraWide SCSI that prevents any write accesses to the connected IDE disk drive. One of many good sources for A-Cards is Microland USA (*www.microlandusa.com*). For the adapter card that prevents data from being written on a disk, locate the model card AEC7720WP that is listed with a write-blocker feature.

With an EISA Firewire card, a Firewire-to-EIDE interface, or a SCSI card with an IDE A-Card adapter, you can manually change the CHS on any EIDE disk drive from a 486 PC.

Examining the IDE Host Protected Area

In 1998, T13 created a new standard for ATA disk drives (ATA or ATAPI-5 AT Attachment with Packet Interface-5). This new standard provides a reserved and protected area of an IDE disk drive, which is out of view of the operating system. This feature is called Protected Area Run Time Interface Extension Service (PARTIES). Many disk manufactures also refer to it as Host Protected Area (HPA) in their documentation.

Service technicians use this protected area to store data created by diagnostic and restore programs. Using the protected area eliminates the need for a CD disaster recovery disk. Accessing the protected area might require a password, and always requires special commands that can only be run from the computer's BIOS level. A disk partition utility such as FDISK cannot see a protected area of a disk because it is only accessible at the BIOS level, not the operating system level.

One commercially available tool that creates and writes data to a protected area is called Area 51 from StorageSoft, Inc. With Area 51, you can create a protected area with the ATA-4 specification. This protected area is referred to as a BIOS Engineering Extension Record (BEER) data structure.

Another product called BIOS, XBIOS Direct Access Reporter (BXDR) from Sanderson Forensics in England (*www.sandersonforensics.co.uk*) can count the sectors on a disk drive. This tool can also access the protected area of a disk drive.

Exploring Hidden Partitions

You can use disk-editing tools to disable disk partitions, which hides them from view of the operating system. Disabling partitions can hide evidence that could be vital to your investigation. You can manually reinstate the hidden partition by manually correcting the modified bit settings in the disk partition table.

Because the hard disk you are investigating might have a hidden partition, use bit-streaming imaging tools that can access unpartitioned areas of a disk drive. This potential problem is covered in Chapter 10 of this book.

Understanding RAID

Redundant Array of Independent Disks (RAID) is a computer configuration involving two or more disks. Originally RAID was developed to minimize data loss due to a disk drive failure by providing data redundancy. As technology improved, RAID also provided larger data-storage capabilities.

TIP   RAID is known as Redundant Array of Independent or Inexpensive Disks per the IEEE.

Several levels of RAID can be implemented through software or special hardware controllers. For Microsoft Windows XP, 2000, and NT servers and workstations, RAID 0 or 1 is available. For a high-end data-processing environment, RAID 5 is very common, and is often based in special RAID towers. These high-end RAID systems often have their own integrated controllers that connect to high-end servers or mainframes. These types of RAIDs provide redundancy, high-speed data access, and can make many small disks appear as one very large disk drive.

TIP   Other variations of RAID besides 0, 1, and 5 are specific to their vendor or application.

RAID 0 provides very fast access and increased data storage. In RAID 0, two or more disk drives become one large volume, so that the computer views the disks as a single disk. The tracks of data on this mode of storage cross over to each drive. The logical addressing scheme makes it appear that each track of data is continuous throughout all disk drives. That is, if you have two disks configured as a RAID 0, track one starts on the first physical disk and continues to the second physical disk. When viewed from a booted operating system such as Windows XP, the two disk drives appear as one large disk drive (see Figure 4-11).

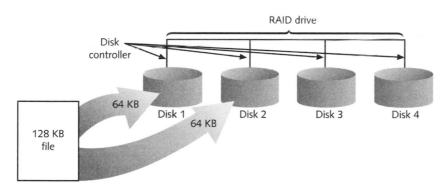

Figure 4-11   RAID 0: Striping

The advantage of RAID 0 is speed and increased data-storage capability. Its biggest disadvantage is lack of redundancy if a disk fails for continuous availability.

RAID 1 is made up of two disk drives for each volume, and is designed for data recovery in the event of a disk drive failure. The content of the two disks in RAID 1 are identical. When data is written to a volume, the operating system writes the data twice, that is, once to each of the drives at the same time. If one drive fails, the operating system switches to the other disk drive. Figure 4-12 shows a RAID 1 drive.

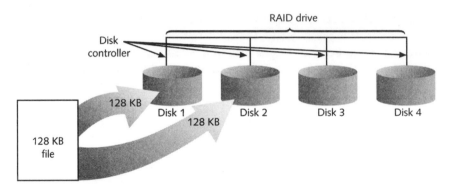

Figure 4-12   RAID 1

RAID 1 ensures that data is not lost and helps prevent computer downtime. The only disadvantage of RAID 1 is the extra cost of purchasing disk drives that support this type of RAID.

Like RAID 1, RAID 2 provides for very fast access and increased data storage by configuring two or more disk drives as one large volume. The difference with RAID 2 is that data is written to disk on a bit level. An error correcting code (ECC) is used to verify whether the write is successful. RAID 2 therefore has better data integrity checking than RAID 0. Because of the bit–level writes and the ECC, RAID 2 is slower than RAID 0. Figure 4-13 shows a RAID 2 volume.

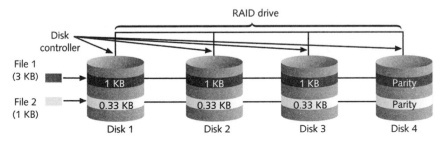

Figure 4-13   RAID 2: Striping (bit level)

RAID 3: Data striping, dedicated parity requires at least three disk drives. Similar to RAID 0, RAID 3 stripes tracks across all disk drives that make up one volume. RAID 3 also implements dedicated parity of the data. Dedicated parity provides recovery in the event of corrupt data. Dedicated parity is stored on one disk drive in the RAID 3 array of disk drives.

RAID 4: Data striping, dedicated parity (block writing) is similar to RAID 3 except data is written in blocks rather than bytes.

RAID 5: Distributed data, distributed parity is similar to RAIDs 0 and 3 in that it stripes data tracks across all disks within the RAID array. But unlike RAID 3, RAID 5 places parity recovery data on each drive. If a disk in a RAID array has a data failure, the parity on the other disk drives automatically rebuilds the corrupt data when the failed drive is replaced. Figure 4-14 shows RAID 5.

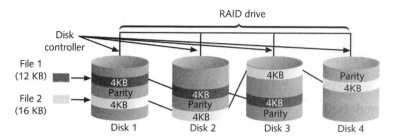

Figure 4-14   RAID 5: Data striping, dedicated parity (block writing)

RAID 6: Distributed data, distributed parity (double parity) functions the same way as RAID 5 except it has redundant parity on each disk drive within the RAID array. The advantage of RAID 6 over RAID 5 is that it recovers any two disk drives that fail because of the additional parity stored on each disk.

RAID 10: Mirrored striping, also known as RAID 1+0, is a combination of RAID 1 and RAID 0. This provides fast access and redundancy of data storage.

RAID 15: Mirrored striping with parity, also known as RAID 1+5, is a combination of RAID 1 and RAID 5. This provides the most robust data recovery capability and speed of access of all RAID configurations. It is more costly than any of the other RAID configurations.

 Windows 2000, NT, and XP also support RAID 0, 1, and 5.

Investigating RAID Disks

When you examine a RAID computing system, you need extra storage to copy all the data. If you are attempting to create a bit-stream image of a large amount of data, such as a terabyte, try retrieving data in smaller chunks.

You might not be able to create bit-stream image backups for very large RAID server configurations. In these special cases, consult with vendor engineers to determine how to best capture data from a RAID array.

CHAPTER SUMMARY

❑ The Macintosh uses a hierarchical file system (HFS) where files are stored in folders, which can be nested in other folders. The File Manager handles the reading, writing, and storage of data to physical media. It also collects data to maintain the HFS, and manipulates files, folders, and other items. The Finder works with the operating system to keep track of files and maintain each user's desktop.

❑ In the Mac OS, a file consists of two parts: a data fork and a resource fork. The resource fork contains a resource map and resource header information for each file, window locations, and icons. The data fork typically contains data that the user creates, such as text or spreadsheets. Application programs also read and write to the data fork. When you are working with an application file, the resource fork contains additional information such as the menu, dialog boxes, icons, executable code, and controls.

❑ A volume is any storage media that is used to store files. In the Mac OS, while a volume can be all or part of the storage media for hard disks, a volume on a floppy disk is always the entire floppy. For larger disks, the user or administrator defines a volume.

❑ Volumes have allocation blocks and logical blocks. A logical block is a collection of data that cannot exceed 512 bytes. An allocation block is a group of consecutive logical blocks. When you save a file, the File Manager assigns the file to an allocation block. On a floppy disk, an allocation block is often one logical block. As volumes increase in size, one allocation block may be composed of three or more logical blocks.

❑ For older Macintosh operating systems, the first two logical blocks on each volume (or disk) are the boot blocks, which contain information about the system startup. The startup block contains information about the system configuration. Optional executable code for the system file can also be placed within the boot blocks. Typically system startup instructions are stored in the HFS System File rather than the boot blocks.

❑ The Linux second extended file system (Ext2fs) uses inodes. When the internal link count reaches "0", a file is considered to be deleted. The superblock on a Linux system keeps track of the geometry and available space on a disk along with the list of inodes.

❑ The Linux file structure is made up of meta-data and data. Meta-data includes items such as the user ID (UID), group ID (GID), size, and permissions for each file. An inode contains the modification/access/creation (MAC) times, not a filename. What they have instead is an inode number that is linked with the filename in the directory called "file_name." The pairing of the inode number with the filename is how Linux keeps track of files and data. The data portion of the Linux file structure contains the contents of the file.

❑ Compact discs (CDs) and digital video discs (DVDs) are optical media used to store large amounts of data. They are regulated by the International Organization of Standards (ISO) 9660 and ISO 13346, respectively. A unit of storage is called a frame, which contains 24 17-bit symbols.

❑ Small Computer System Interface (SCSI) connectors are used for a variety of peripheral devices. They offer unique challenges to the forensic investigation such as finding the proper device drivers and interfaces.

KEY TERMS

Advanced SCSI Programmer Interface (ASPI)—Provides several software drivers that allow for communications between the OS and the SCSI component.

allocation blocks—The number of logical blocks assembled in the Macintosh file system when a file is saved.

Amorphic—A condition achieved when a laser heats the Metal PC layer to 600 degrees Celsius.

bad block inode—In the Linux file system, the inode that tracks the bad sectors on a drive.

B★-tree—A file system used by the Mac OS that consists of nodes, which are objects, and leaf nodes, which contain data.

Berkeley Software Design (BSD) UNIX—A variation of UNIX created at the University of California at Berkeley.

catalog—An area the Macintosh file system uses to maintain the relationships between files and directories on a volume.

clump—In the Macintosh file system, a contiguous allocation block. Clumps are used to keep file fragmentation to a minimum.

compact disc (CD)—Optical media that stores information and typically holds up to 640 MB.

constant angular velocity (CAV)—CD players 12X or faster use this system to read CDs.

constant linear velocity (CLV)—CD players 12X or slower use this method to read CDs.

data—The contents of a file in the Linux file structure.

data block—In the Linux file system, a cluster of hard disk sectors, normally 4096 or 8192 bytes in size.

data fork—The part of the Macintosh file structure that contains the actual data of a file.

digital video disc (DVD)—Optical media that stores information and movies.

double-indirect pointers—The pointers in the second layer or group of an OS.

extents overflow file—Used by the Macintosh File Manager when the list of contiguous blocks of a file becomes too long. The overflow of the list is placed in the extents overflow file. Any file extents not in the MDB or VCB are contained here.

File Manager—In the Macintosh file system, handles the reading, writing, and storage of data to physical media. It also collects data to maintain the HFS along with manipulation of files, folders, and volumes.

Finder—Works with the Macintosh OS to keep track of files and maintain the user's desktop.

GNU General Public License (GPL)—An agreement that defines Linux as open source software, meaning that anyone can use, change, and distribute the software without owing royalties or licensing fees to another party.

header node—Stores information about the B★-tree file in the Macintosh file system.

hierarchical file system (HFS)—The system used by the Mac OS to store files, consisting of folders and subfolders, which can be nested.

index node—Stores link information to the previous and next node in the Macintosh file system.

indirect pointers—The pointers in the first layer or group of an OS.

inode—A key part of the Linux file system that contains UIDs, GIDs, modification, access, creation times, and file locations.

International Organization of Standards (ISO)—An organization set up by the United Nations to ensure compatibility in a variety of fields including engineering, electricity, and computers. The acronym is the Greek word for equal.

lands—Flat areas on a compact disc.

leaf node—A node of the B★-tree system that contains data in the Macintosh file system.

logical blocks—In the Macintosh file system, a collection of data that cannot exceed 512 bytes. These are assembled in allocation blocks to store files.

logical EOF—In the Macintosh file system, the number of bytes that contain data.

map node—Stores the node descriptor and a map record in the Macintosh file system.

Master Directory Block (MDB)—On older Macintosh systems, the location where all information about a volume is stored. A copy of the MDB is kept in the next to the last block on the volume.

meta-data—In Linux, the part of the inode that contains critical data including UIDs, GIDs, size, permissions, and other critical information.

phase change alloy—The Metal PC layer of a CD-RW that allows it to be written to several times.

physical EOF—In the Macintosh file system, the number of allocation blocks assigned to the file.

pits—Lower areas on a compact disc not burned by the laser.

Redundant Array of Independent Disks (RAID)—A computer that has two or more hard drives with redundant storage features so that if one drive fails, the other drives can take over.

resource fork—The part of the Macintosh file system that contains the resource map, header information for the file, window locations, and icons.

second extended file system (Ext2fs)—The file system most used by Linux today.

Small Computer System Interface (SCSI)—An input/output standard protocol device.

triple-indirect pointers—The pointers in the third layer or group of an OS.

volume—Refers to any storage media in the Macintosh file system. A volume can be a single floppy disk, a partition on a hard drive, the entire drive, or several drives.

Volume Bitmap—A system application used to track blocks that are in use and blocks that are available.

Volume Control Block (VCB)—Contains information from the MDB and is used by the File Manager in the Macintosh file system.

Volume Information Block (VIB)—Another name for the Master Directory Block.

4

5

THE INVESTIGATOR'S OFFICE AND LABORATORY

After reading this chapter, you will be able to:

♦ Understand forensic lab certification requirements

♦ Determine the physical layout of a computer forensics lab

♦ Select a basic forensic workstation

♦ Build a business case for developing a forensics lab

♦ Create a forensic boot floppy disk

♦ Retrieve evidence data using a remote network connection

This chapter details what you need to set up an effective computing-forensics laboratory, which is where you examine most of the evidence data that you acquire for an investigation. Adjacent to the lab, most computer forensics investigators have a private office where they manage their cases. Whether you are new to computer forensics or are an experienced examiner, your goal is to make your office and lab work smoothly and efficiently for all casework.

Computer forensics examiners must update their labs to keep pace with computer technology changes. The workflow and processes that you establish directly affect the quality of evidence you discover. You must balance cost, quality, and reliability when determining the kind of equipment, software, and other items you do and do not need to add to your lab. This chapter provides a foundation for organizing, controlling, and managing a safe, efficient computing-forensics laboratory.

UNDERSTANDING FORENSIC LAB CERTIFICATION REQUIREMENTS

A computing-forensics lab is where you conduct your investigations, store evidence, and do most of your work. You use the lab to house your instruments, current and legacy software, and computing-forensics workstations. In general, you need a variety of computer forensic hardware and software to do your work.

The **American Society of Crime Laboratory Directors (ASCLD)** (*www.ascld.org*) provides guidelines for managing a forensics lab and for acquiring official crime-lab certification. ASCLD certifies forensics labs that analyze other criminal evidence, such as fingerprints and deoxyribonucleic acid (DNA) samples. Note that this type of forensics lab is different from a computing-forensics lab and performs different types of analysis. As mentioned in Chapter 1, the use of the word "forensics" as applied to computing investigations is currently being debated. Some police agencies and other government organizations have removed the word "forensics" from the names of their computing investigation labs to avoid confusion with crime labs. However, many of the goals and management practices in a computing-forensics lab are the same as those for a crime lab.

The ASCLD provides a detailed and extensive certification program known as ASCLD/LAB (*www.ascld-lab.org*) that regulates how crime labs are organized and managed. The ASCLD/LAB program includes specific audits on all functions to assure that lab procedures are being performed correctly and consistently for all casework. These audits can be applied to computing-forensics labs to maintain quality and integrity.

ASCLD has defined what constitutes a professional crime laboratory. The following sections discuss several key guidelines from the ASCLD/LAB program that you can apply to managing, configuring, and auditing your computing-forensics lab.

Identifying Duties of the Lab Manager and Staff

The ASCLD states that each lab should have a specific set of objectives set by a parent organization and the director or manager of the lab. The lab manager sets up the processes for managing cases and reviews these procedures regularly. Besides performing general management tasks such as promoting group consensus in decision making, maintaining fiscal responsibility for lab needs, and encouraging honesty among staff members, the manager of a computing-forensics lab plans updates for the lab, such as new hardware and software purchases.

The lab manager also establishes and promotes quality-assurance processes to be used by the lab's staff, such as what to do when a case arrives, including logging evidence, specifying who can enter the lab, and establishing how to file reports. The lab manager also ensures the lab's efficiency by setting reasonable production schedules for processing work.

A typical case for an internal corporate investigation involves seizing a hard disk, making forensic copies of the disk, evaluating evidence, and filing a report. Performing a forensic analysis of a disk 20 GB or larger can take several days and often involves running imaging software overnight and on weekends. This means that one of the forensic computers in the lab is occupied for that time. Evaluating such a disk can take 80 hours or more. Based on past experience, the lab manager can estimate how many cases each investigator can handle and estimate when a preliminary and final report for each case can be expected.

The lab manager creates and monitors lab policies for staff, and provides a safe and secure workplace for staff and evidence. Above all, the lab manager accounts for all activities conducted by the lab's staff to complete its work. Tracking cases such as e-mail abuse, Internet misuse, and illicit activities can justify the funds spent on a lab.

Staff members in a computing-forensics lab should have training sufficient for completing their tasks. Staff skill sets include hardware and software knowledge, including operating system (OS) and file types, and deductive reasoning. Their work is reviewed regularly to ensure quality. The staff is also responsible for continuing technical training to ensure that they update their investigative and computer skills, and maintain a record of the training they have completed. Many vendors and organizations hold annual or quarterly training seminars that provide certification exams.

The ASCLD Web site summarizes the requirements of managing a computing-forensics lab, handling and preserving evidence, performing laboratory procedures, setting personnel requirements, and encouraging professional development. They also provide a user license for a printed and online manual of lab management guidelines, which is available at *www.ascld.org*.

ASCLD stresses that each lab maintain an up-to-date library of resources in their field. For computer forensics, this includes software, hardware information, and technical journals.

Balancing Costs and Needs

To conduct a professional computing investigation, you need to balance the cost with the tools you need to perform the investigation, including computer hardware and software, facility space, and trained personnel. When creating a budget, start by estimating the number of computer cases your lab expects to examine and identifying the types of computers you are likely to examine, such as Windows personal computers (PCs) or Linux workstations.

For example, suppose you work for a state police agency that is planning to provide computing investigation services for the entire state. You could start by collecting state crime statistics for the current year and several previous years. As you examine these statistics, determine how many computers were used to commit a crime. Also identify the types of computers used in these crimes. Criminal behavior often reflects the sales trends for specific computing systems. Because more than 90% of all consumers use Intel and AMD PCs, and 90% of these computers are running a version of Microsoft Windows, the same is likely true of computers used in crimes. Verify this trend by determining how frequently each type of system is used in a crime. List the number of crimes committed using a DOS or Windows computer, Linux or UNIX system, and Macintosh computer.

If you cannot find detailed information that identifies the types of computers and operating systems used in a computer crime, gather enough information to make an educated guess. Your goal is to build a baseline for the types and numbers of systems that you can expect to investigate. In addition to the historical data you compile, identify any future trends that could affect your lab, such as a new version of an operating system or an increase in the number of computers involved in crime.

After you compile these statistics, estimate how many investigations you might conduct involving computer systems that are used less frequently. Doing so helps determine how many tools you need to examine these systems. For example, if you learn that on average, one Macintosh computer running OS 9 or earlier is involved in a criminal investigation each month, you probably need only one or two software tools to perform a forensic analysis on Macintosh file systems.

Figure 5-1 shows a trend analysis from a **Uniform Crime Report** that identifies the number of hard disk types, such as Integrated Drive Electronics (IDE) or Small Computer System Interface (SCSI), and the specific operating system used to commit crimes. Uniform Crime Reports are generated at the federal, state, and local levels to show the types and frequency of crimes committed. For federal reports see *www.fbi.gov/ucr/ucr.htm,* and for a summary of crimes committed at various levels during the 1990s, see *http://fisher.lib.virginia.edu/crime.*

You can also identify which crimes used a computer with specialized software. For example, if you find that many counterfeiters use a certain type of check-writing software, consider adding this specialized software to your inventory.

If you are preparing to set up a computing-forensics lab for a private company, you can easily determine your needs because you are working in a contained environment. Start by obtaining an inventory of all known computing systems used in the business. For example, an insurance company often has a network of Intel PCs and servers. A large manufacturing company might use Intel PCs, UNIX workstations running a Computer-Automated Design (CAD) system, super minicomputers, and mainframes. A publishing company might have a combination of Intel PCs and Apple Macintosh systems.

Next, check with your Management, Human Resource, and Security departments to determine the types of complaints and problems reported in the last year. For example, most companies that have Internet connections receive complaints about employees accessing the Web excessively or for personal use, which generate investigations of Web use. Be sure to distinguish investigations concerning excessive Web use from inappropriate Web site access involving porn sites or hate sites and e-mail abuse.

Your budget should also provide for future developments in computing technology because disk drive storage capabilities improve constantly. When examining a disk, recall that you need a target disk to which you copy your evidence data. The target disk should be at least one and one-half times the size of the evidence (suspect) disk. For example, a lab equipped with 60 GB disks can effectively analyze 20 GB or 40 GB disks. If your company upgrades its computer to 120 GB disks, however, you need disks that are 200 GB or larger or a central secure server with one or more terabytes of storage.

Many businesses replace their desktop computer systems every 18 months to three years. You must be informed of computer upgrades and other changes in the computing environment so you can prepare and submit your budget for needed resources.

	IDE Drive	SCSI Drive	Intel PC Platform		MS Other O/S	Linux	Apple Platform		UNIX H/W	Other H/W	Total Systems Examined	Total HDD Examined
			Win9x	WinNT / 2k / XP			OS 9.x & older	OS X				
Arson	5	3	3	1		1					5	8
Assault— Aggravated	78	5	31		1	14			1		47	83
Assault- Simple	180	3	77	6	1	32	44	2		1	163	183
Bribery	153		153								153	153
Burglary	1746		1487	259							1746	1746
Counterfeiting & Forgery	1390	4	543	331		309	21	186			1390	1394
Destruction, Damage, & Vandalism	976	48	142	45	29	127	325	90	217	1	976	1024
Drug, Narcotic	1939	24	1345	213		158	213	10			1939	1963
Embezzlement	1023		320	549		23	87	41		3	1023	1023
Extortion & Blackmail	77		2	61		10	3	1			77	77
Fraud	2002		638	932	9	173	55	190		5	2002	2002
Gambling	4910	5	1509	2634		136	138	498			4915	4915
Homicide	36		5	11	9	1	3	7			36	36
Kidnapping & Abduction	2		1	1							2	2
Larceny Theft	7342	56	2134	3093	5	935	127	982	1	21	7298	7398
Motor Vehicle Theft	1747		231	1508		5	1	2			1747	1747
Child Porn	593	2	98	162		68	105	160	2		595	595
Robbery	33		23	7			2	1			33	33
Sex Offense— Forcible	80		21	45		1	5	8			80	80
Sex Offense— Non-Forcible	900		324	437		6	90	43			900	900
Stolen Property Offenses	2711	10	800	1634	3	169	53	37	1	9	2706	2721
Weapons Violations	203	1	43	89	2	11	28	31			204	204
Totals Per System	28126	161	9930	12018	59	2179	1300	2289	222	40	28037	28287
			HDD FAT/NTFS	22007				HDD Mac O/S X/Linux/ UNIX	2511			

Figure 5-1   Uniform Crime Report trend analysis

Like computer hardware, operating systems also change periodically. If your current computer forensic tool does not work with the next release of a Microsoft operating system or file system, you must upgrade your software tools. Also monitor vendor product developments to learn about upgrades. For example, the release of Windows NT caused problems for computer forensics examiners. Windows NT hard disks can use both FAT12 and New Technology File System (NTFS). Windows NT 3.0 through 3.5 can also access IBM O/S-2 High Performance File System (HPFS) file system disk drives. When Windows NT was released, computing-forensics software vendors did not have tools that could analyze and extract data from NTFS or HPFS disks. Microsoft released a disk editor called DiskProbe that allowed users to view NTFS disks on Windows 3.5 through Windows XP systems. However, DiskProbe cannot write-block a suspect's disk, making it usable only on copied disks. In such a case, monitor the updates to forensics tools to find a tool that works with Windows NT and NTFS and HPFS disks.

Acquiring Certification and Training

To continue a career in computing investigations and forensics analysis, you need to upgrade your skills through appropriate training. Several organizations are currently developing certification programs for computer forensics that usually test you after you have successfully completed one or more training sessions. The certifying organizations range from non-profit associations to vendor-sponsored groups. All of these programs charge fees for certification, and some require the candidate to take vendor- or organization-sponsored training to qualify for the certification. More recently, some state and federal government agencies are looking into establishing their own certification programs that address the minimum skills needed to conduct computing investigations at various levels.

Before enlisting in a certification program, thoroughly research the requirements, cost, and acceptability in your chosen area of employment. Most certification programs require continuing education credits or reexamination of the candidate's skills, which can become costly.

International Association of Computer Investigative Specialists (IACIS)

The **International Association of Computer Investigative Specialists (IACIS)** is one of the oldest professional computing forensic organizations. It was created by police officers that wanted to formalize credentials in computing investigations. IACIS restricts membership to sworn law-enforcement personnel or government employees working as computer forensic examiners. This restriction might change, so visit the IACIS Web site (*www.cops.org*) to verify the requirements.

IACIS conducts an annual two-week training course for qualified members. Students must interpret and trace e-mail, acquire evidence properly, identify operating systems, recover data, and understand encryption theory and other topics. Students have to take and pass a written exam before continuing to the next level. Passing the exam earns the status of **Certified Electronic Evidence Collection Specialist (CEECS)**.

The next level of training is completed through a five- to six-month correspondence course. The IACIS certification process for this level of training consists of examining six floppy disks and one hard disk drive in sequence, submitting a thorough report of each examination, and completing a written test. The first four floppy disks must be examined using a command-line tool. (You cannot use a graphical user interface [GUI] tool to examine the floppy disks.) The testing agency plants files on the disks that you must find, including items that are easy to find, data in unallocated space, Random-Access Memory

(RAM) slack, file slack, and deleted files. Other topics include data hiding, determining file types of disguised files, and accessing password-protected files. You might also be asked to draw conclusions on a case based on the evidence found on the disks. Proficiency in the use of technical tools and deductive reasoning are necessary. A full and thorough report demonstrating accepted procedures and evidence control must be submitted with each disk before proceeding to the next disk. Candidates who successfully complete all parts of the IACIS test are designated as **Certified Forensic Computer Examiners (CFCE)**. For the latest information about IACIS and how to apply for a CFCE certification or membership in IACIS, visit the IACIS Web page at *www.cops.org*.

High-Tech Crime Network (HTCN)

The **High-Tech Crime Network (HTCN)** also provides several levels of certification for applicants. Unlike IACIS however, HTCN requires a review of all related training, including training in one of their approved courses, a written test for the specific certification, and a review of the candidate's work history. HTCN certification is open to anyone meeting the criteria in the profession of computing investigations. At the time of this writing, the HTCN Web site (*www.htcn.org*) specified the following four levels of certification and the requirements for each.

Certified Computer Crime Investigator, Basic Level

- Candidates have two years of law-enforcement or corporate-investigative experience or a bachelor's degree and one year of investigative experience.

- Eighteen months of the candidate's experience directly relates to the investigation of computer-related incidents or crimes.

- Candidates have successfully completed 40 hours of training from an approved agency, organization, or training company.

- Candidates must provide documentation of at least 10 cases in which they participated.

Certified Computer Crime Investigator, Advanced Level

- Candidates have three years of law-enforcement or corporate-investigative experience in any area or a bachelor's degree and two years investigative experience.

- Four years of the candidate's experience directly relates to the investigation of computer-related incidents or crimes.

- Candidates have successfully completed 80 hours of training provided by an approved agency, organization, or company.

- Candidates served as lead investigator in at least 20 separate cases during the past three years and were involved in at least 40 other cases as a lead investigator, supervisor, or in a supportive capacity.

The third level of certification, **Certified Computer Forensic Technician, Basic Level**, is similar to the Certified Computer Crime Investigator's, Advanced Level certification with three major differences: the 18 months of experience must be directly related to computer forensics, a written exam is required, and the 10 cases must be computer forensics applications. In addition, the fourth level of certification, **Certified Computer Forensic Technician, Advanced Level**, requires that the cases and direct experience be in computer forensics.

EnCE Certification

The EnCE certification program is sponsored by Guidance Software, the creators of EnCase, a computer forensic utility. EnCE certification is open to both the public and private sector, and is specific to the use and mastery of EnCase computer forensics analysis.

Requirements for taking the EnCE certification exam do not depend on taking the Guidance Software EnCase training courses. For more information on the EnCE certification requirements, visit *www.encase.com* or *www.guidancesoftware.com*.

Other Training and Certifications

Other organizations are also either considering certifications or have related training programs. Non-profit high-technology organizations for public and private-sector investigations that offer certification and training include the following organizations:

- High Technology Crime Investigations Association (HTCIA), *www.htcia.org*
- SysAdmin, Audit, Network, Security Institute (SANS), *www.sans.org*
- Computer Technology Investigators Northwest (CTIN), *www.ctin.org*
- New Technologies, Inc. (NTI), *www.forensics-intl.com*

Law-enforcement-only organizations for training and certification include the following:

- National Cybercrime Training Partnership (NCTP), *www.nctp.org*
- National White Collar Crime Center (NW3C), *www.cybercrime.org*

DETERMINING THE PHYSICAL LAYOUT OF A COMPUTER FORENSICS LAB

After you have sufficient training to become a computer forensic investigator, you conduct most of your investigations in a lab. This section discusses the physical requirements of a basic computer investigation and forensics lab. The correct layout of a lab can make it more safe, secure, and productive.

Your lab facility must be physically secure so that evidence is not lost, corrupted, or destroyed. Workspaces should also be set up to prevent or alleviate work-related injuries, such as repetitive-motion injuries. As with hardware and software costs, you must balance physical lab expenses with what you need to maintain a safe and secure environment.

You must also use inventory control methods to track all your computing assets. This means that you should maintain a complete and up-to-date inventory list of all major hardware and software items you have in the lab. For consumable items such as cables and media, including floppy disks, compact discs (CDs), and tapes, maintain an inventory list so you know when to order more supplies.

Identifying Lab Security Needs

All computing investigation and forensic labs need an enclosed room where a forensic computer workstation can be set up. You should not use an open cubicle because doing so allows easy access to your evidence. You need a room that you can lock to control your evidence and attest to its integrity. In particular, your lab should be secure during data analysis, even if it takes several weeks to analyze a disk drive. To preserve the integrity of evidence data, your lab should function as an evidence locker or safe, making it a **secure facility** or a secure storage safe.

The following are the minimum requirements for a computer investigation and forensic lab of any size:

- Small room with true floor to ceiling walls
- Door access with a locking mechanism, which can be either a regular key lock or combination lock; the key or combination must be limited to you and your manager
- Secure container such as a safe or heavy-duty file cabinet with a quality padlock that prevents the drawers from opening
- Visitors log listing all persons who have accessed your lab

For daily work production, several examiners can work together in a large open area as long as they all have the same level of authority and access need. This lab area should also have floor to ceiling walls and a locking door. In many public and private organizations, several investigators share a door to the lab that requires an ID card and an entry code.

As a security practice, computing investigators and forensic examiners must be briefed on the lab's security policy. Share information about a case investigation only with other examiners and personnel who need to know about the investigation.

Conducting High-Risk Investigations

High-risk investigations, such as those involving national security or murder, for example, demand greater security than the minimum lab requirements provide. As technology improves and information circulates among computer hackers, keeping your investigation secure may become more difficult. For example, detecting computer eavesdropping is difficult and expensive, but sophisticated criminals and intelligence services in foreign countries can use equipment that detects network transmissions, wireless devices, phone conversations, and the use of computer equipment. Instructions for building a sniffing device that can illegally collect computer emanations are available online, and are therefore available to anyone. Anything you type on your computer can be picked up by such devices.

Most electronic devices emit electromagnetic radiation (EMR). Certain kinds of equipment can intercept EMR, and the EMR can be used to determine the data that the device is transmitting or displaying. According to Webopedia (see *www.webopedia.com/DidYou Know/Computer_Science/2002/vaneck.asp*), the EMR from a computer monitor can be picked up as far away as a half mile.

To protect your investigations, consider how defense contractors during the Cold War were required to shield sensitive computing systems and prevent electronic eavesdropping of any computer emissions. The U.S. Department of Defense calls this special computer emission-shielding **TEMPEST**. (For a brief description of TEMPEST, see the National Industrial Security Program Operating Manual (NISPOM) DoD 5220.22-M, Chapter 11, Section 1, Tempest, *http://nsi.org/Library/Govt/Nispom.html*.)

In paragraph 11-100, NISPOM states, "TEMPEST is an unclassified short name referring to investigations and studies of compromising emanations. Compromising emanations are unintentional intelligence-bearing signals that, if intercepted and analyzed, will disclose classified information when it is transmitted, received, handled, or otherwise processed by any information processing equipment." NISPOM further states that countermeasures are applied to block these emanations.

Constructing a TEMPEST lab requires lining the walls, ceiling, floor, and doors with specially grounded conductive metal sheets. Typically copper sheeting is used because it conducts electricity well. TEMPEST facilities must include special filters for electrical power that prevent electrical power cables from transmitting computer emanations. All heating and ventilation ducts require special baffles to trap the emanations. Likewise, telephones inside the TEMPEST facility must have special line filters.

A TEMPEST facility usually has two doors separated by dead space. The first exterior door must be shut before the interior door can be opened. Each door also has special copper molding to enhance electricity conduction.

Because a TEMPEST-qualified lab facility is expensive and requires routine inspection and testing, it should be considered only for large regional computing investigations, forensic labs, and significant cases that demand absolute security from illegal eavesdropping. To avoid these financial and maintenance costs, some vendors have built low-emanating workstations instead of TEMPEST facilities. These individual workstations are more expensive than an average workstation, but cost less than a TEMPEST lab.

Considering Office Ergonomics

Because computing investigations often require hours of processing disk drives for evidence, your workspace should be as comfortable as possible to prevent repetitive-motion injuries and other computer work-related injuries.

Ergonomics is the study of designing equipment to meet the human need of comfort while allowing for improved productivity. Ergonomics involves psychology, anatomy, and physiology. Understanding psychology helps designers create equipment that people can easily understand how to use. Ergonomic design considers anatomy to make sure the equipment correctly fits the person using it. It also considers physiology to determine how much effort or energy is required by the person using the equipment.

To ensure an ergonomic workspace, review the following questions when arranging your workspace and selecting lab furniture:

- *Desk or workstation table*—Is the desk placed at the correct height for you? Do you need a chair that is lower or higher than normal to make the desktop easy and comfortable for you? Are your wrists straight when sitting? Is this position comfortable? Are the heels of your hands in a comfortable position? Do they exert too much pressure on the desktop? Do you need a pad under the heels of your hands?

- *Chair*—Does your chair allow you to adjust its height? Is the back of the chair too long or too short for the length of your back? Is the bench portion of the chair too long or too short for the length of your thigh? Is the bench and back of the chair padded enough to be comfortable for you? Can you sit up straight when viewing the computer monitor? Are your elbows in a comfortable position while working? How do your shoulders and back feel while sitting and working at the workstation? Is your head facing the computer's monitor or is it off-center because you can't position the chair correctly in front of the desk? See Figure 5-2.

- *Workbench*—Is the workbench for your lab facility at the correct height for you when you are standing in front of it? Can you easily reach the back of the bench without having to stand on a stool?

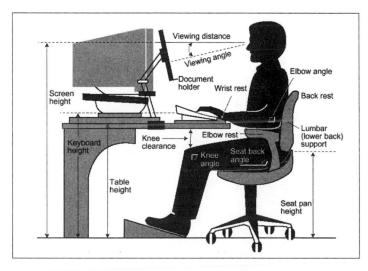

Figure 5-2   Proper ergonomics at a desk

Besides furniture, also consider the ergonomics of your keyboard and mouse. These two items probably contribute to more repetitive-motion injuries than any other device, primarily because they were designed for moderate but not extensive use. Using the keyboard for several hours at a time can be painful and cause physical problems. As shown in Figure 5-3, make sure that your wrists are straight when you are working with a keyboard or mouse, even if they are ergonomically designed.

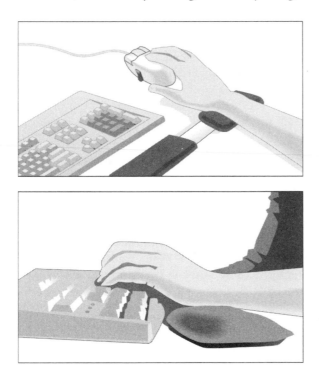

Figure 5-3   Hand and wrist positioning with a wrist pad

If you work with computers for hours in one position, you will injure yourself. No matter how well the furniture, keyboard, or mouse is designed, always take breaks to stretch and rest your body.

Environmental Conditions

Just as the chair, desk, keyboard, and mouse affect your comfort and health, the ventilation and temperature of your lab also contribute to your comfort and productivity. Although the typical desktop computer uses standard household electricity, computers get warm as they run. Unless you invest in a liquid-cooled computer case for your forensic workstation, the standard desktop computer generates heat. The more workstations you are running, the hotter your lab. Therefore, you need adequate air conditioning and ventilation for the room. You should consult with your building's facility coordinator to determine whether the selected room can be upgraded to handle your current and expected computing needs.

Use the following checklist of Heating, Ventilation, and Air Conditioning (HVAC) system questions when planning your computing-forensics laboratory:

- How large is the room, and how much air moves through it per minute?
- Can the room handle the increased heat generated by the workstations?
- What is the maximum number of workstations the room can handle?
- How many computers will be located in this room immediately?
- Will the room handle a small Redundant Array of Inexpensive Disk (RAID) server's heat output?

Lighting

An overlooked environmental issue for any computer forensic facility is the lighting. Most offices have too many lights at the wrong illumination, causing headaches or eyestrain. Several vendors provide natural or full-spectrum lighting, which is less fatiguing than standard incandescent or fluorescent lights, though it does not improve health.

TIP

In 1986, the Food and Drug Administration (FDA) issued a Health Fraud Notice regarding "false and misleading" claims and "gross deceptions" by light bulb and lamp manufacturers to consumers on the benefits of full-spectrum lighting (FDA Enforcement Report: Health Fraud Notice, 1986, WL 59812 (F.D.A.)).

If the lighting in your computer forensics lab is a problem, consult with your facility's management and find out what products are currently available that can best meet your needs.

Kyle Roderick at *www.thirdage.com/features/tech/ouch/index02.html* recommends making the following changes to help minimize eyestrain:

- Make sure your chair is high enough so that you are looking down at the monitor.
- For most people, placing the monitor about two feet from your eyes is most comfortable.
- To minimize the range of focus for your eyes, place any material you are looking at while working on the computer at the same angle as the screen of the monitor.
- If it is difficult to see the fine print or details on the screen, change the zoom or view setting in your active program to enlarge the print or graphic.
- If overhead lights reflect on your computer, move your monitor so that it is clear of any glare. Place a filter screen over the monitor to reduce or eliminate the glare. If glare is still a problem, lower the lighting illumination in your lab.
- Always use some lighting when working at your computer.

- Try to eliminate any direct lighting on your monitor.

- Have regular eye exams and if necessary buy a pair of prescription glasses for computer use.

- Take breaks often and let your eyes focus at distant objects.

Structural Design Considerations

In addition to ergonomic and environmental concerns, including lighting, consider the physical construction of your computer forensics laboratory. Your lab should be a safe, secure, lockable room. Because it can take anywhere from a few hours to several days or weeks to process a computer disk, your lab needs to be secure for the same amount of time. Evidence on larger disk drives takes even longer to analyze and sort. You often need to leave computer evidence, such as a suspect's hard disk drive, connected to your workstation overnight to complete a bit-stream image backup, which can take several hours. You need to leave your unattended evidence in a secure location, a room that no unauthorized person can access without your direct control.

TIP

NISPOM, Chapter 5, Section 8, page 1, Construction Requirements provides an overview of on how to build a secure lab. See *nsi.org/Library/Govt/ Nispom.html* for details.

To ensure the security of your lab, examine the hardware, walls, ceiling, floors, and windows of the facility. Use only heavy-duty building material in the construction of your lab. All hardware such as hinges on doors that are on the outside of the lab should be peened, pinned, brazed, or spot-welded to prevent removal.

Walls can be constructed of plaster, gypsum wallboard, metal panels, hardboard, wood, plywood, grass, wire mesh, expanded metal, or other materials offering resistance to and evidence of any unauthorized entry to the lab. If you use insert panels, you also need to install material that shows evidence of any attempt to gain entry.

Ceilings, like walls, can be constructed of plaster, gypsum wallboard material, panels, hardboard, wood, plywood, ceiling tile, or other material that offers some sort of resistance that allows for detection if access is attempted. For false ceilings or drop ceilings where the walls do not extend to the true ceiling because of hanging ceiling tile, the false ceiling must be reinforced with wire mesh or 18-gauge expanded metal that extends from the top of the false wall to the actual ceiling. This wire mesh or expanded metal must overlap adjoining walls and should provide resistance that allows for detection if access is attempted.

If you have raised floors such as those often found in data centers, look for large openings in the parameter walls. If you find openings, provide the same types of material as described for ceilings to make sure the material provides sufficient resistance and shows evidence of someone attempting to access the lab.

Avoid windows on your lab exterior. If you are assigned a room that has exterior windows, include additional material such as wire mesh on the inside to improve the security of the windows. If you are working in an office building and need to place your lab on an exterior wall, locate the lab on an upper floor, not a ground floor.

Also make sure that all computer monitors of your forensic workstations are facing away from the windows. This will prevent anyone who is unauthorized from spying on you while you are working on a case.

Doors can be wood (solid core) or metal and preferably should not have windows. If your door does have a window, it should have wire mesh in the glass to provide sufficient resistance to prevent and detect an attempted entry. The locking device on the door should have a heavy-duty built-in combination device or a high-quality key-locking doorknob. If you are using a key-locking doorknob, only authorized personnel should have a copy of the key.

Depending on your lab's location, you might need to install intrusion-detection systems and fire alarms. Consult and contract with a bonded alarm company.

Electrical Needs

You need sufficient electrical power to run your workstations and other equipment; 15- and 20-amp service is the preferred setup for electrical outlets. In addition, you should have enough electrical outlets spaced throughout the lab for easy access, eliminating the need for extension cords or electrical plug strips, which are potential fire hazards.

If you have adequate electrical power for your operation, power fluctuations are usually not a problem unless you are located in an area that has poor electrical service. Most computers are fairly tolerant of power fluctuations, though these fluctuations do cause electrical wear and tear on your computer's components. However, all electrical devices eventually fail, usually because of accumulated electrical voltage spikes, where voltage increases rapidly, or surges, or where voltage decreases suddenly. If your lab equipment experiences unexplained failures, consult with your facilities manager to check for problems in electrical power.

One way to reduce electrical problems is to install an Uninterruptible Power Supply (UPS). A UPS allows you to continue working in the event of a power failure until you can shut down your computer. Most UPS systems block electrical fluctuations and help prevent electrical problems from corrupting or destroying evidence.

Communications

When planning voice and data communications, consider that each examiner needs a telephone. Unless you are working within a TEMPEST environment, which has special voice and data access requirements, you can install a multiline Integrated Services Digital Network (ISDN) phone system in the lab. The ISDN provides the easiest way to allow lab personnel to handle incoming calls.

You also need access to the Internet through a dial-up Internet service provider (ISP). Computer forensic software vendors often provide software updates and patches on a Web site, so you need to be able to download that software. You also need Internet access to conduct research on evidence that you find and to consult with other forensics professionals.

However, do not keep your workstation connected to the Internet while performing your analysis unless it is absolutely required. Internet connections can compromise the security of your system.

Networking workstations in a computer forensic lab lets you easily transfer data to another examiner. Having an internal local area network (LAN) provides for ease of operations. For example, you can easily share a RAID file server and printers on a LAN. This is especially useful when you have specialty printers connected to a print server. Using a central lab RAID server also saves time and energy when you are copying large data files such as bit-stream image files.

If your organization is part of a wide area network (WAN), consider having a separate computer that is used only to connect to your WAN to protect the security of your computer forensics workstations. By keeping your forensics workstations physically separate from the WAN, you eliminate any intentional or unintentional access to your evidence or output from your evidence. For example, although workstations on a WAN can receive notices to upgrade software, doing so while your forensics workstation is connected to your WAN can corrupt evidence. Isolating systems prevents this corruption.

Fire-suppression Systems

Fire can be a disaster in a computing-forensics lab. Any electrical device can cause a fire, although this is not common in computers. On rare occasions an electrical short in a computer might destroy a cable. If the power is sufficient on a low-voltage cable, it could ignite other combustible items nearby.

Computers can also cause fires if a hard disk's servo-voice-coil actuators freeze due to damage to the drive. If these actuators are frozen, the head assembly cannot move. The internal programming of the disk's circuit card will then apply more power to the servo-voice-coil actuators to provide more electrical power to move the head assembly correctly, passing too much electrical power through the disk. The components in the disk can handle only so much power before they fail and overload power to the cables connecting the drive to the computer. These cables, especially the ribbon type, do not respond well to excessive power. When too much power is applied to these low-voltage cables, especially ribbon cables, sparks can fly, causing a fire.

Most offices are equipped with fire sprinkler systems and dry chemical fire extinguishers (B rated) as shown in Figure 5-4. For most computing forensic lab operations, these fire-suppression systems work well. The standard desktop workstation used for most forensic analysis does not require additional protection systems. However, if your lab facility has raised floors, you might need to install a dry chemical fire-suppression system. If you have any concerns regarding your fire-suppression needs, contact your facility's coordinator or local fire marshal.

Figure 5-4   Chemical fire extinguishers

Evidence Lockers

The storage containers that you use to store your evidence must be secure so that no unauthorized person can easily access your evidence. You must use high-quality locks such as padlocks with limited duplicate-key distribution.

Also routinely inspect the content of your evidence storage containers to make sure that they store only current evidence. The evidence for closed cases should be moved to other remote secure facilities.

NISPOM Chapter 5, Section 3 (*http://nsi.org/Library/Govt/Nispom.html*) describes the characteristics of a safe storage container. Consult with your facility management or legal counsel, such as corporate or prosecuting attorneys, to determine what your lab should do to maintain evidence integrity. The following are recommendations for securing storage containers:

- The evidence container should be located in a restricted area that is only accessible to lab personnel.

- The number of people authorized to open the evidence container should be kept to a minimum. Maintain records on who is authorized to access each container.

- All evidence containers should remain locked when they are not under the direct supervision of an authorized person.

If a combination locking system is used for your evidence container, implement the following practices:

- Provide same level of security for the combination as the content of the container. Store the combination in another container that is as secure.

- Destroy any previous combinations after setting up a new combination.

- Allow only authorized personnel to change lock combinations.
- Change the combination every six months, when any authorized personnel leave the organization, and immediately after finding an unsecured container, that is, one that is open and unattended.

If you are using a keyed padlock, use the following practices:

- Appoint a key custodian responsible for distributing keys.
- Stamp sequential numbers on each duplicate key.
- Maintain a registry listing which key is assigned to which authorized person.
- Conduct a monthly audit to ensure that no authorized person has lost a key.
- Take an inventory of all keys when the custodian changes.
- Leave keys in the lab—do not remove them.
- Maintain the same level of security for keys as for the evidence container.
- Change locks and keys annually; if a key is missing, replace all associated locks and key.
- Do not use a master key for several locks.

The storage container or cabinet should be made of steel and include either an internal cabinet lock or external padlock. If possible, acquire a safe, which provides superior security and protects your evidence from fire damage. Look for specialized safes that are designed to protect electronic media, called media safes. Media safes are rated by the number of hours it takes before the contents are damaged from a fire. The higher the rating, the better the safe protects evidence.

An evidence storage room is also convenient, especially if it is part of your computing-forensics lab. Security for an evidence room must integrate the same construction and securing devices as the general lab does. Large computer forensic operations also need an evidence custodian and a service counter with a securable metal roll-up window system to control evidence. Using a secure evidence room lets you store large computer components such as computers, monitors, and any other large peripheral devices.

Be sure to maintain a log that indicates every time an evidence container is opened and closed. The log should indicate the date the evidence container was opened and the initials of the authorized person each time the container is accessed. These records should be maintained for at least three years or longer as prescribed by your prosecuting or corporate attorneys. Logs are discussed in more detail in Chapter 8.

Facility Maintenance

Your lab should be properly maintained at all times to ensure the safety and health of the lab personnel. If damage occurs to the floor, walls, ceilings, or furniture, they should be repaired immediately. Floors and carpets should be cleaned at least once a week to help minimize dust that can cause static electricity. Be sure to monitor cleaning crews as they work.

Because static electricity is a major problem when handling electrical devices such as computer parts, consider placing special anti-static pads around electronic workbenches and workstations.

Maintain two separate trash containers, one to store items unrelated to an investigation, such as discarded CDs or magnetic tapes, and the other for waste that is sensitive and requires special handling to ensure that the waste is destroyed. This maintains the integrity of criminal investigation processes and protects trade secrets and attorney-client privileged communications in a private corporation. Several commercially bonded firms specialize in disposing sensitive materials. Your lab should have access to such services to maintain the integrity of your investigations.

Physical Security Needs

In addition to the physical design and construction of your lab, you need to enhance your lab's security by setting security policies. How much physical security you implement depends on the nature of your lab. If your lab is a regional computer crime lab, your security needs are high because the lab risks losing, corrupting, or otherwise damaging evidence. The physical security needs of a large corporation are probably not as high because the risk of evidence loss or compromise is much lower. Determining the risk for your organization dictates how much security you integrate into your computer forensics lab.

Regardless of the security risk to your lab, maintain a sign-in log for all visitors. The log should list the visitor's name, date and time of arrival and departure, employer's name, the purpose of the visit, and the name of the lab member receiving the visitor. Consider anyone who is not assigned to the lab as a visitor, including janitors, facility maintenance personnel, friends, and family. All visitors should be escorted by an assigned authorized staff member throughout their visit to the lab to ensure that they do not accidentally or intentionally tamper with an investigation or evidence. As an added precaution, provide a visible or audible alarm, such as a visitor badge, letting all investigators actively working on cases know that a visitor is in the area.

If possible, hire a security guard or an intrusion alarm system with a guard force to ensure your lab's security. The alarm systems with guards can be used after business hours to monitor your lab.

Auditing a Computer Forensics Lab

To ensure that all security policies and practices are followed, conduct routine inspections to physically audit your lab and evidence storage containers. Audits should include but are not limited to the following facility components and practices:

- Inspect the ceiling, floor, roof, and exterior walls of the lab at least once a month, looking for anything unusual or new.
- Inspect doors to make sure they close and lock correctly.
- Check locks to see if they need to be replaced or changed.

- Review visitor logs to see if they are properly completed.

- Review log sheets for evidence containers to determine when they have been opened and closed.

- Secure at the end of every workday any evidence that is not being processed on a forensic workstation.

Computer Forensics Lab Floor Plan Ideas

How you configure the work area for your computing-forensics lab depends on your budget, the amount of available floor space, and the number of computers you might assign to each computing investigator. If you are a small operation handling two or three cases a month, one forensic workstation should handle your workload. One workstation only requires the area of an average desk. If you are handling many more cases per month, you probably can process two or three computing investigations at a time, which requires more than one workstation. The ideal configuration for multiple workstations is to have two forensic workstations plus one non-forensic workstation that has Internet access.

Because you need plenty of room around each workstation, a work area that contains three workstations requires approximately 150 square feet of space, meaning that the work area should be about 10 feet by 15 feet. This amount of space allows for two chairs so that the computing investigator can brief another investigator on the case.

Small labs usually consist of two forensics computers, a research computer, a workbench (if space allows), and storage cabinets, as shown in Figure 5-5.

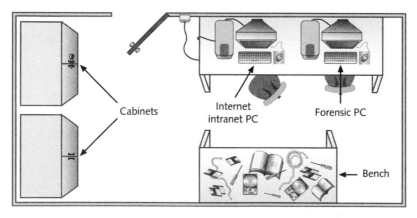

Figure 5-5   Small or home-based lab

Mid-size computer forensic labs, such as those in a private business, have more workstations. For safety reasons, the lab should have at least two exits, as shown in Figure 5-6. If possible, cubicles or even individual offices should be part of the layout to enforce the need-to-know policy. These labs also have more library space for software and hardware storage.

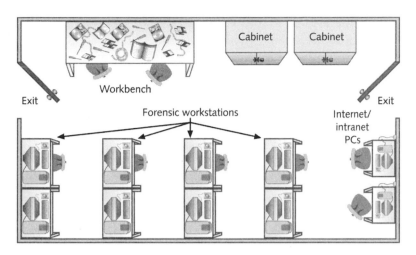

Figure 5-6   Mid-sized computer forensic lab

State law enforcement or the Federal Bureau of Investigation (FBI) most likely runs large or regional computer forensics labs. As shown in Figure 5-7, these labs have a separate evidence room as is typical with police investigations, except that the room is limited to digital evidence. One or more custodians may be assigned to manage and control the traffic in and out of the evidence room.

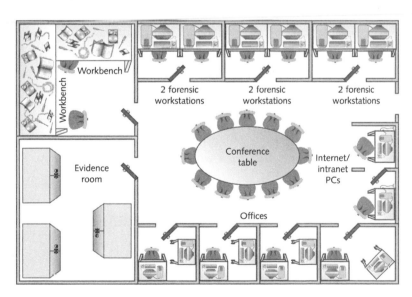

Figure 5-7   Regional computer forensics lab

As discussed earlier, the evidence room needs to be secure. The lab should have at least two controlled exits and no windows. Individual offices for supervisors and cubicles for the investigators are more practical in this configuration. Remember that the forensic computers are connected to an isolated LAN and only a few machines are connected to the outside WAN or metropolitan area network (MAN).

SELECTING A BASIC FORENSIC WORKSTATION

The computer workstation you use as a forensic analysis system depends on your budget and specific needs. Many well-designed computer forensic workstations are available that can handle most computing investigation needs.

Consider, however, that when you start processing a case, you use a workstation for the duration of the examination. Use less powerful workstations for mundane tasks and the multipurpose workstations for the higher-end analysis tasks. Chapter 6 lists several known forensic workstation vendors and the features that make them unique.

Selecting Workstations for Police Labs

Police departments in major cities probably have the most diverse needs for computing investigation tools because the community they serve uses a wide assortment of computing systems. Not all computer users have the latest technology, so police departments need older machines and software to match their community, such as a Commodore 64, an Osbourne I, or Kaypro computer running CP/M or Minix.

One way to investigate older and unusual computing systems is to keep track of the **Special Interest Groups (SIGs)** that still use these old systems. SIGs can be a valuable source of support on recovering and analyzing uncommon systems. (Search for SIGs on the Web as necessary.) When investigating cases involving unusual computer systems, you can also coordinate with or subcontract to larger computer forensic labs. Like large police departments, a regional computer forensic lab must have diverse systems to serve its community. Regional labs often receive work from smaller labs that involve unusual computers or operating systems.

For small, local police departments, the majority of work involves Windows PCs and Apple Macintosh systems. The computer forensic lab of a small police department can be limited to one multipurpose forensics workstation with one or two basic workstations.

The computing systems in a lab should be able to process typical cases in a timely manner. The time it takes to process a typical case usually depends on the size and type of industries in the region. For example, suppose your lab is located in a region with one or more large manufacturing firms that employ 50,000 or more people. Ten percent of those employees might be involved in criminal behavior. One Fortune 500 company investigates an average of one to two murders a year where information on the employee's work computer is used as evidence by law enforcement.

As a general rule there should be at least one law-enforcement computer investigator for every 250,000 people in a geographic region. For example, if your community has 1,000,000 people, the regional computer forensic lab should have at least four computer investigators. Each investigator should have at least one multipurpose computer forensic workstation with one general-purpose workstation.

Selecting Workstations for Private and Corporate Labs

For the private sector, such as a business conducting internal investigations or a commercial business service providing computer forensic services to private parties, equipment resources are generally easy to determine.

Commercial services providing computer forensic analysis for other businesses can tailor their services to specific markets. They can specialize in one or two platforms such as an Intel PC running a Microsoft operating system. They can also gather a variety of tools to meet a wider market. The type of equipment they need depends on their specialty, if any. For general computer forensic facilities, the multipurpose forensic workstation is sufficient.

Private companies with their own Internal Computing Investigation departments can determine the type of forensics workstation they need by identifying the types of computers their company uses. If a business is only running Windows PCs, the internal investigators do not need much specialized equipment. If the business uses many kinds of computers, the Internal Forensic department needs systems and equipment that support the same types of computers. Some of the leading computer forensic programs let you work from a Windows PC and examine both the Windows and Macintosh disk drives.

Stocking Hardware Peripherals

In addition to workstations and software, all labs should have a wide assortment of cables and spare expansion slot cards. Consider stocking your computer forensics lab with the following peripheral devices:

- 40-pin 18-inch and 36-inch IDE cables, both ATA-33 and ATA-100 or faster
- Ribbon cables for floppy disks
- Extra SCSI cards, preferably ultra-wide
- Graphic cards, both Peripheral Component Interconnect (PCI) and Accelerated Graphics Port (AGP) types
- Extra power cords
- A variety of hard disk drives (as many as you can afford)
- At least two 40- to 44-pin laptop computer IDE converter connectors
- Computer hand tools, such as a Philips screwdriver, socket wrench, flat screwdriver, and small flashlight

Maintaining Operating Systems and Application Software Inventories

Operating systems are a necessary part of your lab's inventory. You should maintain licensed copies of as many legacy operating systems as possible to handle cases involving unusual systems.

Microsoft operating systems should include Windows XP, 2000, NT 4.0, NT 3.5, 3.11, and Microsoft DOS 6.22. Apple Macintosh operating systems should include Mac OS X, 9.x, and 8 or older. Linux operating systems can include Red Hat Linux 8 and earlier, Caldera Open Linux, Slackware, and Debian.

Although most high-end computer forensic tools can open or display data files created with popular programs, they don't support all programs. Your software inventory should include current and older versions of the following programs. If you deal with both Windows PCs and Apple Macintosh systems, you should have programs for both.

- Office XP, 2000, 97, and 95
- Quicken (if you deal with a lot of financial investigations)
- Programming languages such as Visual Basic and Visual C++
- Specialized viewers such as QuickView, ACDC, ThumbsPlus, and Irfan
- Corel Office suite
- StarOffice/OpenOffice
- Peachtree accounting applications

Using a Disaster Recovery Plan

Besides planning for equipment needs, you also need to plan for disasters, such as hard disk crashes, lightning strikes, and power outages. A disaster recovery plan makes sure that you can restore your workstations and investigation file servers to their original condition if a catastrophic failure occurs, such as a fire or a head crash to an important disk drive.

A disaster recovery plan also specifies how to rebuild an investigation workstation after it has been severely contaminated by a virus from a disk drive you are analyzing. Central to any disaster recovery plan is a system for backing up investigation computers. Tools such as Norton Ghost are useful for directly restoring files. As a general precaution, consider backing up your workstation once a week. You can restore programs from the original disks or CDs, but it is difficult to recover lost data without up-to-date backups.

Store your system backups where they are easily accessible. You should have at least one copy of your backups on-site, and either a duplicate copy or a previous copy of your backups stored in a safe off-site facility. Off-site backups are typically rotated on a predefined schedule that varies according to your needs, such as every day, week, or month.

In addition to performing routine backups, record all the updates you make to your workstation using a process called **configuration management**. Some companies record updates in a configuration management database to maintain compliance to lab policy. Every time you add or update software on your workstation, enter the change in the database to explain the change. You can also record system updates and other configuration changes in a log, such as in a notebook.

A disaster recovery plan can also address how to restore a workstation that you reconfigured for a specific investigation. For example, if you install a suite of applications, you might not have enough disk space for normal processing needs. Problems may be encountered during the reconfiguration or even during simple upgrades. The disaster recovery plan should outline how to uninstall software and delete any files the uninstall program has not removed so you can restore your system to its original configuration.

Planning for Equipment Upgrades

Risk management involves determining how much risk is acceptable for any process or operation, such as replacing equipment. Identify the equipment on which your lab depends, and create a schedule to replace that equipment. Also identify equipment that you can replace when it fails.

Recall that computing components are designed to last 18–20 months in normal business operations, and new, larger versions of operating systems and applications are released frequently. Therefore, systems periodically need more RAM, disk space, and processing speed. To keep your lab current, schedule hardware replacements at least every 18 months.

Using Laptop Forensic Workstations

Recent significant advances in hardware technology provide more flexibility to computer forensics. You can now use a laptop PC with a Firewire (IEEE 1394 standard) or USB hard disks to create a lightweight, mobile forensic workstation. Improved throughput speeds of data transfer on laptops also make it easier to create bit-stream copies of suspect disk drives.

However, laptops are still limited as forensic workstations. Even with improved data transfer rates, acquiring data with a data compression-imaging tool such as EnCase or SafeBack creates a bottleneck. The speed of the processor determines how quickly you can acquire an image file of a hard disk. The faster the CPU on your laptop (or other PC), the faster the image is created in a compressed mode.

BUILDING A BUSINESS CASE FOR DEVELOPING A FORENSICS LAB

Before you can set up a computer forensics lab, you must enlist the support of your managers and other team members. To do so, you build a **business case**, a plan that you can use to sell your services to your management or clients. In the business plan, you justify acquiring newer and better resources to investigate computer forensics cases.

How you develop your business plan depends on the organization you support. If you are sole proprietor, making a business case is fairly simple. If you need money to buy the tools, you can save your money for the purchase of the tools or you can negotiate with your bank for a loan.

For a public entity such as a police department, the business requirements change significantly because budgets are planned a year or more in advance. Public agency department managers present their budget proposals to upper managers. If approved, the department makes money available to acquire resources outlined in the budget. Some public organizations might have other funds available that can be spent immediately for special needs. Managers can divert these funds in the case of emergency or unforeseen needs.

Keep in mind that a private-sector business, especially a large corporate environment, is motivated by the need to make money. A business case should demonstrate how computing investigations could save money and avoid risks that can damage profits, such as by preventing litigation involving the company. For example, recent court decisions have defined viewing pornographic images in the workplace as creating a hostile environment for other employees, which is related to employee harassment and computer abuse. An employer is responsible for preventing and investigating harassment between employees and non-employees associated with the workplace. A company is also liable if it does not actively prevent the creation of a hostile workplace, such as by providing employee training and investigating allegations of computer abuse.

The Internet makes it difficult for employers to provide a safe and secure environment for employees. In particular, employees can easily abuse free e-mail services available on the Web. These free services provide a sender with anonymity, enabling an employee to transmit inappropriate e-mail messages, which is a form of sexual harassment. Because training rarely prevents this type of inappropriate behavior, an employer needs to institute an investigation program that involves collecting network logs such as proxy server logs and examining computer disks to locate traces of message evidence. Chapter 11 discusses e-mail abuse and using e-mail server and network logs in detail.

A lawsuit, regardless of who wins, can cost an employer several hundred thousand dollars. In your business case, compare the cost of training and conducting computing investigations with the cost of a lawsuit.

Your business case should show how computing investigations can improve profits, such as by protecting intellectual property, trade secrets, and future business plans. For example, when employees leave one company for a competing company, they can provide their new employer with vital competitive information.

Suppose a fictitious company called Skateboard International (SI) has invested research and development into a new product that improves the stability of skateboards. Their main competitor is Better Skateboard, who contacts Gwen Smith, a disgruntled SI employee, via e-mail and offers her a job. When Gwen leaves SI, she takes with her the plans to a new product. A few months later, Better Skateboard introduces a product similar to the skateboard Gwen had been researching at SI.

SI recognizes that the new improved skateboard is similar to the one Gwen had been developing, and consults the non–compete agreement Gwen signed when she was hired. SI feels that the new technology Gwen provided to Better Skateboards belongs to their company. It suspects that Better Skateboard stole their trade secret and intellectual property.

SI can now sue Better Skateboard and demand discovery on internal documents. Because Gwen and Better Skateboard corresponded via e-mail, a computing investigator needs to find data relating to both the hiring and the research engineering at Better Skateboard. Better Skateboard can also demand discovery on SI's research records to determine whether any discrepancies in product design could disprove the lawsuit.

In this fictitious scenario, computing investigations can allow one company to generate revenue from a new product, and prevent the other company from doing so. Information related to profits and losses makes a persuasive argument in a business case.

CREATING A FORENSIC BOOT FLOPPY DISK

Recall that your goal when conducting a computer forensic examination is not to alter any portion of the original data on a disk when making a copy or examining the data. The preferred way to avoid modifying evidence data is to never examine the original evidence disk. In Chapter 2 you learned how make a copy of floppy disk so that you could recreate and then examine it. The same principle applies when examining hard disks—you must preserve the original disk and not alter its contents during your examination.

In the following section, you make a boot floppy disk that will be your forensics boot floppy disk. Whenever a computer is started, it accesses files on the hard disk, even if the computer boots from a floppy disk that contains system files. When the boot process accesses the files on the hard disk, it changes the date and time stamps for these files, which can jeopardize an investigation, especially if a goal in the investigation is to determine when the computer was last used. By booting the computer without a specially configured floppy disk, you destroy information important to an investigation. Windows 9x can also alter other files, especially if DriveSpace is implemented on a FAT16 disk drive. The boot floppy disk that you create is specially configured so that the boot process does not alter any files on the hard disk when the computer is powered on, thus preserving the suspect's disk drive.

Assembling the Tools for a Forensic Boot Floppy Disk

To make a boot floppy disk for forensics data acquisition, you need the following items:

- Disk editor installed on your computer, such as Norton Disk Edit or Hex Workshop

- Floppy disk containing files you no longer need

- MS-DOS operating system such as MS-DOS 6.22, or Windows 95B (OSR2) or Windows 98 running on your computer, not Windows XP, 2000, Me, or NT

- Computer that can boot to a true MS-DOS level, that is, MS-DOS 6.22 or a Windows 95B (OSR2) or Windows 98 computer

- Forensic acquisition tool such as DriveSpy, EnCase, SafeBack, or SnapCopy

- Write-blocking tool to protect the evidence drive

The first task is to make the floppy disk bootable, meaning that it contains the necessary system files to boot the computer. The following steps use a Windows 98 computer to make the boot floppy disk. The process is similar for Windows 95.

To make the floppy disk bootable:

1. Boot into DOS mode. Insert the floppy disk into the floppy disk drive of your computer, which is usually drive A.

2. At the C:\ prompt, format the floppy disk by typing **C:\ Format A: /U /S** and then pressing **Enter**.

3. At the DOS prompt, type **Attrib –r –h A:*.*** and then press **Enter** to remove the read-only and hidden attributes for all the files on the floppy disk.

4. On the A: drive, delete the DRVSPACE.BIN and MSDOS.SYS files by typing **Del A:\DRVSPACE.BIN** and pressing **Enter** and then typing **Del A: \MSDOS.SYS** and pressing **Enter**.

After you create a bootable floppy disk, update the operating system files to remove any reference to the hard disk, which is usually drive C. This ensures that when acquiring a FAT16 or FAT32 evidence disk, your boot floppy disk does not contaminate it. You need to modify the COMMAND.COM file and the IO.SYS file to make a forensic boot disk.

The following steps show you how to use Hex Workshop to create your forensic boot floppy disk. Hex Workshop should already be installed on your computer before you perform these steps. If you are using Norton Disk Edit, first boot your workstation to MS-DOS mode. For further information on how to use Norton Disk Edit, refer to its online help.

To update the COMMAND.COM file:

1. Boot your workstation to Windows.

2. Insert the bootable floppy disk you created in the previous set of steps into the floppy disk drive of your workstation.

3. Start Hex Workshop by double-clicking the **Hex Workshop** icon on your desktop or by clicking **Start**, pointing to **Programs** (**All Programs** in Windows XP), pointing to **Hex Workshop 4.0**, and then clicking **Hex Workshop**. The opening window appears, shown in Figure 5-8. Your Hex Workshop window might be slightly different.

4. Click **File** on the menu bar, and then click **Open**.

5. In the Open dialog box, navigate to the A: drive. Click **Command.com**, as shown in Figure 5-9, and then click **Open**.

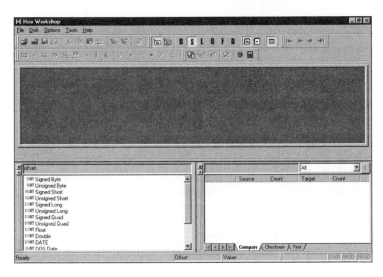

Figure 5-8   Hex Workshop opening window

Figure 5-9   Selecting Command.com

6. To replace references to the hard disk (drive C) in Command.com, start by clicking **Edit** on the menu bar and then clicking **Replace**.

7. In the Replace dialog box, click the **Replace Type** list arrow. A list of data you can replace appears, as shown in Figure 5-10. Click **Text String**.

8. In the Find text box of the Replace dialog box, type **C:** or the letter of your primary hard disk. In the Replace text box, type **A:** in the **Replace** text box (see Figure 5-11.)

9. Click **OK**. The Replace dialog box shown in Figure 5-12 opens, where you can indicate whether you want to find the specified text or replace it. Click the **Replace All** button, and then click **OK**.

10. Click **File** on the menu bar, and then click **Save** to save the changes you made to Command.com on the floppy disk. If a message appears asking if you want to make a back up of Command.com, click the **No** button.

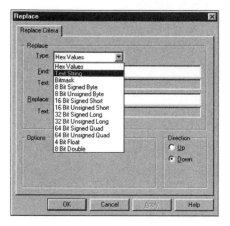

Figure 5-10   Selecting the type of item to replace

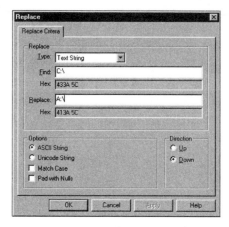

Figure 5-11   Replacing C:\ with A:\

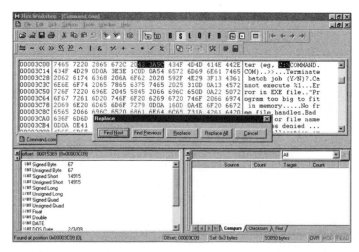

Figure 5-12   Replace dialog box

In the following steps, you modify the IO.SYS file to change all the references to the C: drive and to the DriveSpace utility. You do not want to activate DriveSpace because it can corrupt data.

To update IO.SYS:

1. Click **File** on the Hex Workshop menu bar, and then click **Open**.

2. In the Open dialog box, navigate to the A: drive, and then click **Io.sys** as shown in Figure 5-13.

5

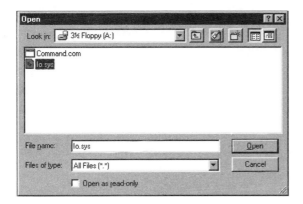

Figure 5-13   Selecting Io.sys

3. Click the **Open** button to open the file in Hex Workshop (sec Figure 5-14).

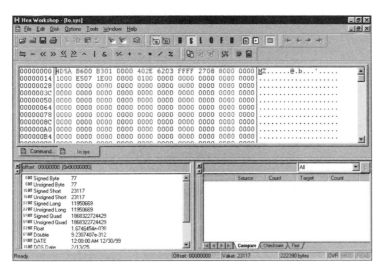

Figure 5-14   Io.sys open in Hex Workshop

4. Click **Edit** on the menu bar, and then click **Replace**.

5. In the Replace dialog box, click the **Replace Type** list arrow, and then click **Text String**, if necessary. In the Find text box of the Replace dialog box, type **C:**. In the Replace text box, type **A:**. Then click **OK**.

6. In the Replace dialog box, click the **Replace All** button, and then click **OK**.

7. Click **Edit** on the menu bar, and then click **Replace**.

8. In the Find text box of the Replace dialog box, delete the current text, and then type **.BIN**. In the Replace text box, type **.ZZZ** (see Figure 5-15). Replacing .BIN with .ZZZ prevents Io.sys from referencing DriveSpace.

Figure 5-15   Replacing .BIN with .ZZZ

9. Click **OK**. In the Replace dialog box, click the **Replace All** button, and then click **OK**.

10. Click **File** on the menu bar, and then click **Save** to save your changes to Io.sys on the floppy disk. If a message appears asking if you want to make a backup of Io.sys, click the **No** button.

11. Click **File** on the menu bar, and then click **Exit** to close Hex Workshop. Store your forensic boot floppy disk in a safe place.

Now you can use the floppy disk to boot a suspect's computer without contaminating the evidence on their hard disk. Next, you add forensic software to the floppy disk so you can use it to acquire an evidence disk. The specific forensic software you add to your forensic boot floppy depends on the tools you have available. In the following steps, you copy the Digital Intelligence software tools to the forensic boot floppy disk.

To add DriveSpy to your forensic floppy disk:

1. Access the command prompt on your computer.

2. Navigate to the **Tools** folder in your work folder.

3. Place your forensic boot floppy disk in the floppy disk drive.

4. At the command prompt, type **Copy DriveSpy.* a:** and press **Enter**.

5. Verify that the files have been copied to the floppy disk by typing **Dir a:** and pressing **Enter**.

6. Exit the command prompt.

5

Now you should make a backup copy of this floppy disk. You can use the MS-DOS Diskcopy command or you can make an image copy with the Digital Intelligence Image utility. You need your original bootable forensic floppy disk and an extra blank floppy disk.

To make a duplicate disk with Diskcopy:

1. Insert the original boot forensic floppy disk in the floppy disk drive, such as drive A.

2. Access a command prompt. Type **Diskcopy A: A:** and then press **Enter**.

3. Follow the prompts to make the duplicate copy, inserting the blank formatted floppy disk when requested.

To make an image copy of the forensics disk using the Image utility:

1. Insert the original boot forensic floppy disk in the floppy disk drive, such as drive A.

2. Access a command prompt and navigate to the **Tools** folder located in your work folder, which is where you originally installed the DriveSpy and Image programs.

3. With the forensic floppy disk in the drive, type **Image a: for_boot.dat** and press **Enter**.

4. When the command prompt reappears, remove the forensic floppy disk and place the blank disk in the drive.

5. Type **Image for_boot.dat a:** and press **Enter** to transfer the files to the new disk.

You now have a copy of your forensic boot floppy on a disk and on your hard disk.

RETRIEVING EVIDENCE DATA USING A REMOTE NETWORK CONNECTION

If you are working on a LAN, you can retrieve bit-stream image copies of disks through a workstation's network connections. An older product called SnapBack originally provided the ability to boot a suspect workstation with a specially configured boot floppy disk that has the appropriate network drivers to connect to a remote server. Other tools such as EnCase version 3 now provide the same feature as SnapBack.

Acquiring a bit-stream image over a LAN can be very time consuming, even with a 100 Mbit connection. However, if you have a direct network interface card (NIC) to NIC connection with a twisted-pair network cable, you can acquire a bit-stream copy through a network connection in a reasonable amount of time. This feature is available with Guidance Software's EnCase version 3 or later.

CHAPTER SUMMARY

- A computer forensics lab is where you conduct your investigations, store your evidence, and do most of your work. You use the lab to house your instruments, current and legacy software, and computer forensics workstations. In general, you need a variety of computer forensic hardware and software to do your work.

- To continue a career in computing investigations and forensic analysis, you need to upgrade your skills through training. Several organizations provide training and are creating certification programs for computer forensics that test you after you have successfully completed training. Some state and federal government agencies are also considering establishing their own certification programs that address minimum skills sets to conduct computing investigations at various levels.

- Your lab facility must be physically secure so that evidence is not lost, corrupted, or destroyed. Workspaces should also be set up to prevent or alleviate work-related injuries, such as repetitive-motion injuries. As with hardware and software costs, you must balance physical lab expenses with what you need to maintain a safe and secure environment. In building a computer forensics lab, you must consider things such as structural integrity, access, fire prevention, HVAC, lighting, and ergonomics.

- Police departments in major cities need a wide assortment of computing systems, including older, outdated technology. Most computer investigations in small, local police departments involve Windows PCs and Apple Macintosh systems. As a general rule, there should be at least one law-enforcement computer investigator for every 250,000 people in a geographic region. Commercial services providing computer forensics analysis for other businesses can tailor their services to specific markets.

- Before you can set up a computer forensic lab, you must enlist the support of your managers and other team members by building a business case, a plan that you can use to sell your services to your management or clients. In the business plan, you justify acquiring newer and better resources to investigate computer forensics cases.

- Creating a bootable forensic floppy disk is necessary to make sure you do not contaminate digital evidence. Use a boot floppy disk that is specially configured so that the boot process does not alter any files on the hard disk when the computer is powered on, thus preserving the suspect's disk drive.

- If you are working on a LAN, you can retrieve bit-stream image copies of disks through a workstation's network connections.

KEY TERMS

American Society of Crime Laboratory Directors (ASCLD)—A national society that sets the standards, management, and audit procedures for labs used in crime analysis including computer forensic labs used by the police, FBI, and similar organizations.

business case—Justification to upper management or a lender for purchasing new equipment, software, or other tools when upgrading your facility. In many instances a business case show how the upgrades will benefit the company.

Certified Computer Crime Investigator, Basic Level—A certificate awarded by the HTCN upon successful completion of the appropriate exams. Requires a BS, two years of investigative experience and 18 months of experience relating to computer crimes.

Certified Computer Crime Investigator, Advanced Level—A certificate awarded by HTCN upon successful completion of appropriate exams. Requires a BS, three years of investigative experience, and four years of experience relating to computer crimes.

Certified Computer Forensic Technician, Basic Level—A certificate awarded by the HTCN upon successful completion of their requirements. Same requirements as the Certified Computer Crime Investigator, Basic Level, but all experience must be related to computer forensics.

Certified Computer Forensic Technician, Advanced Level—A certificate awarded by the HTCN upon successful completion of their requirements. Same requirements as the Certified Computer Crime Investigator, Advanced Level, but all experience must be related to computer forensics.

Certified Electronic Evidence Collection Specialist (CEECS)—A certificate awarded by IACIS upon completion of the written exam.

Certified Forensic Computer Examiners (CFCE)—A certificate awarded by IACIS upon completion of the correspondence portion of testing.

configuration management—The process of keeping track of all upgrades and patches you apply to your computer's OS and applications.

ergonomics—The proper placement of machinery, office equipment, and computers to minimize physical injury or injuries caused by repetitious motions. It is also the study of designing equipment to meet the human need of comfort while allowing for improved productivity.

High Tech Crime Network (HTCN)—A national organization that provides certification for computer crime investigators and computer forensic technicians.

International Association of Computer Investigative Specialists (IACIS)—One of the oldest professional computing forensic organizations, IACIS was created by police officers who wanted to formalize credentials in computing investigations. IACIS restricts membership to only sworn law-enforcement personnel or government employees working as computing forensics examiners.

risk management—Involves determining how much risk is acceptable for any process or operation, such as replacing equipment.

secure facility—A facility that can be locked and provides limited access to the contents of a room.

Special Interest Groups (SIGs)—Associated with various operating systems, these groups maintain Listservs and may hold meetings to exchange information about current and legacy operating systems.

TEMPEST—An unclassified term that refers to facilities that have been hardened so that electrical signals from computers, the computer network, and telephone systems cannot be easily monitored or accessed by someone outside the facility.

Uniform Crime Report—Information collected at the federal, state, and local levels to determine the types and frequencies of crimes committed.

6

CURRENT COMPUTER FORENSICS TOOLS

After reading this chapter, you will be able to:

♦ Evaluate your computer forensics software needs

♦ Use command-line forensics tools

♦ Explore graphical user interface (GUI) forensics tools

♦ Explore other useful computer forensics tools

♦ Explore computer forensics hardware

Whereas Chapter 5 outlined how to set up an effective computer forensics laboratory, this chapter explores the software and hardware tools you use during computing investigations and forensic analysis. You can stock your lab with computer forensics software designed for MS-DOS, DOS shells, and Windows, and hardware such as workstations and peripheral devices. Remember that many new vendor products are being developed and marketed almost daily, and that current products are also being revised. Routinely check vendor Web sites to see what new features and improvements are available. These improvements might address a special problem that has been difficult to solve.

EVALUATING YOUR COMPUTER FORENSICS SOFTWARE NEEDS

Maintaining a computer forensics lab involves creating a software library containing older versions of computer forensics utilities, operating systems, and other programs. You should maintain all older versions of software that you have used and retired, such as older versions of Windows and Linux. If a new version of software fixes one bug but introduces another, you can use the previous version.

Recall from Chapter 5 that when you are acquiring computer forensics tools, you must first identify what you need for most investigations. As part of business planning for your lab, determine which tools provide the most flexibility, reliability, and future expandability to do the job. The software tools you select should be compatible with the next generation of operating systems (OSs). For example, when Microsoft upgraded from Windows 9x to Windows NT, computing investigators had difficulty examining the disks because they used the newly developed New Technology File System (NTFS). When FAT32 was introduced with Windows 95B, forensic software vendors revised their software for the new file system. Seek information on the changes included with a new release of hardware or software and for those planned for the next release. Because operating system vendors do not always provide adequate information about future file system upgrades, it is your responsibility to research and prepare for these changes. Develop your own sources on where to obtain new specifications if the vendor fails to provide them.

Another concern for selecting computer forensics tools is to determine which tool can save time or is more reliable. You often trade speed for reliability. For example, many new GUI forensics tools are resource intensive. They demand more memory than your workstation might have. Other applications running in the background on the forensic workstation, such as an antivirus program, might also compete with the operating system for resources. In these cases, a GUI forensic application can stop running, causing delays in your investigation. When planning business purchases, determine what a new computer forensics tool does better than the one you are using. In particular, research how well the software performs in validation tests, which verify the integrity of the results that data-analysis tools produce.

Using National Institute of Standards and Technology (NIST) Tools

To make sure the evidence you recover and analyze with computer forensics software can be admitted in court, you must test and validate the software. The **National Institute of Standards and Technology (NIST)** is actively publishing articles, providing tools, and creating procedures for testing and validating computing-forensics software. This software should be verified to enhance computer forensics evidence admissibility in judicial proceedings. NIST is sponsoring a project called **Computer Forensics Tool Testing (CFTT)** to manage the research on computing-forensics tools. For additional information on the testing project at NIST, visit *www.cftt.nist.gov*.

NIST has created a general approach for testing computer forensics tools. These general testing criteria are included in an article titled "General Test Methodology for Computer Forensic Tools," (version 1.9, November 7, 2001), available at *www.cftt.nist.gov/testdocs.html*.

The article addresses "the lack of standards or specifications that describe what forensics tools should do and the need for these tools to survive the scrutiny of a judicial process."

The criteria listed in the NIST article are based on standard testing methods and ISO 17025 criteria for testing items for which no standards exist. Your lab must meet the following criteria and keep accurate records so that when new software and hardware become available, the standards are in place for your lab:

- *Establish categories for computer forensics tools*—Group computer forensics software according to categories specified by expert users, such as forensics tools designed specifically to retrieve and trace e-mail.

- *Identify computer forensics category requirements*—For each group, describe the technical features or functions a computer forensics tool in that category must have.

- *Develop test assertions*—Based on the requirements, create tests that prove or disprove the ability of the tool to meet the requirements. For example, a data-recovery tool should be able to retrieve data from RAM slack.

- *Identify test cases*—Find or create types of cases to investigate with the forensics tool. Identify information to retrieve from a sample disk or other media. For example, use the image of a closed case file created with a trusted computing-forensics tool to test a new tool in the same category and see if it produces the same results.

- *Establish a test method*—Considering the purpose and design of the tool, specify how to test the forensics tool and the instructions that ship with the product.

- *Report test results*—Describe the test results in a report that complies with ISO 17025, which requires that test reports must be accurate, clear, unambiguous, and objective.

Another standards document, ISO 5725, demands accuracy for all aspects of the testing process, meaning that the results must be repeatable and reproducible. Repeatable results mean that if you work in the same lab on the same machine, you generate the same results. Reproducible results mean that if you are in a different lab and working on a different machine, the tool still retrieves the same information.

NIST has also developed several tools that evaluate disk drive imaging tools. The following tools are posted on the CFTT Web site at *www.cftt.nist.gov* in a single Zip file named FS-TST10.zip, which contains the **Forensic Software Testing Support Tools (FS-TST)** for testing the imaging capability of a computer forensics tool. The CFTT states that the following testing programs, which are written in Borland C++ 4.5, can be run in MS-DOS 6.3:

- *DISKWIPE*—Initializes the test disk drive to a predefined value for the test

- *BADBLOCK*—Simulates a bad sector on a disk drive by replacing Interrupt 13

- *BADX13*—Creates a bad sector on an extended BIOS disk drive; sectors are listed in logical block addressing (LBA) format

- *CORRUPT*—Corrupts one bit in a specified file to see if it is detected by the forensics tool

- *ADJCMP*—Compares sector by sector two drives that are not the same size, that is, it adjusts and compares sectors for drives that have different geometries

- *DISKCMP*—Compares two disk drives to determine whether they are actually identical when copied with a forensics imaging tool

- *PARTCMP*—Produces a Secure Hash Algorithm 1 (SHA-1) hash for an entire partition

- *DISKHASH*—Produces an SHA-1 hash for an entire disk drive

- *SECHASH*—Produces an SHA-1 hash for a specified sector

- *LOGCASE*—Logs the case information into a file

- *LOGSETUP*—Provides setup information about a source test disk's configuration

- *PARTAB*—Prints the partition table of the test drive

- *DISKCHG*—Alters data on a drive to determine whether it is detected by the forensics tool being tested

- *SECCMP*—Compares sectors to each other to help validate a data copy

- *SECCOPY*—Allows you to copy a specific sector

Another program created by NIST is the **National Software Reference Library (NSRL)** project. The goal of the NSRL project is to collect all known hash values for commercial software applications and operating system files. The primary hash used by NSRL is the **Secure Hash Algorithm 1 (SHA-1)**, which is also called the Reference Data Set (RDS). SHA-1 provides for a much higher degree of accuracy than any other hashing method such as MD5 or CRC-32.

The purpose of the NSRL project is to reduce the number of known files in the forensic examination of a disk drive. Identifying known good files, such as operating system files or application software programs, allows you to significantly reduce the number of files you need to inspect for evidence.

In addition to identifying known files on a disk, you can also use the RDS to identify known bad files, including illegal images such as child pornography or computer viruses. By using this feature on a suspect's hard disk, you can quickly identify and locate known bad files.

Using National Institute of Justice (NIJ) Methods

The **National Institute of Justice (NIJ)** has also developed methods and training programs for computing investigations and forensic analysis. NIJ works with NIST and other federal partners to develop methods to test commercial computer forensics software and establish minimum expected performance standards.

Recall that NIJ created the reference library of the SHA-1 values of all known commercial software. You use SHA-1 to match hash values of known files with those on an evidence disk. For example, if a suspect replaces the filename of an incriminating file with a known filename such as VB3600.dll, the SHA-1 indicates that the hash values do not match, alerting you to investigate VB3600.dll.

NIJ provides several publications specific to electronic crime (e-crime) as quick references. The quick reference manuals developed or being considered concern the following topics:

- Managing technology in law enforcement
- Investigating e-crime scenes for first responders
- Analyzing computer evidence
- Using technology to investigate e-crimes
- Investigating technology crimes
- Creating a digital evidence library
- Presenting digital evidence in a courtroom
- Using best practices when seizing electronic evidence

NIJ has contributed significantly in developing best practices for seizing electronic evidence. They have collected and tested methods that ensure the proper preservation of electronic evidence, and produce a handy quick reference pocketsize notebook that is designed as a field manual for police officers. Visit *www.ojp.usdoj.gov/nij* for more information.

Validating Computer Forensics Tools

After retrieving and examining evidence data using one tool, you should verify your results by performing the same tasks with other similar forensic software. You need at least two tools to validate software or hardware upgrades. After you use one forensic analysis tool to retrieve disk data, you use another to see whether you retrieve the same information. The analysis tool that you use to compare results should be well tested. Reliable test utilities include disk editors such as Norton Disk Edit, Hex Workshop, and WinHex. A disk editor allows you to view data on a disk in its raw form, showing files, file headers, file slack, RAM slack, and any other data on the disk.

However, while a disk editor provides you with the most flexibility in testing, it might have trouble examining the content of a compressed file such as a Zip file or Microsoft Outlook PST file.

In addition to verifying your results by using two disk-analysis tools, you must also test all operating system patches and upgrades to make sure they are reliable and do not corrupt your evidence data. These operating system changes can affect the way your forensics tools perform. The vendors of computer forensics tools also issue upgrades and patches to respond to user requests. Use these upgrades only after you have completed the validation testing described in the previous sections. If you determine that a patch or upgrade is not reliable, you can file a problem report with the vendor. The vendor will then address the problem and provide a new patch, which prompts another round of validation testing.

To test patches and upgrades you need to build a test hard disk to use as part of a validation test. You can then store data on the test disk in file slack, for example, and use a forensics software tool to retrieve it. If you can retrieve the data with the forensics tool, you know the tool is reliable. To build a test disk, you need the following tools. You can modify these recommendations as necessary to meet any situation you may encounter.

- *Hard disk*—Small hard disk (1 to 10 GB capacity) installed with the operating system that you typically investigate

- *Disk editor*—Tools such as Norton Disk Edit, Hex Workshop, or WinHex to view the raw data on a disk

- *MD5 utility*—Forensic software such as DriveSpy or a disk editor such as WinHex that contains an MD5 function

- *Forensic boot floppy disk*—Floppy disk like the one you created in Chapter 5 so you do not boot from the hard disk

- *Write-blocker device on the test disk*—A **write-blocker** can be a physical device that prevents the system from recording data on an evidence disk, or a software utility such as PDBlock from Digital Intelligence—you can use either instead of a forensic boot floppy

- *Computer forensics software*—The software you want to test, installed on the computer forensics workstation

The following steps outline how to build a test disk on FAT16 or FAT32 disks. You don't need to perform these steps now; they provide an overview for the steps you perform later in the chapter.

1. Install an operating system on the test hard disk, if necessary.

2. Connect the test disk to the forensic workstation.

3. Use a disk editor such as Norton Disk Edit to locate the file slack area.

4. Write sample text in the slack area, such as Test Slack Area 00001.

5. Note the exact absolute sector and cluster location on the disk drive.

6. Repeat the sample text with incrementing number values for other file slack space and disk free space.

7. Create two or three text files containing sample text.

8. Close the disk editor.

Building a test disk on an NTFS disk minimizes slack space more effectively because files can reside in the Master File Table (MFT). It is better to write the sample test data on an NTFS disk to the disk free space than to the file slack space.

NOTE

More recent versions of NTFS disks allow for varying sizes of files stored directly in the MFT. Check the online manuals for complete details.

The following steps outline how to build a test disk on NTFS disks. You don't need to perform these steps now; they provide an overview for the steps you perform later in the chapter.

1. Install an operating system on the test hard disk, if necessary. Convert and format a drive using NTFS.

2. Connect the test disk to the forensic workstation.

3. Use a disk editor such as WinHex or Hex Workshop to locate disk free space.

4. In the disk free space, create test files that contain text such as Test Free Area 00001 and Test Free Area 00002.

5. Note the absolute sector and cluster location for each sample text file you created.

6. Close the disk editor.

In the following steps, you create a sample test disk with Hex Workshop 4.0. You store data in the file slack, and then validate AccessData Forensic Toolkit (FTK) by using it to find this data. You generally create a test disk for new software by using a small spare hard disk (1 to 10 GB) or a floppy disk. To save time in the following steps, use a floppy disk with data you no longer need. You also need Hex Workshop installed on your computer to complete the following steps. See Chapter 3 for instructions on installing Hex Workshop, if necessary.

To store data in file slack space:

1. Insert a floppy disk in the floppy disk drive, and then perform a full format of the disk.

   In Windows 2000 and XP: Display the floppy disk icon in a Window Explorer or My Computer window, right-click the **3½ Floppy (A:)** icon, and then click **Format**. Make sure the Quick Format check box is not selected in the Format A: dialog box, and then click Start. Click **OK** to start, click **OK** when finished, and then click **Close**.

   From the command line on Microsoft OS: Type **format a: /u** and then press **Enter** to perform an unconditional format. Then return to Windows.

   If you are creating a test hard disk, use the DriveSpy Wipe command or any wipe utility available from AccessData or other vendors to prepare the hard disk.

2. Use Notepad or another text editor to create a new file. Type **This is a test for a search. The test phrase is ZZZZ.** Save the file as **C6InChp1.txt** on your test floppy disk, and then close Notepad.

3. Start Hex Workshop by clicking **Start**, pointing to **Programs** (**All Programs** in Windows XP), pointing to **Hex Workshop**, and then clicking **Hex Workshop**.

4. Click **Disk** on the menu bar, and then click **Open Drive**. In the Open Drive dialog box, click **(A:)**, if necessary. Then click **OK**. The single tab in the upper pane of the Hex Workshop window displays the boot sector of Drive A, as shown in Figure 6-1.

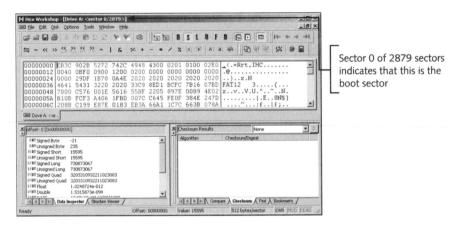

Sector 0 of 2879 sectors indicates that this is the boot sector

Figure 6-1   Floppy disk boot sector in Hex Workshop

5. Click **File** on the menu bar, and then click **Open**. In the Open dialog box, navigate to the floppy disk drive, and then double-click **C6InChp1.txt**. A second tab appears in the upper pane of the Hex Workshop window. The C6InChp1.txt tab includes three columns, with the text you entered in Step 2 appearing in the right column, as shown in Figure 6-2. The settings in your window might be slightly different.

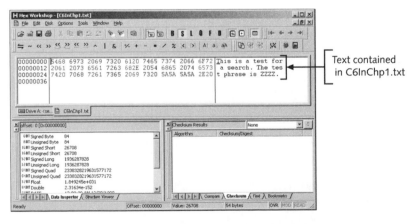

Text contained in C6InChp1.txt

Figure 6-2   Opening C6InChp1.txt in Hex Workshop

Next, you find part of the text you entered in C6InChp1.txt and the sector where it's located. You will search for ZZZZ to find the exact sector in which the file is located.

6. Click the **Drive A:** tab to display the contents of the disk again, and then click at the beginning of the upper-right column. Click **Edit** on the menu bar, and then click **Find**. In the Find dialog box, click the **Type** list arrow, and then click **Text String**, if necessary. In the Value text box, type **ZZZZ**. Click the **Either** option button in the Options area, and then click **OK**. Hex Workshop highlights the ZZZZ text in the right column and the corresponding hexadecimal value in the middle column, and the title bar displays the sector containing the text. (If Hex Workshop does not find ZZZZ after you click OK, repeat this step.)

Next, you enter text in the bottom of the current sector, which is empty space in that sector, or file slack.

7. Scroll to the end of the right column, click the next-to-last line (the one corresponding to 0000001E6 in the left column), and then type **I'm hiding ainsworth** as shown in Figure 6-3.

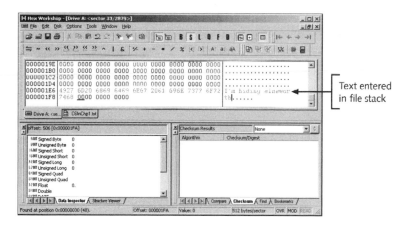

Text entered in file stack

Figure 6-3   Placing text in the file slack area of C6InChp1.txt

8. Click **File** on the menu bar, and then click **Save**.

9. Click the **C6InChp1.txt** tab. It shows only the original sentence, "This is a test for a search. The test phrase is ZZZZ," not "I'm hiding ainsworth."

10. Close Hex Workshop.

Now that you have inserted text in the file slack space on your floppy disk, you can validate a forensics tool by using it to find that text.

To use AccessData FTK to find the text in the file slack space:

1. Use Windows Explorer or My Computer to create a Chap06\Chapter folder in your work folder, if necessary.

2. Start AccessData FTK by clicking **Start**, pointing to **Programs** (**All Programs** in Windows XP), pointing to **AccessData**, pointing to **Forensic Toolkit**, and then clicking **Forensic Toolkit**. If a dialog box appears stating that the KFF Hash Library file was not found, click **OK** to continue. (You don't need the KFF Hash Library for any project in this chapter.)

   When the FTK Startup dialog box opens, click the **Start a new case** option button, if necessary, and then click **OK**.

3. In the New Case dialog box, type your name as the investigator. Type **001** in the Case Number text box, and type **Hiding** in the Case Name text box. Click the **Browse** button, select **Chap06\Chapter** as the Case path, and then click **OK**. Then click **Next**.

4. In the Case Log Options dialog box, make sure all the check boxes are selected, and then click **Next**. In the Evidence Processing Options dialog box, click **Next** to select all but the SHA Hash check box. In the Refine Case – Default dialog box, click **Next** to accept the default selections. In the Refine Index – Default dialog box, click **Next** to accept the default selections.

5. In the Add Evidence to Case dialog box, click the **Add Evidence** button. Click the **Local Drive** option button, and then click **Continue**. In the Select Local Drive dialog box, make sure A: (- FAT) appears in the list box, and the Logical Analysis option button is selected, and then click **OK**. In the Evidence Information dialog box, click **OK** to accept A: as the Evidence Display Name, and then click **Next**. In the Case Summary dialog box, click **Finish**.

   The main FTK window opens, scans the data on the evidence floppy disk, and lists the evidence disk on the lower pane, as shown in Figure 6-4. The settings in your FTK window might differ slightly.

   The Overview tab is open in the main FTK window, showing that the evidence disk contains three total items with one in the file slack or free space.

6. To index the words in the files, click **Tools** on the menu bar, and then click **Analysis Tools**. In the Analysis Tools dialog box, click the **Full Text Indexing** check box as shown in Figure 6-5.

7. Click **OK**, and then click the **Search** tab in the main FTK window. In the Search Term text box, type **ainsworth** and press **Enter**. The search text, "ainsworth," appears in the Search Items list. Close FTK.

If FTK finds "ainsworth" on the evidence floppy disk, you can verify that it can find data in file slack space when you are using your current operating system. If FTK did not find "ainsworth," and you are working on a Windows 9x computer, use a different tool to try to find this data. The following steps show you how to use DriveSpy to find data in file slack space.

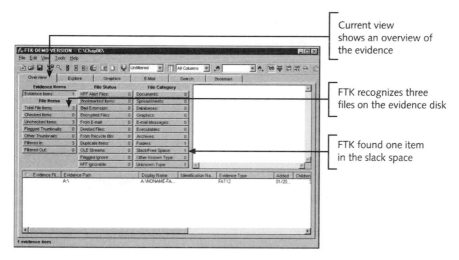

Figure 6-4 Test disk open in FTK

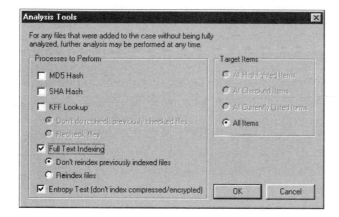

Figure 6-5 Indexing the text in the evidence files

To use DriveSpy to find data in file slack space:

1. Use Windows Explorer to navigate to the folder containing your DriveSpy files, which you installed in the Tools folder in your work folder. (If you have reinstalled or moved the DriveSpy files, navigate to that location.) Right-click **DriveSpy.ini** and then click **Properties**. If the Read only box is checked, click the check box to deselect it, and then click **Apply**. Click **OK** and close Windows Explorer.

2. Start Notepad, and then open DriveSpy.ini from the Tools folder (or other folder as explained in Step 1.) Scroll to the end of the file, press **Enter** to insert a new line, type **[Search Test]** and press **Enter**, and then type **100: "ainsworth"** and press **Enter**, as shown in Figure 6-6. Save DriveSpy.ini, and then close Notepad.

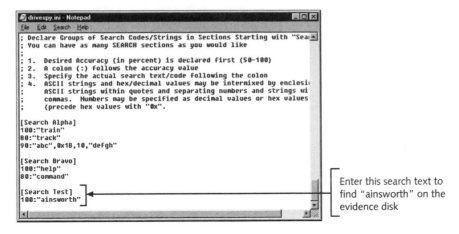

Figure 6-6   Adding search text to DriveSpy.ini

3. Open a Command Prompt window and change to the Tools folder in your work folder. At the command prompt, type **Toolpath** and press **Enter** to run the Toolpath.bat file so you can start DriveSpy from any directory. Then type **DriveSpy** at the command prompt and press **Enter** to start DriveSpy.

4. At the DriveSpy SYS prompt, type **DA** and press **Enter**. Then type **P1** to access the partition area. Create an output file by typing **Output C:\ chap06\Chapter\ ch6_out.txt** and press **Enter**.

5. At the DAP1 prompt, type **Search Test** and press **Enter**. DriveSpy asks whether you want to disable Page mode to avoid lengthy output. Type **y**. DriveSpy then scans Drive A and displays the "I'm hiding ainsworth" text that you entered in the file slack area.

6. Type **q** and press **Enter** to close DriveSpy.

If you are using a Windows 9x computer and you verified that DriveSpy can find data in file slack space, repeat the preceding set of steps on a Windows 2000 or Windows XP computer to verify that DriveSpy also works in those operating systems.

No matter which version of Windows you are using, the next step in creating a test disk is to add data to the disk slack area. Use the same floppy disk that you used in the previous steps, because you know that disk contains information only in the C6InChp1.txt file and in the boot sector.

To add information to the disk slack on the evidence floppy disk:

1. Start Hex Workshop by clicking **Start**, pointing to **Programs** (**All Programs** in Windows XP), pointing to **Hex Workshop**, and then clicking **Hex Workshop**.

2. Click **Disk** on the menu bar, and then click **Open Drive**. In the Open Drive dialog box, click **(A:)**, if necessary. Then click **OK**.

3. Click **Disk** on the menu bar, and then click **First Sector** to make sure you are working with the boot sector of the floppy disk.

4. Hex Workshop shows free space as a series of zeros in the middle column of the window. To find the free space, you need to find a sector that shows only zeros.

5. Click **Disk** on the menu bar, and then click **Next Sector** until only zeros appear in the middle column of the window, as shown in Figure 6-7.

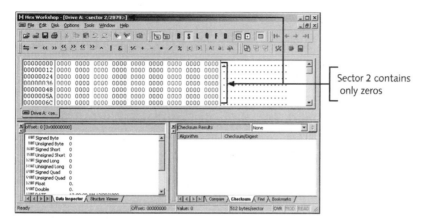

Sector 2 contains only zeros

Figure 6-7   Empty sector

To verify that this sector is empty and has unallocated disk space, or free space, scroll the upper pane to make sure the middle column includes only zeros. Record the sector number shown in the title bar. If you were working with a full disk, you risk writing data to a linked sector. It is a good idea to keep a table that records which sectors contain information, which would appear as hexadecimal numbers other than zero in the middle column.

6. Scroll toward the end of the sector and type **This is where I am hiding financial information** in the right column, as shown in Figure 6-8. Note that you can type this text a line or two before the end of the sector.

7. Click **File** on the menu bar, and then click **Save**. Close Hex Workshop.

You need to generate an MD5 hash value for the disk as a **baseline** to ensure that the test disk is not altered or corrupted. You use the **MD5 hash value** to verify that the test disk is not altered when you examine it using the upgraded or new forensics tool. Recall that the MD5 hash value is generated by an industry-accepted algorithm.

Using DriveSpy from Digital Intelligence or another hashing tool, you would normally run an MD5 hash on the entire hard disk. In the steps in this chapter, you work with floppy disks; however, in live investigations you almost always use a hard disk. The following steps outline the procedure for using a hard disk. To ensure accuracy, run the MD5 hash by using a forensics boot floppy disk or by connecting your test drive to a write-blocker device.

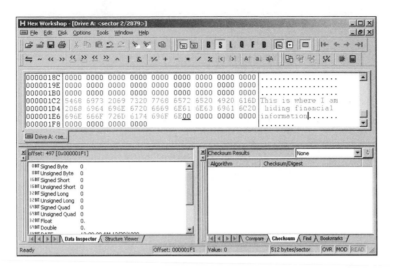

Figure 6-8   Inserting information in free space

To obtain an MD5 hash for a hard drive test disk with DriveSpy:

1. Connect the test disk to your forensic workstation.

2. Insert the forensics boot floppy disk in the floppy disk drive, and then start the forensic workstation with the forensics boot floppy disk.

3. At the DOS prompt, change to the Tools folder in your work folder and type **Toolpath** and press **Enter** to run Toolpath.bat, if necessary. Then start DriveSpy by typing **DriveSpy** at the command prompt and pressing **Enter**.

4. At the SYS prompt, create an output file to collect the MD5 hash values by typing **Output a:\Testmd5.txt** and then pressing **Enter**.

5. Select the test drive by typing **Drive 1** and then pressing **Enter**. If the test drive is the second disk connected to your workstation, it is typically Drive 1.

6. At the DriveSpy D1 prompt, type **MD5** and then press **Enter**. DriveSpy generates an MD5 hash value on the disk and stores the results in a file named Testmd5.txt on the floppy disk. Depending on the size of your test drive, generating the MD5 hash value can take from several minutes to several hours to complete.

7. Type **q** and press **Enter** to close DriveSpy.

After you generate the MD5 hash value, copy the file containing the value to another disk, and store it in a safe place. As an added precaution to prevent altering the MD5 hash value, you can create a bit-stream image backup copy of the test disk. If the test disk is damaged, you can easily restore it from the bit-stream image backup.

USING COMMAND-LINE FORENSICS TOOLS

As mentioned in Chapter 1, computers used several operating systems before MS-DOS dominated the market, though computer forensics was not a major concern at the time. After people began to use personal computers (PCs) to commit crimes and civil infractions, software developers began to release computer forensics tools. The first tools that analyzed and extracted data from floppy disks and hard disks were MS-DOS tools for IBM PC file systems.

The first MS-DOS tool used for a computer investigation was probably Norton Disk Edit. As needs evolved, programs specifically designed for computing forensics were developed for MS-DOS. These early programs could extract data from a file slack and free space. Current programs can search for specific words or characters, or perform a **keyword search**. Most of these tools, however, must run in a true MS-DOS mode, also called the command line, not in an MS-DOS shell window in any recent version of Microsoft Windows such as Windows NT, 2000, or XP.

One advantage of using command-line MS-DOS tools for an investigation is that they require few system resources because they are designed to run in minimal configurations. In fact, most tools fit on a bootable floppy disk. Conducting an initial inquiry or complete investigation using a floppy disk can save time and effort. Most tools also produce a text report that also fits on the forensic boot floppy disk. In addition, some command-line DOS tools prompt you for a new disk if one fills up.

Command-line MS-DOS tools are limited in some ways; they typically cannot search archive files such as Zip (.zip) files or Cabinet (.cab) files. They often work only on Microsoft FAT file systems, although one MS-DOS tool can extract data from NTFS file systems.

Command-line forensics software includes tools from New Technologies, Inc. (NTI) and Ds2dump from DataLifter.

Exploring NTI Tools

NTI provides a full product line of MS-DOS computer forensics tools that are small enough to fit on a floppy disk. NTI is reportedly also developing a GUI tool for Windows. Command-line DOS tools from NTI include AnaDisk, which is specifically designed to analyze floppy disks.

CopyQM is a robust floppy disk-copying utility that can read corrupt areas of a floppy disk and makes a best effort to lift data from damaged areas. The CRCMD5 utility calculates the Cyclic Redundancy Check (CRC), also known as CRC-32, and the MD5 hash value of individual files. CRCMD5 allows for wildcards—asterisks or question marks—to calculate groups of files.

To ensure that no data remains on a disk drive, NTI created DiskScrub, which overwrites all sectors of a hard disk. DiskScrub allows you to overwrite a disk more than once, and meets the U.S. Department of Defense (DoD) requirements.

Some data-recovery software can recover overwritten data from a disk drive platter, usually by using an electron microscope, which can identify bit patterns. This, however, can be a difficult, expensive, and time-consuming process.

NOTE

The DiskSearch 32 program performs keyword searches on Microsoft FAT12, FAT16, and FAT32 file systems. DiskSearch Pro is designed to perform keyword searches on all Microsoft FAT and NTFS file system disk drives. DiskSearch Pro only runs in MS-DOS.

The Disk Signature (DiskSig) program provides CRC-32 and MD5 hash values for an entire disk drive. DiskSig can also include the disk drive boot sector in the hash value check.

FileList is an NTI tool you use to create a data file that has a compressed output file. The FileCNVT program will convert the FileList output file into a dBase III format. FileList also creates a catalog of all files both allocated and deleted that are listed in a disk's FAT.

Filter Intelligence (Filter_I) provides features that few other vendors offer; it aids investigators by filtering nonprintable characters from large mixed data files such as the collected file slack or free space. For investigations that involve non-Microsoft e-mail messages or other text documents, the Filter_I tool saves time by reducing large evidence data files to a readable format. Filter_I provides the following options:

- *Filter*—Replaces nonprintable characters with spaces (Char 20)
- *Intel*—Searches for possible keyboard entries; the output for this feature can be used to create a possible password list
- *Names*—Locates known English surnames
- *Words*—Finds groups of words, typically fragments or complete sentences

The GetFree tool extracts unallocated space from any Microsoft FAT file system disk. GetFree creates files that contain data from unallocated space. GetSlack extracts file slack space from any Microsoft FAT file system disk, and creates volume set files that contain data from file slack space.

The Graphic Image File Extractor carves graphic picture image files from slack or free space data. Graphic Image File Extractor reconstructs BMP, GIF, and JPG graphic image formats. To **carve** data means to locate a deleted file either in its entirety or through fragments by searching for any occurrence of the known file's header information. When the matching header information is located, the file data can be carved out of the file slack or unallocated area. You can copy the deleted file by starting at the located header position and then copying each following sector for a specified number of bytes. Outside of North America this technique is sometimes referred to as salvaging rather than carving.

Net Threat Analyzer is a handy tool for extracting data such as e-mail addresses and Uniform Resource Locator (URL) data from a disk. Net Threat Analyzer works like DiskSearch 32 and DiskSearch Pro, but only locates Internet-related data sets on a suspect disk. Recent upgrades to Net Threat Analyzer now deal with investigations involving terrorist threats.

The M-Sweep Pro tool is designed to erase individual files from a disk. This tool only overwrites files and the associated slack space on Microsoft FAT and NTFS file system disks. Once you have used this tool on a file, there is no way to recover it. M-Sweep Pro is one of several tools that meets U.S. DoD requirements.

SafeBack is one of the original disk drive bit-stream imaging tools and is still considered one of the most reliable. SafeBack performs a sector-by-sector copy of the original disk drive and creates an image file or a disk copy to a target disk drive. SafeBack allows you to recreate the original disk drive to another larger drive, automatically adjusting the target drive's geometry to match the original disk drive. SafeBack can create a bit-stream image file that can be segmented into predefined volume sizes, or it can copy all sectors disk to disk.

SafeBack is an MS-DOS tool that can only be run from a true MS-DOS mode. It will not work from a Windows MS-DOS shell, because it requires direct access to the computer's BIOS, specifically Interrupt 13. Many of the recent GUI computer forensics tools can read SafeBack image files, which saves time and minimizes the need for rebuilding a suspect disk.

The Text Search Plus tool was the original keyword search tool developed by NTI, and must be run from a forensic boot floppy disk. Text Search Plus allows you to search for one or many keywords on a Microsoft FAT file system. Text Search Plus lets you search files, file slack space, and unallocated disk free space.

NTI also provides DOS-based NTFS forensic analysis tools. For more information on NTI products, training, and services, visit *www.forensics-intl.com*.

Exploring Ds2dump

The Ds2dump program from DataLifter collects data from free and slack space. Ds2dump allows you to copy all file slack space and unallocated free space from a Microsoft FAT file system disk. The data from both of these areas are collected into one file. This collected output file can then be analyzed by DataLifter, which is a carving tool. For more information about Ds2dump, visit *www.datalifter.com*.

Reviewing DriveSpy

DriveSpy from Digital Intelligence is an MS-DOS shell program that is small enough to fit on a forensic boot floppy disk. Some of the many features in DriveSpy include using MS-DOS 6.22 to access disk drives that are larger than 8.4 GB. DriveSpy runs in MS-DOS 6.22 or any Windows 9x DOS mode, including DOS shells, although it might occasionally conflict with Windows.

DriveSpy is a full-featured tool that provides forensic analysis for all Microsoft FAT12, FAT16, and FAT32 file systems. It does not analyze other file systems such as NTFS, UNIX, or Linux Ext2fs or Ext3fs. However, you can access disks that use these other file systems in the DriveSpy physical Drive mode, though not at a logical level.

A unique feature of DriveSpy is the Output command, which lets you copy all of your forensic examination activity to a text file. You can then integrate this text file into a formal report on your forensic analysis. You can also use the DriveSpy Unerase command to examine the FAT and attempt to recover files that have been deleted. The Output report lists the deleted files and all known associated clusters. DriveSpy also copies the last known clusters for each deleted file into a new file.

Recall from Chapter 3 that file slack is made up of RAM slack and disk slack. With the DriveSpy GetSlack command, you can collect all slack for specified files. You can also collect only RAM slack or disk slack into separate data files.

For more information about DriveSpy, visit *www.digitalintel.com*.

Exploring PDBlock

Digital Intelligence has created a software-based write-blocker called PDBlock, which disables the write capability of Interrupt 13 in the BIOS of an Intel PC. When a system attempts to write data on a disk, PDBlock prevents the disk from recording the data and displays warning messages that data did not copy. PDBlock is small enough to fit on your forensic boot floppy disk. For more information about PDBlock, visit *www.digitalintel.com*.

Exploring PDWipe

Computing investigators often need to make sure data has been completely removed from a disk. For example, you might want to ensure that sensitive data is completely removed from a disk you need to use for another task, or that the disk you plan to use as a target drive contains no data. To delete all data on a disk, or to wipe the disk, you can use the Digital Intelligence PDWipe program, which deletes all data on a disk, including the partition tables. After you run PDWipe on a disk, you must reinitialize the disk's partition tables with FDisk or another disk-management tool. For more information, visit *www.digitalintel.com*.

Reviewing Image

In previous chapters you used the floppy disk bit-stream copying utility from Digital Intelligence called Image, which is an especially useful tool when you need to analyze data on many floppy disks. In addition to making a compressed bit-stream image copy of a floppy disk, Image can create an uncompressed data file of a floppy disk. You can create an image of each floppy disk in an uncompressed file, and store each uncompressed file in one folder on your investigation workstation where you can examine the contents of each uncompressed floppy file. This feature saves time because you do not have to load each evidence floppy disk individually. For more information on Image, visit *www.digitalintel.com*.

Exploring Part

In an effort to make their forensic workstations more versatile, Digital Intelligence developed a startup boot manager program called Part. This program allows you to have multiple Microsoft operating systems installed on your forensic workstation. For more information about Part, visit *www.digitalintel.com*.

Exploring SnapBack DatArrest

SnapBack DatArrest from Columbia Data Products performs a bit-stream image copy from a suspect's disk to a tape drive or from a network connection to a remote server. Included with SnapBack DatArrest is a disk-to-disk utility called SnapCopy. You use SnapCopy to duplicate a suspect's disk to a target disk of equal or larger size. SnapCopy forces the disk geometry of the suspect's small disk onto your target disk, making the target disk's characteristics identical to the original suspect disk. That is, if you have an IBM 20 GB laptop suspect disk and 30 GB Maxtor desktop disk, SnapCopy successfully copies all data and reconfigures the 30 GB Maxtor disk to be the same as the IBM 20 GB disk. For more information, visit *www.cdp.com*.

Exploring Byte Back

Byte Back from Tools That Work has several features that can be applied to computing investigations. Byte Back runs on DOS 5.0 or greater, and provides the following computer forensics features:

- Clone and image physical sectors of a disk drive
- Recover files automatically on FAT and NTFS file systems
- Rebuild partitions and disk boot records on all FAT and NTFS disks
- Wipe disks
- Edit disks by viewing and modifying disk data for FAT16 and FAT32 file systems
- Scan the surface of disk drives to diagnose problems

For more information on Byte Back, visit *www.toolsthatwork.com*.

Exploring MaresWare

MaresWare, created by Danny Mares, a pioneer in computing investigations, develops many useful tools for all aspects of computing investigations. Mares has developed tools that work at the DOS level as well as tools that work on UNIX and Linux systems. The following are some of the tools available from MaresWare:

- *Catalog programs*—CRCKIT, DISKCAT, HASH, and MD5
- *Disk wiping program*—DECLASFY
- *Locking boot program*—DISABLE

- *Floppy disk imaging program—DISIMAG*

- *CRC and MD5 hashing program—DISCK_CRC*

- *Hex editor program—HEX_SECT*

- *Hashing compare program—HASHCMP*

- *Multiple data stream NTFS directory program—MDIR*

- *File and directory deletion and wiping programs—RM and RMD*

- *Sector keyword search program—SS*

- *Keyword search program—STRSRCH*

For more information on MaresWare tools, visit *www.dmares.com*.

Exploring DIBS Mycroft v3

DIBS USA, Inc., provides a DOS tool called DIBS Mycroft v3 that searches disks and fits on a boot floppy disk. Mycroft can lock disks to prevent any write access to the suspect disk drive it is examining. When you start Mycroft, it opens a DOS shell window that allows you to enter search terms and specify the area of the disk to examine. You can store results from the keyword search on the boot floppy disk for follow-up analysis. For additional information about DIBS Mycroft, visit *www.dibsusa.com*.

EXPLORING GRAPHICAL USER INTERFACE (GUI) FORENSICS TOOLS

Several software vendors have recently introduced computing-investigation tools that work in Windows. The command-line DOS tools you explored in the previous section require a strong understanding of MS-DOS and the various file systems. Because GUI forensics tools do not require the same level of knowledge, they can simplify computer forensics investigations. These GUI tools have also simplified training for beginning examiners in computer forensics. However, you should continue to learn about and use DOS forensics tools. In some cases, one tool might find critical evidence whereas another might miss it.

Exploring AccessData Programs

AccessData has been in business since 1987, when they introduced their Password Recovery Toolkit (PRTK). In recent years AccessData has expanded into computer forensics, including Windows tools. Besides PRTK and the Forensic Toolkit, AccessData publishes other computer forensics programs, including SecureClean, a wipe utility you can use to remove data from a disk.

Password Recovery Toolkit (PRTK)

PRTK was originally a DOS password cracker, but has evolved into a GUI application for Windows. PRTK can interpret the passwords or hashes of passwords in products such as Office 2000, WinZip, and several leading office application products.

One new concern is the advance encryption function now being provided in Microsoft Office XP, Internet Explorer, and Netscape Navigator. Office XP has several levels of data protection, with the uppermost levels using RSA encryption, a public encryption technology developed by RSA Data Security, Inc. The algorithm used is so powerful that the U.S. government has restricted exports containing this algorithm. RSA encryption creates new challenges for the computing investigator because it requires capabilities beyond the skills and computing resources of most examiners.

A recent feature added to PRTK is the Distributed Network Attack (DNA) application. With DNA you can crack the passwords of several networked workstations, reducing the number of hours required to crack the most difficult passwords. DNA might become the solution for recovering data files that have used RSA encryption.

Forensic Toolkit (FTK)

FTK is an easy-to-use, intuitive computer forensics tool. FTK is compatible with PRTK, so you can create password lists, which are collections of words that appear to be standalone character strings. A password-list generator collects these standalone character strings to create a list that PRTK uses to crack passwords. Unique features in FTK include the following:

- Text indexing to produce instant search results
- Data recovery from file systems including NTFS, NTFS compressed, all FAT, and Linux Ext2fs and Ext3fs
- E-mail recovery from the leading e-mail services and products along with the recovery of deleted messages
- Data extraction from PKZip, WinZip, WinRAR, GZIP, and TAR archive files
- File filtering that eliminates known files and bad files, based on NIST, NSRL and HashKeeper

For more information on AccessData products, visit *www.accessdata.com*.

Exploring Guidance Software EnCase

Guidance Software defines the standard of function and quality in computer forensics software, and their EnCase program has pioneered GUI forensics tools for computing investigations. In addition, Guidance Software has developed a DOS disk acquisition and preview tool called En.exe, which is part of the EnCase product. En.exe is small enough to fit on a forensic boot floppy disk.

The En.exe program is one of the best compression options currently available, though it does not perform a disk-to-disk copy, as other computer forensics acquisition tools do. The GUI EnCase and the DOS En.exe programs only create images of a suspect's disk drive. EnCase can also acquire a suspect's disk drive on a network. The suspect's computer can be set up so that you can perform your bit-stream copy to a server disk.

 En.exe searches for predefined keywords on a suspect disk. You use EnCase in Windows to create the keywords on a floppy disk.

TIP

The following are some of the most recent advanced features available on EnCase:

- Extracts messages from Microsoft PST files
- Spans multiple Redundant Array of Inexpensive Disk (RAID) volumes
- Supports NTFS compression and Access Control List (ACL) of files
- Provides advanced language support

EnCase also has many more features. For more information, visit *www.encase.com*.

Exploring Ontrack

Ontrack is one of the world leaders in recovering data from disk drives that become inaccessible due to hardware or software failure. Ontrack has data-recovery facilities in the United States and Europe. If you have a disk drive that has failed due to damage from disk circuit-card failure or a head crash, Ontrack can extract data from the surface of the disk platters. If you encounter older media, including magnetic and optical, and cannot extract data from it, Ontrack may have a solution. Visit Ontrack's Web site at *www.ontrack.com* for more information about contacting them by phone or e-mail regarding your particular problem.

Ontrack has developed many useful disk maintenance tools, and have recently produced their own computer forensics applications.

CaptureIt

CaptureIt is a data acquisition tool for FacTracker (discussed in the next section). CaptureIt runs from a boot floppy disk and creates 600 MB image volumes on a target disk of the source (suspect) disk. When using CaptureIt, you need a target disk larger than your suspect's disk because CaptureIt does not compress the saved image files. One unique feature of CaptureIt is that it can run a mechanical diagnostic test on a selected disk to identify whether it has any hardware problems.

FacTracker

FacTracker is a GUI forensic analysis tool that analyzes data acquired with CaptureIt. FacTracker performs the following tasks:

- Restores files that have been deleted
- Runs keyword searches
- Identifies file signatures for files with altered extensions
- Generates a summary report of findings

For more information about these products and other products and services offered by Ontrack, visit *www.ontrack.com*.

Using BIAProtect

BIAProtect was developed to recover data from RAID computers. BIA produces both hardware and software tools for computing investigations. Much of their hardware uses Firewire and USB connectors, which makes them hot-swappable. Their portable forensics unit is shown in Figure 6-9, and comes complete with extra bays, preloaded software, and plenty of storage. (The camera shown in the figure is not standard equipment with the portable forensics unit.) For more information about BIA, visit *www.biaprotect.com*.

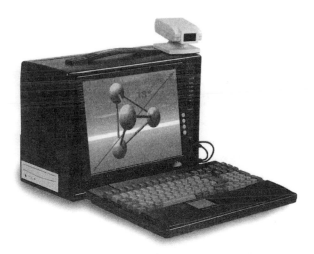

Figure 6-9   BIAProtect portable forensics unit

Using LC Technologies Software

LC Technologies is another data-recovery firm that now develops both software and hardware tools for computing investigations. They specialize in data-recovery tools that can be applied to severely corrupted disk drives. The three main software tools that they have developed are RecoverNT, FileRecovery, and PhotoRecovery.

RecoverNT runs in Microsoft Windows 9x, Me, NT, 2000, and XP, and recovers deleted data from all FAT and NTFS file systems. It is designed to work on Integrated Drive Electronics (IDE), Small Computer System Interface (SCSI), and RAID drives, including striped, spanned, and mirrored drives. RecoverNT also recovers files from disks that have been accidentally formatted and repairs damaged files. Figure 6-10 shows the RecoverNT window with files recovered from an accidentally formatted disk.

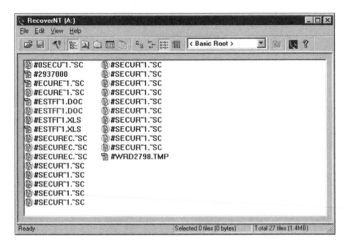

Figure 6-10   RecoverNT window with recovered files

The FileRecovery program from LC Technologies is a powerful undelete utility that you can run in Microsoft Windows 9x, Me, NT, 2000, and XP. It can recover deleted files from all FAT and NTFS file systems. Figure 6-11 shows deleted files recovered in FileRecovery.

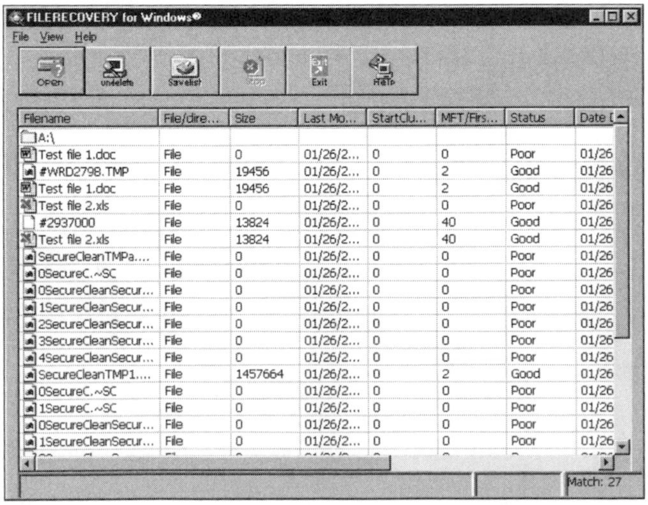

Figure 6-11   Deleted files recovered in FileRecovery

The PhotoRecovery tool from LC Technologies is specifically designed for digital camera images. It can restore deleted images from digital camera storage media such as Memory Sticks and CompactFlash cards, and digital media storage devices. Figure 6-12 shows the main PhotoRecovery window.

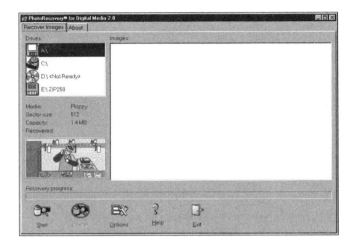

Figure 6-12   PhotoRecovery main window

LC Technologies offers all three of their recovery products in one package called The Forensic Utility Suite. For more information about LC Technologies, visit *www.lc-tech.com*.

Exploring WinHex Specialist Edition

WinHex is a powerful disk-editing tool that has evolved into three versions. The Specialist edition is best suited to the computing investigator because it provides many basic computer forensics functions in addition to the standard disk editor capabilities. You can use WinHex to inspect and repair data files on a disk, as shown in Figure 6-13.

Unlike other disk editors, WinHex can access compact discs (CDs), allowing you to visually inspect how data is written on them. WinHex also provides the following features:

- Disk cloning
- Disk sector imaging with or without compression, an encryption option, and a save set volume size
- Saving to a separate data file all file slack space and unallocated space
- Keyword searching and text gathering

For more information on WinHex Specialist edition, visit *www.sf-soft.de/winhex/index-m.html*.

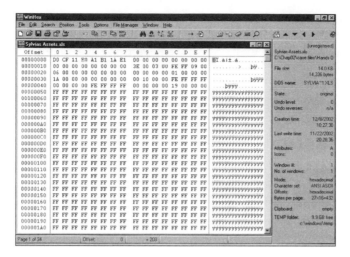

Figure 6-13   WinHex

Exploring DIBS Analyzer Professional Forensic Software

The DIBS Analyzer Professional Forensic Software is made up of individual modules for specific computer forensics analysis, including the core and satellite modules, such as a core module for FAT32 disks and one for FAT16 disks. Specific tasks developed for analysis are called satellite modules. For more information about Analyzer Professional Forensic Software, visit *www.dibsusa.com*.

Exploring ProDiscover DFT

Created by Technology Pathways, ProDiscover DFT provides a full line of services for the computing investigator. ProDiscover DFT performs the following tasks:

- Creates an image file of the suspect's disk, and can read the image files it creates
- Reads images created with the UNIX or Linux dd command
- Accesses a suspect disk through a write-blocking device for previewing purposes
- Displays alternative data streams for Windows NT and 2000 NTFS file systems
- Integrates Bates numbers for your evidence for recovered data lists

NOTE

Bates numbering is used by attorneys for indexing documents used as evidence. Having an automated Bates numbering system for your digital evidence output can save a lot of time and help you organize your evidence. Technology Pathways publishes a white paper describing how Bates numbers work. For more information on Bates numbering, visit *www.techpathways.com*.

For more information on ProDiscover DFT, visit *www.techpathways.com*.

Exploring DataLifter

DataLifter is a collection of several useful tools to aid in your computing investigations, and are often sold separately by a variety of vendors. The most useful program is the File Extraction tool, which carves known files from recovered file slack and unallocated free space of a suspect's disk drive. DataLifter routinely sends updates of new known file signatures and header information to licensed users. As you recall from Chapter 3, file headers let the computer determine file types with or without a file extension. Other useful tools included are:

- Disk cataloging of all files with date and time values
- Image Linker that identifies and allows you to link to any images stored on a Web site
- Internet cache and history viewer of a suspect's Internet history file for Netscape and Internet Explorer
- File signature generator
- E-mail retriever
- Network ping, traceroute, and whois commands
- Recycle Bin history viewer
- Screen capture function
- File slack and free space acquisition tool

For more information about DataLifter and its latest features, visit *www.datalifter.com*.

Exploring ASRData

ASRData has been a pioneer in the development of GUI computer forensics tools. Their first product, Expert Witness, was developed specifically for data recovery of Macintosh disk drives using the HFS file system. More recently, they added another computer forensics tool called SMART that can be run from Linux or BeOS, an open-source OS similar to Linux.

Expert Witness for Macintosh

The current version of Expert Witness for Macintosh reads and analyzes the following file systems:

- HFS and HFS+
- All Microsoft FAT file systems
- ISO 9660 (CDs), UFS, and CDFS

You can also perform the following tasks with Expert Witness for Macintosh:

- Span evidence acquisitions over several different target disk drives
- Generate reports, including file lists and abstracts, network architecture, e-mail, and communications software
- Export data findings to Microsoft Excel to perform additional analysis

SMART

To meet the needs of computer forensics workstations that run a non-Microsoft operating system, SMART was developed to run under BeOS and Linux. SMART is a full-featured computer forensics tool that can acquire and analyze a suspect's disk. SMART can read several different compressed image files such as the UNIX or Linux gzip or the BZ2. Some of the file systems SMART can analyze include:

- All Microsoft FAT
- NTFS
- Linux Ext2fs and Ext3fs
- Reiser
- HFS

Probably the most powerful feature integrated into SMART is its ability to use Linux shell commands. For example, you can use the full syntax and intelligent rules that are allowed in the UNIX and Linux grep command.

For more information on SMART and Expert Witness for Macintosh, visit *www.asrdata.com*.

Exploring the Internet History Viewer

Scott Ponders created the Internet History Viewer, a useful tool in the analysis of Netscape and Internet Explorer history files. With this tool, you can examine and print the URL addresses a browser recently accessed, including date and time stamps. In addition to the URL values, this tool reads the Info and Info2 files for Windows 9x, NT, and 2000, which are created in and maintain records about the Windows Recycled folder, including when these files are permanently deleted or restored. For more information on Internet History Viewer, visit *www.phillipsponder.com/histviewer.htm*.

EXPLORING OTHER USEFUL COMPUTER FORENSICS TOOLS

In addition to the DOS and GUI tools mentioned in previous sections, you can also use computer forensics tools that are available as open source, freeware, and shareware software. Many of these tools are freeware, though some are restricted to law enforcement only.

Exploring LTOOLS

LTOOLS originally evolved from work done by Jason Hunter and David Lutz at Willamette University in Salem, Oregon. They created the tool called lread that allowed you to read data from a Linux disk while working in DOS. In 1996, Werner Zimmermann from the University of Applied Sciences in Esslingen, Germany continued with this original work.

With LTOOLS you can connect a Linux Ext2fs or Ext3fs disk drive to a Microsoft Windows 9x, Me, NT, 2000, or XP workstation, and maintain full access to the Linux drive. If you are examining a Linux file system disk, remember to connect it to a write-blocker device. LTOOLS can read and write data to the Linux disk from your Windows workstation.

Zimmermann created a command-line and a GUI version of LTOOLS. The command-line version is a collection of several programs that can be run from DOS or a DOS shell in Windows. At the DOS level you can enter a variety of commands that directly access the Linux disk. With the GUI version, called ltoolgui, you can run a Windows Explorer version of LTOOLS. Ltoolgui also lets you access other Linux workstations and servers.

For more information about LTOOLS, visit: *www.it.fht-esslingen.de/~zimmerma/software/ltools/ltools.html*.

Exploring Mtools

Linux and Solaris users accessing FAT and OS/2 file system disk drives can use mtools for computer forensics. Mtools is currently maintained by Alain Knaff and David Niemi, and provides several shell commands that allow you to perform many of the standard DOS functions from a Linux shell. Most of the commands are prefaced with the letter "m" to designate them as an mtools command. For example, mdir is equivalent to the DOS directory command, and mcopy is equivalent to the DOS copy command.

For more information about mtools, and for a detailed manual on how to compile and use the mtools, visit *www.mtools.linux.lu*.

Exploring R-Tools

The primary purpose of R-Tools products is for data recovery. You can also use several R-Tools, such as R-Studio, R-Undelete, R-Linux, and R-Mail, for computing investigations.

R-Studio

R-Studio can recover data from all FAT, NTFS, and Ext2fs disks, and can recover corrupt data on RAID systems. You can use R-Studio remotely through a network connection to recover data. R-Studio runs on Windows 9x, Me, 2000, and XP, and recognizes UNIX partitions in addition to NTFS RAID Levels 0, 1, and 5.

If your operating system does not detect a corrupted RAID volume, R-Studio creates a virtual RAID from data it finds on the corrupted disks. With this virtual RAID volume, you can copy data to a backup disk, allowing you to recover all or most of the data.

You can also search for deleted files with R-Studio. R-Studio examines the MFT of an NTFS or FAT disk and restores it. If a disk is formatted from an NTFS to a FAT format, and sufficient information is available, you might be able to rebuild the damaged partition.

R-Undelete

Another tool available from R-Tools is R-Undelete, which you use to restore any FAT, NTFS, and Ext2fs files. This tool recovers altered data streams and encrypted or compressed files. With R-Undelete, you can create a disk image that can be processed by R-Studio for further data recovery.

R-Linux

For corrupted Ext2fs drives, you can use R-Linux to create a disk image. After you have created a disk image of the damaged Linux drive, you can then run R-Studio to correct or recover data from the failed drive.

R-Mail

R-Mail is specially designed to recover damaged .dbx folders for Microsoft Outlook Express versions 5.0 through 6.0. R-Mail recovers the content of the .dbx folder messages and then creates individual messages in the .eml format. These recovered messages can be imported into Outlook Express.

For more information on R-Tools, visit *www.r-tt.com*.

Using Explore2fs

Another good tool for examining Linux Ext2fs disk drives is Explore2fs created by John Newbigin. Explore2fs looks like Windows Explorer and runs on Windows 9x, Me, NT 4.0, 2000, and XP. You can do the following with Explore2fs:

- Move files by dragging and dropping
- Export and import files and directories
- View and execute files
- View and create symbolic links
- Delete files and directories
- Create directories
- Rename and modify file modes
- Change the user ID and group ID of files and directories

For more information on Explore2fs, visit *uranus.it.swin.edu.au/~jn/linux/explore2fs.htm*.

Exploring @stake

@stake has been a major contributor to open-source programs in computing and network security. The following sections describe some of the tools they offer. For more information on products and current research available at @stake, visit *www.atstake.com*.

TASK

The organization @stake provides an open-source utility called TASK, a computer forensics tool that runs in Linux. Because it is open-source software, the computing investigator can customize and verify all actions the program performs. TASK is designed to be used with the open-source graphical interface browser called Autopsy Forensic Browser. You can perform the following tasks in TASK:

- Analyze dd image files of a suspect's drive
- Analyze all FAT, NTFS, FFS, and Ext2fs file systems
- Use fourteen command-line tools that are organized into layers to identify the tool's function
- Create timelines of files and directories for analysis purposes

For more information on TASK, visit *www.atstake.com/research/tools/task*.

Autopsy Forensic Browser

As an open-source alternative to Windows forensics tools, Autopsy Forensic Browser was created to work with TASK. Autopsy Forensic Browser is a Hypertext Markup Language (HTML) graphic interface tool that manages files. With Autopsy Forensic Browser you can view allocated and deleted files on a suspect's disk image data. You can perform the following tasks with Autopsy Forensic Browser:

- Add reference notes to any findings you encounter
- Search on keywords
- Validate using MD5 hash values
- Generate reports in ASCII format
- Inspect a UNIX system in real-time

Examining a UNIX system in real-time allows you to access the system when a hacker is attacking it. When a network or computing system is under attack from a hacker, responding and investigating as quickly as possible, that is, in real-time, can prevent significant damage to the system. Inspecting a system during an intrusion can be very beneficial to an investigation and for creating an intrusion response plan for network security.

For more information on Autopsy Forensic Browser, visit: *www.atstake.com/research/tools/autopsy/index.html*.

Exploring TCT and TCTUTILs

The Coroner's Toolkit (TCT) was developed by Dan Farmer and Wietse Venema as a post-mortem analysis tool for UNIX servers and workstations. TCT's specific purpose is to analyze a UNIX system when a network break-in has occurred. Using TCT requires strong programming and UNIX systems administration skills. TCT collects various system values that might contain information about a system break-in from a hacker. For more information on TCT, visit *www.porcupine.org/forensics/tct.html*.

To handle and process data collected from an system intrusion, you can use TCTUTILs, which lets you examine the file structures on a disk drive and display deleted files to see what efforts a hacker has taken to cover his or her tracks. By combining TCT and TCTUTILs with Autopsy Forensic Browser, you can easily examine the output from these tools. For more information on TCTUTILs, visit: *www.cerias.purdue.edu/homes/carrier/forensics/tctutils/tctutils-1.00.readme.txt*.

Exploring ILook

A forensic examiner named Elliot Spencer from the London, England Metropolitan Police Constabulary created his own computer forensics analysis tool called ILook. It is free to any law-enforcement agency throughout the world, but it is not available for use by any private person or for-profit organization. To acquire a copy of this tool, you need a written request on official letterhead from a police or other government enforcement investigative agency. If you are a police officer or detective, consider acquiring and learning how to use this program, because ILook is one of the most effective computer forensics tools currently available. For licensing information and acquisition of ILook, visit *www.ilook-forensics.org*.

Exploring HashKeeper

The National Drug Intelligence Center calculated the CRC-32 and MD5 hash values of nearly every known application and operating system file. They also calculated the CRC-32 and MD5 hashes of known illegal images of child pornography. All filenames and their hash values are now stored in a database called HashKeeper, which is the forerunner to the National Software Reference Library (NSRL) created by NIST and the NIJ.

With the development of HashKeeper, computer investigators can start to eliminate the good files from the suspect files. By comparing these known hash values, the investigator can quickly identify what files are known files and what files require further examination.

Using Graphic Viewers

Many of the newer GUI computer forensic tools now provide internal viewers of graphic images of a suspect's disk drive. To help manage graphic images you acquire from your investigations, use a reliable graphics viewer program that can open many formats, including motion-picture graphics. A graphics viewer should also be able to create thumbnail images of your images. Some viewers allow you to create contact sheets of the thumbnail images. You can save these contact sheets as an image file and then import it into your final case report.

The following are popular multipurpose graphic viewers:

- Quick View Plus (*www.jasc.com*)
- Lview Pro (*www.lview.com*)
- ACDSee (*www.acdsystems.com*)
- ThumbsPlus (*www.cerious.com*)
- IrfanView (*www.irfanview.com*)

Periodically search Web sites for the latest graphic viewers so you know which ones can solve your graphic needs.

6

EXPLORING HARDWARE TOOLS

This section discusses computer hardware vendors that provide workstations and other tools for the computing investigator. Manufacturers have designed most computer components to last about 18 months between failures. For this reason, schedule replacements for your computer hardware periodically, every 18 months if you use the hardware full time. Most computer forensics operations use a workstation 24 hours a day for a week or longer between complete shutdowns.

Computing-Investigation Workstations

Many computer vendors currently offer a wide range of computer forensics workstations that you can tailor to meet your specific investigation needs. The more diverse your investigation environment, the more options you need. In general, forensic workstations can be divided into the following categories:

- *Stationary workstation*—A tower with several bays and many peripheral devices
- *Portable workstation*—Laptop computers with a built-in liquid crystal display (LCD) monitor with almost as many bays and peripherals as a stationary workstation
- *Lightweight workstation*—Usually a laptop computer that is built into a small carrying case with a small selection of peripheral options

When considering options to add to a basic workstation, keep in mind that PCs have limitations on how many peripherals they can handle. The more peripherals you add, the more potential problems you might encounter, especially if you are using an older version of Windows 9x. You must learn to balance what you actually need with what your system can handle.

If you are operating a computer forensics lab for a police agency, you need as many options as possible to handle any investigation. If possible, use two or three configurations of PCs to handle diverse investigations. On the other hand, in the private corporate environment, consider streamlining your workstation to meet the needs of only the types of systems used in your business.

Building Your Own Workstation

If you have the time and skill to build your own computing-forensics workstation, you can customize it to your exact needs and save money, though you might have trouble finding support for problems that develop. For example, peripheral devices might conflict with one another or components might fail. Having a vendor-supplied workstation can save you time and frustration when you encounter problems.

Using a Write-blocker

You can use software or hardware writer-blockers to protect evidence disks. The software-enabled blockers, such as PDBlock from Digital Intelligence, run in DOS. PDBlock changes Interrupt 13 of the workstation's BIOS, preventing any writing to the specified drive, and signals when you attempt to write data to the disk drive you have blocked. PDBlock can only be run from a real DOS mode, not a Windows MS-DOS shell.

If you use a hardware write-blocker, you can connect your evidence disk drive to your workstation and boot to any version of Windows. These write-blockers prevent any attempt of Windows or Linux from writing data to the blocked disk. In Windows, the write-blocker gives the appearance that you have written data to a blocked disk because the write-blocker tells the operating system that the write was successful. When you access the blocked disk with Windows Explorer, it shows the data has copied successfully. However, the write-blocker actually discards the written data. When you reboot the workstation and examine the blocked disk, you will not see the data or file you previously copied to it.

Many vendors have developed write-blocking devices that connect to a computer through Firewire, USB 2.0, and SCSI controllers. Most of these write-blockers allow you to remove and reconnect disk drives without having to shut down your workstation, saving you time while processing the evidence disk.

Using LC Technology International Hardware

In addition to creating data-recovery software tools, LC Technology International has created a line of hardware products for computing investigations. They offer a very powerful forensic workstation and several Firewire peripheral devices, including the DRAC 2000 workstation.

DRAC 2000 Workstations

The DRAC 2000 workstation has two high-capacity disk drives. One drive is the boot disk, and the other is the acquisition disk for your evidence. Also included is a removable

IDE disk caddy connected to the workstation via a Firewire controller. This Firewire caddy allows you to hot-swap your disk drive.

Firewire Peripherals

In addition to the DRAC 2000, LC Technology has a line of internal and external Firewire devices. The following are some current Firewire products:

- *Read-only IDE drive bays*—A hot-swappable write-blocker device
- *Drive imaging stations*—A setup of two IDE bays, one with an integrated write-blocker, and the other for reads and writes, and a 60-watt power supply with cooling fans
- *Firewire*—Assorted Firewire controller cards and Firewire write-blocker internal interface devices

For more information about these products, visit *www.lc-tech.com*.

Forensic Computers

Forensic Computers builds several models of forensic workstations, including the following types of computer workstations:

- Original forensic tower
- Portable forensic workhorse
- Forensic steel tower
- Forensic Air-Lite

All of these workstations come with a list of peripheral options, allowing you to select components to integrate into a forensic workstation. For more information on Forensic Computers, visit *www.forensic-computers.com*.

DIBS

DIBS provides the following computing-forensics hardware:

- Forensic workstation
- Mobile forensic workstation
- Permanent investigation unit
- Rapid action imaging device (RAID)

For more information on these and other DIBS products, visit *www.dibsusa.com*.

Digital Intelligence

Digital Intelligence provides forensic workstations and peripheral devices for the computing investigator, including three basic models of forensic workstations in the Forensic

Recovery Evidence Device (FRED) series. In addition to the FRED series of systems, Digital Intelligence provides peripheral devices along with a Forensic Recovery of Evidence Data Center (FREDC). See Figure 6-14.

Figure 6-14   Forensic Recovery of Evidence Data Center

The FRED forensic workstations include peripherals that address most computing-investigations needs. You can customize a FRED as necessary. The following FRED forensic workstations are available:

- *FRED*—A tower PC that can be equipped with a cart for portability
- *FREDDIE*—A portable LCD screen equipped FRED unit
- *FRED Sr*—A stationary server case workstation that has three power supplies and an extensive list of peripherals to meet almost any computing-investigation need
- *FREDC*—A modularized RAID system with up to eight separate forensic processors with up to 20 terabytes of disk storage

Figure 6-15 shows a FRED unit.

Figure 6-15   FRED unit

The peripheral devices provided by Digital Intelligence are:

- *FireBlock*—A Firewire IDE bay device write-blocker that can be ordered as an internal bay or an external bay device with its own power supply

- *SCSIBlock*—A SCSI write-blocker device that can be ordered as an internal bay or an external bay device with its own power supply

- *FireChief*—A Firewire IDE dual bay external device that has an IDE write-blocker in the top bay and a read/write in the bottom bay

For more information about all of Digital Intelligence products, visit *www.digitalintel.com*.

Image MASSter Solo

Image MASSter has developed several disk-duplicating systems for commercial disk duplication applications. In addition to the standard disk duplication tools, they develop computer forensic computers, disk duplicating devices, and software.

The Image MASSter Solo-2 Forensics system is a small device that duplicates a disk drive at speeds up to 1.8 GB per minute. With the increased number of large disk drives being used, this device can save time for forensic data acquisitions. Some of the features available for the Solo-2 are:

- Signature generator that produces a CRC-32 hash

- Ability to copy a source disk's Host Protected Area to the target disk

- Device Configuration Overlay (DCO) detection that forces a sector-by-sector copy of a suspect's disk to the target disk

- CD backup and restore capability allowing you to backup and restore a disk to a CD

- Audit trail report that can be printed out to a special thermal printer from the unit

A new product available soon is a USB 2.0 write-blocker device. For more information about Image MASSter products, visit *www.ics-iq.com*.

FastBloc

Guidance Software, creator of EnCase, has developed a SCSI-based write-blocking device that is hot-swappable. This product is designed to allow for data acquisitions of a suspect's hard disk drive from Windows using EnCase. The advantage to performing the acquisition from Windows is the improved data throughput, meaning that acquiring disk data from Windows is significantly faster than from DOS. For more information about FastBloc, visit the Guidance Software Web page *www.encase.com* or *www.guidancesoftware.com*.

Acard

Acard, a computer peripheral manufacturer in Taiwan, has developed a series of interface cards that allow you to connect IDE devices such as disk drives and CD-ROMs to SCSI cards. Two of their SCSI-to-IDE interface cards are called AEC-7720UW and the AEC-7720WP.

The AEC-7720UW interface card connects to a standard SCSI ultra-wide controller so that you can connect any IDE device, such as a disk drive or CD-ROM, to your workstation. The AEC-7720UW has a jumper setting that allows you to designate the SCSI port number. The IDE drive must be set to single mode or master mode for it to work correctly with this interface card.

The AEC-7720WP interface card is the same as the AEC-7720UW interface card but it is configured as a write-blocker. The SCSI port number settings and the IDE jumper settings are the same as the AEC-7720UW.

Of all the write-blocker products, Acard's interface cards are the least expensive. To locate the nearest vendor, search the Web using the Acard card's model number. One of many reliable Internet sales Web site for Acard products is MicrolandUSA (*www.microlandusa.com*).

NoWrite

Technology Pathways may have been the first company to introduce a hardware write-blocker. Their NoWrite write-blocker lets you hot-swap a disk drive. It connects to USB, Firewire, or IDE cables, and is advertised as a true IDE-to-IDE connection. It can also identify any host protected area on a suspect's disk drive. It can be used with DOS, Windows, or Linux to acquire data. For more information on NoWrite, visit the Technology Pathways Web site at *www.techpathways.com*.

Wiebe Tech Forensic DriveDock

Wiebe Tech has developed one of the smallest Firewire IDE devices currently available, including a Firewire IDE write-blocker in addition to regular Firewire IDE disk devices. Their Forensic DriveDock transfers data up to 35 MB per second. All of their Firewire devices are external and require a separate power supply. They are ideal for laptop computers if you need to have a compact field-acquisition system.

For more information about Forensic DriveDock and other Firewire products from Wiebe, visit *www.wiebetech.com*.

Recommendations for a Forensic Workstation

Before you purchase or build your own forensic workstation, determine where will you acquire data. If you acquire data in the field, consider streamlining the tools you use. With the newer Firewire and USB 2.0 write-blocker devices, you can easily acquire data with Digital Intelligence FireChief and a laptop computer. If you want to further reduce the hardware you carry, consider using the Wiebe Tech Forensic DriveDock with their regular DriveDock Firewire bridge.

If you acquire data in a lab, review the various vendor offerings for forensic workstations included in this chapter.

CHAPTER SUMMARY

- ❑ Maintaining a computer forensics lab involves creating a software library for older versions of computer forensics utilities, operating systems (OSs), and application programs. You should maintain all older versions of software that you have used and retired, such as older versions of Windows and Linux.

- ❑ Before upgrading to a new version of a computer forensics tool, you need to run validation testing on the new version. The National Institute of Standards and Technology (NIST) has standard guidelines for verifying forensic software.

- ❑ Many computer forensics tools run in MS-DOS, including those that find file slack and free space, recover data, and search by keyword. Most of these tools run only in MS-DOS, not an MS-DOS shell window. They are also designed to run in minimal configurations, and can fit on a bootable floppy disk. Norton Disk Edit and WinHex are MS-DOS tools that allow you to find file slack and unallocated space on a drive.

- ❑ Computer forensics tools that run in a Windows Command Prompt window include DriveSpy and Image. Computing-investigation tools that run in Windows and other graphical user interface (GUI) environments do not require the same level of computing expertise as MS-DOS tools, and can simplify training and investigations. These GUI tools have also simplified training for beginning examiners in computer forensics.

❏ In addition to the DOS and GUI tools, you can also use computer forensics tools that are available as open source, freeware, and shareware software, though some are restricted to only law enforcement use.

❏ Hardware required for computer forensics include workstations and blockers such as write-blockers needed to prevent contamination of evidence. Before you purchase or build your own forensic workstation, consider where will you acquire data, which determines the type of configuration you need.

KEY TERMS

baseline—An established standard for measurement or comparison.

carve—To locate a deleted file either in its entirety or through fragments by searching for any occurrence of the known file's header information.

Computer Forensics Tool Testing (CFTT)—A project created by the National Institute of Standards and Technology to manage research on computing-forensics tools.

Forensic Software Testing Support Tools (FS-TST)—A collection of programs that analyze the capability of disk imaging tools.

keyword search—Finding files or other information by providing characters, words, or phrases to a search tool.

MD5 hash value—A cryptographic algorithm used to create digital signatures. It creates a one-way hash function, meaning that it can convert data into a fixed string of digits (also called a message digest). With a one-way hash function, you can compare the calculated message digest against the message digest that is decrypted with a public key. This indicates whether the data has changed.

National Institute of Justice (NIJ)—The research, development, and evaluation agency of the U.S. Department of Justice dedicated to researching crime control and justice issues.

National Institute of Standards and Technology (NIST)—A unit of the U.S. Commerce Department. Formerly known as the National Bureau of Standards, NIST promotes and maintains measurement standards.

National Software Reference Library (NSRL)—A project supported by the National Institute of Justice, federal, state, and local law enforcement, and the National Institute of Standards and Technology to promote efficient and effective use of computer technology in the investigation of crimes involving computers.

Secure Hash Algorithm (SHA-1)—A hashing algorithm that creates a 160-bit message digest that a digital signature algorithm (DSA) can process to generate or verify the signature for the message.

write-blocker—A physical device that prevents a computer from recording data on an evidence disk.

7

DIGITAL EVIDENCE
CONTROLS

After reading this chapter, you will be able to:

♦ Identify digital evidence

♦ Secure digital evidence at an incident scene

♦ Catalog digital evidence

♦ Store digital evidence

♦ Obtain a digital signature

This chapter explains how to systematically handle digital evidence so that you do not inadvertently alter data. Even if you are collecting evidence for different types of cases, you must handle all evidence the same way. You should apply the same security controls to evidence for a civil lawsuit as evidence obtained at a major crime, such as a murder. Civil and criminal evidence are governed by the rules of evidence, which are similar in English-speaking countries because they are derived from the British Parliamentary laws, which date back centuries.

IDENTIFYING DIGITAL EVIDENCE

Digital evidence can be any information that is stored or transmitted in digital form. Because you cannot see or touch digital data directly, it is difficult to explain and describe. Is digital evidence real or virtual? Does data on a disk or other storage medium physically exist, or does it merely represent real information? U.S. courts define all digital evidence as physical evidence, which means that digital data is a tangible object, like a weapon, document, or visible injury, that is related to a criminal or civil incident. Groups such as the **Scientific Working Group for Digital Evidence (SWGDE)** and the **International Organization on Digital Evidence (IOCE)** set standards for recovering, preserving, and examining digital evidence. (Note that the IOCE was originally called the International Organization on Computer Evidence, and has retained its original acronym.)

TIP

For more information about digital evidence, visit *www.ojp.usdoj.gov/nij/pubs-sum/187736.htm* to download the document "Electronic Crime Scene Investigation – A Guide for First Responders," which provides guidelines for law enforcement and other responders who protect an electronic crime scene and search for, collect, and preserve electronic evidence.

Following are the general tasks investigators perform when working with digital evidence:

- Identify digital information or artifacts that can be used as evidence

- Collect, preserve, and document the evidence

- Analyze, identify, and organize the evidence

- Rebuild evidence or repeat a situation to verify that you can obtain the same results every time

Figure 7-1 summarizes these four tasks, which are the basis for working with all digital evidence.

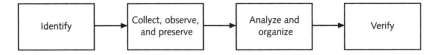

Figure 7-1   Four tasks for working with digital evidence

Collecting computers and processing a criminal or incident scene must be done systematically. To minimize confusion, reduce the risk of losing evidence, and avoid damaging evidence, only one person should collect and catalog digital evidence at a crime scene or lab. If there is too much evidence for one person to collect and process, all examiners must follow the same established standard operating procedures. You should also use standard forms, which are discussed later, for tracking evidence to ensure that you consistently handle evidence in a safe, secure manner.

Understanding Evidence Rules

Consistent practices generally help to verify your work and enhance your credibility as a professional. You must consistently handle all evidence the same way. Apply the same security and accountability controls for evidence in a civil lawsuit as for evidence obtained at a major crime scene to comply with your state's rules of evidence or with the Federal Rules of Evidence. Also keep in mind that findings from evidence admitted in a criminal case can be used in a civil suit and vice versa. For example, suppose someone is charged with murder and acquitted at the criminal trial because the jury is not convinced beyond a reasonable doubt of the person's guilt. If there is sufficient evidence that negligence by the accused contributed to a wrongful death, the evidence can be used in the civil lawsuit by the victim's relatives to collect damages.

As part of your professional growth, keep current on the latest rulings and directives required for collecting, processing, storing, and admitting digital evidence. The following section discusses some of the key concepts of digital evidence. You can find additional information at the United States Department of Justice Web site (*www.usdoj.gov*), and by using a search engine such as Google (*www.google.com*) to search for "electronic" and "best evidence rule" or "hearsay" to obtain the latest postings. Be sure to consult with your prosecuting attorney, crown attorney, or corporate general counsel so that you can gain more knowledge on how to manage evidence for your investigation.

In Chapters 2 and 5, you learned how to make a bit-stream image copy of an evidence disk. Physical evidentiary data you discover from your forensic examination falls under the rules of evidence as applied by your state or the federal rules. However, electronic evidence is unlike other physical evidence because it can easily be changed. The only way to detect these changes is to compare the original data to a duplicate. Furthermore, the duplicate and the original are electronically indistinguishable. Digital evidence therefore requires special legal consideration.

Most federal courts have interpreted computer records as hearsay evidence. Hearsay is secondhand or indirect evidence, such as an overheard conversation or any statements made out of court and not under oath, including letters, diaries, and notes. Because it cannot be proven that the contents of such conversations or documents are true, they are not admissible in court at trial, unless they fall under one of several exceptions to the hearsay rule. The business-record exception allows "Records of regularly conducted activity," such as regular business memos, reports, records, or data compilations. Business records are authenticated by verifying that they were created "at or near the time by, or from information transmitted by, a person with knowledge…" and are admissible "if the record was kept in the course of a regularly conducted business activity, and it was the regular practice of that business activity to make the record." (Federal Rules of Evidence, 803(6). See Section V, "Evidence," in Searching and Seizing Computers and Obtaining Electronic Evidence in Criminal Investigations, *www.usdoj.gov/criminal/cybercrime/s&smanual2002.htm*.)

Computer records are generally considered admissible if they qualify as a business record. Typically, computer records are divided into **computer-generated records** and **computer-stored records**. Computer-generated records are data the system maintains for itself, such as system log files and proxy server logs. They are not usually created by a person, but are output generated from a computer process or algorithm. Computer-stored records, however, are electronic data that a person creates and saves on a computer, such as a spreadsheet or word processor document. Some records combine both computer-generated and computer-stored evidence, such as a spreadsheet that contains mathematical operations (computer-generated records) that were generated from a person's input (computer-stored records).

Computer records must be shown to be authentic, or reliable and trustworthy, to be admitted into court. Computer-generated records are considered authentic if the program that created the output is functioning properly. Computer-generated records are usually considered exceptions to the hearsay rule, as shown in the following ruling from a state supreme court in a case involving telephone records.

"The printout of the results of the computer's internal operations is not hearsay evidence. It does not represent the output of statements placed into the computer by out of court declarants. Nor can we say that this printout itself is a 'statement' constituting hearsay evidence. The underlying rationale of the hearsay rule is that such statements are made without an oath and their truth can not be tested by cross-examination. Of concern is the possibility that a witness may consciously or unconsciously misrepresent what the declarant told him…or that the declarant may consciously or unconsciously misrepresent a fact occurrence. With a machine, however, there is no possibility of a conscious misrepresentation, and the possibility of inaccurate or misleading data only materializes if the machine is not functioning properly."

To admit computer-stored records into court, they must also satisfy an exception to the hearsay rule, usually the business-record exception. They must therefore be authentic records of regularly conducted business activity. To show that computer-stored records are authentic, the person offering the records (the offeror—the prosecutor, plaintiff, or defense) must demonstrate that a person created the data and that the data is reliable and trustworthy—in other words, that it was not altered when it was acquired or afterwards. Collecting the evidence according to the proper steps of evidence control helps to ensure that the computer evidence is authentic, as does using established computer-forensics software tools. Courts have consistently ruled that computer forensics investigators do not have to be subject-matter experts on the tools they use. In other words, if you have to testify about your role in the acquisition, preservation, and analysis of evidence, you do not have to know the inner workings of the tools you used, though you should understand their purpose and operation. For example, Message Digest 5 (MD5) and Secure Hash Algorithm, version 1 (SHA-1) software tools involve complex mathematical formulas. During a cross-examination, an opposing attorney might ask you to describe how these forensics tools work. You can safely testify that you do not know how the formula works, but do know how to use the tools that implement the formula. In *United States v. Salgado*, 250 F.3d 438, 453 (6th Cir. 2001) the Supreme Court stated, "It is not necessary that the computer programmer testify in order to authenticate computer-generated records." In other words, the witness must only have firsthand knowledge of the facts relevant to the case. You should therefore know how to describe the steps involved with using the MD5 function in DriveSpy, for example, not how the MD5 hash algorithm works.

When opposing attorneys challenge digital evidence, they raise the issue of whether the computer-generated records were altered or damaged after they were created. Attorneys might also question the authenticity of the computer-generated records by challenging the program or utility that created them. To date, courts have been skeptical of unsupported claims from opposing attorneys about digital evidence. Asserting that the data changed without specific evidence to show otherwise is not sufficient grounds to discredit the authenticity of digital evidence. Most federal courts that evaluate digital evidence from computer-generated records typically assume the records contain hearsay. Federal courts then apply the business-records exception to hearsay as it applies to digital evidence.

Recall that one test to prove that computer-stored records are authentic is to demonstrate that a person created the records. Establishing who created the digital evidence you recover from your investigation can be a challenge because records you recover from slack space or unallocated disk space usually do not identify the author. The same is true for other records such as anonymous e-mail messages or Internet Relay Chat (IRC) text messages. To establish authorship of the digital evidence in these cases, attorneys can apply circumstantial evidence, which requires finding other clues associated with the suspect's computer or location. The circumstantial evidence might be that the computer has a password consistent with the password used by the suspect on other systems, that a witness saw the suspect at the computer at the time the offense occurred, or that additional trace evidence associates the suspect with the computer at the time of the incident.

In addition to demonstrating that a person created computer-stored records, the records must be proven as authentic, which is the most difficult requirement to prove to qualify as an exception to the hearsay rule. Establishing the trustworthiness of digital evidence originated with written documents and the best evidence rule, which states that to prove the content of a written document, recording, or photograph, the original writing, recording, or photograph is ordinarily required. (See Federal Rules of Evidence, 1002.) In other words, an original copy of a document is preferred to a duplicate version. The best evidence then is the document created and saved on a computer hard disk.

Agents and prosecutors occasionally express concern that a printout of a computer-stored electronic file might not qualify as an original document according to the best evidence rule. In its most fundamental form, the original file is a collection of 0's and 1's; in contrast, the printout is the result of manipulating the file through a complicated series of electronic and mechanical processes. (See Federal Rules of Evidence, 803(6). Page 152, in "Searching and Seizing from Computers and Obtaining Electronic Evidence in Criminal Investigations.") To address this concern about the original evidence, the Federal Rules of Evidence state the following:

"[I]f data are stored in a computer or similar device, any printout or other output readable by sight, shown to reflect the data accurately, is an 'original'." Therefore, instead of producing hard disks in court, attorneys can submit printed copies of files as evidence.

The Federal Rules of Evidence, 1001(4), further allows duplicates instead of originals when the duplicate is "a counterpart produced by the same impression as the original...by mechanical or electronic re-recording...or by other equivalent techniques which accurately reproduce the original." Therefore, as long as bit-stream copies of data are properly made and maintained, the copies can be admitted in court, though they are not considered best evidence. The copied evidence can be a reliable working copy, but it is not considered original.

Courts understand that the original evidence might not be available. For example, you could successfully make one bit-stream copy of the evidence drive, but lose access to the original drive when it has a head crash as you attempt to make a second backup bit-stream copy. Your first successful bit-stream copy then becomes secondary evidence. The attorney needs to explain to a judge that circumstances within reasonable control could not preserve the original evidence.

Another situation might be an investigation that involves a network server. Removing the server from the network to acquire evidence data on the disk could cause harm to a business or its owner, who might be an innocent bystander to a crime or civil suit. In this situation you may not have the authority to create a bit-stream copy or remove the original disk drive. Instead, make your best effort to acquire the digital evidence using any possible method. This becomes the best evidence due to the circumstances.

In summary, computer-generated data such a system log or the results of a mathematical formula in a spreadsheet is not hearsay. Computer-stored records that a person generates are subject to rules governing hearsay evidence. To qualify as a business-record exception to the hearsay rule, a person must have created the computer-stored records, and the records must be original. The Federal Rules of Evidence treat printouts of digital files and bit-stream image copies as original evidence.

SECURING DIGITAL EVIDENCE AT AN INCIDENT SCENE

The evidence you acquire at an incident scene depends on the nature of the case and the alleged crime or violation. For a criminal case involving a drug dealer's computer, for example, you need to take the entire computer along with any peripherals and media in the area, including floppy disks, CDs, DVDs, printers, and scanners. On the other hand, if you are investigating an errant employee, you might only need the hard drive.

Before you obtain digital evidence, ask your supervisor or expert the following questions:

- Do you need to take the entire computer, all peripherals, and media in the immediate area? Do you need to protect the computer or media while transporting it to your lab? For example, should you place a floppy disk into the floppy disk drive to protect the drive heads?

- Is the computer powered on when you arrive to take control of the digital evidence? (This is discussed in more detail later in this chapter.)

- Is the suspect you are investigating in the immediate area of the computer? Is it possible that the suspect damaged or destroyed the computer and its media? Will you have to separate the suspect from the computer?

For example, suppose a company employee named Edward Braun is suspected of using the company computer at his desk to write a book. You suspect that Edward is saving personal files on the hard disk of the company computer. Using imaging software, such as Norton Ghost from Symantec, you can copy the hard disk onto another drive, install the duplicate hard drive in the computer, and take the original drive to your forensics lab for examination.

Because Edward's supervisors do not want him to know that he is being investigated, you must work with the drive when he is not at his desk and is not expected to return. This means you should copy Edward's hard disk on a weekend or late on a weeknight. Because most people notice when something is out of order on their desk, before you begin working with Edward's computer, you should photograph the scene, measure the height of his chair, and record the position of sticky notes, pens, and other items on his desk that you must move before you can remove the hard drive. After you create an image of his hard drive and substitute the copy, return Edward's belongings to their original location.

Standard items to pack when you arrive at a scene are shown in Figure 7-2 and include a digital camera, sketchpad, pencils, tape, gloves, a variety of screwdrivers, evidence bags, needle-nose pliers, and bolt cutters.

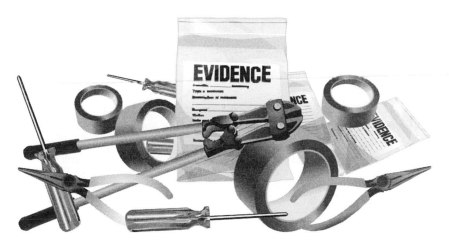

Figure 7-2 Typical equipment for collecting evidence

When handling digital evidence on a computer that is powered on, first photograph the screen contents and save active data to removable media. Do not try to create disk images, but first preserve the data by performing an orderly shutdown on Windows 2000, XP, UNIX, and Linux computers. On older Windows 9x machines, turning off the power typically preserves the data on the drive.

Record the crime or incident scene using still and video imaging. Make sure you take close-ups of all cable connections. Some devices look like a normal hookup to the keyboard, but actually record every keystroke (see Figure 7-3). Dongle devices are also used with specific software as part of the licensing agreement. Computer owners who suspect that someone will investigate their computer might set the computer to delete the contents of the hard disk if a certain component or knob is not turned a particular way or by modifying a common command such as DIR. On older DOS systems, you can change command names. For example, a knowledgeable person can change DIR to FORMAT C: /u, which would format the hard disk, producing catastrophic results, especially if you are in the middle of an investigation.

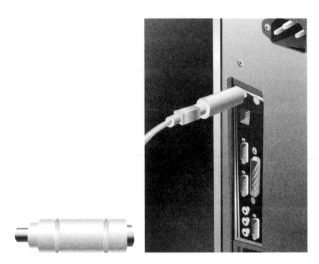

Figure 7-3   Keystroke recording device

Remember that electronic media is sensitive and easily damaged, altered, or destroyed, so you must take care when obtaining, transporting, and copying digital evidence. In addition to photographing the scene and the computer, perform the following tasks to make sure you are preserving the evidence with as much integrity as possible:

- Use antistatic evidence bags for small pieces of evidence such as disks and magnetic tapes, and use adhesive seals to secure the openings on the computer cabinet.

- Look for manuals and software such as the operating system and application programs at the scene. Collect these items as part of the evidence.

- Determine whether the environment is safe for your evidence. If you have to take the computer outside, freezing or very hot temperatures can damage digital media. If you are transporting digital media, make sure your vehicle is heated or air-conditioned as appropriate for the weather. Also determine whether electrical transformers are located near your digital evidence. They can interfere with the magnetic disk coating and damage evidence.

CATALOGING DIGITAL EVIDENCE

After you determine that an incident scene has digital evidence to collect, you visit the scene. First you need to catalog it, or document the evidence you find. Your goal is to preserve evidence integrity, which means that you do not modify the evidence as you collect and catalog it. Keep in mind the rules of evidence discussed in the previous section. First locate the computing asset you need to examine and collect. If the computer is turned off, observe the following guidelines to catalog digital evidence and preserve its integrity:

1. Identify the type of computer you are working with, such as a Windows PC or laptop, a UNIX workstation, or a Macintosh. Do not turn on a suspect computer if it is turned off. Recall that various operating systems overwrite files as a standard part of their boot process.

2. Use a digital camera to photograph all cable connections, and then label the cables with evidence tags. Photograph or videotape the scene, and create a detailed diagram, noting where items are located.

3. Assign one person to collect and log all evidence. Minimize the number of people handling evidence overall to ensure its integrity.

4. Tag all the evidence you collect with the current date and time, serial numbers or unique features, make and model, and the name of the person who collected it.

5. Maintain two separate logs of collected evidence to use as a backup checklist to verify everything you have collected.

6. Maintain constant control of the collected evidence and the crime or incident scene.

If the suspect computer is turned on when you go to collect the digital evidence, as shown in Figure 7-4, you need to perform the following additional steps, which are discussed in greater detail later in this chapter.

Figure 7-4   Typical crime scene

1. If practical, copy any application data displayed on the screen, such as text or a spreadsheet document. Save this RAM data to removable media, such as a floppy disk, Zip, or Jaz disk, using the Save As command. If this is not possible, take a close-up photograph of the screen. Then close the application without saving data.

2. After you copy the RAM data, you can safely shut down the computer. Use the manufacturer's appropriate shutdown method. If you are not familiar with the method, find someone who is.

3. To access the suspect system, use an alternate operating system to examine the hard disk data. On Intel computers, use a specially configured boot disk, which you learned how to create in Chapter 5. For UNIX workstations, remove the drive and inspect the hard drive from another UNIX or Linux system.

4. Acquire the suspect drive with bit-streaming imaging tools.

5. Verify the integrity of your bit-stream image copy of the original disk.

For example, suppose that you have been assigned to collect the evidence at the home of a suspected drug dealer. When you visit the crime scene, you notice a laptop and a desktop in the front room. The computers appear to be networked together by a network cable. First, review the search warrant and make sure you have the proper authority to conduct a search or seizure. Then take photos and sketch the precise locations of the cables between the computers. Also indicate that the machines are running. You photograph the scene to recreate the physical configuration of the computer hardware. You can also use the photographs to prove the condition of the equipment in case it must be returned to the suspect. Next, tag the cables if the cabling is complicated so that you can recreate the system configuration reliably. Then check the computer setup for anything unusual.

Record the RAM data on both machines to your removable media, and then systematically shut down the computers. Record the item number for each cable and tag each with the same number. Finally, disassemble the computers and components, bag and label them, and prepare them for transport.

Lab Evidence Considerations

After you collect digital evidence at the crime or incident scene, you transport it to a forensics lab. The lab environment should be a controlled environment that ensures the security and integrity of your digital evidence. In any investigative work, be sure to record your activities and findings as you work. To do so, you can maintain a journal. Use a journal to record the steps you performed as you process the evidence. Your goal is to produce the same results when you or another investigator repeats the steps you took to collect the evidence.

If you produce different results when you repeat the steps, the credibility of your evidence becomes questionable. At best, the value of the evidence is compromised; at worse, the evidence will be disqualified. Because of the nature of electronic components, failures do occur. For example, you might not be able to repeat a data recovery due to a hardware failure such as a disk drive head crash. Be sure to report all facts as they occur.

Besides verifying your work, a journal provides a reference that documents the methods you used to process digital evidence. You and others can use it for training and guidance on other investigations.

Processing and Handling Digital Evidence

When in the lab, you must maintain the integrity of the digital evidence as you do when you are collecting it in the field. Your first task is to preserve the disk data. If you have a suspect computer that has not been copied with a bit-stream imaging tool, you must create a copy. As you create a copy, be sure to make the suspect drive read-only (typically by using a write-block device), and document this step. If the disk has been copied with a bit-stream imaging tool, you must preserve the image files. When using most bit-stream imaging tools, you can create smaller, compressed volume sets to make archiving your data much easier.

In Chapter 6 you learned how to use bit-stream imaging tools, and in Chapter 2, you examined the steps you should perform to preserve your digital evidence as applied to chain-of-custody controls. Complete the following steps to create bit-stream image files:

1. Copy all bit-stream image files to a large disk drive.

2. Start your desired forensics tool to analyze the evidence.

3. Run an MD5 hash check on the bit-stream image files.

4. When you finish copying bit-stream image files to the larger disk, secure the original media in an evidence locker.

A forensics lab typically has several machines set up with disk imaging software and multiple hard drives that can be exchanged as needed for your cases. These resources enable you to copy the image files to large disk drives.

You run a **Message Digest version 5 (MD5) hash** to get a digital signature. At the end of this chapter, you will see how to compare the MD5 hash to make sure the evidence has not changed.

Do not work with the original media, which should be stored in a locker that has a chain-of-custody form. Be sure to fill out the chain-of-custody form and date it.

STORING DIGITAL EVIDENCE

When securing digital evidence, consider how and on what type of media to save it. Also consider what type of storage device is recommended to secure it. The media you use to store digital evidence usually depends on how long you need to keep the evidence. If you are involved with criminal casework, store the evidence as long as you can. The ideal media on which to store digital data are a Compact Disc - Recordable (CD-R) or DVD. Historically these media systems have long lives. Their disadvantage is that it takes a long time to copy data to them. The larger disk drives on the market today demand larger storage capacity. For example, a DVD can store up to 17 GB of data.

You can also use magnetic tape to preserve evidence data. The popular **4-mm DAT** magnetic tapes store about 4 GB of data, but like the CD-Rs, they are slow to read and write data. The 4-mm DAT is the least robust media currently available. If you are using 4-mm DAT tapes, test your data by copying the contents from the tape back to a disk drive. Then verify that the data is good by accessing it with your computing forensics tools or with an MD5 hash comparison between the original data set to the newly restored data set.

If a 30-year life span for data storage is acceptable for your digital evidence, the older DLT magnetic tape cartridge systems are a good choice. Figure 7-5 shows a 4-mm DAT and a DLT tape.

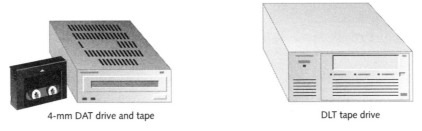

4-mm DAT drive and tape   DLT tape drive

Figure 7-5   4-mm DAT and a DLT tape drive

DLT systems have been used with mainframe computers for several decades, and are reliable data-archiving systems. Depending on the size of the DLT cartridge you obtain, one cartridge can store up to 80 GB of data in compressed mode. Speed of data transfer from your hard disk drive to a DLT tape is also faster than transferring data to a CD or DVD.

The only significant drawback to a DLT drive and its tapes is cost. A drive can cost from $400-$800, and each tape is about $40. However, with newer extremely large disk drives now on the market, the DLT system does provide significant labor savings compared to other systems.

Recently, manufacturers such as Quantum have introduced a high-speed capacity tape cartridge drive system called SDLT. These systems are specifically designed for large RAID data backups. Smaller external SDLT drives can connect to a workstation through a SCSI card.

Do not rely on one media storage method to preserve your evidence—be sure to make two copies of every bit-stream copy of your data to prevent data loss. Also create the two separate bit-stream images with different forensic imaging tools. For example, you can make one bit-stream copy using the Linux dd command, and then use DriveSpy's SavePart or SaveSect bit-stream imaging commands to create the second bit-stream copy.

As mentioned earlier, another consideration when securing your evidence is to run an MD5 digital signature of all media. By maintaining the digital signature values of your digital evidence, you have an added method of verifying its integrity.

Evidence Retention and Media Storage Needs

You must maintain the chain of custody of your digital evidence so that it is accepted in court or by arbitration. Restrict access to your lab facility and the area where you store your digital evidence. These areas must be under constant supervision by authorized personnel when open for operations. When closed, at least two security staff should protect all evidence storage cabinets and lab facilities.

As a practice, your lab should have a sign-in roster for all visitors. For the evidence storage containers, most labs use a manual log system that is initialed by the authorized technician when it is opened and closed. These logs should be maintained forever and should be made available for routine inspection by upper management. A log file for each piece of evidence, your evidence form, should contain space for entry of every person who has handled the evidence (see Figure 7-6).

Item description:				
Item tag number:				
Person	Date logged out	Time logged out	Date logged in	Time logged in

Figure 7-6 Sample log file

If you are supporting a law enforcement agency, you might need to retain your evidence forever, depending on the level of the crime. Check with your local prosecuting attorney's office or state laws to ensure you are in compliance. For the private sector or corporate environment, check with the legal department (the general counsel) of your company. It is their responsibility to set the standards for evidence retention for your organization.

Documenting Evidence

To document your evidence, create or use an evidence form, as shown in Chapter 2. Because of the constant changes in technologies and methods used for acquiring data, update your evidence form to ensure it addresses these changes. An evidence form serves the following functions:

- Identifies the evidence
- Identifies who has handled the evidence
- Lists the dates and times the evidence was handled

After you have established these items, you can add other pieces of information to your form, such as a section that lists the MD5 checksum values. Include any detailed information that you might need to reference.

Evidence bags also include labels or evidence forms that you can use to document your evidence. Commercial companies provide a variety of sizes and styles of paper and plastic evidence bags. Be sure to write on the bag when it is empty, not when it contains digital evidence.

Create an evidence form that you can modify as you progress from one investigation to another, as shown in Figure 7-7. Keep an electronic copy of your form and make adjustments and additions as needed.

OBTAINING A DIGITAL SIGNATURE

To maintain data integrity, various methods of obtaining a unique identity of file data have been developed. One of the first methods was the **Cyclic Redundancy Check (CRC)**, which uses a mathematical algorithm to determine whether the contents of a file have changed. The most recent version of the CRC is the CRC-32. The most common algorithm used today for computing investigations and forensics is the MD5. Like the CRC, the MD5 is a mathematical formula that translates a file into a unique hexadecimal code value, or a hash value. If a bit or byte in the file changes, it alters the **digital signature**, a unique value that identifies a file. Before you process or analyze a file, you can use a software tool to produce a digital signature of the file. After you process the file, you produce another digital signature. If it is the same as the original signature, you can verify the integrity of your digital evidence with mathematical proof that the file did not change.

Corporation X Security Investigations This form is used for one to ten pieces of evidence			
Case No.:		Investigating Organization:	
Investigator:			
Nature of case:			
Location where evidence was obtained:		MD5 hash value:	
Description of evidence	Vendor Name	Model No./Serial No.	
Item #1			
Item #2			
Item #3			
Item #4			
Item #5			
Item #6			
Item #7			
Item #8			
Item #9			
Item #10			
Evidence Recovered by:		Date &Time:	
Evidence Placed in Locker:		Date &Time:	
Item#	Evidence Processed by #	Disposition of Evidence #	Date/Time
			Page__of__

Figure 7-7 Modified evidence form

The newest digital signature method developed by the **National Institute of Standards and Technologies (NIST)** is the **Secure Hash Algorithm, version 1 (SHA-1)**. SHA-1 is slowly replacing MD5 and CRC-32, though MD5 is still widely used.

You use MD5 to obtain the digital signature (also called a digital fingerprint), which is unique identity code of a file or an entire disk. Digital signature hashes vary. Most forensic computing hash needs can be satisfied with a **non-keyed hash set**, which is a unique hash number generated by a software tool such as the DriveSpy MD5 command. The advantage of this type of hash is that it can identify known files such as executable programs or viruses that hide themselves by changing their names. For example, many people who view or transmit pornographic material change the names and extensions of files to obscure the nature of the contents. However, even if the name and extension of a file change, the hash value does not.

The alternative to a non-keyed hash is the **keyed hash set**, which is created by an encryption utility's secret key. You could use the secret key to create a unique hash value (a digital signature) for a file. While a keyed hash set cannot identify files as the non-keyed hash methods can, it can provide a unique fingerprint hash set for your digital evidence.

You can use the MD5 command in DriveSpy to obtain the unique digital signature of a file and an entire disk. In the following steps, you use a floppy disk, though you often work with hard disks in actual investigations. You will work at the command line, though you can apply the same principles to a GUI environment.

You will first create a test file and then generate an MD5 hash value for the file. Then you change the file and produce another MD5 value, this time noting the change in the hash signature. You need a blank, formatted floppy disk and a Windows 98 computer to complete the following steps:

1. Power on your forensic workstation, booting it to the MS-DOS prompt.

2. Write "Chapter 7" on the label of a blank, formatted floppy disk.

3. Change to the A: drive by typing **a:** and then pressing **Enter**. To create a text file named InChap07.txt on the floppy disk, type **Edit InChap07.txt** and press **Enter**. When the edit screen appears, type **This is a test to see how an MD5 digital signature works**, as shown in Figure 7-8.

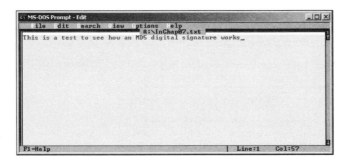

Figure 7-8   Creating a file in the DOS editor

4. To save the file, first press **Alt+F** to open the File menu, and then type **s** to save the file as shown in Figure 7-9.

Figure 7-9   Saving the file

5. Press **Alt+F** to open the File menu again, and then type **x** to exit.

Next you can use DriveSpy to generate an MD5 hash value for the file you just created.

To use DriveSpy to generate an MD5 hash value:

1. Make sure you are working at the DOS prompt. Change to your hard disk drive, such as C:, by typing **c:** and pressing **Enter**. Navigate to your work folder by typing **cd** and pressing **Enter** to change to the root directory, and then typing **cd*work folder*** and pressing **Enter**. (Replace *work folder* with the name of your work folder as necessary.)

2. Create a Chap07 folder in your work folder by typing **md Chap07** and pressing **Enter**. Change to this directory by typing **cd Chap07**. Then type **md Chapter** and press **Enter** to create a Chapter folder in the Chap07 folder.

3. To run Toolpath.bat so that DriveSpy is available from any directory, navigate to your work folder as you did in Step 1, change to the Tools folder by typing **cd Tools** and pressing **Enter**, and then type **Toolpath.bat** and press **Enter**.

4. Change to Drive A by typing **A:** and pressing **Enter**.

5. At the DOS prompt, start DriveSpy by typing **DriveSpy** and pressing **Enter**.

6. At the SYS prompt, type **Output C:*work folder*\Chap07\Chapter\ InChplog.txt** and then press **Enter** to send the output to a log file, as shown in Figure 7-10.

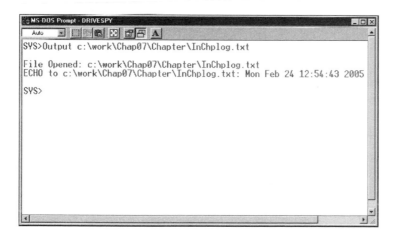

Figure 7-10   Sending output to a log file

7. At the SYS prompt, type **Drive A** and press **Enter** to access the physical level of the floppy disk, as shown in Figure 7-11.

8. At the DA> prompt, type **Part 1** and press **Enter** to access the partition level of the drive, as shown in Figure 7-12.

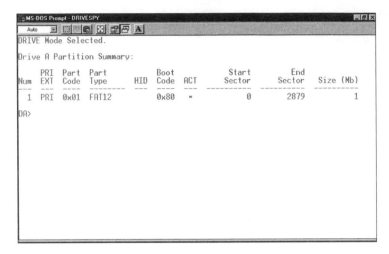

Figure 7-11   Drive level of DriveSpy

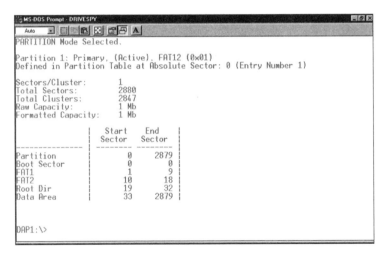

Figure 7-12   Partition level of DriveSpy

Recall that you are working with a floppy disk that uses FAT12 and has 2880 sectors. The partition level also shows where the boot sector and root directory are located, and where the data begins.

9. At the DAP1 prompt, type **Dir** and press **Enter** to view the data on the disk, as shown in Figure 7-13. The Dir command lists the date the file was created and the last time it was accessed.

10. At the DAP1 prompt, type **MD5 InChap07.txt** and press **Enter** to produce the MD5 hash value. Figure 7-14 shows the hash value, or checksum, for the file.

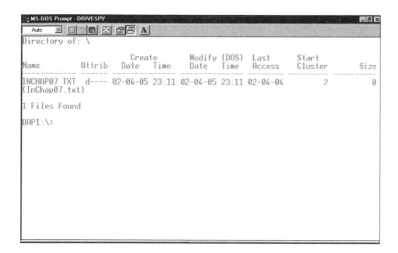

Figure 7-13   Results of the Dir command

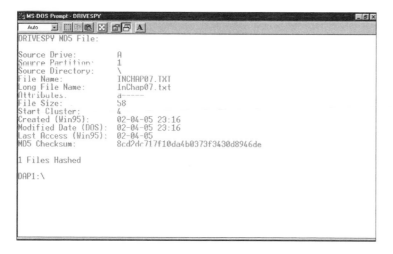

Figure 7-14   MD5 hash value for InChap07.txt

11. To be thorough and to verify that the contents of the disk do not change, you can also create an MD5 hash value for the disk. At the DAP1 prompt, type **Drive A** and press **Enter**. At the DA prompt, type **MD5** and press **Enter** to generate the hash value for the disk. Note that it takes several minutes to generate the hash value of a floppy disk. The results are shown in Figure 7-15. You can also run the MD5 hash for the disk from the DAP1 prompt.

12. To exit DriveSpy, type **Exit** and press **Enter**.

Note that many antivirus programs use checksums to determine whether a file has been altered.

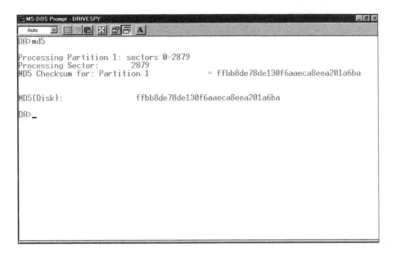

Figure 7-15   MD5 hash value for the floppy disk

In the previous steps, you navigated to the disk's logical level, or the partition mode, to run the MD5 function on your test file. You used the Part command to move into this mode. You then navigated back to the drive mode to run the MD5 function on the entire disk. You used the Drive command to move into this mode.

After you produce an MD5 hash value, you typically review the output you saved in the log file, which is especially useful for cases that involve large disks because it documents all the commands you used. You can open this file using Notepad or another text editor. Pay special attention to the MD5 output you created for your file and disk.

CHAPTER SUMMARY

- Digital evidence is anything that is stored or transmitted on electronic or optical media. It is extremely fragile and easily altered.

- To work with digital evidence, start by identifying digital information or artifacts that can be used as evidence. Collect, preserve, document, analyze, identify, and organize the evidence. Then rebuild evidence or repeat a situation to verify that you can obtain the same results every time.

- You must consistently handle all evidence the same way every time you handle it. Apply the same security and accountability controls for evidence in a civil lawsuit as for evidence obtained at a major crime scene to comply with your state's rules of evidence or with the Federal Rules of Evidence.

- After you determine that an incident scene has digital evidence to collect, you visit the scene. First you need to catalog it, or to document the evidence you find. Your goal is to preserve evidence integrity, which means that you do not modify the evidence as you collect and catalog it. An incident scene should be photographed and sketched, and then each item labeled and put in an evidence bag if possible.

- The media you use to store digital evidence usually depends on how long you need to keep the evidence. The ideal media on which to store digital data are CD-Rs or DVDs. You can also use magnetic tape to preserve evidence data, such as 4-mm DAT and DLT magnetic tapes.

- Digital evidence needs to be copied using bit-stream imaging to make sure that sector-by-sector mapping takes place.

- Digital signatures should be used to make sure that no changes have been made to the file or storage device. The current standards are CRC, MD5 hash, and SHA-1.

KEY TERMS

4-mm DAT—Magnetic tapes that store about 4 GB of data, but like the CD-Rs, are slow to read and write data.

computer-generated record—Data that is generated by the computer such as system log files or proxy server logs.

computer-stored records—Digital files that are generated by a person.

Cyclical Redundancy Check (CRC)—A mathematical algorithm that translates a file into a unique hexadecimal code value.

digital signature—A unique value that identifies a file.

International Organization on Digital Evidence (IOCE)—A group that sets standards for recovering, preserving, and examining digital evidence.

keyed hash set—A value created by an encryption utility's secret key.

Message Digest version 5 (MD5) hash—A mathematical algorithm that translates a file into a unique hexadecimal code value.

National Institute of Standards and Technologies (NIST)—One of the governing bodies responsible for setting standards in the United States for various industries.

non-keyed hash set—A hash set used to identify files or viruses.

Scientific Working Group on Digital Evidence (SWGDE)—A group that sets standards for recovering, preserving, and examining digital evidence.

Secure Hash Algorithm, version 1 (SHA-1)—A new digital signature method developed by the NIST. It is slowly replacing MD5 and CRC.

7

8

PROCESSING CRIME
AND INCIDENT SCENES

After reading this chapter, you will be able to:

♦ Process private-sector incident scenes

♦ Process law enforcement incident scenes

♦ Prepare for a search

♦ Secure a computer incident or crime scene

♦ Seize digital evidence at the scene

♦ Collect digital evidence

♦ Review a case

In this chapter, you will learn how to process a computer investigation scene. Because this chapter discusses only investigation needs relating to computing systems, you should supplement your training by studying Police Science or United States Department of Justice (USDOJ) procedures to understand the field-of-evidence recovery tasks.

This chapter describes the differences between the needs and concerns of a business (private entity) and a law enforcement (public entity) organization, and then discusses incident-scene processing for both the corporate investigator and the law enforcement investigator. Private-sector security officers often begin investigating corporate computer crimes, and then coordinate with law enforcement to complete the investigation. Law enforcement examiners should therefore understand how to process incident scenes and take a leadership role in these technical investigations. Because public agencies usually do not have the funding to continuously train sworn officers in the latest advances in computing systems, they must learn to work with private-sector investigators, whose employers can often afford to maintain computing skills in technologies such as advanced databases or Web-based applications. Law enforcement investigators should therefore learn how to manage private computer examiners when processing a computing investigation.

This chapter also discusses the Fourth Amendment and how it relates to corporate and law enforcement computing investigations in the United States. In particular, this chapter explains how to apply standard crime-scene practices to corporate and law enforcement computing investigations. You learn how to apply the rules of evidence, which were defined in Chapter 7, to the crime scene. Recall that the corporate investigator must secure and document evidence from a computer abuse case as carefully as a police detective does for a homicide case.

PROCESSING PRIVATE-SECTOR INCIDENT SCENES

Private-sector organizations include businesses and government agencies that are not involved in law enforcement. Non-law enforcement government organizations in the United States must comply with state public disclosure and federal Freedom of Information Act (FOIA) laws, and make the documents they find and create available as public records. State public disclosure laws define state public records as open and available for inspection. For example, divorces recorded in a public office such as a courthouse become matters of public record unless a judge orders the documents sealed. Anyone can request a copy of the public divorce decree. Figure 8-1 shows an excerpt of a public disclosure law for the state of Idaho.

9-338. PUBLIC RECORDS -- RIGHT TO EXAMINE.

(1) Every person has a right to examine and take a copy of any public record of this state and there is a presumption that all public records in Idaho are open at all reasonable times for inspection except as otherwise expressly provided by statute.

(2) The right to copy public records shall include the right to make photographs or photographic or other copies while the records are in the possession of the custodian of the records using equipment provided by the public agency or independent public body corporate and politic or using equipment designated by the custodian.

(4) The custodian shall make no inquiry of any person who applies for a public record, except to verify the identity of a person requesting a record in accordance with section 9-342, Idaho Code, to ensure that the requested record or information will not be used for purposes of a mailing or telephone list prohibited by section 9-348, Idaho Code, or as otherwise provided by law. The person may be required to make a written request and provide their name, a mailing address and telephone number. [The custodian shall make no inquiry of any person who applies for a public record, except that the person may be required to make a written request and provide a mailing address and telephone number, and except as required for purposes of protecting personal information from disclosure under chapter 2, title 49, Idaho Code, and federal law.]

(5) The custodian shall not review, examine or scrutinize any copy, photograph or memoranda in the possession of any such person and shall extend to the person all reasonable comfort and facility for the full exercise of the right granted under this act.

Figure 8-1 Idaho public disclosure law

While state public disclosure laws apply to state records, the FOIA allows citizens to request copies of public documents created by federal agencies. The FOIA was originally enacted in the 1960s, and several subsequent amendments have broadened its laws. Some Web sites now provide copies of publicly accessible records for a fee. If you work in a government organization, consult with an attorney assigned to support public employee law.

A special category of private-sector businesses includes Internet service providers (ISPs) and other communication companies. ISPs can investigate computer abuse committed by their employees, not customers. ISPs must preserve customer privacy, especially when dealing with e-mail. However, newer federal regulations related to the Homeland Security Act could redefine how ISPs and large corporate Internet users operate and maintain their records. These regulations could allow computer forensic examiners to investigate computer abuse by ISP customers and employees.

Investigating and controlling computer incident scenes in the corporate environment is much easier than in the criminal environment. In the private sector, the incident scene is often a workplace, such as a contained office or manufacturing area, where a policy violation is being investigated. Therefore, everything from the computers used to violate a company policy to the surrounding facility is under a controlled authority. Furthermore, because businesses determine the make, model, operating system (OS), and programs running on their systems, computer investigators can use forensic tools developed for these computing platforms. Knowing which resources were used when a company's rules were violated also speeds an investigation. For example, most companies use a single Web browser, such as Microsoft Internet Explorer, Netscape Navigator, or Konqueror. Knowing which browser a suspect used lets you develop standard examination procedures to identify data downloaded to the suspect's workstation.

However, if a company does not publish a policy stating that they reserve the right to inspect computing assets at will, employees have an expectation of privacy. When investigating a suspected employee, this expected privacy prevents the employer from legally conducting an intrusive investigation. A well-defined corporate policy states that an employer has the right to examine, inspect, or access any company-owned computing asset. If a company issues a policy statement to all employees, the employer can investigate computing assets at will without any privacy-right restrictions.

A corporate policy statement regarding computing assets lets corporate investigators perform covert surveillance with little or no cause to investigate employees suspected of improper use of company computing assets. An employer can freely initiate any inquiry necessary to protect the company or organization. Being able to access company computing systems without a warrant is an advantage for the corporate investigator. Law enforcement investigators cannot do the same without sufficient reason for a warrant.

In addition to making sure that a company has a policy statement regarding the right to inspect company computers, corporate investigators should also know under what circumstances they can examine an employee's computer. Every business or organization must have a well-defined process that describes when an investigation can be initiated. At a minimum, most corporate policies require that employers have a "reasonable suspicion" that a law or policy is being violated. For example, if a policy states that employees may not use company computers for outside business and a supervisor notices a change in work behavior, that could indicate an employee is using an office computer to conduct another business, and is generally enough to warrant an investigation.

If a corporate investigator finds that an employee is committing or has committed a crime, the employer can file a criminal complaint with the police. The employer must turn over all evidence to the police for prosecution, according to the silver platter doctrine discussed in Chapter 1. If collected by a sworn law enforcement officer, this same evidence would require a warrant, which would be difficult to obtain without sufficient probable cause. In the next section, you learn more about probable cause and how it applies to a criminal investigation.

Employers are usually interested in enforcing company policy, not seeking out and prosecuting employees. The only reason an employer approves a computer investigation is to identify employees who are abusing or misusing company assets. Corporate investigators are therefore primarily concerned with protecting company assets. Finding evidence of a criminal act during an abuse investigation escalates the investigation from an internal civil matter to an external criminal complaint. See Figure 8-2.

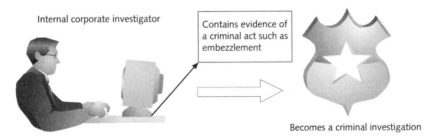

Figure 8-2   Internal civil matter becoming a criminal complaint

While cooperating with law enforcement officers, corporate investigators should avoid becoming an agent of law enforcement, which can happen when an investigation becomes a criminal complaint without the proper safeguards that are required under the Fourth Amendment to the U.S. Constitution. Being an agent of law enforcement can expose corporate investigators to civil liability. To avoid becoming an agent of law enforcement, keep all documentation of evidence collected to investigate an internal company rules violation. Later in this chapter, you will learn more about affidavits and how to apply them to an internal investigation in the private sector.

If you discover evidence of a crime during a company policy investigation, first determine whether the incident meets the elements of criminal law. You might have to consult with your corporate attorney to determine whether the situation is a potential crime. Next, inform your management of the incident; they might have other concerns such as protecting competitively sensitive business data that might be included with the criminal evidence. In this case, coordinate with your management and the corporate attorney to determine the best way to protect commingled data. Once you submit to the police criminal evidence that contains sensitive information, it becomes public record. Public record laws include exceptions for protecting sensitive corporate information, but a judge ultimately decides what to protect.

After you discover illegal activity in a company and document and report the crime, stop your investigation to make sure you do not become an agent of the police and investigate an employee without safeguards required by the Fourth Amendment. If the information you provide is specific enough to meet the criteria of a search warrant, the police are responsible for obtaining a warrant that requests any new evidence. If you follow police instructions to gather additional evidence after you have reported the crime, you run the risk of becoming an agent of the police. Instead, consult with your corporate attorney for direction on how to respond to a police request for information. The police and prosecutor should issue a subpoena for any additional new evidence, which minimizes your exposure to potential civil liability.

One example of a company rules violation involves employees observing another employee accessing pornographic Web sites. If your organization's policy requires you to determine whether any evidence supports this accusation, you could start by extracting log file data from the proxy server and conducting a forensic examination of the subject's computer. Organizations use a **proxy server** to connect their local area network (LAN) to the Internet. Suppose that during your examination, you find adult and child pornography. Further examination of the subject's hard disk reveals that the employee has been collecting child pornography in separate folders on his workstation's hard disk. In the U.S., possessing child pornography is a crime under federal and state criminal statutes.

You survey the remaining content of the subject's disk and find that he is a lead engineer for the team developing your company's latest high-tech bicycle. He has placed the child pornography images in a subfolder where the bicycle plans are stored. By doing so, he has commingled contraband with company's competitive sensitive design plans for the new high-tech bicycle.

Your discovery poses two problems about how to deal with this contraband evidence. First, you must report the crime to the police. Many states require reporting evidence of the sexual exploitation of children. The second problem is that you must also protect the sensitive company information. Letting the high-tech bicycle information become part of the criminal evidence might make it public record, and the design work will then be available to the competitors. Your first step is to notify your corporate attorney to receive directions on how to deal with the commingled contraband data and the engineering plans.

Your next step is to work with the corporate attorney to write an affidavit affirming your findings. The attorney should indicate in the affidavit that the evidence is commingled with company secrets, and that releasing the information will be detrimental to the financial health of the company. When the affidavit is complete, you sign it before a notary, and then deliver the affidavit and the recovered evidence with log files to the police where you make a criminal complaint. At the same time, the corporate attorney goes to court and requests that all evidence recovered from the hard disk that is not related to the complaint and is a company trade secret that should be protected from public viewing. You and the corporate attorney have reported the crime and taken steps to protect the sensitive data.

Now suppose that you receive a call from the police detective assigned to the case. In the evidence you have turned over to the police, the detective notices that the suspect is collecting most of his contraband from e-mail attachments. The prosecutor instructed the detective to ask you to collect more evidence to determine whether the suspect is transmitting contraband pictures to other potential suspects. In this case, you should immediately inform the police detective that collecting more evidence might make you an agent of law enforcement. Before collecting any additional information, consult with your corporate attorney or wait until you receive a subpoena or other court order.

PROCESSING LAW ENFORCEMENT CRIME SCENES

To process a crime scene properly, you must be familiar with criminal rules of search and seizure. You should also understand how a search warrant works and what to do when you process one.

For all criminal investigations in the U.S., the Fourth Amendment to the Constitution limits how governments search and seize evidence. A law enforcement officer may only search for and seize criminal evidence with **probable cause**, which are facts or circumstances that would lead a reasonable person to believe a crime has been committed or is about to be committed. Probable cause requires meeting the following criteria:

- A specific crime was committed or is about to be committed

- Evidence of the specific crime exists

- The place to be searched includes evidence of the specific crime

With probable cause, a police officer can obtain a **search warrant** from a judge that authorizes a search and seizure of specific evidence relating to the criminal complaint. The judge must be neutral and detached from the complaint, and must determine whether there is sufficient probable cause to issue a warrant. Furthermore, a witness under oath or affirmation must assert that a particular location contains specific evidence of criminal activity.

Recall that the Fourth Amendment to the U.S. Constitution states, "The right of the people to be secure in their persons, houses, papers, and effects, against unreasonable searches and seizures, shall not be violated, and no Warrants shall issue, but upon probable cause, supported by Oath or affirmation, and particularly describing the place to be searched, and the persons or things to be seized."

Note how this excerpt uses the word "particularly." The courts have determined that "particularly describing the place to be searched, and the persons or things to be seized," means a warrant can only authorize a search of a specific place for a specific thing. Without *specific* evidence and the description of a particular location, a warrant may be weak and create problems later during prosecution. For example, stating that the evidence is in a house located on Elm Avenue between Broadway and Main Street is too general because a dozen houses might be located on both sides of Elm Avenue between Broadway and Main Street. Instead, provide specific information, such as the exact address of the house. Most courts have allowed more generality regarding computer evidence. For example, you can state that you want to seize a "computer" rather than a "Dell Optiplex GXA." Figure 8-3 shows sample search warrant language for computer evidence that the state of Maryland makes available for computer crime investigators (see *http://ccu.mdsp.org*).

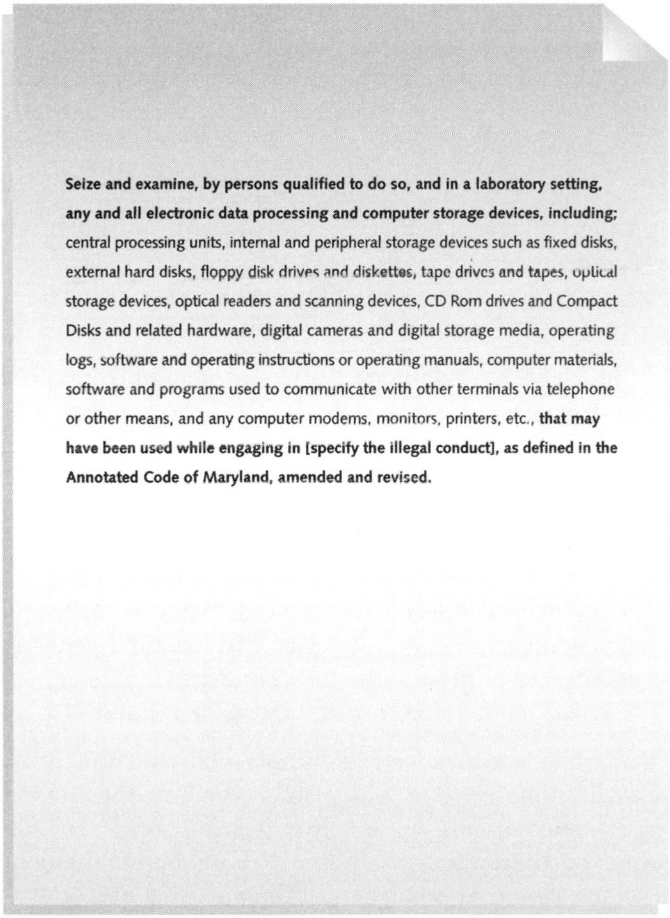

8

> **Seize and examine, by persons qualified to do so, and in a laboratory setting,** **any and all electronic data processing and computer storage devices, including:** central processing units, internal and peripheral storage devices such as fixed disks, external hard disks, floppy disk drives and diskettes, tape drives and tapes, optical storage devices, optical readers and scanning devices, CD Rom drives and Compact Disks and related hardware, digital cameras and digital storage media, operating logs, software and operating instructions or operating manuals, computer materials, software and programs used to communicate with other terminals via telephone or other means, and any computer modems, monitors, printers, etc., **that may** **have been used while engaging in [specify the illegal conduct], as defined in the** **Annotated Code of Maryland, amended and revised.**

Figure 8-3 Sample search warrant wording

Although several court cases have allowed latitude when searching and seizing computer evidence, it is a good practice to make your warrant as specific as possible to avoid challenges from defense attorneys. Typically, a warrant is written and issued in haste because of the nature of the investigation. Law enforcement officers might not have the time to research the correct language to use when stating the nature of the complaint to meet the requirements of probable cause. However, because a judge can exclude evidence obtained from a poorly worded warrant, you should review these issues with your local prosecutor before investigating a case.

Understanding Concepts and Terms Used in Warrants

You should be familiar with warrant terminology that governs the type of evidence that can be seized. Many computing investigations involve large amounts of data that you must sort through to find evidence. Unrelated information is often included with the evidence you are trying to recover. This unrelated information might be personal and private records of innocent people, or sensitive information such as the design plans for a high-tech bicycle. When you find a mix of information, judges typically issue a **limiting phrase** to the warrant allowing the police to separate the **innocent information** from the evidence. The warrant must list the items to seize.

While approaching or investigating a crime scene, you might find evidence that is related to the crime but not in the location specified by the warrant. You might also find evidence of another unrelated crime. In these situations, the evidence related or unrelated to the crime you are investigating is subject to the **plain view doctrine**. The sixth edition of Black's Law Dictionary defines the plain view doctrine as follows:

"In search and seizure context, objects falling in plain view of an officer who has the right to be in position to have that view are subject to seizure without a warrant and may be introduced in evidence. *Harris v. U.S.,* 390 U.S. 234, 236, 88 S.Ct. 992, 993, 19 L.Ed.2d 1069. Under 'plain view doctrine,' warrantless seizure of incriminating evidence may be permitted when police are lawfully searching a specified area if it can be established that police had prior justification for intrusion into the area searched, that police inadvertently came across item seized and that it was immediately apparent to the police that the item seized was evidence. *Washington v. Chrisman,* 455 U.S. 1, 5, 102 S.Ct. 812, 816, 70 L.Ed2d 778. However, the plain view doctrine may not be used to extend a general exploratory search from one object to another until something incriminating at last emerges. *Coolidge v. New Hampshire,* 403 U.S. 443, 466, 91 S.Ct. 2022, 2038, 29 L.Ed2d 564."

All warrants require that officers knock and announce their identity when executing a warrant. Exceptions to this rule include when officers expect the suspect to destroy evidence or when officers encounter a suspect that is armed and dangerous. In most computing investigations, the destruction of evidence is an important concern. When creating a warrant, the judge should be informed of the potential loss of evidence if you must "knock and announce." Evidence can also be seized as part of an inventory search of a suspect's residence.

PREPARING FOR A SEARCH

Preparing for a computer search and seizure is probably the most important step in computing investigations. The better you prepare, the smoother your investigation will be. The following sections discuss the tasks you should complete before you search for evidence. To complete the tasks, you might need to find answers from the victim (the complainant) and an informant, who could be a police detective assigned to the case, a law enforcement witness, or a manager or co-worker of the person of interest to the investigation.

Identifying the Nature of the Case

When you're assigned a computing investigation case, start by identifying the nature of the case, including whether it involves the private or public sector. For example, a corporate investigation might involve an employee abusing his Internet privileges by excessively surfing the Web or an equal employment opportunity (EEO) or ethics complaint. Serious cases might involve an employee abusing company computing assets to acquire or deliver contraband. Law enforcement cases could range from a check fraud ring to a homicide. The nature of the case dictates how you proceed and what types of assets or resources you need to apply in the investigation.

Identifying the Type of Computing System

After you identify the type of investigation, determine the type of computing systems involved in the investigation. For law enforcement, this may be a difficult step because the crime scene is uncontrolled. You might not know where or what kinds of computers were used to commit a crime. In this case, you must draw on your skills, creativity, and knowledge to deal with the unknown.

If you can identify the computing system, determine the size of the disk drive on the suspect's computer and how many computers you have to process at the scene. Also determine which operating systems and specific hardware might be involved, and whether the evidence is located on a Microsoft, Linux, UNIX, Macintosh, or mainframe computer (see Figure 8-4). For corporate investigators, configuration planning makes this an easy step to perform. Consultants to the private sector or law enforcement officers might have to investigate more thoroughly to determine these details.

Figure 8-4   Determining the operating system

Determining Whether You Can Seize a Computer

The ideal situation for all incident or crime scenes is to seize computers and take them to your lab for further processing. However, the type of case and location of the evidence determine whether you can remove the computers from the scene. Law enforcement investigators need a warrant to remove computers from a crime scene and transport them to a lab. If removing the computers will irreparably harm a business, the computers should not be taken off site.

If you are not allowed to take the computers to your lab, determine the resources you need to acquire the digital evidence. Consider which tools can speed data acquisition. With the use of large disk drives, such as a 200 GB drive, acquisition times can increase to several hours. In Chapter 9, you will examine data acquisition software and learn which ones meet specific needs to acquire disk images.

Obtaining a Detailed Description of the Location

The more information you have about the location of a computer crime, the better you can gather evidence from a crime scene. Environmental and safety issues are your primary concerns when you are working at the scene to gather information about an incident or crime. Before arriving at an incident or crime scene, identify potential hazards to your safety, as well as those of other examiners.

Some computer cases involve dangerous settings, such as a drug bust of a methamphetamine lab or terrorist attack using biological, chemical, or nuclear contaminates. For these types of investigations, you must rely on the skills of the **hazardous material (HAZMAT)** teams to recover the evidence from the scene. The recovery process might include decontaminating computing components needed for the investigation, if possible. If the decontamination procedure might destroy electronic evidence, a HAZMAT specialist or an investigator in HAZMAT gear should make a bit-stream image copy of a suspect's hard disk. If you have to rely on a HAZMAT specialist as shown in Figure 8-5, to acquire data, coach the specialist on how to connect cables between the computer and the hard disks and then how to run the software. In this case, you must be exact and articulate in your instructions. Ambiguous or incorrect instructions could destroy that vital evidence. Ideally, a computer forensic investigator trained in dealing with HAZMAT environments should acquire the disk images. However, not all organizations have funds available for such training.

For example, suppose you need to acquire a suspect's hard disk located in a biologically contaminated office. The windows and doors are sealed so that no air can freely pass through the office. The HAZMAT personnel have built a decontamination threshold that allows the HAZMAT technicians to enter and exit the room. The suspect computer in this room contains key evidence that must be examined as soon as possible, but the computer is also contaminated and must be decontaminated before it can leave the crime scene. The lead HAZMAT technician informs you that decontaminating the computer involves scrubbing it with a caustic chemical cleaner that will neutralize the biocontaminates. The cleaner is caustic enough to melt plastic. You learn that the computer is a standard desktop tower with

Figure 8-5 HAZMAT specialist

several ventilation slots for the cooling fans in the central processing unit (CPU) cabinet. Because the computer was running at the time of the contamination, you can assume that the biocontaminates are circulating inside the computer cabinet.

In this extreme situation, you can acquire a bit-stream image copy of the evidence disk drive in a few ways. You could give the HAZMAT technician a hard disk with a forensic boot floppy disk along with detailed instructions on connecting the target disk drive to the suspect's computer. Then you could explain how to run the bit-stream imaging tool. Before doing so, the HAZMAT technician might suggest that you put the target disk drive into a special HAZMAT bag (see Figure 8-6), leaving the Integrated Drive Electronics (IDE) cable out of the bag, but providing an air-tight seal around the cable to prevent any contaminates from entering the bag and the target drive. When the data acquisition is complete, the IDE cable can be cut from the target hard disk and the bag can be decontaminated. When dealing with extreme conditions such as biological or chemical hazardous contaminates, you often need to sacrifice equipment such as IDE cables and 12-volt power cables. To prevent contamination to a disk drive, you should cut the cables that protrude from the HAZMAT bag. Then squeeze the open end of the HAZMAT bag shut so that air or HAZMAT material does not enter the bag. Your goal when dealing with the target disk in a HAZMAT environment is to keep it sterile so that you can handle it after the exterior of the bag is decontaminated.

Figure 8-6   HAZMAT bag

If the temperature in the contaminated room is 80 degrees or higher, you should prevent the target disk from overheating. For example, an 80 GB 7200 rpm Maxtor hard disk heats as it runs. Because the contamination bag cannot circulate air, the target hard disk could quickly overheat.

In this case, consider cooling the target drive by using sealed ice packs or bags of ice that are double wrapped so that moisture does not leak out and damage your drive. When confronting extreme conditions, consider the risks the conditions pose to the evidence and your equipment, and brainstorm solutions to overcome them.

Determining Who Is in Charge

Corporate computing investigations usually require only one person to respond to an incident or crime scene. Processing evidence involves acquiring a bit-stream data image of a subject's disk drive. In law enforcement, however, many investigations require additional staff to collect all evidence quickly. In any type of large-scale investigation, investigators must promote a team approach to process an incident or crime scene.

During a computing investigation, one person should be the designated leader of the investigation. Anyone assigned to the investigation should cooperate with the designated leader to ensure that the team addresses all details when collecting evidence at the scene.

Using Additional Technical Expertise

After you collect evidence data, determine whether you need specialized help to process the incident or crime scene. For example, suppose you are assigned to process a crime scene at a data center running Microsoft Windows XP servers with several Redundant

Array of Inexpensive Disk (RAID) 5 disk drives and high-end UNIX servers. If you are the leader of this investigation, you must identify the additional skills needed to process the crime scene, such as enlisting help with a high-end operating system. Other concerns are how to acquire data from the RAID servers, and how much data you can acquire. RAID servers typically run several terabytes of data, and standard bit-stream imaging tools might not be able to handle such large data sets.

When working with high-end computing facilities, identify the applications the suspect uses, such as Oracle databases. In this case, you might need to recruit an Oracle specialist or site support staff to help extract data for the investigation. Locating the right person may prove to be an even bigger challenge than conducting the investigation.

If you do need to recruit a specialist who is not an investigator, develop a training program to educate the specialist in proper investigative techniques. This also applies to specialists you plan to escort during the search and seizure tasks. When dealing with computer evidence, an untrained specialist can easily and unintentionally destroy evidence no matter how careful you are in providing instructions and monitoring his or her activities.

Determining the Tools You Need

After you have obtained as much information as possible about the incident or crime scene, you can start listing what you will need at the scene. It is better to be overprepared than underprepared, especially when you determine that you cannot transfer the computer to your lab for processing.

To manage your tools, consider creating an initial-response field kit and an extensive-response field kit. Using the right kit makes processing an incident or crime scene much easier, and minimizes how much you have to carry from your vehicle to the computers.

Your initial-response field kit should be lightweight and easy to transport. This kit allows you to arrive at a scene, acquire the data you need, and return to the lab as quickly as possible. Figure 8-7 shows some of the items you might need, and Table 8-1 lists all the tools you might need in an initial-response field kit.

An extensive-response field kit should include all the tools that you can afford to take to the field. When you arrive at the scene, you should extract only those items that you need to acquire evidence. Doing so protects your equipment and minimizes how many items you have to track at the scene. Table 8-2 lists all the tools you might need in an extensive-response field kit, including a Digital Linear Tape (DLT) drive and cartridge, which you examined in Chapter 7. Recall that you can use a DLT tape drive and cartridge to store digital evidence. Figure 8-8 shows a Zip drive and disks, which you can also use to store digital evidence.

Tables 8-1 and 8-2 list only recommended items to include in initial-response and extensive-response field kits. You need to analyze your specific needs in your region or organization to determine the tools you need when responding to an incident or crime scene.

Computer forensics kit

Laptop computer

Digital camera

Flashlight

Figure 8-7   Items in an initial-response field kit

Table 8-1   Tools in an Initial-Response Field Kit

Number needed	Tools
1	Small computer tool kit
1	Large-capacity disk drive
1	IDE ribbon cable, 36 inches or longer (ATA-33 or ATA-100)
1	Forensic boot floppy disk containing your preferred acquisition utility
1	Laptop IDE 40- to 44-pin adapter
1	Laptop personal computer (PC)
1	Firewire or Universal Serial Bus (USB) dual write-protect external bay IDE disk drive box
1	Flashlight
1	Digital camera or photographic camera with film and flash
10	Evidence log forms
1	Notebook or dictation recorder
10	Computer evidence bags (anti-static bags)
20	Evidence labels, tape, and tags
1	Permanent ink marking pen
10	Floppy disks

Table 8-2   Tools in an Extensive-Response Field Kit

Number needed	Tools
Varies	Assorted technical manuals ranging from operating system references to forensic analysis guides
1	Initial-response field kit
1	Portable PC with Small Computer System Interface (SCSI) card for DLT tape drive or suspect's SCSI drive
1	DLT or Super Digital Linear Tape (SDLT) portable tape drive
10	DLT or SDLT tape cartridges
1	DLT or SDLT tape cleaning cartridge
2	Electrical power strips
1	Additional hand tool including bolt cutters, pry-bar, and hacksaw
1	Gloves (leather) and disposable latex gloves (assorted sizes)
1	Hand truck and luggage cart
10	Large garbage bags and large cardboard boxes with packaging tape
1	Rubber bands of assorted sizes
1	Magnifying glass
1	Ream of printer paper
1	Small brush for cleaning dust from suspect's interior CPU cabinet
1	Iomega 250 MB Zip drive
1	Iomega 750 MB Zip drive
1	Iomega 2 GB Jaz drive
10	Iomega 100 MB Zip cartridges
10	Iomega 250 MB Zip cartridges
10	Iomega 750 MB Zip cartridges
10	Iomega 1 GB Jaz cartridges
10	Iomega 2 GB Jaz cartridges
5	Additional assorted hard disk drives for data acquisition

Figure 8-8   External Zip drive and disks

Preparing the Investigation Team

Before you initiate the search and seizure of digital evidence at an incident or crime scene, you must review all of the available facts, plans, and objectives with the investigation team you have assembled. The goal of scene processing is to successfully collect and secure digital evidence from the incident or crime scene. The better prepared you are, the fewer problems you will encounter when you execute the plan to collect data.

Keep in mind that digital evidence is volatile. Develop the skills to quickly assess the facts, make your plan, gather the needed resources, and collect data from the incident or crime scene. Responding slowly may cause the loss of important evidence for the case.

SECURING A COMPUTER INCIDENT OR CRIME SCENE

Investigators secure an incident or crime scene to preserve the evidence and to keep information about the incident or crime confidential. Information made public could easily jeopardize the investigation. If you are in charge of securing a computer incident or crime scene, use yellow barrier tape to prevent bystanders from accidentally entering the scene. Use legal authority such as police officers or security guards to prevent others from entering the scene. Legal authority for the corporate incident scene includes trespassing violations; for a crime scene, legal authority includes obstructing justice or failing to comply with a police officer. Access to the scene should be restricted to only those persons who have a specific reason to visit the scene.

The standard practice of securing an incident or crime scene is to expand the area of control beyond the immediate area of the actual scene. In this way, you avoid overlooking an area that might be part of the scene. It is easier to shrink the scene's parameter than it is to expand it.

For major crime scenes, computer investigators are usually not responsible for defining the security parameter of a scene. These types of cases involve other specialists and detectives who are collecting physical evidence and recording the scene.

For incidents primarily involving computers, computers can be a crime scene within a crime scene. In other words, the computer is a crime scene that contains evidence to be processed. The evidence is virtual data in the computer, but is considered physical evidence by the courts. Computers can also contain actual physical evidence, such as DNA evidence on computer keyboards. Crime labs can use special vacuums to extract DNA residue from a keyboard to compare to other DNA samples. In a major crime scene, law enforcement usually retains the computer keyboard.

A common way to lose or corrupt evidence stems from **professional curiosity**, which involves police officers and other professionals examining an incident or crime scene to see what happened. Inevitably, their presence contaminates the scene directly or indirectly. Even those authorized and trained to search crime scenes can inadvertently alter the scene or evidence.

For example, during one homicide investigation, the lead police detective obtained one very good latent fingerprint from the crime scene. After he collected the print, he compared it to the victim's fingerprints and to those of others who knew the victim. He could not find a fingerprint that matched the latent fingerprint from the scene. The detective suspected that he had the fingerprint of the murderer and kept it with him for several years, until his police department purchased an **Automated Fingerprint Identification Systems (AFIS)** computer. During acceptance testing, the software vendor processed sample fingerprints to see how quickly and accurately the system could match fingerprints in the database. The detective offered the fingerprint he found at the homicide scene, hoping that the murderer's fingerprints were in the AFIS database. Within minutes, AFIS made a near perfect match of the latent fingerprint, and identified that the fingerprint belonged to the detective.

Professional curiosity can destroy or corrupt evidence, including digital evidence. When working at an incident or crime scene, be aware of what you are doing and what you have touched, either physically or virtually. Although a police detective can take elimination prints of everyone who had access to the crime scene to identify the fingerprints of known people, computer evidence does not have an equivalent elimination process. Make sure that no one begins to examine a suspect's computer before you can preserve and capture a bit-stream image copy of the hard disk. Recall that you must protect all digital evidence. Starting the computer without a forensic boot floppy disk alters significant information such as the date and time stamps of last accessed files, destroying vital information on when a suspect or victim used the computer.

SEIZING DIGITAL EVIDENCE AT THE SCENE

With proper search warrants, law enforcement can seize all computing systems and associated peripherals. In corporate investigations, however, you might not have authority to seize computers. Civil litigation cases often provide the authority only to make a bit-stream image copy of the disk drive of interest to the investigation. Rarely does the corporate investigator have the authority to seize all computers.

When seizing computer evidence in criminal investigations, follow the standards outlined in a document the USDOJ provides about how to seize digital data. Civil investigations follow the same rules, though they do not require as many detailed procedures or documentation. A civil computer investigation usually involves less work and equipment for processing an incident or crime scene than a criminal investigation. For example, suppose that you must recover an e-mail message from a plaintiff's or defendant's computer. Creating a crime scene only introduces conflict for you and the attorneys. For most civil cases, an attorney presents a demand for discovery with specific directions on what you can and cannot do. If you have any questions, doubts, or concerns, consult with your attorney for additional guidance.

Processing a Major Incident or Crime Scene

The following guidelines present suggestions on how to process an incident or crime scene. As you gain experience in performing searches and seizures, you can add to or modify these guidelines to meet the needs of your specific case. Use your own judgment to determine what steps to take when processing a civil or criminal investigation.

Keep a journal to document your activities. Include the time you arrive on the scene, the people you encounter, and notes on every significant task you perform. Routinely update the journal as you process the scene.

To secure the scene, use whatever is practical to make sure only authorized people can access the area. Recall that you should secure more area than necessary. Make sure nothing in this area moves until you have had time to record it, including computer evidence.

For any curious onlookers, be professional and courteous, but do not offer information about the investigation or the incident. Refer journalists to a public information officer or the public relations manager of your organization.

Remove anyone who is not investigating the scene unless they must help process the scene. For example, the local computing administrator might need to help you collect and recover data.

Take video recordings of the computer area. Start by recording an overall view of the scene, and then record the details with close-up shots. Record the area around the computer, including the floor and ceiling, and all access points to the computer, such as doors and windows. Be sure to look under any tables or desks for anything taped to the underside of a table, desk drawer, or on the floor out of view. Slowly pan or zoom the camera to prevent blurring in the video image. Always maintain a written camera log for all shots you take.

When you finish videotaping or photographing the scene, sketch the incident or crime scene. Make your sketch a rough draft with notes on the dimensions of objects and the distances between fixed objects. For example, a note might read, "The suspect's computer is on the south wall, three meters from the southeast corner of the room." When you prepare the report, you can make a clean, detailed drawing from your sketch, preferably using a computer-automated drawing program so that the sketch is in electronic form.

Because computer data is volatile, check the state of each computer at the scene as soon as possible. Determine whether the computer you are investigating is powered on or off. If it is off, proceed with the data acquisition. If it is on, save data in any current applications as safely as possible and record all active windows or shell sessions. Do not examine folders or network connections or press keys unless doing so is necessary for the investigation.

For systems that are powered on and operating, photograph the screens. If windows are open but minimized, it is safe to expand them so that you can photograph them individually. As a precaution, write down the content of each window verbatim. Do not cut electrical power to a running system unless it is an older Windows 9x or MS-DOS system.

After you record the screen content of the suspect computer, save the content of each window to external media. For example, if one window shows a Word or Excel file, save the file to a floppy disk. Keep in mind that the suspect might have changed the file since last using the Save command. If another window is a Web browser, take a screenshot of that page or save the Web page to a floppy disk. If a large database file is open but will not fit on a floppy disk, determine how to save the file so that it does not overwrite existing data on the suspect computer's hard disk. If the suspect computer has an Iomega Zip or Jaz drive, use the appropriate media to save the data. If the suspect computer has an active connection to a network server with sufficient storage, you can save the large file to a folder on the server. To do so, you need the cooperation of the computing support administrator to help direct you to the correct server and folder for storing the file.

If you cannot save an open application to an external media device, save the open application to the suspect drive using a new name to avoid overwriting an existing file that may not have already been updated. This is not the ideal method, but remember that your goal is to always preserve as much evidence as possible.

After you have saved all active files on the suspect computer, you can close all applications. If the application prompts you to save before closing, do not save the files. When all applications are closed, perform an orderly shutdown. If you are not familiar with the proper shutdown method for the computer you are examining, find someone who is.

After you record the scene and shut down the system, bag and tag the evidence. If the nature of the case does not permit you to seize the computer, create a bit-stream image copy of the hard disk, which you will learn to do in Chapter 9.

Either during the data acquisition or after you have collected the evidence, look for information related to the investigation, such as passwords, passphrases, Personal Identification Numbers (PINs), and Swiss bank account numbers. This information might be in plain view, in a drawer, or in a trash can. When at the scene, collect as much personal information about the suspect or victim as possible that is related to the facts about the crime or incident, particularly anything that connects the suspect to the victim.

To complete your analysis and processing of an incident or crime scene, collect all documentation and media relevant to the investigation, including the following material:

- Hardware, including peripheral devices
- Software, including operating system and applications programs
- All media such as backup tapes and disks
- All documentation, manuals, printouts, and handwritten notes

Processing Data Centers with an Array of RAIDs

Computer investigators sometimes perform forensic analysis on RAID systems or disk farms, which are rooms filled with extremely large disk systems (usually RAID drives) devices, and are typical for very large business data centers, including government agencies, such as the Department of Motor Vehicles (DMV), banks, insurance companies, and ISPs. Performing disk analysis on these types of devices is beyond the scope of this book. One technique you can use to extract evidence from large systems is called **sparse evidence file** recovery. Sparse evidence file recovery extracts only data relating to the evidence of your case from allocated files. Doing so minimizes how much data you will need to analyze. A drawback to sparse evidence file recovery is that it does not recover residual data in free or slack space. If you have a computer forensic tool that accesses the unallocated space on a RAID system, first work with the tool on a test system to make sure it does not corrupt the RAID computer.

Using a Technical Advisor at an Incident or Crime Scene

When working with advanced technologies, recruit a technical advisor who can help you list the tools you need to process the incident or crime scene. For large data centers, the technical advisor is the person guiding you about where to locate data and then helping you extract log records or actual evidence from large RAID servers. In law enforcement cases, the technical advisor can help to create the search warrant by itemizing what you need for the warrant. At the scene, the technical advisor can help direct other investigators as necessary to collect evidence properly.

The technical advisor has the following responsibilities:

- Know all aspects of the system being seized and searched
- Direct investigators on how to handle sensitive media and systems to prevent damage
- Help to ensure security of the scene
- Help to document the planning strategy for the search and seizure
- Perform ad hoc training for investigators on the technologies being seized and searched
- Document activities during the search and seizure
- Help to execute the search and seizure

Sample Civil Investigation

Most cases in the corporate environment are considered **low-level investigations**, or non-criminal cases. This does not mean that the corporate computing investigations are less important, but that they require less effort than a major criminal case. An example of this would be an e-mail investigation that resulted in a lawsuit between two businesses. Suppose that Mr. Jones at Company A claims to have received an order for $200,000 in widgets from the purchasing manager, Mr. Smith, at Company B. Company A manufactures the widgets and notifies Company B that they are ready for shipment. Mr. Smith at Company B replies that they did not order any widgets and will not pay for them. Company A locates an e-mail that appears to be from Mr. Smith at Company B requesting the widgets. Company A informs Company B about the e-mail. Company B tells Company A that the e-mail did not originate from them and that they will not pay for the widgets.

Company A, the widget manufacturer, files a lawsuit against Company B based on the widget order in Mr. Smith's e-mail message. The lawyers for Company A contact the lawyers for Company B and discuss the lawsuit several times. The lawyers for Company A make discovery demands to have a computer forensic analysis performed on Mr. Smith's computer in hopes of finding the original message that caused the problem. At the same time, Company B's lawyers demand discovery on Mr. Jones' computer because they believe the e-mail is a fake.

As a computing investigator and forensics examiner, you receive a call from your boss directing you to fulfill the discovery demands from Company B's lawyers to locate and determine whether the e-mail message on Mr. Jones' computer is real or fake. Because this is an e-mail investigation, not a major crime such as a homicide that involves computers, you are dispatched to Company A. When you get there, you are taken to Mr. Jones' computer, which you find powered on and running Outlook.

You are authorized under the discovery order only to recover Mr. Jones' Outlook e-mail folder, the PST file. You are not authorized to do anything else. You would take the following steps in this scenario:

1. Close the Outlook program on Mr. Jones' computer.

2. Use Windows Explorer to locate the Outlook PST file that contains his business e-mail. You might need to use the Windows Search feature to find files ending in .pst.

3. Determine how large the PST file is and connect the appropriate media device such as USB Zip drive to Mr. Jones' computer.

4. Copy the PST file to your external USB drive.

5. Remove your USB drive with the disk cartridge.

6. Fill out your evidence form stating where on Mr. Jones' disk you located the PST file along with the date and time you performed this task.

7. Leave Company A and return to your computer forensic lab. Place the Zip disk into your evidence safe.

For most civil incident scenes, you collect only specific items that have been determined germane by lawyers or Human Resource departments.

Other activity that is common in the corporate computing environment is the need to perform **covert surveillance** of employees who are abusing their computing and network privileges. Covert surveillance of employees has to be well defined in company policy before such activity can be conducted. If a company does not have a policy that informs employees that they have no privacy rights using company computers, no surveillance can be performed without exposing the company to civil or even criminal liability. The company must create a policy and notify all employees about the new rules. Your legal department should create the language in the policy appropriate for your state or country. The legal department will also define the rights and authority the company has in conducting surveillance of employees according to the appropriate provincial, state, or country privacy laws.

For covert surveillance, you set up monitoring tools that record a suspect's activity in real time. Real-time surveillance requires **sniffing** data transmissions between a suspect's computer and a network server. Sniffing software allows network administrators and others to determine what data is being transmitted over their network. Other data-collecting tools are screen capture programs such as Spector and WinWhatWhere that collect most or all screens and keystrokes on a suspect's computer. Most of these tools run on Microsoft Windows, and usually collect data through remote network connections. The programs run so that they do not reveal themselves in any of the process logs.

Another product from Guidance Software, the makers of EnCase, is EnCase Enterprise edition. The Enterprise edition is a centrally located server that can activate servlets to access network workstations. Computing investigators can then perform forensic examinations in real time. One significant advantage of EnCase Enterprise edition is that it can locate and recover temporary files such as print spooling files, which are deleted automatically when the computer is shut down. You can also use EnCase Enterprise edition to extract evidence from large RAID servers without having to shut them down, as you have to do when working with regular analysis tools.

Sample Criminal Investigation

Crime scenes involving computers range from fraud cases to homicides. Because high-quality printers are now available, one of the most common crimes is check fraud. Many check fraud cases also involve making and selling of false identification (ID) cards such as drivers licenses.

In one recent case, the police received a tip that a check-forging operation was active in an apartment building. After the detective contacted a reliable informant, he had enough information for a search warrant, and asked the patrol division to assist him in serving the warrant. When the detective entered the suspected apartment and conducted a preliminary search, he found a network of six high-end computer workstations with cables connected to devices in the adjacent apartment through a hole in the wall (see Figure 8-9). Unfortunately, the warrant specified a search of only one apartment.

The detective contacted the deputy prosecutor, who instructed him to stand guard at both apartments until she could have a judge issue an additional warrant for the neighboring apartment. When he received the second search warrant, the detective entered the adjoining apartment and continued his search, finding more computers, high-quality color laser printers, checks, and stolen blank state driver's license ID cards.

The outcome of the investigation revealed that the perpetrators were three enterprising high school students that were selling fake IDs to fellow students. The check fraud scheme was a new sideline they were starting to develop to improve their cash flow.

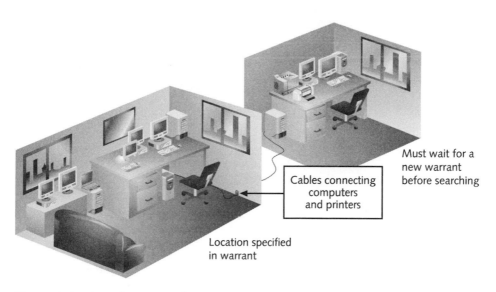

Figure 8-9 Search warrant limits

COLLECTING DIGITAL EVIDENCE

As you collect digital evidence, guard against physically destroying or contaminating the evidence. In particular, take precautions to prevent static electricity discharge to electronic devices. Several vendors sell grounding wristbands, static electricity resistant floor mats, and other anti-static devices. Depending on your environment, it might be worth adding these devices to your extensive-response field kit. For example, northern regions of the continent in the winter months produce very dry air, making static electricity easy to produce by walking across a floor. Whenever you have to handle electronics, always touch a grounded device first, including devices that are wrapped in an anti-static bag. Static electricity can easily destroy media and components.

If possible, bag or box digital evidence and any hardware you collect from the incident or crime scene. Do not carry the evidence unprotected unless you have no other choice.

When preparing for any incident or crime scene, you need bags in various sizes, boxes, and packing tape for the storage and transport of evidence. Use a permanent ink marking pen when working with evidence tags, which should have plastic connecting straps, not wire ones. You also need log forms to record each piece of evidence so that you can account for all the items you have collected from the scene.

As you collect the hardware, sketch the equipment, including exact markings of where components were located. Tag each wire, port, and hookup and record its number and description in a log, as described in Chapters 1 and 2.

REVIEWING A CASE

Chapter 2 introduced the tasks for planning your investigation, some of which are repeated in the following list. In this section, you apply each of these tasks to your investigation to create a preparation plan for searching an incident or crime scene. The broad tasks you perform in any computer forensic case are:

- Identifying the case requirements
- Planning your investigation
- Executing the investigation
- Completing the case report
- Critiquing the case

Suppose you are investigating a case that begins when a manager in a small business, Tony Montoya, notices something unusual with two employees. Ten days ago, Martha Heiser, a shipping clerk, began a one-week emergency leave from the company without informing anyone where she was going or how to contact her. Tony is concerned because she should have returned from her leave three days ago.

A supervisor in the Accounts Payable department, George Popson, has also been missing from work for the past five days. Until now, George has been punctual and dedicated to his work, informing Tony about personal activities that might cause him to be away from the office. Tony talks to other employees, but no one knows why George and Martha are not at work.

To learn where Martha might be, Tony searches the surface of Martha's desk, and notices travel brochures for European tours. Tony also looks around George's office, and finds notes about a Swiss supplier Tony once used and a floppy disk with the former supplier's name on the label. Tony inserts the disk into the floppy disk drive of his computer. At the MS-DOS prompt, he types dir a: and presses Enter to find the information shown in Figure 8-10.

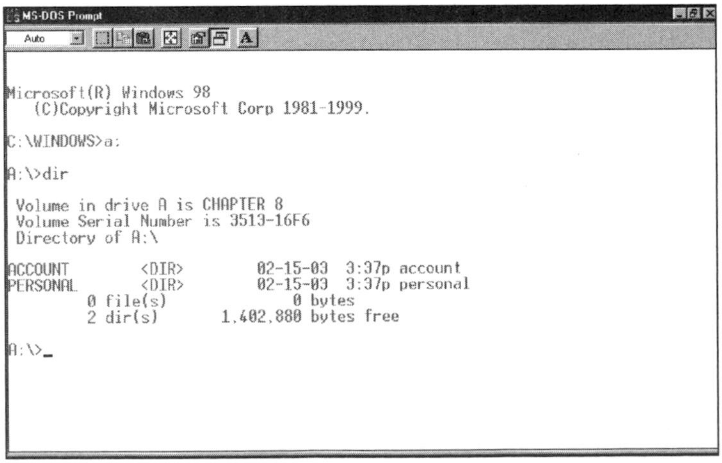

Figure 8-10   Contents of George's disk

Tony suspects that the disk contains more information, and he calls you, the computing investigator for his company. He describes Martha and George's absence from the company, and asks you to examine the floppy disk to see if it identifies their whereabouts.

Identifying the Case Requirements

Before you analyze the floppy disk, answer the following basic questions to start your investigation:

- What is the nature of the case?

   Two people are missing or overdue at work.

- What are their names?

   George Popson and Martha Heiser.

- What do they do?

   George is a supervisor in the Accounts Payable department, and Martha is a shipping clerk.

- What is the operating system of the suspect computer?

   Microsoft Windows 98.

- What type of media needs to be examined?

   One floppy disk drive.

In addition, you need to know the type of computer George used so you can determine the best way to analyze the floppy disk. Tony reports that George used a Pentium III with a 500 MHz processor and a 1 GB Western Digital hard disk drive.

Planning Your Investigation

To find information about George and Martha's whereabouts, list what you can assume or already know about the case.

- George and Martha's absences might or might not be related.

- George's computer might contain information explaining their absence.

- No one else has used George's computer since he disappeared.

- You need to make an image of George's computer and attempt to retrieve evidence related to the case.

In the following steps, you use DriveSpy to extract and analyze the image of a floppy disk. Note that in an actual case, you would acquire and analyze the image of a floppy, Zip, or hard disk.

TIP

If you did not install DriveSpy in Chapter 2, follow the instructions in that chapter to install DriveSpy and Image and to create Toolpath.bat.

You are now ready to create an image of the suspect disk and then extract evidence. You should work on a Windows 98 computer where Microsoft Office is installed. You also need a blank, formatted floppy disk to complete these steps.

To create an image of the suspect disk using DriveSpy:

1. Access a command prompt. Change to the Tools folder in your work folder, and run Toolpath.bat.

2. In your work folder, create a **Chap08** folder. In the Chap08 folder, create a **Chapter** folder. Navigate to the Chap08\Chapter folder and copy **C8InChap.img** from your Data Files (available for download from *www.courseptr.com*) to the Chap08\Chapter folder.

3. To prepare for the retrieval, create additional subfolders in the Chap08\ Chapter folder called **Files**, **Deleted**, **Slack**, **Free**, and **Hidden**. Create a blank text file in Notepad and save it as **hfiles.txt** in the Hidden subfolder.

4. Label a blank, formatted floppy disk "Chapter 8 In Chapter" and insert it in the floppy disk drive. At the prompt, type **Image C8InChap.img a:** and press **Enter** to create an image of George's disk on your floppy disk. Image displays the checksum value to verify that the C8InChap.img file is identical to the original disk, as shown in Figure 8-11.

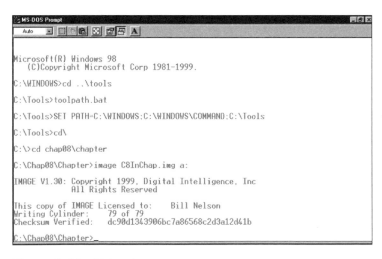

Figure 8-11 Using Image

Now you can start DriveSpy and use it to recover files and analyze the disk.

To use DriveSpy to analyze the evidence disk:

1. Start DriveSpy by typing **DriveSpy** at the command prompt and pressing **Enter**.

2. At the SYS prompt, type **Drive A** and press **Enter** to examine the floppy disk. At the DA prompt, type **Part 1** and press **Enter** to switch to the Partition level of the disk.

3. At the DAP1 prompt, type **Copy *.*   C:*work folder*\\Chap08\\Chapter\\ Files /S** at and press **Enter** to recover any files stored on the disk. (Replace *work folder* with the name of the work folder on your system.) If you are prompted to disable Page mode, type **Y** for yes.

4. In this case, seven files are copied. To recover deleted files from the evidence disk, type **Unerase *.*   C:\\Chap08\\Chapter\\Deleted   /S** and press **Enter**. If prompted to disable page mode, type **Y** for yes. Use Windows Explorer to examine the contents of the Chap08\\Chapter\\Deleted folder in your work folder—it should contain six recovered files. Double-click each file to open it. In a text file or notebook, list the name of each file, describe its contents, and record your assumptions and conclusions.

5. To recover the free space, type **SaveFree C:\\Chap08\\Chapter\\Free\\free** and press **Enter**. After DriveSpy recovers data in free space, use a word processing program such as WordPad to open the FREE file generated, and then record your findings as you did in Step 4.

6. To save the RAM slack and file slack, type **SaveSlack   C:\\Chap08\\ Chapter\\Slack\\slack** and press **Enter** (see Figure 8-12).

Figure 8-12   Using SaveSlack

7. Finally, you need to look for hidden files. Type **dbexport *.* c:\Chap08\ Chapter\Hidden\hfiles /h/s** and press **Enter**.

8. Type **exit** to close DriveSpy. Then close the Command Prompt window.

9. Examine the files recovered and note that George and Martha have embezzled money from the business.

You can now meet with Tony and present your findings, including evidence that George and Martha embezzled money and are now in Zurich.

CHAPTER SUMMARY

❑ In the private sector, an incident scene is often a place of work, such as a contained office or manufacturing area. Because everything from the computers used to violate a company policy to the surrounding facility is under a controlled authority, it is easier to investigate and control the scene than in a criminal environment.

❑ Companies should publish policies stating that they reserve the right to inspect computing assets at will; otherwise, the employees' expectation of privacy prevents an employer from legally conducting an intrusive investigation. A well-defined corporate policy states that an employer has the right to examine, inspect, or access any company-owned computing asset. If the policy statement is issued to all employees, the employer can investigate computing assets at will without any privacy right restrictions.

❑ Proper procedure needs to be followed even in private-sector investigations, because civil litigations can become criminal investigations very easily. As a corporate investigator, you must ensure that sensitive company information does not become commingled with criminal evidence.

❑ If an internal corporate case is turned over to law enforcement because of criminal activity, the corporate investigator must avoid becoming an agent of law enforcement because at that time, affidavits and search warrants are needed.

❑ Criminal cases require a properly executed and well-defined search warrant. A specific crime and specific location must be spelled out in the warrant. For all criminal investigations in the United States, the Fourth Amendment to the Constitution specifies that a law enforcement officer may only search for and seize criminal evidence with probable cause, which are facts or circumstances that would lead a reasonable person to believe a crime has been committed or is about to be committed.

❑ The plain view doctrine applies when items that are evidentiary and not specified in a warrant or under probable cause are in plain view.

❑ When preparing for a case, you need to describe the nature of the case, identify the type of operating system (OS), determine whether you can seize the computer, and obtain a description of the location.

❑ If dealing with a hazardous material (HAZMAT) situation, you may need to have someone else obtain the evidence or you may need to be certified in HAZMAT.

❑ Always take pictures or use a digital camera to document the scene. Then methodically record what exists at the scene. Prevent professional curiosity from contaminating evidence by limiting who enters the scene.

❑ As you collect digital evidence, guard against physically destroying or contaminating it. Take precautions to prevent static electricity discharge to electronic devices. If possible, bag or box digital evidence and any hardware you collect from the incident or crime scene. As you collect the hardware, sketch the equipment, including exact markings of where components were located. Tag and number each cable, port, and other connection and record its number and description in a log.

KEY TERMS

Automated Fingerprint Identification Systems (AFIS)—A computerized system for identifying fingerprints that is connected to a central database for identifying criminal suspects and reviewing thousands of fingerprint samples at high speed.

covert surveillance—Observing people or places without being detected, often using electronic equipment such as video cameras or key and screen capture programs.

hazardous material (HAZMAT)—Chemical, biological, or radiological substances that can cause harm to one or more people.

innocent information—Data that does not contribute to the evidence of a crime or violation.

limiting phrase—A phrase in a search warrant that limits the scope of a search for evidence.

low-level investigations—Corporate cases that require less effort than a major criminal case.

plain view doctrine—When conducting a search and seizure, objects in plain view of a law enforcement officer who has the right to be in position to have that view are subject to seizure without a warrant and may be introduced in evidence.

probable cause—Indication that a crime has been committed, evidence of the specific crime exists, and the evidence for the specific crime exists at the place to be searched.

professional curiosity—The motivation for law enforcement and other professional personnel to examine an incident or crime scene to see what happened.

proxy server—A server computer that connects a local area network (LAN) to the Internet.

search warrant—An order signed by a judge that directs owners of private property to allow the police to enter and search for items named in the warrant.

8

sniffing—Detecting data transmissions to and from a suspect's computer and a network server to determine the type of data being transmitted over a network.

sparse evidence files—Creating files from separate large portions of data to streamline data analysis.

DATA ACQUISITION

After reading this chapter, you will be able to:

♦ Determine the best acquisition method

♦ Plan data recovery contingencies

♦ Use MS-DOS acquisition tools

♦ Use GUI acquisition tools

♦ Acquire data on Linux computers

♦ Use other data acquisition tools

In this chapter, you will learn how to acquire digital evidence from disk drives. Recall that your goal when acquiring data is to preserve the digital evidence. You usually have only one chance to create a reliable copy of disk evidence with a data acquisition tool. Although these tools are generally dependable, you should still take the necessary steps to make sure you obtain a verifiable bit-stream copy of the evidence.

Because all software tools can fail, you must learn how to use tools and methods besides your standard tools. In this chapter, you will work with three data acquisition tools: DriveSpy (an MS-DOS tool from Digital Intelligence), Forensic Toolkit (FTK) Explorer (a GUI tool from AccessData), and the Linux dd command. Other data acquisition tools are described in the last section of this chapter. You can accomplish most digital evidence acquisitions for your investigations using a combination of the tools covered in this chapter.

DETERMINING THE BEST ACQUISITION METHOD

You can acquire digital evidence from disk drives in three ways: creating a bit-stream disk-to-image file, making a bit-stream disk-to-disk copy, or creating a sparse data copy of a folder or file.

Creating a bit-stream disk-to-image file is the most common data acquisition method and provides the most flexibility for your investigation. Using this method, you can make one or many duplicate copies of a suspect's disk drive. In other words, you can replicate the original disk bit for bit on another disk. In addition to recreating the original disk, you can use other forensic analysis tools, such as EnCase, FTK, Smart, Task, and ILook, to read the most common types of bit-stream image files you create. These programs read the image file as if it were the original disk so you do not have to rebuild the bit-stream image file on a target disk drive. This feature saves you time and disk resources. Because these tools automatically adjust the target drive's geometry to match the original drive, you do not need an investigation disk that is identical to the original suspect disk.

In some cases, you cannot make a bit-stream disk-to-image file because of hardware or software errors or incompatibilities. In these situations, you might have to create a disk-to-disk bit-stream image copy of the suspect's disk drive to acquire data. While several bit-streaming programs can copy data exactly from one disk to another, only a few can adjust the target disk's geometry cylinder, head, and track configuration so that it matches the original suspect drive. These disk-to-disk imaging tools include SafeBack, SnapCopy, and Norton Ghost 2002 or later. All of these tools must run in MS-DOS. See the vendor's manual for instructions on using these tools for bit-stream disk-to-disk copying.

If you are using bit-streaming disk-to-disk tools that do not adjust the geometry of the target drive, such as WinHex Specialist edition, DriveSpy, or the Linux dd command, you must manually configure the target drive to match the geometry of the original drive. You need the right hardware tools to perform this task correctly. Chapter 4 explained how to manually configure a drive using a 486 PC. The 486 BIOS allows you to manually change the geometry of the drive. As an alternative, you can acquire a Firewire card or install an ISA SCSI card. It is generally easier to find a used ISA SCSI card at a surplus computer store than it is to find a new one. You also need to purchase an Acard AEC-7720U SCSI-to-IDE adapter card to connect the target IDE drive to the SCSI card. Be sure the SCSI works with the Acard by testing the setup. If you use an ISA SCSI card on a 486 PC, you can connect IDE drives that exceed 486 BIOS limitations. By connecting your target drive to a 486 PC, you can manually define the target drive's geometry. Depending on the 486 BIOS and the peripheral card you are using, such as a SCSI controller, you might have a problem with the maximum size that the BIOS can access. An older BIOS typically can only access up to 8.1 GB of disk drive. Test the SCSI card to see if it can handle large drives before performing a data acquisition for your case.

Recall that it can take several hours to collect evidence from a large disk drive when performing a bit-stream disk-to-disk copy of a suspect's disk drive. If your time is limited, consider using the sparse data copy method, which lets you create exact copies of files or folders. Use this method only when you do not need to examine the entire disk drive, such as when you want to acquire a Microsoft Outlook Express PST or OST mail file or are working with a RAID server. If you have to recover data from a RAID server with several terabytes of data storage, the sparse method may be the only way you can acquire the evidence. Many data recovery experts believe that the sparse data copy method will become the preferred method as data storage continues to grow.

To determine which data acquisition method to use for an investigation, consider the size of the source disk drive, whether you can retain the source disk drive as evidence or must return it to the owner, how much time you have for the data acquisition, and where the evidence is located.

If the source disk is very large, such as 200 GB or more, make sure you have a target disk that can store a bit-stream image file of the large disk. If you don't have a target disk of the right size, review alternatives for reducing the size of the data to create a verifiable copy of the suspect drive. Older Microsoft disk compression tools such as **DoubleSpace** or **DriveSpace** only eliminate slack disk space between files. Other compression methods use an **algorithm**, which is a short mathematical procedure that solves a recurrent problem, to reduce file size. Data acquisition and compression tools use either **lossless compression**, which does not discard data when it compresses files, or **lossy compression**, which can lose data but not perceptible quality when a file is restored. Both compression methods are discussed in more detail in Chapter 12. Many bit-stream imaging tools use lossless data compression to save disk space. The advantage of using lossless compression when making a bit-stream image file is that your target disk drive does not have to be as large as the suspect's disk drive. For example, suppose you need to make a bit-stream image of a Western Digital Drivezilla 120 GB suspect disk. By using the compression option available in several acquisition tools, you might be able to create the image on an 80 GB disk. On a typical target disk, you can compress files to reduce the size of the original disk by 50%. However, if the suspect disk already contains compressed data such as several large WinZip files, the bit-stream image tool cannot compress the data any further.

For computer forensic data acquisition, using a lossless compression method is acceptable, but the lossy compression is not. WinZip and PKZip are lossless compression tools and restore compressed data to its original form. That is, after you decompress data, they do not alter the data when they reconstruct it. If you run a Message Digest 5 (MD5) hash on a file before and after you compress it with WinZip, both versions have the same MD5 hash value. However, if the compressed file becomes corrupt due to a hardware or software error, the MD5 hash value will be different. When you compress data, you should run a Cyclic Redundancy Check (CRC-32), MD5, or Secure Hash Algorithm, version 1 (SHA-1) hash on the original data to compare the decompressed output to the compressed image file and make sure that the data has not changed.

Therefore, when working with large disks, consider using a data acquisition tool that can compress the original drive into a bit-stream image file, such as EnCase or SafeBack. You could also use a DLT or Super-DLT (SDLT) tape drive to save large volumes of data quickly.

If you cannot retain the original evidence disk drive and must return it to the owner, as in a discovery demand for a civil litigation, determine how to acquire the data as quickly and reliably as possible. Make sure you have a good copy, because most discovery demands provide only one chance to capture the data. Use a forensics tool you know is reliable.

If you cannot take a computer off-line for several hours, determine the best way to copy the evidence drive as quickly as possible, whether by creating an image of the entire drive or by using the sparse data copy method. You might also need to develop or rely on your personal negotiation skills to persuade a hostile party to give you more time to copy a drive. The better negotiator you are, the better your chances of obtaining a good image copy of the evidence.

PLANNING DATA RECOVERY CONTINGENCIES

Because you are working with electronic data, you need to take precautions to protect your bit-stream digital evidence. You should also make contingency plans in case software or hardware doesn't work or you encounter a failure during an acquisition. The most common and time-consuming technique to preserve evidence is creating a duplicate copy of your evidence image file. Many computer investigators do not make duplicate copies of their evidence because they don't have enough time or resources to make a second bit-stream image copy of the evidence. However, if the first copy of your evidence does not work correctly, having a duplicate is worth the effort and resources. Be sure you take whatever steps are necessary to minimize the risk of failure in your investigation.

As a standard practice, make at least two bit-stream image copies of the digital evidence you collect. If you have more than one bit-streaming tool such as EnCase and SafeBack, use both to obtain the two copies. If you only have one tool such as DriveSpy, consider making one copy using the disk-to-disk method, and another copy using the disk-to-image file method. The more critical the investigation, the more you need two copies of the evidence.

Use at least two data acquisition tools to create bit-stream image copies of evidence in case one of your preferred data acquisition tools does not recover data correctly. Many acquisition tools do not copy data that resides in a host-protected area of a disk drive. For these situations, consider using a hardware acquisition tool that can access the drive at the BIOS level, such as Image MASSter Solo, which can copy the host-protected area of a disk drive.

Another area of concern is the environment where the evidence is located. In Chapter 8, you learned to consider possible hazardous materials (HAZMAT) risks or threats when processing an incident or crime scene. In addition to addressing HAZMAT concerns, answer the following questions:

- Does the evidence location have adequate electrical power?
- Is there enough light at the evidence location or do you have to bring flood-lights, flashlights, or other kinds of lighting?
- Is the temperature of the evidence location too warm, too cold, or too humid?

USING MS-DOS ACQUISITION TOOLS

The original software tools developed for computing investigations and forensics were created for MS-DOS. Many of these tools are still commercially available and are easy to use. Because they fit on a forensic boot floppy disk, they require fewer resources to make a bit-stream disk-to-image file or disk-to-disk copy of the evidence. Computer forensic examiners should know how to use DOS tools such as DriveSpy and its commands. This section focuses on DriveSpy, though other DOS data acquisition tools are similar.

DriveSpy provides two types of commands that allow you to save digital evidence from a source disk and write to a target disk: data preservation commands and data manipulation commands. Each type has special applications for acquiring and recreating digital evidence.

Before you learn more about DriveSpy data acquisition commands, you should understand how DriveSpy refers to and accesses sector ranges.

Understanding How DriveSpy Accesses Sector Ranges

DriveSpy provides two methods of accessing disk sectors. The first method defines the absolute starting sector followed by a comma and the total number of sectors to read on a drive. For example, if the starting sector is 1000 on the Primary Master drive (Drive 0) of the computer and you want to copy the next 100 sectors, DriveSpy uses the following format:

```
0:1000,100
```

When you specify that you want to copy sectors 0:1000,100, DriveSpy copies from absolute sector 1000 to absolute sector 1099 because sector 1000 is the first sector and sector 1099 is 100 sectors after that. DriveSpy uses this format for designating disk sectors with the CopySect, WriteSect, SaveSect, and Wipe commands, which are explored later in this chapter.

The second way of specifying sectors is to list the absolute starting and ending sectors. Note that an absolute sector starts at the beginning of a disk, while a relative sector starts at the beginning of the current partition. The concept is similar to absolute and relative cell referencing in a spreadsheet. To designate a start and end sector value, you include a dash between the sector values. For example, if the starting sector is 1000 on the Primary Master drive (Drive 0) of the computer and you need to copy through absolute sector 1100, (the next 101 sectors), the format is:

```
0:1000-1100
```

Some DriveSpy commands allow you to direct data from a specified sector range to another sector, which can be on the same disk or a different disk. For example, if you are recovering data from a damaged part of a disk, you can transfer the data to a good part of the disk. To designate the target location, you list the drive number followed by a colon and the starting absolute sector number. For example, to copy data from absolute sectors 1000–1099 on the Primary Master drive to absolute sectors 2000-2099 on a secondary drive, use the following CopySect command:

```
CopySect 0:1000,100 1:2000,100
```

9

If you are working in the DriveSpy Partition mode, the DriveSpy screen shows a logical sector number and an absolute sector number. Be sure to use the absolute sector number.

In the following steps, you use DriveSpy to examine absolute and logical sectors. Use a Windows 98 computer, and boot into DOS.

To view absolute sectors and logical sectors:

1. Access a command prompt and navigate to the **Tools** folder of your work folder.

2. At the command prompt, type **DriveSpy** and press **Enter** to start DriveSpy.

3. At the SYS prompt, type **D0** and press **Enter** to access your hard disk.

4. Note the numbers for the start and end sectors of the disk and select a number between those, such as 2344.

5. At the D0 prompt, type **Sector 2344** and press **Enter**. A sector map appears, as shown in Figure 9-1.

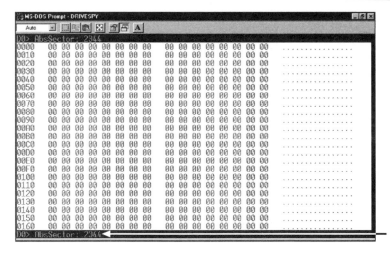

Absolute sector of Drive 0

Figure 9-1   Sector map in Drive mode

6. Press **Esc** to return to the D0 prompt.

7. Type **P1** and press **Enter** to use Partition mode.

8. At the D0P1 prompt, type **Sector 2344** and press **Enter**. (Replace "2344" with the sector number you used in Steps 4 and 5, if necessary.) A map of sector 2344 in Partition 1 appears, as shown in Figure 9-2.

Note that DriveSpy displays a relative sector (RelSector) and an absolute sector (Abs Sector).

NOTE

9. Press **Esc** to return to the D0P1 prompt, and then type **exit** to exit DriveSpy.

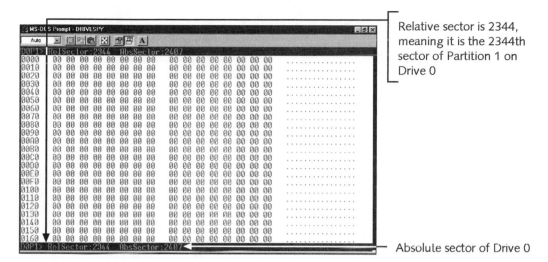

Relative sector is 2344, meaning it is the 2344th sector of Partition 1 on Drive 0

Absolute sector of Drive 0

Figure 9-2   Sector map in Partition mode

Compare the sector numbers in the two figures. Notice that in Figure 9-1, the absolute sector is 2344, while in Figure 9-2, the relative sector is 2344. Also note that the absolute sector in Figure 9-2 is not the same as the one in Figure 9-1.

Data Preservation Commands

You can preserve and recreate digital evidence using the DriveSpy SavePart and WritePart commands. These two commands restore only FAT16 or FAT32 disk partitions. When restoring a FAT16 saved partition, use a partition utility such as FDisk to partition the target drive as a FAT16. For a FAT32 saved partition, use a partition utility to partition the target drive as a FAT32.

The SavePart command acquires partition data regardless of the file system. In other words, the SavePart command acquires an image of a non-DOS partition such as an NTFS or Linux partition. The WritePart command recreates the saved partition file in its original form.

Note that restoring a non-DOS partition to a DOS partition recreates the data, though the partition's format is not exactly the same as the original non-DOS partition. The partition contains the data, but appears to be a DOS FAT file system partition that has unreadable file and directory structures.

Using the SavePart Command

Use the SavePart command in the DriveSpy Partition mode to create an image file of a specified disk partition of a suspect's drive. For example, the following command sends an image of the current partition to the Chap09.img file in the Chap09\Chapter folder:

```
SavePart \Chap09\Chapter\Chap09.img
```

DriveSpy uses lossless data compression to reduce the size of the saved image file. It then saves every sector of the disk partition in the image file you specify. You can redirect the output of the image file to another disk to preserve the image file. If the target disk for the image file is too small for the entire image, DriveSpy automatically requests another disk. For example, if you have a 40 GB suspect disk and two 20 GB target disks connected to your forensic workstation, you can use the SavePart command to write data to the first 20 GB disk. When space runs out on the first disk, DriveSpy asks for another disk. You can then specify the drive and folder path to redirect the image file output to the second 20 GB disk.

You can also use the SavePart command to save image data to removable media such as a 2 GB Jaz disk. SavePart creates image volumes on removable disks, requesting additional disks as necessary. After saving a partition, DriveSpy generates an MD5 hash and stores it in the image file. When the image is restored, the MD5 hash is verified.

In the following steps, you use DriveSpy to save a partition. Normally, you use the SavePart command on a hard disk that has multiple partitions. However, because it can take several hours to perform a SavePart command on a large partition, you will examine your hard disk and save a partition from a floppy disk. You need a floppy disk that contains a few files to complete these steps.

To save a partition using the SavePart command:

1. Start your computer in MS-DOS mode. Navigate to the **Tools** folder in your work folder, and then run Toolpath.bat by typing **Toolpath.bat** and pressing **Enter**. If necessary, create a folder called **Chap09** in your work folder and a subfolder called **Chapter** in the Chap09 folder.

2. Change to the Chap09\Chapter folder in your work folder.

3. At the command prompt, type **DriveSpy** and press **Enter** to start DriveSpy.

4. At the SYS prompt, type **Output Chap9rp1.txt** and then press **Enter** to create an output file to record your actions and results.

5. At the SYS prompt, type **Drives** and then press **Enter** to list all the drives connected to your investigation workstation. Figure 9-3 shows a system with one hard drive. The drives and partitions on your system might be different.

NOTE

The computer illustrated in Figure 9-3 has an older 1.0 GB drive that does not show the logical block allocation (LBA). Newer disks show the LBA along with the CHS values. Your computer forensic tool can interpret these older drives in the same way as it interprets newer drives.

6. At the SYS prompt, type **D0** and then press **Enter** to select the disk drive containing the partition you want to copy, such as Drive 0. The partitions on Drive 0 appear on the screen, as shown in Figure 9-4.

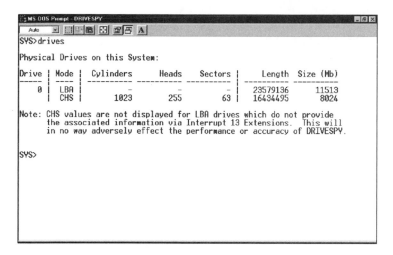

Figure 9-3   Listing the drives on your system

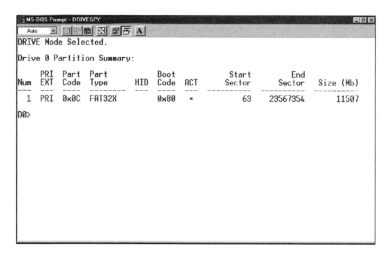

Figure 9-4   Listing the partitions on a drive

7. At the D0 prompt, type **Part 1** and then press **Enter** to select the partition you want to save, such as Partition 1. The contents of Partition 1, including sectors, appear on the screen, as shown in Figure 9-5.

   Although you normally use the SavePart command at this point to save the contents of the current hard disk partition, you will switch to a floppy disk and acquire its partition to save time.

8. Insert a floppy disk that contains a few files into the floppy disk drive. At the D0P1 prompt, type **Drive A** and press **Enter** to access the floppy disk.

9. At the DA prompt, type **Part 1** and press **Enter** to access the partition level.

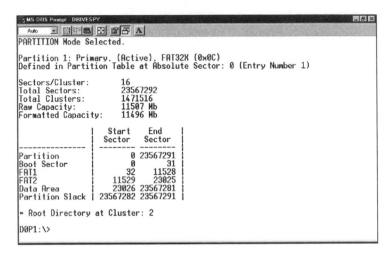

Figure 9-5   Listing the contents of a partition

10. At the DAP1 prompt, type **SavePart C:*work folder*\\Chap09\\Chapter\\Case_9sp.ima** and press **Enter** to copy the partition on the floppy disk to an image file named Case_9sp.ima on your hard disk. (Replace the drive letter and *work folder* with the names of the hard drive and work folder you are using.)

DriveSpy creates the image file, listing details about the partition and displaying a progress indicator. It may take a few minutes to create the image file. When finished, DriveSpy generates an MD5 hash value, as shown in Figure 9-6.

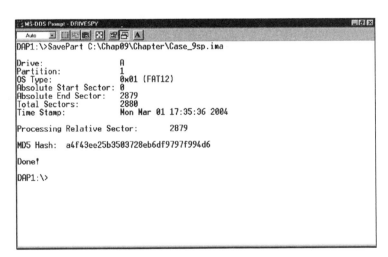

Figure 9-6   Using SavePart to create an image file

11. At the DAP1 prompt, type **exit** and then press **Enter** to close DriveSpy.

Drives with multiple partitions have a gap between each partition. This **inter-partition space**, also called a **partition gap**, is the space between the end of one partition and the start of another. For example, suppose one disk has three partitions. The first partition, Partition 1, ends on absolute sector 8610839, as shown in Figure 9-7. Partition 2 starts on absolute sector 8610903 and ends on absolute sector 17221679. Partition 3 starts on absolute sector 17221743 and ends on absolute sector 400000. Each partition ends on one sector and the next partition starts 64 sectors later. On this system, 64 sectors between each partition are not used by the file system.

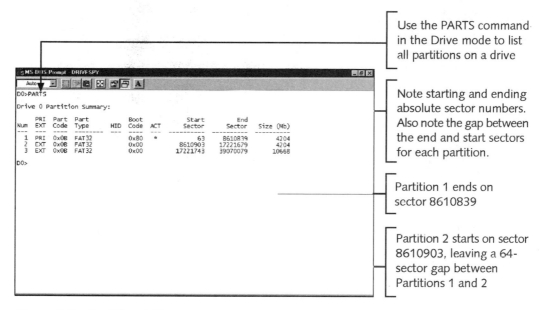

Figure 9-7   Partition table

You cannot use the SavePart command to inspect or extract data from partition gaps, though you can use other DriveSpy commands to do so. You will learn how to use other DriveSpy commands later in this chapter.

In the early days of computer crime, criminals attempting to hide data would use these partition gaps to store incriminating evidence. In Chapter 10, you will learn how to deal with these situations when processing evidence.

Using the WritePart Command

The counterpart to the SavePart command is WritePart, which you use in the DriveSpy Partition mode to recreate the saved partition image file created with the SavePart command. For example, the following command restores the Case_9sp.ima image file to the Case_9 folder on the D: drive:

```
WritePart D:\Case_9\Case_9sp.ima
```

The WritePart command decompresses the SavePart image file and writes it to a specified disk drive. WritePart checks the target drive and only writes to that drive if it is equal to or larger than the original disk. When WritePart creates the partition on the target drive, it changes the partition number to match the source drive. If the image file spans more than one volume (disk), DriveSpy prompts you in the same manner as the SavePart command for the location of the next image volume.

In the following steps, you restore the Case_9sp.ima file you created with the SavePart command. If you were doing this on an actual hard disk with multiple partitions, you would have to be extremely careful that you were working on the correct drive and the correct partition.

Note that you cannot use the WritePart command with Windows running. Reboot to an MS-DOS prompt, if necessary. The following steps demonstrate how to use the WritePart command using a floppy disk. Typically you would use the WritePart command for a hard disk partition.

To perform the following steps, you can use a blank floppy disk. However, because the WritePart command was developed for use on a hard disk, your system might lock if you do use a floppy disk. If your system locks during the following steps, create a small hard disk partition that is larger than the floppy disk, and then restore the image to that partition. Use a partition tool such as FDisk, Partition Magic, or Norton's Gdisk to create a 1.5 MB partition, for example. Then substitute all references to Drive A (or DA) in the following steps with the newly created drive and partition, such as D1P1.

To restore the Case_9sp.ima image file:

1. At an MS-DOS prompt (not in a Command Prompt window), navigate to the **Tools** folder of your work folder, type **Toolpath.bat**, and then press **Enter**. Then type **cd C:*work folder*\\Chap09\\Chapter** and press **Enter** to navigate to the Chap09\\Chapter folder in your work folder. (Replace the drive letter and *work folder* with the names of the hard drive and work folder you are using.)

2. At the command prompt, type **DriveSpy** and press **Enter** to start DriveSpy.

3. At the SYS prompt, type **Output Chap9rp2.txt** and press **Enter** to create an output file.

4. At the SYS prompt, type **Drive A** and press **Enter** to access the floppy disk drive. (If you are using a hard disk partition, use the partition number, as in **Drive 1**.) At the DA prompt, type **Part 1** and press **Enter** to access the partition level of the floppy disk.

5. At the DAP1 prompt, type **WritePart Case_9sp.ima** and press **Enter** to restore the image file you created in the Chap09\\Chapter folder in your work folder to a floppy disk. When a warning appears, type **y** to continue. DriveSpy takes a few minutes to restore the image file. Figure 9-8 shows the output from using the WritePart command.

6. At the DAP1 prompt, type **exit** and then press **Enter** to close DriveSpy. Reboot your machine to Windows.

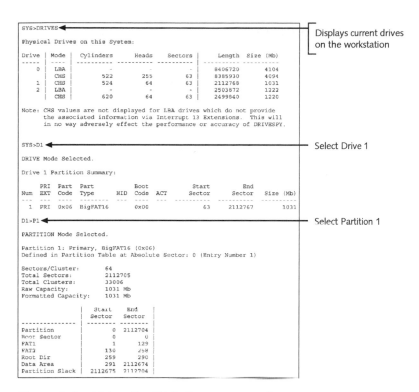

Figure 9-8   Using the WritePart command

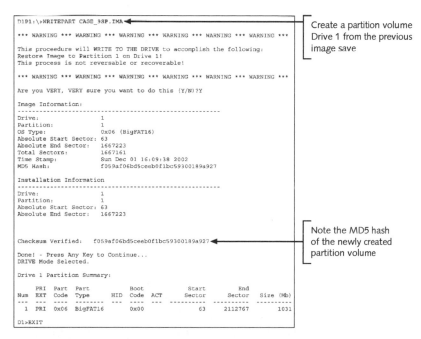

Figure 9-9   Using the WritePart command (continued)

Using the CopySect Command

The CopySect command lets you copy an absolute sector range from one disk to another, making it a powerful command. However, if you specify a destination disk that contains data of value to you or the operating system, such as your system's page file, the CopySect command can overwrite the sector.

You can use the CopySect command in the DriveSpy System, Drive, or Partition mode. For example, in the following command, the source drive (Drive 0) has a total of 214890124 sectors. Data from Drive 0 will start writing data to Sector 0 of the target drive (Drive 2).

```
CopySect  0:0,214890124  2:0
```

The following command copies the source drive (Drive 1) from absolute sector 10000 through absolute sector 20000 to the target drive (Drive 2) starting at absolute sector 50000. By listing the absolute beginning sector of a disk and the absolute ending sector or total number of sectors for a drive, you can make a complete bit-stream copy of a disk drive.

```
CopySect  1:10000-20000  2:50000
```

Of all the programs available in the DOS environment, DriveSpy's CopySect command provides the same bit-stream copy capability as the Linux dd command, which you learned about in Chapter 4. Using the CopySect command, you can preserve only selected sectors by specifying a limited number of sectors to copy. You can also copy every bit on a suspect's drive to a target drive.

The CopySect command is limited when trying to match source and target disks. To make an exact copy of a suspect's disk drive, you need a disk of the identical make, model, and size. CopySect does not adjust the geometry of the target disk drive to match the original source drive. Instead, use the SavePart and WritePart commands to duplicate partitions for FAT 16 and FAT 32 disks. For all other file systems, see "Using the SaveSect Command" and "Using the WriteSect Command" later in this chapter.

In the following steps, you use the CopySect command to copy sectors from one drive to another. You need to work on a Windows 98 workstation that has at least two drives you can access.

To copy sectors from one drive to another:

1. Access a command prompt and navigate to the **Tools** folder of your work folder.

2. At the command prompt, type **DriveSpy** and press **Enter** to start DriveSpy.

3. At the SYS prompt, type **Output C:*work folder*\Chap09\Chapter\\
   Chap9rp3.txt** and press **Enter** to record the commands you use and the results. (Replace the drive letter and *work folder* with the names of the hard drive and work folder you are using.)

4. At the SYS prompt, type **Drives** and press **Enter** to list all the drives connected to your workstation. Figure 9-10 shows that the system used in this example has four drives.

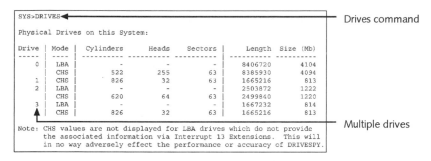

Figure 9-10   Drives command showing multiple drives

5. At the SYS prompt, type **CopySect 1:0,1665216 3:0** and press **Enter** to copy Drive 1 from absolute sectors 0 to 1665216 to Drive 3 starting at absolute sector 0. (Replace the drive numbers as necessary to match the drives on your system.)

6. When a warning appears showing the source and destination drives, verify that they are correct by typing **y** to continue. Copying the sectors may take a few minutes. When it has finished, DriveSpy displays **Done!** and returns to the SYS prompt, as shown in Figure 9-11.

7. At the SYS prompt, type **exit** and then press **Enter** to close DriveSpy. Then reboot your computer.

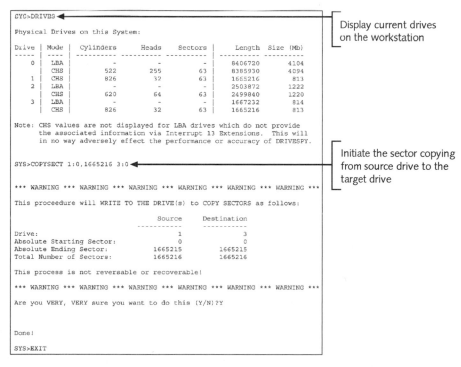

Figure 9-11   Using the CopySect command

Using DriveSpy Data Manipulation Commands

DriveSpy provides two additional commands that help you collect and preserve data. In the previous section, you learned how to acquire a disk partition with the SavePart and WritePart commands. You also learned how to copy specified sectors from one location to another with the CopySect command. DriveSpy also provides two sector-copying commands that you use to acquire specific sectors: SaveSect and WriteSect. With these two commands, you can isolate specific areas of a disk and preserve them for later examination.

Using the SaveSect Command

Use the SaveSect command to copy specific sectors on a disk to a file. SaveSect copies the sectors as a bit-stream image so that the file is an exact duplicate of the original sectors. Because the created file is not compressed, it is called a flat file. In Chapter 10, you will examine the contents of flat files with a variety of evidence recovery tools. You can also use SaveSect to collect sector data that might be located in partition gaps. If a partition is hidden or deleted, use this command to copy the entire hidden section or deleted partition to a flat file.

You can use the SaveSect command in the DriveSpy Drive and Partition modes, using a syntax similar to the CopySect command, except that you list only the source sector values and you specify a file as the target. For example, the following command saves sectors 40000 to 49999 to a file named Part_gap.dat:

```
SaveSect 1:40000-49999 C:\Chap09\Chapter\Part_gap.dat
```

To save a sector in DriveSpy:

1. Access a command prompt and navigate to the **Tools** folder of your work folder. At the command prompt, type **DriveSpy** and press **Enter** to start DriveSpy.

2. At the SYS prompt, type **Output C:*work folder*\Chap09\Chapter\ Chap9rp4.txt** and press **Enter** to create an output file to record your actions and results. (Replace the drive letter and *work folder* with the names of the hard drive and work folder you are using.)

3. At the SYS prompt, type **Drives** and press **Enter** to determine which drive to copy.

4. At the SYS prompt, type **D3** and press **Enter** to access the drive you want to copy. Substitute the number for your drive as necessary.

5. At the D3 prompt, type **P1** and press **Enter** to select the partition that contains the sectors you want to copy. (Note that typing P1 is the same as typing Part 1.)

6. At the D3P1 prompt, type **SaveSect 3:0-415232 C:*work folder*\Chap09\ Chapter\Case_9s.dat** and press **Enter** to copy sectors 0 to 415232 to a data file named Case_9s.dat. (Replace the drive letter and *work folder* with the names of the hard drive and work folder you are using.) See Figure 9-12.

7. At the D3P1 prompt, type **exit** and then press **Enter** to close DriveSpy.

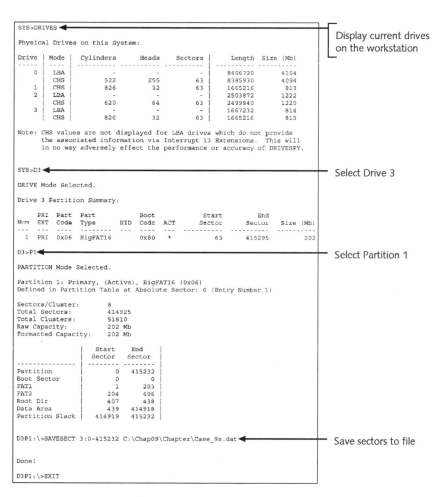

```
SYS>DRIVES ◄─────────────────────────────────────────────────────────────┐  Display current drives
                                                                          │  on the workstation
Physical Drives on this System:                                           ┘

Drive | Mode | Cylinders      Heads      Sectors  |   Length  Size (Mb)
----- | ---- | ----------   ---------  ----------  | ---------- ----------
   0  | LBA  |     -            -           -      |  8406720    4104
      | CHS  |    522          255          63     |  8385930    4094
   1  | CHS  |    826           32          63     |  1665216     813
   2  | LBA  |     -            -           -      |  2503872    1222
      | CHS  |    620           64          63     |  2499840    1220
   3  | LBA  |     -            -           -      |  1667232     814
      | CHS  |    826           32          63     |  1665216     813

Note: CHS values are not displayed for LBA drives which do not provide
      the associated information via Interrupt 13 Extensions.  This will
      in no way adversely effect the performance or accuracy of DRIVESPY.


SYS>D3 ◄──────────────────────────────────────────────────────────────────  Select Drive 3

DRIVE Mode Selected.

Drive 3 Partition Summary:

      PRI  Part  Part                 Boot              Start        End
Num   EXT  Code  Type       HID       Code  ACT         Sector     Sector   Size (Mb)
---   ---  ----  ---------  ---       ----  ---        ----------  ----------  ----------
  1   PRI  0x06  BigFAT16             0x80   *              63      415295         202

D3>P1 ◄────────────────────────────────────────────────────────────────────  Select Partition 1

PARTITION Mode Selected.

Partition 1: Primary, (Active), BigFAT16 (0x06)
Defined in Partition Table at Absolute Sector: 0 (Entry Number 1)

Sectors/Cluster:        8
Total Sectors:      414925
Total Clusters:      51810
Raw Capacity:       202 Mb
Formatted Capacity:  202 Mb

                 | Start    End    |
                 | Sector   Sector |
--------------   | -------- -------- |
Partition        |      0   415232 |
Boot Sector      |      0        0 |
FAT1             |      1      203 |
FAT2             |    204      406 |
Root Dir         |    407      438 |
Data Area        |    439   414918 |
Partition Slack  | 414919   415232 |

D3P1:\>SAVESECT 3:0-415232 C:\Chap09\Chapter\Case_9s.dat ◄────────────────  Save sectors to file

Done!

D3P1:\>EXIT
```

Figure 9-12   Using the SaveSect command

Using the WriteSect Command

With the WriteSect command, you can recreate the data acquired through the SaveSect command. You use the WriteSect command in DriveSpy Drive or Partition mode to recreate an absolute sector range from a SaveSect file to a target disk drive. For example, the following command writes a flat file named Part_gap.dat starting at absolute sector 10000 on Drive 2.

```
WriteSect C:\Chap09\Chapter\Part_gap.dat 2:10000
```

The disadvantage of using the WriteSect command is that if you are not careful, you can easily overwrite data on a target disk. Always review commands to verify where you are sending data.

To write a sector data file in DriveSpy:

1. Access a command prompt and navigate to the **Tools** folder of your work folder. At the command prompt, type **DriveSpy** and press **Enter** to start DriveSpy.

2. At the SYS prompt, type **Output C:*work folder*\Chap09\Chapter\ Chap9rp5.txt** and press **Enter** to record the commands you use and their results in an output file. (Replace the drive letter and *work folder* with the names of the hard drive and work folder you are using.)

3. At the SYS prompt, type **Drives** and press **Enter** to list the drives the system recognizes. Select the drive to which you want to copy data, and verify that it does not contain any vital data.

4. At the SYS prompt, type **D3** and press **Enter** to access the drive you want. Substitute the number for your drive as necessary.

5. At the D3 prompt, type **WriteSect C: *work folder*\Chap09\Chapter\ Case_9s.dat 3:0** and press **Enter** to start transferring data to absolute sector 0 on Drive 3. Substitute drive and folder names for those on your system as necessary. See Figure 9-13.

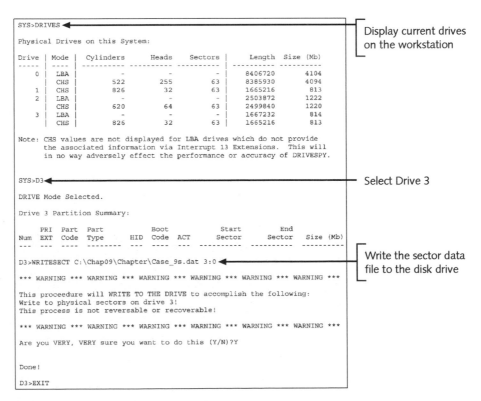

Figure 9-13 Using the WriteSect command

6. Type **y** when a warning appears.

7. At the D3 prompt, type **exit** and then press **Enter** to close DriveSpy.

Like the SavePart command, SaveSect can save an entire disk drive to a data file. The SaveSect and WriteSect commands are useful if you need to acquire a disk image from a non-Microsoft FAT file system. For example, you can use the SavePart and WritePart commands on a Linux Ext2fs disk. Make sure that the target drive where you plan to save the SavePart output file is larger than the source drive.

USING WINDOWS ACQUISITION TOOLS

Many computer forensics software vendors have developed data acquisition tools that you can run in Microsoft Windows. These tools add convenience to the task of acquiring evidence from a suspect's disk, especially when you use the tools with hot-swappable devices that use USB-2 or Firewire to connect hard disks to your workstation.

However, Windows data acquisition tools do have some drawbacks. Because Windows can easily contaminate your evidence drive, you must protect it with a well-tested write-blocking hardware device. (Chapter 6 contains information about using a write-blocking device.) Another drawback is that Windows tools cannot acquire data from the host-protected area on a disk. If you know or suspect that the evidence disk drive contains evidence in the host-protected area, use an MS-DOS tool to acquire the disk.

AccessData FTK Explorer

FTK Explorer is a typical data acquisition program for Windows, and is included with a licensed copy of the AccessData Forensic Toolkit. FTK Explorer, like all Windows data acquisition tools, requires that you use a device such as a USB or parallel port dongle for licensing. Learning how FTK Explorer acquires data can help you understand how other Windows acquisition tools work. If you are using only the demonstration version of FTK that you downloaded from the AccessData Web site, you do not have a copy of FTK Explorer. In that case, read the steps and examine the figures, but do not perform the steps in this section.

FTK Explorer was originally designed to examine evidence disks and bit-stream disk-to-image files created using other forensic software such as EnCase and SafeBack. FTK Explorer also lets you read a connected disk drive directly. FTK Explorer provides a window similar to Windows Explorer with an additional pane that shows the contents of the selected file, as shown in Figure 9-14.

FTK Explorer can make bit-stream disk-to-image copies of evidence disks, and lets you acquire the evidence disk from a logical partition level or a physical drive level. You can also define the size of each bit-stream image file volume, called save-set volumes, allowing you to segment the image you save into one or many volumes. For example, you can specify that each save-set volume is 100 MB if you plan to store the volumes on 100 MB Zip disks, or you can specify the save-set volumes as 650 MB so you can record the volumes on CD-Rs.

9

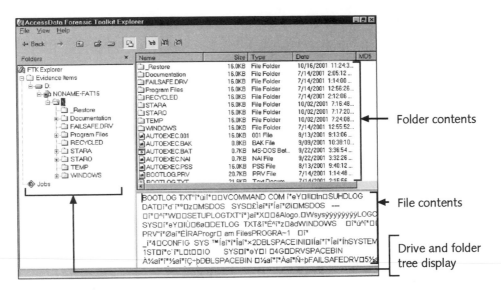

Figure 9-14   FTK Explorer main window

Because FTK Explorer is designed to run on versions of Windows from 9x through XP, the evidence disk from which you are acquiring data must have a hardware write-blocker device between your investigation workstation and the evidence drive. This ensures that you do not contaminate your evidence while using a Windows program. Any USB, Firewire, or SCSI write-blocker protects your evidence when using FTK Explorer.

Like all Windows tools, FTK Explorer cannot acquire the host-protected area of an evidence drive. Recall from Chapter 4 that you should compare actual sectors displayed in a disk editor to the computer's BIOS settings. In other words, if the disk drive's specifications indicate that it has 11,000,000 sectors and the BIOS displays 9,000,000, a host-protected area, or 2,000,000 sectors, might be assigned to the drive. If you suspect an evidence drive has a host-protected area, you must use an advanced MS-DOS tool such as SafeBack or SnapBack or the Linux dd command to include the host-protected area of a disk in the data acquisition. With MS-DOS tools, you might have to define the exact sector count to make sure you include more than what the BIOS shows as the number of known sectors on the drive. Review the specific vendor product manuals to determine how to account for the host-protected area of a drive.

The following sets of steps show you how to use FTK Explorer to make a forensic bit-stream disk-to-image file. The FTK Explorer Image command makes a bit-stream image file of a suspect's disk drive or partition volume. To perform this acquisition, you need a write-blocker device such as Digital Intelligence FireChief, the suspect disk drive, and a target disk drive to receive the acquisition. The FireChief is a Firewire device that allows you to connect disk drives while your workstation is running, which is called hot-swapping. When you connect the disk drives, Windows makes the drive accessible.

NOTE

Recall that if you do not have a licensed copy of FTK, you should read, but not perform, the following steps.

To prepare for a data acquisition with FTK Explorer:

1. Boot a forensic workstation to Windows using an installed write-blocker such as Digital Intelligence FireChief.

2. Connect the evidence disk to a write-blocking device or the FireChief write-block bay.

3. Connect the target disk to the FireChief writeable bay.

To acquire an evidence disk with FTK Explorer:

1. Click the **Start** button, point to **Programs** (**All Programs** in Windows XP), point to **AccessData**, point to **Forensic Toolkit**, and then click **FTK Explorer** to start FTK Explorer.

2. Click **File** on the menu bar, and then click **Image Drive**. The Select Local Drive dialog box opens, as shown in Figure 9-15.

9

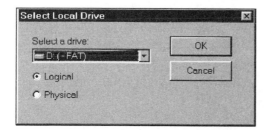

Figure 9-15   Selecting the image drive

3. Click the **Select a drive** list arrow, and then click the drive for which you want to create an image, such as **D: (MS-DOS_6-FAT)**. If your workstation is running Windows 98 and the drive you are acquiring is an NTFS or Ext2fs drive, click the **Physical** option button to access the drive for the acquisition. Then click **OK**. The Export Disk Image dialog box opens, shown in Figure 9-16, which describes what happens when you create an image.

4. Click **Next** to accept these settings. The Image Destination dialog box opens, shown in Figure 9-17.

5. Click **Browse** to select a location for the image file. The Save As dialog box opens. Navigate to the Chap09\Chapter folder in your work folder, use **Case_9** as the name of the file, and then click **Save**. The Image Destination dialog box opens, shown in Figure 9-18, so you can verify the name and location of the image file.

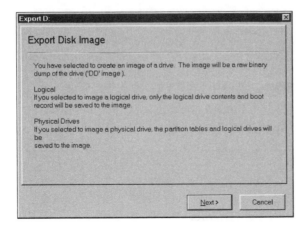

Figure 9-16   Export Disk Image dialog box

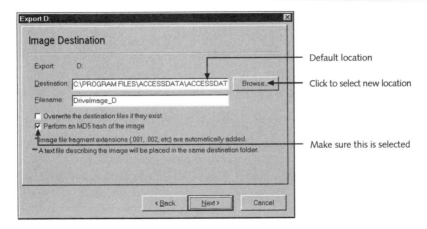

Figure 9-17   Selecting where to save the image file

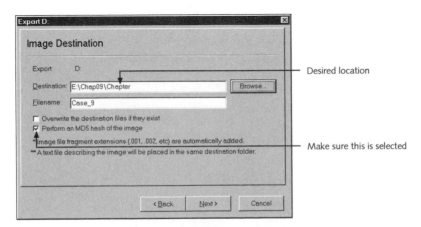

Figure 9-18   Verifying the name of the image file

6. Click **Next**. The Image Segment Size dialog box opens, where you can specify the size of the volumes that you save. To create volumes of 200 MB each to store on 250 MB Zip disks, click the **Custom MB** button. Drag the slider until the Segment Info displays 200 MB, as shown in Figure 9-19. Then click **Next**. The Summary dialog box opens, listing information such as the source and destination locations and the size and number of the saved volumes.

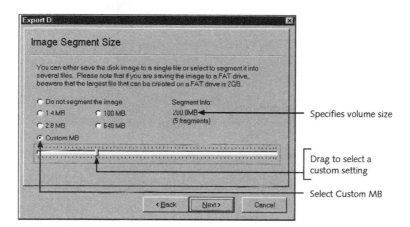

Figure 9-19   Selecting the volume size

 NOTE   The volume size you select should be slightly smaller than the size of the media you plan to use, such as 200 MB for 250 MB Zip disks. Due to the way many acquisition tools calculate volumes, the actual volume size might be slightly larger than what you estimate. For example, if you define the volume size as 250 MB, the actual size of the volume will require 255 or 260 MB of storage. It is much easier and requires less rework to understate the volume size by 50 MB. For CD-R or CD-RW, it is better to acquire volumes at 600 MB rather than 650 or 700 MB. The actual volume file will be larger than the capacity of the CD.

7. Click **Finish** to start the acquisition. A dialog box opens to display the progress of the acquisition.

When the acquisition completes, leave FTK Explorer open for the next set of steps.

You can now use FTK Explorer to view the saved bit-stream disk-to-image file you just created.

To use FTK Explorer to view an image file:

1. Click **File** on the menu bar, and then click **Open Drive**. The Open evidence image file dialog box opens, shown in Figure 9-20.

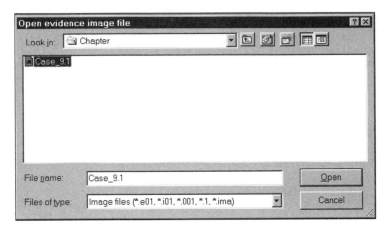

Figure 9-20   Selecting the image file

2. Click the image file you just created, such as **Case_9.1**. Then click the **Open** button. The file opens in the lower-right pane of the FTK window, as shown in Figure 9-21.

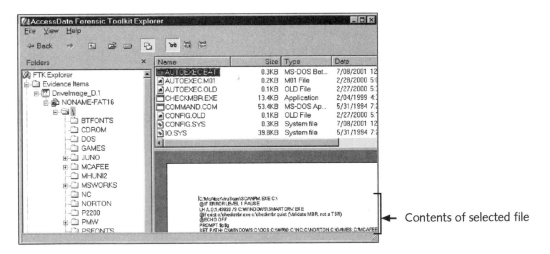

Contents of selected file

Figure 9-21   Viewing image file contents

From the FTK Explorer main window, you can navigate through the folders and files in the image file.

3. When you are finished examining the image file, close FTK Explorer.

ACQUIRING DATA ON LINUX COMPUTERS

Linux is an extremely powerful operating system, especially when you are working at the shell command prompt. You can use the built-in dd command to copy data from a disk drive. The options for the dd command provide flexibility when you are copying the data. With the dd command, you can make a bit-stream disk-to-disk file, a disk-to-image file, block-to-block copy, or block-to-file copy. (Recall from Chapter 4 that in UNIX and Linux file systems, blocks are the same as sectors in a Microsoft file system.) You can also use the dd command to write directly to a tape drive. You can then use the gzip command to compress the image files and minimize your storage needs.

The main advantage of using the dd command is that it is freely available as part of Linux. Other advantages are that it copies data from any disk Linux can mount and access. The dd command can make images of Ext2fs, Ext3fs, most UNIX file systems, FAT12, FAT16, FAT32, NTFS, HFS, and HPFS file systems disks. The dd command copies any data on any disk or tape media that Linux can access. Note that AccessData FTK and ILook can read dd image files.

You should know how to use the dd command in case you encounter UNIX and Linux systems that may not be compatible with other MS-DOS or Windows tools.

The following are the disadvantages of using the dd command:

- You need to know advanced UNIX shell scripting and commands.

- You must specify the number of blocks per save-set volume to create a volume save-set.

- You might not be able to use the dd command on your PC, depending on the distribution and version of Linux you are using.

- You cannot use the dd command to automatically adjust drive geometry to match the target drive, as with the DriveSpy CopySect command.

To use the dd command as a data acquisition tool for computer forensics, you must build a bootable Linux floppy disk. To do so, you can use several freeware Linux boot packages available on the Web. One of the easiest Linux boot utilities to use is Tom's Root Boot Kit, which is available for both Linux and DOS. (If you are using a Microsoft Windows operating system, you can download the DOS version.) To download this boot utility for Linux, visit *www.tux.org/pub/distributions/tinylinux/tomsrtbt/start_here.html* or *www.tux.org/pub/distributions/tinylinux/tomsrtbt*.

If you plan to use this utility, you should routinely go to the Web site and download the latest updates.

Tom's Root Boot Kit is available for Windows, Linux, and other popular UNIX operating systems. The following section describes how to download and then use Windows to create a floppy disk containing Tom's Root Boot Kit.

To download a DOS version of Tom's Root Boot Kit:

1. Start a Web browser such as Internet Explorer, type **www.tux.org/pub/distributions/tinylinux/tomsrtbt** in the Address text box and then press **Enter**. The Tux.org Web page opens.

2. Click the most recent version of tomsrtbt for DOS, such as
tomsrtbt-2.0.103.dos.zip. If the File Download dialog box opens,
click **OK** to save the file. If the Unknown File Save dialog box opens, click
Save File.

3. In the Save As dialog box, navigate to a folder on your system where you usually download files and click **Save**.

4. After the file downloads, close the File Download dialog box, if necessary, and
then close your Web browser.

After you download Tom's Root Boot Kit, you need to configure a floppy disk. Tom's
Root Boot Kit includes an Install.bat program, which automatically formats a floppy disk
and loads the Linux kernel (the core of the Linux operating system). WinZip or PKZip
must be installed on your system to complete the following steps.

NOTE

If you downloaded a version of Tom's Root Boot Kit other than tomsrtbt-
2.0.103.dos.zip, the installation instructions might be different. For additional
information about Tom's Root Boot Kit, visit *www.toms.net/rb*.

To successfully create a Tom's Root Boot Kit, you need a Windows 9x or MS-DOS 6.22
operating system. The Install.bat file does not run from a DOS shell in Windows.

To prepare and load a boot floppy disk for Tom's Root Boot Kit:

1. In Windows Explorer, navigate to the folder where you downloaded the
file containing Tom's Boot Root Kit. Double-click the zip file, such as
tomsrtbt-2.0.103.dos.zip. Extract the files to a folder containing temporary files, such as C:\Temp. If you are using PKUnzip from a DOS shell to
extract the files, as shown in Figure 9-22, type **Pkunzip Tomsrt~1** and press
Enter. Because you are limited to eight characters for DOS filenames, the file
Tomsrtbt-2.0.103.dos.zip is shortened to Tomsrt~1.zip

```
 MS-DOS Prompt                                                      _ □ ×
 T  9 x 15       A
TOMSRT~1 ZIP      2,242,580  09-05-02 12:39p tomsrtbt-2.0.103.dos.zip
        1 file(s)     2,242,580 bytes
        2 dir(s)      1,225.99 MB free

C:\Temp>pkunzip tomsrt~1

PKUNZIP (R)    FAST!    Extract Utility    Version 2.04g  02-01-93
Copr. 1989-1993 PKWARE Inc. All Rights Reserved. Registered version
PKUNZIP Reg. U.S. Pat. and Tm. Off.

■ 80486 CPU detected.
■ EMS version 4.00 detected.
■ XMS version 3.00 detected.
■ DPMI version 0.90 detected.

Searching ZIP: TOMSRT~1.ZIP
  Inflating: initrd.img
  Inflating: install.bat
  Inflating: license.html
  Inflating: loadlin.exe
  Inflating: tomsrtbt.FAQ
  Inflating: tomsrtbt.lsm
  Inflating: zimage

C:\Temp>
```

Figure 9-22   Extracting Tom's Root Boot Kit using PKUnzip

2. Reboot your workstation to MS-DOS.

3. Change to the folder where you unzipped Tom's Root Boot Kit, such as C:\Temp.

4. At the DOS prompt, type **install.bat** and then press **Enter**.

5. Follow the prompts as they are displayed on the screen, and insert a floppy disk into Drive A. Press **Enter** to continue with the installation.

6. After a message "Try again / do another? y/n?" appears, type **n** and then press **Enter** to exit the installation. Your computer reboots to Tom's Root Boot Kit.

Before you use the Tom's Root Boot Kit floppy disk to acquire data from Linux disks, you should understand how Linux and UNIX label disk drives. Depending on the type of controllers installed on the computer, Linux and UNIX designate drives on an IDE hard disk using abbreviations shown in Table 9-1.

Table 9-1   Linux Drive Designations on IDE Hard Disks

IDE disk drive	Abbreviation
Primary Master	hda
Primary Slave	hdb
Secondary Master	hdc
Secondary Slave	hdd

For each drive, the partitions are numbered starting at 1. The first partition for the Primary Master drive is hda1. The second partition then becomes hda2, and so on. Partition hda1 is equivalent to the C partition in DOS.

Table 9-2 shows the abbreviations Linux and UNIX use to designate drives on a SCSI hard disk.

Table 9-2   Linux Drive Designations on SCSI Hard Disks

SCSI disk drive	Abbreviation
First SCSI drive	sda
Second SCSI drive	sdb
Third SCSI drive	sdc

Similar to the IDE drives, the partitions on a SCSI hard disk start at 1. The first partition for the first SCSI drive is sda1, the second partition on this drive is sda2, and so on.

To use Tom's Root Boot Kit for a data acquisition, you must boot the PC with the floppy disk. Before starting the PC, connect the source and target disk drives, noting on which controller each drive is located. For example, the suspect's disk might be connected to the

Primary Master IDE controller, and the target drive might be connected to the Primary Slave IDE controller.

Before you install your target disk drive, make sure that a MS-DOS FAT16 or FAT32 partition has been configured on the target disk drive. The partition must also be formatted so that data can be copied to the target drive.

To boot your PC with Tom's Root Boot Kit floppy disk:

1. If the PC is not already shut down, perform an orderly shutdown. If you are working in Tom's Root Boot Kit, press **Ctrl+Alt+Del** to shut down the Linux operating system.

2. Make sure your source disk is connected to the Primary Master IDE controller on your forensic workstation. This requires you to remove the original operating system disk from your workstation to perform the acquisition of the suspect disk.

3. Connect the target disk to the next controller, such as the Primary Slave IDE cable connector.

4. Insert your Tom's Root Boot Kit floppy disk, and power on the PC.

5. As the PC is powering up, access the BIOS to make sure you can boot from the floppy disk drive. Watch for a splash screen or refer to the motherboard manual of your workstation to determine what key to press during the bootstrap to access the BIOS. Change the appropriate setting to boot from the floppy disk drive, if necessary.

6. Restart the computer.

7. When the "boot:" prompt appears, press **Enter**.

8. At the login prompt, type **root** (be sure to use all lowercase letters), and then press **Enter**.

9. At the password prompt, type **xxxx** and then press **Enter**.

Now you are ready to initiate the disk acquisition. The dd command has several options or switches that provide flexibility for copying data. Table 9-3 lists the options you can use when copying data.

To use the dd command to acquire data from an evidence disk:

1. After you boot the PC with the Linux boot floppy disk, create a mount point for the source hard disk (such as the C: disk). At the shell prompt (#), type **mkdir /mnt/hda1** and then press **Enter**.

2. At the shell prompt (#), create a mount point for the Primary Slave disk drive (such as the D: disk) by typing **mkdir /mnt/hdb1** and then pressing **Enter**.

3. Mount the Primary Master disk by typing **mount –t msdos /dev/hda1 / mnt/hda1** and then pressing **Enter**.

Table 9-3   dd Command Switches

Switch	Description
if=	Input filename or device such as a disk drive
of=	Output filename or device such as a disk drive
bs=	Block size in bytes (optional: bs=1M is one megabyte)
count=	Number of blocks to transfer at a time
seek=	Block position to start the next block segment write location, this switch advances the position to the next location where to start writing data
skip=	Block position to start the next block segment read location, this switch advances the position to the next location where to start reading data
conv=	Changes data output to a different format such as American Standard Code for Information Interchange (ASCII) to Extended Binary-Coded Decimal Interchange Code (EBCDIC)

4. Mount the Primary Slave disk by typing **mount −t msdos /dev/hdb1 / mnt/hdb1** and then pressing **Enter**.

5. To create a one-volume dd image file (disk-to-image file), type **dd if=/dev/ hda of=/mnt/hdb1/image-file.img** and then press **Enter**.

NOTE   Linux and UNIX commands do not describe their actions or results unless you specify a switch to use verbose mode. When you use dd command, the computer may seem to hang as it copies data. Depending on the size of your source drive, it may take several hours to copy the data to the target disk. If your workstation has a disk LED indicator, check to see if it is on or flashing. If it is not on steady or flashing, review and repeat the data acquisition steps. Linux is not compatible with all computer hardware, and drives on the Linux boot disk might only be able to access less common or older Intel computers.

To make multiple volumes of a disk with the dd command, you must first perform some calculations. First you need to determine the number of bytes per volume, that is, a save-set which are the individual volumes when combined that make a copy of the entire source disk. Then you calculate the number of save-sets you need to create to successfully copy all the blocks on the disk. For example, suppose a disk drive is 4.8 GB and you plan to archive the volume save-sets to 700 MB CD-Rs. To determine the number of volume save-sets necessary to collect all blocks on the source drive, you perform the following calculations:

1. Determine how many bytes you want to store on the CD-Rs, such as 600 MB, leaving at least 50 MB free in case the actual size of the final volume save-set is larger than 650 MB. Recall that this is a common problem when determining the maximum size of a save-set volume. You should underestimate the size of a save-set volume to ensure it will fit on your target storage or archive media such as a CD-R or CD-RW.

2. Divide the number of bytes you plan to store (600,000,000) by the total number of bytes on the suspect's disk, such as 48 MB:

4,800,000,000/ 600,000,000 = 4 volume save-sets

3. For disks that produce a remainder, add one extra volume save-set to your calculation. For a 10 GB source disk, the calculation is 10,000,000,000 / 600,000,000 = 16.67, meaning you need 16 full volumes and one partial volume, or 17 volume save-sets.

Instead of typing individual commands with various options at the shell prompt, you can create a Linux script file, similar to a batch file in DOS. Linux reads the script file and performs the commands as specified. Creating a script file is possible only if you are running a fully configured Linux system with a text editor such as vi. Entering and executing each command for each volume save-set is difficult and prone to typing errors. Creating a script that lists all dd save-set volumes will save time and eliminate mistakes.

To use the dd command, you need to define the input source, the output source, the block size, and the number of blocks to save to each save-set volume. The following script includes commands for creating an image, that is, a volume save-set of a 10 GB disk drive that will be divided into 17 save-set volumes. Note that each command starts one block after the last block of the previous command line. For example, the first command line reads from block 0 through block 600, which is defined with the count=600 switch. The input file is defined as a disk, such as the entire Primary Master disk drive with the if=/dev/hda switch. The output file in this example is defined as a specific target disk, path, and filename with the of=/mnt/hdb1/hda_vol_01. Note that each block is defined as 1 MB in size with the bs=1M switch. With this configuration each volume will be 600,000,000 MB, which will easily fit on to a CD-R or CD-RW disk.

The next command line skips to block 601 and reads from the source drive, /dev/hda, and writes the next volume save-set, /mnt/hdb1/hda_vol_02, to the target disk drive. The following commands continue to increment to the next set of 600 blocks on the disk drive:

```
dd if=/dev/hda of=/mnt/hdb1/hda_vol_01 bs=1M count=600
dd if=/dev/hda of=/mnt/hdb1/hda_vol_02 bs=1M count=600 skip=601
dd if=/dev/hda of=/mnt/hdb1/hda_vol_03 bs=1M count=600 skip=1201
dd if=/dev/hda of=/mnt/hdb1/hda_vol_04 bs=1M count=600 skip=1801
dd if=/dev/hda of=/mnt/hdb1/hda_vol_05 bs=1M count=600 skip=2401
dd if=/dev/hda of=/mnt/hdb1/hda_vol_06 bs=1M count=600 skip=3001
dd if=/dev/hda of=/mnt/hdb1/hda_vol_07 bs=1M count=600 skip=3601
dd if=/dev/hda of=/mnt/hdb1/hda_vol_08 bs=1M count=600 skip=4201
dd if=/dev/hda of=/mnt/hdb1/hda_vol_09 bs=1M count=600 skip=4801
dd if=/dev/hda of=/mnt/hdb1/hda_vol_10 bs=1M count=600 skip=5401
dd if=/dev/hda of=/mnt/hdb1/hda_vol_11 bs=1M count=600 skip=6001
dd if=/dev/hda of=/mnt/hdb1/hda_vol_12 bs=1M count=600 skip=6601
dd if=/dev/hda of=/mnt/hdb1/hda_vol_13 bs=1M count=600 skip=7201
dd if=/dev/hda of=/mnt/hdb1/hda_vol_14 bs=1M count=600 skip=7801
```

```
dd if=/dev/hda of=/mnt/hdb1/hda_vol_15 bs=1M count=600 skip=8401
dd if=/dev/hda of=/mnt/hdb1/hda_vol_16 bs=1M count=600 skip=9001
dd if=/dev/hda of=/mnt/hdb1/hda_vol_17 bs=1M count=400 skip=9601
```

Note the last dd command's count=400 value copies the remaining data on the drive.

After you create the volume save-sets of a source disk using the dd command, you can copy each volume save-set to a CD-R or a CD-RW. The purpose of this is to preserve the data as part of your evidence retention for your investigation.

If you need to recreate the source disk from the dd volume save-sets, you need an identical disk drive. The dd command does not adjust for disk drive geometry differences because it writes the data to the target drive in the same order it used when reading the data from the original disk drive or a volume save-set. The DriveSpy CopySect and WriteSect commands work the same way as the dd command in that the target drive must have the same geometry as the original source disk. You can copy data acquired from a source drive or image file to a different target drive, but the logical data structures, such as directories, will not link correctly. You will only be able to read the drive at a physical level rather than at a logical level—the data will be on the target drive, but you will not be able to determine the filename, its path, or any other related data such as date and time values.

Restoring a dd volume save-set requires changing the input (if=) values with the output (of=) values and changing the skip= option to the seek= option. The following is a script for restoring the previous dd command save-set:

```
dd if=/mnt/hdb1/hda_vol_01 of=/dev/hda bs=1M count=600
dd if=/mnt/hdb1/hda_vol_02 of=/dev/hda bs=1M count=600 seek=601
dd if=/mnt/hdb1/hda_vol_03 of=/dev/hda bs=1M count=600 seek=1201
dd if=/mnt/hdb1/hda_vol_04 of=/dev/hda bs=1M count=600 seek=1801
dd if=/mnt/hdb1/hda_vol_05 of=/dev/hda bs=1M count=600 seek=2401
dd if=/mnt/hdb1/hda_vol_06 of=/dev/hda bs=1M count=600 seek=3001
dd if=/mnt/hdb1/hda_vol_07 of=/dev/hda bs=1M count=600 seek=3601
dd if=/mnt/hdb1/hda_vol_08 of=/dev/hda bs=1M count=600 seek=4201
dd if=/mnt/hdb1/hda_vol_09 of=/dev/hda bs=1M count=600 seek=4801
dd if=/mnt/hdb1/hda_vol_10 of=/dev/hda bs=1M count=600 seek=5401
dd if=/mnt/hdb1/hda_vol_11 of=/dev/hda bs=1M count=600 seek=6001
dd if=/mnt/hdb1/hda_vol_12 of=/dev/hda bs=1M count=600 seek=6601
dd if=/mnt/hdb1/hda_vol_13 of=/dev/hda bs=1M count=600 seek=7201
dd if=/mnt/hdb1/hda_vol_14 of=/dev/hda bs=1M count=600 seek=7801
dd if=/mnt/hdb1/hda_vol_15 of=/dev/hda bs=1M count=600 seek=8401
dd if=/mnt/hdb1/hda_vol_16 of=/dev/hda bs=1M count=600 seek=9001
dd if=/mnt/hdb1/hda_vol_17 of=/dev/hda bs=1M count=400 seek=9601
```

To make a duplicate copy of a disk drive, you can use the following dd command. Recall that dd does not adjust the drive geometry.

```
dd if=/dev/hda of=/dev/hdc
```

If you have a tape drive mounted to the system from which you are acquiring data, use the following dd command to copy the contents of the entire drive:

```
dd if=/dev/hda of=/dev/rst0
```

Earlier you learned how to use the mount command to access disks. In Linux and UNIX, you must also unmount the disks using the umount (not unmount) command to disable the connection between the operating system and the disk drive, as in the following command:

```
umount /mnt/hdb1
```

When you have finished your data acquisition from the Linux floppy boot disk, be sure to perform an orderly shutdown using the shutdown command. If you do not shut down properly, open files could be corrupted, which could damage your evidence data. Due to the limited amount of space on a floppy disk, the shutdown command is not available with Tom's Root Boot Kit. To shut down Tom's Root Boot Kit, press Ctrl+Alt+Del. To shut down a Linux computer, you use the following command:

```
shutdown -h 0
```

USING OTHER FORENSICS ACQUISITION TOOLS

In addition to DriveSpy, FTK Explorer, and the Linux dd command, you can use other data acquisition tools that are commercially available, including SnapBack DatArrest from Columbia Data Products and SafeBack from NTI. The cost of these tools ranges from $600 to $2500.

Exploring SnapBack DatArrest

SnapBack DatArrest from Columbia Data Products is an old, reliable MS-DOS forensic data acquisition tool that can perform a bit-stream data copy of an evidence drive in three ways: disk to SCSI drive (magnetic tape or Jaz disk), disk to network drive, and disk to disk. Each method is a separate program that fits on a forensic boot floppy disk. SnapBack DatArrest provides network drivers so you can boot from a forensic boot floppy disk and access a remote network server disk. You can then save a data acquisition image directly to a remote networked server drive.

You can restore image files created on a network drive or removable media to a new target drive for follow-up examination and analysis. SnapCopy is a disk-to-disk utility that adjusts the target drive geometry to match the original suspect's disk drive. SnapCopy is the only automated disk-to-disk tool that allows you to copy data to a slightly smaller target drive than the original suspect's drive.

SnapBack DatArrest is sold separately or with AccessData FTK.

Exploring SafeBack

SafeBack is another reliable MS-DOS data acquisition tool, and is small enough to fit on to a forensic boot floppy disk. SafeBack performs a CRC-32 calculation for each sector copied to ensure data integrity. During the data acquisition, SafeBack creates a log file of all the transactions it performs. The log file includes a comment field where you can identify the investigation and the data you collect. SafeBack does the following:

- Creates disk-to-image files
- Copies from a source disk to an image on a tape drive
- Copies from a source disk to a target disk (disk-to-disk copy), adjusting the target drive's geometry to match the source drive
- Copies from a source disk to a target disk using a parallel port laplink cable
- Copies a partition to an image file
- Compresses acquired files to reduce the volume save-set sizes

SafeBack provides the following four programs:

- Master.exe, the main SafeBack utility program
- Remote.exe, for connecting two computers and transferring data with a parallel port laplink cable
- Restpart.exe, for restoring a partition that is saved separate from the entire suspect's disk
- Taspi.exe, for connecting SCSI devices for your data acquisition

AccessData FTK and ILook can read SafeBack image files.

Exploring EnCase

EnCase is a Windows forensics tool from Guidance Software that you can use to create a forensic boot floppy disk. EnCase loads a program called En.exe on the floppy disk, which is a reliable forensic data acquisition tool that compresses data to reduce the amount of storage space required for the save-sets. In fact, the En.exe program has one of the best compression algorithms of the data acquisition tools.

You must use EnCase to restore images created with En.exe. You can acquire data disk to disk, disk to network server drive, or through the parallel port with a laplink cable to another computer's disk drive. EnCase, FTK, and ILook can read EnCase image files.

9

CHAPTER SUMMARY

❑ You can acquire digital evidence from disk drives in three ways: creating a bit-stream disk-to-image file, making a bit-stream disk-to-disk copy, or creating a sparse data copy of a specific folder path or file.

❑ Several tools on the market allow you to restore disks that are larger or smaller than the suspect source drive.

❑ Lossless compression is an acceptable method for computer forensics because it does not alter the data in any way. Lossy compression alters the data and is not acceptable.

❑ Because you are dealing with electronic data, you need to protect your bit-stream digital evidence and make contingency plans in case software or hardware doesn't work, or you encounter a failure during an acquisition. The most common and time-consuming technique to preserve evidence is creating a duplicate copy of your evidence image file. Also make sure that you make at least two data acquisitions using two different methods.

❑ The partition gap is an area where information can be stored. DriveSpy's SavePart command can retrieve this information.

❑ Some command-line tools can be dangerous, such as the CopySect command. It will not notify you that it is about to write over critical information. You must keep a careful log of what sectors you are writing to and from.

❑ Windows data acquisition tools add convenience and ease of use to the forensics investigation. They also enable you to use hot-swappable devices such as Zip and Jaz drives. However, you must write-protect your evidence and access the host-protected area of a disk.

❑ You can use a built-in Linux command called dd to make a bit-stream disk-to-disk copy, disk-to-image file, block-to-block copy, or block-to-file copy. You can also use the dd command to write directly to a tape drive. You can use the gzip command to compress the image files and minimize your storage needs.

❑ In addition to DriveSpy, FTK Explorer, and the Linux dd command, you can use other data acquisition tools that are commercially available, including SnapBack DatArrest from Columbia Data Products and SafeBack from NTI.

KEY TERMS

algorithm—A short mathematical procedure that solves a recurrent problem.

DoubleSpace—An MS-DOS disk compression utility distributed with MS-DOS 6.0 and 6.20.

DriveSpace—An MS-DOS disk compression utility distributed with MS-DOS 6.22 and Windows 9x.

gzip—A Linux program that compresses image files and minimizes your storage needs.

inter-partition space—The space between the end of one partition and the start of another.

lossless compression—A compression method in which no data is lost. With this type of compression, a large file can be compressed to take up less space, and then decompressed without any loss of information.

lossy compression—A compression technique that can lose data but not perceptible quality when a file is restored. Files that use lossy compression include JPEG and MPEG.

partition gap—*See* inter-partition space.

9

10

COMPUTER FORENSIC ANALYSIS

After reading this chapter, you will be able to:

♦ Understand computer forensic analysis

♦ Use DriveSpy to analyze computer data

♦ Use other Digital Intelligence computer forensics tools

♦ Use AccessData's Forensic Toolkit (FTK)

♦ Perform a computer forensic analysis

♦ Address data-hiding techniques

This chapter explains how to apply your computer forensics skills and techniques to a computing investigation. You learn how to refine the organization of an investigation and use data-analysis tools and practices to process digital evidence. The first section of this chapter explains the basic concepts of processing data to recover digital evidence. The second section describes how to use utilities such as Digital Intelligence DriveSpy and AccessData Forensic Toolkit (FTK) to analyze recovered evidence. You also learn how to systematically investigate specific operating systems and discover where data is often intentionally hidden.

Later, in Chapters 13 and 14, you learn how to assemble the data you found and analyzed, and then present it in court or to a board of inquiry either as a technical expert or as an expert witness.

UNDERSTANDING COMPUTER FORENSIC ANALYSIS

Examining and analyzing digital evidence depends on the nature of the investigation and the amount of data that you have to process. For most law enforcement-related computing investigations, the investigator is limited to working with data defined in the search warrant. The private-sector investigator is also limited when working under the direction of a court order for discovery. The goal in either investigation often involves locating and recovering one or two items, which simplifies and speeds processing.

In the corporate environment, however, especially if the case involves litigation, the investigator is often directed by the company attorney to recover as much information as possible. Satisfying this demand becomes a major undertaking involving many hours and days of tedious work. These types of investigations can involve **scope creep**, where every piece of new evidence prompts the attorney to demand that you examine other areas to recover more evidence, widening the scope of the investigation. This increases the amount of time and resources needed to extract, analyze, and present all the evidence.

Recent criminal investigations required more detailed examination of evidence just before trial to help prosecutors fend off attacks from defense attorneys. Defense attorneys typically have the right of full discovery of the digital evidence being used against their clients. However, new evidence found while complying with the defense request for full discovery is often not revealed to the prosecution. Its purpose is only to help the defense attorney better defend the accused. This applies only to criminal cases in the United States; civil cases are handled differently.

Refining the Investigation Plan

Recall from Chapter 2 that you begin any computer forensic case by creating an investigation plan that defines the goal and scope of the investigation, the materials needed, and the tasks you will perform. The scope of the investigation is determined by the nature of the case such as a criminal case with a search warrant or a civil litigation subpoena. For these types of cases, you can recover only data that is specified in the search warrant or subpoena. Other cases, such as business employee abuse investigations, might not specify limitations in recovering data. When a supervisor or attorney requests that you recover and analyze digital data, refine the investigation plan by determining the elements of the case described in the following list. If refining the plan raises concerns about the case, such as not having enough resources to complete the investigation on time, inform your management or attorney of the problem.

- Determine the scope of the investigation.
- Estimate the number of hours it will take to complete the case.
- Determine whether you should collect only what is relevant to the investigation if you are investigating a large system with a lot of data (sparse evidence).
- Determine whether you must investigate further if you find more clues than anticipated (scope creep).

- Determine whether you have adequate resources to complete the investigation.

- Establish the deadline for completing the investigation.

After you refine the description of the investigation and acquire the disk you need to analyze, you are ready to search for evidence on the disk. In general, you systematically perform the following tasks:

- Examine file and folder (or directory) date and time stamps.

- Locate and extract all log files.

- Locate and recover any temporary print spool files.

- Locate and recover any encrypted or archived (e.g., Zip or Cabinet) files.

- Perform a keyword search on all data within the digital evidence.

- Examine Windows shortcut, Internet, Recycle Bin, and Registry files.

As computer hardware, operating systems, and software applications evolve, review the latest releases of hardware and software to determine how they store data. Determine whether they use new methods to store data and whether current forensic tools can access the data.

USING DRIVESPY TO ANALYZE COMPUTER DATA

In previous chapters, you used DriveSpy to find digital data. In this chapter, you will examine other features of DriveSpy. Before you learn these additional features of DriveSpy, download a copy of the DriveSpy user manual from *www.digitalintel.com/support.htm*.

To use DriveSpy, you need DriveSpy.exe, DriveSpy.ini, and the help file, DriveSpy.hlp, which is included with your data files. Recall that you installed DriveSpy in Chapter 2; the DriveSpy.hlp file should be stored in the Tools folder of your work folder. You also need to work with the DriveSpy.ini file, which is a simple text file that specifies licensing, file, and search features. You customize DriveSpy.ini by modifying its settings to suit a particular disk forensic examination.

The DriveSpy.ini file is divided into four sections: License, File Type, File Group, and Search. Comment fields begin with a semicolon (;) and describe each section and function. The **[License]** section contains the following information, as shown in Figure 10-1:

- Owner's name (the licensee)

- Organization's name

- E-mail address of the owner

- Level of functionality of the DriveSpy release

- Number of licenses issued to the owner

- Notes and comments

- Expiration date for the license
- License key, a twelve-digit hexadecimal number

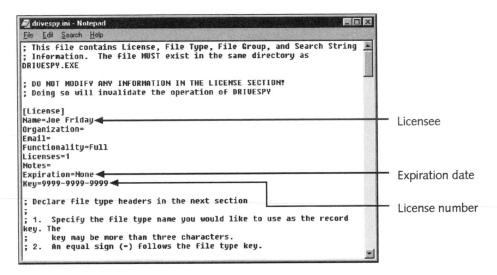

Figure 10-1   License section of DriveSpy.ini

 NOTE You received the license key with your copy of DriveSpy. Do not modify the license section of DriveSpy.ini. Doing so corrupts the license and prevents DriveSpy from running. You can modify all other sections of this file, but be sure to save it as a plain text file with the .ini extension.

The **[File Headers]** section contains the hexadecimal number values for many known file types. These hexadecimal numbers are the header data contained in the first several bytes of all specialized data files such as Microsoft Word documents or Excel spreadsheets and any associated templates. The file header uniquely identifies the file type.

You can use the file header information in DriveSpy to search for specific files that might have had their extensions changed. If someone changes an Excel file named FootballBets.xls to Report.wpt, DriveSpy can identify Report.wpt as an Excel file by reading the hexadecimal values in the file header. For example, suppose you are involved in a case where law enforcement seized a computer during a raid on an illegal gambling operation. The suspect knows he has a high-risk operation that is subject to a police investigation and raid, so he probably hides or changes files containing gambling evidence. The detective handling this case informs you that the suspect has a temporary employment service called Acme Personnel Quick Help.

You are instructed to perform a forensic analysis on the suspect's computer and look for specific evidence of the bookmaking operation. You create a bit-stream image copy of the original evidence drive as described in Chapter 9. Then you shut down your investigation workstation and secure the original evidence disk drive. Now you are ready to start your disk examination.

Your first task is to examine and locate all known files in the folders on the duplicated evidence disk drive. You use DriveSpy to list all allocated files. (You will learn how to do this using the Dir /S command later in this chapter.) You note that Microsoft Office is installed on the evidence drive, but do not find any Excel (.xls) files. After talking to the detective you find out that the suspect used Excel and might have saved Excel files on the C: partition. You can use the DriveSpy.ini File Header information to search for a specific file type. One way to hide data is to change the extension of a sensitive or incriminating file. Later in this chapter you will learn about other techniques for hiding evidence.

To search for files of a particular type, you can use DriveSpy to read the header section of a specific group of files or all files on an evidence disk drive. DriveSpy uses the information listed in the beginning of the File Header section of DriveSpy.ini, shown in Figure 10-2.

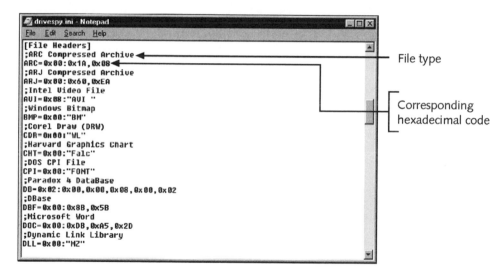

Figure 10-2   File Header section of DriveSpy.ini

Digital Intelligence routinely updates the File Header section as new file types are created. You can download the latest File Type and File Group Information from the Digital Intelligence Web site at *www.digitalintel.com/support.htm*.

TIP

In the File Header section, the file type is specified in a comment field—a line beginning with a semi-colon (;). The line after the file type is the corresponding header value. The header for Microsoft Excel is

XLS=0x00:0xD0,0xCF,0x11,0xE0,0xA1,0xB1,0x1A,0xE1,0x00,0x00.

The 0x before each value is the **designator** that tells DriveSpy that the next value is a hexadecimal number. Without a 0x, DriveSpy treats the value as a decimal number or ASCII character value. The first ten bytes of an Excel file are therefore the hexadecimal values D0, CF, 11, E0, A1, B1, 1A, E1, 00, and 00.

Also note the first hexadecimal number (0x00) followed by a colon. This first hexadecimal number is called the **offset**, which is the first byte where the actual header starts. In an Excel file, the offset starts at the first byte position of zero (0x00). Other types of files use different offsets. For example, in an .avi file, the header starts at byte eight from the beginning byte (0) of the file. Figure 10-3 shows an .avi file open in Hex Workshop.

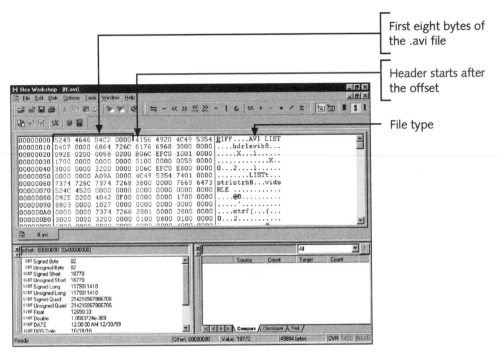

Figure 10-3   Offset of .avi file

Based on the information in the File Header section of DriveSpy.ini, you can search for any file with the Excel spreadsheet header value of 0xD0, 0xCF, 0x11, 0xE0, 0xA1, 0xB1, 0x1A, 0xE1, 0x00, 0x00 and an offset of 0x00. You will perform steps that apply this type of search technique later in this chapter.

You can also add your own file headers to the DriveSpy.ini file. If you encounter a special file, use a tool such as Hex Workshop, WinHex, or Norton Disk Edit to find the file header and offset values. Examine several files with the same extension so that you can determine whether this file type has a common offset. Then add the file header and offset information to DriveSpy.ini in the File Headers section.

The **[File Groups]** section is a convenient place to consolidate similar file types under one group heading. For example, the Graphics file group in DriveSpy.ini lists the extensions of the graphic file types defined in the File Header section, as shown in Figure 10-4.

For a particular file group, you can list file types of interest to the investigation, and then search for several header types at one time.

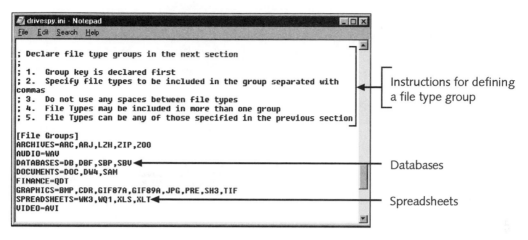

Figure 10-4 File Groups section of DriveSpy.ini

In the case of the gambling suspect's computer, you could look for all known spreadsheets in addition to Excel spreadsheets, such as Quattro Pro, Lotus 123, Quicken, Superbase 4, or all-in-one products such as Microsoft Works, OpenOffice, and StarOffice. An important exception to this recommendation is when you are analyzing a disk under the authority of a search warrant that limits your search to certain types of files. For example, if the warrant explicitly states that you can recover only Excel files, you cannot look for other spreadsheet formats such as Quattro Pro. If the warrant allows you to recover spreadsheet files, you can search for all spreadsheet formats. Consult with the investigator or prosecutor in charge of the case for guidance.

If necessary, you can define your own file groups. For example, suppose you are investigating an intellectual property case involving Microsoft Word documents, Harvard Graphics images, TIFF graphic files, and Waveform audio files. First find the label names for each of these file types in the File Type section of DriveSpy.ini.

- Microsoft Word: DOC

- Harvard Graphics 3.0: SH3

- Harvard Graphics Show File: SHW

- TIFF file: TIF

- Waveform Audio: WAV

For example, "Microsoft Word" is the name of the DOC file type. To create a new group for your intellectual property investigation, insert the following text in the DriveSpy.ini File Group section:

INTEL_PROP=DOC,SH3,SHW,TIF,WAV

Note you can give the file group any unique name. Use descriptive, meaningful names, such as those that specify the case number and suspect name, to clarify the purpose of the file group. Do not use short cryptic labels.

The **[Search]** section in DriveSpy.ini can include one or many keywords. Recall from Chapter 6 that you can create your own search group and keywords. The Search section is the last section in DriveSpy.ini, and is the section computer forensic investigators use most often. The Search section is shown in Figure 10-5.

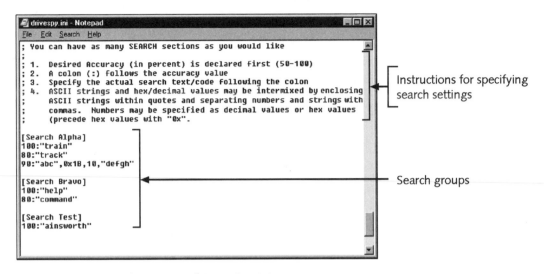

Figure 10-5   Search section of DriveSpy.ini

To improve the data search, you can define the level of accuracy for the search from 50 to 100 percent. The accuracy is defined by entering the percentage value with a colon (:) between the percentage number and the keyword. For example if you want to search for the word BOOKMAKING, you enter 100:"bookmaking". Because the search is not case sensitive, DriveSpy will search the specified evidence disk or data set for text that exactly matches "bookmaking" except for the case. For example, it would find Bookmaking, BOOKMAKING, and bookmaking.

If you think the evidence disk might contain misspelled words, you can lower the accuracy of comparison. For example, if you set the accuracy to 50 percent by entering 50:"bookmaking" in the Search section of DriveSpy.ini, DriveSpy finds any word that contains at least five letters that match any of the ten letters in bookmaking, such as bookkmaking and bookmakeing, which are possible misspellings of bookmaking.

However, a 50 percent search can produce **false–positive hits**, which means that it finds matches that do not apply to the case. In this example any sequential combination of ten letters will provide a successful match. False-positive hits include bookie, maker, lookie, booking, kmake, bokzmake7, and so on.

To minimize the false-positive hits, increase the percentage value. It is best to start high at 100 percent and decrement 10 percent at a time to minimize the number of matches found.

DriveSpy interprets keywords that are enclosed by quotation marks, such as "bookmaking", as literal keywords. That is, when quotation marks are used, DriveSpy searches for those values exactly. You can search for any character that you can type on a keyboard, such as: "1a2b[}\" or "^&87 2%20".

One character you cannot search for literally is the quotation mark because DriveSpy interprets the quotation mark as the start and end of the literal string. Entering """" produces errors. Instead, you can use the hexadecimal value (a decimal value can be used, but not recommended) of a quotation mark. You can find hexadecimal equivalents of characters in an ASCII chart or in Hex Workshop—click Help on the menu bar, click Contents, select the Index tab, if necessary, and then click ASCII Character Set and Display. The hexadecimal value for a quotation mark is 22, and the decimal is 34. To search for quotation marks, use 0x22 in the search text where you expect quotation marks to appear. For example, suppose you want to search for "place bets by Friday", including the quotation marks. You could enter `100:0x22,"place bets by Friday",34` in the Search section of the DriveSpy.ini file.

This line starts with 100 to specify that DriveSpy search for text that exactly matches the keyword after the colon. Following the colon is the 0x22 value, which is the hexadecimal equivalent of a quotation mark. A comma then separates the hexadecimal value from the literal "place bets by Friday" followed by another comma. The last value, 34, is the ASCII decimal equivalent of a quotation mark. You can use either the hexadecimal or the decimal values in the Search label section.

An alternate method to search for specific values such as uppercase letters requires that you list all ASCII uppercase hexadecimal values. For example, to search for the word BOOKMAKING, use the following search string:

100:0x42,0x4F,0x4F,0x4B,0x4D,0x41,0x4B,0x49,0x4E,0x47

To search for the capitalized word Bookmaking, use its hexadecimal value of

0x42,0x6F,0x6F,0x6B,0x6D,0x61,0x6B,0x69,0x6E,0x67,

as shown in Figure 10-6.

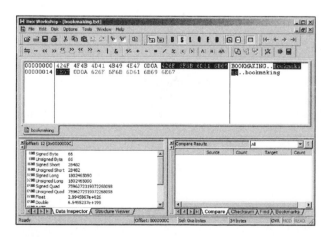

Figure 10-6 Hex conversion of "Bookmaking"

When you have finished updating DriveSpy.ini, save it in the same location as the DriveSpy.exe and DriveSpy.hlp file. As a standard practice, before you change DriveSpy.ini, you should make a backup copy of this file and store it in a safe location.

DriveSpy Command Switches

DriveSpy provides several switches, or parameters, to make its shell commands flexible. Most of these switches are similar to DOS command switches. Appendix C contains a list of most commonly used switches for DriveSpy. Note that the wildcards commonly used in DOS and Windows such as the asterisk (*) and the question mark (?) are also used in DriveSpy.

DriveSpy Keyword Searching

You use the DriveSpy Search command to search a drive at the physical level (Drive mode) or the logical level (Part mode). You can also use Search to analyze specific files and folders by specifying one or more keywords that the files are likely to contain. To record results from the search, create an output file using the Output command before using the Search command. You can then examine the results of the search thoroughly. (If you do not create an output file, the search results will scroll off the screen and you will not be able to see the results.) Always use the Output command to create a log of your work.

The Search command has a variety of switches that allow you to specify which files or folders to search. Refer to Appendix C for more details on Search command switches. Before using the Search command, update the DriveSpy.ini file by adding the keywords you want to use to search the evidence drive.

The Search command is extremely reliable in locating keywords in a formatted file. In Drive mode, Search can analyze other file systems such as NTFS, HFS, and UNIX/Linux, as well as search the inter-partition gap areas of a disk drive. In Partition mode, you can streamline Search to search specific files and folders. The only disadvantage to the Search command is that it cannot analyze archive files such as Zip or encrypted files.

DriveSpy Scripts

With DriveSpy, you can use the Script command to launch predefined commands. The **Script command** runs a script file that lists DriveSpy shell commands. A script is a plain text file that contains the commands you want to run. Consider using a script file to ensure consistent processing of an investigation that may involve more than one disk media such as several hard disks. By using scripts, you ensure that you have not left out any important commands or steps that you need to perform for each disk.

To use the Script command, specify the name of the script and the associated path, as in the following example:

```
Script C:\Chap10\Chapter\Scr_File.scr
```

You can then run the Script command from the DriveSpy System, Drive, or Partition prompts.

To create a script file, use a text editor such as Notepad to enter the commands that you want to execute in their proper syntax. As in a DOS batch file, you enter each command line by line, and DriveSpy runs each command in the order in which they are listed. The following is an example of a simple script file:

```
Output C:\Chap10\Chapter\Case_10.log
Page Off
Drive A
Part 1
DBExport C:\Chap10\Chapter\CaseDBexp.txt
DIR *.xls /s
Search Spreadsheets
COPY *.* /S /T:xls C:\Chap10\Case_10\XLS_File
QUIT
```

This script records in a log file the output of the commands, turns off Page mode, switches to Drive A, then Partition 1, exports a detailed list of all files, lists the .xls files in the partition, searches for spreadsheets as specified in the Search section of DriveSpy.ini, copies the spreadsheets to the XLS_File folder, and then exits DriveSpy.

If necessary, you can run other scripts from any script. That is, you can nest script calls from one script to another script file. When the called script file completes its commands, it returns control to the previous script. For example, suppose you need to create two file listings of all Microsoft Excel files on a disk. The output for both files should be stored in different folders for further analysis. One folder will contain all allocated (files not deleted) Excel files. The other folder will contain all deleted Excel files. You can create a nested script file to automate these tasks.

To list all the Excel files on the suspect's disk, use the Dbexport command to write the recovered Excel files in descending order to a folder, as in *work folder*\Chap10\Case_10\ Xls_File. Then write the deleted Excel files in ascending order to *work folder*\Chap10 \Case_10\Xls_Del. To do this, you can create three separate script files. The first script launches the initialization commands for your investigation. The next two scripts contain the additional command to extract the Excel files.

To create the main script file:

1. In Windows, start Notepad.

2. Type the following DriveSpy commands, substituting the appropriate drive for C: and the appropriate folder name for *work folder*:

```
Output C:\work folder\Chap10\Chapter\Case_10\Case_10.log
Page off
Drive 1
Part 1
Dbexport  C:\work folder\Chap10\Chapter\Case_10\Dbexp_10.txt
C:\work folder\Chap10\Chapter\Case_10\Script Scr_file.scr
```

10

```
C:\work folder\Chap10\Chapter\Case_10\Script Scr_del.scr
Quit
```

3. Save this script file as **Scr_main.scr** in the Chap10\Chapter folder in your work folder.

NOTE

The DriveSpy manual specifies using .scr for script files. However, Windows might associate .scr files with a Windows program, making it awkward to manually edit the file in Windows. If necessary, you can use a different extension for DriveSpy scripts to minimize conflicts. For example, use .txt or .spt.

Now that you completed the main script for your investigation, you can create the two other scripts that are called from the main script.

To create the other two script files:

1. Start a new document in Notepad.

2. Type the following command, substituting the appropriate drive for C: and the appropriate folder name for *work folder*:

```
Copy *.xls /S /-O C:\work folder\Chap10\Chapter\Case_10\
Xls_file
```

3. If necessary, create a subfolder called Case_10 in the **Chapter** subfolder of the **Chap10** folder. Save this Notepad file as **Scr_file.scr** in the Chap10\Chapter\Case_10 folder in your work folder.

4. Start a new document and then type the following command:

```
Unerase *.xls /S /O C:\work folder\Chap10\Chapter\Case_10\
Xls_del
```

5. Save this file as **Scr_del.scr** in the Chap10\Chapter\Case_10 folder in your work folder.

6. Close Notepad.

Each script can include one or more commands. As a standard practice, consider building a library of several scripts to keep track of what you have done and to reuse during other investigations.

DriveSpy Data-Integrity Tools

This section examines three commands you have already used in the text: Wipe, MD5, and Dbexport. These commands ensure integrity of the disk media in a variety of ways.

Use the **Wipe command** to overwrite possibly sensitive data from a disk or data that could corrupt any output data to the disk. You can overwrite data on a specific sector, partition, or drive, or eliminate data from unallocated space such as file slack space, unallocated free space on a logical partition, or the master boot record. You can use Wipe at the DriveSpy Drive or Partition level. Appendix C lists the common switches for the Wipe command.

Because Wipe can remove all the data from a disk, including your system disk, carefully check the switches and specified drives before pressing Enter to run the Wipe command.

Another data-integrity feature that DriveSpy provides is an RFC-Compliant **Message Digest version 5 (MD5) hash function**. Use the MD5 command to collect the MD5 hash signatures for any data on a disk. Recall that you use an MD5 hash signature to verify that the file has not changed, serving as a fingerprint to the file. You can obtain the hash value of specific files, a partition, or an entire disk. MD5 operates at the Drive or Partition level.

You can use the following switches with the MD5 command. (These switches are described in Appendix C.)

/S   Examines all subdirectories recursively

/A   Hashes files with specific attributes

/O   Sorts output

/T   Hashes files of a specified type

/G   Hashes files in a specified group

To hash an entire drive or partition depending on current mode, use the following command:

    MD5

To hash all files in a partition, use the following command:

    MD5 *.* /S

To hash Myfile.doc, use the following command:

    MD5 Myfile.doc

When you use the MD5 command in Partition mode for FAT file system disks, MD5 lists the boot sector, first FAT, second FAT, root directory, and then the data area of the partition. In Drive mode, MD5 provides one hash signature value for the entire physical disk, whether the disk uses a FAT file system or not.

The third data-integrity DriveSpy command is Dbexport, which creates a text file of all specified data in the selected file or disk. Dbexport also lists all deleted files in addition to current allocated files on a disk drive. The Dbexport output file includes the following data fields:

- File path
- Filename
- File extension
- File long name
- File size
- Starting cluster position on the partition

10

- Attribute settings:
- File archive switch setting
- Directory switch setting
- Volume switch setting
- System switch setting
- Hidden switch setting
- Read-only switch setting
- Erased pseudo-attribute setting
- File date values:
- Creation date
- Modification date
- Last access date
- MD5 file hash signature (/MD5 switch must be used)
- Header values of each file (/HDR switch must be used)

You can import the text file that Dbexport produces into most spreadsheet or database programs such as Excel or Access.

You can use Dbexport only in DriveSpy Partition mode with any of the following switches. (The first five switches are described in Appendix C.)

/S   Exports files in all subdirectories recursively

/A   Exports files with specific attributes

/O   Sorts output

/T   Exports files of a specified type

/G   Exports files in a specified group

/MD5   Generates a Message Digest version 5 hash file signature for each file

/HDR   Lists the first twelve bytes for each file in the output

To list all files within a partition, use the following command:

```
Dbexport
```

To list all Excel files in the current default directory, use the following command:

```
Dbexport *.xls
```

To list all Excel files in the current directory and all subdirectories with an MD5 hash signature for each file, use the following command:

```
Dbexport *.XLS /S /MD5
```

DriveSpy Residual Data Collection Tools

Deleted files on a Microsoft FAT file system disk become residual data. Recall that residual data resides in unallocated or slack space of the partition. DriveSpy provides the **SaveSlack** and **SaveFree** commands to copy this residual data and save it in a file that you can analyze.

The SaveSlack command allows you to copy all slack space from individual files or all files on a partition. The destination file must have an 8.3 filename because it will be created from a DOS program. As it will contain formatted and unformatted binary data, .dat is an appropriate extension. To copy all file slack space on the current partition to an output file named Slack_10.dat in the Chap10\Chapter\Case_10 folder on drive C, use the following command:

```
SaveSlack C:\Chap10\Chapter\Case_10\Slack_10.dat
```

To save all file slack space for all Excel files in the current default directory to a file named Xls_slk.dat in the Chap10\Chapter\Case_10 folder on drive C, use the following command. (Recall that the /S switch indicates that SaveSlack should retrieve data from slack space in all subdirectories.)

```
SaveSlack *.xls C:\Chap10\Chapter\Case_10\Xls_slk.dat /S
```

You can use SaveSlack only in DriveSpy Partition mode. (The first five switches in the following list are described in more detail in Appendix C.)

/S   Copies data from file slack in all subdirectories recursively

/A   Copies file slack files with specific attributes

/O   Sorts output

/T   Copies file slack files of a specified type

/G   Copies file slack files in a specified group

/RAM   Collects only RAM slack area of a file

/FILE   Collects only disk slack area of a file

The SaveSlack command is one of the few tools that allows you to separate RAM slack from disk slack in different data files.

Similar to the SaveSlack command, the SaveFree command collects all unallocated disk space on a partition. It works only in Partition modes, and does not have any switches. To save data in the unallocated space on the current partition to a file named Free_10.dat in the Chap10\Chapter\Case_10 folder on drive C, use the following command:

```
SaveFree C:\Chap10\Chapter\Case_10\Free_10.dat
```

The advantage of using this command is that it collects all unallocated space from a disk partition and saves it to a data file for follow-up analysis. You can examine deleted files and even RAM slack from this data.

Other Useful DriveSpy Command Tools

In addition to the Wipe, MD5, and Dbexport data-integrity commands and the SaveSlack and SaveFree residual data-collection commands, DriveSpy provides several other useful commands including FAT interrogation commands and navigation and viewing tools.

The **Get FAT Entry (GFE)** command displays the FAT entry for a specified cluster, and works only at the DriveSpy Partition level. The primary advantage of the GFE command is that it provides the next cluster link for a specified FAT entry, which helps you rebuild fragmented deleted files. For example, if you locate data of evidence value for your investigation in an unallocated cluster, you can check the FAT to see where the next link is located. Using the GFE command with the cluster number of the evidence fragment, you can determine the location of the next cluster associated with the first fragment of evidence. By using this command for unallocated disk space, you can piece together the remaining fragmented clusters of a deleted file.

You must supply the cluster number of the FAT entry you want to display. For example, the following command displays the FAT entry for cluster 230:

```
GFE 230
```

The disadvantage in using the GFE command is that it provides only the next higher numbered cluster location. Because of the limitations of FAT, it does not locate the beginning cluster.

The **Chain FAT Entry (CFE)** command displays all clusters after a cluster you specify. Use the CFE command to list all known FAT entries on all cluster positions for residual file data in unallocated disk space. Like GFE, the CFE command works only in the Partition mode of the disk, and you have to designate the starting cluster. For example, the following command lists all FAT cluster links starting with the cluster number you have specified until it runs out of FAT links:

```
CFE 230
```

The CFE command only works forward from the cluster number you provide. It does not list previous cluster positions of a deleted file.

Like the CFE command, **Chain Directory Entry (CDE)** displays all directory cluster positions, and works only in the Partition mode. You must specify the directory you are searching. For example, the following command displays directory cluster positions in MyDocuments:

```
CDE MyDocuments
```

The **Trace Directory Cluster (TDC)** command helps you rebuild a directory on a disk partition. It provides the name of the directory that resides in the specified cluster position. You can use the TDC command only in Partition mode. For example, to determine the directory in cluster 1111, use the following command:

```
TDC 1111
```

The **Cluster command** displays a specified cluster in a hexadecimal view, letting you quickly examine a specified cluster area of a partition. You can use the Cluster command only in Partition mode. Figure 10-7 shows the output of the Cluster command.

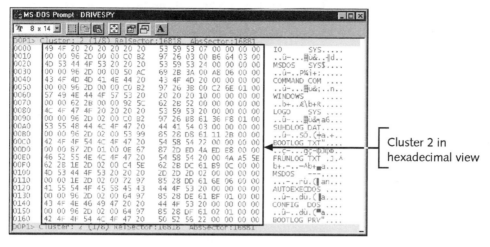

Figure 10-7   Using the Cluster command

The **Boot command** allows you to examine the boot sector area of a disk partition, and displays the boot sector statistics for the specified partition. You can use the Boot command only in Partition mode. Figure 10-8 shows the output of the Boot command.

```
DOP1:\>BOOT

Bootsector at Absolute Sector: 63 - Type 0x0B (FAT32)

OEM & Version ID:     MSWIN4.1      Sectors Per FAT:       8393
Bytes Per Sector:     512           Extended Flags:        0x0000
Sectors Per Cluster:  8             File System Version:   0x0000
Reserved Sectors:     32            Root Dir at Cluster:   2
Number of FATs:       2             FileSys Info Sector:   1
Root Dir Entries:     0             Backup Boot Sector:    6
Media Descriptor:     0xF8          Reserved[0]:           0x0000
Sectors Per Track:    63            Reserved[1]:           0x0000
Number of Heads:      255           Reserved[2]:           0x0000
Hidden Sectors:       63            Reserved[3]:           0x0000
Total Sectors:        8610777       Reserved[4]:           0x0000
Drive Number:         0x80          Reserved[5]:           0x0000
Boot Signature:       0x29          Ext Boot Signature:    0x41615252
32 bit Volume ID:     0x276212F5    FSINFO Signature:      0x61417272
Volume Label:         NO NAME       Free Clusters:         399250
File System:          FAT32         Next Free Cluster:     2

Clusters:    1074245
FAT1 @Sect: 32                      FAT2 @Sect: 8425
Data @Sect: 16818                   Root @Sect: 16818
```

Figure 10-8   Using the Boot command

The **PartMap command** provides a sector map of a partition, listing the start and ending sector positions of each component of the partition. You can use the PartMap command only in Partition mode. Figure 10-9 shows the Partition information.

```
D0P1:\>PARTMAP

Partition 1: Primary, (Active), FAT32 (0x0B)
Defined in Partition Table at Absolute Sector: 0 (Entry Number 1)

Sectors/Cluster:        8
Total Sectors:          8610777
Total Clusters:         1074244
Raw Capacity:           4204 Mb
Formatted Capacity:     4196 Mb

                    |   Start     End   |
                    |   Sector   Sector |
----------------    | --------  -------- |
Partition           |       0   8610776 |
Boot Sector         |       0        31 |
FAT1                |      32      8424 |
FAT2                |    8425     16817 |
Data Area           |   16818   8610769 |
Partition Slack     | 8610770   8610776 |

* Root Directory at Cluster: 2
```

Figure 10-9   Using the PartMap command

The **Tables command** provides a sector map of a partition, listing each partition table for all partitions on a disk drive. You can use the Tables command in Drive and Partition mode. Figure 10-10 shows the partition table for the drive outlining everything from the CHS begin and end along with the partition offset and length. (Recall that Chapter 3 discusses CHS.)

```
D0P1:\>TABLES

Absolute Sector: 0 - Partition Table 1

Part Part        Boot     |    Start    |    End      |
Code Type    Hid Code Act |  C   H   S  |  C   H   S  |   Offset     Length
---- -------- --- ---- --- | ---- --- -- | ---- --- -- | ---------- ----------
0x0B FAT32       0x80  *  |    0   1   1 |  535 254 63 |        63    8610777
0x0F ExtendX     0x00     |  536   0   1 |  383 254 63 |   8610840   30459240
0x00 Unused      0x00     |    0   0   0 |    0   0  0 |         0          0
0x00 Unused      0x00     |    0   0   0 |    0   0  0 |         0          0


Absolute Sector: 8610840 - Partition Table 2

Part Part        Boot     |    Start    |    End      |
Code Type    Hid Code Act |  C   H   S  |  C   H   S  |   Offset     Length
---- -------- --- ---- --- | ---- --- -- | ---- --- -- | ---------- ----------
0x0B FAT32       0x00     |  536   1   1 |   47 254 63 |        63    8610777
0x05 Extended    0x00     |   48   0   1 |  383 254 63 |   8610840   21848400
0x00 Unused      0x00     |    0   0   0 |    0   0  0 |         0          0
0x00 Unused      0x00     |    0   0   0 |    0   0  0 |         0          0


Absolute Sector: 17221680 - Partition Table 3

Part Part        Boot     |    Start    |    End      |
Code Type    Hid Code Act |  C   H   S  |  C   H   S  |   Offset     Length
---- -------- --- ---- --- | ---- --- -- | ---- --- -- | ---------- ----------
0x0B FAT32       0x00     |   48   1   1 |  383 254 63 |        63   21848337
0x00 Unused      0x00     |    0   0   0 |    0   0  0 |         0          0
0x00 Unused      0x00     |    0   0   0 |    0   0  0 |         0          0
0x00 Unused      0x00     |    0   0   0 |    0   0  0.|         0          0
```

Figure 10-10   Partition table

USING OTHER DIGITAL INTELLIGENCE COMPUTER FORENSICS TOOLS

In addition to DriveSpy, Digital Intelligence provides other tools to perform computer forensics. These tools are compact enough to fit on a forensic boot floppy disk, and are sold individually. They are not included with your data files, but are described here for your reference. For more information on any of these programs, visit *www.digitalintel.com*.

Using PDBlock and PDWipe

The **PDBlock** program is designed to prevent data from being written on a disk drive, and can only be used in a true MS-DOS environment. Running PDBlock from a Windows DOS shell causes unpredictable errors.

PDBlock works at the BIOS level by turning off the write capability of Interrupt 13. It is designed to work with all IDE, EIDE, and some SCSI disk drives. Test PDBlock and any other write-blocker utility before you use it for investigation data acquisitions.

The **PDWipe** program is designed to overwrite hard disk drives, cleaning all data from the drive. Use PDWipe to overwrite all sectors of a disk, which then means you must repartition and format the disk to make it usable. Use PDWipe in a computer forensic investigation to sanitize a disk used in a previous investigation.

10

USING ACCESSDATA'S FORENSIC TOOLKIT

The **Forensic Toolkit (FTK)** from AccessData is a data-analysis tool that provides you with more forensic examination features than most other tools. FTK is a GUI-based utility that runs in Windows XP, 2000, Me, or 9x operating systems. AccessData provides a demo version of their FTK tool, which has most of the same features as the full-licensed version, except it only allows you to examine up to 5000 files. In addition to examining image files from other vendors, FTK also allows you to directly access a target evidence disk (i.e., the bit-stream copy), folder (directory), or specific file.

Demo copies of FTK are available at *www.accessdata.com*. To test this product, be sure to download and install the latest release of the FTK demo and the Known File Filter (KFF).

FTK can perform forensic analysis on the following file systems:

- Microsoft FAT12, FAT16, and FAT32
- Microsoft NTFS (for Windows NT, 2000, and XP)
- Linux Ext2fs and Ext3fs (licensed version only)

FTK provides flexibility in analyzing data from several sources, including bit-stream imaging files from other vendors. It can also read entire evidence drives or subsets of data on specific evidence drives, allowing you to consolidate large volumes of data from many sources when processing a computer forensics analysis. An example of this might be when you have several workstations and servers where suspects might have stored incriminating evidence. With FTK you can store everything from bit-stream image files to recovered server folders on one investigation drive. FTK analyzes the following bit-stream image file types:

- EnCase image files
- Linux or UNIX dd image files
- New Technologies, Inc. (NTI) SafeBack image files
- FTK Explorer dd image files
- DriveSpy's SaveSect output files

AccessData provides a separate program called the **Known File Filter (KFF)**, which integrates only with FTK. KFF filters known application software files from view, such as MSWord.exe, and identifies known illegal images such as child pornography. KFF compares known file hash digital signatures to files on your evidence disk drive or bit-stream image file to see if it contains contraband images. Periodically AccessData updates the known digital signatures and posts an updated KFF.

FTK also produces a Case Log file, where you can maintain a detailed log of all activities during your examination. All transactions such as keyword searches or data extractions are recorded in the log file for the current case. This log is also handy for reporting errors to AccessData.

FTK provides two options for searching for keywords. One option is the live search, which you have performed in previous chapters. Another option, an indexed search, provides for rapid search results, though it does have some shortcomings. For example, performing an indexed search does not let you search for hexadecimal string values. Also, depending on how the data is stored on the evidence disk drive, indexing might not catalog every word.

To facilitate keyword searches, FTK can index words on an evidence drive. Indexing catalogs all words on the evidence disk so that FTK can find them quickly. After you have FTK index all word data, locating keywords is instantaneous. Note, however, that indexing an evidence disk or bit-stream image file takes several hours to complete. Running this feature is best done overnight.

FTK provides a live search feature to overcome the shortcomings of an indexed search. You can use the live search feature to search for alphanumeric and hexadecimal values on the evidence disk. This feature also accesses and compares all data on the evidence drive or bit-stream image file.

During the data-analysis processing, FTK opens compressed file systems, including Microsoft Cabinet (.cab) files, Microsoft personal e-mail folders (.pst or .ost), and .zip files. FTK indexes any compressed data files that it can open.

You can generate FTK reports using the FTK Report Wizard. To generate a report, you first need to **bookmark** specific findings of evidence during an examination. FTK and other computer forensics programs use bookmarks to tag and document discovered digital evidence. As you are analyzing an evidence disk, you designate a bookmark when you find data you want to note, such as evidence relevant to your investigation. When you are using the FTK Report Wizard, you can select the bookmarked data you want to include in a report. FTK then integrates all the specified bookmarks and related case information in a Hypertext Markup Language (HTML) document. Each bookmark appears as a hyperlink in the HTML document, allowing the reader to view the report in a browser. The FTK Report Wizard also allows you to insert external documents such as a Microsoft Word report into the HTML file. Before printing an FTK report, you might need to use Adobe Acrobat or a conversion program to convert the HTML code to a Portable Document Format (PDF) file.

A password recovery program available from AccessData is the Password Recovery Toolkit (PRTK), which is designed to accept possible password lists from many sources, allowing investigators to open password-protected files. You can create a password list in many ways, including using FTK to generate a password list, as shown in Figure 10-11, or creating a text file of passwords yourself, as shown in Figure 10-12. You can download a free demo version of PRTK from the AccessData Web site at *www.accessdata.com*.

10

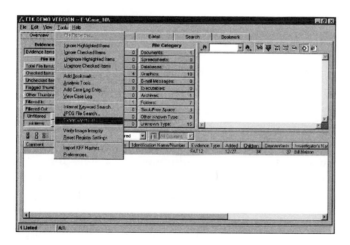

Figure 10-11   Using FTK to generate a password list

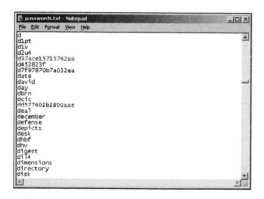

Figure 10-12   Partial list of possible passwords

FTK identifies known encrypted files and those that seem to be encrypted. For example, a simple encrypted file is a password-protected WinZip file or PGP file. For WinZip password-protected files, FTK displays the filenames contained in the compressed file, as shown in Figure 10-13.

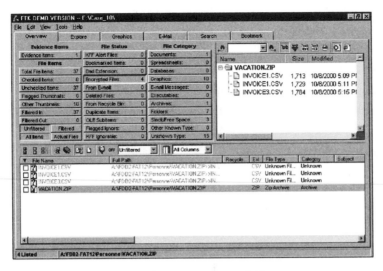

Figure 10-13   FTK displaying encrypted files

PERFORMING A COMPUTER FORENSIC ANALYSIS

As a standard practice, you should perform the following basic steps for all computing-forensics investigations. For more information on basic processes and recommendations, visit the International Association of Computer Investigative Specialists (IACIS) Web site at *www.cops.org*.

1. Before starting an investigation use only recently wiped media (disks), for the target drive that have been reformatted and inspected for computer viruses. For example, use the Digital Intelligence PDWipe or the DriveSpy Wipe command or SecureClean from AccessData to clean all data from the target disk drive you plan to use.

2. Inventory the hardware on the suspect's computer and note the condition of the computer when seized. Document all physical hardware components as part of your evidence acquisition process.

3. On a PC, remove the original disk drive, and then check the date and time values in the system's CMOS.

4. Record how you acquired data from the original disk—note, for example, that you performed a bit-stream image copy or a disk-to-disk bit-stream copy.

5. When examining the forensic bit-stream image copy of the disk's contents, process the data methodically and logically.

6. List all directories (folders) and files on the copied bit-stream image or disk. For example, use the DriveSpy Dbexport command with a switch appropriate to the needs of the investigation.

7. If possible, examine the contents of all data files in all directories starting at the root directory level of the volume partition.

8. For all encrypted files that might be related to the investigation, make your best effort to recover the contents of each file. For example, use a password recovery tool such as AccessData's PRTK or NTI's Password Recovery.

9. Create a document that lists the directories and files on the evidence drive. Note where specific evidence is found, indicating the relationship to the investigation.

10. Identify the function of every executable (binary or .exe) file that does not match known hash values. For example, after you perform a negative hash search that shows no listing for a specific executable file, examine the file to see what it does and how it works.

11. Always maintain control of all evidence and findings, and document everything as you progress through your examination.

Setting Up Your Forensic Workstation

Chapter 5 discussed setting up an investigator's lab. This chapter extends that discussion by explaining how to set up your forensic workstation in your lab. Before you can start an investigation, your computer forensic workstation must be properly configured and ready to process the investigation. The following lists provide general descriptions of the minimum components and software necessary to install on your investigation workstation. Adjust these lists to your specific investigation needs. You need the following computer hardware for your computer forensic workstation:

- PC with color monitor, keyboard, mouse, and rewriteable compact disc (CD-RW) drive

- Cables and tools including IDE ribbon cables (preferably 36 inches), extra 12-volt power extenders and splitters, assorted tools such as screwdrivers, an IDE 40-to-44-pin adapter bridge for notebook computer drives, and an optional SCSI card with cables

- One or more spare target drives to collect and analyze evidence

- Anti-static wrist strap and pad

You also need to have the following software installed on your computer forensic workstation:

- Windows 9x or more recent operating system installed on the C: drive and a forensic boot floppy disk. If you are using Windows 9x, configure the MSDOS.SYS file to allow you to boot to a MS-DOS prompt or to Windows. (Refer to Chapter 2 for specific instructions.)

- Bit-stream acquisition tool such as DriveSpy (you can use the SavePart, SaveSect, and CopySect commands). You can also use programs such as EnCase's EN.EXE DOS, Ontrack's CaptureIt, FTK Explorer, or Linux dd to acquire data.

- A computer forensic analysis tool such as DriveSpy, FTK, or EnCase, and a write-blocker utility.

Besides the specified hardware and software, you also need the following types of media:

- Recordable compact discs (CD-Rs)

- Floppy disks

- Evidence forms and labels

Install all necessary and available hardware and software components before you start your forensic analysis to ensure that you do not overlook a necessary step or file. Add any other hardware components that can contribute to your investigation, such as Zip drives or Jaz drives. Remember to test each component, both hardware and software, before applying it to an actual investigation. Become familiar with all the tools prior to the actual disk examination.

Performing Forensic Analysis on Microsoft File Systems

When analyzing digital evidence on Microsoft file systems, perform the following general steps, adapting them as necessary to suit the needs of your investigation:

1. Before connecting a disk-to-disk bit-stream copied evidence disk to the investigation workstation, run an antivirus program to scan all forensic workstation disk drives for viruses.

2. After connecting the disk-to-disk bit-stream copied evidence disk, run an antivirus program again on all disks including the copied evidence drive.

   Note that you should run an antivirus utility for copied suspect disks, not on bit-stream image files such as EnCase, dd, and SaveSect save-set volumes.

3. For the copied suspect disk, examine all boot files located in the root directory for primary boot drive. Determine if a boot manager utility is installed, and then identify all separate boot volumes.

4. Recover all deleted files and save them to a specified location on an investigation work drive. For example, create a subfolder on the investigation workstation to store all recovered data. Use the DriveSpy UnErase command with the appropriate switches to do so.

5. Recover all file slack and unallocated (free) space to an investigation subfolder. For example, use the DriveSpy SaveSlack and SaveFree commands with the appropriate switches to do so.

FAT Disk Forensic Analysis

When analyzing a FAT disk, your first step is to make a bit-stream image copy of the evidence disk. Preserve the evidence disk by creating image volumes that can be stored on CDs. Then recreate the original evidence volume from the CDs to an evidence disk that you use for the forensic analysis. Determine whether to copy the entire drive or each partition volume separately. If your target disk is not identical to the evidence disk, copy each partition with the DriveSpy SavePart command, for example. If your target disk is identical to the evidence disk, you can use the DriveSpy CopySect command. The following steps outline how to acquire evidence from a FAT disk.

To acquire evidence from a FAT disk:

1. Prepare the investigation target drive as outlined in the preceding steps.

2. In DOS, create a case folder for storing your evidence. If you have not already done so, create Chap10\Chapter folders in your work folder for this book. For a live investigation, you might use a folder name that reflects the case number, such as Case_10-2. If the target disk is drive E:, for example, and you are working at the DOS command line, type **md e: *work folder*\\Chap10\\ Chapter** and then press **Enter**. This is the main folder to store your evidence.

3. Change to the Chap10\Chapter directory by typing **cd e:*work folder*\\ Chap10\\Chapter** and then pressing **Enter**. Then use the DOS md command to create the following subfolders in your work folder:

   Chap10\Chapter\Unerase   Folder (to store all recovered deleted files)

   Chap10\Chapter\Allocate   Folder (to store all allocated files)

   Chap10\Chapter\Image   Folder (to store all bit-stream image files)

   Chap10\Chapter\Residual   Folder (to store all slack and free space data)

   Chap10\Chapter\SSheets   Folder (to store any special files, such as spreadsheets or graphics)

   Note that the name of the SSheets folder changes depending on the kinds of files you are seeking. For example, if you are searching for graphic files, you could name this folder Graphics. Figure 10-14 shows these folders created for a live investigation.

4. Connect the suspect evidence disk and target (investigation) disk to the investigation workstation. If a hardware write-blocker is available (such as the Acard AEC-7720WP), use it on the suspect disk.

5. Boot the investigation workstation to DOS using the forensic boot floppy disk or Windows 9x DOS mode. If no hardware write-blocker is installed, use a software write-blocker such as Digital Intelligence PDBlock.

10

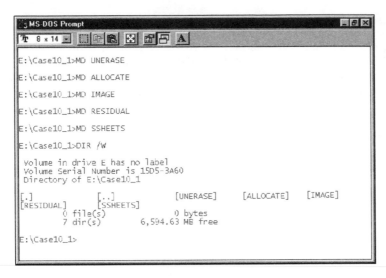

Figure 10-14   Using the md command

6. Run a data acquisition tool such as DriveSpy (using the SavePart command) or FTK Explorer on the suspect disk drive. If you are using the DriveSpy SavePart and WritePart commands, create a partition on the target evidence drive that is the same size as on the original evidence drive.

7. When you are finished, archive the bit-stream image data to a CD-R or other media such as tape or Jaz cartridges.

8. Secure the evidence drive and any archive media in an appropriate evidence storage container, maintaining appropriate evidence controls.

After you have completed the acquisition steps of the computer evidence, you can process and analyze the data.

Processing and Analyzing Computer Evidence

This step requires attention to detail. Keep the processing and analysis of your investigation free from any intentional or unintentional interference to maintain the integrity of your findings. To process digital evidence from a computer, you must extract all relevant data from the acquired evidence. In this section, you learn how to examine an entire disk. Remember to tailor your processing and analysis to the specific needs of the investigation, such as one governed by a search warrant that specifies what you can locate and recover only Excel spreadsheets. If you find a Quicken file, for example, you cannot recover it because of the restrictions of the warrant. However, recall that in civil litigation cases, the attorney you are working for may direct you to recover everything.

The following steps are recommendations; how you apply each step depends on the investigation. Each computer forensic examination should include most if not all of these tasks, which use DriveSpy. You can also use other tools such as FTK or EnCase; refer to their user guides for instructions.

To prepare to use DriveSpy:

1. If the evidence disk was saved with the DriveSpy SavePart command, restore all partitions of the original evidence drive to a target drive. Reboot the investigation workstation after you have restored each partition to make the newly created partition on the target drive visible to the operating system.

2. Boot the investigation workstation to DOS (MS-DOS 6.22 or Windows 9x DOS mode).

3. If available, run PDBlock on the target evidence drive. For example, type **PDBlock 1** (the 1 assumes the target evidence drive is the second drive on your forensics machine) and press **Enter**. This command write-blocks the second drive on the machine.

4. At the DOS prompt, change to the investigation work drive where you had previously created the folders. To change to the Chap10\Chapter folder in your work folder on the investigation drive (drive E:), type **E:** and press **Enter** to change to the E: drive, and then type **cd** *work folder***Chap10\ Chapter** and press **Enter** to change to the Chap10\Chapter folder in your work folder.

5. Using a text editor such as the DOS Edit tool or Windows Notepad, update the DriveSpy.ini search keyword values. (In Windows Explorer, make sure that the read-only attribute for DriveSpy.ini is unchecked in the Properties dialog box for the DriveSpy.ini file first.) For example, if you stored DriveSpy.ini in a special folder on the C: drive called Tools, you can use the DOS Edit utility by typing **Edit C:**work folder**\Tools\DriveSpy.ini** and then pressing **Enter**. The DriveSpy.ini file opens so you can edit it, as shown in Figure 10-15. The contents of your file may be different.

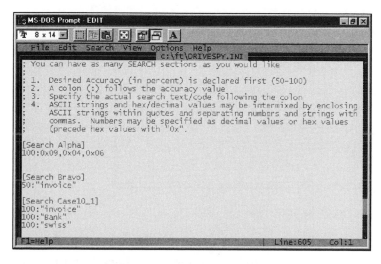

Figure 10-15 Updating the DriveSpy.ini file

10

At the end of the DriveSpy.ini file, type the following lines:

```
[Search Case10_1]
100:"invoice"
100:"Bank"
100:"swiss"
```

6. Save and exit DriveSpy.ini.

After updating the DriveSpy.ini file and creating the necessary folders, your next task is to recover the evidence from the target evidence drive. The following steps assume that the evidence drive is the second hard disk on your system.

To access the evidence using DriveSpy:

1. At the DOS prompt, change to the Tools folder in your work folder, and then run **Toolpath.bat**.

2. On your primary disk, create a subfolder to the Chap10\Chapter folder called Case10_1. This subfolder should be located on your primary disk, not the evidence disk.

3. Navigate to the folder E:*work folder*\Chap10\Chapter\Case10_1, type **DriveSpy**, and then press **Enter** to start DriveSpy.

4. At the SYS prompt, create an output file to record your actions and findings by typing **Output Case10_1.log**, as shown in Figure 10-16, and then pressing **Enter**.

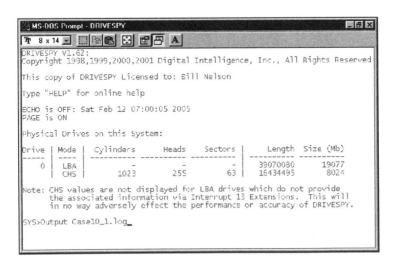

Figure 10-16   Creating an output file

5. At the SYS prompt, type **Drive 1** and then press **Enter** to examine the partition on the target drive. At the D1 prompt, type **Part 1** and press **Enter**.

NOTE

If the target evidence disk has more than one partition, repeat Steps 1-3 to recover all evidence. Use your preferred disk partition utility, such as FDisk, Gdisk, or Partition Magic.

The next task is to establish an integrity baseline for the evidence. To do this, use the Dbexport command with the MD5 switch to create an output file that provides a record of all file data on the evidence disk. You can run Dbexport again at the end of the examination to compare the final output to the first Dbexport listing and ensure that no data on the evidence drive has been altered.

To create an evidence integrity baseline:

1. At the D1P1 prompt, type **Dbexport Dbexp_10.Txt /MD5 /Hdr /S** and press **Enter**.

2. To create a baseline for the first and second FAT, boot sector, root directory, and combined data area of the partition, run the MD5 command from the partition mode by typing **MD5** at the D1P1 prompt and pressing **Enter**. DriveSpy processes the disk, as shown in Figure 10-17.

```
MS-DOS Prompt - DRIVESPY                                    _ |6|X|
|T  8 x 14 ▼|  ☐ |🗐🗐| 🖶 | 🗐🖶 | A |
Processing Boot Record: sectors 0-0
Processing Sector:             0
MD5 Checksum for: Boot Record          = c1cd33d115698825bda6b638fcfda108

Processing First FAT: sectors 1-9
Processing Sector:             9
MD5 Checksum for: First FAT            = 16f61d49dd0e8ee2fdbd80b45f3d630d

Processing Second FAT: sectors 10-18
Processing Sector:            18
MD5 Checksum for: Second FAT           = 16f61d49dd0e8ee2fdbd80b45f3d630d

Processing Root Directory: sectors 19-32
Processing Sector:            32
MD5 Checksum for: Root Directory       = 1c22241b32bca53684526055d93cb2cf

Processing Data Area: sectors 33-2879
Processing Sector:          2879
MD5 Checksum for: Data Area            = 74054f5998f3fba2841d69aa78793322

------------------------------------------------------------------
MD5 Checksum for: DOS Logical Drive    = 078748a97dd23dc641e77ef0370620c1
DAP1:\>
```

Figure 10-17 Producing the MD5 hash with no switches

NOTE

Running MD5 with no switches or parameters produces a hash value for all major sections of a disk partition.

After creating a data integrity baseline, collect all recoverable deleted files and residual data from the target evidence disk. In the following steps, you do so using the DriveSpy Copy, Unerase, SaveSlack, and SaveFree commands.

10

To recover residual data:

1. At the D1P1 prompt, type **Copy *.* /S E:***work folder***\\Chap10\\Chapter\\Case10_1\\Allocate** and then press **Enter** to copy all allocated data from the target evidence partition to the Allocate folder. Type **y** to disable Page mode.

2. At the D1P1 prompt, type **Copy *.* /S /T:xls E:***work folder***\\Chap10\\Chapter\\Case10_1\\SSheets** and then press **Enter** to recover only specific allocated file types such as Microsoft Excel spreadsheets and store them in the SSheets folder. Type **y** to disable Page mode.

3. At the D1P1 prompt, type **Unerase *.* /S E:***work folder***\\Chap10\\Chapter\\Case10_1\\Unerase** and then press **Enter** to recover all deleted files with the Unerase command and store them in the Unerase folder. See Figure 10-18. Then type **y** to disable Page mode.

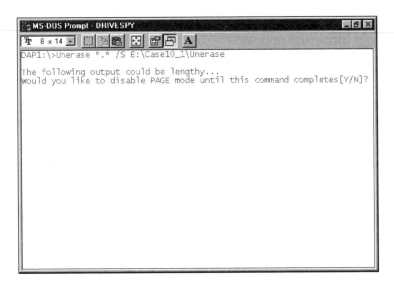

Figure 10-18   Using the Unerase command

4. At the D1P1 prompt, type **Unerase *.* /S /T:xls E:***work folder***\\Chap10\\Chapter\\Case10_1\\SSheets** and then press **Enter** to recover only specific deleted files, such as Microsoft Excel spreadsheets, and store them in the SSheets folder. Type **y** to disable Page mode.

5. At the D1P1 prompt, type **SaveSlack E:***work folder***\\Chap10\\Chapter\\Case10_1\\Residual\\Slack_10.dat** and then press **Enter** to use the SaveSlack command to collect all residual data located in file slack space and store it in a file named Slack_10.dat in the Residual folder. Type **y** to disable Page mode.

6. At the D1P1 prompt, type **SaveFree E:***work folder***\\Chap10\\Chapter\\Case10_1\\Residual\\Free_10.dat** and then press **Enter** to use the SaveFree command to collect all residual data located in unallocated disk space and store it in a file named Free_10.data in the Residual folder. Type **y** to disable Page mode.

Your responsibility is to collect as much information about the case as possible (within the bounds of the search warrant or subpoena). The more information you have, the better you can identify keywords that might help you locate evidence. In the next section, you apply the DriveSpy Search command to the investigation. Recall that the Search command only searches for words that you have listed in the DriveSpy.ini file.

To run keyword searches with DriveSpy:

1. At the D1P1 prompt, type **Search Case10_1** and then press **Enter** to start searching for the keywords you entered earlier. Type **y** to disable Page mode.

2. At the D1P1 prompt, change from Partition mode to Drive mode by typing **D1** and then pressing **Enter**. Data might reside on the interpartition gap that will not show up on the logical level.

3. At the D1 prompt, type **Search Case10_1** and press **Enter** to run the search pattern again.

4. At the D1 prompt, type **Quit** and then press **Enter** to exit DriveSpy.

Some considerations when analyzing MS-DOS and Windows 9x operating systems are the use of older compression utilities such as DriveSpace or DoubleSpace. If you encounter partition volumes compressed with DriveSpace or DoubleSpace, you must reconstruct the evidence partition on a target investigation drive. After you have duplicated the original evidence drive, you must reboot your forensic workstation with the target evidence drive so you can access the compressed partition.

DriveSpace and DoubleSpace partition volumes compress disks by eliminating file slack space, so these volumes do not have file slack space.

NOTE

Other ways to acquire data with DriveSpy range from searching for unique file headers to recovering residual fragments of files that are partially overwritten. By using the Search command to find hexadecimal values and the GFE, CFE, CDE, and TDC commands, you can piece together parts or whole file fragments.

After you have collected all the data you need, analyze its content to find evidence related to your investigation. Analyzing digital evidence is the most time-consuming and sometimes difficult investigation task. Recent GUI tools, such as FTK, EnCase, FacTracker, and ProDiscover DFT, make analysis faster than DOS tools such as DriveSpy. No matter which tool you use, learn how to maximize its capabilities to make the analysis task successful.

For example, suppose you need to recover Microsoft Word documents that are located in unallocated free space of a suspect's disk drive. With DriveSpy, you can recover specific deleted Word files by searching for unique keywords that those files are likely to contain. If the keywords appear in unallocated space, you can use the SaveSect command to extract the appropriate sectors to a data or text file. Suppose you are looking for Word documents that contain the phrase "pay off" and the name "Joe." You can create a search section in DriveSpy.ini with the following keywords:

10

```
[Search CASE10_1A]
100:"pay off"
100:"Joe"
```

In DriveSpy Partition mode, you can then run a logical search by typing Search Case10_1a at the D1P1 prompt. To restrict the search to only .doc files, you can type Search *.doc Case10_1a at the D1P1 prompt. Similarly, to conduct a physical (Drive mode) search, type Search Case10_1a at the D1 prompt. In Drive mode, DriveSpy searches the entire drive including data areas within and between partitions. You can use Drive mode to search non-FAT file system drives such as NTFS, Linux Ext2fs and Ext3fs, and UNIX drives. Figure 10-19 shows the results of the search reviewed above.

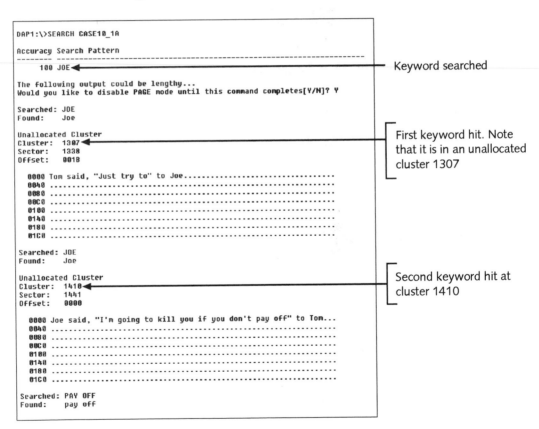

Figure 10-19 Using Search parameters

When you locate the keyword from a logical (Partition mode) search that is in unallocated space, use the Cluster command to examine it for evidentiary value. For physical (Drive mode) searches, use the Sector command to examine it for evidentiary value. You can then use the SaveSect command to extract the evidence to an external data file. You need to obtain the starting absolute sector number where the evidence is located to use the SaveSect command. Estimate how many sectors to copy by examining the clusters following the initial cluster for each keyword found. In Cluster or Sector view, scroll through the data area to determine where the data ends. When you have located the possible ending cluster area, note the absolute sector number.

To recover unallocated evidence data:

1. In DriveSpy, locate the cluster position from the keyword search results. For example, Figure 10-19 indicates that the name Joe first appears at cluster position 1307.

2. At the D1P1 prompt, type **Cluster 1307** and then press **Enter** in the cluster command with the cluster position. See Figure 10-20.

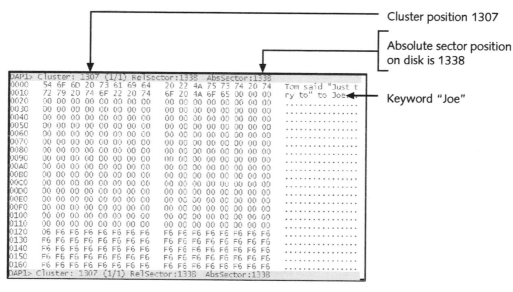

Figure 10-20 Location of Joe at cluster position 1307

3. Note that the absolute sector value (AbsSector) of cluster 1307 is absolute sector 1338.

4. Press the **Pg Dn** key to scroll to the end of cluster listing, and look for the last absolute sector value, or the ending absolute sector, which is also 1338 because this is a short file.

5. Press the **Esc** key to exit the Cluster view and return to the DriveSpy shell prompt. Now you can use the SaveSect command to extract the data from unallocated disk space and save it in a text file. Recall from Chapter 9 that with the SaveSect command, you specify the starting sector and then the number of sectors to read.

6. At the D1P1 prompt, type **Savesect 1 1338,1 E:*work folder*\\Chap10\\Chapter\\Kw_Joe.Txt** and then press **Enter**.

In an actual investigation, you would repeat these steps until you have completed the evidence recovery. Next, you must sort through the evidence to determine what is of value to the case. Consider the following guidelines as you examine the evidence:

- Create separate folders to store evidence, such as one folder for spreadsheets and another for e-mail. You can further subdivide these folders into subjects or persons of interest.

- For complex investigations maintain a log, preferably in a database that allows you to collect relevant information and notes of your observations. Create as many fields as necessary to sort the data more easily.

- Periodically review the data you have collected to refresh your knowledge of the facts you gathered.

- Apply deductive reasoning to your findings to help build new leads. Determine new keywords you can use to search for related evidence. Become skilled at building on the little pieces of information to create bigger pieces of the investigation puzzle.

- Research data that you are not familiar with, such as unknown file types. This data might be evidence that will solve the case.

NTFS Forensic Analysis

Performing computer forensics on an NTFS file system is similar to performing computer forensics on FAT file systems. Most computer forensics tools allow you to analyze NTFS disks. Some are easy to use while others will challenge your technical ability and knowledge of NTFS file structures. DOS-based tools include DriveSpy and NTI NTFS suite, while GUI-based tools include FTK, EnCase, Pro Discover DLT, FactFind, and ILook.

NTFS DOS Analysis

The current release of DriveSpy (version 1.62) provides limited analysis capability for NTFS disks. To use DriveSpy, you must access the target evidence NTFS drive in Drive mode (at the physical level). DriveSpy does not let you directly examine the data structures on an NTFS partition, such as directories and filenames, or the dates and times that directories and files were created, modified, and last accessed, as you can a FAT file system.

On an NTFS disk, you can perform a keyword search in both an ASCII version and a Unicode version of the keyword. (Refer to Chapter 3 for instructions on performing ASCII and Unicode searches.) For example, the following entries in the DriveSpy.ini file search for "Joe" as ASCII text and as Unicode ("J",0x00,"o",0x00,"e",0x00):

```
[Search CASE10_1B]
100:"Joe"
100:"J",0x00,"o",0x00,"e",0x00
```

You use the null (0x00) values between each literal character because Unicode is a 16-bit code, whereas ASCII is only an 8-bit code.

The NTFS analysis tools from NTI are easier to use than DriveSpy when accessing NTFS disks from DOS. The NTFS suite of tools allows you to list the contents of the MFT, and copy specific files from the NTFS drive to a DOS FAT partition. You can also copy file slack space and unallocated space to a data file for additional analysis. DiskSearch NT is a tool in the NTI suite that allows you to perform keyword searches on the target evidence disk.

SysInternals (*www.sysinternals.com*) offers an additional product for NTFS investigations called NTFSDOS, which runs on MS-DOS and Windows 9x systems. The freeware version only reads NTFS drive partitions from Windows 9x systems. This read-only feature makes it ideal for performing forensic analysis. For NTFS data recovery, an ideal combination of DOS tools is DriveSpy to perform physical level searches and NTFSDOS to examine NTFS file structures.

NTFS GUI Analysis

Using GUI tools such as FTK, EnCase, Pro Discover DFT, FactFind, and ILook makes viewing and locating evidence on NTFS disks much easier than with DOS tools. In particular, the GUI tools show directory and file structures, which speeds up processing time for the analysis.

With a tool such as FTK, you can view an NTFS disk (see Figure 10-21) or a variety of bit-stream image files on an NTFS disk partition. FTK provides a Windows Explorer-type of viewer that includes allocated files, deleted files, and unallocated disk space.

10

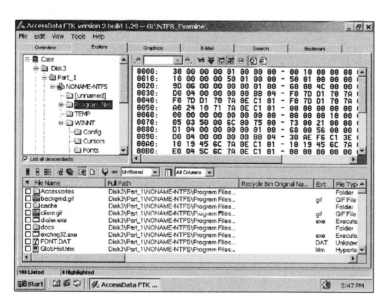

Figure 10-21   Exploring an NTFS disk with FTK

UNIX and Linux Forensic Analysis

Most computer forensics tools have been developed for Microsoft file systems. However, to respond to the recent popularity of Linux, several computer forensics software programs now let you examine Ext2fs and Ext3fs Linux file systems. Organizations such as @stake have also contributed to the development of freeware UNIX file system analysis tools. While this section introduces you to computer forensics tools you can use with UNIX and Linux file systems, you should also obtain additional training in UNIX system administration to enhance your ability to analyze data and determine its evidentiary value to the investigation.

Windows Forensics Tools for Analyzing UNIX and Linux Data

Many of the leading GUI computer forensics tools can analyze UNIX and Linux files systems, including EnCase, FTK, and iLook. You do not need advanced UNIX system knowledge to use these tools on a UNIX or Linux file system. You can perform the same forensic analysis as you do with FAT and NTFS file systems.

Figure 10-22 shows an example of a Linux Ext2fs file system in FTK, which configures the directories, files, and unallocated space in the same manner as it does for NTFS or FAT file systems.

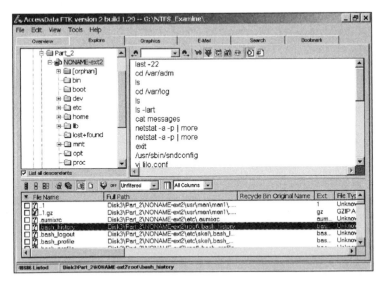

Figure 10-22 Linux Ext2fs file using FTK

Note that the naming conventions used in a Linux or UNIX environment are more cryptic at first glance than DOS and Windows filenames. Understanding how UNIX systems work and the purpose of each file and directory helps when investigating these types of systems.

UNIX and Linux Forensics Tools

UNIX forensics tools were originally designed to help UNIX system administrators identify hacker activities on systems and network servers. The freeware tools TCT, TCTUTILs, and TASK provide analysis ability from several UNIX and Linux platforms. These tools have been designed to perform analysis on imaged systems as well as live systems. For additional information on these tools and others, visit the following Web sites:

- Freeware UNIX and Linux data analysis: Purdue University, *www.cerias.purdue.edu/homes/carrier/forensics*
- The Coroner's Toolkit (TCT): *www.porcupine.org/forensics/tct.html*
- TCTUTILs: *www.incident-response.org/tct-utils.htm* or *www.atstake.com*
- TASK: *www.atstake.com*

Because high-end UNIX and Linux systems are often used as Web servers, investigating these computers involves working with a live system. Depending on the use of a UNIX or Linux server, you might not be able to shut down the computer to perform a data acquisition. For example, UNIX servers are used to provide services as critical as a Shuttle launch for NASA.

As a standard practice for all UNIX or Linux systems, your first task is to preserve any data temporarily stored in volatile memory. That is, determine which applications are running, including those running in the background such as batch jobs, and save the active data. Preserving active data often results in evidence that can make your case.

For all UNIX and Linux systems, use the following checklist to help preserve volatile data. This list is ranked in order of importance:

- Running processes
- Network connections
- System memory
- Swap space
- Console messages

UNIX and Linux systems can also have multiple user accounts. To investigate intrusion incidents on these systems, you must examine system log files to help identify which accounts were used to compromise the system. You might need to recover data if skilled hackers have deleted log files to cover their tracks.

If you are working on a live system, always use the redirect output parameter to redirect the results of your analysis work to an external media device such as a floppy disk. For example, to preserve the output from the UNIX ps (process status) command to a text file, first mount the floppy disk by typing `mount /dev/fd0 /mnt/floppy` and pressing Enter, and then save the output of the ps command to a text file named psdata.txt on the floppy disk by typing `ps -aux > /floppy/psdata.txt` and pressing Enter.

10

For intrusion investigations, examine the following data areas on UNIX and Linux systems:

- All running processes
- All network connections
- All deleted files
- File system
- Current status of memory
- Contents of the swap file
- Backup media to compare to the current system
- All background processes

Reconstruct all events to see what happened to a system after it was attacked. Look for discrepancies in time-based components, such as system files, password files, and log files. Examine the files that were created or modified during the period of the incident. Then analyze and hypothesize how the incident occurred.

- *System*—Registers, peripheral memory, and cache files.
- *Physical memory*—Use the dd command to copy the contents of RAM to a file.
- *Network state*—Use the netstat command to identify the computer's network accesses and connections.
- *Current running processes*—Use the ps command to find the names of all current processes.
- *Terminate current processes*—Use the kill command to terminate current processes without overwriting current file space.
- *Disk data acquisition*—Run an MD5 or SHA1 hash on all files and directories. Before shutting down the computer, copy all logs and other system accounting files to external media.

Some useful UNIX commands to use when analyzing disk content are included in Appendix C, which also lists the log and data files to inspect on Solaris, HP-UX, AIX, and IRIX UNIX systems and on Linux systems.

It is always a good idea to examine /etc/syslog.conf, /etc/inetd.conf, and shell history data files.

If the system you are investigating has been attacked, determine whether a RootKit has been installed on it. A **RootKit** is a hacker tool that allows for backdoor access to a system. For the latest information on RootKits, visit the Computer Emergency Response Team (CERT) Web page at *www.cert.org*.

Macintosh Investigations

Investigating newer Macintosh systems that have implemented the Berkely Standard Distribution (BSD) UNIX file system are no different from investigating any other type of UNIX or Linux disk. To investigate older Macintosh systems, Mac OS 9 or later, use one of the Windows, UNIX, or Linux forensics tools such as EnCase, ILook, SMART, or TASK. ASR Data (*www.asrdata.com*) sells Expert Witness, which is specifically designed for the older Macintosh file systems.

You use EnCase or ILook on older Macintosh file systems the same way you examine a FAT or NTFS disk partition.

ADDRESSING DATA HIDING TECHNIQUES

Data hiding involves changing or manipulating a file to conceal information. People can hide data by changing the extension of a filename, setting a file's attribute to hidden, or using encryption to keep the contents secret.

One skill many early home computer users developed was programming in the specific computer manufacturer's assembly language. Assembly programming involves cryptic system commands called mnemonics. Listing these commands in a program allows programmers to use a computer's CPU to directly manipulate functions and data. With these skills, some computer users developed programming tools that could change data. They could create a low-level encryption program that shifted binary data, making the altered data unreadable when accessed with a text editor or word processor. They accomplished this by shifting or rearranging bits for each byte within a specified file. To secure a file that might contain sensitive or incriminating information, programmers could run the assembler (also called a macro) program on the file to scramble the bits. To access the file, the programmers ran another program to restore the scrambled bits to their original settings.

Some low-level encryption programs are still used today, and can make it difficult for an investigator to analyze the data for a suspect disk drive. To examine such as disk, start by identifying as many files as possible to find some with which you are not familiar that might lead to new evidence. Obtaining training in one or more programming languages such as Visual Basic, Visual C++, or Perl is also helpful.

Hiding Partitions

One way to hide partitions is to create a partition on a disk, and then use a disk editor such as Norton Disk Edit to manually delete any reference to it. To access the deleted partition, users can edit the partition table to recreate the links. When users reboot the computer, the hidden partition reappears.

Another way to hide partitions is to use a disk-partitioning utility such as PartitionMagic, System Commander, or Linux Loader (LILO), which provide a start-up menu that allows

10

you to select an operating system to use. When you select an operating system, the system ignores other bootable partitions.

To circumvent these techniques, be sure to account for all disk space when examining an evidence disk. Analyze any areas of the disk that contain space for which you cannot account to determine whether these areas contain additional evidence. For example, in Figure 10-23, DriveSpy lists all the starting and ending sectors for each partition on the drive. Note that Partition 1 ends at sector 205631 and Partition 2 starts at sector 248031. This leaves a 42400–sector gap between these two sectors.

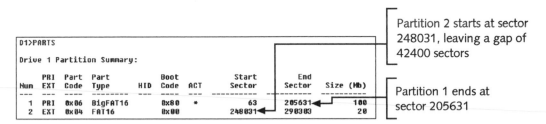

Figure 10-23   DriveSpy showing starting and ending sectors

To access the partition gap area of a disk with DriveSpy, you need to work in Drive mode. To view the content of the data area, set DriveSpy to Drive mode, and then examine and analyze a partition gap area using the Sector, Search, CopySect, and SaveSect commands.

For example, using the DriveSpy SaveSect command, you can copy the contents of the sector gap shown in Figure 10-23 to a data file for further examination. To determine the sector range for the SaveSect command, add one to the ending sector number of Partition 1, and subtract one from the beginning sector number of Partition 2. If the first Partition ends at sector 205631, the beginning sector position of the partition gap is 205631 + 1, or 205632. If the second partition starts at sector 248031, the ending sector position of the partition gap is 248031 − 1, or 248030. The partition gap ranges from sector 205632 to sector 248030. To copy the sector gap to a data file, at the DriveSpy D1 prompt, type `SaveSect 205632-248030 E:`*`work folder`*`\Chap10\Chapter\Part_gap.dat` and press Enter.

With Hex Workshop you can examine the contents of the partition gap as shown in Figure 10-24.

To carve (or salvage) data from the recovered partition gap, apply other computer forensics tools such as FTK, as shown in Figure 10-25.

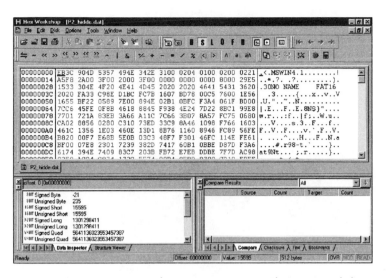

Figure 10-24 Viewing the partition gap with Hex Workshop

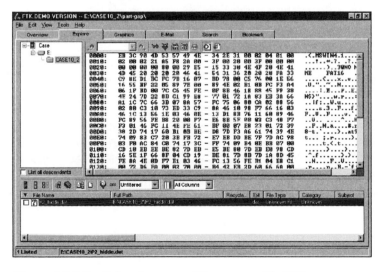

Figure 10-25 Salvaging a partition gap with FTK

Marking Bad Clusters

Another data-hiding technique is to place sensitive or incriminating data in free space on disk partition clusters. This method of hiding data is more common with FAT file systems. By using a disk editor such as Norton Disk Edit, the good clusters can be marked as bad clusters. The operating system then considers these clusters as unusable. The only way they can be accessed from the operating system is by changing them to good clusters with a disk editor.

To mark a good cluster as bad using Norton Disk Edit, you must first update the first FAT table for the specific cluster or clusters you want to mark as bad. Then you type the letter B in the FAT cluster location, as shown in Figure 10-26.

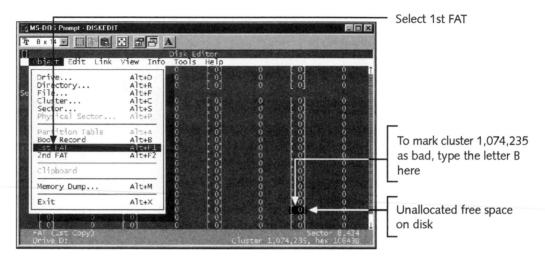

Select 1st FAT

To mark cluster 1,074,235 as bad, type the letter B here

Unallocated free space on disk

Figure 10-26   Marking a good cluster as bad

To access the alleged bad cluster, you can use any DOS disk editor to write and read data to it.

NOTE   If a FAT partition containing clusters marked as bad is converted to an NTFS partition, the bad clusters remain marked as bad on the NTFS partition. Hence, if data is hidden in these marked bad clusters the conversion to NTFS does not affect their content. Most GUI tools such as BCWipe skips clusters marked as bad for FAT and NTFS file systems.

Bit-Shifting

To hide data, you can also shift bit patterns to alter the byte values of data. This technique has been around for many years. By altering the bit pattern, data can be changed from readable code to something that looks like binary executable code. Hex Workshop provides simple switches that allow you to alter the bits or byte patterns of specified data and entire files.

To shift bits in a text file:

1. In Windows, start Notepad, and then type the text shown in Figure 10-27.

2. Save it as **Bit_Shift.txt** in the Chap10\Chapter folder in your work folder. Close Notepad.

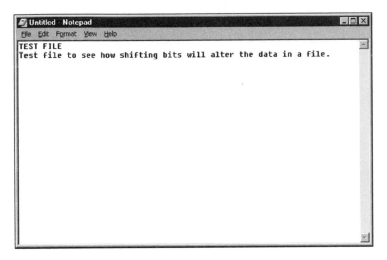

Figure 10-27   Creating Bit_Shift.txt

3. Start Hex Workshop. Click **File** on the menu bar, and then click **Open**. Navigate to the Chap10\Chapter folder in your work folder, and then double-click **Bit_Shift.txt**. See Figure 10-28.

10

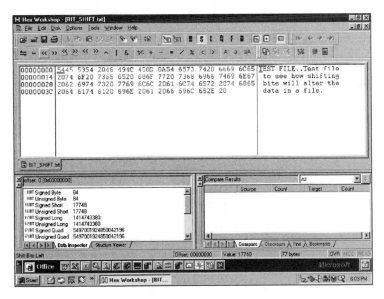

Figure 10-28   Bit_Shift.txt open in Hex Workshop

4. Click the **Shift Left** button (<<) on the Operations toolbar. The Shift Left Operation dialog box opens, as shown in Figure 10-29.

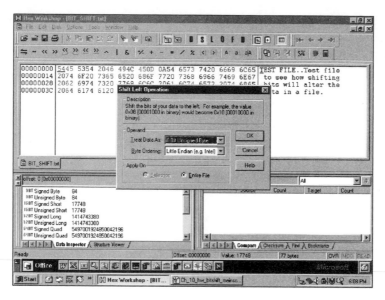

Figure 10-29   Shift Left Operation dialog box

You use this dialog box to specify how you want to treat the data, the ordering scheme to use for bytes, and whether you shift the bits for selected text or the entire file.

5. Click **OK** to accept the default settings and shift the bits in Bit_Shift.txt to the left.

6. To save the updated file, click **File** on the menu bar, and then click **Save As**. Use the Save As dialog box to save the file as **Bit_shift_left.txt** in the Chap10\Chapter folder in your work folder. See Figure 10-30. Notice the "@" symbols in the far right screen.

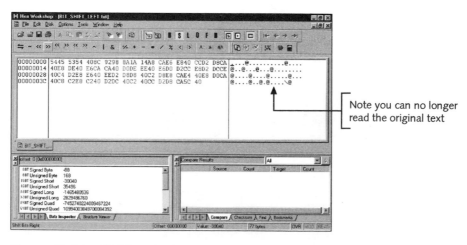

Note you can no longer read the original text

Figure 10-30   Shifting the bits

7. To return the file to its original configuration, you can shift the bits back to the right by clicking the **Shift Right** button (>>) on the Operations toolbar. Then click **OK** to accept the default settings in the Shift Right Operation dialog box. The file appears in its original format, as shown in Figure 10-31.

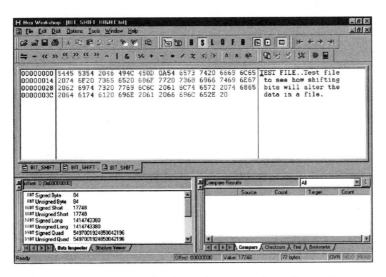

Figure 10-31 Shifting back to the original configuration

8. Click **File** on the menu bar, and then click **Save As**. Use the Save As dialog box to save the file as **Bit_shift_right.txt** in the Chap10\Chapter folder in your work folder.

Now you can use Hex Workshop to test these three files to find their MD5 hash values to determine whether Bit_shift.txt is different from Bit_shift_right.txt. Note that you can also use DriveSpy to find MD5 hash values.

To check the MD5 values:

1. With Bit_shift_right.txt open in Hex Workshop, click **File** on the menu bar, and then click **Open** to open **Bit_shift.txt**, and then **Bit_shift_left.txt**.

2. Click the **Bit_shift.txt** tab in the upper pane to make that the active file.

3. Click **Tools** on the menu bar, and then click **Generate Checksum**. The Generate Checksum dialog box opens, shown in Figure 10-32. You use this dialog box to select the type of algorithm you want to use to generate a value, such as an MD5 hash value.

4. In the Select Algorithms list, click **MD5**, and then click **Generate**. The Checksum tab opens in the lower-right pane of the Hex Workshop window, displaying the MD5 hash value of Bit_shift.txt. Write down the MD5 hash value that is displayed for this file for future comparison to other changes to the file.

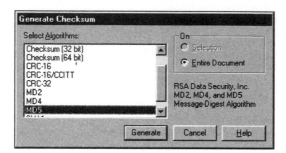

Figure 10-32   Generate Checksum dialog box

5. Repeat Steps 3 and 4 for Bit_shift_left.txt and Bit_shift_right.txt.

6. Examine the Checksum window for each file and compare each MD5 hash value for each file.

7. Close Hex Workshop.

Instead of shifting bits, marking bad clusters, and hiding partitions, people who want to hide data can use advanced encryption products such as PGP or BestCrypt.

Using Steganography

Many **steganography** tools were created to protect copyrighted material by inserting digital watermarks into a file. When viewing a stenographic file, such as a text document or graphic, the digital watermark is not visible. If you examine a graphics file such as a bitmap (.bmp) file with a disk editor such as Hex Workshop, it is difficult to find a water-mark. A non-steganographic .bmp file is the same size as an identical steganographic .bmp file, and they look the same when you view both files in a graphic viewer utility such as IrfanView. However, if you run a CRC-32, MD5, or SHA-1 hash comparison on both files, you will find that the hashes are not equal. Chapter 12 discusses a few steganography utilities that are available for lossy graphic files. These tools insert data into the graphic file, but often alter the original file in size and clarity.

To hide data, people can use steganography programs to insert covert information into a variety of data files. One Web site that provides several freeware and shareware steg-anography programs is *http://members.tripod.com/steganography/stego/software.html*. (This site might not always be available; to locate this or other Web sites with steganography programs use your favorite Internet search engine. In your search engine type "steganog-raphy" to locate additional information and resources.) If someone wanting to secure a message encrypts a plain text file using a program such as PGP, and inserts the encrypted text into the steganography file, the file becomes extremely difficult to crack. However, most steganography programs can insert only small amounts of data into a file, and usually require a password to restrict accessing the inserted data.

To detect steganography in evidence, you need prior information about the case; oth-erwise you cannot detect files that might have been used to hide data. During your examination, look for steganography programs such as of S-Tools, DPEnvelope, jpgx, and tte. If you locate any of these programs, look for files that might have been used to hide data—specifically graphic files, but even text documents can be used for steganography. To help identify steganography output files, perform the following tasks:

1. Locate the modified date and time stamp of the steganography program.

2. If you are using DriveSpy, use the Dbexport command with the MD5 switch and transfer the output into a text file that you can open in a spreadsheet or database program. For example, at the D1P1 prompt, type **Dbexport E:***work folder***\Chap10\Chapter\Dbexport.Txt /MD5** and press **Enter**.

3. In a spreadsheet or database program, sort all files in the Dbexport output file by modified date and time.

4. Generate a list of all files that have a date and time equal to or after the modified date and time of the steganography application.

5. Carefully examine each file in the generated listing.

If you locate files, especially graphic files such as .bmp files, that appear to have been created by the steganography program, attempt to reverse-engineer the file by recreating known non-steganographic images in the steganographic image files. This is a trial-and-error process and may not be practical unless the investigation is extremely important. Try building a timeline of possible output files that match the last used date of the steganography utilities. You can build a timeline with tools such as the DriveSpy DBExport command, FTK, and EnCase.

Examining Encrypted Files

Recall that encrypted files are those encoded to prevent unauthorized access, and can be difficult to examine for forensic evidence. To decode an encrypted file, users provide a password or passphrase that indicates they are authorized to decrypt the file. Without the passphrase, it is difficult to recover the contents of encrypted data. Many commercial encryption programs use a technology called **key escrow**, which is designed to recover encrypted data if users forget their passphrase or if the user key is corrupted due to a system data failure. Forensics examiners can use the key escrow to attempt to recover encrypted data. Although some vendors are developing key recovery tools, the amount of resources needed typically require national institutions to apply experts and powerful computer systems to crack encryption schemes.

If you do encounter encrypted data in your investigation, make an effort to persuade the suspect or person of interest to reveal the passphrase.

Recovering Passwords

Password recovery is probably the easiest of tasks to overcome during a computer forensic analysis. Several vendors have produced password crackers such as Password Recovery Tool Kit (PRTK), Advanced Password Recovery Software Tool Kit, and @stake's LC4

(L0phtCrack). These tools crack passwords by guessing the password, which is called a dictionary attack, or performing a brute force attack. In a dictionary attack, the program generates common words found in the dictionary and provides them as passwords. Some password-cracking programs allow you to import additional unique words that are typically extracted from evidence. Recall that FTK, for example, allows you to export a word list that you can import into the PRTK companion tool.

Brute force attacks use every possible letter, number, and character found on a keyboard. Eventually, a brute force attack can crack any password, though it might take several days or weeks.

Other programs help you build profiles of a suspect to help determine the suspect's password. These programs consider information such as the names of relatives, pets, favorite colors, and schools attended. The principle behind these multiple input programs is that people have a habit of using things they are comfortable with, especially if it requires memorizing something secret like a password.

CHAPTER SUMMARY

- When conducting computer forensic analysis, you must guard against scope creep so that you remain focused on the primary job. When looking at a case, you should consider how much time it will take, what information is actually relevant, if there are adequate resources, and if there is a deadline.

- For all operating systems, you need to determine where the digital evidence most likely will be stored by examining date and time stamps, log files, temporary spool files, encrypted or archived files, shortcuts, Recycle Bins, and Registry files.

- The DriveSpy.ini file contains critical information regarding your license in the [License] section. You can update the remaining sections as needed for your investigation. For example, in the [Search] section, you can specify one or more keywords of files you want to examine are likely to contain. Use the [File Headers] section to keep a list of common file headers and their hexadecimal representation for file types such as spreadsheets, word processors, and databases, making it easier to locate files using almost all of the popular computer forensics tools.

- Other useful features of DriveSpy are script files, which are text files that contain a sequence of commands that a program such as DriveSpy can perform to automate repetitious tasks. DriveSpy also provides other tools that retrieve residual data such as free space and slack space, and others that can help retrieve clusters associated with deleted files.

- The PDBlock program is designed to prevent data from being written on a disk drive. PDWipe is designed to overwrite all sectors on a disk, cleaning all data from the drive. The Forensic Toolkit (FTK) is a data analysis tool that allows you to examine image files and directly access a target evidence disk, folder, or specific file.

◻ For any computer forensic investigation, prepare the disks where you will store images of your evidence by wiping the disks and inspecting them for computer viruses. Inventory the hardware on the suspect's computer and note the condition of the computer when seized. Remove the original disk drive, and then check the date and time values in the system's CMOS. Record how you acquired data from the original disk. List all folders and files on the copied bit-stream image or disk, and examine the contents of all data files in all folders starting at the root folder of the volume partition. Research the function of every executable file that does not match known hash values. Maintain control of all evidence and findings, and document everything as you progress through your examination.

◻ UNIX and Linux machines are still commonly used as Web servers. You need to collect volatile data, log files, swap files, and a variety of others when investigating these systems. You may also be required to perform a live system analysis.

◻ Data hiding involves changing or manipulating a file to conceal the file or its contents from anyone other than the owner of the file. For example, bit-shifting allows you to alter files easily. Encryption can be used to protect data as can passwords. Some tools are available for password cracking.

◻ Steganography was created to protect the copyrights of art placed online. People have since used it to hide data. You can use tools such as DriveSpy MD5 to identify known files that contain steganographic data.

10

KEY TERMS

bookmark—A marker or address that identifies a specific place or location for subsequent retrieval.

Boot command—A DriveSpy command that examines the boot sector area of a disk partition.

Chain Directory Entry (CDE)—A DriveSpy command that displays all directory cluster positions.

Chain FAT Entry (CFE)—A DriveSpy command that lists all known FAT entries.

Cluster command—A DriveSpy command that displays the cluster in hexadecimal view.

designator—The 0x before each value that tells DriveSpy that the following value is a hexadecimal number.

false-positive hits—When a system incorrectly provides a positive validation when in fact it is false.

[File Groups]—The section of DriveSpy.ini that allows you to list all the extensions or files headers for graphics files or spreadsheets.

[File Headers]—The section of DriveSpy.ini that contains the hexadecimal number values for many known file types. These hexadecimal numbers are the header data contained in the first several bytes of all specialized data files such as Microsoft Word documents or Excel spreadsheets and any associated templates.

Forensic Toolkit (FTK)—A GUI software tool used for forensic examination.

Get FAT Entry (GFE)—A DriveSpy command that displays the FAT entry for a specified cluster.

key escrow—A technology designed to recover encrypted data if users forget their passphrase or if the user key is corrupted due to a system failure.

Known File Filter (KFF)—A program database that is updated periodically by AccessData that contains the hash values of known files such as MSWord.exe or illicit items floating on the web. It is used to quickly identify the files for evidence or eliminate them from the investigation if they are legitimate files.

[License]—The section of the DriveSpy.ini file that contains the product license code and owner's name for DriveSpy.exe.

Message Digest version 5 (MD5) hash function—Generates the MD5 hash for a file. This value will be the same unless the file is altered. Even changing the filename will not alter the hash value.

offset—A value added to a base address to produce a second address.

PartMap command—A DriveSpy command that lists a sector map of a partition.

PDBlock—A program designed to prevent writes to a disk drive.

PDWipe—A program used to overwrite hard disk drives, overwriting all data on the drive.

RootKit—A prebuilt package of programs that allows an intruder to install a network sniffer and obtain user IDs and passwords to your most sensitive systems.

SaveFree—A DriveSpy command that saves the free space of the default partition.

SaveSlack—A DriveSpy command that saves the slack space of the default partition.

scope creep—A situation or condition that increases the level of work not originally expected.

Script command—A DriveSpy command that runs a script file that contains sequences of DriveSpy shell commands. A script is a plain text file that contains the commands you want to run.

[Search]—The section of the DriveSpy.ini file that allows you to specify what keywords you want to search for in an image file or document.

Steganography—A cryptographic technique for embedding information into something else (like an image or sound file) for the sole purpose of hiding that information from the casual observer.

Tables command—A DriveSpy command that lists a sector map of a partition.

Trace Directory Cluster (TDC)—A DriveSpy command used to rebuild a subdirectory on a disk partition.

Wipe command—A DriveSpy command used to reduce a disk to all zeros and erase all traces of files that were there.

10

E-MAIL INVESTIGATIONS

After reading this chapter, you will be able to:

♦ Understand Internet fundamentals

♦ Explore the roles of the client and server in e-mail

♦ Identify e-mail crimes and violations

♦ Investigate e-mail crimes and violations

♦ Understand e-mail servers

♦ Use specialized e-mail computer forensics tools

This chapter explains how e-mail works to send and retrieve messages via the Internet. It also discusses how you can trace, recover, and analyze e-mail messages. In particular, this chapter covers Transmission Control Protocol/Internet Protocol (TCP/IP) protocols related to e-mail, e-mail client software, such as Outlook and Eudora, and e-mail servers, such as Exchange and Sendmail. You also examine network device logs to find e-mail information, and examine software tools used to recover e-mail files.

Over the last decade, e-mail has become a primary means of communication, and most computer users employ e-mail programs to receive, send, and manage their e-mail messages. These programs, known as e-mail clients, differ in how and where they store and track e-mail messages. Some e-mail clients are installed separately from the operating system and thus require their own directories and information files on the local computer. Other e-mail clients take advantage of your existing software such as your Web browser, and install no additional software on the client machine. Throughout this chapter you will see how e-mail programs on the server interact with the e-mail programs on the client and vice versa. You will also learn how to recover deleted e-mail from a client machine, regardless of which type of software has been used on the client, and how to trace an e-mail back to the sender.

UNDERSTANDING INTERNET FUNDAMENTALS

Because e-mail programs usually employ some protocols used with the Internet to exchange messages, you need to understand the fundamentals of the Internet to understand how e-mail works. For example, you should be familiar with Internet connection methods, technical rules, and similarities among e-mail applications.

As you probably know, the Internet is a huge collection of networks containing multiple forms of information. To access this information, you need to connect, or log on, to a server that is a member of a network that participates on the Internet. A common way to do so is to use a modem on your computer to connect to an **Internet service provider (ISP)**, which provides a service or membership that allows you to access the information available on the Internet. When you use a modem to connect to an ISP, you are creating a **dial-up connection** on a standard telephone line. While connecting, you hear a variety of tones being generated by the modem speaker. These tones are a good indicator that your computer (the client) and the ISP server are communicating and agreeing on how fast and how long to communicate and how to address one another. The client and server computers also exchange other technical information necessary to maintain their connection. In Windows, you can set the volume of the speaker for the connection process by opening the Control Panel and selecting the Modems icon (or the Phone and Modem Options icon in Windows XP). The volume can be adjusted using a slider as shown in Figure 11-1.

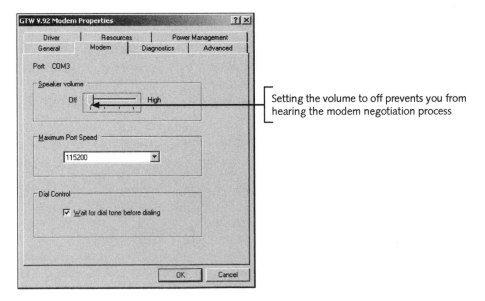

Setting the volume to off prevents you from hearing the modem negotiation process

Figure 11-1   Modem Properties dialog box

Other ways of connecting to the ISPs in home and business environments include using a Digital Subscriber Line (DSL), cable modem, or satellite. Although these methods use different devices to connect to an ISP, they all communicate in a similar manner.

After the modems in the client and ISP server computers agree to communicate, you can log on to the server by providing your user name, such as your e-mail address, and your password. If you provide the correct information, the ISP allows you to join its network, which is connected to the Internet. You can then access the Internet using a Web browser or e-mail program, for example.

After you connect to an ISP and the Internet, you can access information such as e-mail messages, Web pages, files, instant messages, and games. This information is available through various Internet services. For example, you can use the File Transfer Protocol (FTP) service to retrieve files stored on a Web site. Each service communicates using its own protocol or standard. A protocol sets the parameters or rules of how one computer communicates with another. Generally, each service used on a computer, such as e-mail, uses its own protocol or protocols.

In addition, computers need **code**, or programs, to take advantage of the protocols for a particular service. A computer can then communicate with the same service on another computer. By combining protocols with code, you can create a viable means of communication. For example, to read information on the Internet, you need to use a program that interprets the service's protocol and code to view a Web page—a **Web browser**, such as Netscape Navigator or Internet Explorer. The Web browser lets you view a formatted Web page without seeing the code, **Hypertext Markup Language (HTML)**, used to create the page.

For example, if you use a Web browser to visit *www.msn.com*, you see the home page for the MSN Web site, including graphics, headings, and other formatted text. To see the HTML used to create the Web page, as shown in Figure 11-2, you can right-click the page and then select View Source in Internet Explorer.

To read your e-mail messages, you use an e-mail program such as Pine, Eudora, or Outlook. E-mail programs provide a service similar to Web browsers, except they interpret and display e-mail messages. When you use an e-mail program to compose a message, the program encodes the message according to an e-mail standard such as Multipurpose Internet Mail Extensions (MIME), a type of coding that contains information for sending messages from point to point.

In addition to MIME, e-mail programs can also use another type of coding method called uuencode. MIME is the enhanced version of coding used for e-mail messages. Although some people attempt to hide information by using uuencode for e-mail messages, UNIX, DOS, and Windows all have a uudecode utility that you as an investigator can use to decode the message. Request For Comment (RFC) 2045 and 2046 describe the MIME format in technical detail.

Source code

Web page

Figure 11-2   HTML source code and resulting Web page

Understanding Internet Protocols

Just like the spoken language, the Internet has standards and rules that it must follow to make information available to different programs. Every computer that participates on the Internet must observe a protocol, or a set of standards, to communicate with other computers on the Internet. The Internet uses TCP/IP, a suite of protocols that addresses specific tasks in the electronic communication process.

Each computer that accesses the Internet is assigned an IP address that other computers use to find it. An IP address is 32 bits long, and the bits are divided into four groups of eight bits, called octets. At their most basic level, computers interpret data as combinations of zeros and ones. Each bit is represented with a 0 or 1 for off or on, respectively. Knowing that the bit is either on or off, an IP address would look like 11001011.00110111.00011 101.10101010 in binary, which is 203.55.29.170 in dotted decimal form.

Because most people do not easily remember numerical values, various servers on the Internet provide an interpreter service called the **Domain Name Service (DNS)**, which converts IP addresses into named addresses such as *www.yahoo.com*. These addresses have different forms, but they all reference the same Web site being hosted on a single machine.

Because each IP address is unique, it's almost as good as the physical home address to identify the suspect in a computer forensics investigation. Using the IP address, you can trace e-mail back to its origin, which is discussed in detail in the "Investigating E-mail Crimes and Violations" section of this chapter.

Recall that each protocol in the TCP/IP suite performs specific tasks and each protocol corresponds to a particular standard identified in the **Open Systems Interconnect (OSI)** model created by the International Organization for Standardization (ISO) for use in evaluating networks and network communications. Not all of the protocols in the TCP/IP suite work the same way or at the same levels of the OSI model.

TIP

Examining the OSI model is beyond the scope of this book. For more information on the OSI model, see *Network+ Guide to Networks*, 2nd Edition, by Tamara Dean.

The TCP/IP protocols associated with e-mail are **Simple Mail Transfer Protocol (SMTP)**, **Post Office Protocol version 3 (POP3)**, and the **Internet Message Access Protocol version 4 (IMAP)**. In most cases, an e-mail program uses MIME to encode messages, and then uses SMTP, POP3, or IMAP to transport the messages. Each protocol has characteristics that differentiate it from other types of encoding and protocols. Because an e-mail program can use one or all three protocols to exchange e-mail messages, you can track the messages based on the characteristics of each protocol.

E-mail is easily recognizable because it includes a header at the beginning of every message that provides information such as the IP address of the server sending the message, the names of any attachments included with the e-mail, and the time and date the e-mail was sent and received. The computer forensics tool you use to investigate e-mail should be able to identify e-mail messages based on their structure. (Computer forensics tools used for e-mail investigation are discussed later in this chapter.)

11

EXPLORING THE ROLES OF THE CLIENT AND SERVER IN E-MAIL

You can send and receive e-mail in two environments: via the Internet or a local area network (LAN). Both environments distribute data, such as e-mail messages, from one central server to many connected client computers, a configuration called client-server architecture. The server computer uses a server operating system, such as Windows Server 2003, Novell Netware, or UNIX, and runs an e-mail server program, such as Exchange Server 2000, GroupWise, or Sendmail, to provide e-mail service. Client computers run an operating system such as Windows or Linux, and use e-mail programs such as Eudora or Outlook to contact the e-mail server and send and retrieve e-mail messages. See Figure 11-3.

Regardless of operating system or e-mail program, each user accesses his or her e-mail based on the permissions granted by the administrator in charge of the e-mail server. These permissions prevent others from accessing your e-mail. To retrieve your messages

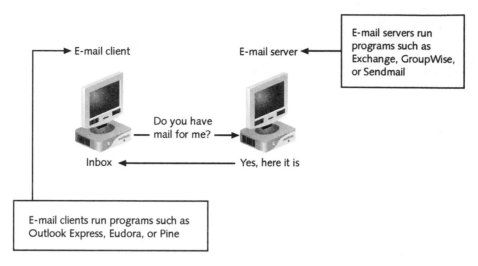

Figure 11-3 E-mail in client-server architecture

from the e-mail server, you identify yourself to the server, as you did when you logged on to the network. Then the e-mail messages are delivered to you.

While e-mail services on the Internet and a LAN both use client-server architecture, they differ in how the client accounts are assigned, used, and managed and how users access their e-mail. Overall, a LAN e-mail system is for the private use of the LAN users, and Internet e-mail systems are for public use. On a LAN, the e-mail server is generally part of the local network and an administrator is dedicated to managing the server and the services it supplies. In most cases, a LAN e-mail system is specific to a company, only used by its employees, and is regulated by its business practices, which usually involves strict security and acceptable use policies. For example, LAN e-mail does not allow users to create their own accounts. E-mail addresses on a LAN follow a **Universal Naming Convention (UNC)**, meaning that all accounts follow a standard account-addressing scheme. For example, John Smith at Some Company would use *jsmith@somecompany.com*. The network administrator who is responsible for the e-mail server determines the UNC.

In an e-mail address, everything after the @ symbol represents the domain name. You need to know the domain information when you investigate e-mail.

TIP

In contrast, a company that provides e-mail services, such as AOL, Hotmail, or Juno, owns the e-mail server on an Internet-based e-mail system. They accept everyone who signs up for their service. E-mail companies provide their own servers and administrators. Anyone can receive Internet e-mail services by connecting to the Internet, signing up for an e-mail account, and providing a user name and password. After users sign up, they can access their e-mail from any machine that is connected to the Internet. In most cases, Internet e-mail users are not required to follow a UNC.

For computer investigators, it is easier to trace LAN e-mail because the accounts use UNC names established by the network or e-mail administrator. For example, *jane.smith@mycompany.com* would be easily mapped and recognized as the e-mail address for an employee named Jane Smith. Tracking Internet e-mail users, on the other hand, is more difficult because those user accounts do not use UNC names, and the e-mail administrator is not familiar with all the users with e-mail accounts on their servers. For example, *itty_bitty@hotmail.com* does not easily identify the owner of the e-mail account.

INVESTIGATING E-MAIL CRIMES AND VIOLATIONS

Investigating crimes or policy violations involving e-mail is similar to investigating other types of computer abuse and crimes. Your goal is to find out who is behind the crime, collect the evidence, and build a case.

Identifying E-mail Crimes and Violations

E-mail crimes and violations depend on the city, state, and in some cases, country in which the e-mail originated. For example, in the state of Washington, it is illegal to send an unsolicited e-mail, also known as spam. However, in other states, spam is not considered a crime. Consult with an attorney for your organization to determine what specifically constitutes an e-mail crime.

In addition to committing crimes by sending e-mail, other crimes are supported by e-mail. For example, people use e-mail when committing other crimes such as selling narcotics, extortion, sexual harassment, stalking, fraud, child abductions, and child pornography. Because e-mail has become a major communication medium, any crime can involve e-mail.

Examining E-mail Messages

Once you have determined that a crime has been committed using e-mail, first access the victim's computer to recover the evidence contained in the e-mail. If possible, physically access the victim's computer, and then use the e-mail program on that computer to find a copy of an offending e-mail message that the victim received. Ask the victim for user names and passwords, if necessary, to log on to the e-mail service and access any files or directories that are protected or encrypted. If you cannot physically access the computer, guide the victim on the phone to open and print a copy of an offending message, including the header, as you will do in the following steps. The header of the e-mail message contains unique identifying numbers, such as the IP address of the server that sent the message. This information will help you to trace the e-mail to the suspect.

TIP

Before you work with a victim on the phone, create written procedures for opening and printing an e-mail header and message text using a variety of e-mail programs according to your state, county, or company's laws or policies. These steps will help you provide consistent instructions and can be helpful when training new forensic investigators.

11

In some cases, you might have to recover e-mail after the suspect of a crime has deleted it and tried to hide it from you. You will see how to recover those messages at the end of this chapter.

Copying an E-mail Message

Before you start an e-mail investigation, you need to copy and print the e-mail message involved in a crime or policy violation. You may want to forward the message to another e-mail address as well, depending on your department's guidelines.

The following steps explain how to use Microsoft Outlook to copy an e-mail message. Outlook is a Windows program included in the Microsoft Office suite of programs. You use a similar procedure to copy messages in other e-mail programs, including Outlook Express and Eudora. If Microsoft Outlook or Outlook Express is installed on your computer, perform the following steps and copy any e-mail message in your Inbox folder to a floppy disk.

To copy an e-mail message using Microsoft Outlook or Outlook Express:

1. Insert a formatted floppy disk into the floppy disk drive, such as Drive A. Use Windows Explorer or My Computer to open a window showing the floppy disk icon.

2. Start Outlook, if necessary, by clicking **Start**, pointing to **Programs** (**All Programs** in Windows XP), and then clicking **Microsoft Outlook**. The Outlook window opens.

3. Make sure the Folder List is open, as shown in Figure 11-4. In the Folders pane, click the folder that contains the message you want to copy. For example, click the **Inbox** folder. A list of messages in that folder appears in the right pane of the Outlook window.

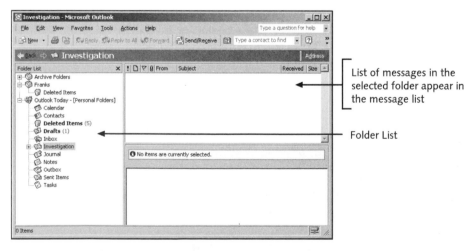

Figure 11-4   Folders pane in Outlook

4. Resize the Outlook window so that you can see the message you want to copy and the icon for the floppy disk.

5. Drag the message from the Outlook window to the floppy disk icon.

TIP

Instead of dragging, you can also click a message in the Inbox, click File on the menu bar, and then click Save As. The Save As dialog box opens. Click the Save in list arrow to navigate to the disk or folder where you want to copy the message, make sure that you select the .msg format if you want to make a duplicate of the message. If you select the text format, you will only get the contents of the message. Once you have selected a storage location and the desired format, click the Save button.

All GUI e-mail programs let you copy an e-mail message by dragging the message to a storage medium, such as a folder or disk, or by using a Save dialog box to save the message in a different location. For e-mail programs that you run from the command line, however, such as Pine used with UNIX, open the message, and then use the option to copy the e-mail message. The key used for the copy option usually appears at the bottom of the screen.

After you copy an e-mail message, work only with the copy, not the original version of the message.

Printing an E-mail Message

After you acquire a copy of the e-mail message, you should print the e-mail message. The following steps explain how to print an e-mail using Outlook or Outlook Express. If you are using a different e-mail program, read but do not perform the following steps.

To print an e-mail message using Outlook or Outlook Express:

1. Use Windows Explorer or My Computer to navigate to the location where you stored a copy of the e-mail message, such as a floppy disk.

2. Double-click the message you want to print. The message opens in an e-mail program, such as Outlook.

3. Click **File** on the menu bar, and then click **Print**. The Print dialog box opens.

4. Select settings as appropriate in the Print dialog box, and then click the **Print** button.

If you are using Pine or another command-line e-mail client, open the e-mail message and select the print option as indicated at the bottom of the screen.

Viewing E-mail Headers

After you copy and print an e-mail message, use the e-mail program that created the message to find the e-mail header. This section includes instructions for viewing an e-mail header using a variety of different e-mail clients, including Microsoft Outlook, Outlook

11

Express, and Eudora, which are Windows programs that use a GUI, a command-line e-mail client used with UNIX called Pine, common Internet e-mail providers using a Web interface such as AOL, Hotmail, Yahoo!, and an unusual Web-based client called WebTV. After you open the e-mail headers, copy and paste them into a text document, such as a Notepad or a Pico file. You will examine the headers in the next section.

Whether you are working on this chapter in a computer lab or elsewhere, perform as many of the following sets of steps as possible. More than one e-mail program is often installed on a single computer. The following steps assume that you know how to open the e-mail program.

To retrieve e-mail headers using Microsoft Outlook:

1. Start Outlook as you usually do, and then display the message you copied in the previous section.

2. Right-click the message, and then click **Options** on the shortcut menu. The Message Options dialog box opens. The Internet headers text box at the bottom of the dialog box contains the message header, as shown in Figure 11-5.

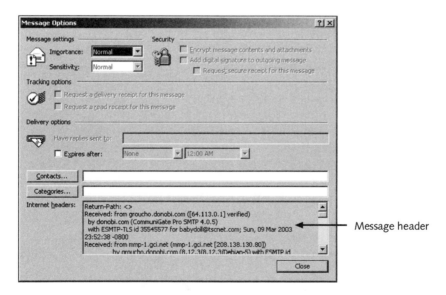

Figure 11-5 Microsoft Outlook e-mail header

3. Drag to select all of the message header text, and then press **Ctrl+C** to copy the text to the Clipboard.

4. Start a text editor, such as Notepad, and then press **Ctrl+V** in a new document window to paste the message header text.

5. Save the message header document as **Outlook Header.txt** in the Chap11\ Chapter folder in your work folder. Then close Outlook Header.txt.

6. Close Outlook.

To retrieve an Outlook Express e-mail header:

1. Start Outlook Express as you usually do, and then display the message you want to examine in the Outlook window.

2. Right-click the message, and then click **Properties** to open a dialog box showing general information about the message.

3. Click the **Details** tab to display the header for the e-mail message. See Figure 11-6.

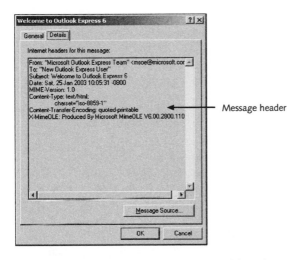

Figure 11-6   Outlook Express e-mail header

4. To see a detailed version of the header, click the **Message Source** button. See Figure 11-7.

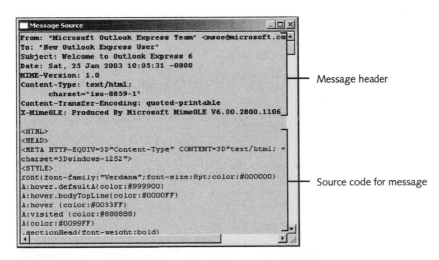

Figure 11-7   Detailed Outlook Express e-mail header

5. Drag to select all of the message header text, and then press **Ctrl+C** to copy the text to the Clipboard.

6. Start a text editor, such as Notepad, and then press **Ctrl+V** in a new document window to paste the message header text.

7. Save the message header document as **Outlook Express Header.txt** in the Chap11\Chapter folder in your work folder.

8. Close all open windows and dialog boxes, and then close Outlook Express.

To retrieve the e-mail header in Eudora:

1. Start Eudora as you usually do.

2. Open the Inbox.

3. Double-click the e-mail message to open it.

4. Click the **BLAH BLAH BLAH** button on the toolbar above the message. The e-mail header appears, as shown in Figure 11-8.

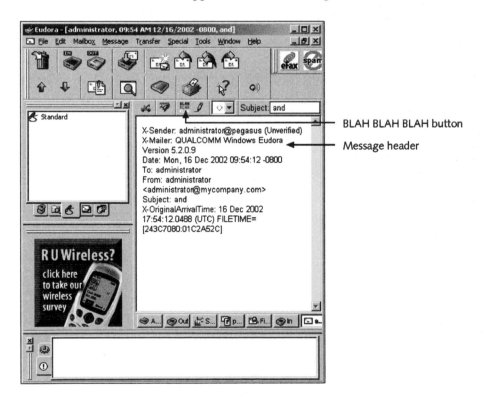

Figure 11-8 Eudora e-mail header

5. Drag to select all of the message header text, and then press **Ctrl+C** to copy the text to the Clipboard. Start a text editor, such as Notepad, and then press **Ctrl+V** in a new document window to paste the message header text.

6. Save the message header document as **Eudora Header.txt** in the Chap11\ Chapter folder in your work folder. Then close Eudora Header.txt.

7. Close Eudora.

The previous steps used a GUI to help you find the header information. Now you will see how to find this same information using e-mail software provided at the command prompt using UNIX.

To retrieve e-mail headers using Pine for UNIX:

1. Start Pine by typing **Pine** at the command prompt and then pressing **Enter**. The Pine e-mail screen appears with the options available shown at the bottom of the screen.

2. Press **S** to display the setup options.

3. Press **C** to configure the e-mail configuration options.

4. Scroll the list of options, and then use the arrow keys to highlight the **[ ] enable-full-header** option. Then type **X** to select the option.

5. Type **E** to exit the configuration mode.

6. When asked if you want to save the changes, type **Y** to save the changes. You return to the Pine main options.

7. Use the arrow keys to select an e-mail message and then select **O** from the options at the bottom of the screen. See Figure 11-9.

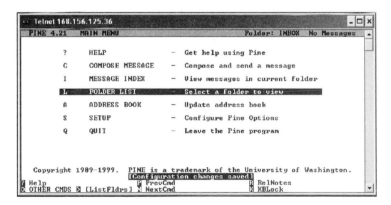

Figure 11-9 Pine e-mail options

8. Type **H** to open the e-mail header for this message. See Figure 11-10.

9. Type **Q** to quit Pine.

These steps also work with (ELM), another command-line e-mail program for UNIX and Linux. For older UNIX applications such as mail or mailx, you can print the e-mail headers by using the print command. When the e-mail message is open, type an uppercase P to

Figure 11-10   Pine e-mail header

use the `print` command. You can also save the e-mail message into a directory and use the command `type >type saved e-mail >>printer` where *saved e-mail* is the name of the saved e-mail message and *printer* is the name of the printer. For example, if you had an e-mail message called Nightmare and a printer called MyPrinter, you could print this e-mail message by typing at the command prompt:

```
type Nightmare >> MyPrinter
```

AOL, Hotmail, Juno, and Yahoo! are popular Internet e-mail service providers. Recall that using an Internet e-mail service lets you use any computer connected to the Internet to send and receive e-mail, making these messages more difficult to trace.

To view AOL e-mail headers:

1. Start AOL as you usually do.

2. Double-click the e-mail message to open it.

3. Click the **DETAILS** link below the subject line. The header appears, as shown in Figure 11-11.

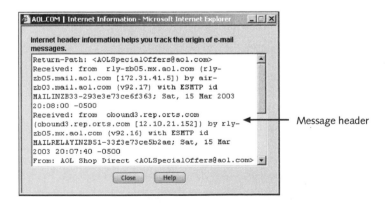

Figure 11-11   AOL e-mail header

4. Drag to select all of the message header text, and then press **Ctrl+C** to copy the text to the Clipboard. Start a text editor, such as Notepad, and then press **Ctrl+V** in a new document window to paste the message header text.

5. Save the message header document as **AOL Header.txt** in the Chap11\ Chapter folder in your work folder.

6. Close AOL.

To view e-mail headers in Hotmail:

1. Start Hotmail as you usually do.

2. Click the e-mail message to open it.

3. Click **Options** on the menu bar, and then click **Preferences**. (In MSN/ Hotmail 8, click **Mail Display Settings**.)

4. Click **Advanced Headers**. (In MSN/Hotmail 8, click the **Advanced** option in **Message Headers**.) The header appears in the Hotmail window, as shown in Figure 11-12.

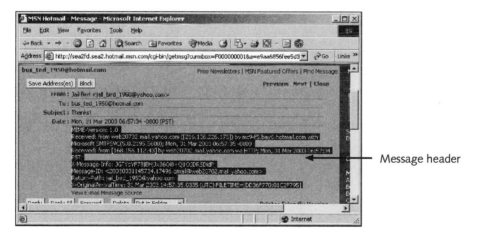

Figure 11-12   Hotmail e-mail headers option

5. Drag to select all of the message header text, and then press **Ctrl+C** to copy the text to the Clipboard. Start a text editor, such as Notepad, and then press **Ctrl+V** in a new document window to paste the message header text.

6. Save the message header document as **Hotmail Header.txt** in the Chap11\ Chapter folder in your work folder.

7. Close Hotmail.

To view e-mail headers in early versions of Juno:

1. Start Juno as you usually do.

2. Double-click a message to open it.

3. Click **File** on the menu bar, and then click **Save as**. The Save As dialog box opens.

4. In the File name text box, type **Juno Header**.

5. Click the **Save as type** list arrow, and then click **Text**.

6. Use the **Save in** list arrow to navigate to the Chap11\Chapter folder in your work folder. Then click the **Save** button.

7. Use My Computer or Windows Explorer to go to the Chap11\Chapter folder in your work folder.

8. Double-click **Juno Header.txt** to open it in Notepad. The e-mail header appears, as shown in Figure 11-13.

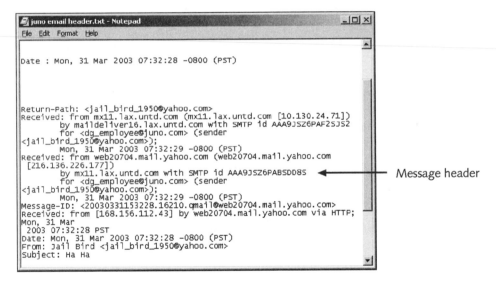

Figure 11-13 E-mail message header for early versions of Juno

9. Close Notepad, and then close Juno.

To view an e-mail header in a more recent version of Juno:

1. Open Juno as you normally do.

2. Click the **Go to E-mail** tab at the top of the page.

3. Click **Options**.

4. Select **Show Headers** under Preferences by clicking the empty box.

5. Click **Save**.

6. Scroll back to the top, if necessary, and click the **Inbox** tab.

7. Open a message and the header appears, as shown in Figure 11-14.

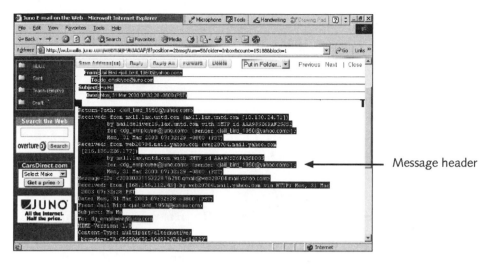

Figure 11-14   E-mail message header for recent versions of Juno

To view e-mail headers in Yahoo!:

1. Log onto your Yahoo! mail account.

2. Click the **Options** link on the left navigation bar (In newer versions of Yahoo! click the **Mail Options** link on the right). The MAIL options window opens.

3. Click the **Mail Preferences** link (or the **General Preferences** link in newer versions).

4. In the Show Headers dialog box, click **All**. (In newer versions, scroll the General Preferences page, and then click **Show All headers on incoming messages**.)

5. Click the **Save** button to put your new settings into effect. Any e-mail messages you open will include the header. (Figure 11-15 later in this chapter shows a sample Yahoo! e-mail header.)

6. Drag to select all of the message header text, and then press **Ctrl+C** to copy the text to the Clipboard. Start a text editor, such as Notepad, and then press **Ctrl+V** in a new document window to paste the message header text.

7. Save the message header document as **Yahoo Header.txt** in the Chap11\ Chapter folder in your work folder.

8. Close Yahoo!

WebTV (now called MSN TV) is a specialized TV with computer-like accessories. This combination allows you to use the Internet and e-mail and view messages and Web pages on your TV. To view the headers of a WebTV e-mail message, you must forward a copy of the message to yourself, enter a special symbol in the Subject line, and then send the message to another e-mail address.

If you do not have a copy of WebTV, read but do not perform the following steps.

To view a WebTV e-mail header:

1. Start WebTV as you usually do.

2. Open the e-mail message by using the arrow keys to highlight the e-mail message and then press the **Enter** or **Return** key.

3. Scroll down with arrow keys if necessary, select the **Forward** button on the e-mail toolbar, and then press **Enter** or **Return** to forward a copy of the message.

4. In the To text box, type your e-mail address to send the message to yourself.

5. In the message area, press **Enter** or **Return** three or four times to insert a few blank lines.

6. Press and hold the **Alt** key, type **1234**, and then release the **Alt** key to insert a unique symbol or characters such as a square □ or 123¢ in the message.

7. Drag to select the square symbol or other unique characters, and then press **Ctrl+C** to copy the symbol to the Clipboard.

8. Click in the **Subject** text box, and then press **Ctrl+V** to paste the symbol.

9. Click **Send** and then press **Enter** or **Return** to send the e-mail to your e-mail account.

10. Start your e-mail program, if necessary, and open the message you just sent to yourself. The message includes the header text.

11. Drag to select all of the message header text, and then press **Ctrl+C** to copy the text to the Clipboard. Start a text editor, such as Notepad, and then press **Ctrl+V** in a new document window to paste the message header text.

12. Save the message header document as **WebTV Header.txt** in the Chap11\ Chapter folder in your work folder, if possible.

13. Close your e-mail program and WebTV.

All of the e-mail clients that you reviewed supply you with the same information in the e-mail header. Keep in mind that not all e-mail clients are included here, and as new e-mail clients and versions emerge, they will have different options to obtain the e-mail header. In most cases, however, you can find information about display message headers in the program's help files.

Examining an E-mail Header

In the previous steps, you used as many e-mail programs as possible to open and then save the header for an e-mail message. Now you can open one of the headers you saved and examine it to gather information about the e-mail message. As mentioned before, you can use the e-mail header to gather supporting evidence and ultimately track the suspect to the originating location of the e-mail. The primary piece of information you are looking for is the originating e-mail domain address or an IP address. Also helpful are the date and time the message was sent, the filenames of any attachments, and the unique message number for the message, if it is supplied. When you find the originating e-mail address, you can track the message to a suspect by doing reverse lookups, which are covered later in the chapter.

To open and examine an e-mail header:

1. Use My Computer or Windows Explorer to navigate to the Chap11\Chapter folder in your work folder.

2. Double-click a file containing message header text, such as **Outlook Header.txt**. The message header opens in Notepad.

Figure 11-15 shows a sample message header copied from a fictitious Yahoo e-mail message. (The e-mail addresses, for example, are not real addresses.) Line numbers have been added for reference.

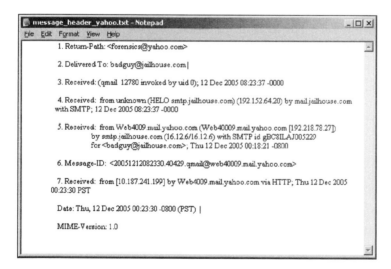

Figure 11-15   Sample e-mail header with line numbers added

The message header shown in Figure 11-15 provides a significant amount of information. Lines 1–5 identify from where your e-mail server received the message. Line 1 shows the return path, or the e-mail address an e-mail program would use to send a reply. Do *not* rely on the return path to show the source account of the e-mail message. It is easy to fake, or spoof, an e-mail address in the Return-Path line, otherwise known as the Reply to.

Line 2 identifies the recipient's e-mail address, which is *badguy@jailhouse.com* in Figure 11-15. When you are investigating e-mail involved in a crime or company policy violation, you should verify this address by confirming it with the e-mail service provider. Request a bill or a log to make sure that the account name identified in Line 2 is being used by the victim. (Check with your Attorney General's office to determine the type of documentation you need.)

Line 3 indicates the type of e-mail service that sent the e-mail, such as qmail (UNIX e-mail), and includes an identifying number, such as 12780. Later, you match this number to one on the appropriate e-mail log. For the message shown in Figure 11-15, once you have located the UNIX e-mail server physical location, you will access the e-mail log for that UNIX e-mail server and match the identification numbers.

Line 4 identifies the IP address of the e-mail server that sent the e-mail message, such as 192.152.64.20. Line 4 also identifies the name of the server sending the e-mail message, smtp.jailhouse.com.

TIP

A good indicator of a spoofed e-mail address is if the Received from server (shown in Line 4) and reply to or Return-Path server (shown in Line 1) are different.

Line 5 contains the name of the e-mail server that was responsible for connecting to the victim's e-mail server.

The next two lines provide information important for the e-mail investigator. Line 6 shows a unique message number that the sending e-mail server assigned to the message. In the sample e-mail header shown in Figure 11-15, this is 20051212082330.40429. You can use this number to track the e-mail on the originating e-mail server through the e-mail logs.

Line 7 identifies the IP address of the server sending the e-mail and provides a date and time that the offending e-mail was sent. For example, 10.187.241.199 is the IP address of Web40009.mail.yahoo.com, the sending server, and Thu 12 Dec 2005 00:23:30 PST is the date the message was sent. Line 7 might also identify the e-mail as being sent through a Hypertext Transfer Protocol (HTTP) client, as it does in Figure 11-15.

The e-mail message header shown in Figure 11-15 does not include a Line 8, which usually identifies any attachment included with the e-mail. An attachment is a file that is sent with an e-mail message. The attached file can be just about any type of file, from a program to a picture. If a message includes an attachment, investigate the attachment as a supporting piece of evidence. If you are working with the victim, in most cases, the attachment will still be attached to the e-mail. If you are investigating a suspect's machine, remember to work with the copied version and start searching for the attached file by using the Search or Find feature of the computer's operating system (or a computer forensics tool) to determine whether the file was saved and still exists on the hard disk. In most cases, if you supply the name of the attachment, you will find it on the computer. If you do not find the attachment on the hard disk, use the tools and skills learned earlier in this book to recover the missing attachment. Once you find the file, copy it to a working directory to prevent any accidental changes of the original data.

If you are investigating an e-mail that has an attachment with an unfamiliar file extension, such as .mdf, you can use the Internet to research the file to find out what program creates a file of this type. Visit *www.whatis.com* to check file extensions and match the file to a program.

TIP

When searching a suspect's computer, you will want to use computer forensics tools to look for specific files. Using these tools allows a more thorough search of the machine for the file based on the structure of the file rather than the name of the file. Computer forensics tools also allow you to recover deleted files and folders.

Examining Additional E-mail Files

E-mail programs either save e-mail messages on the client computer or leave them on the server. The storage of e-mail files depends on the settings on both the client and server computers. With the client computer you could save all your e-mail in a separate folder for record keeping. For example, Microsoft Outlook allows a user to save sent, drafted, deleted, and received e-mails in a personal file with a file extension of .pst or off-line files in a file with a file extension of .ost.

If you are using Microsoft Outlook as your e-mail client, you can attach a personal e-mail file (.pst) or off-line e-mail file (.ost) to your Outlook program. You can then read the e-mail messages contained in these files without logging on to the user's e-mail account. Each e-mail program lets you open a certain type of data file that contains a collection of e-mails. In the previous example, this collection of e-mails would be contained in the PST file.

Each e-mail program also maintains an electronic personal address book for the user. A suspect's personal address book can contain valuable information to link criminal e-mail abuse to other participants as well as the suspect's physical address and his or her involvement in a crime.

After seeing how Microsoft Outlook operates, UNIX e-mail might seem a little easier. In UNIX, e-mail is handled per user. However, UNIX allows the administrator to create groups for e-mail distributions. As a member of a group, you get all the messages for that group. A UNIX e-mail server allows the members of an e-mail group to view the same messages. If the UNIX administrator adds you to the same group as the suspect, you can read the e-mail messages of the suspect without logging on as the suspect.

When an online e-mail program uses a Web browser to connect to the e-mail server, as with AOL, Hotmail, and Yahoo!, the e-mail messages are Web pages. Like any other Web page, these e-mail messages leave files on the computer that include information about the e-mail message. These files are stored in different folders, including the History, Cookies, Cache, Temp, Temporary Internet folders, and any folders created by the client computer for the use of the e-mail program such as AOL. Scan the folder lists or use computer forensics tools to find the folders used for the appropriate e-mail client.

Once you have found these folders, you can view and open the folders and the files they contain, which often provides valuable information for your investigation. The files contained in these directories will be helpful to you in most cases when you have seized a suspect's drive. When you are working on the victim's machine, these files help you document the offensive material.

11

For some of these files, you need to download a program to read the data. For example, you might need to download a cookie reader to read the cookies. You will, however, be able to pick out key phrases and words without using a specialized reader. These cookies are used by Web sites to track your activity.

Tracing an E-mail Message

After you read the suspect e-mail, determine a crime has been committed, check for, find, and open an attached file, and open the e-mail header to record the IP address from the originating source, you can track down the source of the e-mail abuse.

For example, if you are investigating the source of the e-mail message shown in Figure 11-15, you can look up the Web site *www.jailhouse.com* on the Internet to find out who is responsible for that domain name. Some popular sites to use to find the owner of the Web address are described in the following list:

- *www.arin.net*–Use the American Registry for Internet Numbers (ARIN) to map an IP address to a domain name and the point of contact for the domain name.

- *www.internic.com*–Like *www.arin.net*, you use *www.internic.com* to find the IP address of a domain name and the point of contact for the domain name.

- *www.freeality.com*–A comprehensive Web site that has options for searching for a suspect, including by e-mail address, phone numbers, and names.

- *www.google.com*–A general search engine you can use to search for all the information on the Web and additional postings on discussion boards.

Using one of these Web sites, you can find the suspect's full e-mail address, such as *badguy@jailhouse.com* as well as all of suspect's contact information from the Web. Keep in mind that the suspect may have posted false information as well. Make sure you verify your findings by checking the network logs with the e-mail addresses.

Using Network Logs Related to E-mail

After you identify the contact person at the various domain names in the header, it may be necessary to confirm the route e-mail made. To verify the path with the header information, you need to use the device log that identifies the e-mail as having taken the path. The networking devices to focus on are the **routers**, which pass network traffic on the Internet. Network administrators maintain a log of the traffic handled by their routers. In general, a log is a text file that tracks the events that happen on that device. The log files for a router can track all inbound and outbound traffic on its ports. The router will have rules on them to allow or disallow traffic onto their network based on the destination address. In most cases, a router will be set up to track all traffic that flows through its ports. The network administrator that manages routers can provide the log files you need. Review the router logs on behalf of your victim's offending e-mail looking for that identifying message ID number.

Network administrators also often maintain logs for firewalls, devices that filter Internet traffic that can help verify whether or not the e-mail message passed through that device. Firewalls such as WatchGuard, CISCO Pix, and Checkpoint maintain log files that track the traffic on the Internet that is either destined for other networks or for the network the firewall is protecting. The network administrator can also provide firewall log files, which you can open in a text editor such as Notepad in Windows or Vi in UNIX. Figure 11-16 shows a typical log file for a WatchGuard Firebox II. Although Figure 11-16 shows the log file open in Notepad, some devices also use special programs to read log files.

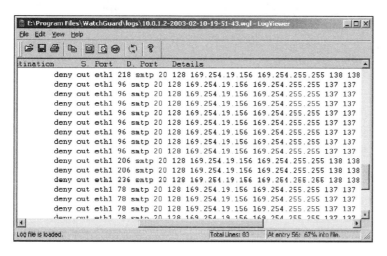

Figure 11-16   Firewall log

UNDERSTANDING E-MAIL SERVERS

Now that you understand how e-mail programs work in general, you can examine the tasks that e-mail servers perform and how you might use them in your investigation. An e-mail server is a computer that is running an operating system such as UNIX, and the computer is loaded with a software package that uses the e-mail protocols for its services. As a computer forensic investigator, you cannot know everything about all e-mail servers. Your focus is not to learn how a particular e-mail server works, but how to retrieve information about e-mail messages for an e-mail investigation. In most cases, you must work closely with the network administrator or the e-mail administrator of the network. (In some instances, they are the same person.) Administrators are usually willing to help you find the data or files that you need and may even offer new ways to find this information. If you cannot work with an administrator, perform research on the Internet or use the computer forensics tools discussed later in this chapter to investigate the particular e-mail server software and operating system being used.

To investigate e-mail abuse, you should know how an e-mail server records and handles the e-mail that it receives. Some e-mail servers are databases that store multiple users' e-mails while others are a flat file system. All e-mail servers can maintain a log of all the e-mails that are processed. Some e-mail servers are set up to log e-mail transactions by default. Others provide the option for logging, but must be configured to do so. Most e-mail administrators log the system operations and message traffic on their e-mail server to recover e-mail messages in case of a disaster, to make sure the firewall and e-mail filters are working properly, and to enforce company policy. However, the e-mail administrator can turn off logging or use circular logging, which allocates space for a log file on the server, and then starts overwriting from the beginning when the logging reaches the end of the time frame or log size. Circular logging saves valuable server space. However, you cannot recover a log after it is overwritten. For example, on Monday the e-mail server records e-mail traffic in a file named Mon.log. For the next six days, the e-mail server uses a log for each day, such as Tues.log, Wed.log, etc. On Sunday at midnight, the e-mail server starts recording e-mail traffic information in Mon.log, overwriting the information logged the previous Monday. The only way to access the log file information would be from a backup file, which many e-mail administrators create before a log file is overwritten.

As shown in Figure 11-17, e-mail logs generally identify the e-mail messages an account received, the IP address from which they were sent, the time and date the e-mail server received them, the time and date the client computer accessed the e-mail, the IP addresses, the contents of the e-mail, system-specific information, and any other information the e-mail administrator wants to track. These e-mail logs are usually formatted in plain text and can be read using a basic text editor, Notepad or Vi.

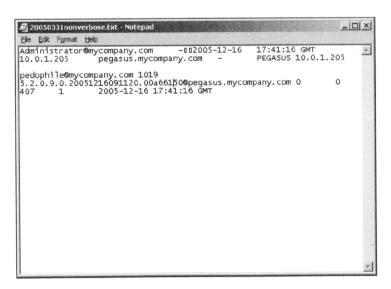

Figure 11-17   E-mail server log file

In most cases, administrators set e-mail servers to continuous logging mode. The administrator can also log all of the e-mail information in the same file, or use one log file for date and time information, for example, the size of the e-mail, and IP address. This is extremely useful when you have the e-mail header from the client that has a date and time stamp and an IP address and you want to filter or sort the log files to narrow your search.

Once you have identified the source of the offending e-mail, contact the network or e-mail administrator of the offending e-mail owner's network as soon as possible. Some e-mail providers, especially Internet e-mail providers, do not keep their logs for long, and their logs might contain key information for your investigation.

In addition to logging e-mail traffic, e-mail servers help your investigations by maintaining a copy of a client's e-mail, even if the user has deleted the messages from the Inbox. Some e-mail servers do not completely delete an e-mail message from the server until the system is backed up. Even if the suspect deletes the e-mail, in some cases the e-mail administrator can recover the e-mail without restoring the entire e-mail system. With other systems, however, the e-mail administrator will have to recover the entire e-mail server to recover one deleted message.

This is similar to the deletion of files on a hard drive; the file is marked for deletion, but it is not truly deleted until another piece of data is written in the same place. With e-mail servers, it waits to overwrite the area until the server has been backed up. If you have a date and time stamp for an e-mail message, the e-mail administrator should be able to recover the message from backup media if the message is no longer available on the e-mail server.

Examining UNIX E-mail Server Logs

UNIX is an operating system that has been used for over thirty years. It has several different versions and spin-offs. UNIX supports different e-mail servers, including mail, mailx, qmail, Pine, and Sendmail to name just a few. This section focuses on the log and configuration files that the Sendmail e-mail server creates by default. Other UNIX e-mail servers produce similar log files in similar locations.

The files that provide helpful information to an e-mail investigation are log files and configuration files. Sendmail creates a number of files on the server to track and maintain the e-mail service. The first one to be aware of is /etc/sendmail.cf, which contains the configuration information for Sendmail allowing the investigator to determine where the log files reside.

Sendmail uses the sendmail.cf file as an instruction page. Sendmail refers to the sendmail.cf file to find out what to do with an e-mail message once it is received For example, if a server receives an e-mail from an unsolicited site, a line in the sendmail.cf file can tell the Sendmail server to discard the unwanted e-mail.

Similar to the sendmail.cf file, the syslogd file includes e-mail logging instructions—it specifies how and which events Sendmail should log. Viewing the syslogd will allow you to determine how Sendmail is set up to log e-mail events. The syslogd configuration file can be located in /etc/syslog.conf and contains three bits of information: the event, the priority level of concern, and the action taken when it was logged. By examining this log, you can see what happened to an e-mail message when it was logged. By default, Sendmail can display an event message, log the event message to a log file, or send an event message to a remote log host. Figure 11-18 shows a typical syslog.conf file. Note that the lines that begin with pound signs (#) are comments describing the purpose of the commands.

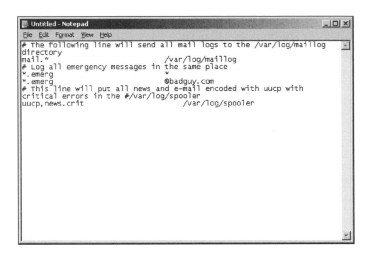

Figure 11-18   Typical syslog.conf file

The syslog.conf file simply specifies where to save different types of e-mail log files. The first log file it configures is /var/log/maillog. This log file usually contains SMTP communications used between servers. Figure 11-19 shows a sample of a log that is monitoring the SMTP protocol.

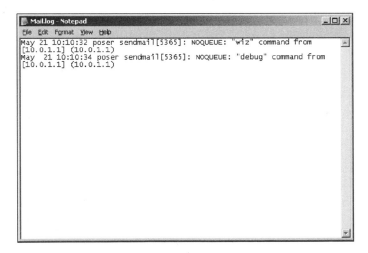

Figure 11-19   Sample mail log with SMTP information

As shown in Figure 11-19, IP addresses (10.0.1.1) and a date and time stamp (May 21 10:10:34) identified in the mail log are important information in an e-mail investigation. Use the mail log IP address and date and time stamp to compare with the client e-mail header to confirm the originator of the e-mail.

The maillog file also contains information about POP3 events. Figure 11-20 shows the first two lines of a POP3 event.

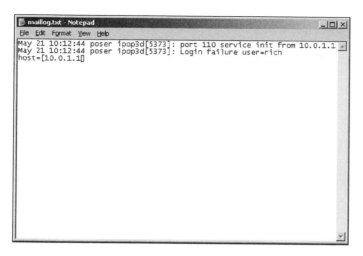

Figure 11-20   Sample mail log with POP information

The POP3 event information also includes an IP address and a date and time stamp to make your comparisons against the victim's e-mail message.

Typically, UNIX installations are set to store logs such as maillog in the var/log directory. However, an administrator can change the log location, especially when an e-mail service specifies a different location. If you are examining a UNIX computer and do not find the e-mail logs in var/log, you can find log files by using the find or locate command. For example, type locate *.log at the UNIX command prompt.

Note that UNIX and Linux use the forward slash (/) in file paths, while Windows uses the backslash (\ ) in file paths.

TIP

If you need further assistance on where a file is created by default, you can use the manual pages for the type of e-mail service running on the machine. Be aware that a new directory is created on the client when the user logs in for the first time and runs Pine or Elm (UNIX e-mail clients). The directory is created in the /home/username/mail. If the server has been configured to deliver the e-mail messages to the client machines, and has not been configured to maintain a copy of the e-mail on the server, the only copy of the e-mail will be on the client in the user's mail folder.

If the UNIX e-mail server is set to keep all messages on the server, you can access e-mail messages by requesting that the UNIX administrator create e-mail groups and add yourself to the same group as the suspect. UNIX e-mail servers do not usually use groups to prevent users from accidentally viewing e-mail that does not belong to them. However, e-mail groups can be useful for investigative purposes with the appropriate warrants.

Examining Microsoft E-mail Server Logs

Microsoft Exchange 2000 Server, generally called Exchange, is the most recent version of the Microsoft e-mail server. Exchange is a database, as are many other e-mail servers, and is based on the Microsoft Extensible Storage Engine (ESE), which uses several files in different combinations to provide e-mail service. The files most useful to a computer forensic investigator are EDB and STM database files, checkpoint files, and temporary files.

In older versions of Exchange, EDB files were the only database files associated with Exchange, while Exchange 2000 Server uses both the EDB file and the STM database files. An EDB file is responsible for messages formatted with the Message Application Protocol Interface (MAPI), a newer format being used with e-mail, while the STM database file is responsible for messages that are not formatted with the MAPI properties. These two files constitute the Information Store, a storage area for e-mail messages.

As a database server, Exchange logs information about changes to its data, also called transactions, in a transaction log. To prevent a loss of data from the last backup, a checkpoint file or marker is inserted in the transaction log to mark the last point at which the database was written to disk. These files allow the e-mail administrator to recover lost or deleted e-mail messages in the event of a disaster, such as a power failure.

Exchange also creates TMP, or temporary files when it becomes busy converting the binary data to readable text. Again, these files are used by Exchange to prevent data loss.

Like UNIX e-mail servers, Exchange maintains logs to track e-mail communication. For example, RESx.logs track information about database overflow. They are used to make sure that the database can keep up with the changing environment without losing data.

Microsoft Exchange servers can also maintain a log called tracking.log that tracks e-mail messages. If the Message Tracking feature has been turned on and the e-mail administrator selects verbose (detailed) logging as shown in Figure 11-21, you will see the contents of the message.

With this option selected, you will see the date and time stamp, IP address of the sending computer, and the contents or body of the e-mail message. Outside of special computer forensics tools, the message tracking log shown in verbose mode provides the most information about e-mail messages sent and received by Exchange.

Another log you need to be aware of that is used for troubleshooting and investigating the Exchange environment is the troubleshooting log. You can read this troubleshooting log, also known as the diagnostic log, using the Windows Event Viewer, shown in Figure 11-22, which is included in the Administrative Tools window. Each event logged has an ID number with a severity level.

To examine the details about an e-mail event, double-click the event to open its Event Properties dialog box, shown in Figure 11-23. This dialog box provides information that may be useful if you suspect the e-mail server has been tampered with to alter its contents.

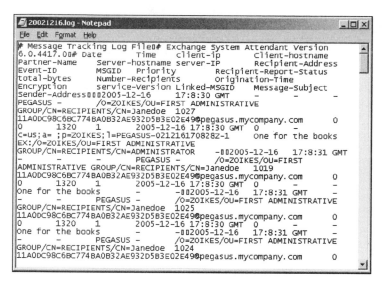

Figure 11-21   Message tracking log in verbose mode

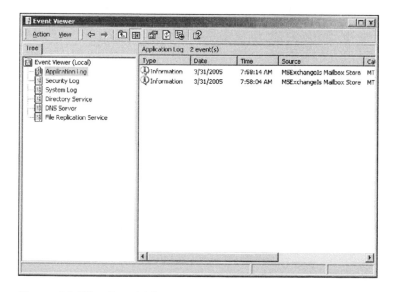

Figure 11-22   Event Viewer

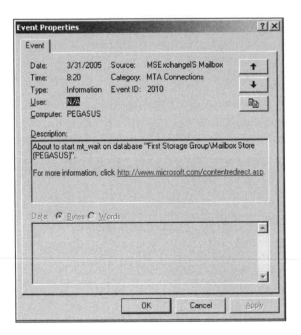

Figure 11-23   Event Properties dialog box

Examining Novell GroupWise E-mail Logs

Novell is a network operating system that is not used as often as UNIX/Linux and Windows. The Novell e-mail server software is called **GroupWise**, which is a database server like Microsoft Exchange and UNIX Sendmail. GroupWise has up to 25 databases for user e-mails. Each database is stored in the OFUSER directory object, (Netware refers to all of the entries in its structure as objects to include directories and users) and is referenced by a user name followed by the unique identifier and a .db file extension.

TIP In addition to the 25 databases GroupWise has for user e-mails, it uses another database called NGWDFR.DB for delayed or deferred e-mail delivery. By default, this database is stored in the OFMSG directory object. This is similar to how the Microsoft Exchange Server uses TMP directory.

GroupWise shares resources with the e-mail server, as do the Microsoft and UNIX e-mail servers. GroupWise gives the first folder to be shared at the post office or on the e-mail server as the filename PU020101.DB, regardless of who shares the folder. GroupWise then names the next folder to be shared by changing the filename to the next sequential number, PU020102.DB, and so on, increasing in sequence by one. These files contain information such as user files that have been shared for other users to view.

These files are important if the user has shared an address book on the GroupWise server. In this case, if the user who created the PUxxxxxxx.DB files shares those files, they are available for searching on the server. If the user has decided not to share an address book, then the data is stored in a file called USER.Db. In either case, you will be able to view the user's personal address book using one of the two files.

GroupWise mailboxes make recovering data easy. GroupWise has two ways of organizing the mailboxes on the server. The first is with the permanent index files identified with an IDX file extension. These files are updated and renamed at the end of everyday. It puts the mailboxes in order. Microsoft and UNIX also can sort mailboxes in order, but they do not use a specific index file to do so.

The second organizing method involves the GroupWise QuickFinder action. The incremental indexing files are used to maintain the changes to the e-mail server. Then any changes are written to the IDX file at the end of the day by the QuickFinder.

The GroupWise folder and file structure can be complex because it takes advantage of the directory structure provided by Novell. As such, GroupWise has a number of files scattered within the post office directory, but maintains control of the e-mail service and the files associated using a specialized database, called the Guardian database.

With GroupWise, administrators manage the e-mail server in a centralized manner using the guardian database, NGWGUARD.Db. The Guardian database is a directory of every database in the GroupWise environment. As its name suggests, the Guardian database tracks changes in the GroupWise environment, and protects the database against all processes that want to change the GroupWise databases. The Guardian database must first clear these processes before they can change a GroupWise database. Although the Guardian database protects the e-mail server data, it is also considered a single point of failure. If it is erased or becomes corrupt, you must recover the database from a backup and begin your forensic investigation again. The Guardian database does include some built-in safeguards against data loss. The NGWGUARD.FBK, NGWGUARD.RRL, and NGWGUARD.Db files contain backup copies and log files from the Guardian database. They prevent the total loss of the Guardian database and allow it to track changes without affecting the performance of the server.

Similar to the other e-mail servers, GroupWise generates log files. The GroupWise logs are maintained in a standard log format in the GW\volz\ *.log directory. Use these logs to match the e-mail header of an e-mail with the IP address of a suspect.

USING SPECIALIZED E-MAIL FORENSICS TOOLS

For many e-mail investigations, you can rely on e-mail message files, e-mail headers, and e-mail server log files to investigate e-mail crimes. However, if you cannot find an e-mail administrator willing to participate in the investigation, or you encounter a highly customized e-mail environment, you can use data-recovery tools and computer forensics tools specially designed to recover e-mail files.

As technology has progressed for the use of e-mail and other services, so too have the tools used to recover the information lost or deleted from a hard drive. In previous chapters, you reviewed many tools available for data recovery, such as AccessData's Forensic

11

Toolkit (FTK) and EnCase. You can also use these tools in the investigation and recovery of e-mail files. Other tools are specifically built for e-mail recovery, including recovering deleted attachments from the hard drive. These tools include FINALeMAIL, Sawmill-GroupWise, and Audimation for logging.

When you use one of these third-party programs to search the machine for a .db file, for example, you can find where the administrator stores the .db files for the e-mail server. To find log files, use *.log as the search criteria. You are likely to find at least two logs specific to e-mail—one listing logged events for messages, while the other lists logged events for accounts accessing the e-mail.

FTK, EnCase, and other computer forensics tools, allow you to find e-mail database files, personal e-mail files, off-line storage files, and log files. Some tools allow you to view the messages and other files with a special viewer, while others require you to use a text editor to begin comparing information such as the date and time stamp, user name, domain name, and contents of the e-mail to determine whether this information matches what was found on the victim's machine.

One advantage of using data-recovery tools is that you do need to know about the e-mail server or client to extract the data from these computers. Data-recovery tools do the work for you and allow you to view the evidence on the machine.

After you compare the e-mail logs with the e-mail messages, verify the e-mail account, message ID, IP address, and date and time stamp, and determine that there is enough evidence for a warrant, you can obtain and serve your warrant for the suspect and his or her computer equipment. When serving your warrant and collecting the suspect's computer, remember to follow the evidence-handling rules and control measures appropriate for your agency, as described in previous chapters.

When requesting a search warrant, consider whether you are looking for more than one topic area. The warrant should then cover all areas of interest. For example, if your suspect is currently being investigated for harassment, but you believe he or she is also distributing narcotics over the Internet, request two separate warrants.

TIP

Once all the evidence has been bagged and tagged, you need to begin copying it to another source for further investigation. As you are copying evidence data, document everything you are doing. For example, if you create a bit-stream image of the evidence, document the procedure and tool that you use. You are then ready to proceed with the forensic data acquisition and analysis, as you learned in Chapter 9.

For example, suppose you have the FINALeMAIL tool. You can use FINALeMAIL to scan e-mail database files on the suspect's Windows computer and locate any e-mail messages that the suspect has deleted—these are message that do not have data location information associated with them—and restore the messages to their original state. When you run FINALeMAIL, you can search the computer for lost or deleted e-mail messages, and for other files associated with e-mail. Figure 11-24 shows two e-mail databases that FINALeMAIL found—one database for Outlook Express and one for Eudora.

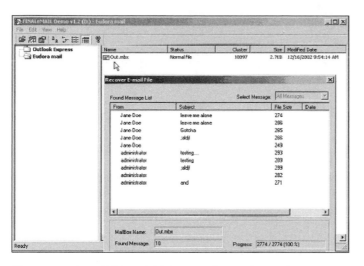

Figure 11-24   FINALeMAIL e-mail search results

To examine the Eudora Mail database, select it in the left pane and then click the Out.mbx in the right pane. When you double-click the Out.mbx, the Recover E-mail file dialog box opens. As shown in Figure 11-24, there are five Jane Doe messages and five administrator messages. By double-clicking the message you want to view, you can see the contents of the message as shown in Figure 11-25. In this case, the subject line and the body of the e-mail message are the same.

Figure 11-25   FINALeMAIL message contents

11

FINALeMAIL is not as flashy as the other tools, but it is quick, fairly intuitive to use, and affordably priced. It lets you see if there were any attachments sent with the e-mail and lets you view them as necessary.

Another tool to consider is FTK, an all-purpose program that is used for all file discoveries. It is not task or file specific and indexes drives for faster data retrieval, allowing you to investigate the drive more thoroughly.

As with the FINALeMAIL product, FTK can find files that are specific to e-mail clients and servers. FTK has the ability to filter or find only those files found that are specific to e-mail. FTK allows you to provide these filters by simply supplying the information in the search parameters.

Other tools available for investigating e-mail servers include EnCase, a general data-recovery tool; Sawmill, which reads logs generated by Netware's GroupWise e-mail server; and the Coroner's Toolkit, a UNIX toolset that can help recover e-mail messages from a UNIX e-mail server. These tools provide features similar to the ones you've worked with in FINALeMAIL and FTK.

Chapter Summary

- ❑ Because e-mail programs usually employ some protocols used with the Internet to exchange messages, you should understand the fundamentals of the Internet to understand how e-mail works, including Internet connection methods, technical rules, and similarities among e-mail applications.

- ❑ You can send and receive e-mail in two environments: via the Internet or a local area network (LAN). Both environments distribute data, such as e-mail messages, from one central server to many connected client computers, a configuration called client-server architecture. The server computer uses a server operating system to provide e-mail service. Client computers run an operating system such as Windows or Linux, and use e-mail programs to contact the e-mail server and send and retrieve e-mail messages.

- ❑ Investigating crimes or policy violations involving e-mail is similar to investigating other types of computer abuse and crimes. Your goal is to find out who is behind the crime, collect the evidence, and build a case.

- ❑ Once you have determined that a crime has been committed using e-mail, first access the victim's computer to recover the evidence contained in the e-mail. If possible, physically access the victim's computer, and then use the e-mail program on that computer to find a copy of an offending e-mail message that the victim received.

- ❑ Before you start an e-mail investigation, you need to copy and print the e-mail message involved in a crime or policy violation. You may want to forward the message to another e-mail address as well, depending on your department's guidelines.

❑ After you copy and print an e-mail message, use the e-mail program that created the message to find the e-mail header. You can use the e-mail header to gather supporting evidence and ultimately track the suspect to the originating location of the e-mail by finding the originating e-mail domain address or an IP address. Also helpful are the date and time the message was sent, the filenames of any attachments, and the unique message number for the message, if it is supplied. When you find the originating e-mail address, you can track the message to a suspect by doing reverse lookups.

❑ To investigate e-mail abuse, you should know how an e-mail server records and handles the e-mail that it receives. Some e-mail servers are databases that store multiple user's e-mails while others are a flat file system. All e-mail servers can maintain a log of all the e-mails that are processed. Some e-mail servers are set up to log e-mail transactions by default. Others provide the option for logging, but must be configured to do so.

❑ For many e-mail investigations, you can rely on e-mail message files, e-mail headers, and e-mail server log files to investigate e-mail crimes. However, if you cannot find an e-mail administrator willing to participate in the investigation, or you encounter a highly customized e-mail environment, you can use data-recovery tools and computer forensics tools specially designed to recover e-mail files.

KEY TERMS

client-server architecture—A network architecture in which each computer or process on the network is either a client or a server. Clients are the systems that request services from the server. A server has systems that process the request from clients.

code—A group of specialized characters combined in a sequence to provide instructions to a program on how to perform a specific action.

dial-up connection—A connecting device to a network via a modem or a public telephone network. Dial-up access acts just like a phone connection, except that the two connecting parties are computers instead of people.

Domain Naming Service (DNS)—An Internet service that translates domain names (i.e. *www.microsoft.com*) to IP addresses (i.e. 10.0.1.10).

Electronic Communications Privacy Act (ECPA)—A law that prohibits phone tapping, interception of e-mail, and other privacy violations.

GroupWise—The Novell e-mail server software, a database server like Microsoft Exchange and UNIX Sendmail.

Hypertext Markup Language (HTML)—The authoring language used to create documents (pages) on the World Wide Web (WWW). It defines the structure and layout of a Web document by using a variety of tags and attributes.

Internet Message Access Protocol version 4 (IMAP4)—A protocol for retrieving e-mail massages. It is similar to POP3 but supports additional features such as the ability to search for keywords while messages are still on the mail server.

Internet service provider (ISP)—Provides a service or membership that allows you to access the information available on the Internet.

Open Source Interconnect (OSI)—A standard for worldwide communications that defines a networking framework for implementing protocols in seven layers.

Post Office Protocol version 3 (POP3)—A protocol used to retrieve e-mail messages from an e-mail server.

print—A command used in Unix to print a file.

router—A network device that connects a number of local area networks together.

Simple Mail Transfer Protocol (SMTP)—A protocol used for sending e-mail messages between servers.

Universal Naming Convention (UNC)—A PC format that specified the location of resources on a local area network. It uses the following format: \\servername\ shared-resource-pathname.

Web browser—A software program used to locate and display Web pages.

12

RECOVERING IMAGE FILES

After reading this chapter, you will be able to:

♦ Recognize image files

♦ Understand data compression

♦ Locate and recover image files

♦ Analyze image file headers

♦ Identify copyright issues with graphics

Many computing-forensics investigations involve graphic images, especially those downloaded from the Web and circulated via e-mail. To examine and recover image files successfully, you need to understand the basics of computer graphics, including image file characteristics, common image file formats, and compression methods that image files often use to reduce file size. This chapter begins with brief introductions to computer graphics and data compression, and then explains how to locate and recover image files based on information stored in image file headers. You will identify image file fragments, repair damaged file headers, and reconstruct file fragments. In addition, you will analyze image file headers, including those from unknown graphic file formats.

This chapter also explores tools you can use to view the images you recover and discusses two computer graphics issues that are receiving attention and discussion: steganography and copyrights. Steganography involves hiding data in files, including images, and copyrights determine the ownership of media, such as images downloaded from a Web site.

RECOGNIZING AN IMAGE FILE

An image file contains a graphic, such as a digital photograph, line art, three-dimensional image, or scanned replica of a printed picture. You might have used a program to create or edit an image, such as Microsoft Paint or Adobe Photoshop for Windows. A graphics program creates and saves one of three types of image files: bitmap, vector, or metafile. **Bitmap images** are collections of dots, or pixels, that form an image. **Vector images** are mathematical instructions that define lines, curves, text, ovals, and other geometric shapes. **Metafiles** are combinations of bitmap and vector images.

You can use two types of programs to work with image files: graphic editors and image viewers. You use graphic editors to create, modify, and save bitmap, vector, and metafile image files. You use image viewers to open and view image files, but not change their contents. When you use either a graphic editor or image viewer, you can open a file in one of many image file formats, which is indicated by the file extension, such as .bmp, .gif, or .eps. Each format has different qualities, including the amount of color and compression it uses. If you open an image file in a graphics program that supports multiple file formats, you can save the file in a different file format. However, converting image files this way can change the quality of the image.

Understanding Bitmap and Raster Images

Bitmap images store graphic information as grids of individual **pixels**, short for picture elements. **Raster images** are also collections of pixels, but store these pixels in rows to make the images easy to print. In most cases, printing an image converts, or **rasterizes**, the image to print the pixels line by line instead of processing the complete collection of pixels.

The quality of a bitmap image displayed on a computer monitor is governed by **screen resolution**, which determines the amount of detail displayed in the image. **Resolution** is related to the density of the pixels on your screen and depends on a combination of hardware and software. Monitors can display a range of resolutions; the higher the resolution, the sharper the image. Computers also use a hardware component called a video card that contains a certain amount of memory and electronic parts for displaying images. The more advanced the electronics and the higher the memory on the video card, the more detailed instructions your video card can accept, resulting in higher quality images.

For example, the monitor and video card on your Windows computer might support an 800×600 resolution. If so, the Display Properties dialog box looks similar to the one shown in Figure 12-1. This means that your monitor and video card display 800 pixels horizontally and 600 pixels vertically. The higher the number of pixels, the smaller the pixels must be to fit in the area of the monitor, thus the smaller your pictures are displayed. Because a bitmap image is defined by the pixel size, those displayed at a higher resolution are smaller than bitmap images displayed at a lower resolution.

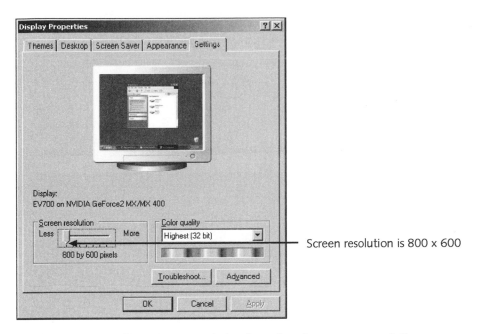

Screen resolution is 800 x 600

Figure 12-1   Display Properties dialog box showing screen resolution

In addition to hardware, software contributes to the quality of displayed images. Software includes drivers, which are coded instructions that set the parameters of what the video card can display. Software also includes the programs you use to create, modify, and view images on the computer. Some programs, such as IrfanView, allow you to view many types of images, while other programs only allow you to view or work with the image files that were created by that program.

Computer graphics professionals can use programs that support high resolutions to achieve a greater level of control over the presentation of the bitmap images they create and edit. However, bitmap graphics, especially those with low resolution, usually lose quality when you enlarge them.

As shown in Figure 12-1, the other setting that affects image quality is the number of colors the monitor displays in an image. Image files can contain different amounts of color per pixel, but each must support the colors with bits of space. The following list indicates the number of bits used per colored pixel:

- 1 bit = 2 colors
- 4 bits = 16 colors
- 8 bits = 256 colors
- 16 bits = 65,536 colors
- 24 bits = 16,777,216 colors

Bitmap and raster image files use as much of the color palette as possible. However, when you save a bitmap or raster image file, the resolution and color may change depending on the colors contained in the original file and whether the file format supports those colors.

Understanding Vector Images

Vector files are different from bitmap and raster files; a raster image uses dots and the vector format uses lines. A vector file stores only the mathematics for drawing lines and shapes; a graphics program converts the calculation into the appropriate image. Because vector files store mathematical calculations and not images, vector files are generally smaller than bitmap files, thereby saving disk space. You can also enlarge a vector image without affecting the image quality—to make an image twice as large, a graphics program multiplies by two instead of manipulating pixels. CorelDraw, Adobe Illustrator, and other draw-type programs create vector files. Although you can save vector graphics in a bitmap file format, you should not save photos, scanned graphics, and other bitmap or raster images in a vector format.

Metafile Graphics

Metafile image files combine raster and vector graphics, and can have the characteristics of both image types. For example, if you scan a photograph (a bitmap image) and then add text or arrows (vector drawings), you create a metafile.

While metafile images provide the features of both bitmap and vector files, metafiles also share their limitations. For example, if you enlarge a metafile image, the area that was created with a raster format loses some resolution, while the vector formatted area remains sharp and clear.

Understanding Image File Formats

Image files are created and saved in a graphic editor, such as Microsoft Paint, Macromedia Freehand or Adobe Photoshop for Windows and the Macintosh, or The GIMP for Linux. Some graphic editors, such as Paint, only work with bitmap graphics; others, such as Freehand, only work with vector graphics; and some programs, such as Photoshop, work with both.

Most graphic editors let you create and save files in one or more of the **standard image file formats**. Standard bitmap image file formats include the Graphics Interchange Format (.gif), Joint Photographic Experts Group (.jpg or .jpeg), Tagged Image File Format (.tif or .tiff), and Windows Bitmap (.bmp). Standard vector image file formats include Encapsulated Postscript (.eps) and Hewlett Packard Graphics Language (.hpgl).

Nonstandard image file formats include uncommon formats such as Targa (.tga) and Raster Transfer Language (.rtl), proprietary formats such as Photoshop (.psd), Illustrator (.ai), and Freehand (.fh9), emerging formats such as Scalable Vector Graphics (.svg), and those related to old or obsolete technology, such as Paintbrush (.pcx). Because you can open standard image files in most or all graphics programs, they are easier to work with during a computing-forensics investigation. If you encounter files in nonstandard formats, you might need to rely on your investigative skills to first identify the file as an image file, and then find the appropriate tools for viewing the file.

To determine whether a file is an image file and to find a program you can use to view a nonstandard image file, you can search the Web using a search engine or a dictionary Web site. For example, suppose you find a file with a .tga extension during an investigation. None of the programs on your investigation computer can open the file, and you know that this file could provide crucial evidence. To uncover the file contents, you must first identify a program that can open the file and let you view it.

To find the program used to create the TGA file:

1. Start a Web browser, such as Internet Explorer.

2. In the Address text box, type **www.webopedia.com**. The Webopedia home page opens.

3. In the Search area, type **tga** in the By keyword text box, and then press **Enter**. Webopedia lists pages on its Web site that describe the TGA file format.

4. Click the first **Webopedia: Data Formats and Their File Extensions** link. A page opens listing file formats that begin with "T."

5. Scroll down to .tga and record the description in a text file or sheet of paper. Now you can compare this description to one included on another dictionary Web site.

6. Click the Address text box of your browser, and then type **whatis.techtarget.com/fileformatA/** and press **Enter**. The Every File Format in the World Web page opens.

7. In the Browse File Formats Alphabetically section, click the **T** link. Scroll down to find the TGA file format, and record the descriptions of the Targa bitmap files.

   Also list the applications that can be used to create and view the file.

12

UNDERSTANDING DATA COMPRESSION

Most image file formats, including GIF and JPEG, compress their data to save disk space and to reduce the amount of time it takes to transfer the image from one computer to another. Other formats, such as BMP, rarely compress their data or do so inefficiently. In this case, people can use compression tools to compact data and reduce file size. You need to understand how compression schemes work in order to understand what happens when an image is altered.

Data compression is the coding of data from a larger form to another smaller form. Image files and most compression tools use one of two data compression methods: lossless or lossy.

Reviewing Lossless and Lossy Compression

Recall from Chapter 9 that lossless compression techniques reduce the size of a file without removing data. When you uncompress a file that uses lossless compression, you restore all of its information. GIF and Portable Network Graphics (PNG) are image file formats that reduce file size by using lossless compression.

Lossless compression saves file space by using mathematical formulas to represent the data contained in a file. These formulas generally use one of two algorithms: the Huffman Coding or Lempel-Ziv Coding algorithm. (Recall that an algorithm is a short mathematical procedure that solves a recurrent problem.) Each algorithm uses a code to represent redundant bits of data. For example, if a text file contains 60 instances of the phrase, "As a matter of fact," lossless compression replaces the 152 bits in "As a matter of fact" with the single bit of 1. When the file is uncompressed, the algorithm converts all single bits of 1 to "As a matter of fact."

Lossy compression is significantly different from lossless compression because it compresses data by permanently discarding bits of information contained in the file. Some of the discarded bits are redundant while others are not. When you uncompress an image file that uses lossy compression, you lose information, though most people do not notice the difference unless they print the image on a high-resolution printer or increase the size of the image. In either case, the removed bits of information reduce the quality of the image. JPEG is one graphics file format that uses lossy compression. If you open a JPEG file in a graphics program, for example, and save it as a JPEG file with a different name, the file automatically uses lossy compression, which reduces image quality. The JPEG format reapplies the lossy file compression, removing more bits of data, when you create a file by saving an existing file with a new name. If you simply rename a file using Windows Explorer or the command line, the file does not lose any further data.

Another form of lossy compression uses vectors and is known as **vector quantization (VQ)**. VQ uses complex algorithms to determine the data to disregard based on vectors in the image file. In simplistic terms, VQ discards bits similar to the way rounding off decimal values discards numbers.

In Chapter 9, you learned that popular lossless compression utilities include WinZip, PKZip, and FreeZip. Lzip is a lossy compression utility. You use these compression tools to compact folders and files for data storage and transmission. Remember that the difference between lossless and lossy compression is the way that the data is represented *after* it has been uncompressed. Lossless compression produces an exact replica of the original data after it has been uncompressed, whereas lossy compression typically produces an altered replica of the data after it has been uncompressed.

LOCATING AND RECOVERING IMAGE FILES

If a computer forensics investigation involves image files, you need to locate and recover all of the image files on a drive and determine which ones are pertinent to your case. Because images are not always stored in standard image file formats, you should examine files that your computer forensics tools find even if they are not identified as image files.

Windows and DOS provide tools to recover image files, but using these tools is time-consuming and their results are difficult to verify. Instead, you can use computer forensics tools dedicated to analyzing image files. As you work with these tools and those that Windows and DOS offer, develop standard procedures for your organization and continue to refine them so that other investigators can benefit from your experience. You should also follow the standard procedures for each case to provide a thorough analysis.

You can use computer forensics investigative tools to analyze images based on information contained in the image file itself. In Chapter 11, you learned that e-mail message headers contain a significant amount of hidden information. An image file also contains a header with instructions for displaying the image. Each type of image file has its own header, and examining the header helps you identify the file format. Because the header is complex and difficult to remember, you can compare a known good file header with that of a suspected file. For example, if you find an image that you suspect is a JPEG, but cannot display the image using a bitmap graphics program, check the file header to verify its contents. You can determine whether the header has been altered by comparing that header to another JPEG file header. You could then use the information in the good JPEG file header to supply the instructions necessary to display the picture. In other words, you use the good JPEG header information to create a baseline analysis.

Before you can examine an image file header, you often need to reconstruct a fragmented image file. To do so, you will need to identify the data patterns the image files use. If some of the file header has been overwritten with other data, you may also need to repair the damaged header. By rebuilding the image file header, you can then perform a forensic analysis on the image file.

12

Identifying Image File Fragments

If an image file is fragmented across different areas on a disk, you must first recover all the fragments to recreate the image file. Recovering pieces of a file is called **salvaging**, also known as **carving** in North America. To carve an image file data from file slack space and free space, you should be familiar with the data patterns of known image file types. Most computer forensics programs recognize these data patterns so you can identify image file fragments, which is the first step in recovering deleted data. After you recover the pieces of a fragmented image file, you restore the data fragments to continue your computer forensics examination. You will use DriveSpy later in this chapter to carve known data sets from residual data that you recover, and then restore this information to view the image file.

Repairing Damaged Headers

When you are examining recovered data remnants from files in slack or free space, you might find data that appears to be a header for a common image file type. If you locate header data that is partially overwritten, you must reconstruct the header. To do this, you compare the hexadecimal values of known image file formats to the pattern of the file header you found to make it readable again.

Each image file type has a unique file header value. If you become familiar with these common image header values, you can spot residual data from partially overwritten headers in file slack or free space. For example, a JPEG file has a hexadecimal header value of FF D8 FF E0 00 10. Most JPEG files also include the letters "JFIF" immediately following these hexadecimal data values, as in FF D8 FF E0 00 10 JFIF. If you find a file fragment with JFIF or some of the header values unique to JPEG files, you can identify the file as a JPEG image.

 To learn more about hexadecimal values for well-known image files, open the Drivespy.ini file and examine the File Headers section, as described in Chapter 10.

TIP

Suppose you are investigating a possible intellectual property theft from a contract employee of the Exotic Mountain Tour Service (EMTS). EMTS has just completed an expensive marketing and customer service analysis. Based on this analysis, EMTS plans to release advertising for their latest tour service. Unfortunately, EMTS suspects that a contract travel consultant might have given their sensitive marketing data to a competitor. An EMTS manager found a floppy disk that the contract travel consultant used. Your task is to determine whether the floppy disk contains proprietary EMTS data to include brochures with images.

As you examine the file slack, or free space, of the contract consultant's floppy disk, you find the letters FIF. You document that these letters are located at the beginning of cluster 499 on the floppy disk. You know that JPEG file headers always include "JFIF," so you suspect that you found a fragment of a JPEG file header. You find several other JPEG files in allocated disk space on the floppy disk, and you also document these files.

Carving Data from Unallocated Space

After you identify fragmented data, you can use a computer forensics program to recover the fragmented file. In this section, you use DriveSpy to locate and carve data from unallocated space, and then use the SaveSect command to save a file as an external file. You continue examining the floppy disk that the EMTS manager found.

To begin the carving task, perform the standard data preservation steps of creating a duplicate bit-stream copy of the original floppy disk. Use Digital Intelligence's Image program to copy the original evidence floppy disk to a target investigation floppy disk. In the following steps, you restore the file Ch12hdfx.sav from your Data Files to a blank, unformatted floppy disk that will serve as the EMTS target investigation floppy disk.

To restore a saved image file:

1. Insert a blank, unformatted floppy disk in the floppy disk drive (drive A), and then open a DOS Command Prompt window. Then navigate to the directory containing Image.exe on your system.

2. Copy the **Ch12hdfx.sav** file from the Chap12\Chapter folder in your Data Files (which can be downloaded from *www.courseptr.com*) to the **Tools** folder in your work folder. In the following step, change the drive letter as necessary to reflect the location of your Data Files.

3. At the DOS prompt, type **image c:*work folder*\Tools\Ch12hdfx.sav A:** and then press **Enter** to create an image file on the floppy disk.

4. Type **exit** to close the Command Prompt window.

Before you start DriveSpy, you must update the Drivespy.ini file to add a search label for the keyword JFIF. (Recall that JPEG headers always include JFIF.)

To update the Drivespy.ini file:

1. Start Notepad or another text editor as you usually do.

2. Click **File** on the menu bar, and then click **Open**. In the Open dialog box, navigate to where Drivespy.ini is stored, such as the Tools folder in your work folder. Then double-click **Drivespy.ini** to open it.

3. Scroll to the end of the file, and press **Enter**, if necessary, to create a new line. Insert new search text by typing **[Search Chap12]** and pressing **Enter**. Then type **70:"JFIF"** and press **Enter**.

4. Recall that you include quotation marks around JFIF because you are searching for a literal value on the floppy disk.

5. Save Drivespy.ini, and then close Notepad.

Note that you set a sensitivity level of 70 to search for values that contain at least three of the four specified letters. This setting lets you locate partially overwritten data, such as JFFF or FIF. If you wanted a perfect match, you would enter 100:"JFIF". Because the keyword JFIF contains four letters, each letter is 25% of the total. To reduce the acceptable hit rate by 25%, round off the percentage value to 70%. (DriveSpy only works in 10% increments, so always round down.) If DriveSpy finds too many hits, you can increase the sensitivity level and run the keyword search again to help minimize the number of hits.

After you update the search text in Drivespy.ini, you are ready to use DriveSpy to locate all possible JFIF keywords. If necessary, first use Windows Explorer or My Computer to create a folder named Chap12 in your work folder. Then create a folder named Chapter in the Chap12 folder. To complete the following steps, you need your EMTS investigation floppy disk.

To locate JPEG files on a disk:

1. Open a DOS Command Prompt window, and then change to the Tools folder in your work folder. Type **Toolpath.bat** to run the Toolpath batch file so you can use DriveSpy from any directory.

2. Navigate to the Chap12\Chapter folder, and then start DriveSpy by typing **DriveSpy** and pressing **Enter**.

3. At the DriveSpy SYS prompt, type **Output Hdr_find.log** and then press **Enter** to record the output of the commands you use in a text file named Hdr_find.log.

4. Make sure the EMTS target investigation floppy disk is in drive A. At the SYS prompt, type **Drive a** and then press **Enter** to navigate to drive A.

5. At the DA prompt, type **Part 1** and then press **Enter** to display partition information for the floppy disk.

6. At the DAP1 prompt, type **Search Chap12** and then press **Enter** to start the keyword search you specified in the previous set of steps. When a message appears asking if you want to turn off Page mode, type **y**.

   DriveSpy searches the floppy disk for data that matches the search criteria and records this data in Hdr_find.log.

   Leave DriveSpy open for the next set of steps.

Now you can examine the Hdr_find.log output file to identify possible unallocated data sets that contain the full or partial JPEG header values.

To examine Hdr_find.log:

1. Start Notepad or another text editor as you usually do.

2. Click **File** on the menu bar, and then click **Open**. In the Open dialog box, navigate to the Chapter12\Chapter folder in your work folder, and then double-click **Hdr_find.log** to open it. See Figure 12-2.

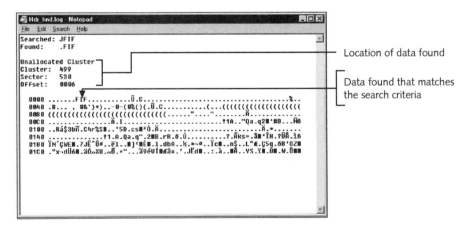

Figure 12-2   Hdr_find.log open in Notepad

Note that the log file shows that DriveSpy searched the floppy disk for JFIF and found one piece of data consisting of the letters FIF at beginning cluster position 499, sector 530, with an offset of 6 bytes. The offset is the amount of data between the beginning of the sector 530 and the beginning of the text DriveSpy found, or the first letter "F".

Now that you have located the potential JPEG file, you can carve it from the floppy disk. First you must determine which sectors to carve on the disk by examining the contents of the EMTS floppy disk.

3. Close Notepad.

4. At the DAP1 prompt, type **Dir** and then press **Enter** to list the files on the first partition of the floppy disk. See Figure 12-3. DriveSpy shows that the disk contains four files in allocated space: sawtooth_1.jpg, stream_1.jpg, stream_2.jpg, and east_side_1.jpg.

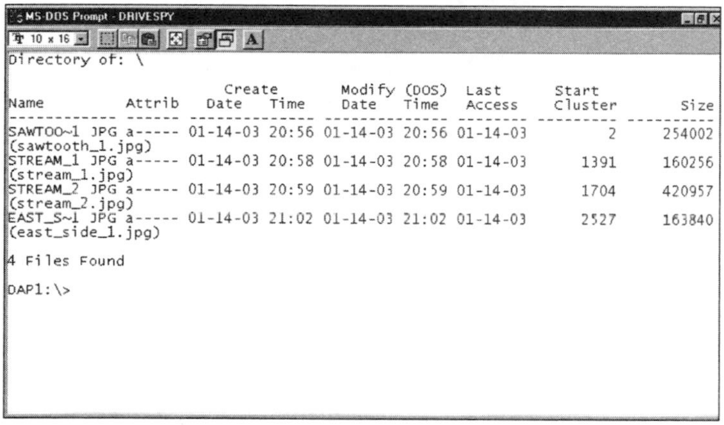

```
MS-DOS Prompt - DRIVESPY                                          _ 8 x
 10 x 16                A
Directory of: \

                        Create       Modify (DOS)  Last      Start
Name          Attrib    Date    Time  Date    Time  Access    Cluster    Size
-----------   ------    -------------- --------------  --------  --------  --------
SAWTOO~1 JPG a----- 01-14-03 20:56 01-14-03 20:56 01-14-03         2    254002
(sawtooth_1.jpg)
STREAM_1 JPG a----- 01-14-03 20:58 01-14-03 20:58 01-14-03      1391    160256
(stream_1.jpg)
STREAM_2 JPG a----- 01-14-03 20:59 01-14-03 20:59 01-14-03      1704    420957
(stream_2.jpg)
EAST_S~1 JPG a----- 01-14-03 21:02 01-14-03 21:02 01-14-03      2527    163840
(east_side_1.jpg)

4 Files Found

DAP1:\>
```

Figure 12-3   Files on the EMTS disk

5. Leave DriveSpy open for the next set of steps.

The results of the keyword search reveal that the EMTS disk might contain a JPEG file starting at cluster 499. As shown in Figure 12-3, the first file listed starts at cluster 2, and the second file starts at cluster 1391. Because you are examining a floppy disk, you know that it contains exactly 512 bytes per sector and that one sector is assigned for every cluster. Remember from Chapter 3 that the larger the FAT disk, the higher the number of sectors per cluster. If this were a 2 GB disk drive, you would need to calculate how many 512-byte sectors it contained per cluster.

You can calculate the total cluster size by multiplying the number of sectors per cluster. Then you divide the file byte size by total cluster size and round up the result to the next integer. Table 12-1 shows the number of maximum clusters, clusters used, and the maximum volume size for FAT12, FAT16, and FAT32 disks.

The disk contains 1389 clusters between the starting position of the first file, Sawtoo~1.jpg, which starts at cluster 2, and the second file, Stream_1.jpg, which starts at cluster 1391. Because Sawtoo~1.jpg is 254,002 bytes long, you can determine its ending position by using the following formula:

```
Ending_cluster = start_cluster + total_clusters - 1.
Ending_cluster = 499 + 892 - 1
Ending_cluster = 1390
```

Table 12-1   Calculating total cluster size

Attribute	FAT12	FAT16	FAT32
Number of clusters (max)	4086	65,526	~268,435,456
Cluster size used	0.5 KB to 4 KB	2 KB to 32 KB	4 KB to 32 KB
Maximum volume size	16,736,256	2,147,123,200	About 2^41

Another method you could use would be as follows:

```
(file_byte_size ÷ 512) ÷ the_number_of_sectors_per_cluster =
total_number_of_clusters_assigned
```

To locate the exact ending cluster position of a file (assuming the file is contiguous), add the total number of clusters assigned to the starting cluster position. To determine each assigned cluster to the starting cluster, use the DriveSpy Cluster Link End (CLE) command to list all forward cluster links.

For example, the total bytes in the Sawtoo~1.jpg file is 254,002 with 512 bytes per sector and 1 sector per cluster. You can determine the ending cluster position by using the following formula:

```
(254002/512)/1 = 496.1
```

Therefore, the Sawtoo~1.jpg file ends at cluster 496, leaving a significant amount of data unaccounted for from cluster 497 through cluster 1390. You can determine this because you know that the second file, Stream_1.jpg, starts at cluster 1391. Because the keyword search revealed a potential JPEG header at cluster 499, a deleted JPEG file probably starts at cluster 499 and ends near or on cluster 1390.

TIP

Remember that when a user deletes a file it is not necessarily completely deleted. In most cases, only the first bit of the first sector is removed and the area is marked in the FAT Master File Table (MFT) to indicate that user can write to the cluster again.

To recover the deleted data that is not listed as a deleted file in the FAT, you need to determine the absolute sector starting position for the beginning and ending clusters. By using DriveSpy and the SaveSect command, you can obtain the absolute values. Keep in mind that the SaveSect command only interprets the absolute sector value. If you use the relative sector number, you collect the wrong data. You need to use the absolute sector number to obtain the correct sector values.

To determine absolute sectors for carving:

1. At the DAP1 prompt in the DriveSpy window, type **Cluster 499** and then press **Enter** to determine the beginning absolute sector number. See Figure 12-4.

2. On a separate sheet of paper, record the AbsSector (absolute sector) number, which is located at the top and bottom of the DriveSpy window (absolute sector 530).

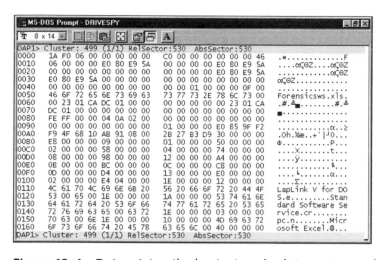

Figure 12-4 Determining the beginning absolute sector number

3. Press **Esc** to close the cluster view.

4. At the DAP1 prompt, type **Cluster 1390** and press **Enter** to determine the ending absolute sector number, which is one less than the next file's cluster starting number. See Figure 12-5.

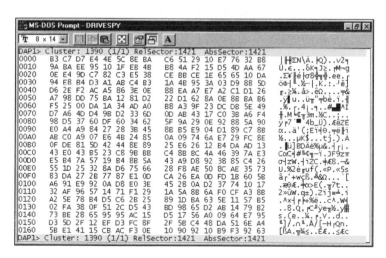

Figure 12-5 Determining the ending absolute sector number

Note the AbsSector (absolute sector) number that is located at the top and bottom of the DriveSpy shell window (absolute sector 1421).

5. Press **Esc** to exit the cluster view. Leave DriveSpy open for the next set of steps.

You determined that the beginning absolute sector is 530 and ending absolute sector number is 1421 for the possible JPEG file. Next you need to isolate, or carve, these sectors and save them in a file.

To carve data from a disk:

1. At the DAP1 prompt in the DriveSpy window, type **SaveSect 530-1421 Bad_hdr.jpg** and then press **Enter**. DriveSpy extracts the data in sectors 530-1421 and saves it in a file named Bad_hdr.jpg on the floppy disk.

2. At the DAP1 prompt, type **Exit** and then press **Enter** to close DriveSpy.

You carved the potential JPEG file that you located with the JFIF keyword search. The next step is to rebuild the JPEG header with the correct hexadecimal values. To perform this task, you will use Hex Workshop to manually insert the correct hexadecimal codes. Then you save the repaired file as a new file so you can test whether the values you placed in the header are the appropriate values. To test the repaired file, you simply need to see whether you can view the image using an image viewer.

Rebuilding File Headers

Before attempting to edit an image file that you recovered, first try to open it with an image viewer such as Microsoft Photo Editor. To test whether you can view the image, you can double-click the recovered file in its current location in Windows Explorer. If you can open and view the image, you have successfully recovered the image file. If the image does not appear in the image viewer, you must manually inspect and correct the header data values.

If some of the data you recovered from the image file header is corrupt, you might need to recover more pieces of the file before you can view the image. You will learn how to recover the other pieces later in this chapter.

Figure 12-6 shows a dialog box that might appear when you attempt to open Bad_hdr.jpg because it is a damaged image file.

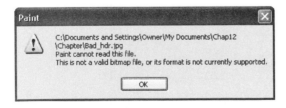

Figure 12-6   Damaged image file

If you cannot open an image file in an image viewer, your next step is to examine the header data of the file to see if it matches the header in a good JPEG file. If the header does not match, you must manually insert the correct hexadecimal values using a tool such as Hex Workshop. You can then inspect and correct the hexadecimal values within a file.

To inspect a file with Hex Workshop:

1. Start Hex Workshop. Click **File** on the menu bar, and then click **Open**. Navigate to the Chap12\Chapter folder in your work folder, and then double-click **Bad_hdr.jpg**. See Figure 12-7.

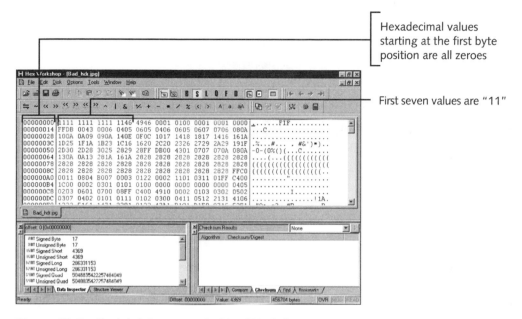

Figure 12-7   Bad_hdr.jpg open in Hex Workshop

2. In the upper-left column of the Hex Workshop window, note that the hexadecimal values starting at the first byte position are all zeros (00000000), and that the first seven bytes all contain the number eleven (11). Leave Hex Workshop open for the next set of steps.

Recall that the correct hexadecimal characters for a JPEG file are FF, D8, FF, E0, 00, 10, JFIF. The first seven bytes of the Bad_hdr.jpg file are all 11, indicating that this file header data is not appropriate for a JPEG file. You must convert the first seven bytes to the correct hexadecimal characters for a JPEG image so you can continue to repair the file.

To repair a file header:

1. In Hex Workshop, click to the left of the first hexadecimal value of 11. Then type **FF D8 FF E0 00 10**, which are the correct hexadecimal values for the first six bytes of a JPEG file. See Figure 12-8.

2. In the upper-right column, click to the left of "FIF" and then type **J**.

   In Hex Workshop, when you type a keyboard character in the upper-right column, the corresponding hexadecimal value appears in the upper-middle pane. When you type the letter J in the right column, the hexadecimal value 4A appears in the middle column.

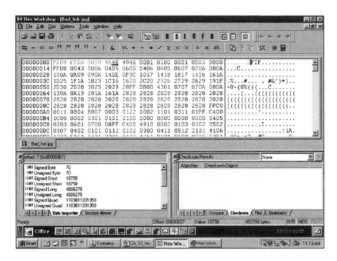

Figure 12-8   Inserting correct hexadecimal values for a JPEG file

3. Click **File** on the menu bar, and then click **Save As**. In the Save As dialog box, navigate to the Chap12\Chapter folder in your work folder, type **Good_hdr.jpg** as the filename, and then click the **Save** button.

4. Close Hex Workshop.

Note that every two hexadecimal values you entered in the previous steps are equivalent to one ASCII character. For example, the uppercase letter "A" has a hexadecimal value of 41, while the lowercase letter "a" has a hexadecimal value of 61. Most disk editors provide a reference chart that converts hexadecimal values to ASCII characters. For example, Hex Workshop provides a useful ANSI (ASCII) Character Set, shown in Figure 12-9.

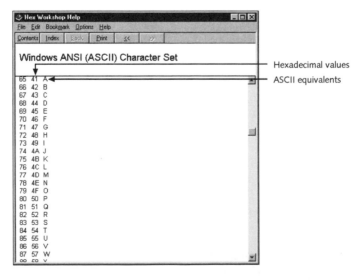

Figure 12-9   ASCII equivalents to hexadecimal values

After you repair an image file header, you can test the updated file by opening it in an image viewer such as Microsoft Photo Editor, IrfanView, Thumbs Plus, Quick View, or ACDSee.

To test the repaired JPEG file:

1. In Windows Explorer, navigate to the Chap12\Chapter folder in your work folder. Then double-click **Good_hdr.jpg**. The file opens in your default image viewer, such as Microsoft Photo Editor, as shown in Figure 12-10.

Figure 12-10   Good_hdr.jpg open in Microsoft Photo Editor

12

2. Close the image viewer.

By viewing the Good_hdr.jpg you have verified that you successfully carved the file out of the slack space.

The process of repairing file headers is not limited to JPEG files. You can apply the same technique to any file for which you can determine the header value, including Microsoft Word, Excel, and PowerPoint documents as well as other image formats. You only need to know the correct header format for the type of file you are attempting to repair.

Reconstructing File Fragments

You might occasionally encounter corrupt data that prevents you from properly recovering data fragments for files such as image files. Whether the data corruption is accidental or intentional, you need to know how to examine a suspect disk and extract possible data fragments to reconstruct files for evidentiary purposes. In this section, you learn how to identify files that have been intentionally corrupted and recover them with DriveSpy.

In some computing-forensics investigations, the suspect has intentionally corrupted cluster links in a FAT table of a disk. Anyone can use a disk-editing tool such as Norton Disk Edit to access the FAT and mark specific clusters as bad by typing the letter B at the specific cluster. After you mark the cluster as bad, it appears with a zero value in the disk editor. As Figure 12-11 shows, cluster position 156 has a zero value, which indicates that this cluster does not link to any other clusters on the disk.

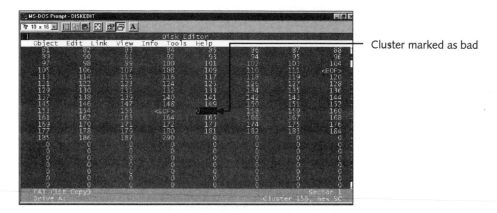

Figure 12-11   Bad cluster appearing as zero in Norton Disk Edit

To locate files of a particular type, such as JPEG image files, you can use the DriveSpy Search command to locate potential JPEG files with a corrupt cluster. If you are searching for other types of files, update the Search section in Drivespy.ini to add the specific header string of the file type. In an actual investigation, you usually copy a bit-stream image of the original evidence drive to a target investigation disk. In the following steps, you use a floppy disk.

To create the floppy disk for the following steps:

1. Open a DOS Command Prompt window. Make sure Ch12Frag.sav is in the Chap12\Chapter folder in your work folder. Insert a floppy disk in the appropriate drive.

2. Type **Image c:*work folder*\Chap12\Chapter\Ch12Frag.sav a:** where *work folder* is the name of your work folder, and then press **Enter**. (Replace the drive letter as necessary.)

To locate potential unallocated files:

1. In the Command Prompt window, change to the Tools folder in your work folder. Type **Toolpath.bat** to run the Toolpath batch file so you can use DriveSpy from any directory.

2. Navigate to the Chap12\Chapter folder, and then start DriveSpy by typing **DriveSpy** and pressing **Enter**.

3. At the SYS prompt, type **Output Ch12frag.log** and then press **Enter** to create an output file to record the results of the commands you use.

4. At the SYS prompt, type **Drive A** and then press **Enter** to navigate to the floppy disk drive.

5. At the DA prompt, type **Part 1** then press **Enter**.

6. At the DAP1 prompt, type **Search Chap12** and then press **Enter** to search for JPEG files on the floppy disk. Type **Y** when prompted to disable page mode. Leave DriveSpy open for the next set of steps.

   Now you can examine the output file to determine whether DriveSpy identified recoverable files.

7. Start Notepad as you usually do, and then open the log file **Ch12frag.log** in the Chap12\Chapter folder in your work folder. Scan the file to find any occurrences of the letters JFIF. See Figure 12-12. Ch12frag.sav contains five potential JPEG headers.

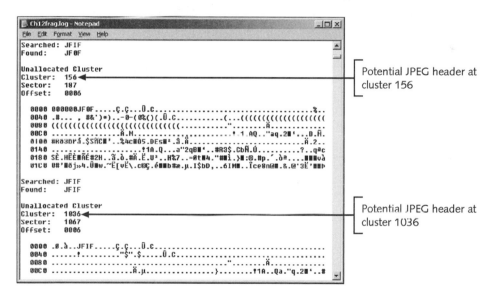

Potential JPEG header at cluster 156

Potential JPEG header at cluster 1036

Figure 12-12   Two of five potential JPEG headers

Some of the data containing three or more of the letters in JFIF might be JPEG headers, but some might not. You need to examine file type characteristics such as other hexadecimal characters in this data to determine which ones are actual JPEG headers.

As you examine Ch12frag.log, note that Ch12frag.sav contains five potential JPEG headers at cluster positions 156, 1036, 2835, 448, and 1287. All the clusters are in unallocated disk space. Your next task is to determine whether other file fragments are linked to these clusters. To do so, you can use the DriveSpy Chain FAT Entry (CFE) command.

To confirm the cluster content:

1. At the DAP1 prompt in the DriveSpy window, type **Cluster 156** and then press **Enter** to examine the data at cluster 156.

   Note that the header appears corrupt because it does not reflect the appropriate header information for a known JPEG.

2. Press the **Page Down** key to inspect cluster 156 and the next cluster to determine whether the file continues past cluster 156. Additional data appears.

3. Press **Esc** to exit the cluster view and return to the DAP1 prompt. Leave DriveSpy open for the next set of steps.

It appears that the corrupted JPEG file extends past cluster 156. The next task is to determine how many other clusters might be linked to the corrupted beginning cluster. These clusters might be part of the JPEG file.

To collect the unallocated file cluster links:

1. At the DAP1 prompt, type **CFE 156** and then press **Enter** to see whether other clusters are linked to cluster 156. See Figure 12-13. DriveSpy reports the results as 156, 0x000, which indicates that no clusters are linked to cluster 156. (For more information on the CFE command, see Chapter 2.)

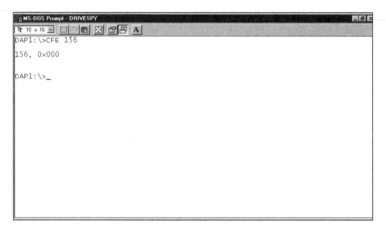

Figure 12-13 Clusters linked to cluster 156

2. At the DAP1 prompt, type **CFE 157** and then press **Enter** to see whether other clusters are linked to cluster 157. Many other clusters are linked to cluster 157, as shown in Figure 12-14, indicating that a number of clusters are used in conjunction to 157 to create a file.

3. At the DAP1 prompt, type **CFE 448** and then press **Enter** to see whether other clusters are linked to cluster 448, which is the next cluster DriveSpy identified as containing a potential JPEG header. DriveSpy reports the results as 448, 0x000.

4. At the DAP1 prompt, type **CFE 449** and then press **Enter.**

5. At the DAP1 prompt, type **CFE 1036** and then press **Enter** to see whether other clusters are linked to cluster 1036, which is the next cluster DriveSpy identified as containing a potential JPEG header. Then type **CFE 1037** and press **Enter**.

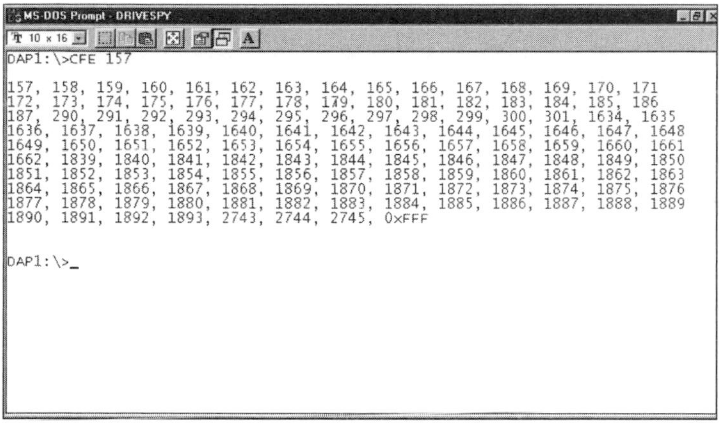

Figure 12-14   Clusters linked to cluster 157

6. At the DAP1 prompt, type **CFE 1287** and then press **Enter**. Then type **CFE 1288** and press **Enter**.

7. At the DAP1 prompt, type **CFE 2835** and then press **Enter** to check the links to the last known cluster. Then type **CFE 2836** and press **Enter**. Note that both clusters 2835 and 2836 have zero values, indicating that they are not linked to other clusters on the disk. Leave DriveSpy open for the next set of steps.

Using the DriveSpy CFE command, you identified all cluster links associated with the unallocated JPEG file headers except the last cluster, 2835. Note that the cluster 2836 has a zero value as does cluster 2835, indicating that you have obtained all the pieces of data for your image, the next task is to determine which specific unallocated cluster might be linked to cluster 2835.

To do so, one method is to use the DriveSpy Get FAT Entry (GFE) command to map all possible cluster links. This task is labor intensive because you must first list all unallocated clusters and then manually run the GFE command on each one to see if the unallocated cluster links to cluster 2835. Usually when you have to examine all unallocated clusters you will spend a significant amount of time obtaining the results. A more effective method is to copy all the sectors immediately after a nonlinked cluster until you reach the cluster immediately before the next allocated or deleted file cluster on the disk.

To continue recovering fragmented unallocated files, you can use the DriveSpy SaveSect command. First create a script file listing all the clusters associated with each unallocated file that you found with the initial keyword search. To accomplish this, you open the log file you created and copy each group of sectors into another text file. Start by determining the absolute sector numbers for each cluster range in the file you want to recover. To do this you will use DriveSpy to view the clusters to obtain the absolute sector numbers. Figure 12-15 shows the cluster numbers associated with clusters 448 and 449 in Ch12svsc.scr.

12

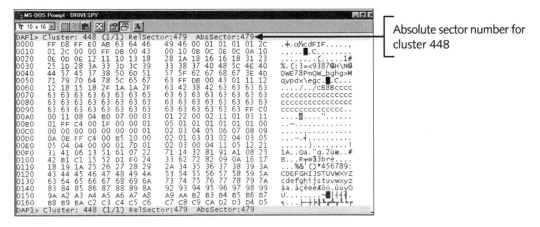

Figure 12-15   Cluster numbers for clusters 448 and 449

To minimize the number of clusters to look up, group the cluster numbers into contiguous blocks. You can look up cluster ranges 449–494, 792–815, and 1194–1280 by finding the absolute sector numbers of the first and last cluster values in each range.

Now you can use DriveSpy to locate the starting and ending absolute sector numbers for each of these cluster ranges.

To locate the absolute sector numbers:

1. At the DAP1 prompt in the DriveSpy window, type **Cluster 448** and press **Enter** to find the absolute sector number of this cluster. As Figure 12-16 shows, the absolute sector number is 479.

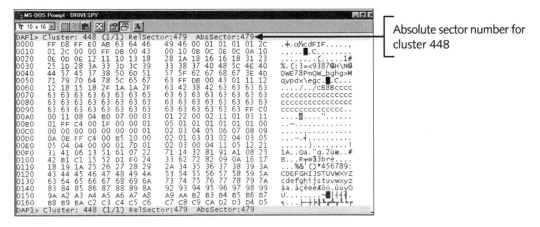

Absolute sector number for cluster 448

Figure 12-16   Absolute sector number for cluster 448

2. Press **Esc** to return to the DAP1 prompt, type **Cluster 494**, and then press **Enter**. As Figure 12-17 shows, the absolute sector number of cluster 494 is 525.

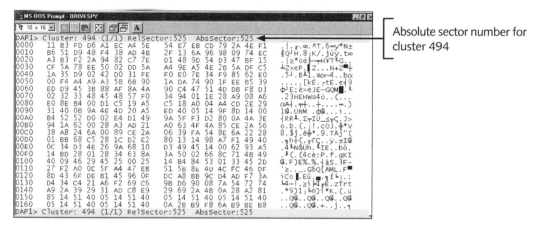

Absolute sector number for cluster 494

Figure 12-17   Absolute sector number for cluster 494

3. Press **Esc** to return to the DAP1 prompt, type **Cluster 792**, and then press **Enter**. As Figure 12-18 shows, the absolute sector number of cluster 792 is 823.

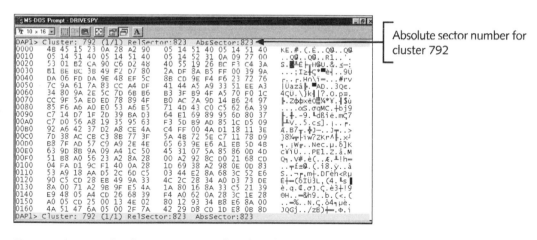

Absolute sector number for cluster 792

12

Figure 12-18   Absolute sector number for cluster 792

4. Press **Esc** to return to the DAP1 prompt, type **Cluster 815**, and then press **Enter**. As Figure 12-19 shows, the absolute sector number of cluster 815 is 846.

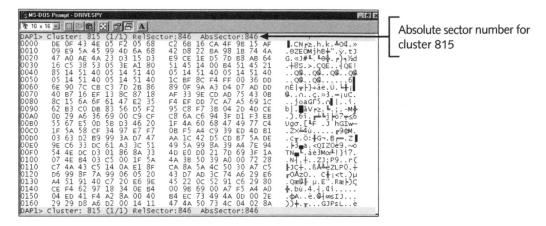

Absolute sector number for cluster 815

Figure 12-19   Absolute sector number for cluster 815

5. Press **Esc** to return to the DAP1 prompt, type **Cluster 1194**, and then press **Enter**. As Figure 12-20 shows, the absolute sector number of cluster 1194 is 1225.

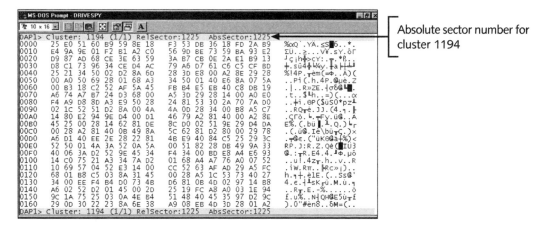

Absolute sector number for cluster 1194

Figure 12-20   Absolute sector number for cluster 1194

6. Press **Esc** to return to the DAP1 prompt, type **Cluster 1280**, and then press **Enter**. As Figure 12-21 shows, the absolute sector number of cluster 1280 is 1311.

7. Press **Esc** to return to the DAP1 prompt, and leave DriveSpy open for another set of steps.

You used the DriveSpy Cluster command to collect the absolute sector numbers for the unallocated file located at cluster 448. The absolute sectors are 479–525, 823–846, and 1225–1311. Now you need to build a script file that copies each group of absolute sectors into three individual files.

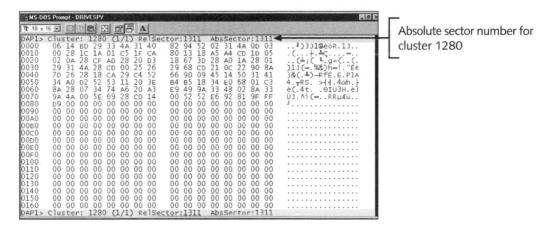

Figure 12-21   Absolute sector number for cluster 1280

To create a SaveSect script for unallocated files:

1. Start Notepad, and in a new document, type the following SaveSect commands:

   SaveSect 479–525 C12_448.jpg

   SaveSect 823–846 C12_448.jpg

   SaveSect 1225–1311 C12_448.jpg

   Be sure that you do not insert blank lines between the commands. This applies to the end of the script as well. Blank lines anywhere in the script will generate errors in DriveSpy.

   When you run this script, DriveSpy extracts the sectors you specified, and asks if you want to Cancel, Overwrite, or Append the sector groups. You can select Append to combine all groups into one file.

2. Save this script as **Ch12svsc.scr** in the Chap12\Chapter folder in your home folder, and then close Notepad.

NOTE

Because the last keyword search for cluster 2835 revealed no additional links, copy all sectors (using the SaveSect command) from sector 2835 to the very last sector, 2848, on the disk. There may be residual data left in this portion of unlinked clusters of the drive.

Now you are ready to run the script in DriveSpy to extract the sectors that contain the JPEG file in unallocated disk space.

To extract the unallocated file:

1. At the DAP1 prompt in the DriveSpy window, type **Script Ch12svsc.scr** and press **Enter**.

2. When the (C)ancel, (O)verwrite, or (A)ppend prompt appears, type **A**. This prompt appears twice—type **A** each time.

3. Type **Exit** and then press **Enter** to close DriveSpy.

The file you recovered from cluster 448 has a corrupt header. You can use Hex Workshop to insert the correct hexadecimal values to see if you can read this file, as you did earlier in the "Rebuilding File Headers" section.

To rebuild the header in Hex Workshop:

1. Start Hex Workshop. Click **File** on the menu bar, and then click **Open**. Navigate to the Chap12\Chapter folder in your work folder, and then double-click **Ch12_448A.jpg**.

2. Click to the left of the first hexadecimal value, and then type **FF D8 FF E0 00 10**, which are the correct hexadecimal values for the first six bytes of a JPEG file.

3. In the upper-right column, click to the left of "FIF," and then type **J**. Your Hex Workshop window should be similar to the one shown in Figure 12-22.

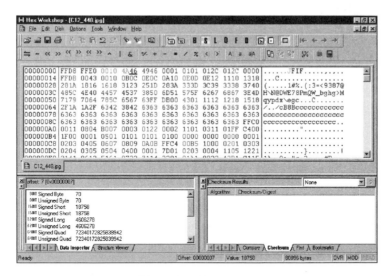

Figure 12-22 Rebuilding the file header

4. Click **File** on the menu bar, and then click **Save**. Click **Yes** to create a backup.

5. Close Hex Workshop.

Now you can test the file by opening it in an image viewer.

6. Use Windows Explorer to navigate to the Chap12\Chapter folder, and then double-click **Ch12_448.jpg**. The file opens, as shown in Figure 12-23.

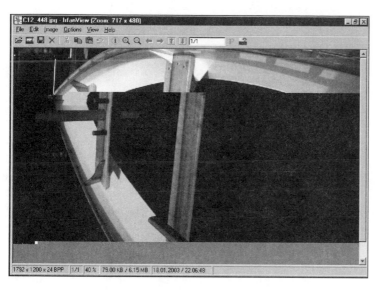

Figure 12-23   Ch12_448.jpg open in IrfanView

7. Close your image viewer.

Note that recovering deleted images is not an exact science. Parts of the recovered image are misaligned. Your success in image recovery varies depending on the quality of the media.

Identifying Unknown File Formats

With the continuing changes in technology and computer graphic products, you will eventually encounter new image file formats with which you are not familiar. In addition, suspects might use older computer systems with programs that create uncommon or obsolete image file formats. In these cases, you must research old and new file types. Knowing the purpose of each format and how it stores data is part of the investigation process.

Recall that when you examined the Ch12frag.sav floppy disk image, the keyword search found a file with a .xif extension. This file, ZPICT0~1.XIF, is in the allocated space of the drive and appeared when you used the DriveSpy Dir command. Because the name of the file has the letters "PICT" as part of its name, it might be an image file, though the XIF file format is not a common image file format. The File Type section of Drivespy.ini does not include a reference to an XIF file format.

Recall that the Internet is the best source for learning more about file formats and their associated extensions. You have already used the Webopedia Web site to research the TGA file format. You can use also any popular search engine to search for "file type" or "file format" and find the latest list of Web sites providing information on file extensions. If you still cannot find a specific file extension, try refining your search by entering the file extension along with the words "file type" in a search engine.

To search for information about XIF files:

1. Start your Web browser, such as Internet Explorer.

2. In the Address text box, type **www.google.com** and then press **Enter**.

3. Type **xif file format** in the text box, and then press **Enter**. A page of links opens.

4. Click links to learn more about the XIF file format.

   You should learn that Xerox Pagis is a scanning program that produces images in the XIF format. The XIF extension is commonly called XIFF and is derived from the more common TIFF file format with some unique modifications. You might also find that Pagis provides a free viewer utility that can display XIF files, and makes it available for download. For more information about XIF files and its associated viewer go to Xerox Pagis Web sites at *www.scantips.com/pagis1.html* and *www.scansoft.com/pagis/support/downloads/pagisviewer.asp*.

The following are three popular sites that provide information to help analyze file formats. Keep in mind that information on the Web changes frequently; use a search engine to find image file information if you cannot access the following Web sites:

- www.digitek-asi.com/file_formats.html

- www.wotsit.org

- http://whatis.techtarget.com/fileFormatA/0,289933,sid9,00.html

ANALYZING IMAGE FILE HEADERS

You should analyze image file headers when you find new or unique file types that computer forensics tools do not recognize. The simplest way to access a file header is to use a hexadecimal editor such as Hex Workshop. You can then record the hexadecimal values in the header and later use them to define a file type in Drivespy.ini.

For example, suppose you encounter a XIFF file. The File Headers section of Drivespy.ini does not define the XIFF file type. To define a file type in the File Headers section, you need know the file's known good header value.

Start by comparing a TIFF file header to a XIFF file header to determine if the header is different or if the TIFF file was simply renamed to have a XIFF extension. The TIFF file format is a well-established format used for transmitting faxes and for printed publications. All TIFF files start at position zero (offset 0 is the first byte of a file) with hexadecimal 49, followed by another 49 and 2A. These hexadecimal values translate to ASCII 11, 11, *. Drivespy.ini defines a TIFF file header as TIF=0x00:"II". Figure 12-24 shows a TIFF file named Sawtooth_050.tif open in Hex Workshop.

For XIFF files, the first three bytes are the same as a TIFF file, followed by other hexadecimal values that distinguish it from a TIFF file. See Figure 12-25.

All TIFF files start at
position zero

TIFF file headers start with
hexadecimal 49, 49, 2A,
which are equivalent to
ASCII II*

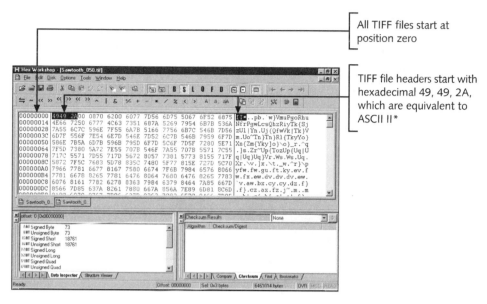

Figure 12-24   TIFF file open in Hex Workshop

XIFF file header

ASCII equivalent defines
this file type as an
extension of TIFF

12

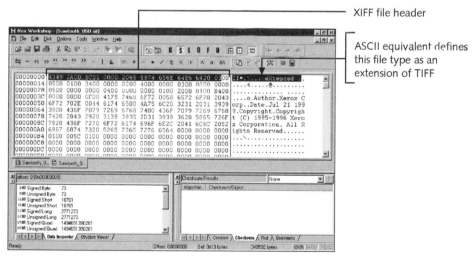

Figure 12-25   XIFF file open in Hex Workshop

As you can see, the XIFF header starts with hexadecimal 49, 49, 2A and has an offset of four bytes of 5C, 01, 00, 00, 20, 65, 58, 74, 65, 6E, 64, 65, 64, 20, 03. With this information about XIFF files, you can define a file header in Drivespy.ini. To insert a new file type in the File Headers section, you specify the starting offset of the header and the actual header code in the proper format, which is defined at the beginning of the Drivespy.ini file, shown in Figure 12-26.

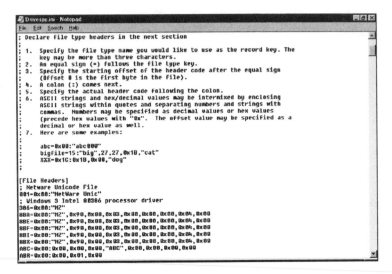

Figure 12-26   Instructions for adding a file type to Drivespy.ini

To insert a new header in the Drivespy.ini file:

1. Start Notepad as you usually do. Click **File** on the menu bar, and then click **Open**. In the Open dialog box, navigate to the folder where Drivespy.ini is located, such as the Tools folder in your work folder. Then double-click **Drivespy.ini** to open it.

2. Scroll down to the bottom of the File Headers section. Press **Enter** to insert a new line, if necessary, type **; XEROX Pagis XIFF Graphic File**, and then press **Enter**.

3. Type the following text and codes on the new line:

   XIF=0x04:0x5C,0x01,0x00,0x00,0x20,0x65,0x58,0x74,0x65,0x6E,0x64, 0x65,0x64,0x20,0x03

4. Click **File** on the menu bar, and then click **Save** to save your changes to Drivespy.ini.

5. Close Notepad.

Now DriveSpy can identify XIFF files. When you find other unknown file types, you can add them to Drivespy.ini in the same way.

Tools for Viewing Images

Throughout this chapter you have been learning about recognizing file formats, using compression techniques, salvaging the header information, recovering image files, and saving your modifications. Recall that after you recover an image file, you can use an image viewer to open and view the graphic. Several hundred image viewers are available that can read many graphic file formats, though no one viewer program can read every file format. Like computer forensics tools, it is best to have as many different viewer programs available for every investigation.

Many popular viewer utilities are shareware programs such as ThumbsPlus, ACDSee, QuickView, and IrfanView that let you view a wide range of image file formats.

Most GUI computer forensics tools such as EnCase, FTK, and ILook integrate image viewers that display only common image formats, especially GIF and JPEG, which are often involved in computing investigations related to Internet cases. However, for unusual file formats such as RAW, TNA, PCX, PPM, or FSH, integrated viewers often only identify the data as an image file or might not recognize the data at all. This inability to view all formats can prevent you from finding the critical evidence for your case. Be sure that you analyze, identify, and inspect every unknown file on a disk drive.

In the following steps, you download IrfanView from the Web, if necessary. If you have already downloaded and installed IrfanView, you only need to download and install the all_plugins.exe file.

To download and start IrfanView:

1. Start your Web browser, such as Internet Explorer.

2. In the Address text box, type **www.irfanview.com** and then press **Enter**. The IrfanView Web page opens.

3. In the left column, click the **Download** link. Two download links appear: one for IrfanView and one for the plug-ins. You need to download both.

4. Click the **TUCOWS Worldwide Network – download IrfanView** link. If the File Download dialog box opens, click the **Save** button. In the Save As dialog box, navigate to a folder where you are allowed to store downloaded files, such as a temporary folder. Then click the **Save** button to download iview380.exe.

5. Return to the IrfanView Web page, and then click the **TUCOWS Worldwide Network – Download IrfanView plugins** link. Save the all_plugins.exe file in the same folder as iview380.exe. Then close Internet Explorer.

6. Use Windows Explorer to navigate to the folder where you downloaded the IrfanView files. Double-click **iview380.exe** to start the IrfanView Setup wizard. Accept the defaults to install the program on your computer.

7. To install the IrfanView plug-ins, double-click **all_plugins.exe**. The IrfanView Plug-ins Setup wizard starts. Click **Next** and then click **OK** to install the plug-ins.

8. To become familiar with the file formats IrfanView supports, start IrfanView by clicking **Start**, pointing to **Programs** (**All Programs** in Windows XP), pointing to **IrfanView**, and then clicking **IrfanView 3.80**.

12

9. Click **File** on the menu bar, and then click **Open**. In the Open dialog box, click the **Files of type** list arrow, and then review the list of image file types. Click a blank area of the Open dialog box to close the list. Then click **Cancel** to close the dialog box.

10. Close IrfanView.

Understanding Steganography in Image Files

When you open some image files in an image viewer, it might appear that they do not contain information related to your investigation. However, someone might have hidden information inside the image using a data-hiding technique called steganography. **Steganography** is a method for hiding data using a host file to cover the contents of the secret message.

Steganography might sound like a relatively new term and technique, but has been used since ancient times. The term itself comes from the Greek words *steganos*, which means covered or secret, and *graphie*, which refers to writing. Ancient Greek rulers used steganography to send covert messages to their diplomats and troops via messengers. To protect the privacy of the message, the rulers shaved the heads of their messengers and tattooed the message on their skull. After the hair grew enough to cover the message, the messengers left for their destinations, where they would shave their heads so that others could read the contents of the message. This was a clever but inefficient way to send and retrieve encrypted information as it took a long time for the messenger's hair to grow back. Also, depending on the shape and size of the messengers head, this method offered only a limited amount of space to write messages. However, it effectively allowed the Greeks to send secret messages until their enemies discovered this early form of steganography and began intercepting the messengers.

TIP
Contemporary steganography is also inefficient because an image file can hide only a certain amount of information before its size and structure changes. However, it effectively allows someone to send covert information to a recipient unless someone else detects the hidden data.

The two major forms of steganography are insertion and substitution. Insertion places data from the secret file into the host file without displaying the secret data when you view the host file in its associated program. The inserted data is hidden unless you review the data structure. For example, if you create a Web page using Hypertext Markup Language (HTML), you can display images and text in a Web browser without revealing the HTML code. Figure 12-27 shows a typical Web page as it was intended to be viewed in a Web browser. This Web page contains hidden text, which is shown in Figure 12-28 along with the source HTML code.

To detect hidden inserted text, you need to compare what the file displays and what the file contains.

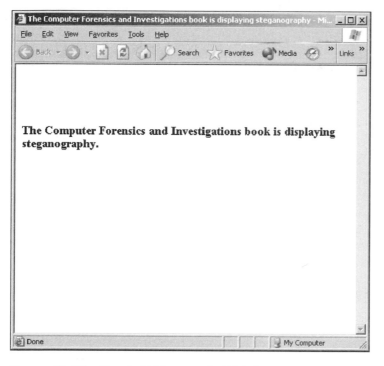

Figure 12-27   Simple Web page in Web browser

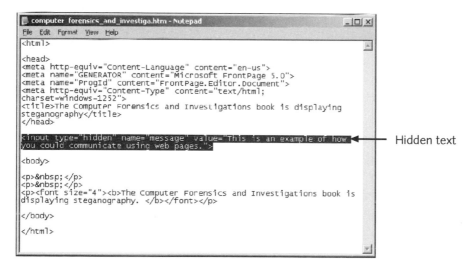

Hidden text

Figure 12-28   HTML code with hidden text

The second type of steganography, substitution, replaces bits of the host file with other bits of data. When using a bitmap image file, for example, you could replace bits used for the pixels and their colors with hidden data. To avoid detection, you need to substitute only those bits that make the least amount of change.

For example, if you use an 8-bit image file, each pixel is represented by 8 bits of data. These 8 bits contain information about the color each pixel displays on the monitor. The bits are prioritized from left to right, as such 11101100. The first bit on the left is the Most Significant Bit (MSB), and the last bit on the right is the Least Significant Bit (LSB). As the names suggest, changing the MSB affects the display of the pixel more than changing the LSB. Furthermore, you can usually only change the last two LSBs in the image without affecting a noticeable change in the shade of color the pixel displays. To detect a change to the last two LSBs in an image file, you need to use a **steganalysis** tool, which is software specifically designed to identify steganography techniques.

For example, if your secret message is converted to binary form to equal 01101100 and you wanted to embed this secret message into a picture, you would alter the last two bits of four pixels. You would break the binary form into sections of two, as in 01 10 11 00, and insert the bits into the last two bits of each pixel, as shown in Table 12-2.

Table 12-2   Bit breakdown of secret message

Original pixel	Altered pixel
1010 1010	1010 1001
1001 1101	1001 1110
1111 0000	1111 0011
0011 1111	0011 1100

The sequence of the two bits was used to substitute the last two bits used for the pixel. This substitution of bits is undetectable by the human eye, which can see only about 6 bits of color.

Figure 12-29 shows an original picture, a simple line drawing on the left, and an altered image on the right.

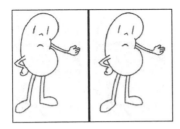

Figure 12-29   Original and altered images

The altered image contains the hidden picture shown in Figure 12-30.

Figure 12-30   Hidden image

Whether using insertion or substitution, image files tend to be the files of choice for steganography because they contain enough bits to manipulate for hiding data. You should therefore always inspect image files for steganography evidence, especially if your suspect is technically savvy.

Steganography can be used with file formats other than image files, such as MPEG and AVI files.

TIP

Finding the hidden data contained in a steganography file can be difficult. You can use several different steganalysis tools to detect, decode, and record the hidden data.

Using Steganalysis Tools

Several steganalysis tools can detect hidden data in image files, even in files that have been renamed to protect their contents. The steganalysis tool must be able to detect the variations of the graphic image. If the image file has been renamed, the steganalysis tool can use the file header to identify the file format and indicate whether the file contains an image.

Although steganalysis tools can help identify hidden data, steganography is generally very difficult to detect. In fact, if steganography is done correctly, in most cases you will not be able to detect the hidden data unless you can compare the altered file with the original file.

As an example of the complexity of detecting steganography, Niels Provos and Peter Honeyman at the University of Michigan conducted a study of over 2 million images obtained from eBay auctions. They reported that they were "…unable to report finding a single hidden message."

Steganography and steganalysis tools are changing as rapidly as some operating systems. Current standard tools include Hashkeeper, the Known File Filter (KFF) in the AccessData Forensic Toolkit, Stegowatch, Outguess, StegDetect, and S-Tools. For a list of other steganography and steganalysis tools, use a search engine to search for "steganography."

All of these tools compare a suspect file to a known good version of the image file or known bad version. Some more recent tools can detect steganography without a known good or bad file. Because the files are binary, these tools make complex mathematical calculations to verify the authenticity of the file by checking the file size and palette color. Other tools compare the hash value of a known good or known bad file to the suspect file to determine if steganography was used on the image file.

You can also use steganalysis tools to determine which sectors of the image hide data. This becomes a lengthy investigation. Your first obstacle is obtaining the original image to compare to the known steganography file. In some cases, you can find the original file on the suspect's computer or can recover it if it was deleted. If the filename has been changed, you might need to view each image file you recover to try and find a match. If you cannot find the original file, you can still analyze the suspect file by using a steganalysis tool such as Stegowatch to detect the hidden data.

IDENTIFYING COPYRIGHT ISSUES WITH GRAPHICS

Recall from Chapter 10 that a form of steganography was originally created to protect copyrighted material by inserting digital watermarks into a file. When working with image files, computer investigators also need to be aware of copyright laws, especially in the corporate environment, to guard against copyright violations.

The following excerpt from the U.S. Copyright Office Web site (*www.copyright.gov*) defines copyright:

Copyright is a form of protection provided by the laws of the United States (title 17, U.S. Code) to the authors of "original works of authorship," including literary, dramatic, musical, artistic, and certain other intellectual works. This protection is available to both published and unpublished works. Section 106 of the 1976 Copyright Act generally gives the owner of copyright the exclusive right to do and to authorize others to do the following:

- *To reproduce* the work in copies or phonorecords;
- To prepare *derivative works* based upon the work;
- *To distribute copies or phonorecords* of the work to the public by sale or other transfer of ownership, or by rental, lease, or lending;
- *To perform the work publicly,* in the case of literary, musical, dramatic, and choreographic works, pantomimes, and motion pictures and other audiovisual works;

- ■ *To display the copyrighted work publicly*, in the case of literary, musical, dramatic, and choreographic works, pantomimes, and pictorial, graphic, or sculptural works, including the individual images of a motion picture or other audiovisual work; and

- ■ In the case of *sound recordings, to perform the work publicly* by means of a *digital audio transmission.*

In addition, certain authors of works of visual art have the rights of attribution and integrity as described in section 106A of the 1976 Copyright Act. For further information, request Circular 40, "Copyright Registration for Works of the Visual Arts."

It is illegal for anyone to violate any of the rights provided by the copyright law to the owner of copyright. These rights, however, are not unlimited in scope. Sections 107 through 121 of the 1976 Copyright Act establish limitations on these rights. In some cases, these limitations are specified exemptions from copyright liability. One major limitation is the doctrine of "fair use," which is given a statutory basis in section 107 of the 1976 Copyright Act. In other instances, the limitation takes the form of a "compulsory license" under which certain limited uses of copyrighted works are permitted upon payment of specified royalties and compliance with statutory conditions. For further information about the limitations of any of these rights, consult the copyright law or write to the Copyright Office.

This excerpt from the U.S. Copyright Office Web site precisely defines how copyright laws pertain to graphics. Copyright laws as they pertain to the Internet, however, are not as clear. For example, a server in another country might host a Web site, which could mean that it is regulated by the copyright laws in that country. Each country has its own copyright laws, making them difficult to enforce. Contrary to what some may believe, there is no international copyright law.

The Copyright Web site identifies what can and cannot be covered in copyright law in the U.S:

Copyright protects "original works of authorship" that are fixed in a tangible form of expression. The fixation need not be directly perceptible so long as it may be communicated with the aid of a machine or device. Copyrightable works include the following categories:

1. literary works;

2. musical works, including any accompanying words;

3. dramatic works, including any accompanying music;

4. pantomimes and choreographic works;

5. pictorial, graphic, and sculptural works;

6. motion pictures and other audiovisual works;

7. sound recordings;

8. architectural works.

These categories should be viewed broadly. For example, computer programs and most "compilations" may be registered as "literary works"; maps and architectural plans may be registered as "pictorial, graphic, and sculptural works."

Anything that would ordinarily be copyrighted through noncomputer means and is now being created on digital media is considered to be copyrighted as long as process has been followed to obtain a copyright.

Chapter Summary

- An image file contains a graphic, such as a digital photograph, line art, three-dimensional image, or scanned replica of a printed picture. A graphics program creates and saves one of three types of image files: bitmap, vector, or metafile. Bitmap images are collections of dots, or pixels, that form an image. Vector images are mathematical instructions that define lines, curves, text, ovals, and other geometric shapes. Metafiles are combinations of bitmap and vector images.

- When you use either a graphic editor or image viewer, you can open a file in one of many image file formats, which is indicated by the file extension, such as .bmp, .gif, or .eps. Each format has different qualities, including the amount of color and compression it uses. If you open an image file in a graphics program that supports multiple file formats, you can save the file in a different file format. However, converting image files this way can change the quality of the image.

- Bitmap images store graphic information as grids of individual pixels, short for picture elements. The quality of a bitmap image displayed on a computer monitor is governed by screen resolution, which determines the amount of detail displayed in the image. Vector files are different from the bitmap and raster files; a raster image uses dots and the vector format uses lines. A vector file stores only the mathematics for drawing lines and shapes; a graphics program converts the calculation into the appropriate image. You can enlarge a vector image without affecting the image quality. Metafile image files combine raster and vector graphics, and can have the characteristics of both image types.

- Most graphic editors let you create and save files in one or more of the standard image file formats, such as Graphic Interchange Format (GIF), Joint Photographic Experts Group (JPEG), Windows Bitmap (BMP), or Encapsulated Postscript (EPS). Nonstandard image file formats include uncommon formats such as Targa (TGA), and Raster Transfer Language (RTL), proprietary formats such as Photoshop (PSD), emerging formats such as Scalable Vector Graphics (SVG), and those related to old or obsolete technology, such as Paintbrush (PCX).

- Most image file formats, including GIF and JPEG, compress their data to save disk space and to reduce the amount of time it takes to transfer the image from one computer to another. Other formats, such as BMP, rarely compress their data or do so inefficiently. In this case, people can use compression tools to compact data and reduce file size. Lossless compression saves file space by using mathematical formulas to represent the data contained in a file. Lossy compression is significantly different from lossless compression because it compresses data by permanently discarding bits of information contained in the file.

❑ If a computer forensics investigation involves image files, you need to locate and recover all of the image files on a drive and determine which ones are pertinent to your case. Because images are not always stored in standard image file formats, you should examine files that your computer forensics tools find even if they are not identified as image files. An image file contains a header with instructions for displaying the image. Each type of image file has its own header and examining the header helps you identify the file format. Because the header is complex and difficult to remember, you can compare a known good file header with that of a suspected file.

❑ When you are examining recovered data remnants from files in slack or free space, you might find data that appears to be a header for a common image file type. If you locate header data that is partially overwritten, you must reconstruct the header. To do this, you compare the hexadecimal values of known image file formats to the pattern of the file header you found to make it readable again. After you identify fragmented data, you can use a computer forensics program to recover the fragmented file.

❑ If you cannot open an image file in an image viewer, your next step is to examine the header data of the file to see if it matches the header in a good JPEG file. If the header does not match, you must manually insert the correct hexadecimal values using a tool such as Hex Workshop. You can then inspect and correct the hexadecimal values within a file.

❑ The Internet is the best source for learning more about file formats and their associated extensions. You have already used the Webopedia Web site to research the TGA file format. You can use also any popular search engine to search for "file type" or "file format" and find the latest list of Web sites providing information on file extensions.

❑ You should analyze image file headers when you find new or unique file types that computer forensics tools do not recognize. The simplest way to access a file header is to use a hexadecimal editor such as Hex Workshop. You can then record the hexadecimal values in the header and later use them to define a file type in Drivespy.ini.

❑ Many popular viewer utilities are shareware programs such as ThumbsPlus, ACDSee, Quick View, and IrfanView that let you view a wide range of image file formats. Most GUI computer forensics tools such as EnCase, FTK, and ILook integrate image viewers that display only common image formats, especially GIF and JPEG, which are often involved in computing investigations related to Internet cases.

❑ Steganography is a method for hiding data using a host file to cover the contents of the secret message. The two major forms of steganography are insertion and substitution. Insertion places data from the secret file into the host file without displaying the secret data when you view the host file in its associated program. The inserted data is hidden unless you review the data structure. The second type of steganography, substitution, replaces bits of the host file with other bits of data.

12

❑ Several steganalysis tools can detect hidden data in image files, even in files that have been renamed to protect their contents. The steganalysis tool must be able to detect the variations of the graphic image. If the image file has been renamed, the steganalysis tool can use the file header to identify the file format and indicate whether the file contains an image.

KEY TERMS

algorithm—A short mathematical procedure that solves a recurrent problem.

bitmap image—A representation of a graphics image in a grid type format.

carving—The process of removing an item from a group of items.

data compression—A complex algorithm used to reduce the size of a file.

metafiles—Combinations of bitmap and vector images.

nonstandard image file format—An uncommon graphic file format, including those that most image viewers do not recognize, proprietary formats, emerging formats, and those related to old or obsolete technology.

pixel—A small dot used to create images.

raster image—A bitmap file that organizes pixels in rows; usually created when a vector image is converted to a bitmap image.

rasterize—To convert a bitmap file to a raster file for printing.

resolution—Density of pixels on the screen.

salvaging—Another term for carving used in the United Kingdom; the process of removing an item from a group of items.

screen resolution—The density of pixels displayed on your monitor.

standard image file format—An image file format that most or all graphics programs can open.

steganalysis—The practice of detecting and decoding steganography.

steganography—Hiding data in a file.

vector image—An image created based on mathematical equations.

vector quantization (VQ)—A form of vector image that uses an algorithm similar to rounding up decimal values to eliminate unnecessary data.

CHAPTER
13
WRITING
INVESTIGATION REPORTS

After reading this chapter, you will be able to:
- Understand the importance of reports
- List procedural and evidence rules requirements
- List types of reports
- Write reports
- Determine what you need to express an opinion
- Express an opinion
- Document a report

This chapter explains the rules of evidence and procedure as they apply to reports and disclosure requirements. You will examine the Federal Rules of Evidence (FRE) and the Federal Rules of Civil Procedure (FRCP) in the United States and learn how they parallel the comparable rules in most states of the United States. You will also learn how to write and document a report.

UNDERSTANDING THE IMPORTANCE OF REPORTS

You write a report to communicate the results of your computing-forensics examination or investigation. A formal report presents evidence as testimony in court, at an administrative hearing, or as an affidavit. Besides presenting facts, reports can communicate expert opinion.

For civil cases, including those involving computer forensics investigations, the United States District Courts require that expert witnesses submit written reports; state courts are also starting to require reports from expert witnesses, although the details of the report requirements vary. Therefore, if you are a computer forensics examiner involved in a civil case, you must write a report explaining your investigation and findings. Specifically, Rule 26, Federal Rules of Civil Procedure, requires that parties who anticipate calling an expert witness to testify must provide a copy of the expert's written report that includes all opinions, the basis for the opinions, and the information that was considered in coming to the opinions (see Figure 13-1). The report must also include related exhibits, such as photographs or diagrams, and the curriculum vitae of the witness that lists all the publications the witness wrote during the preceding ten years. (These publications do not have to be relevant to the case.)

Figure 13-1 Typical court scene

In addition to opinions and exhibits, the written report must specify the fees paid for the expert's services and list all other civil or criminal cases in which the expert has testified, in trial and deposition as an expert, for the preceding four years. This includes all instances of trial or deposition expert testimony, without regard to outcome, but not cases where the expert acted as a consulting expert and did not provide expert testimony, such as criminal cases where you or a police officer testifies as a **lay witness**, who is someone not called as a witness because of their expertise in a technical field. Cases where you or a police officer were qualified or offered testimony as an expert and provided opinion in trial or deposition must be included.

While the requirements for information on the list are not specific, you should keep a copy of any deposition notice or subpoena for reference; either will have the style of the case, e.g. John Smith, Plaintiff v. Paul Jones, Defendant, jurisdiction, date, and cause (court case file) number. There are no requirements that the details of testimony be included.

As an expert witness, you should be aware that lawyers use services called deposition banks or libraries, where they can deposit and withdraw examples of expert witnesses' previous testimony. Some of these services have hundreds of thousands of depositions on file and may have several deposition examples for any expert witness who testifies regularly. After a case is resolved, a lawyer sends copies of the depositions of the opposing expert witnesses to the bank for deposit. In preparation for a trial upon identification of an expert witness by the opposing party, the attorney may request copies of previous testimony by a witness. A lawyer might also request transcripts of previous testimony by his or her own potential experts to assure himself that the expert has not testified to a contrary position previously. As a computer forensics examiner, your testimony and report writing may be stored in a deposition bank or library. Because of this you must maintain the highest standards possible for your writing and testifying.

Limiting the Report to Specifics

You can now submit computing-forensics reports electronically in many courts; the standard format is Portable Document Format (PDF). Do not file a report directly with the court unless you have been so directed to by an attorney or the court.

All reports should first repeat to the client the mission or goal of the investigation, which is usually to find information on a specific subject, recover certain significant documents, or recover certain types of files or files with certain dates and times. The client (who might be an attorney, detective, or investigator) should define the goal or mission. You can then contribute your definition of what you are seeking. Clearly defining the goals reduces the amount of time and cost of the examination. Defining the goal of the investigation is especially important as the size of hard drives now often exceed 100 GB, and networks may encompass terabytes of data, thousands of systems, hundreds of servers, and applications spanning several states or countries.

Types of Reports

Before you begin writing, identify your audience and the purpose of the particular report. If the audience has little technical knowledge, part of your report may have to educate the audience on technical issues.

Reports are usually categorized in two major forms: verbal and written. Within each of these are two major forms, reports are further categorized as formal and informal.

The **verbal formal report** is very structured and often delivered to a board of directors or managers or to a jury. When presenting a verbal formal report in a corporate boardroom, you can organize the report and deliver it at your own pace, but often with time restrictions.

An **examination plan** is a document that lets you know what questions to expect when you are on the stand. In the courtroom, you will be guided by such an examination plan prepared by the attorney to whom you can propose changes, such as those involving clarification or definition. For example, if the attorney misuses an expression or term that indicates that other nonexperts might not understand it. Examination resources should then be used to address the definition of the expression if it has relevance to the testimony. If the expression is not part of relevant testimony, drop it from the examination plan. The changes would normally not be significant, because the attorney structures the examination from your report. You are still operating under a time constraint for presenting your report, but the constraint is less rigid, and ultimately controlled by the judge. The plan allows the attorney to document that testimony has been elicited on each of the points on which you have relevant knowledge. There are multiple sources for questions: the attorney that hired you and the opposing counsel. (Your retaining attorney usually anticipates the paths of cross-examination.) There may be more than one opposing attorney, especially if there is more than one opposing party, and, in many jurisdictions, the jury may submit written questions (each question is subject to evaluation against the same rules of evidence as the questions placed by the attorneys).

Do not include anything in the examination plan that you would not want the jury to see (see Figure 13-2). If opposing counsel asks about the examination plan, acknowledge that you have one. A possible course of action is for retaining counsel to ask to have the plan admitted into evidence. The retaining attorney will have to provide a copy of the plan to opposing counsel prior to the requesting its admission into evidence. If asked on cross-examination if you have a script, you can reply, "No, I have reviewed an examination plan," or something similar. If asked if you rehearsed, you may answer, "No. I have, however, prepared to testify."

A **verbal informal report** is less structured than a formal report. A typical venue is an attorney's office where the attorney requests your consultant's report. As an expert hired into the trial consultant role, you most often use this report form. The attorney often wants as little written down as possible because what does not exist cannot be discovered. Furthermore, others cannot force the attorney to release a verbal informal report, it cannot be mishandled, or inadvertently released. This report is preliminary and mention the areas of investigation that are yet to be completed such as the following:

- Tests may not have been concluded
- Interrogatories
- Document production
- Depositions

Mention also that your factual statement and opinion are at this point still tentative and subject to change as more information comes in.

WITNESS EXAMINATION PLAN

WITNESS:_Karen Stolz_____/Factors:_____Expert and Treating for P.

Direct Examination – Expected Testimony: Objection/Rule/

Testimony on CV

Identity and Address Iowa Bureau of Criminal Investigation

Position (Current) Computer Forensic Examiner

Undergraduate   Iowa State University summa cum laude 1990 BS Computer Engineering

Summer Internship 1989 Des Moines Police Department

Neurology residency, University of Massachusetts MC 86-89

Chief resident in neurology, UM MC 88-89____explain neurology

Fellowship in Electroencephalography and Clinical Neurophysiology, UWMC-Seattle 89-90

Fellowship in Sleep Disorders Medicine, Univ. Michigan MC, 90-91

Academic Appointments

Lecturer, Dept of Computer Science, University of Iowa 1998-Current

Instructor, Iowa Police Academy, 1999-Current

Professional Society Certifications

P.E.   1999

CISSP 2001

Membership

American Society for Industrial Security

Publications

          Journal of the Iowa State Bar Association. May 1999. "Computer Forensics on Raid Servers-Testifying to a Reasonable Certainty"

How many systems have you conducted forensic examination on?

What is your relationship to the Plaintiff?   Retained by his attorney to examine the hard drive of his computer for all financial records. I have never actually met or talked with Mr. Smith.

How long did it take you conduct this examination?

What types of files were you looking for?   Why those file types?   Where did you find those file types?

What condition were the files in?

What is your opinion as to the cause of that condition?

Can you say for a reasonable certainty that the financial data files were deleted intentionally? Yes.

Are you able to state to a reasonable certainty who deleted the financial data files? Yes.

What is your fee for examining the hard drive, preparing a report and testifying?

Cross Examination - Expected Testimony

How many times have you worked for Mr. Sawyer as an expert witness? I've had 16 contracts as consulting expert or expert witness.

Have you ever previously testified that overwrite utilities are not 100% reliable? Yes, but that was in 1994 and utilities are so far as I can tell 100% reliable today.

Figure 13-2   Examination plan

A **written formal report** is frequently an affidavit or declaration. Because this type of report is sworn to under oath (and penalty of perjury or comparable false swearing statute), it demands the greatest attention to detail, careful limiting of what you write, and careful documentation and support of what you write.

When writing a report use a natural language style. Describe yourself in the first person, not the third person; e.g. don't call yourself "Your Affiant" when "I" is appropriate and is clearly more natural. Remember, somebody (probably a judge) will read your report or affidavit. Keep the judge interested in what you have to say. Pay attention to word usage, grammar, and spelling, especially because this is formal writing. Your formal report should also include your curriculum vitae or refer to it. This is the part of the report where you qualify yourself as an expert or technical/scientific witness.

An affidavit may be used to support issuing an arrest warrant or search warrant, and may be used at a probable cause hearing or as evidence in a grand jury hearing.

Federal courts as matter of course, and rule, in civil cases require that all technical, scientific, or expert witnesses provide a report prior to trial. See Federal Rule of Civil Procedure 26 (a) (2) and Federal Rules of Evidence 702, 703, and 705.

Avoid producing a **written informal report** if you can. If you must produce the informal or preliminary report in written form, understand that actions or statements you do not make are as important as what you do and say.

Written informal reports or preliminary reports are **high-risk documents** that opposing counsel may receive in **discovery** if you become a disclosed expert witness. A high-risk document in this context relates to a written informal report that addresses subjects relevant to the cause; you may be examined over the written informal report. If the written informal report states a contrary or more equivocal position than you take in your final report or testimony, you should expect opposing counsel to try to discredit your testimony by using the written informal report. It is simply better if there is not a written informal report to provide. Just as you should use certain important words in a report, you should also avoid using other important words, especially in the written informal report or preliminary report. For example, do not use the words "preliminary copy," "draft copy," "working draft," or any words to this effect. This language offers an opening for opposing counsel, making it appear that the attorney who retained you contributed to what should be your independent professional judgment. Do not produce a written informal report and later destroy it, especially before a final resolution of the case or any discovery issue relating to the report. Destroying the report could be considered destruction or concealing of evidence; among lawyers this is called **spoliation**, and may subject your retaining party or attorney to monetary or evidentiary sanctions.

Instead, include the same information that you would provide in an informal verbal report. First, restate the assignment. This confirms between you and the retaining attorney that the work that you have done is properly focused. Next, summarize what has been accomplished. Identify the systems that you have examined, what tools you have used, and what you have seen. State evidence preservation or protection processes you have implemented. (See Chapters 6 and 9 for more information about these processes.)

- Summarize your billing to date and estimate costs to complete the effort.

- Identify the tentative conclusion (rather than the preliminary conclusion).

- Identify areas of further investigation and obtain confirmation from the attorney on the scope of your examination.

EXPRESSING AN OPINION

The long preferred method for expressing an opinion has been to frame a hypothetical question based on factual evidence that is available. This method is less favored today than in the past, but still has validity, even if not formally used. You can construct the hypothetical to guide and support your opinion. State the facts that are necessary to the question. Do not include any facts that are not necessary, unless they are alternative facts that allow the opinion to remain the same in the event that one set of facts is not supported and the other is. The expert opinion is governed by the FRE under rule FRE 705 and the corresponding rule in many states. The rule FRE 705 states that relates to expert testimony. This will be further discussed in Chapter 14. For more information go to *www.law.cornell.edu/rules/fre/705.html*.

The following text illustrates an exchange between an attorney and a computer forensics expert:

> **Mr. Garcia**: Mr. Noriki, presented with a hard drive of 40 MB, an attached Maxtor manufacturer's data sheet that indicated that it was manufactured in May of 2002, previous testimony by a detective that the notebook computer in which this drive was found was manufactured by Dell Computer Corporation in June of 2002 and purchased by the owner in June of 2002. Based on those assumed facts, do you have an opinion whether this is original equipment on this system?
>
> **Mr. Noriki**: Yes.
>
> **Mr. Garcia**: Mr. Noriki, what is your opinion on whether this hypothetical hard drive would be original equipment with the system?
>
> **Mr. Noriki**: Based on facts that you have provided, it is my opinion that the hard drive would ....

The hypothetical question can be abused and can be made so complex that the finder of fact may not be able to remember enough of the question fact pattern to evaluate the answer. Another abuse of the hypothetical question is that it effectively allows the attorney to recite his or her favored facts to the jury repeatedly and in the order and with the emphasis that he wants to apply.

The law previously required that an expert who does not have personal knowledge regarding the system or the occurrence must give his or her opinions by response to hypothetical questions, which ask you as an expert witness to express an opinion based on hypothetical facts without specifically referring to a particular system or situation. In this regard, you differ fundamentally from the ordinary witness. You did not see or hear the incident in dispute, but give evidence of scientific fact and an opinion based on professional knowledge and experience, though you may subsequently see the system, data, or scene. Although the rules of evidence have relaxed the requirements on the formal structure and requirements of rendering an opinion, privately structuring the hypothetical question is helpful, whether it is asked in court or stated in a report. This ensures that the witness is basing the opinion on facts that are expected to be supported by evidence.

As an expert witness, such as a computer forensics examiner, you may testify to an opinion, or conclusion, if four basic conditions are met:

- The opinion, inferences, or conclusions, depend on special knowledge, skill, or training not within the ordinary experience of lay jurors.

13

- The witness must be shown to be qualified as a true expert in the particular field of expertise (this is why the curriculum vitae is important).

- The witness must testify to a reasonable degree of certainty (probability) regarding his or her opinion, inference, or conclusion.

- It has generally been true that an expert witness must first describe the data (facts) on which his or her opinion, inference, or conclusion, is based or, in the alternative, he must testify in response to a hypothetical question that sets forth the underlying evidence.

Keep the following guidelines in mind as you write your report:

- Don't make any assumptions. If you discover an e-mail, don't assume you know the recipient's name from the e-mail address alone. An e-mail addressed to "Matt," whose e-mail address is *msmith@iex.net*, does not necessarily mean that the recipient's name is Matt Smith. E-mail addresses can be faked easily.

- Don't identify leads. The report is for the case officer, and it is his or her job to identify the leads. If you discover something important during your analysis, write it up so it is obvious to the officer without providing a lead.

- Check your spelling before the report leaves your office; don't wait for a supervisor or the attorney to proofread your report.

- Double-check the media that you have stored findings to. If you create a findings CD, make sure the data is on it before you send it out.

Think about the criteria for assessment of English language skills in a written report. You should criticize and assess the quality of your writing. Consider the following criteria:

- Communicative quality—Is it easy to read?

- Ideas and organization—Is the information appropriate and clearly organized?

- Grammar and vocabulary—Is there a good range of language used so that the meaning is clear and the text is not repetitive? However, always remember that using different words for the same thing may generate questions.

- Surface features—Is the punctuation and spelling accurate? Consider what a report is expected to contain.

The structure of a report should include all of the sections shown in Figure 13-3. The order varies depending on organizational guides or case requirements.

The title for an affidavit that may be used as the submission in response to a discovery and disclosure request or used to support the issuance of an arrest or search warrant. The style shown is that of a criminal case, but as an affidavit it would look very much the same in a civil case.

Adjust the sections shown in Figure 13-3 to suit the purpose of the report. Each section has a particular role. The title tells the reader directly and at first glance what it is that

```
SUPERIOR COURT OF WASHINGTON
COUNTY OF KING

State of Washington, Plaintiff,          |
No. 03-0123456-8-1                       |
                                         |
v.                                       |
                                         |
John Doe Jones, Defendant.               |
                                         |
         Affidavit of John Smith
     Report of Forensic Examination of
     Dell Inspiron 2650 SN: 12345678
```

```
Author(s) see example above and Bona Fides or reference to Curriculum Vitae

  •  Abstract, if the report is long and complex

  •  Summary, also important if the report is long and complex

  •  Table of contents, also important if the report is long and complex

  •  Body of report

  •  Conclusion and if applicable opinion

  •  References

  •  Glossary (if needed)

  •  Acknowledgments (if appropriate)
```

Figure 13-3   Sample formal report structure

you are discussing. Convey the essential point of the paper. Be precise, concise, and use key words. Avoid padding with phrases like "A study of ..." or headline statements.

The abstract or summary and table of contents give the reader an overview of the report and a list of section headings. From these, they can see the points included and decide what you need to look at. Condense the paper into miniature form. A sentence or two summarizing each of the sections of the report should suffice. Provide no new information or supporting material. Limit the details by including just the essential message that explains what you did and found out. The form and function of the abstract of a report include a definition, providing the essence of the report in a few words; an informative form, or descriptive form and impersonal tone; connected writing; with a length around 150–250 words. The abstract is very important because many more people read the abstract than hear or read the entire report. It should not be a mere recital of the subject covered. The abstract should be a condensation and concentration of the essential information in the report. The abstract describes the examination or investigation and presents the main ideas of the report in a summarized form. Informative abstracts do not duplicate references or tables of results. As with any research paper, write the abstract last.

The body consists of the introduction and component sections. The introduction should state the purpose of the report and show that you are aware of its terms of reference. That is, you should state the subject and purpose of the report. You should also state any method(s) used and any limitations and indicate how the report is structured. It is important to justify, or say why you are writing the report. You should also give the reader a map of what you are delivering. Introduce the problem, moving from the broader issues to your specific problem, finishing the section with the precise aims of the paper (key questions).

Craft this section carefully, setting up the processes you used to develop the information in logical order. Refer to *relevant* ideas/theories and related research by other authors. Answer the question, "What is the problem?"

Sections of the report should be organized under headings to reflect how you classify information and to help you remain relevant.

The conclusion starts by referring back to the purpose of the report, states the main points, draws conclusions, and possibly renders an opinion.

References and appendices list the material referred to in your work. Follow any guidelines on format for presentation of references. Appendices provide additional material not included in the text.

Designing the Layout and Presentation

Layout and presentation involves matters ranging from clear title and section headings to accurate spelling and punctuation. Think of your readers and how to make the report appealing to them. Presenting accurate text is equivalent to speaking clearly. Because you cannot be physically present to explain problems to your reader, be sure to edit and check your text.

Numbering structure is part of the layout. An author usually chooses one of the following two layout systems: decimal numbering or legal-sequential numbering. Once a system is chosen, be sure to present this system consistently throughout the report.

A report using the decimal numbering system divides material into sections as follows:

1.0 Introduction
       1.1 Nature of incident
              1.1.1 Victim
2.0 First Incident
       2.1 Witness 1
              2.1.1 Witness testimony
3.0 Location of Evidence
       3.1 Seizure of Evidence
              3.1.1 Transportation of Evidence
4.0 Analysis of Evidence
       4.1 Chain of Evidence
              4.1.1 Extraction of Data
5.0 Conclusion
       5.1 Results
              5.1.1 Expert Opinion

A reader can scan the headings and understand how one part of the report relates to the other. An alternative is to use legal-sequential numbering, as in the following example:

I. Introduction
> 1. Nature of the Incident
> 2. The Victim
> 3. Witnesses to the Crime
> 4. Location of Evidence

II. Examination
> 5. Chain of Evidence
> 6. Extraction of Evidence
> 7. Analysis of Evidence

This system is frequently used in pleadings, where each Roman numeral represents a major aspect of the report, and each Arabic number is a significant piece of supporting information.

The system of legal-sequential organization is meaningful to lawyers, but may not be as effective with nonlawyers. It generally does not provide as strong a set of cues about the organization and relative significance of information in the report.

Including Signposts

Apart from structure, layout, and presentation, your main tool in writing reports is your language. Select language that gives your reader signposts to what you are trying to communicate. A signpost is a guide to the reader to draw their attention to a point or to show them the sequence of a process. It assists the readers in scanning the text quickly by highlighting the main points and the logical development of information. For example, the first substantive section of your report could start with "This is the report of findings from the forensic examination of computer SN 123456." This sentence provides a signpost that shows the purpose of the report.

Within the first section, the steps could be introduced with "The first step in this examination was," or "The second step in this examination was," and so on. In these examples, "first" and "second" are signposts that show the sequence of information or tasks.

When you want to evaluate something, you might include a signpost such as "The problem with this is," or "What is significant about this is." To show that you are drawing a conclusion, introduce the point with, "This means that," or "The result shows that."

Considering Style

Style means the tone of language you use to address the reader. Be sure to avoid repetition and vague language. Repeat only what is necessary, such as key words or technical terms.

Be precise and be specific. Avoid generalizing, as in "There was a problem so we...". Instead, state the problem specifically and describe what you or others did to solve the problem. However, avoid presenting too many details and personal observations. Although

13

it is acceptable and appealing to use "I" or "we" in a report, too many sentences with "I" and "we" become repetitive. The reader may not want to know about everything that happened, but rather your objective assessment of the situation.

When making conclusions and recommendations, read over what you have written and check it against the guidelines. Pay particular attention to punctuation and spelling.

Litigation Support Reports versus Technical Reports

In many technical reports, you can assume that your intended reader has a background similar to yours before you started the project. That is that they have a general understanding of the topic but no specific knowledge of the details. This is not a valid assumption if you are producing a report supporting litigation. In this case, you cannot assume that your reader (the finder of fact) has any significant technical background knowledge to assist them in understanding your report.

WRITING CLEARLY

Good scientific-technical-expert reports share many of the qualities found in other kinds of writing. To write is to think, so a report that lays out ideas in a logical order facilitates the same kind of thinking. Make each sentence follow from the previous one, building an argument piece by piece. Group related ideas and sentences into paragraphs, and group paragraphs into sections. Create a flow from the beginning of the report to the end. The report should be grammatically sound, use correct spelling, and be free of writing errors. Avoid jargon, slang, or colloquial terms. If technical terms must be used, define them in ordinary language (or refer to a glossary). It is particularly important to define acronyms and any abbreviations not used as standard measurement units. If there is any possibility of misinterpreting an abbreviation, define it or use the full expression. As an example, m. or M. are routinely used in scientific-technical writing as abbreviations for meter, but might be confused (especially in the United States) by the nontechnical reader as an abbreviation for mile. Most lawyers (and judges) and jurors are not technically trained.

Most of the report describes what you did, and thus it should be in the past tense, but use present or future tense as appropriate. Employ the active rather than passive voice to avoid boring writing and contorted phrases. For example, "the software recovered the following data" is clearer than "the following data were recovered by the software."

Providing Supporting Material

Use material such as figures, tables, data, and equations to help tell the story as it unfolds. Refer to this material directly in the text and integrate the points they make into your writing. Number figures and tables sequentially as they are introduced (e.g., Figure 1, Figure 2, etc. with another sequence for Table 1, Table 2, etc.).

Provide captions with complete information and not just a simple title. In charts, label all axes and include units. Insert a figure or table after the paragraph in which it is first mentioned, or, gather all supporting material together after the reference section (before any appendices).

Formatting Consistently

Within the report, the exact format of particular items is less important than consistency of application. For example, if you indent paragraphs, be sure to indent them all; use a consistent style of headings throughout (e.g., major headings in bold with initial capitals, minor headings in italics, etc.); write "%" or "percent" but do not mix them. In other words, establish a template and stick to it. Consult other reports for examples.

All sections are important, but each becomes more meaningful at different stages to different readers.

Explaining Methods

Explain how you studied the problem, which should follow logically from the purpose of the report. Depending on the kind of data, this section may contain subsections on examination procedures, materials or equipment used, data collection/sources, analytical or statistical techniques employed, study area, etc. Provide enough detail for the reader to understand what you did.

Data Collection

This is a critical portion of the lab report. Without good data recording in the laboratory notebook or record, completing the lab report beyond this point is futile. If your data collection process becomes a subject of discovery or examination, it will be important that it appear to be well organized. Presentation of data in tables, if practical, allows others to easily follow any data manipulations. Recall that tables should be clearly labeled as to their content and numbered for ease of referral in the discussion section.

Part of the data may involve making observations (color changes, temperature changes, melting point, boiling point, the physical appearance of a chemical substance, etc.). The observations requested in the lab experiment are the bare minimum needed to perform the experiments. Sometimes extra observations you make may provide extra clues.

Including Calculations

In most cases, an investigator or forensic software performs some calculations in the forensic examination of a computer. If you use any calculations, be sure to provide the common name of the calculation, such as Message Digest 5 (MD5) hash. Generally, you should not need to provide examples of each different type of calculation if they are standard tools, you explain generally what they do, and you cite the source that you rely on for using the tool. If you do provide actual calculations, do not include pages full of each and every calculation, it just wastes your time, paper, and the attention of your audience.

Providing for Uncertainty and Error Analysis

In computer forensics, many results can be absolutely true if stated conservatively, but may be a guess if you reach beyond the conservative answer. Therefore, the statement of the limitations of knowledge and uncertainty is necessary to protect your credibility. For example, if you know that the date time stamp for a file from a Windows operating system of a PC indicates it was created at a certain time, you need to state that the clock may easily be reset on a PC and that there is no absolute assurance that a file's date time stamp is a reflection of its creation, but that there may be other reliable indicators relating to that date time stamp.

Explaining Results

Explain your actual findings, using subheadings to divide the section into logical parts, with the text addressing the report objective. Link your writing to figures and tables as you present the results. For each, describe and interpret what you see. Your approach should be that you do the thinking—do not leave this to the reader. If you have many similar figures, select representative examples for brevity and put the rest in an appendix. Mention any uncertainty in observation. Make comments on the results as they are presented, but save broader generalizations and conclusions for later. Answer the question, "What did I find out?"

Discussing Results and Conclusions

Discuss the importance of what you found in light of the overall study aims. Take a step back from the details and synthesize what has (and has not) been learned about the problem, and what it all means. Describe what you actually found, not what you hoped to find. Begin with specific comments and expand to more general issues. Recommend any improvements for further study. Answer the question, "What is the significance of the research?"

This discussion section is often combined with the results or conclusions section. Decide whether understanding and clarity are improved if you include some discussion as you cover the results. The conclusion should restate the objective, aims, and key questions, and summarize your findings using clear, concise statements. Keep the conclusions section brief and to the point.

Providing References

Within the text, cite references by author and year unless instructed otherwise. In the reference section, list alphabetically only the people and publications that you cite in the report (if none, omit the section). Provide sufficient detail to enable somebody to actually track down the information. List all authors in your publications. Follow a standard format such as the following examples and note the distinctions regarding italics, capitalization, volume and page numbers, publisher address, and other style concerns among the various kinds of references.

The Harvard (author-date) system is the one usually encountered in the sciences and social sciences, and it is the system promoted in professional writing and communication subjects. All examples provided are based on the generally accepted author-date system of referencing.

When you write an assignment, you must cite in your text references to all material you have used as sources for the content of your work. These citations must be made wherever and whenever you quote, paraphrase, or summarize someone else's opinions, theories, or data in the text of your report. References may be to any source from books, periodicals, articles, newspapers, and reports to personal communications. A list of references, in alphabetical order based on authors' surnames, should be attached to your report, giving complete details of the references used in the report.

Unless it is clearly stated otherwise in your report, the citation of another's opinions or conclusions often signifies your acceptance of their point of view as your own. The intention of the original text must not be altered, but if the quotation is provided to indicate that you are aware of differences of opinion or interpretation of data, that should be made clear.

The titles of books, journals, and other major works appear in italics (or may be underlined when handwritten), while the titles of articles and smaller works, which are found in a larger work, are placed in single quotation marks.

For the citations in your text, only the author's surname, year of publication for the material cited, and page numbers, if required, should be listed. Page numbers of your references are necessary only in the event you quote or paraphrase particular passages or provide lists or figures from the sources, as in the following examples:

- Personal (unpublished) communications:
  Cited in the text only, e.g., "... x is recoverable using tool A (Koenick, F, pers. comm.)."

- Lecture notes:
  Garcia, C. K., 2000: The Curriculum Vitae. May 1, 2000 lecture CIS 411/511, CTIN and City University.

- Web site:
  Law Office of Christopher K. Garcia, 2003: Internet: *www.garcialaw.com*.

- Single author journal paper:
  O'Herlighy, T. A., S.J., 2001: Development of Relationships on the Internet. Journal of the Advocate 7, 130-142.

- Multiple author journal paper:
  Noriki, H. W., C. K. Garcia and M. D. Clay. 2002: The Frontline Journal of Aviation 8, 150-152.

- Book:
  Clark, Franklin and Diliberto, Ken. "Investigating Computer Crime," CRC Press, New York, 1996.

13

- Government/technical report:
  2000: The EXAMINATION OF COMPUTERS. Report XYZ-001,
  United States Department of Justice.

- Chapter in an edited volume:
  Pellegrino, A., 2003: Investigation of the Automated Backup Copies of
  Microsoft Applications Files. In Noriki, H. W. Pellegrino, A., Garcia,
  C. K., Koenick, F. eds., Computer Forensics. Thompson Technology, Boston.

Including Appendices

If necessary, one or more appendices containing material such as raw data, figures not used in the body of the report, and anticipated exhibits can be included. Arrange appendices in the order referred to in the report. They are considered as additional material to the report, and may not be examined by the reader at all; some portions of the appendices may be considered optional, but others are required, e.g. the exhibits are required under Rule 26 of the Federal Rules of Civil Procedure as is the curriculum vita (unless bona fides are provided as integrated into the report).

Providing Acknowledgments

Acknowledgments are optional, and generally thank people who directly contributed to the report by providing data, for example, assisting with some part of the analysis, or proofreading. Give credit where credit is due. The acknowledgments are not a dedication, which identifies to whom the author dedicates the work.

FORMAL REPORT FORMAT

If you are working for a law firm, computer forensics firm, a research laboratory, or a law enforcement agency, they have previously established formats for reports. Be sure to get samples from them before beginning.

Remember to project objectivity; your calm detached observations must be what you report. Do not become emotionally involved in the investigation. Do not think in terms of catching somebody or proving something; do not develop an agenda, other than finding the truth. Always try to identify the flaws in your thinking or examination; it is better that you should identify the flaws than to allow opposing counsel to do it for you. It is not your job to win the case. Do not become an advocate for anything other than the truth and your honest objective opinion.

WRITING THE REPORT

With many of the computer forensics software tools such as Forensic ToolKit (FTK) Explorer, DriveSpy, ILook, or EnCase, log files and reports are generated when performing analysis. These reports and logs are typically in plain text format, a word processor format, or in a Web page HTML format. In this section, you will learn how to integrate a computer forensics tool log file or report generator into your official investigation report. It is this final product that you will present to your customer, attorney, or client.

As an example of a report from a computing investigation, you will reexamine a previous case from Chapter 8. In the "Planning Your Investigation" section of Chapter 8, you processed and analyzed a floppy disk using DriveSpy. Now you will analyze and process the same sample case using FTK and its Report Wizard. As in Chapter 8, you will be attempting to find the whereabouts of George and Martha. The key facts about this investigation are:

- George and Martha's absences might or might not be related.

- George's computer might contain information explaining their absence.

- No one else has used George's computer since he disappeared.

- You will need to make a bit-stream image of a floppy disk found on George's desk.

- You will then use FTK to examine the data and create a report using the Report Wizard.

In the following steps, you recreate the floppy disk using the Image program as described in Chapter 8. When you have recreated the duplicate floppy disk, proceed to the next section to process it using the FTK Demo version.

To create an image of the suspect disk using Image:

1. Access a command prompt. Change to the Tools folder in your work folder and run Toolpath.bat.

2. In your work folder, create a **Chap13** folder, if necessary. In the Chap13 folder, create a **Chapter** folder, if necessary. Navigate to the Chap13\Chapter folder and copy **C8InChap.img** from your Data Files to the Chap13\ Chapter folder.

3. Label a blank, formatted floppy disk "Chapter 8 In Chapter" and insert it in the floppy disk drive. At the prompt, type **Image C8InChap.img a:** and press **Enter** to create an image of George's disk on your floppy disk. Image displays the checksum value to verify that the C8InChap.img file is identical to the original disk.

Using FTK Demo Version

Recall that AccessData provides a demo version of their FTK. If you have not already done so, obtain a copy of it by going to *www.accessdata.com* and find the link for downloads, then locate FTK and download the latest demo version for the following exercise.

The following steps guide you through the analysis and report creation process using FTK.

To prepare FTK:

1. Write-protect the floppy disk by moving the write-protect tab to the closed position.

2. In Windows Explorer, create a folder in your work folder called Chap13 and a subfolder called Chapter, if necessary.

3. Start FTK: Click the **Start** button, point to **Programs** or **All Programs**, point to **AccessData**, point to **Forensic Toolkit**, and then click **Forensic Toolkit**.

4. When FTK starts, and the Demo warning banner appears, click **OK**. See Figure 13-4.

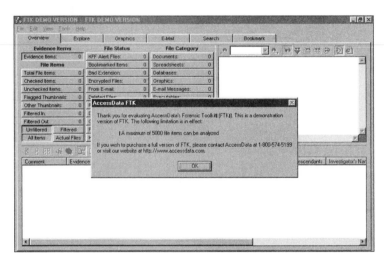

Figure 13-4   AccessData warning banner

5. In the FTK Startup dialog box, click **Start a new case**, and then click **OK** as shown in Figure 13-5.

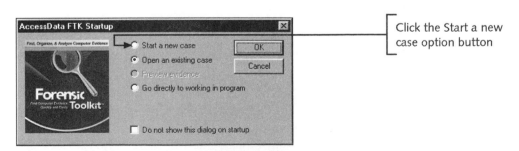

Click the Start a new case option button

Figure 13-5   Starting a new case in AccessData FTK

6. In the New Case dialog box, fill out the appropriate information regarding the case, as shown in Figure 13-6. Then click **Continue**.

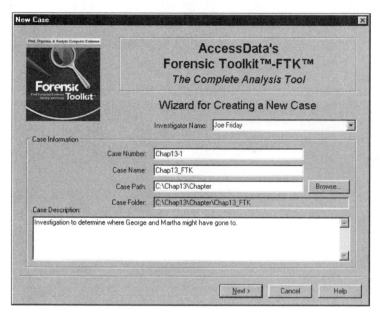

Figure 13-6 New Case window in FTK

7. For the Case Path, click the **Browse** button and navigate to the **Chap13\Chapter** folder in your work folder.

8. In the Case Description text box, type a brief description of the investigation. Then click **Next**.

After you have completed the initial New Case information, you need to complete other specifications about the case before you can start the forensic analysis.

To provide FTK case specifications:

1. In the Case Log Options window shown in Figure 13-7, click **Next**.

2. In the Processes to Perform window shown in Figure 13-8, click **Next**.

3. In the Refine Case – Default window, click **Next**.

4. In the Refine Index – Default window, click **Next**.

5. In the Add Evidence window shown in Figure 13-9, click the **Add Evidence** button.

6. In the Add Evidence to Case dialog box, click the **Local Drive** option button, and then click **Continue**.

13

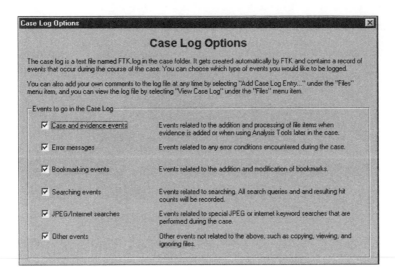

Figure 13-7   Case Log Options window

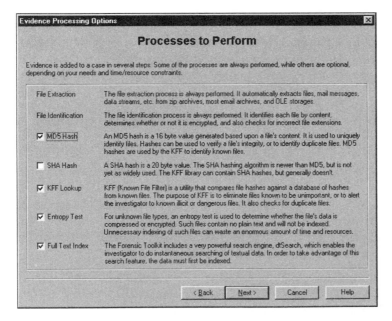

Figure 13-8   Processes to Perform window

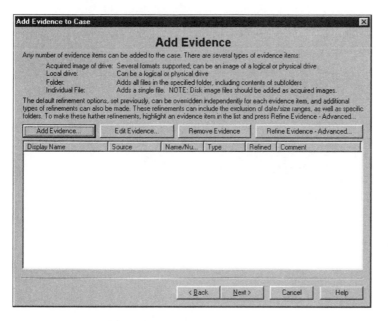

Figure 13-9   Add Evidence window

7. In the Select Local Drive dialog box, make sure the A: drive option and the Logical option button are selected, and then click **OK**.

8. In the Evidence Information window, enter additional comments about this case as shown in Figure 13-10, and then click **OK**.

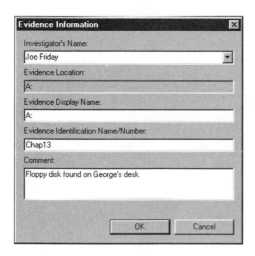

Figure 13-10   Evidence Information window

9. In the Add Evidence window, click **Next**.

10. In the New Case Setup is now Complete window shown in Figure 13-11, verify the specifications. If they are incorrect, click the **Back** button to update the specifications. If they are correct, click **Finish**.

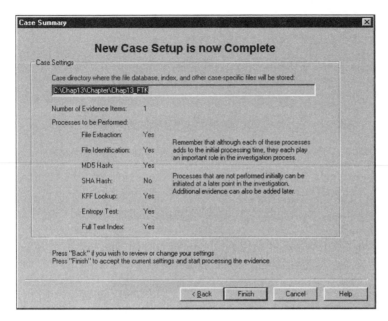

Figure 13-11   New Case Setup is now Complete window

When the FTK Processing Files window shown in Figure 13-12 appears, FTK starts analyzing data on the investigation floppy disk. When it completes, the main FTK window shown in Figure 13-13 appears showing all data sets found from this examination.

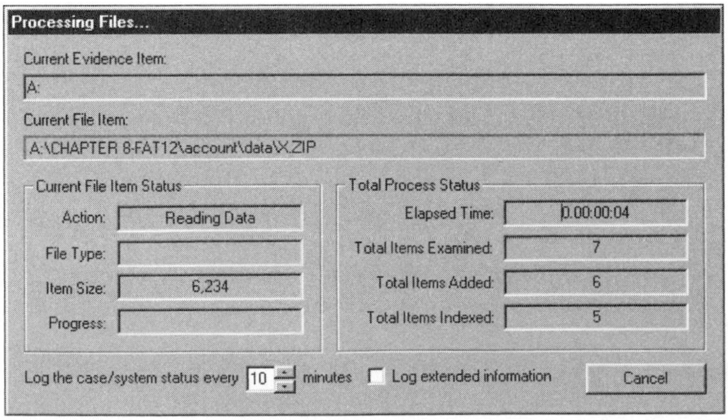

Figure 13-12   Processing Files window

Figure 13-13 FTK main window

Analyzing with FTK

When the processing has completed, locate and extract data from the floppy disk using FTK to process the investigation.

To collect pictures with FTK:

1. In FTK, click the **Graphics** tab, and then check the **List all descendants** box.

2. Click the cat picture in the upper pane, shown in Figure 13-14, and then check the box in the lower pane for the file named **cat.jpg**.

13

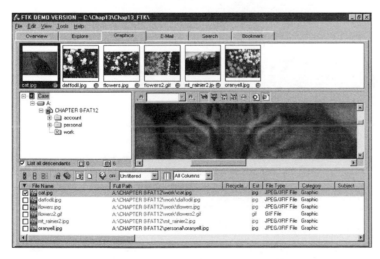

Figure 13-14 FTK graphics on disk

3. Click the mountain picture in the upper pane, shown in Figure 13-15, and then check the box in the lower pane for the file named **mt_rainier2.jpg**.

Figure 13-15   Viewing mt_rainier2.jpg

To locate encrypted files with FTK:

1. Click the **Overview** tab, click the **Encrypted Files** button, shown in Figure 13-16, and then highlight the **X.ZIP** file in the lower pane.

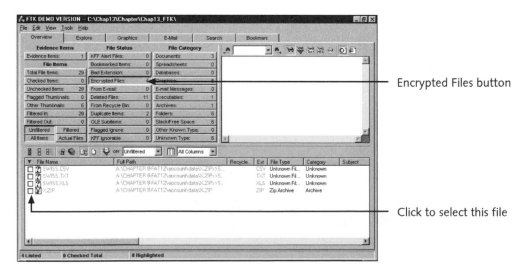

Figure 13-16   Viewing encrypted files

2. Check the box next to file **X.ZIP**.

3. Right-click **X.ZIP** and then click **Export File** on the shortcut menu.

4. Uncheck all boxes located at the bottom of the Export Files dialog box. See Figure 13-17.

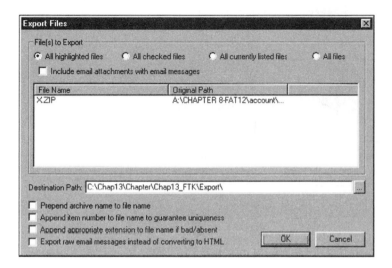

Figure 13-17 Export Files dialog box

5. In the Export Files dialog box, click **OK**, and then click **OK** in the Export Files window message.

Next you will search for any occurrences of specific keywords relating to this investigation. To start searching for the names George and Martha, you will need to access the Search screen of FTK.

To run an indexed search:

1. Click the **Search** tab.

2. In the Search Term text box, type **George** and then click **Add**.

3. In the Search Term text box, type **Martha** and then click **Add**. Your window should resemble Figure 13-18.

4. Click **View Cumulative Results**, and then click **OK** in the Retrieve Search Hits dialog window.

5. In the upper-right window, click the plus sign to expand the search results.

6. Check the three boxes in the lower pane. See Figure 13-19.

In the results of the Indexed Search, examine all text message contents. From this examination, you should find references to Zurich and money. To continue the investigation, try a Live Search for the keyword of Account.

13

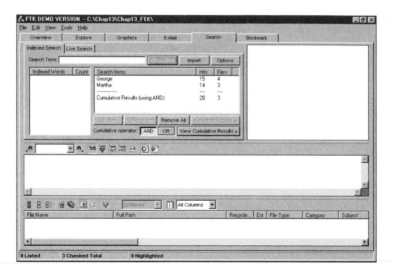

Figure 13-18   Cumulative results for George and Martha

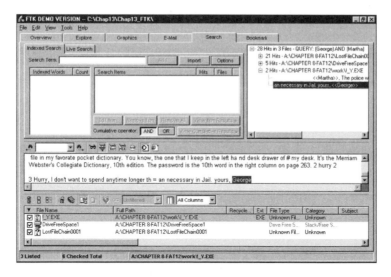

Figure 13-19   Expanded search results

To run a live search:

1. In the Search pane, click the **Live Search** tab.

2. In the Search Term text box, type the keyword **Account** then click **Add**. Click **Search**, and then click **OK** in the Retrieve Search Hits dialog box.

3. When the search completes, click **View Results** in the Live Search Progress dialog box.

4. In the upper-right pane, click all plus signs to expand the search results. See Figure 13-20.

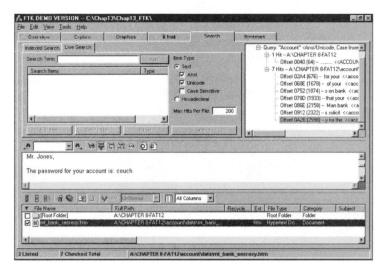

Figure 13-20   Expanded live search

5. Read the contents of these search results to find additional information that might support the investigation.

To minimize the data you are looking at, click "View files in filtered text format." See if you can locate a possible password from this latest keyword search. Next you will learn how to bookmark the data you have checked for your report.

Filter buttons for FTK data viewing are shown in Figure 13-21.

13

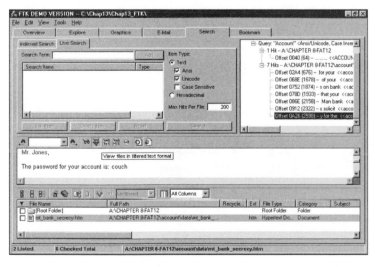

Figure 13-21   Filtered data

To bookmark investigation findings:

1. Right-click any file that has been checked, and then click **Create Bookmark** on the shortcut menu. See Figure 13-22.

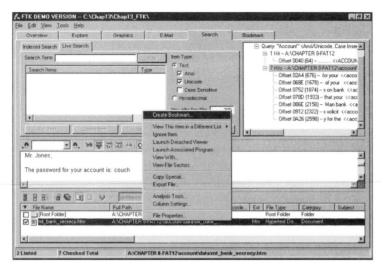

Figure 13-22   Creating a bookmark

2. In the Create New Bookmark dialog box, in the Bookmark name text box, type **Ch13_search_results**. Click **All checked items**, and then check the **Include in report** and **Export files boxes**.

3. In the Bookmark comment window, type any comments that describe this particular bookmark. See Figure 13-23. Then click **OK**.

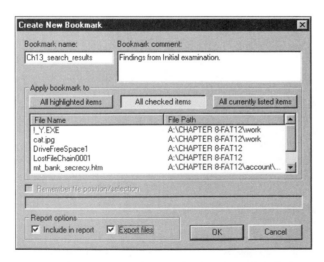

Figure 13-23   Completing the bookmark information

After you have bookmarked specific data of interest to the investigation, you can generate a report of your findings. The FTK Report Wizard has a feature that allows you to insert other documents into the final FTK report. Later in this section, you will learn how to add these other documents, including your narrative report, to the FTK HTML report. Any Web browser such as Netscape and Internet Explorer can read the HTML report created by FTK.

The next step is to write a narrative report of what you found on the floppy disk. This narrative should follow the recommendations previously discussed in this chapter for your report's contents. To review your findings for this investigation follow these recommended steps.

To review case findings in FTK:

1. Click the **Overview** tab of FTK and then click the **Checked Items** button.

2. In the lower pane, click the first file **!_Y.EXE**. See Figure 13-24.

Figure 13-24   Viewing selected items

3. In the upper-right pane, scroll down and read the contents of the bookmark, and make note of its contents for your report.

4. To locate a specific keyword with the data set that is displayed in the upper-right pane, type the keyword value in the Search text box.

5. Repeat Steps 2 and 3 and examine each file. Note the password in the file mt_bank_secrecy.htm, shown in Figure 13-25.

6. To view graphic files, click the **Internet Explorer** icon located above the upper-right pane.

7. To view binary files such as X.ZIP, click the **HEX** icon located above the upper-right pane.

Figure 13-25   Locating a specific keyword

To review your findings, note that you discovered the following facts from this analysis. In the first file you found several text messages that appear to be correspondence between a Martha James and George Jones. In this file you find that there are key elements that will require further examination. Of specific interest are the words:

- Encrypted this file

- Flee when the auditor finds the missing money

- Meet me in Zurich

- Merriam Webster Collegiate Dictionary, as shown in Figure 13-26.

The next data set of interest is LostFileCluster0001, shown in Figure 13-27. This is data located in a cluster that became corrupt for unknown reasons. The link in the File Allocation Table (FAT) has lost any reference to this cluster. Within this lost cluster there is reference to a vacation in the mountains. Words of specific interest for this data set are:

- Vacation

- I have a plan to pay for vacation

- Wait until we can talk in private

Mrge

Dr.

deposits. I encrypted this file so as to prevent an yone from reading

them. If I have to flee when the auditor finds the missing mo ney, you

can meet me in Zurich % on the 19 of January. yours devotedly, Ge +

orge,

Martha, The police will be here any minute. You can f

ind the password for the encrypted

 file in my favorate pocket dictionary. You know, the one that I keep in

the left ha nd desk drawer of # my desk. It's the Merriam Webster's

Collegiate Dictionary, 10th edition. The password is the 10th word in

the right column on page 263. 2 hurry 2

3 Hurry, I don't want to spend anytime longer th = an necessary in

Jail. yours, George

13

Figure 13-26   Text recovered from the floppy disk

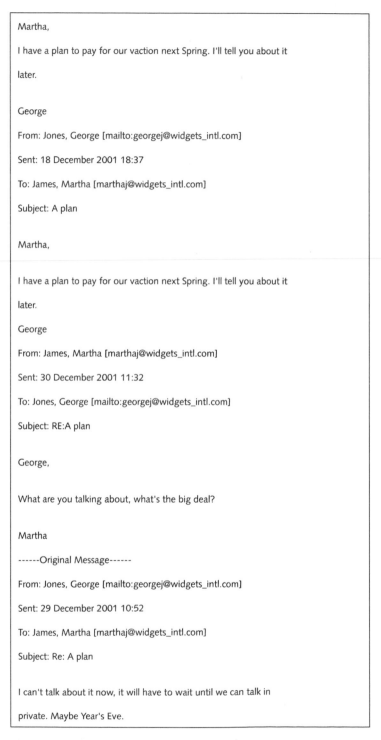

Martha,

I have a plan to pay for our vaction next Spring. I'll tell you about it

later.

George

From: Jones, George [mailto:georgej@widgets_intl.com]

Sent: 18 December 2001 18:37

To: James, Martha [marthaj@widgets_intl.com]

Subject: A plan

Martha,

I have a plan to pay for our vaction next Spring. I'll tell you about it

later.

George

From: James, Martha [marthaj@widgets_intl.com]

Sent: 30 December 2001 11:32

To: Jones, George [mailto:georgej@widgets_intl.com]

Subject: RE:A plan

George,

What are you talking about, what's the big deal?

Martha

------Original Message------

From: Jones, George [mailto:georgej@widgets_intl.com]

Sent: 29 December 2001 10:52

To: James, Martha [marthaj@widgets_intl.com]

Subject: Re: A plan

I can't talk about it now, it will have to wait until we can talk in

private. Maybe Year's Eve.

Figure 13-27 Contents of LostFileCluster0001

The next data set of interest is file mt_bank_secrecy.htm. This appears to be an HTML file that contains a message. Of interest for this data set is reference to a password for an account at Isle of Man Saving & Loan.

```
Mr. Jones,

The password for your account is: couch

Please let us know if you need anything else.

Regards,

Sigor Krautfletz

Isle of Man Saving & Loan
```

The last data set of interest is the file X.ZIP. This is a zip file that contains three files, which have the same name of Swiss but with different extensions. Recall earlier that you had exported this file with FTK. FTK creates a subfolder named Export where it automatically copies exported data for your forensics examination. See Figure 13-28.

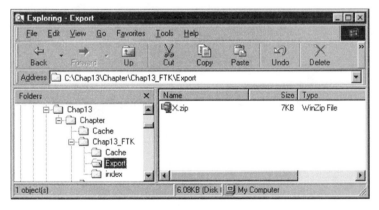

Figure 13-28   Creating a subfolder

Using WinZip or PKUnzip, attempt to extract the content of X.ZIP for your follow-up examination. If an error occurs when extracting this file, you may have forgotten to uncheck the "Prepend archive name to file name" and "Append item number to file name to guarantee uniqueness" boxes in the Export Files window in FTK. If you do encounter an error, open FTK and export X.ZIP again with all boxes unchecked.

File X.ZIP is a password-protected PKZip file. Recall from your examination there was reference to a password for a bank account. Try that password to see if it will successfully open this compressed archive file.

After you have successfully unzipped the password protected file X.ZIP you can continue your examination. At this time you can inspect the content of all three files that were extracted. Depending on the office application you have available, open one of the three files to view their contents. Figure 13-29 shows the contents of file Swiss.xls.

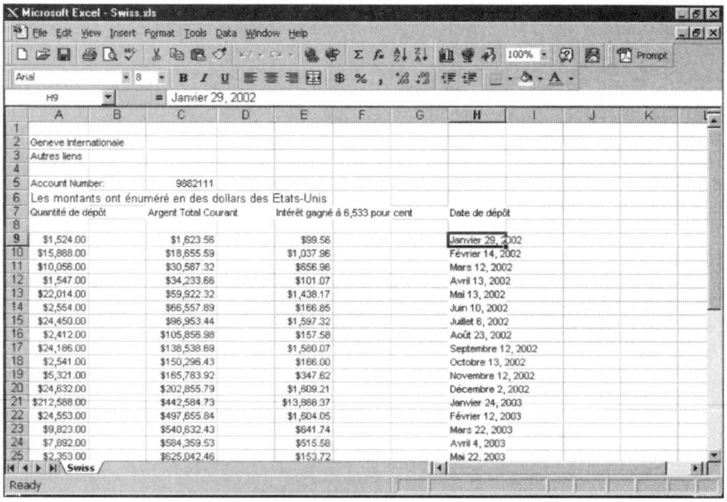

Figure 13-29   Contents of file Swiss.xls

This file is a spreadsheet that appears to contain deposits entries from January 2002 through December 2004. Note also the language appears to be French and the bank name is Geneve Internationale.

Now that you have completed your examination, write a brief narrative of your findings. An example of this might be as follows:

Narrative report:

On January 10, 2005 I examined a floppy disk drive for Widgets International. This examination was predicated on information that management of Widget International were concerned about the whereabouts of two employees that had been absent from work for over two days. No additional information about the circumstances of the missing employees was provided to me.

Widget International security department provided the following information about their concerns. The missing employees are George Popson and Martha Heiser. Mr. Popson works in the Accounts Payable department. Ms. Heiser is the executive secretary for Mr. Thompson, Senior Vice President of Marketing for Widget International.

Upon receiving the floppy disk from Mr. Wilson Smith of Widget International's Security Department, I immediately made a duplicate bit-stream image copy of the floppy using Digital Intelligence Image program. When the image copy was completed, I returned it to Mr. Smith for his retention.

Following the creation of the bit-stream image copy of the floppy disk, I created a working copy of the saved image file. I examined the content of the floppy disk using AccessData Forensics Toolkit (FTK) to determine what was contained on the disk.

With FTK I located several text messages that appear to be e-mail correspondence between a George Jones and Martha James. The date and time stamps of these messages show activity on December 2001. I could not determine whether the computer used to record these messages had the correct time and dates on its internal clock.

Further examination of the contents of the messages revealed that George Jones may have had financial problems. Later messages revealed that he had resolved his financial dilemma but did not state how. Additional messages indicate that George Jones was concerned about the police arresting him due to undisclosed activity.

While examining the disk for other facts I found a hidden Zip file that was password protected. Also found was a Web message from an offshore bank, Isle of Man Saving and Loan, that contained a password. The password in this message is "couch."

I extracted the file X.ZIP with FTK and was successful in extracting all of its contents with the same password from the Web message HTML file, mt_bank_secrecy.htm.

The file X.ZIP contained three files that appear to be different formats of the same spreadsheet. Content of the spreadsheet shows what appear to be deposits to a Swiss bank, Geneve International. The dates in these spreadsheets appear to be French.

The date and time stamps for the file mt_bank_secrecy.htm show that the file was created on February 15, 2003, but the last entry of deposit transaction shows December 2004. The discrepancies of this date and time value along with the date and time stamps for the email messages appear that the computer used to generate these files may not be running correctly. Because of this the accuracy of when these files where created can not be verified.

For additional information on data recovered for this examination see the FTK HTML report.

After completing the narrative of the case, you now must run FTK Report Wizard to integrate all components such as evidence and reports into the final HTML document.

To run the FTK Report Wizard:

1. In the FTK main window, click **File** on the menu bar, and then click **Report Wizard**. The Report Wizard starts and opens the FTK Report Wizard – Case Information window.

2. Enter the appropriate information about the case, as shown in Figure 13-30, and then click **Next**.

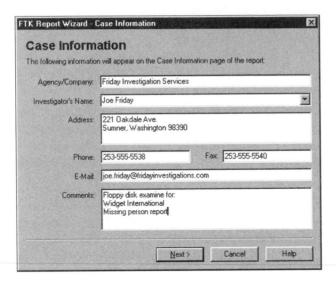

Figure 13-30   Report Wizard - Case Information window

3. In the FTK Report Wizard – Bookmarks – A dialog box, click **Next** to accept the default options.

4. In the FTK Report Wizard – Bookmarks – B dialog box, click **Next** to accept the default options.

5. In the FTK Report Wizard – Graphic Thumbnails dialog box, if you are using FTK version 1.32 or later, check the **Export full-size graphics and link them to the thumbnails** box, as shown in Figure 13-31. Then click **Next**.

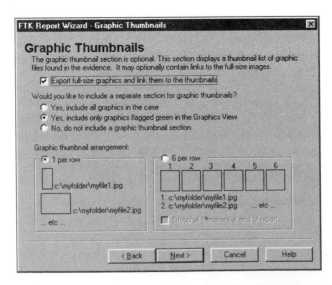

Figure 13-31   Report Wizard - Graphic Thumbnails dialog box

6. In the FTK Report Wizard – List by File Path dialog box, check the **Include a list by file path section in the report** box and the **Include in the report** and **Export to the report** boxes, as shown in Figure 13-32, and then click **Next**.

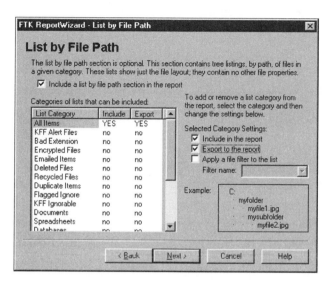

Figure 13-32 Report Wizard - List by File Path dialog box

7. In the FTK Report Wizard – List by File Properties – A dialog box, click **Next** to accept the default options.

8. In the FTK Report Wizard – Case Audit Files dialog box, click **Add Files** and navigate to Chap13\Chapter folder in your work folder.

9. In Windows Explorer, unzip the extracted file, if necessary. Copy **Chap_13_ narrative.rtf** from Chap13\Chapter to the Export folder. In the Open dialog box, press and hold down the **Ctrl** key, click files **Chap_13_narrative.rtf** and **Swiss.xls**, and then click **Open**.

10. In the FTK Report Wizard – Case Audit Files dialog box, click **Next**.

11. In the FTK Report Wizard – Report Location dialog box, click **Finish**.

When the wizard completes processing, click Yes to view the report from your Web browser. To open the report in Windows Explorer, double-click **Index.html** in the Chap13\Chap13_FTK\Report folder in your work folder, as shown in Figure 13-33.

13

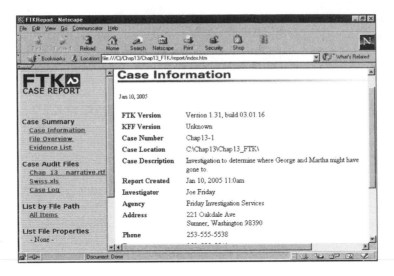

Figure 13-33   Final report

CHAPTER SUMMARY

- Deposition banks or libraries are used by lawyers to see examples of an expert witnesses' previous testimony.

- Reports are critical to your investigations because they communicate your computer forensics findings and other information to the necessary authorities.

- Reports can be formal or informal, verbal or written. Consult with an attorney before creating a report because anything created can be requested for observation.

- You must help the reader by giving signposts.

- Clarity of writing is critical to the success of a report.

- Reports need to be grammatically sound, use correct spelling, and be free of writing errors. Avoid jargon, slang, or colloquial terms.

- Project objectivity; be detached in your observations for your report.

- For your report, stand back from the details and synthesize what has (and has not) been learned about the problem, and what it all means.

KEY TERMS

discovery—The efforts to obtain information before a trial by demanding documents, depositions, questions and answers written under oath, written requests for admissions of fact, and the examination of the scene, for example.

examination plan—The plan laying out the strategy created by the attorney to try a case.

high-risk document—A document that contains sensitive information that could create an advantage for the opposing attorney.

lay witness—A witness not considered an expert in a particular field.

spoliation—Destroying or concealing evidence.

verbal formal report—A structured report delivered in person to a board of directors or managers or to a jury.

verbal informal report—A report that is less structured than a formal report and is delivered in person, usually in an attorney's office.

written formal report—A written report sworn under oath, such as an affidavit or declaration.

written informal report—An informal or preliminary report in written form.

13

14

BECOMING
AN EXPERT WITNESS

> ### After reading this chapter, you will be able to:
> ♦ Compare technical and scientific testimony
> ♦ Prepare for testimony
> ♦ Testify in court
> ♦ Testify during cross-examination
> ♦ Prepare for a deposition
> ♦ Form an expert opinion

The types of testimony by professionals at any trial, deposition, or hearing can be divided into two categories: technical or scientific witness testimony and expert witness testimony. Computer forensic examiners need to be aware of the differences between these types of testimony as they prepare for any type of litigation. This chapter explains how to become an expert witness and how to avoid problems when giving testimony.

COMPARING TECHNICAL AND SCIENTIFIC TESTIMONY

When cases go to trial, you as the forensic expert play one of two roles: you are either called as a **technical witness** or as an **expert witness**. As a technical or scientific witness, you are only providing the facts as you have found them in your investigation. That is, you present any evidence you found that contributes to resolution of the incident or crime. When you provide technical or scientific testimony, you present this evidence and explain what it is and how it was obtained. You do not offer conclusions, only the facts.

However, as an expert, you have opinions about what you observe. You can base these opinions on experience, allowing you to use deductive reasoning with facts found during an investigation or examination of a digital system. In fact, it is your opinion that makes you an expert witness.

Because computer forensics is a relatively new field, it is not yet governed by standards of practice, as is the field of electronics or network protocols. A computer forensics examiner who serves as an expert witness provides opinion on the evidence that contributes to the litigation.

PREPARING FOR TESTIMONY

If you are called as a technical or expert witness in a computer forensics case, you need to thoroughly prepare for your testimony. Establish communication early on with your attorney. Learn the general concepts of the case before you start processing and examining the evidence. Keep in mind that criminal investigations have slightly different requirements than civil litigation needs; your attorney can provide specific guidelines.

As an expert witness, you work for the attorney, not the client (plaintiff or defendant). The attorney and his or her client are dedicated to their case; if you obtain negative findings, communicate them as soon as possible to the attorney.

When preparing to testify for any litigation, substantiate your findings with your own documentation and by collaborating with other computer forensics professionals. Return to the notes you took during your investigation. If you are working with electronic notes, use care in storing them. In your analysis and reporting, develop and maintain a standard method of processing to minimize or eliminate any confusion and to help you prepare for testimony later. Computer forensics is only now developing a peer review process as the number of experts increases. In many instances to get peer review, you either have to search outside of your region or approach the Federal Bureau of Investigation (FBI). Learn to take advantage of your professional network and request peer reviews to help support your findings.

While you should recognize when conflict of interest issues apply to your case and discuss any concerns or issues with the attorney that hires you, also be aware of a practice called conflict out. This is an attempt to prevent you from being used by another attorney on an important case, and is most common in the private sector when you work as an independent consultant. Opposing attorneys might call and discuss the case with you, only to have you excluded from the case by the attorney needing your service. By doing this, they have created a conflict of interest for you and the other attorney trying the case. Avoid agreeing to review a case unless you are under contract and ready to process it. Also avoid conversation with opposing attorneys—there is no such thing as an "off the record" conversation with opposing attorneys.

Documenting and Preparing Evidence

Document your steps; make sure they are repeatable if challenged. When you gather and preserve technical evidence, make sure what you have done can be repeated. Without the ability to repeat your processes, your findings lose credibility as evidence. This applies to all computer evidence. As emphasized in earlier chapters, always preserve the evidence you find and document how you preserved the evidence.

Validate your tools and use Message Digest 5 (MD5) or Secure Hash Algorithm, version 1 (SHA-1) to perform hash checks on evidence before and after to insure its integrity.

Do not create a formal checklist of your procedures or integrate a checklist into your final reports because opposing counsel can easily challenge a checklist.

Keeping Consistent Work Habits

As a practice, collect your evidence and record the tools you used in designated file folders. This helps in maintaining the organization of your evidence and the tools you used. Follow a system in your office or laboratory to record where items are kept for each case and how documentation is stored.

Remember the chain of custody of evidence supports the integrity of your evidence; do whatever you can to prevent contamination of the evidence. Document any lapse in evidence preservation or custody. Lapses do not necessarily result in the inadmissibility of the evidence, but might affect the amount of importance given to the evidence.

You should use research and intelligence-gathering methods to acquire necessary supporting information when preparing your testimony. For example, the Internet can help you find preliminary information to support your investigation and examination.

You can also use the Internet to learn about the opposing expert and to try to find their strengths and weaknesses in previous testimony. See how they present themselves and print their curriculum vita, if possible. Your attorney may be able to obtain copies of depositions that the opposing witness has given in other cases. Many attorneys are members of organizations that maintain **deposition banks** that contain thousands of depositions. Some organizations of digital investigators can also maintain listservs that allow you to query members about various firms or expert witnesses.

When collecting evidence, be careful not to get too little or too much information. Remember that for litigation, you are only responsible for collecting what is asked for, no more. In some circumstances, collecting and identifying evidence or problems unrelated to the case may cause problems for your attorney.

Note the date and time of your forensic workstation when initiating your analysis. Use an Internet clock to verify the accuracy of your workstation's clock.

Processing Evidence

As you process evidence, be sure to always monitor, preserve, and validate your work. Doing so helps to ensure it can be presented in court.

Recall that you should not have a standard checklist that you follow. If you need a checklist to analyze evidence in a case, create the checklist for a specific analysis, not one that can be applied to any other cases. If opposing counsel obtains a checklist through discovery that has been used on previous examinations and analysis, it can be used against you.

Keep only successful output when running analysis tools; don't keep previous runs, such as those missing necessary switch settings or output settings of your software tools.

Whenever possible, use SHA-1 to validate your evidence. Only use MD5 or CRC32 if SHA-1 is unavailable because it uses a higher level of computation. When examining evidence disks or files, perform an MD5 or SHA-1 hash check before and after your examination of the evidence to ensure nothing was altered during your data collection.

When searching for keyword results, rerun searches with well-defined search parameters. You may even want to state how they relate to the case such as a business or personal name or nickname. Narrow the search so that you eliminate any false hits. Eliminate previous search results that contain false-positive hits from your final output.

When taking notes of your findings, keep your notations simple and specific to the investigation. You should avoid any personal comments or ideas in your note taking so as to minimize any need to explain to opposing counsel what you had written. Recall that you only state your "opinion" when appearing as an expert witness in court.

When writing your report, only list evidence findings that are relevant to the case. That is, list only those things that you find; do not include unrelated findings.

Serving as a Consulting Expert or an Expert Witness

Depending on the attorney's needs, you might only need to provide your opinion and technical expertise to the attorney, and not testify in court. You may be initially hired as a consulting expert, but your role may become that of an expert witness later in the case. If that happens, all of your previous work as a consulting expert becomes discoverable.

Because your work might be discovered, or formally requested by a court officer, do not record conversations or telephone calls. Doing so might create more work for you and the hiring attorney to explain than what is necessary for the case.

When presenting yourself to a federal court as an expert witness, federal rules require that you provide the following information as presented in Chapter 13:

- Four years of previous testimony you may have provided, which indicates that you have experience at trial

- Ten years of any published writings

- Previous compensation you may have received when giving testimony

When preparing for your testimony, learn about the victim, the complainant, opposing expert or technical and scientific witnesses, and the opposing attorney as soon as possible. Learn what the basic points of the dispute are. As you learn about the case for which you will testify, take notes, but keep them in rough draft form, recording only the facts and keeping your notations to a minimum.

Define any procedures you use to conduct your analysis as scientific and conforming to the standards of your profession. Pointing to textbooks, technical books, articles by recognized experts, and procedures by responsible and authoritative agencies or companies are common ways to prove your conformity with scientific and professional standards.

When approached to give expert testimony, find out if you are the first one asked. If you are not the first person contacted, find out why other experts may have rejected the assignment.

Creating and Maintaining Your CV

Recall from Chapter 13 that your **curriculum vita (CV)** is used to qualify your testimony and tells your professional life story. As a forensic specialist, it is crucial that you keep this document updated at all times to substantiate your role as an expert. Organize your CV so that it supports your testimony as an expert—it should reflect that you are continuously enhancing your skills through training, teaching, and experience.

In your CV, detail your job tasks to define specific accomplishments and your basic and advanced skills. Also indicate the professional training you received. List your colleagues and fellow trainees as referrals and contacts. (However, you do not need to impress the court by listing important or influential people.) If the list of your training is lengthy or difficult to complete, introduce the list using language such as "Selected Training Attended." Be sure to include course work that was sponsored by government agencies or organizations that train government agencies personnel, or sponsored or approved by professional associations, such as bar associations. Make sure that your CV reflects you professionally and, unlike a job resume, should not be geared for the specific trial.

Keep a separate list of books read on your specialized area of expertise, but don't include your reading list on the CV. Books read and listed on a CV may suggest that you approve of everything written in every book on the list.

Make sure that you include a testimony log in your CV, which records every testimony you have given as an expert. Most of all, keep the CV current and date it for version control. If your CV is more than three months old, you probably need to update it to reflect new cases and additional training.

14

Preparing Technical Definitions

Before you testify in court, prepare definitions of technical material so that you can provide them as answers when questioned by your attorney and the opposing attorney. When preparing your definitions, use your own words and language that the jury, which typically averages an eighth-grade education, can understand. You do not need to make the jury a subject matter expert, but only explain how a tool works.

The following are examples of definitions to prepare ahead of time for your testimony:

- Computer forensics
- CRC32, MD5, and SHA-1 hash functions
- Image and bit-stream backup
- File slack and unallocated (free) space
- File date and time stamps
- Computer log files

TESTIFYING IN COURT

Before you are called to testify in court, become familiar with the usual procedures followed during a trial. First your attorney demonstrates to the court that you are competent as an expert or technical witness. The opposing counsel may attempt to discredit you or may choose not to based on your past record. Your attorney then leads you through the evidence followed by the opposing counsel cross-examining you.

Understanding the Trial Process

The typical order of trial proceedings is as follows:

1. *Motion in Limine*–Special hearing on admissibility of evidence or limitation of evidence, (typically done a day or two before the beginning of trial, but always before formal trial begins). Effectively, this is a written list of objections to certain testimony or exhibits. It allows the judge to examine whether certain evidence should be admitted out of the presence of the jury.

2. *Opening statement*–Provides an overview of case.

3. *Plaintiff*–Plaintiff presents case.

4. *Defendant*–Defendant presents case.

5. *Rebuttal*–Rebuttal from both plaintiff and defense.

6. *Jury instructions*–Instructions proposed by counsel and approved and read to the jury by the judge.

7. *Closing arguments*–Statements that organize the evidence and the law.

There are three types of communications in a trial: visual communications, which are the most significant, voice quality, and verbal skills. To be an expert witness and present opinion testimony, you must possess special skills and knowledge not available to the ordinary person.

Verdicts at trials can be attributed in part to jury character, attorneys' communications skills, jury's instructions, but the most significant factor is evidence presented in trial.

During the trial, be conscious of the jury, judge, and the attorneys; try to learn what their knowledge and attitudes are relating to computers and technology.

If asked a question that you do not have an answer for, respond by saying, "That is beyond the scope of my expertise" or "I was not requested to investigate that." These statements make it clear that you understand your limitations. Everybody has limitations; you will not appear to be less an expert for knowing and expressing your limitations. If anything, expressing your limitations will enhance your standing with a jury.

Qualifying Your Testimony and Voir Dire

Your attorney—usually the plaintiff's attorney—calls you for your testimony. The qualification phase of your testimony is when your attorney demonstrates your expertise that makes you an expert witness. It puts you above your competition and sets you apart from other expert witnesses with the jury. This qualification process is called **voir dire** (from French, literally "to see, to say").

The court may appoint its own expert witnesses. Court-appointed expert witnesses must be neutral in their initial position and opinion, and they must be knowledgeable about their profession. As an expert hired by the defense or plaintiff, you will need to evaluate the court's expert. You will need to brief your attorney on your findings and opinion of the court's expert to help your attorney to better deal with the case and any testimony provided by the court-appointed expert.

A tactic used by opposing attorneys is to attempt to have you disqualified as a witness. At trial the attorney that hired you qualifies you as an expert by guiding you through your CV. After your attorney has completed his or her examination on your qualifications, he or she asks the court to accept you as an expert on computer forensics. However, opposing counsel may object and is allowed to examine you also.

If you have especially strong qualifications and have been qualified as an expert on several occasions, opposing counsel might offer to accept you as an expert without the necessity of formal qualification. Your attorney will generally eschew that opportunity in favor of impressing the jury with your qualifications.

Addressing Potential Problems

Early in direct examination, the attorney should ask you if you were hired to do analysis and to testify. The attorney may ask you how much you charged for your services. He or she will also ask you if you have already been paid; you should receive payment before testifying. If you have not been paid, it may appear that you have a contingent interest in the litigation. Fees and payment schedules are an appropriate subject area for examination. If your attorney does not ask you questions about payment, the opposing counsel will, and will attempt to make the most of it.

Testifying in General

A scientific or technical witness testifies to facts. An expert witness gives an opinion for testifying. When you are serving in either capacity, be professional and polite when presenting yourself to any attorney or the court. If you don't understand a question or find it confusing, simply say, "Can you please rephrase the question?" This will typically get the attorney to reorganize the question. This is one method you can use to control the attorney. When presenting yourself, always pay tribute to the jury. Always put enthusiasm in your testimony, keep the jury interested in what you have to say, be sincere.

Be aware of leading questions, especially from the opposing attorney. An ambiguous question of "Isn't it true that forensics experts always destroy their handwritten notes?" is an attempt to lead you to say something that could be construed as wrong. Leading questions like this are referred to as "set up questions."

When giving expert testimony, avoid over-reaching opinions. Part of what you have to deliver to the jury is a person (you) that they can trust to help them figure out something that is beyond their expertise. To overreach or overstate will create distrust with the jury; like a teacher you should admit your limitations and the limitations of your results.

When testifying, build repetition into your explanations and descriptions for the jury. To enhance your image with the jury, dress in a manner that conforms to the dress code for the community. For example, clothing that is black, dark green, and yellow may not be appropriate. In a small a town, dress like the local bank manager or in clothes that are similar to what the attorneys are wearing. If your testimony is being videotaped, avoid fine stripes in suits or ties.

Presenting Your Evidence

For direct examinations, state your opinion, first identify evidence to support your opinion, and then relate the method you used to arrive at your opinion from your analysis. Restate your opinion, and never carry on with a lengthy build up. Books and other documentation are useful but are not considered authoritative for testimony.

As an expert witness, you have to keep in mind your audience. You have a judge who is well educated, but not necessarily in the field of digital evidence. The juries, as stated earlier, typically average an eighth-grade education. The attorneys may have a thorough background or foundation in the field, but you are the expert with experience. You also may be dealing with an arbiter or mediator who may or may not have a background in computer forensics.

When preparing for trial, make ready your testimony, assist in cross-examination of opposing (hostile) expert witness, and testify yourself. Be prepared to defend your opinion with testifying in trial or deposition. Find out as much as possible about the opposing attorney and expert.

Consider the following questions when preparing your testimony:

- What is my story of the case?
- What can I say with confidence?
- What is the client's overall theory of the case?
- How does my opinion support the case?
- What is the scope of the case? Have I gone too far?
- Have I identified the client's desires?

Recall that you should have definitions ready for MD5, CRC32, checksum, and SHA-1. You should familiarize yourself with the principles of electromagnetic theory to explain how data is stored on a disk drive. Learn how to describe the tools you use as a standardized practice or process flow for your work. Remember to state your descriptions so that a nontechnical person could understand them. Learn how to overwhelm the opposing counsel with answers that they will have difficulty in attacking. Learn the fallibility of computer forensics to better resist counter-attacks from opposing counsel. Lengthy explanation may be good for some jury cases but not for others, so seek your attorney's opinion.

When called upon to provide testimony for a case, prepare it with the attorney that will be trying the case. This will optimize the necessary communications between you and your attorney. The following are specific questions you should prepare for:

- How is data (or evidence) stored on a hard disk drive?
- What is an image or a bit-stream copy of a disk drive?
- How is deleted data recovered from a disk drive?
- What are Windows temporary files and how do they relate to data or evidence?
- What are system or network log files?

When being called to testify, do not talk to anyone during court recess. If the opposing attorney sees you having a conversation with anyone, including the attorney you represent, the opposing attorney could cross-examine you again and demand that you explain and repeat your conversation. However, be aware that your attorney may want to notify you of any updates during breaks.

Using Graphics in Your Testimony

Create graphical exhibits such as charts and tables that illustrate and clarify your findings. Make sure the jury can see your graphics, and face the jury as you present the graphics.

Practice using charts for courtroom testimony. Your exhibits must be clear and easy to understand. Exhibits should be big and bold so the jury can see them easily.

If necessary, make smaller copies of your graphics for each jury member so they can see any details better. When talking about specific areas of your graphic artwork, use a pointer. When creating graphics, provide information the jury needs to know, how the mechanics of the hardware and software work, the role the evidence has in relation to the case, and an explanation of the evidence findings for the case.

Helping Your Attorney

Talk to local attorneys to learn more about the type of people typically serving on a jury, gauge your presentation to the jury's education level, use the jury's education level when giving testimony, and use parallel examples for your explanations.

To help your attorney prepare for the direct examination, prepare a list of questions that you feel are important. This will help the attorney to get your testimony into the trial. It will also help your attorney review and improve on how he or she wants to try the case. It will also provide you the needed practice in your testimony for the direct examination.

When preparing your testimony for direct examination, develop a script and work with your attorney to get right language that will most effectively communicate your message to the jury.

You will never get enough information about the case. After your testimony, you may be called back to critique your work, update your testimony log in your CV, or as a rebuttal witness.

Avoiding Testimony Problems

Always be an impartial expert witness not an advocate, be clear about your opinion, and define your boundaries of knowledge and ethics if necessary. Always build a business case for the justification of such things as graphics that will improve your testimony, which may be considered an unnecessary expense. Build a case outline and summary for the attorney. You and the attorney can use this to review your plan and to make sure he or she understands what your level of knowledge is about the case. Learn how you are expected to perform for the your attorney and how you fit in to the case. Make your best effort to coordinate your testimony with other experts also retained by your attorney in support of the case. Make time with the attorney to ensure that he or she knows all the facts and your opinion. Meet with paralegal to communicate necessary information to your attorney. And, above all, don't lie.

Take time to tutor the attorney on the technology you are an expert on, create memorandums and list important items by bullets, and build a glossary for technical terms.

Testifying During Direct Examination

While many cases never make it to court, you provide direct testimony when you testify on behalf of the attorney who hired you. The direct examination is the most important part of testimony at a trial. Cross-examination is not as important even if the opposing attorney is attempting to discredit you. There are some effective direct testimony techniques to use.

State your background and qualifications relating to why you are an expert able to give testimony. Provide a clear overview of your findings. Create a systematic and easy to follow plan for describing your evidence collection methods. Balance between technical language and layperson language when describing complex matters. Remember to gauge your speech to the education level of the jury.

Be prepared by knowing the following facts and issues before giving testimony.

- *Independent recollection*–Things that you know about this case and others without being prompted.

- *Customary practice*–Things that are traditionally done in similar cases.

- *Documentation of the case*–The actual written records that you have maintained.

When questioned, give the answers you need to bring attention to your factual findings and opinion, looking at the jury to keep them engaged with your answers. Prepare with your attorney for your testimony. When standing in court, keep your elbows bent and hands above your waist. Remember to project your voice when speaking. Always create, before testifying, a list of questions for your attorney. Your attorney will use these questions for his or her direct examination of you. Practice testifying with your graphics and always let the jury see your face when working with your graphics.

If you have to draw something and explain it in detail, do one thing at a time, that is, draw, turn toward the jury and give your explanation. Sometimes opposing attorneys will do this in an attempt to make you look stupid in front of the jury. Keep in mind that you are basically instructing them in what you had to do to obtain the evidence. Play the part of a good teacher for the jury.

When you meet before a trial or deposition to discuss the case, your attorney might advise you to be wary of your inclination to be helpful. This natural trait can hurt you when testifying. You should not volunteer any information or be overly friendly (or hostile) to the opposing attorney. Your attorney might also help you develop a theme to follow when presenting your testimony. Use your own words and phrases when answering questions. If you are asked whether you perform tasks the same way on every case, respond by saying, "That is my practice, to do it that way." In court, the best approach your attorney can take is to ask you, "then what?" and then let you give your expert testimony.

The key to successful cross-examination is to continue selling yourself to the jury no matter how much the opposing attorney tries to discredit you. In addition, be aware that you can't remember everything and don't think you have to.

14

Using Graphics During Testimony

As a general rule, visual information and memory retention is much weaker for audio, slightly stronger for visual, and the most reliable is combined audio and visual. Graphics that you prepare for trial should be big, bold, appealing, simple, and straightforward, with one item per graphic and only two dimensions. Each graphic should contain clear and understandable messages. It is the responsibility of the attorney to ensure that graphical exhibits are admitted into evidence.

Prepare at least two copies of the graphics you use—one for your attorney and one for the opposing attorney. Review all graphics that you prepare for testimony with your attorney before trial. Do not include vendor logos on the charts, and create your own charts rather than use someone else's because you have to explain them yourself.

Some graphics may be for the purpose of general education and others may be evidentiary, such as those shown in Figures 14-1 and 14-2.

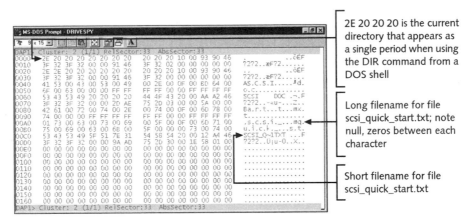

Figure 14-1   DriveSpy directory cluster content

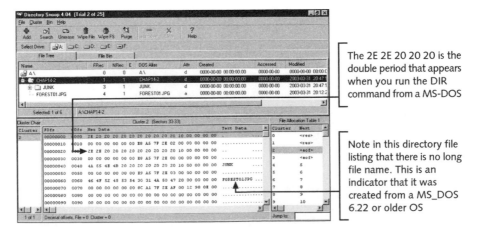

Figure 14-2   Directory Snoop

Display the graphic during your testimony and face the jury to explain it. Use a pointer to direct their attention to the details of each point. If the graphic display is not near the jury box, ask the judge if you can move it so that the jury can see it better. If an attorney asks you questions as you explain the graphic, face the jury and answer the questions in full sentences. If you are right-handed, use your right hand to hold the pointer as you talk. Your left hand should be active too; that is, it should be above the waist with slight movement as you talk. Make sure the jury sees you at all times and also make sure the jury can see what you are pointing at when you are testifying. When standing in front of the jury with your graphics, leave your suit jacket unbuttoned and keep your elbows bent. Wear a blue or dark gray suit with a light blue shirt. Men should wear conservative ties with a base color of red if you have an aggressive opposing attorney. For women who prefer to wear suits, conservative colors are advisable. If you prefer a dress, you should be able to move freely in it.

Use two or more graphics for complex technical descriptions, with the first graphic providing an overview. The subsequent graphics should become more complex as needed to communicate the information.

TESTIFYING DURING CROSS-EXAMINATION

After your attorney has established your credentials and you have presented your evidence, the opposing attorney has an opportunity to ask questions about your testimony and evidence, a process called cross-examination. If the opposing attorney asks you something that you do not know, a good answer is "I don't know." Never guess when asked something that you have no knowledge about.

When answering questions from the opposing attorney, use your own words, not those of the opposing attorney. Certain words have additional meanings that can be easily exploited by an opposing attorney. An example would be to use the word "concerned" rather than "suspicious" when answering a question.

A trick used by opposing attorneys during the cross-examination is to interrupt you as you are answering a question. In a trial, a judge usually does not allow this, but in a deposition there is no independent arbiter of procedure. Be prepared at the end of the deposition to spell any specialized or technical words that you used. To aid court reporters, bring a list of technical or scientific words you frequently use, including definitions and correct spellings.

If the opposing attorney asks you a question such as, "Did you use more than one tool to verify the evidence?" he or she is checking to make sure that you validated the findings from a specific tool using another tool. The following are other questions opposing attorneys often ask:

- What is your standing in the profession of computer forensics?

- What are the tools used and what are their known problems or weak features?

- Are the tools you used reliable, are they consistent and produce the same results?

14

- Are the tools safe to use on the original evidence?

- Have you been called upon as a consultant on how to use the tools from other professionals?

- Do you keep up with the latest technologies applied to computer forensics-journals-papers read or published?

Some questions can cause conflicting answers. Be aware of leading questions that are posed to cause you to give conflicting answers. Your best offense for troublesome questions is to be patient with your answers. Speaking slowly also helps significantly. During examinations, lawyers are not supposed to ask another question until you have finished answering the current question. Shifting or turning toward the jury slowly when you give your response allows you to maintain control over the opposing attorney.

In many instances, the opposing counsel give you rapid-fire questions meant to throw you off. For example, they may ask the following questions:

- Does the vendor certify your tools?

- Are there other tools available that do the same thing?

- How do these tools compare to each other?

Don't be afraid to regroup and redefine your answers if you get confused during your testimony. The jury will sympathize because typically they too are often confused by the opposing attorney's questions. For tricky questions, try to learn how to "tread water" in your response without appearing to be hostile or uncooperative. If the opposing attorney causes you to turn away from the jury, take your time turning back toward the jury to answer the question.

If the opposing attorney declares that you are not answering the questions, consider that he is making an attempt to get you to change your testimony. You are not giving the answer he or she wants or he or she is attempting to get you to say something that contradicts part of your previous testimony. Do not take this personally, but think carefully about what the opposing attorney is trying to do.

Keep eye contact at all times with jury, you may find yourself competing with the opposing attorney, do your best to keep jury attention on you during your testimony. As the opposing attorney asks you questions, avoid flat yes or no answers; add your opinion or additional facts every chance you get. Make it a habit to insert your opinion or facts before the opposing attorney can hit you with the killer question. The killer question is one that you cannot answer or cannot deny. It is a question that can derail your testimony and the case for your client.

Sometimes opposing attorneys ask several questions at one time, causing you to lose track of which question to answer first. Your attorney should object to this question by calling it a compound question or by saying, "Counsel has not allowed the witness to answer the question." If your attorney does not object, you can respond by saying, "Could you please break your last question into individual questions?" Your counter tactic to such methods should challenge the opposing attorney to be more sensible, a response that often plays well with juries. Responding to a question using a full sentence also carries further with the jury than a simple yes or no response.

One tactic used in cross-examinations by opposing attorneys is to make a speech and phrase it as a question. This should draw an objection from your attorney.

When in court or deposition, no questions are hypothetical. Take your time to answer questions—being reprimanded by the opposing attorney can add credence to your testimony. Be courteous in your responses, and expand yes or no answers with qualifying information. Sound interested in what is being asked and said. Short pauses to simple questions create a good impression with the jury.

The more patient you are during the cross-examination, the better you will weather the stormy attack. When the opposing attorney becomes assertive or upset with your testimony, be as professional and courteous as possible. The opposing attorney might continue to lose control, which strengthens your case.

In general, maintain a vigorous demeanor and use energetic speech to make people want to listen to you. Build variety in your presentation to maintain the jury's interest. Be fluent, keep going, and stay comfortable during your testimony. Use extemporaneous speech; do not memorize your testimony. Learn to avoid any glazed eyes among the jury members.

Many factors contribute to your stress on the stand, including the judge, the attorneys, the jury, and the feeling of losing control. Do not feel you are responsible for the outcome. For the opposing attorney, creating stress of a witness will help in getting the favorable answer they want from the expert witness.

At all costs, you want to avoid losing control, which you can do in any of the following ways:

- Being argumentative when being badgered by the opposing attorney; being nervous about testifying
- Having an unresponsive attorney not objecting to the opposing attorney questions
- Having poor listening skills on your part with negative body language
- Being too talkative when answering questions
- Being too technical to the jury
- Acting surprised and unprepared to respond when presented unknown or new information
- If you make a mistake, correct it, do your repairs, and get back on track at the time you realize your mistake.

Some methods used by opposing attorneys to challenge your credibility are putting words into your mouth and summarizing your testimony to fit their needs, creating assumptions or speculation, and controlling the pace of your testimony. Other tactics used to trip you up on the witness stand are stating minor inconsistencies that cause you to make conflicting statements and encouraging you to volunteer information.

14

Never have unrealistic high self-expectations when testifying; everyone makes mistakes. Who controls the testimony is the most important part for the attorney. This applies for both direct examination and cross-examination. You can't remember everything. If you don't remember, simply say so to the attorney during the examination.

Exercising Ethics When Testifying

Be aware of negative influence from attorneys attempting to alter your opinion or fact-finding. Explain yourself technically (using a mechanical approach), not scientifically. If your attorney misunderstands the technology and asks a poorly worded question, reply, "Can you repeat the question?" This will help the attorney fix the question or retract it. (You can avoid this situation by preparing an examination plan that you and the attorney agree on and by reviewing the anticipated testimony.)

If you need to demonstrate something to the jury, move closer to the jury box and talk directly to the jury. Make sure they can see and understand what you are doing. For technical descriptions, the first pass should be general, the second pass should build details. If the demonstration is a standard test or process, tell the jury that it is and on whose authority it is a standard. Identify evidence findings, and then explain how it ties into the case and then how it helped you arrive at your conclusion or opinion.

Understanding Prosecutorial Misconduct

If you are working for a prosecutor in a criminal case and you believe you have found exculpatory evidence (evidence tending to exonerate or diminish the liability of a defendant), you have an obligation to assure that that evidence is not concealed. Initially you should report the evidence (emphasizing its exculpatory nature) to the prosecutor handling the case. If it is not disclosed to the defendant's counsel in a reasonable time, you may report this information to the prosecutor's supervisor if he or she has one. If this still does not result in disclosure, you may report the lack of disclosure to the court (the judge). Do not directly communicate with the defense counsel; reporting evidence to the court fulfills your obligation. Document each of your attempts to induce disclosure, including your reasoning.

If a court reporter is present, that usually means that the hearing is not being audio recorded. If a microphone is present, place the microphone six to eight inches from you, and remember to project your voice so that your words are both recorded and heard by the jury.

If the question asked is awkwardly stated or you are not sure of the intent, ask the attorney for clarification of what he or she is asking. If necessary, insert your comments in the question. In your speech, use simple, direct language to help the jury understand you. For example, use "test" instead of "analyze," as in "I ran a test on the files I found."

Avoid using inappropriate words when giving testimony unless the words are specific to the testimony such as the narrative of recovered evidence. When giving an opinion use a phrase such as: "Based on my examination of the evidence, my opinion is the most reasonable explanation of what happened."

Use chronological order to describe events when testifying, and use hand gestures to help the audience to understand what you are emphasizing. For example, point to graphics while talking. Also make sure you use specific articulate speech when speaking, avoiding contractions such as "can't or don't" instead of "cannot" or "do not."

When asked a question by an attorney or the judge, turn toward the questioner, and then turn back to the jury to give the answer. If you are using technical terms, identify and define all the key terms for the jury, using analogies and graphics as appropriate. List any important technical elements, showing how you verified and validated each element. Repeat information twice to reinforce your message. Speak clearly and loudly enough so the jury can hear you, using a courteous, conciliatory tone. Do not use slang unless you are quoting a fact relating to the case. You are selling yourself to the jury, not the judge or attorneys. With this in mind, make sure the height of the witness chair makes you look presentable to the jury. Turn the chair so that it faces the jury.

When giving an opinion, cite the source of the evidence that the opinion is based on. Then express your opinion and explain your methodology, i.e., how you arrived at your opinion.

PREPARING FOR A DEPOSITION

A **deposition** differs from a trial because there is no jury or judge. Both attorneys are present and the opposing counsel asks you questions. The purpose of the deposition is for your opposing attorney to preview your testimony at trial. The attorney who requests a deposition usually establishes its location, which might be in an office or in your computer forensics laboratory.

There are two types of deposition, discovery and testimony preservation. A **discovery deposition** is part of the discovery process for trial. It is a hostile but open examination under oath before trial with no judge present. The attorney who requested the deposition frequently conducts the equivalent of a direct and cross-examination.

A **testimony preservation deposition** is usually requested by your client to preserve your testimony because of conflicts of schedule or health problems. In some cases, you can set the deposition at your laboratory or have lab facilities available to you, which may make for better testimony and easier demonstrations.

14

Guidelines for Testifying at a Deposition

Overall, stay calm and convey a relaxed, confident appearance during a deposition. Maintain a professional demeanor and try not to be influenced by the opposing attorney's tone, expression, or tactics. Learn the name of the opposing attorney before the deposition so that you can respond to his or her questions using his or her name. Using the opposing attorney's name can help you control the deposition. Look the opposing attorney directly in the eyes, even if he or she attempts to avoid eye contact with you. During a deposition, opposing attorneys often interrupt you before you can complete your answer in an effort to confuse you. Be assertive in your responses, and effect an indifferent manner. If possible, ask your attorney to videotape a practice session of you giving a deposition, and then evaluate your deposition.

When sitting at a table in front of the opposing attorney, try to keep your hands on top of the table. Holding out your elbows appears more open and friendly. Keep your hands away from your face; this shows indecision and weakness. If you wear glasses, keep them on at all times, especially during videotaped depositions. Make sure your chair is at the best height possible to avoid sitting below the eye level of the opposing attorney.

Rules to follow during deposition:

- Be professional and polite.

- Use facts when describing your opinion.

- Understand that being deposed in a discovery deposition is an unnatural process; it is intended to get you to make mistakes.

In general, take your time answering questions, making sure that your answer is correct and that you are stating it clearly. If you prepared a written report, the opposing attorney might attempt to use the report against you by leading you to testify contrary to what you had previously written. If the attorney is concealing the report or any other document from your view, ask to see the document.

If your attorney objects to a question from the opposing attorney, pause and think of what direction your attorney may want you to go in your answer. Keep your answers short, answering questions in phrases and making the answers sound friendly, especially if you are being videotaped. To gain time and control, ask the opposing attorney questions. For example, if you are having trouble answering questions, ask the opposing attorney to repeat the question. When reviewing a report that you have written and are asked about something specific by the opposing attorney, ask what page number he or she is referring to on the report during the questioning.

Recognizing Deposition Problems

Discuss any potential problems with your attorney prior to the deposition. Identify anything that might be negative to your client and could be used by the opposing attorney. If you don't disclose this information, the opposing attorney will use it against you in court. Be prepared to defend yourself if there are possible problems. Avoid omitting information in your testimony; omissions can cause major problems. Although you do not have to volunteer more information than an attorney asks for, make sure you are telling the truth at all times. To respond to difficult questions that may jeopardize your client's case, pause before answering, allowing your attorney to object before you answer.

To avoid having the opposing attorney box you into a corner or lead you to contradict previous statements, only answer the questions that you are asked, answering "yes" or "no" when possible. Recognize that excessively detailed questions from the opposing attorney are an attempt to get you to contradict yourself. Avoid trying to educate the opposing attorney, especially if the questions appear to be misguided. Feel free to provide answers such as "I don't know" or "I don't understand." Keep in mind that you can correct any minor errors you make during your examination and reporting later when you give your deposition. Also, deposition testimony will typically not make it to the jury. However, the stronger your case, the less likely the opposing attorney will want to go to trial.

When asked if you know about an opposing expert witness, your response should be as professional as possible. A good standard answer is, "I have heard Mr. Smith is a competent examiner, but I have not reviewed his work." If you have specific and verifiable information that is damaging to the reputation of the opposing expert, you can note it, but do it in as understated a manner as possible. This works best especially if you have negative information about the skills or competency of the opposing expert.

When accepting a case where the opposing side has its own expert witness, learn as much as possible about the opposing expert. You will need to know this to prepare your testimony to offset their expert. The better expert witness will know what the opposing expert's field is along with their level of expertise.

Public Release: Dealing with Reporters

Any legal action may generate interest from the news media. Avoid contact with the news media, especially during a case. If you are solicited for information or opinions by journalists (or anyone else), minimize your contact with them and avoid saying anything; refer them to your client (the attorney that retained you). If you cannot avoid a journalist, consult with your attorney and learn what not to say. Record any attempted interviews so you have your own record of what occurred. This recording can be important if you are misquoted or quoted out of context. Reporters often look for the sensational sound bite or controversial quote.

Avoid using the expression, "No comment." This phrase attracts more attention than it deflects. Instead, refer questions or requests for information to the attorney that retained you.

You should avoid talking to the news media for the following reasons:

- Your comments could harm the case.

- It creates a record for future testimony that can be used against you.

- Your lack of media training could easily expose you to embarrassing situations.

- You have no control over the context of the information the journalist will publish.

- You cannot rely on a journalist's promises of confidentiality. Journalists have been known to be very aggressive in getting information. Their interests do not coincide with yours or your clients. Be on guard at all times, as your comments may be interpreted in a manner that taints your impartiality in a case and future cases. Questions from journalists can become too big of a distraction from your work on the case. Even after the case is resolved, avoid discussing the details with the press.

14

FORMING AN EXPERT OPINION

This section provides an example of how to provide an expert opinion. For this exercise, you need to review FAT12, FAT16, and FAT32 file systems in Chapter 3. Also refer to the "Overview of FAT Directory Structures" sections in Appendix B for additional information on FAT directory structures. Specifically, you need to learn how to identify the differences from an older Microsoft Disk Operating System (MS-DOS) system verses a newer operating systems (OS) such as Windows XP.

Determining the Origin of a Floppy Disk

In this exercise, you determine whether a floppy disk was created from a MS-DOS 6.22 OS or a Windows 95 or newer operating system. You need the following items:

- Data File C14-ea.ima
- Digital Intelligence Image utility
- Digital Intelligence DriveSpy, Directory Snoop, FTK, or your preferred computer forensics tool

To create the floppy disk:

1. In Windows, use Windows Explorer or My Computer to copy **C14-ea.ima** from the Chap14\Chapter folder in the Data Files to the Chap14\Chapter folder in the work folder on your system.

2. Open a Command Prompt window or boot your computer to MS-DOS.

3. At the DOS command prompt, navigate to the **Tools** folder in your work folder, type **Toolpath** and press **Enter**.

4. Change to the Chap14\Chapter folder in your work folder.

5. Insert a blank floppy disk into drive A.

6. At the DOS command prompt, type **Image C14-ea.ima a:** and press **Enter**.

TIP

If you are notified that you successfully created an image, but cannot find the image file using Windows Explorer, remove the floppy disk from its drive, reinsert it, click View on the Windows Explorer menu bar, and then click Refresh.

Now you are ready to start your preferred computer forensics tool. If you are using DriveSpy, perform the following steps. If you are using another computer forensics tool, refer to the vendor's user manual.

To use DriveSpy to examine a directory's content:

1. Remove the floppy disk you created in the previous set of steps, and then boot your forensic workstation to DOS.

2. Insert the floppy disk you created in the previous set of steps in drive A. At the DOS command prompt, navigate to the **Tools** folder in your work folder, type **Toolpath** and press **Enter**.

3. At the DOS command prompt, navigate to the Chap14\Chapter folder in your work folder. Type **DriveSpy** and press **Enter**.

4. At the DriveSpy SYS prompt, type **DA** and press **Enter**. Then type **P1** and press **Enter**.

5. At the DAP1 prompt, type **Dir** and press **Enter**. Note the cluster number for any directories that appear in the output.

6. At the DAP1 prompt, type **Cluster** *x* where *x* is the number of the directory you want to examine, and then press **Enter** to view the content of a directory.

7. In the cluster output screen, examine each filename listed and determine if there are any long filenames.

After you examine the content of the directory for this floppy disk, write a brief opinion report (one to three pages) of your findings. Give your expert opinion on which type of OS was used to create this floppy disk and the files contained on it.

CHAPTER SUMMARY

□ When cases go to trial, you as the forensics expert play one of two roles: you are either called as a technical witness or as an expert witness. As a technical or scientific witness, you are only providing the facts as you have found them in your investigation. However, as an expert, you have opinions about what you observe. In fact, it is your opinion that makes you an expert witness.

□ If you are called as a technical or expert witness in a computer forensics case, you need to thoroughly prepare for your testimony. Establish communication early on with your attorney. When preparing to testify for any litigation, substantiate your findings with your own documentation and by collaborating with other computer forensic professionals.

□ As you process evidence, be sure to always monitor, preserve, and validate your work. Doing so helps to ensure that it can be presented in court. Then submit to your attorney all evidence you collected and analyzed. When writing your report, only list evidence findings that are relevant to the case.

□ When you are called to testify in court, your attorney demonstrates to the court that you are competent as an expert or technical witness. The opposing counsel may attempt to discredit you or may choose not to based on your past record. Your attorney then leads you through the evidence followed by the opposing counsel cross-examining you. After your attorney has established your credentials and you have presented your evidence, the opposing attorney has an opportunity to ask questions about your testimony and evidence, a process called cross-examination.

14

❑ Know whether you are being called as a scientific-technical witness or expert witness (or both), whether you are being retained as a consulting expert or as an expert witness. Also be familiar with the contents of your curriculum vita (CV).

❑ A deposition differs from a trial because there is no jury or judge. Both attorneys are present and the opposing counsel asks you questions. There are two types of deposition: discovery and testimony preservation.

KEY TERMS

conflict out—When you already have knowledge or have rendered an opinion about a case before you are hired

curriculum vita (CV)—An extensive résumé of your professional history that includes not only where you have worked, but what cases you have worked on, what testimony you have given, what training you have received and from whom, along with details of your other skills.

deposition—A formal meeting where you are questioned in a room in which only the opposing attorneys, your attorney, and the opposing parties are present. There is no judge or jury at this time. A deposition is considered part of discovery.

deposition banks—Libraries kept by various law firms of depositions given in the past.

discovery deposition—A hostile but open examination under oath before trial with no judge present. The attorney setting the deposition will frequently conduct the equivalent of a direct and cross-examination.

expert witness—A person who has knowledge in a field and can offer an opinion in addition to the facts being presented.

technical witness—A person who has performed the actual field work, but does not offer an opinion in court, only the results of their findings.

testimony preservation deposition—A deposition usually set by your client to preserve your testimony because of conflicts of schedule or health issues but also in some cases because having the full features of your laboratory available to you may make for better testimony and easier demonstrations.

voir dire—The process of qualifying a witness as an expert in their particular field.

A

CERTIFICATION
TEST REFERENCES

IACIS CERTIFICATION

The International Association of Computing Investigative Specialist (IACIS) is a non-profit organization that was formed to promote professional standards and to certify computing-forensics examiners. Through IACIS, you can become a Certified Forensic Computer Examiner (CFCE). To qualify to take the CFCE exam, you must be an active law enforcement officer or other person qualified to be an IACIS member. For more information on qualification requirements, visit *www.cops.org*.

IACIS provides an extensive testing program to verify an individual's competence in performing a computing investigation. The examination process is not a training program; it is strictly a testing program. Applicants are screened before acceptance into the certification program. IACIS is the sole decision maker for all applicants. To apply for the certification requires the completion of an application form and a fee of $750 to be paid at the time the application is submitted. If you are rejected for any reason, your fee will be returned to you. If you are accepted into the program, a monitor (an IACIS CFCE member) will direct you through the examination testing.

If you are accepted, you will have to analyze six floppy disks and one hard disk. Requirements for these examinations are:

- All disks must be examined.
- All technical matters must be solved for each disk.
- A report for each disk must be prepared and submitted to the monitor.
- All disks and reports must be submitted to the monitor within five months from the start of the testing process.

Sound forensics practices must be use for all disk examinations. This includes evidence control procedure and detailed written reports. Reports can be submitted to your monitor by e-mail and should be written in Microsoft Word or WordPerfect.

Reports for each disk need to contain the following information:

- Clear explanations of the procedures used to analyze the disks.
- Clear explanation of what was found on each disk.
- Exhibits of evidence recovered from the disks.
- Detailed lists of evidence controls you have implemented for each disk examine.

After you are accepted into this program, your monitor will provide additional requirements such as the type of software that can be used for each disk examination.

IACIS COMPUTER FORENSICS SKILLS EXPECTATIONS

The following table is a list of the skills you will need to master before taking the IACIS CFCE exam. These skills are divided between report writing, analysis, and data acquisition proficiencies. Next to each skill is a chapter where you can find specific information on how to perform these tasks.

Expected skill for report writing	Covered in chapter
Sanitizing target media with a wiping utility	Chapter 2
Chain-of-evidence procedures and documentation	Chapter 7
Narrative report on how evidence was discovered	Chapter 13
A formed conclusion	Chapters 13 and 14
Your stated opinion on the evidence you have found	Chapters 13 and 14

Expected skill for data analysis	Covered in chapter
Understanding bit-shift and data offsets	Chapter 10
Understanding of file slack and unallocated disk space	Chapter 3
Reconstruction of graphic files found in unallocated space	Chapter 12
Identifying files by header value	Chapter 10
Recovery of erased files	Chapter 10
Ability to interpret and form a story line of an investigation	Chapters 10, 13, and 14
File Allocation Table (FAT) file system directory structures and recovery	Chapters 3 and 14
Data compression methods	Chapter 12
Ability to search disk data for specific hexadecimal values	Chapters 10, 12, and 14

Expected skill for data acquisition	Covered in chapter
Making a bit-stream image copy of a suspect disk	Chapter 9
Verifying the bit-stream image copy through hashing algorithms	Chapter 10

Looking Up URLs

An additional skill that is separate from normal computer forensics that is needed for the IACIS CFCE examine is the ability to identify contact persons or owners of Internet Web sites. Part of the investigation and analysis process for the CFCE requires you to search for information that supports the investigation and is not available on the evidence disks provided. The primary source for this additional contributory evidence can be found on the Internet.

With any Internet Web browser such as Netscape, Internet Explorer, or Konqueror, finding a Web site's contact person or owner is very easy. You can use a Whois Web page to obtain registration information about most Web pages. The following information is typically available at a Whois Web page:

- The assigned IP address for the Internet Web site
- The Web site's contact person's name, address, email, telephone and fax number
- Registration date and expiration date for the Web site
- The domain server for the IP address

From the Whois Web page, you can typically search for a site's registration by its domain name, its Internic handle (that is, its identification), or contact person's name. For more information about Web site registrations, go to *www.internic.net*.

Several Internet Web sites provide information about any registration information for all sites. To locate any of these Web sites, from your favorite search engine type in Whois to obtain a current list of Internet registration providers. Some easy to use Whois Web sites are:

- *www-whois.internic.net/cgi/whois*
- *www.whois.net/*
- *http://resellers.tucows.com/opensrs/whois/*

An example of what the output looks like from a Whois inquiry for Course Technology's Web site is shown in Figure A-1.

Figure A-1   Whois search results

APPENDIX
B

COMPUTER FORENSICS REFERENCES

QUICK REFERENCES FOR COMPUTING INVESTIGATORS

This section contains references to the commands used with the software tools described in this book.

DriveSpy Command Switch References

Table B-1   DriveSpy command switches and attributes

Category and switch	Attribute	Description	Example
Wildcards	Asterisk (*)	Stand for one or more characters	To copy all .txt files to the Case_10 folder on Drive D: `Copy *.txt D:\Case_10\`
	Question mark (?)	Stand for a single character	To copy all files named Mydoc that have an extension beginning with "do" such as .doc and .dot: `Dir Mydoc.do?`
File attributes /A	A	Archived files	To list all the attributes of archived files: `Dir *.* /AA`
	D	Directories	To list only directories on a disk partition: `Dir /AD`
	V	Disk volumes or partitions	
	S	System files	
	H	Hidden files	To copy hidden files: `Copy *.* /AH D:\Case_10\`
	R	Read-only files	

Category and switch	Attribute	Description	Example
Sorting /O	N	Sort by name	
	E	Sort by extension	
	G	Sort by directory	
	S	Sort by file size	
	D	Sort by the modification date and time	To get a directory listing sorted by date `DIR *.GIF /OD`
	A	Sort by last access date	
	X	Sort deleted files when using the DIR command	
	-	Before an attribute, reverses the sort order	To display files by date and time in descending order: `Dir *.* /O-A`
Recursion /S		Lets you access subdirectory data when using other DriveSpy commands	To list the files in the current directory and all subdirectories: `DIR /S` To copy specific files from the current directories and all subdirectories: `Copy *.txt \D:\CASE_10\ /S`
File types /T		Select specific file types that are predefined in DriveSpy.ini	To use the Unerase command to recover Excel spreadsheet files: `Unerase *.* /T:xls D:\CASE_10\`
File groups /G		Access or recover predefined groups	To copy files defined in the INTEL_PROP group: `Copy *.* /G:INTEL_PROP D:\CASE_10\`

Table B-2   Wipe command switches

Switch	Description
Sector range, such as WIPE 0-1000	List specific sectors to overwrite
/L	Overwrite only a logical partition
/FREE	Overwrite only unallocated disk space
/SLACK	Overwrite only file slack space
/UNUSED	Overwrite unallocated and file slack space
/C:[value]	Overwrite a specified character value, which can be hexadecimal or decimal, as in /C:0xF6 or /C:246
/RAND	Random characters generated for the overwrite
/MBR	Overwrite the master boot record
/SA	Display the sector addresses while overwriting disk

UNIX and Linux Common Shell Commands

Table B-3   Standard UNIX and Linux commands

Command	Switches	Description
cat file more file		Display the contents of a file (similar to the MS-DOS Type command)
dd	Use the man dd command to list the switch options available for this command	Create a bit-stream copy of a device to another device or image file
df bdf (HP-UX)	-k (Solaris)	Display information about the number of blocks that are allocated, used and available for local and NFS-mounted partitions
find	Use the man find command to list the switch options available for this command	Find files matching a list of attributes such as name, last modification time, and owner
netstat	-a	Display the systems connected via the network interface(s)
ps	-ef (Sys V) -ax (BSD)	Display a list of processes that are currently running
uname	-a	List the current name of system

Table B-4 Log and data files on UNIX and Linux systems

Files	Description
Solaris systems	
/etc/passwd	Local account information
/etc/group	Local group information
/var/adm/sulog	Switch user log data
/var/adm/utmp	Current login information
/var/adm/wtmp /var/adm/wtmpx /var/adm/lastlog	Historical login information
/var/adm/loginlog	Login failure information
Messages	System log file
/etc/vfstab	Static information about file system
/etc/dfs/dfstab /etc/vfstab	Configuration files
HP-UX systems	
/etc/utmp	Current login information
/var/adm/wtmp /var/adm/wtmpx	Historical login information
/var/adm/btmp	Login failure information
/etc/fstab	Static information about file system
/etc/checklist	Static information about file system (version 9.x)
/etc/exports	Configuration files
syslog	System log file
AIX systems	
/etc/filesystems	Static information about file system
/etc/exports	Configuration files
/etc/utmp	Current login information
/var/adm/wtmp /etc/security/lastlog	Historical login information
/etc/security/failedlogin	Login failure information

Files	Description
IRIX systems	
/etc/fstab	Static information about file system
/var/adm/utmp	Current login information
/var/adm/utmpx	
/var/adm/wtmp	Historical login information
/var/adm/wtmpx	
/var/adm/lastlog	
/var/adm/btmp	Login failure information
/etc/fstab	Relevant file
/etc/exports	Configuration files
syslog	System log file
Linux systems	
/etc/exports	Configuration files
/var/run/utmp	Current login information
/var/log/wtmp	Historical login information
/var/log/lastlog	
/etc/fstab	Relevant files

SAMPLE SCRIPT FOR DRIVESPY

With the DriveSpy SaveSect and WriteSect commands, you can create multiple volume save-sets of disk drives and then recreate the saved volumes to a new target disk drive. The sample script files in this section are for a Macintosh running O/S 8.2 disk drive that is 8.0 GB in size.

Figure B-1 shows the output of using the DriveSpy SaveSect command to create multiple volumes of a disk drive.

```
OUTPUT MAC_SAV.LOG
PAGE OFF
DRIVE 1
SAVESECT 00000000-00999999 MAC_SAV.000
SAVESECT 01000000-01999999 MAC_SAV.001
SAVESECT 02000000-02999999 MAC_SAV.002
SAVESECT 03000000-03999999 MAC_SAV.003
SAVESECT 04000000-04999999 MAC_SAV.004
SAVESECT 05000000-05999999 MAC_SAV.005
SAVESECT 06000000-06999999 MAC_SAV.006
SAVESECT 07000000-07999999 MAC_SAV.007
SAVESECT 08000000-08999999 MAC_SAV.008
SAVESECT 09000000-09999999 MAC_SAV.009
SAVESECT 10000000-10999999 MAC_SAV.010
SAVESECT 11000000-11999999 MAC_SAV.011
SAVESECT 12000000-12999999 MAC_SAV.012
SAVESECT 13000000-13999999 MAC_SAV.013
SAVESECT 14000000-14999999 MAC_SAV.014
SAVESECT 15000000-15999999 MAC_SAV.015
SAVESECT 16000000-16957030 MAC_SAV.016
```

Figure B-1   Output of DriveSpy SaveSect command

This script will create volume save-sets that are 512,000,000 bytes each with the exception of the very last volume save-set that is only 489,999,360 bytes. This last save-set is smaller because the end of the drive is at block position 16957030. Remember, each block is 512 bytes.

Figure B-2 shows the output of the DriveSpy WriteSect command to restore multiple volumes from a SaveSect script.

```
OUTPUT MAC_WRT.LOG
PAGE OFF
DRIVE 1
WRITESECT MAC_SAV.000 00000000-00999999
WRITESECT MAC_SAV.001 01000000-01999999
WRITESECT MAC_SAV.002 02000000-02999999
WRITESECT MAC_SAV.003 03000000-03999999
WRITESECT MAC_SAV.004 04000000-04999999
WRITESECT MAC_SAV.005 05000000-05999999
WRITESECT MAC_SAV.006 06000000-06999999
WRITESECT MAC_SAV.007 07000000-07999999
WRITESECT MAC_SAV.008 08000000-08999999
WRITESECT MAC_SAV.009 09000000-09999999
WRITESECT MAC_SAV.010 10000000-10999999
WRITESECT MAC_SAV.011 11000000-11999999
WRITESECT MAC_SAV.012 12000000-12999999
WRITESECT MAC_SAV.013 13000000-13999999
WRITESECT MAC_SAV.014 14000000-14999999
WRITESECT MAC_SAV.015 15000000-15999999
WRITESECT MAC_SAV.016 16000000-16957030
```

Figure B-2   Output of the DriveSpy WriteSect command

OVERVIEW OF FAT DIRECTORY STRUCTURES

When Microsoft first created the MS-DOS operating system (OS) data was stored on floppy disks. Because floppy disks have had a limited evolution in their maximum size, the addressable storage space is small compared to modern hard disks. All floppy disks for Microsoft operating systems use the FAT12 file system (see Chapter 3 for additional information on File Allocation Table; FAT file systems). Because of the limited disk space and memory space on older computers, Microsoft engineered the FAT12 file system so that directory names could only be from one to eight characters in length. For filenames, they could only be up to eight characters long and from zero to three characters for the extension values. The three characters for the extension of a filename is used to identify the file type such as a document file that has a .doc value or a spreadsheet file with a .xls value.

When larger disk drives where developed, Microsoft re-engineered the FAT file system and created FAT16. FAT16 allows for disk drive partitions up to 2.0 GB of addressable storage space. With further advances in disk technologies Microsoft then created FAT32 that can access up to 2.0 terabytes or more of storage space. Under MS-DOS 6.22 the same directory and filename convention was carried over from FAT12 to FAT16. For Windows 95 and newer OSs FAT32 maintains the same eight character maximum for the filename and up to three characters for the file extension.

When Microsoft released Windows 95, they needed to allow for larger filenames under the FAT12 and FAT16 file systems. As a solution to this Microsoft developed Virtual FAT, which is referred to as VFAT. VFAT provides two filenames for every file within the directory file. The first name is the long filename that appears in what looks like a Unicode format. The Unicode format appears in a hexadecimal editor with null (00) values between each character. The second name is the short filename that follows the eight-character name and three-character extension name.

The purpose of providing two filenames for each file in a newer FAT file system, that is Windows 95 or newer, is to keep the file naming convention compliant with MS-DOS. An example of this is what you see in a Windows Explorer window. In Figure B-3 there are two files, one under eight characters long and another that is over eight characters long. The first file is over the eight character maximum length allowed under MS-DOS 6.22.

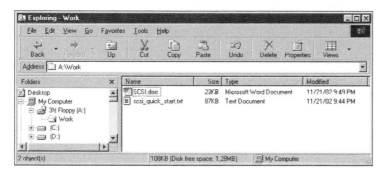

Figure B-3   Windows Explorer

When performing the DIR directory command from a Disk Operating System (DOS) shell these two files appear with a short filename and long filename, as shown in Figure B-4.

```
MS-DOS Prompt

T  9 x 15

A:\>dir /s

 Volume in drive A has no label
 Volume Serial Number is 0178-100B

Directory of A:\

WORK          <DIR>        01-31-05  8:52a work
        0 file(s)              0 bytes

Directory of A:\work

.             <DIR>        01-31-05  8:52a .
..            <DIR>        01-31-05  8:52a ..
SCSI    DOC      23,040   11-21-02  9:49p SCSI.doc
SCSI_Q~1 TXT     88,094   11-21-02  9:44p scsi_quick_start.txt
        2 file(s)        111,134 bytes

Total files listed:
        2 file(s)        111,134 bytes
        3 dir(s)       1,345,536 bytes free

A:\>_
```

Figure B-4   DOS directory

In Figure B-4, the leftmost column shows the file's short name that has six characters followed by a tilde (~), then followed by a number. The extreme right column shows the VFAT long filename.

You can view the directory file and examine its content using such tools as DriveSpy, FTK, EnCase, ILook, and others. An example of using DriveSpy to examine the directory structure will require you to locate the cluster position of the directory of interest. In this example, you can locate the cluster number of the Work folder by using the DIR command in DriveSpy. See Chapter 10 for information on using DriveSpy and the Cluster command. See Figure B-5.

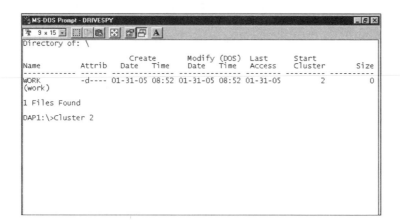

Figure B-5   DriveSpy directory cluster number

Note that the cluster number for the Work folder is 2 in Figure B-5. To view the content of this cluster, type Cluster 2 and Enter. See Figure B-6.

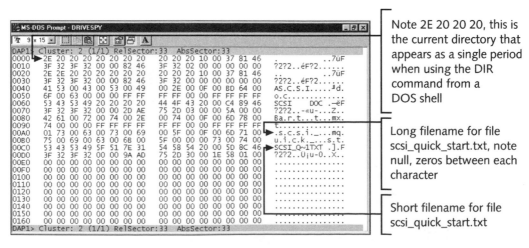

Note 2E 20 20 20, this is the current directory that appears as a single period when using the DIR command from a DOS shell

Long filename for file scsi_quick_start.txt, note null, zeros between each character

Short filename for file scsi_quick_start.txt

Figure B-6   DriveSpy directory cluster content

Another useful tool designed to be run from Windows is the shareware program Directory Snoop from Briggs Software (*www.briggsoft.com*). Directory Snoop is a convenient Graphical User Interface (GUI) tool that allows you to inspect and recover deleted data from disks. At the time of this writing Directory Snoop will only work on FAT file system partitions. See Figure B-7.

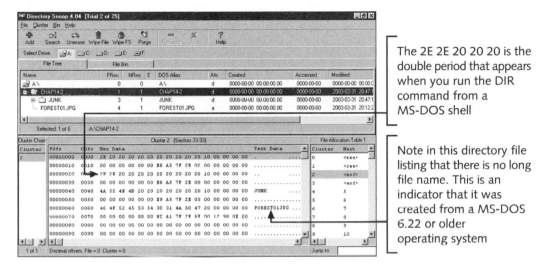

The 2E 2E 20 20 20 is the double period that appears when you run the DIR command from a MS-DOS shell

Note in this directory file listing that there is no long file name. This is an indicator that it was created from a MS-DOS 6.22 or older operating system

Figure B-7   Directory Snoop

In the example shown in Figure B-7, note the missing long filename in the lower center window of Directory Snoop. The lack of a long filename in the directory is an indicator that this floppy was formatted and data written to it from an MS-DOS 6.22 or older OS.

FAT directories contain information about files that have been stored within them. Specific information about each file can be found within the directory file itself. All FAT directories start with the hexadecimal value of 2E followed by several hexadecimal 20 values. The hexadecimal 2E converts to the ASCII value of a period (.) and the hexadecimal 20 are spacebars. See Figure B-8.

Following is the information listed for all files in the directory file:

- Long filename for Windows 95 or newer formatted FAT disks

- Short filename (8.3 convention)

- Attributes assigned to the file

- Case and creation time in milliseconds

- Creation time of the file

- Creation date of the file

- Last access date of the file

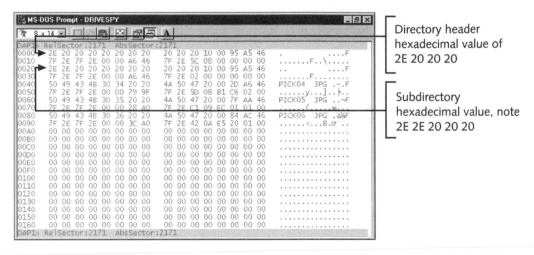

Figure B-8 Showing hexadecimal values

- Starting cluster high word for FAT32 file systems
- Modified time stamp
- Modified date stamp
- Starting cluster of the file (this is assigned by the FAT where all links to the file are listed)
- File size

One feature of FAT directories is what occurs when a file is deleted or renamed. When a file is deleted, a hexadecimal E5 value is inserted in the first character position of the file's name. If the file is renamed, a new entry containing the new name for the file is created and the old filename is marked as deleted with the E5 value the same as if the file was deleted. These previous entries are not typically deleted from the directory file. Several computer forensics tools and disk editing tools can display the content of a directory file. As an example, Figure B-9 shows what a renamed file looks like in the directory file in a FAT12 disk in Directory Snoop.

You can also reverse-engineer the starting cluster position and the file size. Within the directory file these values are listed in hexadecimal format. To convert hexadecimal values to decimal, use the Windows scientific calculator.

To access the Windows scientific calculator:

1. From Windows, click the **Start** button, point to **Programs**, point to **Accessories**, and then click **Calculator**.

2. In the Calculator window, click the View menu and then click Scientific.

3. In the Scientific Calculator window, click the **Hex** button.

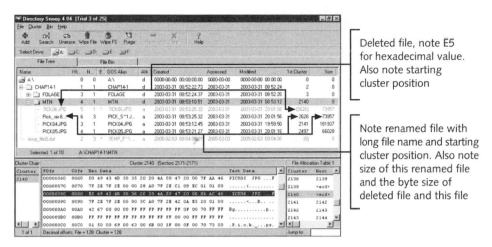

Deleted file, note E5 for hexadecimal value. Also note starting cluster position

Note renamed file with long file name and starting cluster position. Also note size of this renamed file and the byte size of deleted file and this file

Figure B-9   Directory Snoop with a FAT12 disk

4. From either the keyboard or the hexadecimal buttons, enter the desired hexadecimal value.

5. To convert the hexadecimal value to decimal, click the **Dec** button.

   See Figure B-10, which shows the last four hex numbers as the byte size for file PICK_S~1.JPG. When converting this from hex to decimal, read it from right to left. 00 01 20 E5 is how you would type this value in a scientific calculator to obtain the decimal byte size. Note that what is displayed with the DIR command or Windows Explorer might be slightly smaller than what is converted. Figure B-10 also shows the starting cluster number in hex for file PICK_S~1.JPG. Note that to compute this value, read right to left. 0A 42 is how you would type this value in a scientific calculator to obtain the decimal cluster number value.

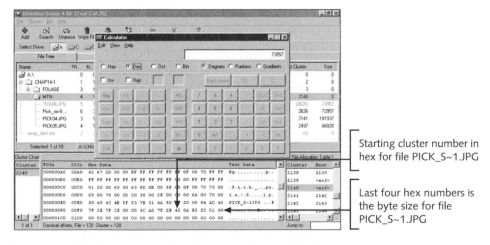

Starting cluster number in hex for file PICK_S~1.JPG

Last four hex numbers is the byte size for file PICK_S~1.JPG

Figure B-10   Converting from hexadecimal to decimal

In Figure B-10, note the decimal value 73957. For all FAT directory entries, the file's starting cluster position is located at offset 1A hexadecimal or 26 decimal. The file's byte size is located starting at offset 1C hexadecimal or 28 decimal. Note that these values are read from right to left.

Converting the decimal value 73957 to hexadecimal will produce a value of 0120E5.

Of special interest for an investigation is trying to determine the size of a file that has been deleted and overwritten by a newer file. Knowing the size of the previously deleted and overwritten file may have investigation value in that it will provide subjective information that might contribute to a copy of the deleted file from another disk. It is subjective but may provide clues for the investigation.

COMPUTER FORENSICS REFERENCES

This book is only the beginning of computer forensics and investigations. To master all levels of computing forensics, you should familiarize yourself with the works of many other authors who have made significant contributions to this profession. Listed here you will find several other books that will help your understanding of computing investigation processes and expand your technical skills.

Clark, Franklin and Ken Diliberto, "Investigating Computer Crime" CRC Press, 1996 ISBN 0-8493-8158-4

Rosenblatt, Kenneth S., "High-Technology Crime" KSK Publications, 1995 ISBN 0-9648171-0-1

Icove, David, Karl Seger, and William VonStorch, "Computer Crime, A Crimefighter's Handbook" O'Reilly & Associates, Inc. 1995 ISBN 1-56592-086-4

Stephenson, Peter, "Investigating Computer-Related Crime" CRC Press, 2000 ISBN 0-8493-2218-9

Sammes, Tom and Brian Jenkinson, "Forensic Computing, A Practitioner's Guide" Springer-Verlag London Limited 2000 ISBN 1-85233-299-9

Casey, Eoghan, ed., "Handbook of Computer Crime Investigation, Forensic Tools and Technology" Academic Press, 2002 ISBN 0-12-163103-6

Caloyhannides, Michael A., "Computer Forensics and Privacy" Artrech House Publishers, 2001 ISBN 1-58053-283-7

Mel, H. X. and Doris Baker, "Cryptography Decrypted" Addison-Wesley, 2001 ISBN 0-201-61647-5

C

PROCEDURES FOR CORPORATE HIGH-TECHNOLOGY INVESTIGATIONS

PROCEDURES FOR INVESTIGATIONS

As an investigator you will need to develop formal procedures and informal checklists to cover all issues that are important to a high-tech investigation. Procedures are necessary to ensure that proper techniques are applied to an investigation. Use informal checklists to make sure that all evidence is collected and properly processed. This appendix lists some sample procedures commonly used in corporate investigations (non-law enforcement) for the computing investigator.

EMPLOYEE TERMINATION CASES

The majority of termination casework performed by a corporate computing investigator is because of employee abuse issues. Incidents such as viewing pornography in the workplace that create a hostile work environment or inappropriate e-mail messages are the predominant types of cases investigated. The following are key points to consider when conducting an investigation that might lead to an employee's termination. It is recommended that you consult with your organization's General Counsel and Personnel Department for specific directions on how to handle these types of investigations. Your organization must have appropriate policies implemented as described in Chapter 1 of this book.

Internet Web Abuse Investigations

The information in this section applies to the internal private networks of a business, not a public Internet Service Provider (ISP). Consult with your General Counsel after reviewing this list and to make changes according to the directions of you organization's attorneys to build your own procedures.

To conduct an investigation involving Web abuse:

- Internet proxy server log
- Suspect computer's IP address; consult with your organization's network administrator

- Suspect computer's disk drive
- Your preferred computer forensic analysis tool such as FTK, EnCase, DriveSpy, etc.

Recommended processing:

1. Use standard forensics analysis techniques and procedures for the disk drive examination as described in this book.

2. Using tools such as Data Lifter or FTK's Internet Keyword Search option under the Tools menu, extract all Web page URL information.

3. If available, contact the firewall network administrator and request a proxy server log for the date range of interest of the suspect computer's IP address. Consult with your organization's network administrator to confirm that such logs are maintained.

4. Compare the output of the forensics analysis Internet Web page data to the proxy server log data to confirm that they match.

5. If the URL data matches both the proxy server log and the forensic disk examination, continue analyzing the suspect computer's disk drive data, and collect any relevant downloaded inappropriate pictures or Web pages that support the allegation. If there are no matches between the proxy server logs and the forensic examination also shows no contributing evidence, then report that the allegation is unsubstantiated.

NOTE

Before conducting an Internet abuse case, research your state or country's privacy laws. Many countries have unique privacy laws that restrict the use of computer log data such as proxy server logs or disk drive cache files for any type of investigation. Some state or federal laws may supercede your organization's employee policies. Always consult with your organization's attorney. For companies that have international business operations, jurisdiction is a problem; what is legal in the United States, such as examining and investigating a proxy server log, may not be legal in Germany, for example.

For investigations where the proxy server log does not match the forensic analysis that found inappropriate data, continue the examination of the suspect computer's disk drive. Determine when inappropriate data was downloaded to the computer and if it was through an organization's intranet connection to the Internet. Employees might have used their employers' laptop computers to connect to their own ISP to download inappropriate Web content. For these situations you will need to consult with your organization's employee policy guidelines for what is appropriate use of the organization's computing assets.

E-mail Abuse Investigations

E-mail investigations typically range from spam to inappropriate and offensive message content to harassment and threats. E-mail is subject to the same restrictions as other computer evidence data in that an organization must have a properly defined policy as described in Chapter 1 of this book.

What you need for an investigation involving e-mail abuse:

- An electronic copy of offending e-mail message that contains message header data; consult with your e-mail server administrator.

- If available, e-mail server log records; consult with your e-mail server administrator to see if they are available.

- For e-mail systems that store users' messages on a central server, access to the server; consult with your e-mail server administrator.

- For e-mail systems that store users' messages on a computer such as an Outlook PST or OST file, access to the computer and perform a forensic analysis on it.

- Your preferred computer forensic analysis tool such as FTK or EnCase.

Recommended procedure:

1. For computer based e-mail data files such Outlook PST or OST files, use standard forensics analysis techniques and procedures for the disk drive examination as described in this book.

2. For server-based e-mail data files, contact the e-mail server administrator and obtain an electronic copy of the suspect and victim's server e-mail folder or data.

3. For Web-based e-mail investigations such as Hotmail or Yahoo! mail, use tools such as FTK's Internet Keyword Search option under the Tools menu, extract all "@" e-mail information.

4. Examine header data of all messages of interest to the investigation.

ATTORNEY-CLIENT PRIVILEGED INVESTIGATIONS

When performing a computer forensic analysis under Attorney-Client Privilege (ACP) rules for an attorney, it is necessary to keep all findings confidential. The attorney you are working for is the ultimate authority over the investigation. For investigations of this nature, attorneys typically request that you extract all data from the disk drive or drives. It is your responsibility to comply with the directions of the attorney. Because of the large quantities of data that can be present on a disk drive, the attorney will want to know about everything on the disk drive or drives of interest.

Many attorneys like to have printouts of the data you have recovered. This presents problems when there are log files that are several thousand pages of data or computer-aided design (CAD) drawing programs that can only be read by proprietary programs. You will need to persuade and educate many attorneys on how digital evidence can be viewed electronically. Teaching attorneys and paralegals on how to sort through data files is a service you need to learn how to do. This is to help them to analyze the huge amounts of data produced from a forensic examination as efficiently as possible.

You can encounter problems if you find data in the form of binary files such as CAD drawings. Examining these types of files requires the use of the CAD program that had created them. Engineering companies often have specialized drafting programs. Discovery demands for lawsuits of a product that caused injury or death requires the extraction of design plans for review by attorneys and expert witnesses. You will be responsible in locating the appropriate programs for these design plans so that these files can be viewable to the attorneys and expert witnesses.

Basic list for conducting an ACP case:

1. Request a memorandum from the attorney directing you to start the investigation. The memorandum must state that the investigation is privileged communication. It must list your name and any other associates', names also assigned to the case.

2. Request a list of keywords that are of interest to the investigation.

3. When you have received the memorandum, initiate the investigation and analysis. Any findings you have prior to receiving the memorandum are subject to discovery by the opposing attorney.

4. For disk drive examinations, make two bit-stream image copies of the disk and one logical copy using a tool such as Norton Ghost. For each bit-stream image copy, use different imaging tools such as EnCase for the first and DriveSpy's SaveSect or SafeBack for the second. If you have large enough storage disk drives, make each bit-stream image uncompressed to make sure that if any of the bit-stream images become corrupt, you can still examine the uncorrupted areas with your preferred forensic analysis tool.

5. If possible, run Message Digest 5 (MD5) or Secure Hash Algorithm (SHA) hashes on all files on the original and recreated disks. Typically attorneys will want to view all data even if it is not relevant to the case. Many Graphical User Interface (GUI) computer forensic tools perform this task during the bit-stream imaging for the disk drive.

6. Methodically examine every portion of the disk drive and extract all data. This applies to both allocated and unallocated data areas of a disk.

7. Run keyword searches on allocated and unallocated disk space. Follow up the search results to determine whether the keyword hit contains information that will support the case.

8. For Microsoft Windows operating systems, use specialty tools to analyze and extract data from the Registry file such as EnCase or one of the many Registry viewer programs such as RegdatXP. Use the Find function in the Registry viewer to search for keywords of interest to the investigation.

9. If necessary, reconstruct the original drive so that you can boot it using the logical image save. It might be difficult to create a bootable drive if you do not have the original computer because many operating systems rely on specific vendor hardware configurations. Reconstructing a computer so that you can boot it can provide additional information that may not be available when examining with a computer forensics tool.

10. For binary data files such as CAD drawings, locate the appropriate software product and if possible make printouts of the binary file content. If the data files are too large, load the specialty application on a separate workstation with the recovered binary files so that they can be viewed by the attorney.

11. For unallocated data (file slack space or free space) recovery, use a tool that removes or replaces nonprintable data such as NTI's Filter_I program.

12. Consolidate all recovered data from the evidence bit-stream image into well-organized folders and subfolders. Store the recovered data output using a logical and easy to follow storage method for the attorney or the assigned paralegal.

Other things to remember for ACP cases are:

- Minimize all written communications with the attorney; use the telephone when you need to ask questions or provide information relating to the case.

- Any documentation written to the attorney must contain a header that states it is "Privileged Legal Communication—Confidential Work Product" as defined under the attorney-work-product rule.

- Provide assistance to the attorney and paralegal on analyzing the data.

If you have difficulty complying with the directions or do not understand the directives from the memorandum contact the attorney and explain your problems. Always keep an open line of verbal communications with the attorney during these types of investigations. If using e-mail to communicating with the attorney use encryption such as PGP or other security e-mail service for all messages.

MEDIA LEAK INVESTIGATIONS

For the corporate computing and network environment, controlling sensitive data can be very difficult. If an organization has disgruntled employees, they might send sensitive data to a news reporter. The reason for media leaks range from an effort to embarrass an organization's management by employees to a rival conducting a power struggle between competing internal organizations. Another concern is the premature release of information about new products, which can disrupt and cause market share lose for a business if it is made public too soon. Media leak investigations can be very time consuming and resource intensive. It is not uncommon to experience scope-creep due to management's desire to find who had leaked the information.

Consider the following for media leak investigations:

- Examine e-mail, both organization's e-mail servers and private (e.g. Hotmail, Yahoo!, etc.) on company owned computers.

- Internet message boards (e.g. Yahoo!); research the Internet for any information about the company or product. Use several of the Internet search engines such as Google, Yahoo!, Lycos, etc. and perform word searches relating to the company, product, or leaked information.

- Proxy server log; examine all log activities that might show use of free e-mail services such as Hotmail or Yahoo! mail. Track back to the specific workstation where these messages had originated from and perform a forensic analysis on the disk drives to help determine what was communicated.

- Known suspects' workstations; perform computer forensics on persons of interest, develop other leads of possible associates.

- Telephone records; review all company telephone records for any calls to known media organizations.

Steps to take for media leaks:

1. Interview management privately to obtain a list of employees that have direct knowledge of the sensitive data.

2. Identify the media source that had published the information.

3. Review company telephone records to see who may have had contact with the news service.

4. Obtain a listing of keywords of interest relating to the media leak.

5. Perform keyword searches on Proxy and e-mail servers.

6. Discreetly make forensic disk acquisitions and analysis of employees of interest.

7. From the forensic disk examinations, analyze all e-mail correspondence and trace any sensitive messages to other individuals who have not been listed as having direct knowledge of the sensitive data.

8. Expand the discreet forensic disk acquisition and analysis for any new persons of interest.

9. Consolidate findings and periodically review to see if new clues can be determined.

10. Routinely report findings to management and discuss with them how much further to continue the investigation.

INDUSTRIAL ESPIONAGE INVESTIGATIONS

Industrial espionage cases, similar to media leaks, can be very time consuming and are subject to the same scope-creep problems. Here are some guidelines on how to deal with economic espionage investigations. Be aware that industrial espionage cases that deal with foreign nationals may be violations of the International Traffic in Arms Regulations (ITAR) or Export Administration Regulation (EAR). For more information on the ITAR regulations, see the United States Department of State's Web site or perform a Web search for "International Traffic in Arms Regulations" using your favorite search engine. For EAR information, see the United States Department of Commerce Web site or perform a Web search for "Export Administration Regulations" using your favorite search engine.

All suspected industrial espionage cases should be treated as criminal investigations. The techniques described here are for the private network environment and internal investigations that have not yet been reported to law enforcement officials. Make sure you do not become an agent of the police by filing a complaint of a suspected espionage case prior to substantiating the allegation. The following list includes staff you might need when planning an industrial espionage investigation. Be creative and apply your talents to improve on these recommendations since this is not an inclusive list.

Industrial espionage investigations staff skills:

- The computing investigator who is responsible for disk forensics examinations.

- The technology specialist who is knowledgeable of the suspected compromised technical data.

- The network specialist who can perform log analysis and set up network sniffers to trap network communications of possible suspects.

- The threat assessment specialist (typically an attorney) who is familiar with federal and state laws and regulations that are related to ITAR and industrial espionage.

Considerations when initiating an international espionage investigation:

- Determine if this is a possible industrial espionage incident, and then determine if it falls under ITAR or EAR.

- Consult with corporate attorneys and upper management if the investigations must be conducted discreetly.

- Determine what information will be needed to substantiate the allegation of industrial espionage.

- Generate a list of keywords for disk forensics and sniffer monitoring.

- Make a list and collect needed resources for the investigation.

- Determine the goal and scope of the investigation; consult with management and the attorneys on how much work you should do.

- Initiate the investigation upon approval from management and make regular reports of your activities and findings.

Planning considerations for industrial espionage investigations:

- Examine all e-mail of suspected persons, both company provided and any free Web-based services such as Hotmail or Yahoo! mail.

- Search the Internet newsgroups for any posting relating to the incident such as the Yahoo message boards.

- Initiate physical surveillance with cameras on person or things of interest to the investigation.

- If available, examine all facility physical access log systems for sensitive areas, this might include secure areas where smart badges are used or video surveillance recordings.

- If there is a suspect, determine his or her location to the vulnerable asset that was compromised.

- Study the work habits of the suspect.

- Collect all telephone logs going in and out of the organization to see if there are any unique or unusual places called.

Conducting an industrial espionage case:

1. Gather all persons assigned to the investigation and brief them on the plan and the concerns.

2. Get the needed resources to conduct the investigation.

3. Start the investigation by placing surveillance systems in at the key locations such as camera surveillance and network sniffers.

4. Gather discreetly any additional evidence such as suspect's computer disk drive and perform a bit-stream image copy of it for follow up examination.

5. Collect all log data from networks and e-mail servers and examine them for unique items that might relate to the investigation.

6. Report regularly to management and corporate attorneys the status and current finding from your investigation.

7. Review with management and corporate attorneys the investigation's scope to determine if it needs to be expanded and more resources added.

INTERVIEWS AND INTERROGATION IN HIGH-TECHNOLOGY INVESTIGATIONS

It can take several volumes and years of training and experience to become a skilled interviewer and interrogator. Typically the corporate computing investigator is a technical person acquiring the evidence for an investigation. Many large corporate organizations have full-time security investigators who have had many years of training and experience in criminal and civil investigations and interviewing techniques. Few of these investigators will have any computing or network technical skills. Because of this you may be requested to assist in the interview or interrogation of a suspect that you have performed a forensic disk analysis on.

An interrogation is different from an interview. Interviews typically are information collection from a witness or suspect about specific facts relating to an investigation. An interrogation is the process of trying to get a suspect to confess about a specific incident or crime. An investigator might change from an interview into an interrogation when talking to a suspect.

Your role as a computing investigator is to instruct the investigator who is conducting the interview on what questions to ask and what the answers should be. As you build rapport with the investigator, he or she might ask you to question the suspect. Watching a skilled interrogator is a unique learning experience on human relation skills.

If you are asked to assist in an interview or interrogation as a computer investigator, prepare yourself by answering the following questions:

- What questions do I need to ask the suspect to get the vital information about the case?

- Do I know what I'm talking about; will I have to research the topic or the technology relating to the investigation?

- Do I need additional questions to cover other indirect issues relating to the investigation?

Common interview and interrogation errors include being unprepared for the interview or interrogation and not having the right questions or enough questions to provide more depth of knowledge. Make sure you do not run out of conversation topics; you need to keep the conversation friendly to gain the suspect's confidence. Avoid doubting your own skills, which might show the suspect you lack confidence in your ability.

Ingredients for a successful interview or interrogation require:

- Being patient throughout the entire session.

- Repeating or rephrasing questions to zero in on the specific facts from a reluctant witness or suspect.

- Being tenacious.

Glossary

4-mm DAT—Magnetic tapes that store about 4 GB of data, but like CD-Rs, are slow to read and write data.

Advanced SCSI Programmer Interface (ASPI)—Provides several software drivers that allow for communication between the OS and the SCSI component.

affidavit—The legal document that an investigator creates outlining the details of a case. In many cases, this document is used to issue a warrant or deal with abuse in a corporation.

algorithm—A short mathematical procedure that solves a recurrent problem.

allegation—A charge made against someone or something before proof has been found.

allocated data—Data on a drive that has not been deleted or written over.

allocation blocks—The number of logical blocks assembled in the Macintosh file system when a file is saved.

American Society of Crime Laboratory Directors (ASCLD)—A national society that sets the standards, management, and audit procedures for labs used in crime analysis including computer forensic labs used by the police, FBI, and similar organizations.

American Standard Code for Information Interchange (ASCII)—A coding scheme using 7 or 8 bits that assigns numeric values to up to 256 characters, including letters, numerals, punctuation marks, control characters, and other symbols.

amorphic—A condition achieved when a laser heats the Metal PC layer to 600 degrees Celsius.

approved secure container—A fireproof container that is locked by key or combination.

areal density—The number of bits per square inch of a platter.

attribute type code—In NTFS, the code assigned to file attributes such as the filename and security information.

authorized requester—In a corporation or company entity, the persons who have the right to request an investigation such as the chief security officer or chief intelligence officer.

AUTOEXEC.BAT—An automatically executed batch file that contains customized settings for MS-DOS, including the default path and environmental variables such as temporary directories.

Automated Fingerprint Identification System (AFIS)—A computerized system for identifying fingerprints that is connected to a central database for identifying criminal suspects and reviewing thousands of fingerprint samples at high speed.

B*-tree—A file system used by the Mac OS that consists of nodes, which are objects, and leaf nodes, which contain data.

bad block inode—In the Linux file system, the inode that tracks the bad sectors on a drive.

baseline—An established standard for measurement or comparison.

Berkeley Software Design (BSD) UNIX—A variation of UNIX created at the University of California at Berkeley.

bit-stream copy—A bit-by-bit copy of the data on the original storage media.

bit-stream image—The file used to store the bit-stream copy.

bitmap image—A representation of a graphics image in a grid format.

bookmark—A marker or address that identifies a specific place or location for subsequent retrieval.

Boot command—A DriveSpy command that examines the boot sector area of a disk partition.

boot.ini—A file used by NTLDR to specify boot requirements for Windows NT, 2000, and XP.

BOOTSECT.DOS—If the machine has a multiple booting system, NTLDR reads BOOTSECT.DOS to determine the address of the sector location of each OS. This is a hidden file.

bootstrap—Information contained in the ROM that the computer accesses during its startup process that tells it how to access the OS and hard drive.

business case—Justification to upper management or a lender for purchasing new equipment, software, or other tools when upgrading your facility. In many instances a business case shows how the upgrades will benefit the company.

carve—To locate a deleted file either in its entirety or through fragments by searching for any occurrence of the known file's header information.

carving—The process of removing an item from a group of items.

catalog—An area the Macintosh file system uses to maintain the relationships between files and directories on a volume.

Certified Computer Crime Investigator, Advanced Level—A certificate awarded by HTCN upon successful completion of appropriate exams. Requires a BS, three years of investigative experience, and four years of experience relating to computer crimes.

Certified Computer Crime Investigator, Basic Level—A certificate awarded by the HTCN upon successful completion of the appropriate exams. Requires a BS, two years of investigative experience, and 18 months of experience relating to computer crimes.

Certified Computer Forensic Technician, Advanced Level—A certificate awarded by the HTCN upon successful completion of their requirements. Same requirements as the Certified Computer Crime Investigator, Advanced Level, but all experience must be related to computer forensics.

Certified Computer Forensic Technician, Basic Level—A certificate awarded by the HTCN upon successful completion of their requirements. Same requirements as the Certified Computer Crime Investigator, Basic Level, but all experience must be related to computer forensics.

Certified Electronic Evidence Collection Specialist (CEECS)—A certificate awarded by IACIS upon completion of the written exam.

Certified Forensic Computer Examiners (CFCE)—A certificate awarded by IACIS upon completion of the correspondence portion of testing.

Chain Directory Entry (CDE)—A DriveSpy command that displays all directory cluster positions.

Chain FAT Entry (CFE)—A command used by DriveSpy that displays all the clusters in a chain that start at a specified cluster.

chain of custody—The route that evidence takes from the time it is obtained by the investigator until the case is closed or goes to court.

client-server architecture—A network architecture in which each computer or process on the network is either a client or a server. Clients are the systems that request services from the server. A server has systems that process the request from clients.

clump—In the Macintosh file system, a contiguous allocation block. Clumps are used to keep file fragmentation to a minimum.

Cluster command—A DriveSpy command that displays the cluster in hexadecimal view.

clusters—Storage allocation units composed of sectors. Clusters are 512, 1024, 2048, or 4096 bytes in length.

code—A group of specialized characters combined in a sequence to provide instructions to a program on how to perform a specific action.

COMMAND.COM—A file that contains the basic commands for MS-DOS, such as Copy, Date, and Time.

compact disc (CD)—Optical media that stores information and typically holds up to 640 MB.

Computer Forensics Tool Testing (CFTT)—A project created by the National Institute of Standards and Technology to manage research on computing-forensics tools.

computer-forensic workstation—A workstation set up to allow copying of forensic evidence whether on a hard drive, floppy, CD, or Zip disk. It typically has various software preloaded and ready to use.

computer-generated records—Data that is generated by the computer such as system log files or proxy server logs.

computer-stored records—Digital files that are generated by a person.

Computer Technology Investigators Northwest (CTIN)—A non-profit group based in the Seattle-Tacoma, Washington, area comprised of law enforcement and private corporations whose aim is to improve the quality of investigations in the Pacific northwest.

computing forensic facility/lab—A computer lab that is dedicated to computing investigations, and typically has a variety of computers, OSs, and forensic software.

computing forensics—Applying scientific methods to retrieve data and/or information from digital evidence.

computing investigations—The detailed examination and collection of facts and data from a computer and its operating system used in an affidavit or warrant.

CONFIG.SYS—A text file containing commands that are typically run only at system startup to enhance the computer's DOS configuration.

configuration management—The process of keeping track of all upgrades and patches you apply to your computer's OS and applications.

conflict out—When you already have knowledge or have rendered an opinion about a case before you are hired.

constant angular velocity (CAV)—CD players 12X or faster use this system to read CDs.

constant linear velocity (CLV)—CD players 12X or slower use this method to read CDs.

covert surveillance—Observing people or places without being detected, often using electronic equipment such as video cameras or key and screen capture programs.

criminal case—A case in which criminal law must be applied.

criminal law—The statutes in your country or jurisdiction that determine what items must be addressed in an investigation.

curriculum vita (CV)—An extensive résumé of your professional history that includes not only where you have worked, but what cases you have worked on, what testimony you have given, what training you have received and from whom, along with details of your other skills.

Cyclical Redundancy Check (CRC)—A mathematical algorithm that translates a file into a unique hexadecimal code value.

cylinders—The intersection of tracks on two or more disk platters.

data—The contents of a file in the Linux file structure.

data block—In the Linux file system, a cluster of hard disk sectors, normally 4096 or 8192 bytes in size.

data compression—A complex algorithm used to reduce the size of a file.

data fork—The part of the Macintosh file structure that contains the actual data of a file.

data recovery—Retrieving files that were accidentally or purposefully deleted.

data recovery lab—An alternate name for a computer-forensic lab.

deposition—A formal meeting where you are questioned in a room in which only the opposing attorneys, your attorney, and the opposing parties are present. There is no judge or jury at this time. A deposition is considered part of discovery.

deposition banks—Libraries kept by various law firms of depositions given in the past.

designator—The 0x before a value that indicates the value is a hexadecimal number.

dial-up connection—A connecting device to a network via a modem or a public telephone network. Dial-up access acts like a phone connection, except that the two connecting parties are computers instead of people.

digital signature—A unique value that identifies a file.

digital video disc (DVD)—Optical media that stores information and movies up to 17 GB.

disaster recovery—Performing real-time backups, monitoring, and data recovery.

discovery—The efforts to obtain information before a trial by demanding documents, depositions, questions and answers written under oath, written requests for admissions of fact, and the examination of the scene, for example.

discovery deposition—A hostile but open examination under oath before trial with no judge present. The attorney setting the deposition will frequently conduct the equivalent of a direct and cross-examination.

Domain Naming Service (DNS)—An Internet service that translates domain names (i.e., www.microsoft.com) to IP addresses (i.e. 10.0.1.10).

DOS protected-mode interface (DPMI)—Used by many computer forensic tools that do not operate in the Windows environment.

double-indirect pointers—The pointers in the second layer or group of an OS.

DoubleSpace—An MS-DOS disk compression utility distributed with MS-DOS 6.0 and 6.20.

drive slack—Any information that had been on the storage device previously. It can contain deleted files, deleted e-mail, or file fragments. Both file slack and RAM slack constitute drive slack.

DriveSpace—An MS-DOS disk compression utility distributed with MS-DOS 6.22 and Windows 9x.

Electronic Communications Privacy Act (ECPA)—A law that prohibits phone tapping, interception of e-mail, and other privacy violations.

Encrypted File System (EFS)—Symmetric key encryption first used in Windows 2000 on NTFS formatted disks.

end user—The person who uses a software package. In most cases this person has less expertise than the software designer.

end-of-file marker—0x0FFFFFFF, the code typically used with FAT file systems to show where the file ends.

enterprise environment—Refers to large corporate computing systems that may include one or more disparate or formerly independent systems.

ergonomics—The proper placement of machinery, office equipment, and computers to minimize physical injury or injuries caused by repetitious motions. It is also the study of designing equipment to meet the human need of comfort while allowing for improved productivity.

evidence bag—A non-static bag used to transport floppy disks, hard drives, and other computer components.

evidence custody form—A printed copy of a form indicating who has signed out and physically been in possession of evidence.

evidence floppy disk—The original disk on which the electronic evidence was found.

examination plan—The plan laying out the strategy created by the attorney to try a case.

exculpatory—Evidence that proves the innocence of the accused.

exhibits—Items used in court to prove a case.

expert witness—A person who has knowledge in a field and can offer an opinion and facts in a legal case.

extents overflow file—Used by the Macintosh File Manager when the list of contiguous blocks of a file becomes too long. The overflow of the list is placed in the extents overflow file. Any file extents not in the MDB or VCB are contained here.

false-positive hits—When a system incorrectly provides a positive validation when in fact it is false.

File Allocation Table (FAT)—The original file structure created by Microsoft. It is written to the outermost track of a disk and contains information about each file stored on the drive. The variations are FAT12, FAT16, and FAT32.

[File Groups]—The section of DriveSpy.ini that allows you to list all the extensions or files headers for graphics files or spreadsheets.

[File Headers]—The section of DriveSpy.ini that contains the hexadecimal number values for many known file types. These hexadecimal numbers are the header data contained in the first several bytes of all specialized data files such as Microsoft Word documents or Excel spreadsheets and any associated templates.

File Manager—In the Macintosh file system, handles the reading, writing, and storage of data to physical media. It also collects data to maintain the HFS along with manipulation of files, folders, and volumes.

file slack—The slack space created when a file is saved. If the allocated space is larger than the file, the remainder is slack and can contain passwords, login IDs, and deleted e-mail.

file system—Provides an OS with a road map to the data on a disk.

Finder—Works with the Macintosh OS to keep track of files and maintain the user's desktop.

forensic copy—A copy of an evidence disk that is used during the actual investigation.

Forensic Software Testing Support Tools (FS-TST)—A collection of programs that analyze the capability of disk imaging tools.

Forensic Toolkit (FTK)—A GUI software tool used for forensic examination.

Fourth Amendment—The Fourth Amendment to the United States Constitution contained in the Bill of Rights. It dictates that you must have probable cause for search and seizure.

free space—Space on a drive that is not reserved for saved files.

geometry—The internal organization of the drive.

Get FAT Entry (GFE)—A DriveSpy command that displays the FAT entry for a specified cluster.

GNU General Public License (GPL)—An agreement that defines Linux as open source software, meaning that anyone can use, change, and distribute the software without owing royalties or licensing fees to another party.

GroupWise—The Novell e-mail server software, a database server like Microsoft Exchange and UNIX Sendmail.

gzip—A Linux program that compresses image files and minimizes your storage needs.

Hal.dll—Hardware abstraction layer dynamic link library. It tells the OS kernel how to interface with the hardware.

hazardous material (HAZMAT)—Chemical, biological, or radiological substances that can cause harm to one or more people.

head and cylinder skew—A method used by manufacturers to minimize lag time. The starting sectors of tracks are slightly offset from each other to move the read-write head.

header node—Stores information about the B*-tree file in the Macintosh file system.

heads—The devices that read and write data to the disk platters.

hierarchical file system (HFS)—The system used by the Mac OS to store files, consisting of folders and subfolders, which can be nested.

High Performance File system (HPFS)—File system used by IBM for their OS/2 OS.

High Tech Crime Network (HTCN)—A national organization that provides certification for computer crime investigators and computer forensic technicians.

High Technology Crime Investigation Association (HTCIA)—A non-profit association for solving international computer crimes.

high-risk document—A document that contains sensitive information that could create an advantage for the opposing attorney.

hostile work environment—An environment in which a person cannot perform his or her assigned duties. In the workplace, this normally includes actions such as sending threatening or demeaning e-mail or a co-worker viewing hate sites.

Hypertext Markup Language (HTML)—The authoring language used to create documents (pages) on the World Wide Web (WWW). It defines the structure and layout of a Web document by using a variety of tags and attributes.

IF—This MS-DOS command tests three possible conditions: ERRORLEVEL, the value of two strings to see if they are equal, and whether a file exists.

image file—A file created by Image tool from Digital Intelligence.

index node—Stores link information to the previous and next node in the Macintosh file system.

indirect pointers—The pointers in the first layer or group of an OS.

industrial espionage—Selling of sensitive company or proprietary information to a competitor.

Info2 file—In Windows NT, 2000, and XP, the control file for the Recycle Bin.

innocent information—Data that does not contribute to the evidence of a crime or violation.

inode—A key part of the Linux file system that contains UIDs, GIDs, modification, access, creation times, and file locations.

International Association of Computer Investigative Specialists (IACIS)—One of the oldest professional computing forensic organizations, IACIS was created by police officers who wanted to formalize credentials in computing investigations. IACIS restricts membership to only sworn law-enforcement personnel or government employees working as computing forensics examiners.

International Organization of Standards (ISO)—An organization set up by the United Nations to ensure compatibility in a variety of fields including engineering, electricity, and computers. The acronym is the Greek word for equal.

International Organization on Digital Evidence (IOCE)—A group that sets standards for recovering, preserving, and examining digital evidence.

Internet Message Access Protocol version 4 (IMAP4)—A protocol for retrieving e-mail messages. It is similar to POP3 but supports additional features such as the ability to search for keywords while messages are still on the mail server.

Internet service provider (ISP)—Provides a service or membership that allows you to access the information available on the Internet.

inter-partition gap—Partition created with unused space or void between the primary partition and the first logical partition.

inter-partition space—The space between the end of one partition and the start of another.

IO.SYS—This MS-DOS file communicates between a computer's BIOS and hardware and with MS DOS code.

journal—A notebook or series of notebooks in which you record the techniques you used and the people who assisted you with specific types of investigations.

key escrow—A technology designed to recover encrypted data if users forget their passphrase or if the user key is corrupted due to a system failure.

keyed hash set—A value created by an encryption utility's secret key.

keyword search—Finding files or other information by providing characters, words, or phrases to a search tool.

Known File Filter (KFF)—A database for the Forensic Toolkit that is updated periodically by AccessData and contains the hash values of known files such as MSWord.exe or illicit items floating on the Web. It is used to quickly identify the files for evidence or eliminate them from the investigation if they are legitimate files.

lands—Flat areas on a compact disc.

lay witness—A witness not considered an expert in a particular field.

leaf node—A node of the B★-tree system that contains data in the Macintosh file system.

[License]—The section of the DriveSpy.ini file that contains the product license code and owner's name for DriveSpy.exe.

limiting phrase—A phrase in a search warrant that limits the scope of a search for evidence.

line of authority—The people or positions specified in a company policy who have the right to initiate an investigation.

litigation—The legal process taken to prove a person's or entity's guilt or innocence in a court of law.

logical address—When files are saved, they are assigned to clusters. The clusters have been given numbers by the OS that start at two. The cluster number defines the logical address.

logical blocks—In the Macintosh file system, a collection of data that cannot exceed 512 bytes. These are assembled in allocation blocks to store files.

logical cluster number (LCN)—Used by the MFT of NTFS. It refers to a specific physical location on the drive.

logical EOF—In the Macintosh file system, the number of bytes that contain data.

lossless compression—A compression method in which no data is lost. With this type of compression, a large file can be compressed to take up less space, and then decompressed without any loss of information.

lossy compression—A compression technique that can lose data but not perceptible quality when a file is restored. Files that use lossy compression include JPEG and MPEG.

low-level investigations—Corporate cases that require less effort than a major criminal case.

map node—Stores the node descriptor and a map record in the Macintosh file system.

Master Boot Record (MBR)—On Windows and DOS computer systems, the boot disk file, which contains information regarding the files on a disk and their locations, size, and other critical items.

Master Directory Block (MDB)—On older Macintosh systems, the location where all information about a volume is stored. A copy of the MDB is kept in the next to the last block on the volume.

Master File Table (MFT)—Used by NTFS to track files. It contains information about the access rights, date and time stamps, system attributes, and parts of the file.

MD5 hash value—A cryptographic algorithm used to create digital signatures. It creates a one-way hash function, meaning that it can convert data into a fixed string of digits (also called a message digest). With a one-way hash function, you can compare the calculated message digest against the message digest that is decrypted with a public key. This indicates whether the data has changed.

Message Digest version 5 (MD5) hash— A mathematical algorithm that translates a file into a unique hexadecimal code value.

meta-data—In Linux, the part of the inode that contains critical data including UIDs, GIDs, size, permissions, and other critical information. In NTFS, this refers to information stored in the MFT.

metafiles—Combinations of bitmap and vector images.

MSDOS.SYS—A hidden text file that contains startup options for Windows 9x.

multi-evidence form—A chain-of-evidence form used to list all items associated with a case.

multiple data streams—Ways in which data can be appended to a file intentionally or not. In NTFS, it becomes an additional data attribute of a file.

National Institute of Justice (NIJ)— The research, development, and evaluation agency of the U.S. Department of Justice dedicated to researching crime control and justice issues.

National Institute of Standards and Technology (NIST)—A unit of the U.S. Commerce Department. Formerly known as the National Bureau of Standards, NIST promotes and maintains measurement standards.

National Software Reference Library (NSRL)—A project supported by the National Institute of Justice, federal, state, and local law enforcement, and the National Institute of Standards and Technology to promote efficient and effective use of computer technology in the investigation of crimes involving computers.

network forensics—Information obtained about which ports were used to access a computer or which ports a computer accessed to commit a crime.

network intrusion detection and incident response—Detecting attacks from intruders by using automated tools and the manual process of monitoring network firewall logs.

New Technology file system (NTFS)—Created by Microsoft to replace FAT. NTFS uses security features, allows for smaller cluster sizes, and uses Unicode, which makes it a much more versatile system. Used mainly on newer OSs such as Windows NT, 2000, and XP.

non-keyed hash set—A hash set used to identify files or viruses.

nonresident attributes—When referring to the MFT of the NTFS, all data that is stored in a location separate from the MFT.

nonstandard image file format—An uncommon graphic file format, including those that most image viewers do not recognize, proprietary formats, emerging formats, and those related to old or obsolete technology.

notarize—To have a document witnessed and a person clearly identified as the source before a notary public.

NT Loader (NTLDR)—A service that loads Windows NT. It is located in the root folder of the system partition.

NTBootdd.sys—A device driver that allows access to SCSI or ATA drives that are not referred to in the BIOS.

NTDetect.com—A command file that identifies hardware components during boot up and sends the information to NTLDR.

Ntoskrnl.exe—The kernel for Windows XP, NT, and 2000.

offset—A value added to a base address to produce a second address.

Open Source Interconnect (OSI)—A standard for worldwide communications that defines a networking framework for implementing protocols in seven layers.

PageFile.sys—At a computer startup, data and instruction code is moved in and out of the PageFile.sys. This is to optimize the amount of physical memory (RAM) that is available during startup.

partition—A logical drive on a disk. It can be the entire disk or a fraction thereof.

partition boot sector—The first data set of an NTFS disk. It starts at Sector [0] of the disk drive and it can expand up to 16 sectors.

partition gap—See inter-partition space.

PartMap command—A DriveSpy command that lists a sector map of a partition.

password cracking software—Software used to match the hash patterns of passwords or simply guess the words by using common combinations or by employing standard algorithms.

password protected—Files and areas of any storage media can have limited access by using a password to prevent unintentional use.

PDBlock—A program designed to prevent writes to a disk drive.

PDWipe—A program used to overwrite hard disk drives, overwriting all data on the drive.

phase change alloy—The Metal PC layer of a CD-RW that allows it to be written to several times.

physical address—The actual sector in which a file is located. Sectors are at the hardware and firmware level.

physical EOF—In the Macintosh file system, the number of allocation blocks assigned to the file.

pits—Lower areas on a compact disc not burned by the laser.

pixel—A small dot used to create images.

plain view doctrine—When conducting a search and seizure, objects in plain view of a law enforcement officer who has the right to be in position to have that view are subject to seizure without a warrant and may be introduced in evidence.

police blotter—A journal of criminal activity used to inform law-enforcement personnel of current criminal activities.

Post Office Protocol version 3 (POP3)—A protocol used to retrieve e-mail messages from an e-mail server.

print—A command used in UNIX to print a file.

private key—In encryption, the key held by the owner of the file.

probable cause—Indication that a crime has been committed, evidence of the specific crime exists, and the evidence for the specific crime exists at the place to be searched.

professional conduct—Behavior expected of an employee in the workplace or other such professional setting.

professional curiosity—The motivation for law enforcement and other professional personnel to examine an incident or crime scene to see what happened.

protected-mode graphical user interface (GUI)—One mode in Windows 9x.

proxy server—A server computer that connects a local area network (LAN) to the Internet.

public key—In encryption, the key held by the system receiving the file.

RAM slack—The slack in the last sector of a file. Any data currently residing in RAM at the time the file is saved can appear in this area whether the information was saved or not. It can contain login IDs, passwords, and phone numbers for dial-ups.

raster image—A bitmap file that organizes pixels in rows; usually created when a vector image is converted to a bitmap image.

rasterize—To convert a bitmap or vector file to a raster file for printing.

recovery certificate—A method used by NTFS so a network administrator can recover encrypted files if the user/creator of the file loses their private key encryption code.

Redundant Array of Independent Disks (RAID)—A computer that has two or more hard drives with redundant storage features so that if one drive fails, the other drives can take over.

Registry—In Windows, the Registry contains information about the hardware, network connections, user preferences, installed software, and other critical information. Using the Regedit or Regedit32 from the Run dialog box lets you access the Registry.

resident attributes—When referring to the MFT, all attributes that are stored in the MFT of the NTFS.

resolution—Density of pixels on the screen.

resource fork—The part of the Macintosh file system that contains the resource map, header information for the file, window locations, and icons.

right of privacy—An employee's right to have their transmissions at work protected.

risk management—Involves determining how much risk is acceptable for any process or operation, such as replacing equipment.

RootKit—A prebuilt package of programs that allows an intruder to install a network sniffer and obtain user IDs and passwords to your most sensitive systems.

router—A network device that connects a number of local area networks together.

salvaging—Another term for carving used in the United Kingdom; the process of removing an item from a group of items.

SaveFree—A DriveSpy command that saves the free space of the default partition.

SaveSlack—A DriveSpy command that saves the slack space of the default partition.

Scientific Working Group on Digital Evidence (SWGDE)—A group that sets standards for recovering, preserving, and examining digital evidence.

scope creep—A situation or condition that increases the level of work not originally expected.

screen resolution—The density of pixels displayed on a computer monitor.

Script command—A DriveSpy command that runs a script file that contains sequences of DriveSpy shell commands. A script is a plain text file that contains the commands you want to run.

[Search]—The section of the DriveSpy.ini file that allows you to specify what keywords you want to search for in an image file or document.

search and seizure—The legal act of acquiring evidence for an investigation. See Fourth Amendment.

search warrant—The legal document that allows law enforcement to search an office, place of business, or other locale for evidence relating to an alleged crime.

second extended file system (Ext2fs)—The file system most used by Linux today.

sectors—Individual sections on tracks, typically made up of 512 bytes.

secure facility—A facility that can be locked and provides limited access to the contents of a room.

Secure Hash Algorithm (SHA-1)—A hashing algorithm that creates a 160-bit message digest that a digital signature algorithm (DSA) can process to generate or verify the signature for the message.

SET command—When used at the command-line prompt with no switches or attributes, this command displays all current system-root paths.

silver-platter doctrine—The policy of submitting acquired evidence to the police by an investigator who is not an agent of the court when a criminal act has been uncovered.

Simple Mail Transfer Protocol (SMTP)—A protocol used for sending e-mail messages between servers.

single evidence form—A form that dedicates a page for each item retrieved for a case. It allows the investigator to add more detail as to exactly what was done to the evidence each time it was taken from the storage locker.

slack space—Space on a disk between the end of a file and the allotted space for a file.

Small Computer System Interface (SCSI)—An input/output standard protocol device.

sniffing—Detecting data transmissions to and from a suspect's computer and a network server to determine the type of data being transmitted over a network.

sparse evidence files—Creating files from separate large portions of data to streamline data analysis.

Special Interest Groups (SIGs)—Associated with various operating systems, these groups maintain Listservs and may hold meetings to exchange information about current and legacy operating systems.

spoliation—Destroying or concealing evidence.

standard image file format—An image file format that most or all graphics programs can open.

steganalysis—The practice of detecting and decoding steganography.

steganography—A cryptographic technique for embedding information into something else (like an image or sound file) for the sole purpose of hiding that information from the casual observer.

Tables command—A DriveSpy command that lists a sector map of a partition.

technical witness—A person who has performed the actual field work, but does not offer an opinion in court, only the results of their findings.

TEMPEST—An unclassified term that refers to facilities that have been hardened so that electrical signals from computers, the computer network, and telephone systems cannot be easily monitored or accessed by someone outside the facility.

testimony preservation deposition—A deposition usually set by your client to preserve your testimony because of conflicts of schedule or health issues but also in some cases because having the full features of your laboratory available to you may make for better testimony and easier demonstrations.

Trace Directory Cluster (TDC)—A DriveSpy command used to rebuild a subdirectory on a disk partition.

track density—The space between tracks on a disk. The smaller the space between tracks, the more tracks on a disk. Older drives with wider track densities allowed wandering.

tracks—The individual concentric circles on a disk platter.

triple-indirect pointers—The pointers in the third layer or group of an OS.

unallocated disk space—The area of the disk where the deleted file resides.

Unicode—A 16-bit character code representation that is replacing ASCII. It is capable of representing over 64,000 characters.

Uniform Crime Report—Information collected at the federal, state, and local levels to determine the types and frequencies of crimes committed.

Universal Naming Convention (UNC)—A PC format that specified the location of resources on a local area network. It uses the following format: \\servername\shared-resource-pathname.

vector image—An image created based on mathematical equations.

vector quantization (VQ)—A form of vector image that uses an algorithm similar to rounding up decimal values to eliminate unnecessary data.

verbal formal report—A structured report delivered in person to a board of directors or managers or to a jury.

verbal informal report—A report that is less structured than a formal report and is delivered in person, usually in an attorney's office.

virtual cluster number (VCN)—When a file is saved in the NTFS, it is assigned both a logical cluster number and a virtual cluster number. The logical cluster is a physical location, while the virtual cluster consists of chained clusters.

voir dire—The process of qualifying a witness as an expert in their particular field.

volume—Any storage media, such as a single floppy disk, a partition on a hard drive, the entire drive, or several drives. On Intel systems, a volume is any partitioned disk.

Volume Bitmap—A system application used to track blocks that are in use and blocks that are available.

Volume Control Block (VCB)—Contains information from the MDB and is used by the File Manager in the Macintosh file system.

Volume Information Block (VIB)—Another name for the Master Directory Block.

vulnerability assessment and risk management—Determining the weakest points in a system, then calculating the return on investment to decide which ones have to be fixed.

warning banner—Text that appears when someone logs on to a company computer that tells them the appropriate use of the machine or Internet access.

Web browser—A software program used to locate and display Web pages.

Wipe command—A DriveSpy command used to reduce a disk to all zeros and erase all traces of files that were there.

write-blocker—A physical device that prevents a computer from recording data on an evidence disk.

written formal report—A written report sworn under oath, such as an affidavit or declaration.

written informal report—An informal or preliminary report in written form.

zoned bit recording—How most manufacturers deal with the fact that the inner tracks of a platter are physically smaller than the outer tracks. Grouping the tracks by zones ensures that the tracks are all the same size.

Index